Lecture Notes of the Institute for Computer Sciences, Social Informatics and Telecommunications Engineering 367

T0211938

More information about this series at http://www.springer.com/series/8197

Anthony Brooks · Eva Irene Brooks ·
Duckworth Jonathan (Eds.)

Interactivity and Game Creation

9th EAI International Conference, ArtsIT 2020
Aalborg, Denmark, December 10–11, 2020
Proceedings

 Springer

Editors
Anthony Brooks 🆔
Department of Software and Media
Aalborg University
Aalborg, Denmark

Eva Irene Brooks 🆔
Aalborg University
Aalborg, Denmark

Duckworth Jonathan 🆔
RMIT University
Melbourne, VIC, Australia

ISSN 1867-8211   ISSN 1867-822X   (electronic)
Lecture Notes of the Institute for Computer Sciences, Social Informatics
and Telecommunications Engineering
ISBN 978-3-030-73425-1   ISBN 978-3-030-73426-8   (eBook)
https://doi.org/10.1007/978-3-030-73426-8

This Springer imprint is published by the registered company Springer Nature Switzerland AG
The registered company address is: Gewerbestrasse 11, 6330 Cham, Switzerland

Preface

The ArtsIT team are delighted to introduce the proceedings of the 9th European Alliance for Innovation (EAI) International Conference on Arts and Technology, Interactivity, and Game Creation (ArtsIT 2020), held as an online virtual conference in Cyberspace, December 10–11, 2020.

ArtsIT is a place where people in the arts, design and technology meet – unfortunately, due to the COVID-19 situation, the 2020 edition of this 'meeting' had to take place remotely via a live video stream of presentations, which is now archived for viewing at the URL https://www.youtube.com/watch?v=vBVugi9RpX8&t=31s.

Opening the proceedings was a first-class keynote given by Portuguese international artist João Martinho Moura. Moura is a media artist and researcher, interested in electronic art and embodiment, virtual environments, computer music, and computational aesthetics. For the past 20 years, he has been adopting new ways to present the body and space in digital media. He has a particular interest in art and science, perception, visualization, and the intersections between art and technology. Since the 2000s, his work has been presented internationally, several times, in more than 18 countries, including some city-scale exhibitions. João has authored numerous publications in and across the fields of media arts, interfaces, embodiment, virtual reality, and visualization. As a media artist, he has collaborated with a number of renowned international institutions, such as the European Space Agency (ESA), the International Iberian Nanotechnology Laboratory (INL), the North Atlantic Treaty Organization (NATO), and the United Nations Educational, Scientific and Cultural Organization (UNESCO), and was selected as an artist in residence for the European Commission's STARTS and MindSpaces initiatives. In 2013, João Martinho Moura received the National Multimedia Art and Culture Award in Lisbon for his contributions to the field of digital arts in Portugal. A feature in João's ArtsIT keynote presentation was his most recent avant-garde works within dance performance and installation where he explores at and beyond the cutting edge of domains by experimenting with virtual and extended realities. Through this it was clear how he is offering and creating new actor and audience experiences, bridging established divides and confines, so as to establish new performer/audience virtual interactive spaces pushing the limits of the state of the art in the field. We are also grateful for and acknowledge the important contribution by João as webmaster for the conference website.

Following the keynote, a full day of paper presentations was broadcast until well into the evening. These are presented herein in their text form and as oral presentations archived at the given URL. Thus, in this edition of the book series Lecture Notes of the Institute for Computer Sciences, Social Informatics and Telecommunications Engineering (LNICST) published by Springer, proceedings from ArtsIT are presented. We sincerely hope that this volume will be well received by those who authored papers as well as others who read the work herein. We also hope that this volume may inspire those who have published in this (near) annual series, now in its eleventh year, to return and encourage other readers to consider the events as worthy in their targeted publications. Hence, we encourage all authors and would-be-authors to regularly check the event web pages for calls to submit for upcoming editions. We, as the managing/organizing/editing team, would like to express our thanks to EAI for the continued support as well as to all delegates who attended the December 2020 event, either as presenting authors or as part of the audience. We express our thanks to Aalborg University which supported us in numerous ways and again sponsored the event. Finally, the ArtsIT 'family' all look forward to physically meeting you at ArtsIT or another academic or social occasion in the future.

Anthony Brooks
Eva Irene Brooks
Duckworth Jonathan

Conference Organization (ArtsIT)

Steering Committee

Imrich Chlamtac (Chair)   University of Trento, Italy
Anthony Brooks (Co-chair)   Aalborg University, Denmark

Organizing Committee

General Chair

Anthony Brooks   Aalborg University, Denmark

Technical Program Committee Chairs

Mark Palmer   University of the West of England, United Kingdom
Irene Mavrommati   Hellenic Open University, Greece
Stephen J. Wang   Hong Kong Polytechnic University

Demos and PhD Track Chair

Anthony Brooks   Aalborg University, Denmark

Web Chair

João Martinho Moura   Polytechnic Institute of Cávado and Ave, Portugal

Panels and Demos Chair

Anthony Brooks   Aalborg University, Denmark

Publications Chair

Jonathan Duckworth   RMIT University, Australia

Workshops Chairs

Thomas Westin   Stockholm University, Sweden
Anton Nijholt   University of Twente, Netherlands
Anthony Brooks   Aalborg University, Denmark

Publicity and Social Media Chair

João Martinho Moura   Polytechnic Institute of Cávado and Ave, Portugal

Sponsorship and Exhibit Chair

Anthony Brooks   Aalborg University, Denmark

Local Chair

Tine Skjødt Andreasen	Aalborg University, Denmark
Anthony Brooks	Aalborg University, Denmark

Technical Program Committee

Margaret Schedel	Stony Brook University, USA
Mel Krokos	University of Portsmouth, UK
Zoi Karageorgiou	Hellenic Open University, Greece
Cecília Sik-Lanyi	University of Pannonia, Hungary
Stuart Cunningham	Manchester Metropolitan University, UK
Sue Gollifer	Brighton University, UK
Chamari Edirisinghe	Imagineering Institute, Malaysia
Stefania Serafin	Aalborg University, Denmark
Bruno Herbelin	Ecole Polytechnique Fédérale de Lausanne (EPFL), Switzerland
Mirian Tavares	University of Algarve, Portugal
Dimitris Grammenos	FORTH, Greece
Antonio Camurri	University of Genoa, Italy
Damianos Gavalas	University of the Aegean, Greece
Jack Ox	University of New Mexico, USA
Christos Bouras	Computer Technology Institute and Press, Greece
Jean Detheux	Independant painter/filmmaker
George Raptis	University of Patras, Greece
Christos Sintoris	University of Patras, Greece
Pirkko Raudaskoski	Aalborg University, Denmark
Dimosthenis Manias	Hellenic Open University, Greece
Spiros Siakas	University of West Attica, Greece
Ioannis Chatzigiannakis	Sapienza Universita di Roma, Italy
Elissavet Georgiadou	Aristotle University of Thessaloniki, Greece
Georgios Mylonas	Computer Technology Institute and Press, Greece
Modestos Stavrakis	University of the Aegean, Greece
Thanos Balafoutis	Hellenic Open University, Greece
Theodora Moulou	Hellenic Open University, Greece
Iro Laskari	Hellenic Open University, Greece

Contents

Design

Intelligence and Creativity in Healthcare, Wellbeing and Aging

Art, Installation and Performance

Digitisation and Vector maps

Embodiment in Virtual Reality Performance

João Martinho Moura[1]([✉]) [iD], Né Barros[2] [iD], and Paulo Ferreira-Lopes[3] [iD]

[1] School of Arts, Universidade Católica Portuguesa, Porto, Portugal
[2] Balleteatro, Porto, Portugal
[3] University of Applied Sciences Mainz - IMG, Mainz, Germany

Abstract. In this publication, we present artistic and technical developments in creating and presenting dance performances in media art, where embodiment is crucial in the artistic process. We study and compare three distinct performances with dancers and one choreographer in the same dance company between 2009 and 2020. The degree of immersion in performance is then compared between the three pieces, created at Balleteatro, in Porto, addressing the transition from the real to the virtual in the performance perspective, with practical cases and direct observations in the way the audience learns different states of body representation through technological means. We initially present the NUVE performance (2010), interpreted by Né Barros, Co:Lateral (2016–2019), a performance that crosses different realities, and, finally, the transition to the UNA work (2020) that takes place in total virtuality. This publication focuses on the developments, the public experience, and the results obtained in more than 20 exhibitions in different locations, either in theater or auditorium and in conference venues.

Keywords: Embodiment · Performance · Virtual reality

1 Introduction

Balleteatro[1], founded in 1983 by Isabel Barros, Jorge Levi, and Né Barros with the designation of *Ballet Teatro Contemporâneo do Porto*, is a performing arts center based in Porto, Portugal (Fig. 1). It is currently composed of an auditorium, a company, a professional school, a training center, and an audiovisual and editing center, currently located in the Coliseu do Porto. Since its beginning, Balleteatro has had the mission of being a center for the development of the performing arts. Having inhabited several spaces in Porto, the Balleteatro is building an artistic community for the contemporary performing arts that until then had never existed. Having as a fundamental area the creation, it generated the first contemporary dance company in Porto, and presents today a vast repertoire. The continuity of this profound work, of contamination between creation and training, allowed that in 1989 the Balleteatro had seen approved its candidacy as a professional school of theatre and dance, the first in the country with these possibilities. From this school, several generations of artists representing the performing arts were formed.

---

[1] https://balleteatro.pt/.

© ICST Institute for Computer Sciences, Social Informatics and Telecommunications Engineering 2021
Published by Springer Nature Switzerland AG 2021. All Rights Reserved
A. Brooks et al. (Eds.): ArtsIT 2020, LNICST 367, pp. 3–20, 2021.
https://doi.org/10.1007/978-3-030-73426-8_1

Fig. 1. The Balleteatro. *Ballet Teatro Contemporâneo do Porto.* Picture: José Caldeira.

In 2009 João Martinho Moura[2] joined Balleteatro as a media artist and researcher, working closely with choreographer Né Barros[3] in the frontier between dance and digital art. Since then, both developed different works, presented in various venues, having the embodiment process in performance in common, exploring further possibilities in the confrontation between the body and virtual environments. In the last ten years, they collaborated. The digital body was thought, and many tests were carried out using different capture and presentation technologies to the general public. This publication will make a straightforward approach to performance and Virtual Reality (VR). It will focus on the developments, public presentation, and embodied comparisons between the three works carried out with an approximate interval of 5 years.

1.1 Performance and Media Art

Among the many intersections, digital art is an expanding domain in dance. Digital Dance refers to dance-making processes and performances that include digital technologies as an integral feature. These projects often involved close collaboration between dance artists and technology specialists, usually artists themselves [1]. Though the appropriation of new technologies can be found in many relevant examples in dance, it is a field with the potential to explore the aesthetic and artistic level [2]. Several contemporary dance companies and artists experiment with new ways to present choreographies and movement using the digital [3]. In a digital performance, where technologies play a relevant role, these can be seen not as tools but as filters for our meetings with other people or us [4]. The integration of VR and interactive technology in dance performances leads to new insights and experiments with choreographic methods that may ultimately take dance in a new direction [5]. Brooks, a pioneer artist in using different performance interfaces, says that many of these artists used the body as a central element of the canvas, often abusing or decorating the flesh and provoking audiences – bringing them into the action [6]. Brooks emphasizes the future interface's concept: the free air space around one's own body, tailored and controllable, maybe from the mind, or by

---

[2] https://jmartinho.net/about/.
[3] https://balleteatro.pt/artistas/ne-barros.

the skin, as in his Virtual Interactive Space (VIS) concept focused on rehabilitation [7]. For Saltz, performance, such as dance and theater, is a visual and auditory event, but, above all, corporeal [8]. For Dixon and Kozel, performance translates into an emerging state, a deep interconnection [4, 9]. For Fred Forest, art maintains close relationships with reality and seeks to use its influence to modify its properties [10]. Contemporary art sets the scenery for a body exploration based on movements, actions, and behaviors.

1.2 Virtual Reality and Embodiment

In the 1960s, Morton Heilig created the Sensorama device, a machine that is one of the earliest known examples of technology [11]. Ivan Sutherland, in paper entitled 'The ultimate display', written in 1965, reinforces the idea of the display connected to a digital computer that gives us the chance to become familiar with concepts not feasible in the physical world, describing a room within which the computer can control the existence of matter [12, 13]. In the 1980s, Scott Fisher, founder and director of NASA's Virtual Environment Workstation Project (VIEW), worked on prototypes to help users, such as pilots, make better estimates of spatial relationships on 2D monitors and developed specific capacitor monitors (HMDs) at the Ames Research Center [14].

Artist and researcher Jaron Lanier claim to have used the term Virtual Reality (VR) for the first time, in the 1980s, during a period of intense creative activity, which narrates how to enter a new world [15]. He described it as a computer-simulated environment with, and within, people interact, classifying it as one of the greatest scientific, philosophical, and technological frontiers of our era [16]. Of the definitions found in the several decades, VR, generally, can consist of three types of systems: virtual environments presented on the screen, environments based on multi-projection rooms (CAVE systems[4]) and visualization devices placed on the heads of people designated as Head Mounted Displays (HMDs) [17–22].

In the last twenty years, and with the evolution of technology, immersive vision devices with sufficient resolution have emerged so that we can visualize generated worlds, and we will probably witness a revolution in human interaction with virtual reality technology and the environment in the next decade [23]. However, the foundations of this technology are more than 50 years old. There are references in 1938 to the term "La realité virtuelle" by Antonin Artaud in theater contexts [24]. This emerging medium's impact is now beginning to be felt more in society in general, since in recent years, computational processing power to render binocular images with resolution and acceptable refresh rate to human beings, without causing nausea, become more possible.

The notion of presence is relevant as a mediating variable between experience and induced emotions [25, 26]. Precisely, what distinguishes VR from other mediums and gives it this status as such, is a sense of presence: the feeling of "being there", within the virtual experience produced by the artifact [17]. The feeling of presence, associated with the high level of emotional involvement, allowed by virtual experiences, makes VR technology a powerful tool for exploring what is possible to imagine, supporting personal and clinical changes [27]. In this sense, this "new" medium can be considered quite distinct from other mediums, such as video, and in this distinction comes the

---

[4] Cave Automatic Virtual Environment.

concept of teleportation, a transition to a remote location [28]. Thus, these devices allow us to consider the hypothesis that mediated perception (with a tool) and non-mediated perception (with a sensory organ) follow similar mechanisms of appropriation [29]. In the following section, we present three different dance pieces involving digital technologies, been developed over the past ten years.

2 Three Performances Exploring the Concept of Embodiment in Virtuality

The three pieces we will explore have something relevant in common for our analysis: they were created by a group of people who worked together, that is, by the same team. However, the three pieces were made at different times and used different technologies that have evolved and are related to varying degrees of immersion inside the performance. We also highlight a growing approach to the immaterial body in a constant virtuality progression in these three pieces. In this way, it makes sense to group the three works in this essay.

The relationship between materiality and immateriality mediated by technology, from the interface, is very well explained by Milgram's research, which proposes the concept of "bilateral continuity" between several layers of abstraction between reality and virtuality (Fig. 2). The different degrees of immersion in the three works will be analyzed, taking as a starting point the concept of Virtual Continuum, postulated by Milgram et al. [30] in his publication "Augmented Reality: A class of displays on the reality-virtuality continuum", written in 1994.

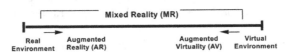

Fig. 2. The concept of *Reality-Virtuality (RV) Continuum* proposed by Milgram et al.

In this essay, Milgram contextualizes the Reality-Virtuality Continuum, which ranges from authentic environments to completely virtual environments, presenting specific taxonomies for each immersion level from the *unmodeled world* (real) to the *completely modeled world* generated by computers (Fig. 3).

Fig. 3. Taxonomies in the *Reality-Virtual Continuum* by Milgram et al. *Extent of World Knowledge.*

The works NUVE[5] [31], introduced in 2010; Co:Lateral[6] [32], presented in 2016; and UNA[7], presented in 2020, will be subject to our analysis.

2.1 Nuve (2010)

NUVE is an artistic project that explores the artistic possibilities offered by the digital dance performances in the interaction between the individual and his virtual double. In NUVE (Fig. 4) we conceptualized, developed, and implemented a digital artifact, resulting in a digital fluid performance based on the analog body's theme versus the digital virtual body [2].

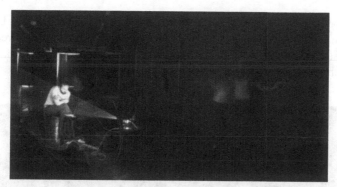

Fig. 4. Rehearsal by Né Barros and João Martinho Moura at the black box of Balleteatro, Porto. 2009.

In NUVE, the body is the principal motor of activity. However, the choreographic body advances into a connection with its own "virtual twofold" in an approach to make a discourse, testing the choreographic limits and adding new measurements to the motion. We were much inspired by pioneering works in the 1980s by Myron W. Krueger [33], Jeffrey Shaw [34], and Maurice Benayoun [35]. In NUVE (Figs. 5, 6), the "virtual body" separates itself from the performer at some phase in the performance, and de-embodiment processes happen. NUVE was created with openframeworks[8], an open-source C++ programming language toolbox. At that time, before the Kinect interface, no depth extraction was easily possible. The work depended on an infrared firewire camera to catch the stage's picture at 25 frames per second. Properly infrared lights were used to get the ideal image of the dancer. The audience could not see the infrared light in the dark. A blend of standard picture handling procedures was then used to catch the outline and the performer's movement [31].

At certain moments during the movement, the dancer's gestures entered in a feedback loop with itself, provoking reactions in the visual environment and sound. This consistent

---

[5] https://jmartinho.net/nuve/.

[6] https://jmartinho.net/colateral/.

[7] https://jmartinho.net/una/.

[8] https://openframeworks.cc/.

Fig. 5. First presentation of NUVE in 2010 at *Quintas de Leitura*, Teatro Municipal do Porto - Campo Alegre. Balleteatro.

cooperation between the full body and the virtual imagery is conceivable by figuring the distinctive speed of the various parts of the body and space. Initially rehearsed in 2009, and firstly presented in 2010, this solo, interpreted by Né Barros, was the motif for several publications [2, 31, 36].

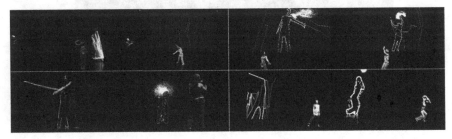

Fig. 6. NUVE. Presentation at Balleteatro auditorium, in Porto, 2010.

2.2 Co:Lateral (2016)

Co:Lateral was developed from the NUVE artwork, a project for performance and digital art. Here, the body was projected and extended itself in a relationship of intimacy with interactive virtual reality. The performative discourse resulting from this connection calls for a poetic moment made of a mixture of realities, made of body, double, and images [37]. Co:Lateral evokes moments of the death of the swan immersed in an immaterial space of light and projection: a phantom of the archive of dance now returns to test itself in a reality of illusory imprisonment. The dialogue between digital art and performance allowed us to generate a communicative space that challenges choreography limits, recapturing gesture and movement, and creating a space for experimentation with new performative possibilities [37].

In Co:Lateral, the body capture is performed through two depth cameras, and tests were performed with different models [38–40] between 2015 and 2019. Specific software was developed for the different scenes, using C++ and openframeworks platform [41], Processing [42], OpenCV [43], applying different computer vision techniques, for example, background subtraction [44] and the optical flow, to capture the different directions where each body parts move, individually. Hence, it is a generative drawing that follows one body in motion, thought space, and time. Using the Lucas-Kanade algorithm [45], accelerations are perceived, and different movement causes appropriate forces in the environment. This visual abstraction causes a noteworthy convergence of generative draws, which makes the idea of the human figure to be seen drawn during the performance [46].

In the first moments, only two-dimensional representations of the moving body (Fig. 7) are projected.

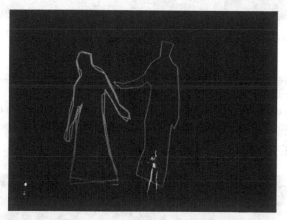

Fig. 7. Co:Lateral. Two-dimensional representations of the moving body. Né Barros and João Martinho Moura. Balleteatro, Porto. 2016.

The piece, initially performed by Sara Marú in 2016 and by Sónia Cunha in the next years, evoked the movement's distorted memory. Let's imagine that someone is drawing a moving figure and that the drawing reflects the current position, but, at the same time, the immediately preceding performer's postures. The software presented a body with minimum connected possible lines and confronted the dancer with herself moments earlier. The image was projected in the middle of the stage, between audience and performer, on a transparent screen called *tulle*. This transparency creates a translucid illusion in the audience that the image is closer. At the same time, the dancer is behind, illuminated by a small light beamer (Figs. 7, 8). When we do not project, the audience sees only the dancer. When the algorithms begin to project images, those appear in her front, physically separated by 2 or 3 m, a poetic visual moment that enhances the dialogue between movement and the imaginary that it represents. This presentation scenario has enabled several possibilities that could not exist in the previous work. In Co:Lateral, the dancer played herself moments ago. The audience watched several moving personas recreated in a continuous loop in the visual environment (Fig. 8).

Later, at certain moments, we turn on the Z depth coordinate, which allows us to obtain more information, such as the body parts closest to the audience. Jaron Lanier was one of the first artists to use gestures in electronic art with a device called Z-Glove, and used the hand in virtual environments to manipulate virtual objects that appeared

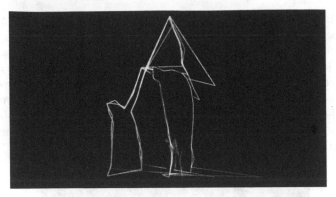

Fig. 8. Co:Lateral. Presentation at Coliseu do Porto, in 2017.

in an image, suggesting, at the time, a broad spectrum of possibilities of representing objects in virtual environments of interaction.

In Fig. 9, we see a moment in which the performer draws, literally in the air, a gesture that materializes the letter N (of the word "no"), projected between the performer and the audience.

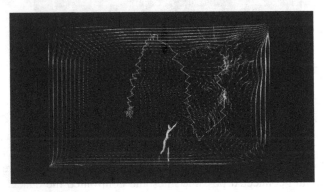

Fig. 9. Co:Lateral. Performer Sónia Cunha drawing letters on screen. Presentation at Teatro Virgínia, Torres Novas, in 2018.

Throughout the performance, gestures are continuously analyzed, and specific scenarios consider the piece's interactive narrative. We opted to process the original camera signal and not processed body points for the output visualization, as is quite traditional in body-tracking techniques for avatars' recreation. We believed that the depth camera's signal is entirely relevant to represent the performer's body, as it is. In computing history, we have accustomed computers to immediately recognize human beings, whether through body detection [47] or facial analysis [48]. These mappings are sometimes not enough to describe the richness of detail in the subtle and artistic movement. There's such rich information between shoulders and arms, harms and hands, head, neck, and chest, that point marking systems cannot catch. Figure 10 shows a relevant moment, where the performer gently 'touches' many white vertical bars, initially well marked, rigid, symbolizing a prison. After the interaction, lines react smoothly to virtual touch, immaterial, in fact, but real in the imaginary of the audience. With timed and more vigorous movements, the bars end up forming a volumetric image of the moving body.

Fig. 10. Co:Lateral. The white bars end up, forming a volumetric image of the moving body. Presentation at Art and Tech Days, in Kosice, Slovakia, in 2019.

In the preparation of the Co:Lateral work, we had the opportunity to explore the three-dimensional body on stage, using multiple depth cameras. With the necessary spatial calibration, the body was recreated and presented volumetrically. Different aggregations of points demonstrate the fragile, even in low detail resolution, of the female body in motion (Figs. 11,12 and 13).

Fig. 11. Volumetric fragile body in Co:Lateral. 2016.

This piece has been active for four years, and so has undergone enough developments in its course of presentations. It was presented in several theaters and stages.

In the various communications we made with the public, we felt that this approach to the stage equipped corporality's performance, difficult to achieve without media art technologies. This volumetric body had more and more enhancement in presentations between 2017 and 2019. Several trials were conducted to show it in its fullness. In the following images, we can see frames of motion sequences obtained from rehearsals and performances. Videos can also be observed online[9].

---

[9] https://jmartinho.net/colateral/.

Fig. 12. Presentation at *Arquipelago*, in Açores, and Temp d'Images, in Lisbon.

Fig. 13. Sequences of motion in Co:Lateral. Presentation at Temp d'Images, in Lisbon, Portugal, 2019.

During Balleteatro's 37 years of existence, Co:Lateral was one of the most presented performance, having been selected for EAI ArtsIT 2018[10] artistic venue, in Braga, celebrating the UNESCO Braga Media Arts initiative, for ISEA 2019[11], in Gwangju, South Korea, as research, for Temp d'Images Festival in Lisbon[12], Portugal, and Art and Tech Days[13] in Košice, Slovakia.

2.3 Una (2020)

In the rehearsals of Co:Lateral, we asked ourselves what if we could see that volumetric body in total immersion in VR. This question was a *leitmotiv* for creating the next work, UNA, planed at Balleteatro in 2018, as a trial in total immersion, and firstly presented in 2020 (Fig. 14). In NUVE, performed by Né Barros in 2010, the relationship between the choreographic body and its artificial double was explored, in the space-time, projected, and extended in an intimate relationship with the virtual. In Co:Lateral (2016), the immaterial space expanded, the image became closer to the public, and between the moving body and the audience, transparent, mixed, embodied realities were presented. UNA is a possible continuation of this immateriality, this time, in total immersion, where the audience (one spectator at a time) witnesses the body in movement, again, expanding. Ten years after NUVE, one goes back to testing, to the laboratory, transforming and

---

[10] https://artsit.eai-conferences.org/2018/program-at-a-glance/.

[11] https://isea2019.isea-international.org/.

[12] https://www.tempsdimages-portugal.com/2019/show-item/colateral/.

[13] https://2019.atdays.sk/.

questioning the performative and embodied space, where the spectator is one, is not in the audience, but in the center, in a space that does not exist, and where different understandings of the performative body are reflected [49].

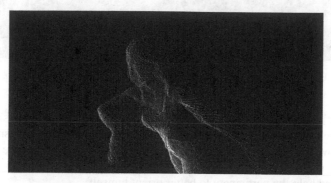

Fig. 14. UNA (2020). Né Barros performing in virtual reality. Balleteatro, Porto. 2019.

When using virtual reality, we noticed that many experimenters needed some initial time to get used to the technology. The performance was announced as an experimental trial. The audience was explicitly told that it would take about 5 to 8 min. Even though this information was made aware by the public, only at the venue, they felt that they would be teleported to another space, one by one. In this way, the spectator enters the Coliseu, stays in a waiting room, an antechamber, waiting for his/her turn. When called, the participant moves into the middle of a selected room, being received by an assistant, who explains that the performance will take place in total immersion and provides assistance in placing the equipment. In this room, Né Barros is positioned laterally, serene, and calm. Silence is total. There's no big audience, only one spectator and one performer, and a room assistant. Headphones with noise cancellation are also correctly placed in the participant's head. These headphones have two microphones that capture all the outside sound, invert the signal, and make the viewer hear nothing except the performance's sounds. When the viewer opens his eyes, an abstract representation of the room appears. This representation is minimal and only serves to place the viewer in space. The participant is still there. In the first experiments, this teleportation happened quickly, and many viewers did not adapt well to the change. So, in a second experiment, we decided to digitize the entire rehearsal room (*Sala Dois*) of the Coliseu do Porto. Thus, when the participant puts on the helmet, the space he sees is an abstract representation of the area where he is, in reality. Looking sideways, they realize themselves inside the Coliseu. This smoother transition between real and digital gives the participant the time needed to adapt to the headset's images. Not everyone feels at ease when experiencing virtual reality, as that equipment cause disorientation or nausea sometimes. So, the assistant is always present. After a minute, the participant is gently elevated to a virtual height of about 1km, thus leaving Porto's city and begins to see a different scenario, the one where performance begins (Fig. 15).

This elevation is accompanied by real wind. We put a fan on stage pointed to the participant, triggered at the elevation moment. This physical sensation caused chills in

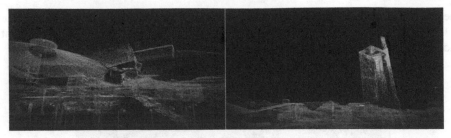

Fig. 15. UNA (2020). City of Porto and Coliseu do Porto. Balleteatro, Porto. 2020.

the participant's skin when they felt taken to immaterial space. Né Barros thus approaches the capture area and places herself in the fetal position (Fig. 16). Its body shape begins to appear, slowly. All movements happen steadily, as the participant has the freedom to look everywhere and may not be in the performer's frontal position (Fig. 17). Indications in spatial sound help the participant to better orient himself.

Né Barros gently approaches the participant and begins to gesture. The participant realizes there is a body nearby. In this scenario, there is no traditional physical barrier between the stage and the audience, as in previous works. The notion of performative space is challenged.

Fig. 16. UNA (2020). Né Barros performing in virtual reality. Balleteatro, Porto. 2020.

The participant can also move in an area of 3 square meters. Furthermore, can approach a few centimeters from the performer or even incorporate her, depending on its position in space. The artist hugs the participant, touching him, virtually, positioning herself in front of the depth sensor (Fig. 18).

At the final moment, the participants return to the place where they started. Né Barros positions herself laterally to the participant and held out her hand (Fig. 19). The

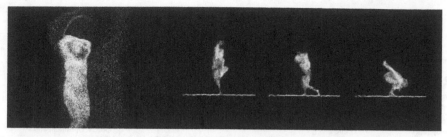

Fig. 17. UNA (2020). Né Barros performing in virtual reality. Frontal view in virtual reality. Balleteatro, Porto. 2020.

Fig. 18. UNA (2020). View from participants' perspectives in different positions. Balleteatro, Coliseu do Porto. 2020.

headset's virtual camera moves smoothly to a side position to capture both the participant and the performer's bodies. She approaches very slowly. And then something unexpected happens, hands touch. The feeling of physical belonging happens. It was a remarkable moment for the Balleteatro, a long journey in this sequence of works related to the digital embodiment. Informal conversations with about 20 participants immediately after the performance presentation show that they felt embrace and bodily involved.

This work was presented two times in 2020[14], the last one happening days before the COVID pandemic lockdown. After March, all the following exhibitions were postponed as embodied virtual reality between participants is very intimate. After the pandemic restrictions, we plan to return to new exhibitions (Table 1).

Fig. 19. UNA (2020). Rehearsals and experiences with participants in virtual reality. Tests with touch between performer and participant. On the right: João Martinho Moura and Né Barros at Coliseu do Porto. Balleteatro. 2020.

---

[14] https://www.dgartes.gov.pt/pt/evento/2966.

Table 1. Comparison between NUVE (2010), Co:Lateral (2016), and UNA (2020).

Parameters	NUVE (2010)	Co:Lateral (2016)	UNA (2020)
Canvas/Display	Wall behind the performer. Frontal or retro video projection	Transparent textile between performer and audience. Frontal video projection	Total immersion inside head-mounted display (HMD)
Computer vision to acquire the performer's body	Infrared lights with one RGB modified camera	Two Microsoft Kinect and/or Intel Realsense	Three Microsoft Kinect Azure
Software platforms for development	Processing. Openframeworks. OpenCV	Openframeworks. OpenCV	Unity3D. Kinect Azure SDK. OpenCV. Openframeworks
Immersion (performer's perspective)	Low (image behind the body, need to use a live auxiliary screen at the stage)	High (image in front of the performer, causing a good sense of embodiment)	Low (when performer dresses HMD, sees his body in VR). Additional debug information necessary to fulfill auto-control
Immersion (audience perspective)	Low	High	Total immersion
Difficulty for the artist to perform	High	Low	Very High
Stage	Auditorium	Auditorium with enough space for a transparent screen between performer and audience	Room, space inside a gallery, or stage
Audience capacity	Auditorium capacity (average of 200 attendees in 5 performances)	Auditorium capacity, with adaption to place transparent screen (average of 100 attendees in 14 performances)	One person for each HMD for each performance. Participants have to stand in line in a waiting room
Attention and focus required by the audience	Medium. Due to the high feeling about auditorium space, other public, noises, security, and low lights	High. Due to total darkness in the auditorium, caused by short distance image, sometimes participants are lost against the physical and holographic reality	Very high. The attendee needs total focus to catch the performance in 360º. Sometimes performance is required to be repeated for the same participant
Maximum duration of performance	45 min	25 min	8 min
Repetition of performance	One time for each date/venue	One time for each date/venue	Several times for each date/venue (average of 30 repetitions per venue)
Milgram Reality-Virtuality Continuum classification	*Augmented Reality (AR).* Digital is superimposed on the real	*Augmented Virtuality (AV) Virtual.* Digital happens from the real	*Virtual Environment.* Total immersion

3   Conclusions

The three pieces presented at the different moments in the last decade have as their central element one body, immaterial, always associated with the physical body that materializes it. Moreover, this body, educated for performance, is crucial for its expressiveness to be transposed to the digital narrative. Looking chronologically at the pieces, we quickly realized the technology itself influenced their creation, and, indeed, also limited or reinforced specific components that we will now analyze. Throughout this process, the body has been dematerializing. Although increasingly digital, it remains well present, and its physicality has never been called into question. The image was approaching the audience more and more to the limit of the senses. If in NUVE the image was behind the dancer, in Co:Lateral was in-between the performer and the audience, and, in UNA, the image became mixed with the audience. The presentation models also changed significantly between NUVE, Co:Lateral, and UNA, the space for the audience decreased, with more space for imagery. We have reached a point where one performance is presented to one participant at a time. The performer's difficulty increased significantly as we entered total virtuality, which was notable in fatigue after presentations. As for the audience, it became increasingly immersed along with the different performance presentations. We noticed that this greater immersion requires a doubled public attention, especially when we advance on virtuality degrees. As the three pieces were created in the same dance company and rehearsed with the same professionals over the last ten years, we managed to have a generalized view of the audience's receptivity. Because Balleteatro houses many students and the local artistic community in Porto, in many cases, some participants attended the three pieces in different years. We obtained continued feedback from these individuals, which reinforces what we mention in this conclusion. In the next table, we group and compare the three works by different parameters:

Returning to the idea presented at the beginning of this publication, the three works converge to Milgram's concept of *Reality-Virtuality Continuum* presented in the 90's, which we associate in this essay with embodied performance in virtual reality. These works were relevant in Balleteatro history, an institution that accompanied many developments and changes in artistic performance over the last four decades.

NUVE, Co:Lateral and UNA allow mapping an evolution of a relationship between performer and visualization. On this map, it is possible to locate the performing body, not in absolute physical presence but performativity's most profound dimension. In other words, the cartography of the choreographic gesture is drawn through its dynamic qualities captured and transformed by the technological device, and recreate new and diverse entities. It is no longer so much about thinking about technoculture through the mutation in the perception of performing arts but about perceiving these entities' impact on the ontology of performance. If in NUVE, the gesture expands and, in doing so, creates a new scenario for the performer, in Co:Lateral, the entire performative space is taken by the visualization of the expanded gesture. There is no scenario, but, rather, a dynamic and interactive place. UNA breaks with the subject's barrier based on a principle of double immersion of the performer and the receiver and the performer with himself. In this virtual dimension, the performer's experience is itself of embodiment: the performer moves through the perception of the movement he generates. There is an experience of duplication, of unfolding between physical body and gesture. If in previous works one could also speak of incorporation, be it through the experience of expanding the scenario to a body (NUVE), or through the recreation of an interactive place where the presence of the physical body gives way to the virtual presence (Co:Lateral), in NUVE the embodiment is revealed through a hypersensitive experience of displacement of the gesture. In UNA, the possibility of mapping the ballast of the gesture is achieved. It is no longer the gesture gathered by the memory of an image, but by a kinesthetic experience of the movement reinforced and offered by a type of visualization that the technological device allows performing.

In addition to these aspects that affect and challenge choreographic thinking, there is another of great importance: memory rewrites time. In any of the projects, the gesture's visualization is the product of adequate control of its execution. Survival, which defines the condition of the gesture's ephemerality, is revealed in this partnership (performer and digital media) as a very concrete condition in the production of a performative discourse. The control of forms that can become chaotic or constructing a choreographic nexus is hostage to a micro dialogue between executed gesture and visualization. There is a strong relationship between micro and macro and the possibility of working with the gesture's memory through decalage effects. In Co:Lateral, the work on the gesture's memory, where present gesture dialogues with the past gesture, reveals the vital principle of constructing the choreographic work. In the end, a kind of death, given by a three-dimensional image, symbolizes a journey of memory, of inner dialogue or, in another perspective, of a monad. All the incursions that these projects promote put performance and performativity necessarily in tension with the notion of presence or interaction, preferring an expanded domain as a territory for exploration and contact.

Acknowledgments. We are grateful to the entire Balleteatro technical and producing team that has supported the three projects described in this paper over the past ten years. To the research center CITAR (Research Center in Science and Technology of the Arts), School of Arts, Universidade Católica Portuguesa. To Casa Rolão in Braga for the space for some rehearsals. To the UNESCO Braga Media Arts organization, for the support in part of some equipment. To the EAI ArtsIT 2018 conference organization, in Braga. We would also like to thank the University of Minho's engageLab laboratory for all the NUVE performance support in 2010. We also acknowledge the Openframeworks, OpenCV and Unity communities always very supportive in the on-line forums. Co:Lateral had the support of Direção Geral das Artes (https://www.dgartes.gov.pt/pt/noticia/2758).

References

1. Blades, H., DeLahunta, S.: Digital aptitude - finding the right questions for dance studies. Routledge Int. Handbook Res. Methods Digit. Human. **31**–45, (2020). https://doi.org/10.4324/9780429777028-4
2. Moura, J.M., Marcos, A., Barros, N., Branco, P.: NUVE: resizing the digital gesture. Int. J. Creative Interfaces Comput. Graph. **5**, 87–100 (2014). https://doi.org/10.4018/ijcicg.2014070106
3. Leach, J.: Choreographic objects: contemporary dance, digital creations and prototyping social visibility. J. Cult. Econ. **7**, 458–475 (2014). https://doi.org/10.1080/17530350.2013.858058
4. Kozel, S.: Closer: Performance, Technologies, Phenomenology. MIT Press, Leonardo Book Series (2007)
5. Cisneros, R.E., Wood, K., Whatley, S., et al.: Virtual reality and choreographic practice: the potential for new creative methods. Body Space Technol. **18**, 1–32. https://doi.org/10.16995/bst.305
6. Brooks, A.L.: Body Electric and Reality Feedback loops: Virtual Interactive Space & Entertainment Potentials. South Korea (2004)
7. Brooks, A.L.: Virtual Interactive Space (VIS): creating a unique dynamic HCI ludic engaging design (apparatus/method) for human performance and (re)habilitation. In: Antona, M., Stephanidis, C. (eds.) UAHCI 2015. LNCS, vol. 9176, pp. 419–427. Springer, Cham (2015). https://doi.org/10.1007/978-3-319-20681-3_39
8. Saltz, D.Z.: The art of interaction: interactivity, performativity, and computers. J. Aesthet. Art Critic. **55**, 117–127 (1997). https://doi.org/10.2307/431258
9. Dixon, S.: Digital Performance: A History of New Media in Theater, Dance, Performance Art, and Installation. MIT Press (2007)

10. Forest, F., Sugarman, D., Weston, J.: Communication esthetics, interactive participation and artistic systems of communication and expression. Des. Issues **4**, 97–115 (1988). https://doi.org/10.2307/1511394

11. Heilig, M.L.: Sensorama U.S. Patent No. 3,050,870. 870 (1962)

12. Sutherland, I.E.: The ultimate display. In: Proceedings of the Congress of the Internation Federation of Information Processing (IFIP), pp. 506–508 (1965)

13. Moura, J.M., Kolen'ko, Y.: Sci-fi Miners: a virtual reality journey to the nanocluster scale. In: Proceedings of the 9th International Conference on Digital and Interactive Arts, pp. 1–10 (2019). https://doi.org/10.1145/3359852.3359912

14. Fisher, S.S.: The NASA ames VIEWlab Project-A brief history. Presence: Teleoperators Virtual Environ. **25**, 339–348 (2016). https://doi.org/10.1162/PRES_a_00277

15. Lanier, J.: Virtually there. Sci. Am. **284**, 66–75 (2001)

16. Lanier, J.: Dawn of the New Everything : A Journey Through Virtual Reality. Bodley Head (2017)

17. Steuer, J.: Defining virtual reality: dimensions determining telepresence. J. Commun. **42**, 73–93 (1992). https://doi.org/10.1111/j.1460-2466.1992.tb00812.x

18. Gigante, M.A.: Virtual reality: definitions. History Appl. Virtual Reality Syst. **3–14**, (1993). https://doi.org/10.1016/b978-0-12-227748-1.50009-3

19. Cruz-Neira, C., Sandin, D.J., DeFanti, T.A.: Surround-screen projection-based virtual reality: the design and implementation of the CAVE. In: Proceedings of the 20th Annual Conference on Computer Graphics and Interactive Techniques, SIGGRAPH 1993, pp. 135–142 (1993). https://doi.org/10.1145/166117.166134

20. Swanson, K.: Second life: a science library presence in virtual reality. Sci. Technol. Libr. **27**, 79–86 (2007). https://doi.org/10.1300/J122v27n03_06

21. Mazuryk, T., Gervautz, M.: Virtual Reality History. Applications, Technology and Future (1999)

22. Grau, O.: On the Visual Power of Digital Arts. For a New Archive and Museum Infrastructure in the 21st Century. Ediciones de la Universidad de Castilla-La Mancha (2016)

23. Shi, J., Honjo, T., Zhang, K., Furuya, K.: Using virtual reality to assess landscape: a comparative study between on-site survey and virtual reality of aesthetic preference and landscape cognition. Sustainability **12**, 1–6 (2020). https://doi.org/10.3390/su12072875

24. Jamieson, H.V.: Adventures in cyberformance - experiments at the interface of theatre and the internet. Queensland University of Technology (2008)

25. Riva, G., Mantovani, F., Capideville, C.S., et al.: Affective interactions using virtual reality: the link between presence and emotions. Cyberpsychol. Behav. **10**, 45–56 (2007). https://doi.org/10.1089/cpb.2006.9993

26. Baños, R.M., Botella, C., Alcañiz, M., et al.: Immersion and emotion: their impact on the sense of presence. Cyberpsychol. Behav. **7**, 734–741 (2004). https://doi.org/10.1089/cpb.2004.7.734

27. Riva, G.: Virtual Reality. The Palgrave Encyclopedia of the Possible **1–10**, (2020). https://doi.org/10.1007/978-3-319-98390-5_34-1

28. Loomis, J.M.: Distal Attribution and Presence. Presence: Teleoperators Virtual Environ. **1**, 113–119 (1992). https://doi.org/10.1162/pres.1992.1.1.113

29. Auvray, M., Hanneton, S., Lenay, C., O'Regan, K.: There is something out there: distal attributtion in sensory substitution, twenty years later. J. Integr. Neurosci. **4**, 505–521 (2005). https://doi.org/10.1142/S0219635205001002

30. Milgram, P., Takemura, H., Utsumi, A., Kishino, F.: Augmented reality : a class of displays on the reality - virtuality continuum. Syst. Res. **2351**, 1–2 (1994). https://doi.org/10.1117/12.197321

31. Moura, J.M., Marcos, A.F., Barros, N., Branco, P.: NUVE: in between the analog and virtual body. In: Proceedings of 5th International Conference Tangible Embedded Embodied Interact TEI 2011 (2011). https://doi.org/10.1145/1935701.1935804

32. Moura, J.M., Barros, N., Ferreira-Lopes, P.: Co: Lateral – realidades e virtualidades incorporadas. In: Vilela, E., Barros, N. (eds.) Performances no Contemporâneo, Coleção Es, pp. 179–198. Faculdade de Letras da Universidade do Porto, Politics and Knowledge Research Group, Instituto de Filosofia, Universidade do Porto, Porto (2018)

33. Krueger, M.W., Gionfriddo, T., Hinrichsen, K.: VIDEOPLACE - an artificial reality. In: Proceedings of the SIGCHI Conference on Human Factors in Computing Systems - CHI 1985, pp. 35–43 (1985). https://doi.org/10.1145/1165385.317463

34. Buscher, M., Hughes, J., O'Brien, J., Rodden, T.: Presence and Representation in Multimedia Art and Electronic Landscapes. The eSCAPE Project (1998)

35. Benayoun, M.: World Skin, A Photo Safari In The Land Of War By Maurice Benayoun - ADA | Archive Of Digital Art. https://www.digitalartarchive.at/database/general/work/world-skin.html. Accessed 6 May 2020

36. Moura, J.M.: A Dança como Performance Digital: O Projeto NUVE. Universidade do Minho (2012)

37. Moura, J.M., Barros, N., Ferreira-Lopes, P.: From real to virtual embodied performance-a case study between dance and technology. In: Park, J., Nam, J., Park, J.W. (eds.) Proceedings of the 25th International Symposium on Electronic Art (ISEA 2019). ISEA International, Gwangju, pp 370–377 (2019)

38. Microsoft: Kinect. https://pt.wikipedia.org/wiki/Kinect(2010)

39. Orbbec: Orbbec – Intelligent computing for everyone everywhere (2018). https://orbbec3d.com/. Accessed 21 Nov 2018

40. INTEL Intel®'s RealSense^{TM}. https://www.intelrealsense.com/. Accessed 21 Nov 2019

41. Lieberman, Z., Castro, A., Community, O.: Openframeworks (2004). https://openframeworks.cc

42. Fry, B., Reas, C.: Processing.org. In: Processing (2001). https://processing.org/

43. Bradski, G.: The OpenCV Library. Dr Dobb's J Softw Tools (2000)

44. OpenCV Community OpenCV: Background Subtraction. https://docs.opencv.org/3.4/db/d5c/tutorial_py_bg_subtraction.html. Accessed 21 Nov 2018

45. Bruhn, A., Weickert, J., Schnörr, C.: Lucas/Kanade meets Horn/Schunck: combining local and global optic flow methods. Int. J. Comput. Vision **61**, 1–21 (2005). https://doi.org/10.1023/B:VISI.0000045324.43199.43

46. Moura, J.M., Sousa, J., Branco, P., Marcos, A.F.: You move you interact : a full-body dance in-between reality and virtuality. In: Barbosa, Á., Marcos, A. (ed.) ARTECH 2008 : Proceedings of the 4th International Conference on Digital Arts. Universidade Católica Portuguesa, pp. 49–54 (2008)

47. Albert, J.A., Owolabi, V., Gebel, A., et al.: Evaluation of the pose tracking performance of the azure kinect and kinect v2 for gait analysis in comparison with a gold standard: a pilot study. Sensors (Switzerland) **20**, 1–22 (2020). https://doi.org/10.3390/s20185104

48. Moura, J.M., Ferreira-Lopes, P.: Generative Face from Random Data, on How Computers Imagine Humans. In: Proceedings of the 8th International Conference on Digital Arts – ARTECH 2017, pp. 85–91 (2017). https://doi.org/10.1145/3106548.3106605

49. Moura, J.M., Barros, N., Ferreira-Lopes, P.: UNA (by Né Barros and João Martinho Moura, 2020) | João Martinho Moura. https://jmartinho.net/una/. Accessed 6 Aug 2020

Designing Context-Aware Mobile Systems for Self-guided Exhibition Sites

Rameshnath Krishnasamy$^{(\boxtimes)}$ ⓘ, Vashanth Selvadurai ⓘ, and Peter Vistisen ⓘ

Department of Communication and Psychology, Aalborg University, Aalborg, Denmark
{krishnasamy,vashanth,vistisen}@hum.aau.dk

Abstract. This study examines the design of digital systems created to support users in self-guided exhibitions (i.e., sites without human personnel to support the users). We developed a location-aware smartphone guide called *Aratag*, which utilizes Bluetooth beacons to serve contextual information at the user's request. Using this guide, we conducted a user study to investigate what types of content institutions perceive as relevant versus the kinds of content users actually find relevant. The study also contributes to our understanding of users' attitudes toward using smartphones to support their self-guidance in exhibitions. Our results provide insights into designing for interplay between the physical setting of the exhibition and the digital platform, so as to inform the utility, desirability, and usability of mobile guides. Based on these findings, we present the following two design insights that should be considered when designing future mobile systems for self-guidance in exhibitions: 1) multi-level content to accommodate individual user interest by scaffolding information layers from glimpses to an increasingly immersive experience and 2) real-time location tracking with clear visual feedback.

Keywords: Mobile guide · Human–computer interaction · Exhibition site · Context-aware · User experience · Self-guided

1 Introduction

Mobile guides have become synonymous with communication technology relevant to exhibitions ever since the first electronic audio guide was presented at Amsterdam's Stedelijk Museum in 1952. This guide was a shortwave radio system that used a handheld receiver with a connected headset, approximately the size of a current-day smartphone, to link the user to the exhibits through voice-recorded expositions of presented items [1]. Since the introduction of such technologies for exhibitions, the long and tempestuous history of technology's role in this context has shaped present-day usage. In some cases, the technologies are perceived as being disruptive for the social experience and thus as detrimental to the overall visiting experience [2, 3]. In other cases, such technologies can provide interactive experiences that support users in social and practical situations [4, 5] and even attract new users with novel ways of experiencing exhibitions [6–8].

© ICST Institute for Computer Sciences, Social Informatics and Telecommunications Engineering 2021
Published by Springer Nature Switzerland AG 2021. All Rights Reserved
A. Brooks et al. (Eds.): ArtsIT 2020, LNICST 367, pp. 21–44, 2021.
https://doi.org/10.1007/978-3-030-73426-8_2

This study began as a collaborative design process among five diverse institutions, namely, cultural heritage sites, museums, zoos, and outdoor nature parks responsible for attractions and exhibition sites around Denmark. One of the (perceived) key challenges articulated by the participating institutions was wayfinding. The desire to devise a wayfinding solution by introducing self-guided systems, such as a mobile application, was tempered by concerns about negatively impacting visitor experience. Many exhibition sites have "so much" content that some users experience it as "noise," which could contribute to physical fatigue [9]. Adding another digital layer could easily be perceived as "more noise." Further, many exhibitions are very authentic and visceral, and the governing institutions do not desire digital tools or experience designs to take center stage. A comparative study [10] addressed visitors' preferences of how to deliver the same content across a mobile phone application, smart cards, and smart replicas: cards and replicas were favored by visitors of all ages over the app [10]. However, interactions featuring tangible objects pose other challenges; their design should take into account the risk of limited lifespan due to wear and tear, replacements, sanitization protocols, and added security, which can add to the workload and cost of exhibitions.

In recent years, smart devices and mobile technologies have attracted much attention because they are context-aware technologies capable of communicating location-specific content through multiple media formats (e.g., text, audio, and video). As such, exhibitions are in a process of deep transformation as a result of these technologically mediated forms of communication [11]. However, the increased focus on new technologies does not come without criticism, as practitioners and scholars are concerned about shifting the focus on the digital technologies instead of the knowledge that is to be communicated [11, 12].

Digital technologies, however, are critical to the latter. As exhibitions have struggled to retain users and their attention throughout a visit, novel mediation techniques with a strong technological focus have been tried and tested as solutions to invite, educate, and entertain visitors. In addition, users are influenced and shaped by the technological advancements in their everyday life, which affects their perceptions and expectations of exhibitions. Thus, the "right" communication strategy at any given time will change because the specifications and requirements associated with it will also change over time, as would human–computer interaction paradigms. Accordingly, communication strategies for today's world must investigate current and future trends in technology to arrive at a new status quo that can support communication for contemporary exhibition visitors.

Studies show that digital technologies can substantiate knowledge acquisition [13–16]; however, knowledge about the educational effect of digital technologies is limited [17], and that about how visitors understand, apply, and respond to new digital technologies, even more so [18, 19]. The research arena for digital mediation in museum exhibitions is expanding, and with novel and emerging technologies, existing mediation, facilitation, and communication strategies are being re-evaluated and explored, thereby indicating the growing interest for knowledge about communication strategies via emerging digital technologies [11, 20, 21].

1.1 Mobile Exploration Systems

Today, the smartphone is a ubiquitous tool in our working and social lives. It is also used for personal entertainment [22]. It can augment, extend, and support the cognitive capacities of humans through computational capabilities that support habit changing, problem solving, learning, or performing a skill, among others [23], spanning areas such as healthcare, education, entertainment, tourism, banking, and governance. The past decade has witnessed a massive worldwide expansion in smartphone use, and the widespread adoption of these devices marks them as one of the most prominent, pervasive, and ubiquitous platforms in the world, which is evident from many recent market reports [24–26].

Lately, many sites and landmarks have experienced severe long-term challenges due to economic and political reasons [27–29]. This has led to the implementation of centralization strategies and efficiency measures, such as decommissioning smaller exhibition sites [30] or reducing the number of personnel in order to free up resources. In response to these rising challenges, institutions have considered automation and self-guided strategies (e.g., introducing mobile guides for extant exhibitions) [30]. Given the rising challenges due to budget cuts and a shift toward more automation and self-guidance, the "BYOD" or "bring your own device" concept has become part of the digital communication strategy that exhibitions are keen on implementing [31, 32]. According to existing surveys, each incremental iteration of mobile technologies helps improve and expand computational capacities and context-sensing capabilities, in turn driving topics on emerging challenges into the research arena on mobile guides [33–35].

Modern mobile phones offer a link between physical places and digital spaces because of their mobility, application ubiquity, and sensitivity to the context in which they are used [36]. This close coupling has enabled the development of many applications, both in the research and the commercial sectors. Games can penetrate the digital–physical barrier to offer new ways of exercising, for instance. A mixed reality, location-based game can target users with sedentary lifestyles to increase their physical activity through pervasive and persuasive play [37, 38]. Such games are referred to as exertion games [39]. Other mobile applications target tourism to assist exploration and guidance [40, 41]. A myriad of smartphone services and systems focus on human–exhibition interaction [42], such as the markerless augmented reality application MovieMaker [43], which uses the exhibition as a backdrop to enable users to shoot a movie with digital augmented layers to enrich their visiting experience through explorative exhibitions.

Guided tours have become an expected visitor service at exhibition sites. Although guided tours are a common feature at most exhibition sites, not nearly as much research has been devoted to this topic compared to visitor and educator studies in the context of exhibitions [44–49]. While particular types of guided tours, such as guided safaris and guided holidays [50, 51], have been explored in detail, guided tours at museums have not been studied to a similar degree [52].

As mentioned in Sect. 1, audio guides were one of the earliest examples of electronically enhanced exhibition technologies. They opened up the future of technological mediation with the change from the analog to the digital format. Although several ways exist to implement and integrate any technology, the mobility aspect continues to be a core component of exhibition-related communication.

The more recent developments in the field of digital technologies mark an aggressive expansion into context-aware guides that retain the mobility aspect while linking the user with the exhibit. Indeed, this expansion is evident in both the literature and practice. For example, the past ten years have seen an increase in research projects that utilize global positioning, Wi-Fi meshes, and Bluetooth beacons to improve or modify the user's experience through location-specific content [1, 4, 35, 52, 53]. Likewise, recent developments in augmented reality, which are supported by technology providers such as Apple and Google, have led to an abundance of mixed reality experiences in the realms of research as well as commercial services.

While the literature advocates guided tours due to their increased learning potential, it also provides critical insights into the drawbacks of such tours, as they limit users' freedom to engage with the exhibition [54, 55]. We notice a gap here that could be bridged with mobile-enabled smart guides, as seen in the system presented by Tallon and Walker [1]. Removing the role of guidance could prove detrimental to the user's experience, whereas shifting away from human-facilitated guidance could be beneficial to users who want to take control of their own visit and choose how and when they want to access information pertinent to the exhibition. Tallon and Walker presented a system that builds on the notion of exhibitions as "free-choice learning environments" [1] for visitors without any specific objectives. This is interesting because the technology imbues the user with freedom; the system offers structure as well as self-facilitated exploration of the exhibition. To the best of our knowledge, past studies on self-guided exploration tended to focus on systems such as REXplorer [56] and Kurio [7]; the technology of the time imposed a learning curve on the user and also required device maintenance. These variables have changed as an increasing number of users now own capable mobile devices and the institution's workload of maintaining devices is eliminated in self-guided situations that facilitate increased automation.

As argued by Best [52], the relevance of facilitation guidance is clearly a required attribute for exhibitions, but it is unclear how the current practice of guided tours can properly support this aspect through digital technologies [52]. It also raises the question of content preference from a user's perspective. The literature is ripe with examples of content designed around testing a specific type of technology; for instance, the past decade has seen a massive resurgence in augmented reality applications for mobiles in the exhibition space [6, 57–59]. However, we are yet to witness an updated articulation of the key aspects affecting self-guidance in exhibitions. Admittedly, a thorough analysis of the challenges presented by many of the existing services and systems could narrow this gap, but no study has investigated this topic thus far. In particular, to the best of our knowledge, none of the previous studies have examined the content preferences or preferred media modalities of content (e.g., long text, short text, audio book, and video snippet) for mobile guides from both sides of the screen; namely, users' actual preferences and the exhibition personnel's perceptions of appropriate content need to be explored. Thus, it is important to generate knowledge about how fact-based content is best delivered and communicated through this type of location-aware and mixed reality media.

1.2 Research Question and Hypotheses

The current state of art in both academia and practice suggest that mobile self-guided exhibition design is still challenging to implement successfully; the challenge lies not in creating the digital component itself, but rather in making it useful, usable, and desirable enough to ensure a widespread use by visitors. This is evident in the growing literature that investigates different mediation techniques in combination with past, current, and emerging technologies. For example, the technical limitations of Bluetooth beacons have been used as a game mechanic to offer a game experience [60]. Personalized guides that provide the user with a tailored visit through context-aware technologies have been developed [35, 61], with some aiming to extend the visiting experience by suggesting a subsequent destination for future visits [8] and others trying to implement learning via mobile systems [7]. However, a limited number of studies have investigated the design and testing of a smartphone guide with content preference. Additionally, investigations of users' attitudes toward using mobile guides in situations that require self-guidance are even more scarce; thus, insights into smartphone use in this situation are highly limited. Consequently, many questions about mobile self-guided guidance remain unanswered. We argue that the following research question is a critical part of the challenge of designing mobile guides for self-guided exhibitions: *How can digital mediation add sufficient value to promote use, and what criteria for exhibition content are preferred by guests in self-guided contexts?* To guide the exploration of these two intersecting problems, we propose the following two hypotheses:

1. The communicated content must, first and foremost, provide the visitor with a more functional dimension to support their visit (e.g., wayfinding, guidance, practical information, and discounts) if self-guidance use is expected.
2. User experiences differ depending on the media modalities of the content (e.g., long text, short text, audio book, and video snippet).

The remainder of the paper will detail how these two hypotheses are qualified through design and user testing of the mobile guiding platform "Aratag," which will be used to explore the content preferences needed to encourage use and provide value to digitally mediated self-guidance.

2 Designing "Aratag"

In 2018, the authors began a collaboration with the company Pangea Rocks to create a shared application platform for cultural heritage and zoological sites. A range of Danish exhibitions participated as "beta clients" in a series of co-design sprints and acted as field testing contexts for the development of the mobile platform [62]. The authors were actively involved throughout the process, from the first ideation workshops and the design sprints, to the first live user testing at one of the participating exhibitions. The initial workshops functioned as a discussion session with the participating organizations, the goal being to identify the requirements for the application. In particular, two potential solutions were discussed; separate applications for each organization and one application for all organizations with dedicated pages. The major disadvantage with the separate applications was the financial burden entailed in developing, updating, and sustaining an application and its content over time. Furthermore, the organizations expressed limitations in their ability to update the content continuously, which particularly underscored our research interest of examining different content preferences among visitors. In contrast, a single-platform solution offered the possibility for the organizations to focus on providing flexibility in updating their content continuously and added practical value for their visitors by enabling features such as wayfinding and the provision of practical information. In general, the single-platform solution offered the potential to leverage economies of scale by increasing the degree of onboarding across organizations.

2.1 The Aratag Application

The Aratag application is a mobile application for iOS and Android with a web-based content management system platform to create, edit, and distribute content across multiple content formats. It also provides location-aware features in exhibition contexts through both Bluetooth beacons and the global positioning system (GPS). The application is created as a multi-attraction platform, where different institutions can create their own individual "shell" to present themselves on the application's start screen.

Fig. 1. Typical user interaction scenario with Aratag in the context of an exhibition.

Aratag is a location-based application that utilizes GPS and Beacon technology to provide location-specific content to users (Fig. 1). In detail, GPS is used to position the device outdoors and trigger location-specific content in the application, while beacon technology triggers location-specific content in indoor areas. Specifically, a beacon emits a unique identification (ID) number at a given distance. This ID number is captured by a smartphone via Bluetooth and can trigger a local action in the application. While GPS technology may be limited in indoor areas, Beacon technology can be used in outdoor areas as well as indoor. Beacons are inexpensive, and battery life typically ranges from 1 to 5 years, making the technology cost-efficient and sustainable.

The Aratag application consists of a main screen presenting the different attractions the user can chose to explore (Fig. 2). Clicking on an institution provides different information to the user. The *Introduction* screen presents "Events," directing the user to select the events they want to attend. "Experiences near you" shows nearby points of interest (POI) along with an approximate distance to the location. The "Explore" tab at the bottom shows all the available experiences. "Near You" brings the users to the "Experiences near you" tab. "Map" contains a map of the location, showing the venues of the experiences in the form of POIs. The users can click on any POI on the map and see the information for that specific location. After reaching a selected POI, the user

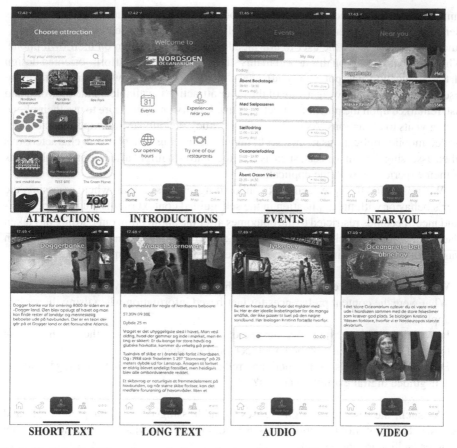

Fig. 2. Designed interfaces for wayfinding and point-of-interest (POI) discovery applications (top panel) and different tested content formats (bottom panel).

can be presented with different content, namely short text, long text, audio, and video (bottom panel in Fig. 2).

Bluetooth beacon technology is used to inform the application about the user's location. When the user approaches a specific beacon location, the distance to that specific POI decreases, and the updated distance is shown under the tab "Near You."

3   Research Design of Aratag in the Wild

The challenge of onboarding users, namely facilitating "the first use" of downloading an application and getting the users to understand and engage with it sufficiently to continue using rather than abandoning it, is an important consideration when designing mobile applications for exhibitions (e.g., [43, 63, 64]). The platform design of Aratag, namely the shell that multiple cultural institutions can share, includes the service design dimension of being usable across a multitude of different sites and attractions, with the same user interface standards, interaction modalities, and conventions for all users. This element potentially overcomes one of the oft-repeated onboarding challenges of self-guided use: persuading the user to download a mobile application on their own phone. While we do not focus on this aspect in this study, we argue the platform-oriented design of the application has potentially affected the outcome of this work, since all of the researched user groups were aware of the other attractions available on the platform and also remarked upon the potential effects this availability on their desire to use their phone during visits to attractions. As such, we do not study the onboarding experience of self-guided mobile applications in this work; rather, we leverage the platform characteristics when assessing certain aspects, such as how the platform might affect users' evaluations of their experiences with the application.

We posit that this pre-facilitated onboarding creates a bias when assessing the user's behavior with the application in the self-guided context of this study, since "self-guidance" becomes restricted to the outcomes after the application onboarding has taken place. However, we seek to account for this aspect when assessing how the evaluation was conducted by limiting our areas of concern to the following questions:

- Which content types engaged the visitor the most during their visit?
- What were the content preferences for fact-based information when using the mobile application?
- How did the visitor experience the use of the mobile app during their visit (e.g., in terms of extension, disturbance, tool, personal vs. shared device etc.)?
- How did the visitor's user experience reflect their requirements with regard to the self-guided digital exhibition design?

As such, the research design focuses on addressing the content preferences and assesses the use of mobile applications as a guiding tool for visitors when no personnel or other facilitators are present.

3.1 Applied Methods and Frameworks

The study on users' application of Aratag was conducted as a field experiment [65] at an authentic exhibition. The goal of this work was to reveal unforeseen consequences of users being allowed only a digital device to support their experience during a visit, and to observe their actual behavior, how they use the content provided, and if and when breakdowns in user experience occur. The application uses four formats to communicate information; short facts, longer text, audio, and video.

In preparation for the user studies, we created a specific experimental setup of different content types (varying text lengths, audio logs, and video presentations) and paired them with different physical locations spread around the exhibition area of the North Sea Oceanarium, one of the participating beta clients in the Aratag project. Each content page was connected to a Bluetooth beacon, prompting the user when they were near the exhibition as well as providing an approximate measure of how far they were from nearby POIs. The beacon points of interest were spread throughout the entire exhibition area to enable assessment of whether the mobile application and the location-dependent content could facilitate the visitors to move around and experience the entire exhibition area (both indoors and outdoors) without any human facilitation or guidance.

Using inputs from the curators of the North Sea Oceanarium, we enlisted seven families to participate in the field test. The enlisted families were a mix of frequent visitors (those who visited the exhibition multiple times each year), infrequent visitors (those who visited the exhibition approximately once a year), and newcomers (first-time visitors to the exhibition). The families consisted of two parents and children of varying ages, but all of them belonged to the age range of the specified target audience for the North Sea Oceanarium (Table 1).

Table 1. Details of the families that participated in the field test.

Family	Adults	Children (age)	Total number of members per family
Family 01	2	2 (6 and 8)	4
Family 02	2	2 (3 and 8)	4
Family 03	2	2 (5 and 7)	4
Family 04	2	2 (3 and 11)	4
Family 05	2	2 (10 and 12)	4
Family 06	2	2 (10 and 13)	4
Family 07	2	1 (3)	3

The families were invited to arrive at the exhibition at different times in the morning. The authors provided them with a brief introduction to the context of the exhibition and a mobile device with the Aratag application installed. The families were invited at a specified time in the afternoon to rejoin the authors for a debriefing focus group interview. Besides the short introduction, none of the families were provided with further information or a detailed walkthrough of the application. This was necessary to facilitate the use of the application and allow the families to devise their own specific strategies for pursuing location-aware content.

When each of the seven families had been briefed and started their respective journeys through the exhibition, two other authors, who were not present at the introduction, conducted contextual shadowing observations [66] by blending in among the visitors and taking field notes about important interactions, behaviors, or conversations concerning the families' interactions with the application in the exhibition. Some of these field notes were based on actual quotes made by visitors, indicating, for instance, frustration or wonder over some aspect of using Aratag. Other instances, however, involved the authors interpreting non-verbal interactions with the application as well as the social interactions of the families being observed.

The debriefing focus group interviews were conducted with four setups, one with only one family of four participating, and the remaining three with two families participating in each discussion. The focus group interviews were based on a semi-structured interview guide, following the funneling principles of Morgan [67]. Initially, open questions were asked to the family about its journey through the exhibition, before honing the discussion to clarify its opinions about specific POIs, content types, and interactions between the application, the family, and the physical exhibition. The initial broad queries were based on the four general research questions mentioned above, which were paraphrased into the interview questions [68]. The interview questions asked in the latter part of the focus group interviews were based on the more specific behaviors and social situations observed during the contextual shadowing, and thus were not part of the interview guide; rather, they were based on the merged field notes of the two authors, which were used to probe the families further about specific details of what they did, said, or omitted from the observations.

3.2 Analytical Approaches and Limitations

The observations and focus group interviews from the user study resulted in 2 h and 15 min worth of empirical material for analysis. The material was transcribed with annotated time codes and labels so that the participants could be identified in their respective family's groupings. They were otherwise anonymized to ensure privacy. The data were further codified into themes within broad categories based on their relation to each other as well as the research questions. Each of the overarching themes were codified into subtopics, which presented more specific instances, such as those pertaining to content preferences or wayfinding guidance through the application. Each instance was counted and visually categorized in an affinity diagram, clustering them into the analytical topics presented covered in Sect. 4.

3.3 Presentation of Data

The topics most relevant to designing the mobile guide are content type and technology use. We identified several themes from our analysis, which were grouped and subsequently "dot-voted" to be either included or excluded in relation to the areas of concern, depending on the functional value that the technologically driven digital mediation could provide and the users' content preferences. These areas were used as "filters" to identify the relevant themes from the focus group interviews to be included in the analysis (Table 2).

Table 2. Ordering of the information that emerged from the focus group interviews into content- and technology-specific themes and further specification into subthemes and topics based on thematic analysis.

THEMES	SUBTHEMES	TOPICS	INSTANCES		
CONTENT	PRACTICAL INFO	Practical problem first, dissemination secondary	18	45	153
		Overview and Planning	17		
		Checklist	20		
	MEDIATION	Apps are not attractions	04	77	
		Content value	11		
		Text	14		
		Audio	20		
		Video	19		
		Mixed content	09		
	EXPERIENCE	Experience over enlightenment	01	14	
		Experience can be enlightenment	04		
		Coherent content over the same communicator	05		
		More experience content	04		
	AMBIGUOUS	Enlightenment vs Experience	07	17	
		Discovery through wayfinding	10		
TECHNOLOGY	MOBILE DEVICE	Self-facilitation	07	96	169
		Social vs Individual	08		
		Disturbance vs Amplification	23		
		Bring your own Device	14		
		Up and Down	27		
		Mostly for Adults – disseminates to children	17		
	WAYFINDING	Usability	06	28	
		Usability enabler	03		
		When does wayfinding give meaning?	19		
	TECHNICAL EVALUATION	Push & Pull messages	16	45	
		Feature Request	10		
		UX & Usability Inhibitor	06		
		More vs less content	13		

4   Analysis and Findings

This section is structured into the two main themes: content and technology. The findings are described through quotations from the focus group interviews and analyzed in relation to the relevant subthemes and topics.

4.1   Content

An exhibition visit starts at the entrance, where pamphlets providing practical information, such as opening times, special event times, and a map of the place showing the POIs, toilets, ice-cream stores, lunch cafes, and playgrounds, can be found. This service is often provided to help visitors access the most essential information. It was evident that the families expected all of this practical information to be provided by the application so that they could dispense with the need to use the pamphlets, visit the exhibition website during the visit, and/or find a tour guide to help them. Thus, the practical information provided by the application was considered valuable by the families, more so because it was provided in one application. However, the families did request additional practical information, such as a calendar with special activities and special deals to help plan their visit accordingly. The importance of planning was also expressed by how the visitors used the "Experience" tab. Consider the example below.

> *"I especially like the 'Experience' tab where you can plan the day's trip, because you cannot remember all those feeding times, so it is better to plan what you want to see." (Man, Family 2)*

Some families marked the locations they wanted to see as "Favorites" in advance, thus making the application experience more personalized for themselves. Others used the same feature to check if they had visited all the places (Fig. 3). Another set of families visited the POIs one by one and never reached the second floor, as none of the POIs were situated there.

| AII EXPERIENCES (A) | FAVORITES (B) | UPCOMING EVENTS (C) | MY DAY (D) |

Fig. 3. Images of the application pages showing (A) a listing of available experiences, (B) favorite experiences, (C) upcoming events, and (D) selected events in the "My Day" tab.

> *"I would probably say that if I went to another attraction in Denmark, where we have not been for a long time, I think we will take it one by one, so we do not miss anything." (Woman, Family 3)*

These families trusted the application to navigate them through the entire exhibition. This finding underscores an important and practical use of such applications from the users' viewpoint and the need to consider the same in the design process. In addition to planning, a notification system was requested by the users to substantiate the planned journey. The families expressed that it would be convenient if they were notified when they were approaching a POI or a location that required their attention. However, they also observed that such information should be provided in reasonable amounts and the feature should be optional. The value of a notification system lies in the extent of support it provides visitors with regard to allocating their time for different activities in the exhibition.

Typically, the families remarked that all of their practical needs should have been met before they were motivated to explore other mediated content. This finding supports the hypothesis that the communicated content must, first and foremost, provide the visitor with more functional dimensions that support their visit.

A set of factors should be considered when selecting the formats to mediate content through a smartphone application in an exhibition context. The Oceanarium is a family-oriented exhibition, and therefore, its primary target group comprises families with children. In this situation, children play a major role in how families interact with a smartphone application during an exhibition visit. With regard to the text format, the families primarily preferred short facts, as longer text was time-consuming to read and already widely available at the exhibition in the form of signages and pamphlets. Moreover, the parents were also increasingly occupied with looking after their children, who were not interested in longer texts (see also the screenshots showing the short and long texts in Fig. 2). If the parents spent too much time reading long texts, they would probably lose track of their children. For instance, one participant remarked,

"No, I will never be able to make time for long texts when I have the kids. But it's fine with the short texts. So you can read more if you want to know more." (Woman, Family 6).

However, some of the visitors did mention that the longer texts were more detailed and therefore preferable for those who wanted to know more. Short texts, which provided the families the most essential facts, were considered important, as some families did not have the time and interest to delve deep into the given information. Longer texts are also probably more appealing to enthusiasts, who have a deep interest and want to know more than just the availability of information at the exhibition. The audio format, which functioned as an audio guide, was appreciated by some parents who visited the aquarium.

"The one that made the best impression on me was the sound file; I stood and looked at the little sharks while she [the voice-over in the audio] talked about them. This gives a really good understanding of what you are looking at." (Man, Family 1)

As expected, the children did not express much interest in listening to the audio descriptions. However, in such situations, the parents could hear the audio while also looking after their children. Most often, if the parents had heard something interesting, they passed on the information to their children. Even though such an experience cannot be described as "shared listening," the passing on of the knowledge from parent to child makes it a shared learning experience. The audio format suffered from one constraint; a less noisy area was preferable when listening to the audio. The families suggested using headphones to solve this problem and also prevent disturbing the other visitors. However, the headphones might limit shared family experiences.

The video format was the most preferable for the families. Notably, the short length of 1–2 min appealed to both the parents and their children. The videos were often watched together, which created a dialogue between the family members about the topics at the exhibition. The parents explained that their children were normally not receptive to signages at exhibitions because they tend to be too long, unappealing, or difficult to follow. For example, one of the participants stated that,

> *"I also think in the long term that not many children bother to stand and read long texts. But to see a small video would appeal more to them, so they can get something more than just looking at a skeleton and only know what it looked like."* *(Woman, Family 7)*

Compared to information posters, children are typically distracted by attractive elements that catch their attention. In contrast, the videos were much more enriching for the children than the usual posters and signages. The families also suggested limiting the videos to approximately 30 s, with the added option of seeing a longer video depending on the user's interest. However, the video format also suffers from the same constraint as the audio format, namely loud areas. The families suggested adding subtitles to the videos to resolve this issue.

> *"It would be good if there were subtitles. Because if you have text and you miss some bits of the narration because of the surrounding sounds, you can still easily follow the video. Subtitles could be the best option to help videos work optimally."* *(Woman, Family 3)*

This idea somehow contradicts some participants' attitudes about longer texts. However, when the longer texts are facilitated through a video format, the families tended to be much more receptive to the information being provided. It can be argued that, by itself, longer text can be characterized as education rather than entertainment, whereas when it is encapsulated in a video substantiating the footage, it offers a balance between education and entertainment, providing optimal circumstances for information enrichment.

Regarding the authors' questions about coherent experiences, the families revealed that they perceived having the same guide in the video and audio as an element of cohesiveness. The guide in the video functioned as a tour guide, taking the families around the exhibition. Continuing with the same person adds a feeling of reliability and coherence to the overall experience, but could also become quite monotonous. For example, one of the participants observed that,

> *"Well, I can see the coherence with having the same person communicate all the information, but it can also be monotonous...so I do not think it necessarily needs to be the same person. But the content must be coherent."* *(Woman, Family 2)*

Therefore, the users typically preferred maintaining cohesiveness throughout the content, in form of its theme, difficulty, and length. According to the majority of the visitors, a human guide still adds a unique value to the exhibition experience, but the participants in this study did not find themselves requiring critical assistance from a guide during their visit on the day of the experiment. For example, one of the participants noted that,

"A guide gives great value during special events, such as when the backstage is opened, because this is a real person who stands in front of you and communicates with you, making the visit memorable. But it is not something you will miss." (Man, Family 2)

Even when the families noticed the guides at the exhibition, they did not feel the need to ask them about anything. As such, there was no immediate need for the visitors to seek information from a guide. They may only approach a guide if they require information.

In general, the participants were satisfied about the amount and difficulty level of content as well as the manner in which the guide mediated the content. The families expressed that the content was well communicated and easy to understand. It was neither too complex nor too simple; rather, it added value for the parents as well as their children. The families who had visited the Oceanarium before also appreciated the fact that previously inaccessible knowledge about the exhibition was communicated through the application:

"It is always better with more info because we can know more. We have been here many times, and this time, we got to know more than we usually do. So, we have learned new things today." (Man, Family 5)

Thus, the participants expressed delight in having learned something new. As such, not only did the families in this research express increased interest toward more POIs throughout the exhibition, but they also reported appreciating the seasonal updates that support revisits. However, they noted that regular updates alone would not encourage them to revisit. This clearly shows that the smartphone application served as an element that supported their experience rather than becoming the experience itself.

In summary, a smartphone application must fulfil the practical needs of the visitors for them to consider using it. The different media formats on a smartphone application in this exhibition context are characterized by different strengths and weaknesses. Short texts provide easily acceptable information for both parents and children, and are easily usable in loud areas. The audio format works best in less noisy areas, while videos can include subtitles, facilitating their use in both quiet and loud areas. These findings support the second hypothesis, namely that differences exist with regard to user experience with different media modalities for information provision, especially in the context of family-oriented exhibitions. In general, the families expressed their interest in being able to choose the content format, length, and difficulty level according to their needs:

"It could be very cool if there were different kinds of content. Because I think some would rather read and others would rather watch a video and vice versa. If you have two children with you, or if there is a lot of noise around you, then it may not be easy to hear, so it will be nice to be able to read it." (Woman, Family 2)

This idea about choosing format options arose through their previous experiences with audio guides; these guides were initially interesting for them, but became boring and redundant over time as the visit progressed. As such, different visitors have different needs, and therefore, the possibility of customizing the content format, length, and level of difficulty was preferred.

4.2 Technology

All of the visitors were familiar with using different technologies during a visit to an exhibition and had also explored different smartphone applications that supported specific exhibition activities. The visitors also presented good insights about the possibilities of improving the smartphone application, given their everyday use of their own devices. As such the technology-related feedback from the visitors originated from these previously acquired experiences.

Given these experiences, it is evident that the visitors also have certain practical information-related expectations that need to be fulfilled by such technologies. One of their major practical expectations involved navigation support with the application. Almost all smartphone users today are accustomed with navigational applications, such as Google and Apple Maps. Thus, the navigational feature is a critical element when considering smartphone applications for exhibitions. Thus, it was not surprising to find that the map in the application was criticized as not supporting either orientation or navigation:

> "The smartphone knows where you are, but you just miss the dot on the map in the application. The outdoors are fine; there are paths you can follow, but inside it is just a square and you do not know where you are and what level you are on in that square." (Man, Family 3)

The map in the application showed the outlines of the halls in the exhibition, but it did not provide any indication of where and which floor the families were on. To compensate for the limited navigational option, some families tried to use the rangefinder in "Near You" as a navigational tool to find POIs. However, they became demotivated by the inaccurate distance provided by the application and the lack of a direction to follow. In contrast, one of the families that had visited the exhibition before conveyed that they had discovered new areas and exhibits they had not seen during their previous visits through the "Rangefinder" feature. For example:

> "That big screen you have, I only discovered it because of the 'Near You' feature. I thought it was a narrative about that location in the aquarium, but I found it was located behind the aquarium because of the 'Near You' feature. It was not there the last time we were here." (Man, Family 1)

However, all the families insisted that it is crucial to know one's location on a virtual map or at least be able to orientate their location during the visit. While the "Rangefinder" was praised as a good feature for exploration, the families felt that it could be more valuable with an orientation feature. All of these observations elaborate the importance of wayfinding in exhibitions, which the visitors expect the application to support through smartphone technologies. This understanding also supports the first hypothesis, namely that the communicated content must, first and foremost, provide the visitor with a more functional dimension to support their visit.

In general, the families reported having prior experience in using applications in the exhibition context. Therefore, the use of Aratag was not perceived as disruptive by the families during their visit. Even though the visitors had tried similar products at certain other locations, they noted that the functionalities of the Aratag application were the most numerous of all the applications they had tried so far. The advantage of this application lay in its ability to communicate through different formats, which was particularly useful in an exhibition. They especially preferred the video and audio formats over information-heavy signages typically seen at exhibitions. Some visitors did not feel particularly interested in exploring aquariums and fishes, but they expressed that the application motivated them to learn more about these locations, as they were very interested in using the new technology. However, the attention that visitors would need to pay while gleaning the information provided by the application could cause them to lose track of their children, and thus, this was viewed as a disadvantage of Aratag. The Oceanarium was also very noisy, which prevented the visitors from hearing all of the content. The instability of some of the features and the few POIs were also demotivating factors for most of the visitors:

"If you want people to have the application open all the time, you have to provide something all the time. Well...otherwise you will be lost in this zapper generation."
(Woman, Family 4)

The visitors also expressed that in a normal-use scenario, they would have put away their mobile devices due to these disadvantages. Thus, it was important that the technology be stable and flawless. Moreover, the technology should provide a consistent flow of content throughout the exhibition instead of limiting this information for certain areas. Thus, it is clear that users want the freedom to choose the type of content as well as not be restricted by limited information.

In general, exhibitions tend to provide visitors with technologies to support visitor experiences. However, the families preferred using their own devices rather than borrowing one for several reasons. First, users are more familiar with their own devices. Second, when using ones' own device, visitors need not be concerned about data privacy (e.g., sensitive personal photos taken by their children). However, the families also expressed their concern about conflicting interests if everyone in the family were to use the application simultaneously. This shows that the parents prioritize a shared family experience over individual experiences. Typically, the visitors would like to shun using mobile devices on family tours, but when they require to use an application for a specific purpose, they are motivated to use it and do not feel that it diverts them from their focus. In contrast, they revealed that the application amplified their accessibility to information, as they did not need to queue or wait for other visitors to move away from the signages or info-screens in the exhibition. As such, the content provided by the application was the primary reason for the families to continuously use the mobile device during their visit. Encouragingly, they expressed that they would likely use the application for the entire duration of a first-time visit to explore the exhibition:

"We went through the exhibition with the application open all the time, to see what appeared. I did not put it away but kept it open to look for something new. It was more about exploring the exciting things it [the application] could tell me about that I was not bothered to read up on." (Man, Family 1)

Notably, one family did mention that the intense use of the application might be attributed to its participation in this experiment; on a normal visit, they might have used it to a lesser extent. Currently, the application interface is mainly designed for adults. The families concurred that the application should appeal to all age groups, with different interface designs for different age groups.

In summary, these results prove the importance of practical functionality for smartphone applications and the possibility of identifying their requirements in the context of exhibitions. People are accustomed to using mobile devices and applications, which has created a set of predefined requirements; thus, users expect a well-designed application using these technologies.

5   Discussion

The Aratag project followed previous studies with regard to the design and implementation path to create a mobile guide for exhibitions. It also extended previous work by investigating users' content preferences for a location-based, context-aware application for self-guided exhibitions. Content preparation for museum visitor guides is a time-consuming and laborious task [1, 69], but the Aratag prototype resulted in a robust method for configuring mixed media modalities. The platform offers a unique tool for exhibitions to share experiences and provides users a more streamlined application across multiple exhibitions. This study was guided by the following two hypotheses:

1. The communicated content must, first and foremost, provide the visitor with a more functional dimension to support their visit (e.g., wayfinding, guidance, practical information, and discounts) if self-guidance use is expected.
2. User experiences differ depending on the media modalities of the content (e.g., long text, short text, audio book, and video snippet).

The first hypothesis was related to the functional dimension (e.g., wayfinding, guidance, practical information, and discounts) in order for the user to initially perceive the value of the system. Our experiment showed that first-time as well as returning visitors found the access provided by the application to be useful because of the different levels of information. This result hinted that multi-level content is favorable, as the user is able to glimpse important information or immerse themselves into more detailed content that captures their individual interests. This finding aligns with research that emphasizes user modeling in design to personalize the visitor's experience and sustain individual user interest [70, 71].

The backbone of the system lies in its "Wayfinding" feature, which provides the user with precise information about locations to support their navigation within the exhibition. For example, the map in the application shows the outlines of the halls in the exhibition. However, at this time, it does not provide any indications of where and which floor the families are located on. This shortcoming was pointed out several times by the participants. As many people use smartphones for daily activities and tasks, they are well aware of the map function provided by the Apple/Google Map apps, and when Aratag failed to deliver the same functionalities, the users expressed frustration with the application. This shortcoming impacted user experience negatively. Examples of desired interactions with the application map include rotating and scaling functions, which were unavailable at the time of the experiment. However, this shortcoming is more usability-specific and has been tackled in an updated version that was tested recently.

The second hypothesis was related to how different media modalities affect user experience. In self-guided exhibitions, the smartphone application assumes the role of the guide. In such cases, several modalities may be used to mediate content. The different media formats presented various strengths and weaknesses. Short texts were preferred by both parents and children, and were more helpful in loud areas in particular. The audio format worked best in less noisy areas, whereas the video format was the most preferable of all. The inclusion of subtitles was suggested to add value to the video format in both quiet and loud areas. These findings supported the second hypothesis. In generally, the families expressed their interest in being able to choose the content format, length, and difficulty level according to their needs. Typically, the visitors would like to avoid using mobile devices on family tours, but if they are offered an application customized for the purpose, they are more receptive to using mobile devices. This is because the application amplifies accessibility to information and/or provides additional content that is inaccessible at the exhibition. Therefore, it is very likely that mobile guides will not be rejected by visitors to exhibitions in favor of other tools, such as smart cards and smart objects; in fact, users prefer bringing their own devices to exhibitions as they are readily accessible. This point aligns with recent studies that focused on different types of interaction frames (i.e., ways in which users can interact with digital media technologies at exhibitions) and showed that user preferences are highly dependent on the content [20]. The users' content preferences revealed a predilection toward shorter texts and more video, but these findings do not imply that the institutions should "dumb down" on information; in fact, they should make information accessible, but at the user's request and not by adding to their cognitive load as is typically the case with the content displayed in the physical space at exhibitions. In this regard, a notification system could alleviate the cognitive load by pinging for the user's attention, in relation to the user's interests and location in the exhibition.

Our findings align with those of existing studies as well as extend our knowledge with design insights that are central to the development of interactive mobile systems for self-guided situations in exhibitions. The first finding of this work points to the importance of content personalization through **multi-level content formats** to accommodate an individual user's interest. Moreover, the information should be scaffolded such that the user may have varied types of access, from glimpsing the content to immersing themselves within a particular subject should they wish to. This design insight should be investigated further in order to understand how a user's curiosity can be triggered (e.g., by prioritizing knowledge acquisition). The second design insight provided by this work concerns the pragmatic features that are key to creating reliable, robust, and precise mobile guides capable of **real-time location tracking.** The implementation of location tracking was inadequate in the current study, and the participant's feedback points to a clear desire for this functionality in the application. In other words, this feature is critical for users to want to use mobile guides for self-guided exhibitions.

6 Conclusion

Smartphones with context-aware applications can potentially support exhibition experiences, particularly since visitors are more likely to be accustomed users of these devices. The rapid technological development in this field and the lessons learnt with context-aware applications in exhibitions will expand practitioners' knowledge about creating self-guided smartphone applications. As the technology matures along with its users, research in this field continues to expand; the potential and implications of self-guided exhibition experiences with smartphones must be explored continuously.

In line with the two hypotheses discussed in the previous section, this study was guided by the following research question: *How can digital mediation add sufficient value to promote use, and what criteria for exhibition content is preferred by guests in self-guided contexts?* We found that users' attitudes were positive toward the use of smartphones at exhibitions, and on several occasions, they voiced that they would indeed have preferred to use the application on their own devices. Thus, the users signaled their openness toward institutions implementing the BYOD strategy. Users' content preferences varied, but in general, they agreed that the entry-level content should be just sufficient for them to sample whether or not the information interests them. If it does, they should be offered additional in-depth information on specific content. We see this outcome as an indication of users' desire to be able to explore more content of their own volition instead of having it thrust upon them by the institution. Removing unnecessary signage and labels will allow the exhibition to benefit as well, as it would lower the cognitive load on the user and possibly create more explorative and immersive environments.

Our experimental results also show that the video format was preferred from among all content types, because it could engage with both the children and the adults, thus enabling situations where the operator of the mobile guide could share information with the other members of the family. These insights relate back to the desirability and utility dimensions. We did not investigate the latter in this study, but our results did provide some insights about the use of beacons. Bluetooth beacons (which were not under scrutiny in this study) were chosen based on market reports and trending consumer technologies. This specific type of technology is highly unreliable at this time, as signal strength between different types of smartphones is inconsistent.

Our findings point to the need to study the extent of content and its types on the mobile guide so as to calibrate these aspects for actual implementation of the application. Conversely, the physical space at the exhibition must be designed to avoid overloading users' cognition with a plethora of information. A balance will provide the user with the freedom they need to experience the exhibition as they see fit, while still being enticed to explore the site. The proposed technology can alleviate the cognitive load experienced by the user by facilitating content selection by them. Thus, future work should aim to better balance the content, user, and physical signage of the exhibition with the mobile exploration system. This is a very challenging topic, however, and the results of this research will assist to this end. Thus, we recommend conducting a comprehensive quantitative study as a follow-up on this qualitative study. This future work should include tracking people's activity on the smartphone and triangulating the data with user preferences to reinforce and explore the possibilities and widen the area of application. Future work should be scaled up by using a mix methods approach and increasing the number of participating families and exhibitions. It will also be possible to explore the potential and challenges of using one application for multiple exhibitions. It would be interesting to understand how exhibitions can collaborate to promote each other and create a coherent experience across different event spaces. Furthermore, the advent of new location-aware technologies and improvements in existing ones will help developers improve user experience with such applications. Thus, a more focused study on location-aware technologies will provide a comprehensive picture for designing context-aware mobile systems for self-guided exhibitions.

References

1. Tallon, L., Walker, K. (eds.): Digital Technologies and the Museum Experience: Handheld Guides and Other Media. AltaMira Press, Lanham (2008)
2. Damala, A., Cubaud, P., Bationo, A., Houlier, P., Marchal, I.: Bridging the gap between the digital and the physical: design and evaluation of a mobile augmented reality guide for the museum visit, no. 8 (2008)
3. Petrelli, D., O'Brien, S.: "Mobiles for museum visit should be abolished": a comparison of smart replicas, smart cards, and phones. In: Proceedings of the 2016 ACM International Joint Conference on Pervasive and Ubiquitous Computing: Adjunct, pp. 1513–1519. ACM, New York (2016). https://doi.org/10.1145/2968219.2974049
4. Abowd, G.D., Atkeson, C.G., Hong, J., Long, S., Kooper, R., Pinkerton, M.: Cyberguide: a mobile context-aware tour guide. Wirel. Netw. **3**, 421–433 (1997). https://doi.org/10.1023/A:1019194325861
5. Ballagas, R., Kuntze, A., Walz, S.P.: Gaming tourism: lessons from evaluating REXplorer, a pervasive game for tourists. In: Indulska, J., Patterson, D.J., Rodden, T., Ott, M. (eds.) Pervasive 2008. LNCS, vol. 5013, pp. 244–261. Springer, Heidelberg (2008). https://doi.org/10.1007/978-3-540-79576-6_15
6. Vlahakis, V., et al.: Archeoguide: an augmented reality guide for archaeological sites. IEEE Comput. Graphics Appl. **22**, 52–60 (2002)
7. Wakkary, R., et al.: Kurio: a museum guide for families. In: Proceedings of the 3rd International Conference on Tangible and Embedded Interaction, pp. 215–222. ACM (2009)
8. Wecker, A.J., Kuflik, T., Stock, O.: AMuse: connecting indoor and outdoor cultural heritage experiences. In: Proceedings of the 22nd International Conference on Intelligent User Interfaces Companion, pp. 153–156. ACM, New York (2017). https://doi.org/10.1145/3030024.3040980
9. Bitgood, S.: Museum fatigue: a critical review. Visitor Stud. **12**, 93–111 (2009). https://doi.org/10.1080/10645570903203406
10. Petrelli, D., O'Brien, S.: Phone vs. tangible in museums: a comparative study. In: Proceedings of the 2018 CHI Conference on Human Factors in Computing Systems, pp. 112:1–112:12. ACM, New York (2018). https://doi.org/10.1145/3173574.3173686

11. Drotner, K., Dziekan, V., Parry, R., Schrøder, K.C.: The Routledge Handbook of Museums Media and Communication. Routledge, Abingdon (2018)
12. Drotner, K., Laursen, D.: Introduction . J. Media Commun. Res. **27**, 1–6 (2011)
13. Apostolellis, P., Bowman, D.A.: Small group learning with games in museums: effects of interactivity as mediated by cultural differences. In: Proceedings of the 14th International Conference on Interaction Design and Children, pp. 160–169. ACM, New York (2015). https://doi.org/10.1145/2771839.2771856
14. Danielak, B.A., Mechtley, A., Berland, M., Lyons, L., Eydt, R.: MakeScape lite: a prototype learning environment for making and design. In: Proceedings of the 2014 Conference on Interaction Design and Children, pp. 229–232. ACM, New York (2014). https://doi.org/10.1145/2593968.2610459
15. Falk, J.H., Dierking, L.D.: Enhancing visitor interaction and learning with mobile technologies. In: Tallon, L. (ed.) Digital Technologies and the Museum Experience: Handheld Guides and Other Media, pp. 19–33. Rowman Altamira (2008)
16. Muise, K., Wakkary, R.: Bridging designers' intentions to outcomes with constructivism. In: Proceedings of the 8th ACM Conference on Designing Interactive Systems, pp. 320–329. ACM, New York (2010). https://doi.org/10.1145/1858171.1858229
17. Tallon, L.: Introduction: mobile, digital, and personal. In: Tallon, L. (ed.) Digital Technologies and the Museum Experience: Handheld Guides and Other Media, pp. Xiii–XXV. Rowman Altamira (2008)
18. Heath, C., vom Lehn, D.: configuring "interactivity": enhancing engagement in science centres and museums. Soc. Stud. Sci. **38**, 63–91 (2008)
19. Olsson, T., Svensson, A.: Reaching and including digital visitors: Swedish museums and social demand. In: Pruulmann-Vengerfeldt, P., Viires, P. (eds.) The Digital Turn: User's Practices and Cultural Transformations, pp. 45–57. Peter Lang GmbH, New York (2013)
20. Hornecker, E., Ciolfi, L.: Human-Computer Interactions in Museums. Synthesis Lectures on Human-Centered Informatics, no. 12, p. i–153 (2019). https://doi.org/10.2200/S00901ED1V01Y201902HCI042
21. Vermeeren, A., Calvi, L., Sabiescu, A. (eds.): Museum Experience Design Crowds, Ecosystems and Novel Technologies. SSCC, Springer, Cham (2018). https://doi.org/10.1007/978-3-319-58550-5
22. Harper, R. (ed.): Being Human: Human-Computer Interaction in the Year 2020. Microsoft Research, Cambridge (2008)
23. Rogers, Y.: Moving on from Weiser's vision of calm computing: engaging UbiComp experiences. In: Dourish, P., Friday, A. (eds.) UbiComp 2006. LNCS, vol. 4206, pp. 404–421. Springer, Heidelberg (2006). https://doi.org/10.1007/11853565_24
24. Gartner, G.: Gartner Says Worldwide Sales of Smartphones Returned to Growth in First Quarter of 2018. (2018)
25. Ericsson, R.: Ericsson Mobility Report - MWC. 28 (2019)
26. Statista, S.: Number of mobile phone users worldwide 2015–2020 (2016)
27. Lindqvist, K.: Museum finances: challenges beyond economic crises. Museum Manag. Curatorship **27**, 1–5 (2012). https://doi.org/10.1080/09647775.2012.644693
28. Skot-Hansen, D.: Museerne i den danske oplevelsesøkonomi. Samfundslitteratur (2008)
29. Skot-Hansen, D.: Digital formidling i danske museer – udfordringer for oplevelsessamfund og oplevelsesøkonomi. In: Digital formidling af kulturarv: fra samling til sampling, pp. 43–63. Multivers, København (2009)
30. Our Museum, V.M.: Project 07: Self-facilitation in Automated Exhibition Sites (2016). https://ourmuseum.dk/projects/programme-projects/unmanned-exhibition-sites/
31. Horizon Report: 2015 Museum Edition (2015)

32. Sayre, S.: Bring it on: Ensuring the success of BYOD programming in the museum environment. https://mw2015.museumsandtheweb.com/paper/bring-it-on-ensuring-the-success-of-byod-programming-in-the-museum-environment/. Accessed 16 July 2020

33. Kenteris, M., Gavalas, D., Economou, D.: Electronic mobile guides: a survey. Pers. Ubiquit. Comput. **15**, 97–111 (2011). https://doi.org/10.1007/s00779-010-0295-7

34. Kosmopoulos, D., Styliaras, G.: A survey on developing personalized content services in museums. Pervasive Mob. Comput. **47**, 54–77 (2018). https://doi.org/10.1016/j.pmcj.2018.05.002

35. Vahdat-Nejad, H., Navabi, M.S., Khosravi-Mahmouei, H.: A context-aware museum-guide system based on cloud computing. IJCAC. **8**, 1–19 (2018). https://doi.org/10.4018/IJCAC.2018100101

36. Jensen, K.L., Larsen, L.B.: The challenges of evaluating the mobile and ubiquitous user experience, no. 11 (2008)

37. Jensen, K.L., Krishnasamy, R., Selvadurai, V.: Studying PH.A.N.T.O.M. in the wild: a pervasive persuasive game for daily physical activity. Presented at the 22nd Conference of the Computer-Human Interaction Special Interest Group of Australia on Computer-Human Interaction (2010). https://doi.org/10.1145/1952222.1952228

38. Kan, A., Gibbs, M., Ploderer, B.: Being chased by zombies!: understanding the experience of mixed reality quests. In: Proceedings of the 25th Australian Computer-Human Interaction Conference: Augmentation, Application, Innovation, Collaboration, pp. 207–216. ACM, New York (2013). https://doi.org/10.1145/2541016.2541038

39. Mueller, F., Khot, R.A., Gerling, K., Mandryk, R.: Exertion games. Found. Trends Hum.-Comput. Interact. **10**, 1–86 (2016). https://doi.org/10.1561/1100000041

40. Inversini, A., Schegg, R. (eds.): Information and Communication Technologies in Tourism 2016. Springer, Cham (2016). https://doi.org/10.1007/978-3-319-28231-2

41. Kerr, C.: Niantic partners with United Nations to boost tourism using AR games. https://www.gamasutra.com/view/news/331088/Niantic_partners_with_United_Nations_to_boost_tourism_using_AR_games.php. Accessed 21 Nov 2018

42. Wang, N., Xia, L.: Human-exhibition interaction (HEI) in designing exhibitions: a systematic literature review. Int. J. Hosp. Manag. **77**, 292–302 (2019). https://doi.org/10.1016/j.ijhm.2018.07.009

43. Vistisen, P., Østergaard, C.P., Krishnasamy, R.K.: Adopting the unknown through the known supporting user interaction of non-idiomatic technologies in exhibitions through known idioms of conventional technologies. Des. J. **20**, S3696–S3706 (2017). https://doi.org/10.1080/14606925.2017.1352875

44. Friedman, A.J.: The great sustainability challenge: how visitor studies can save cultural institutions in the 21st century. Visitor Stud. **10**, 3–12 (2007). https://doi.org/10.1080/10645570701263396

45. Hooper-Greenhill, E.: The Educational Role of the Museum. Psychology Press, London (1999)

46. Hooper-Greenhill, E., Hooper-Greenhill, E.: Museums and Their Visitors. Routledge, London; New York (1994)

47. Munley, M.E., Roberts, R.: Are museum educators still necessary? J. Museum Educ. **31**, 29–39 (2006)

48. Tran, L.U.: Teaching science in museums: the pedagogy and goals of museum educators. Sci. Educ. **91**, 278–297 (2007). https://doi.org/10.1002/sce.20193

49. Yalowitz, S.S., Bronnenkant, K.: Timing and tracking: unlocking visitor behavior. Visitor Stud. **12**, 47–64 (2009). https://doi.org/10.1080/10645570902769134

50. Hughes, K.: Tourist satisfaction: a guided, "cultural" Tour in North Queensland. Aust. Psychol. **26**, 166–171 (1991). https://doi.org/10.1080/00050069108257243

51. Weiler, B., Ham, S.H.: Tour guide training: a model for sustainable capacity building in developing countries. J. Sustain. Tour. **10**, 52–69 (2002). https://doi.org/10.1080/096695802 08667152
52. Best, K.: Making museum tours better: understanding what a guided tour really is and what a tour guide really does. Museum Manag. Curatorship **27**, 35–52 (2012). https://doi.org/10. 1080/09647775.2012.644695
53. Sumi, Y., Etani, T., Fels, S., Simonet, N., Kobayashi, K., Mase, K.: C-MAP: building a context-aware mobile assistant for exhibition tours. In: Ishida, T. (ed.) Community Computing and Support Systems: Social Interaction in Networked Communities, vol. 1519, pp. 137–154. Springer, Heidelberg (1998). https://doi.org/10.1007/3-540-49247-X_10
54. Dindler, C., Iversen, O.S.: Motivation in the museum - mediating between everyday engagement and cultural heritage, no. 11 (2009)
55. McCaw, C., Oliver, M., Glen, L.: Restaging a garden party: sharing social histories through the design of digital and material interactive experiences. NODEM (2014)
56. Ballagas, R.A., et al.: REXplorer: a mobile, pervasive spell-casting game for tourists. In: CHI 2007 Extended Abstracts on Human Factors in Computing Systems, pp. 1929–1934. ACM, New York (2007). https://doi.org/10.1145/1240866.1240927
57. Damala, A., Schuchert, T., Rodriguez, I., Moragues, J., Gilleade, K., Stojanovic, N.: Exploring the affective museum visiting experience: adaptive augmented reality (A2R) and cultural heritage. Int. J. Heritage Digit. Era **2**, 117–142 (2013). https://doi.org/10.1260/2047-4970.2. 1.117
58. Aluri, A.: Mobile augmented reality (MAR) game as a travel guide: insights from Pokémon GO. JHTT. **8**, 55–72 (2017). https://doi.org/10.1108/JHTT-12-2016-0087
59. Arth, C., Grasset, R., Gruber, L., Langlotz, T., Mulloni, A., Wagner, D.: The history of mobile augmented reality. arXiv preprint arXiv:1505.01319 (2015)
60. Nilsson, T., Blackwell, A., Hogsden, C., Scruton, D.: Ghosts! A location-based bluetooth LE mobile game for museum exploration. arXiv:1607.05654 [cs] (2016)
61. Kang, J.H., Jang, J.C., Jeong, C.: Understanding museum visitor satisfaction and revisit intentions through mobile guide system: moderating role of age in museum mobile guide adoption. Asia Pac. J. Tour. Res. **23**, 95–108 (2018). https://doi.org/10.1080/10941665.2017.1410190
62. Simonsen, J., Robertson, T.: Routledge International Handbook of Participatory Design. Routledge, Abingdon (2012). https://doi.org/10.4324/9780203108543
63. Khan, S., Krishnasamy, R., Germak, C.: Design challenges in promoting inclusion for cultural heritage contents through low cost technology. In: DS 91: Proceedings of NordDesign 2018, Linköping, Sweden, 14th–17th August 2018 (2018)
64. Vistisen, P.: Applied Gamification in Self-guided Exhibitions. In: Proceedings From the 1st Gamescope Conference (2018)
65. Koskinen, I.K. (ed.): Design Research Through Practice: From the Lab, Field, and Showroom. Morgan Kaufmann/Elsevier, Waltham (2011)
66. Quinlan, E.: Conspicuous invisibility: shadowing as a data collection strategy. Qual. Inq. **14**, 1480–1499 (2008). https://doi.org/10.1177/1077800408318318
67. Bloor, M., Frankland, J., Thomas, M., Robson, K.: Focus Groups in Social Research. SAGE Publications Ltd., London (2001). https://doi.org/10.4135/9781849209175
68. Aratag, I.G.: Interview Guide – Aratag (2018). https://www.dropbox.com/s/ppi5rim8ulwff4f/ Interview%20Guide.docx?dl=0
69. Kuflik, T., et al.: A visitor's guide in an active museum: presentations, communications, and reflection. J. Comput. Cult. Heritage **3**, 1–25 (2011). https://doi.org/10.1145/1921614.192 1618
70. Falk, J.H.: Identity and the Museum Visitor Experience. Left Coast Press, Walnut Creek (2009)
71. Csikszentmihalyi, M., Hermanson, K.: Intrinsic Motivation in Museums (1995)

Designing the Exhibition Modus of Virtual Experiences: Virtual Reality Installations at Film Festivals

Camilla Jaller[1,2]([envelope])

[1] Multisensory Experience Lab, Aalborg University Copenhagen,
2450 Copenhagen, Denmark
caja@create.aau.dk
[2] Makropol ApS, Helgesensgade 12, 2100 Copenhagen, Denmark
camilla@makropol.dk

Abstract. We are currently witnessing an increase of virtual reality sections at several major film festivals exhibiting a growing number of experiences combining cinema and VR (this field is also known as cinematic virtual reality (CVR)). However, we are still lacking a homogeneous exhibition modus for these hybrid experiences. Moreover, the installation's context is further complicated when some CVR experiences make use of additional media including scenography, spatial sound, and live performance to transition their audience into the virtual experience. As such, special attention is given to the exhibition modus of the work, and therefore the installation must be considered part of the experience design. This paper investigates some trends within installation design at film festivals exemplified by a selection of six works exhibited at the Venice 2019 VR selection. These works are initially divided according to the design strategies of 'the story room', 'the attraction window' and 'the performance space'. Through interviews with industry professionals about their retrospective thoughts on the installation design for the experiences, the paper uncovers some design considerations and strategies, including consideration of installations as a transitional element of the audience experience design, how to approach audience put-through and spectatorship, ways to ensure transportability and distribution of design, and dealing with venue specificity and adaptability of the installation, among others.

Keywords: Cinematic virtual reality · Film festivals · Exhibition design

1 Introduction

Throughout its history, once commercialized and institutionalized, film has done well in describing its exhibition and viewing modus. When films were increas-

This work was supported by the Innovation Fund Denmark under the Industrial Ph.D. program with grant 9065-00137B and by the Nordisk Film Fonden under the Isbjørn Project Scheme 2019.

A. Brooks et al. (Eds.): ArtsIT 2020, LNICST 367, pp. 45–63, 2021.
https://doi.org/10.1007/978-3-030-73426-8_3

ingly found in venues specifically built to screen them, the exhibition practice of cinema started to gain special attention from theorists including Baudry and Williams [1], Metz and Guzzetti [14], Deleuze [8], and Bellour [2] who sought to explore the combinatory effect of film viewing technologies and spatial architecture creating a homogenous relationship between the spectator and the film. Today, as we are noticing an increase of virtual reality sections emerging at several major film festivals showcasing a growing number of experiences combining cinema and VR, it becomes evident that we still lack a homogenous exhibition modus for these hybrid experiences and that discussions of CVR spectatorship are only at their infancy. To the present, a formal definition of CVR is still being developed, but several studies, e.g. [9,10], adhere to the definition formulated by John Mateer. According to Mateer, CVR refers to "(...) a type of immersive VR experience where individual users can look around synthetic worlds in 360 degrees, often with stereoscopic views, and hear spatialized audio specifically designed to reinforce the veracity of the virtual environment" ([13] p. 15). However, it remains unknown what will become the future venues of CVR and how virtual technologies and spatial architecture may be combined in these venues. A common approach among festivals has been to install so-called 'VR theatres' consisting of a number of seats in a neutral room in which people experience either the same or a number of different works through HMDs.

Fig. 1. Traditional 'VR theatre' exhibition modus at Venice Film Festival 2017. Photo copyright by Venice Film Festival.

We are, however, starting to see other potential solutions to the challenge of facilitating virtual experiences in physical space by designers in the industry. In installation contexts, including that of film festivals, some CVR experiences are making use of additional media including scenography, spatial sound, and live performance to transition their audience into the virtual experience. As such, special attention is given to the exhibition modus of the work, and therefore the installation must be considered part of the experience design although it may vary and change across venues during the touring life of the experience.

This design focus on the exhibition modus of virtual experiences has been largely overlooked within academia but contributes with some important perspectives at the intersections of film theory, human-computer interaction research, and industrial design training. Focusing on this specific viewing context as one possible exhibition outlet for CVR experiences will provide the fields with a stronger conceptual approach to the connection between CVR productions and their exhibition contexts leading towards future discussions of CVR spectatorship. Furthermore, documenting and discussing current design solutions in the industry will aid designers in their future development for particular channels of semi-public distribution (e.g. festivals and museums) but will also prove valuable to the work of the venues themselves in their continued curatorial work of facilitating audience engagement helped by spatial design. Furthermore, contributing to the larger notion of media in 'attraction phases' [18] with the characteristics of unassimilated, interdisciplinary, seamed, and participatory works, focusing on CVR installations will help illuminate design approaches and document works in such an early phase. As a result, the works and their installation designs will be taken seriously and not be understood as "naive or embryonic forms of some forthcoming standardized form" [18], which tends to be the norm when framing emerging media experience design.

Therefore, this paper aims to investigate three trends within installation design at film festivals exemplified by a selection of works exhibited at the Venice 2019 VR selection. Through several interviews with industry professionals about their retrospective thoughts on installation development and design, the paper will uncover a number of design strategies that answer the question: how are virtual experiences facilitated in a physical space?

2   Materials and Methods

2.1   Materials

This paper analyzes a small selection of works exhibited at the Venice 2019 VR selection (see Fig. 2.). All experiences were selected since they had a distinctive installation part but varied in design strategies for audience and spectator approach across three initial categories with different characteristics that will now be briefly defined.

The first design strategy is termed the "story room". This installation space is completely enclosed and allows no clues for passing spectators on what might be happening behind the white walls. However, once inside the room, the space

	The story room		The attraction window		The performance space	
Name of the work	Battlescar: Punk was invented by girls	The Key	Porton Down	A Life in Flowers	Cosmos Within Us	The Collider
Interviewee(s)	Director Nico Casavecchia & installation designer Mercedes Arturo	Producer Gloria Bradbury	Director Callum Cooper	Creative director Armando Kirwin	Creative director Tupac Martir	Director Amy Rose
Venice category	Competition - Linear	Competition – Interactive (Winner of the Grand Jury Prize for Best VR immersive Work)	Competition - Interactive	Competition - Interactive	Competition - Interactive	Best of VR - out of competition

Fig. 2. Overview of the chosen experiences from Venice 2019 and their initial categorization.

starts transitioning its audience into the narrative even before entering the HMD. This is done through extensive use of set-design through additional media often in a way that corresponds with the mood and aesthetic of the VR world but not necessarily represented 1:1 or with tracked surfaces and objects. In some cases, this set-design furthermore includes the use of human performers to ensure this narrative transition into and out of the experience.

The second design strategy is termed the "attraction window". Similarly, to the "story room", this type of experience is characterized by having an installation space with a distinctive design often including physical props (e.g. furniture, decorations, etc.). However, whereas the "story room" is a singular experience with only one audience member attending at a time on a scheduled time slot, the "attraction window" provides an additional layer of experience. The spatial design includes a big window towards the general audience area (which mainly consisted of hallways where people pass by) and thus allows spectators to catch a glimpse of what the experience might entail. As such, this window might even be described as a 'suspenseful interface' strategy [15] aiming at anticipation and excitement before trying the experience yourself.

The third design strategy is termed "the performance space". Here, the installation space itself consists of several "parts". In some cases, these parts do no refer to something physical but to differing experiential qualities within the same space. In one of the cases, this results in two different audience experiences, where one person enters the enclosed room and experiences the work from inside the HMD, whereas another four persons enter the room as audience members to watch the experience of the person that interacts. In another case, the "parts" refer to a series of adjacent rooms with different experiential qualities; a preparation room, an experience room, and a debriefing room. A shared characteristic for these types of works is that the audience is considered somehow performative in that they are supposed to do something and to enact the story themselves, either with or without an audience.

2.2 Method

Through retrospective interviews with the industry professionals involved in the conceptualization and design of the installations, the paper will illuminate a diverse range of design approaches to the challenge of facilitating virtual experiences in a physical space. The reason for focusing on the design process and asking the designers is twofold. Firstly, there has already been a heavy focus on the user experience within the area of experiences mixing real and physical spaces, such as the trajectory framework [3–5], the notion of blended spaces [6,7], spectator interfaces [15], and performative 'frictions' [16].

Secondly, the immersive technologies themselves have also had the center of attention. This attention has mainly been divided into two categories, according to Rouse et al. (2015, p. 176) [17]: "(1) research on the development of the enabling technologies, computer graphics, and tracking, and (2) evaluation of users' abilities to accomplish discrete tasks in various applications, which are often specifically designed to test the effectiveness of AR/MR tools ([11,20]." Both categories do, however, tend to be rather medium-centric where especially immersion is regarded as an inherent quality of a medium resulting from its technical properties.

This means, that the voice of the mixed reality designer or creator is still rather unexplored. One important exception includes Rouse and Barba, who in their paper "Design for Emerging Media: How MR Designers Think About Storytelling, Process, and Defining the Field." (2017) conducted semi-structured interviews with fifteen designers in the field on their design processes and the medium of MR. Their motivation for conducting this study stems from their argument that "Despite a wealth of scholarship on mixed reality (MR) from many disciplinary perspectives, a comprehensive account of design practices for MR remains elusive. The choice to focus on the MR design process sets this study apart from the majority of work in the field, which commonly analyzes these experiences as discrete artifacts and discusses the effects of design choices in summative evaluations that sometimes obscure the pathways that led to those final results." ([19] p. 245). Therefore, this paper intends to add to this work and to do so in the specific design context of film festivals as exhibition and distribution venues.

For this paper, a total of six experiences from Venice 2019 were chosen because of their distinctive spatial design compared to the more traditional exhibition modus of the 'VR theatre'. Individuals or teams involved in the design process of these experiences were contacted and invited for online interviews conducted via Zoom. A total of six semi-structured interviews were conducted, and before the start, all interviewees were provided a consent form allowing for the interviews to be filmed and transcribed. Furthermore, all interviewees were asked specifically as to if and how they wished to be cited in this paper. They were briefed that the subject of the interview was the specific installation in Venice

2019, but they were also encouraged to reflect on earlier or later installations of the work. They were asked about how the physical component became part of the overall concept and how the design process developed. Furthermore, they were asked about the general aspect of film festivals as distribution and exhibition venues and the potential future for location-based experiences outside of this context.

3 How Are CVR Installations at Film Festivals Designed?

This section will present a selection of the findings from the interviews. While I have previously argued for the function of installations as a transitional element of the experience design [12], this was confirmed in the majority of the interviews. However, several additional design considerations surfaced in the interviews regarding how to design installations for the exhibition context of film festivals and a conceptual and experiential link between physical and virtual elements. These considerations included audience put-through and spectatorship, transportability, and distribution of the design, venue specificity, and adaptability of the installation, among others. While there are many ways to structure these findings, I have chosen to keep the initial design strategy categories for this section, before opening up the discussion on more general perspectives in Sect. 4.

3.1 Designing the Story Room

To summarize, the "story room" strategy is described as an enclosed installation space making use of additional media and set-design to transition the audience into the experience before entering the HMD.

This section covers two different installations, both of which I have categorized under the name "story room". The first one, *Battlescar - Punk was invented by girls*, is directed by Martin Allais and Nico Casavecchia, and produced by ATLAS V, Fauns, 1stAveMachine, RYOT, Arte France and Kaleidoscope [22]. The experience is 28 min long and follows the story of Lupe, a Puertorican-American living in the late 1970s New York City. She is introduced to the punk scene by Debbie whom she meets in the cell of the juvenile detention center, and through the story, you witness her entry into the secret worlds in the Lower East Side scene. The first episode, consisting of 9 min, premiered at the 2018 Sundance Film Festival in the New Frontier category and the experience furthermore went to Tribeca Film Festival later the same year. In Venice, the 28 min version was nominated for the Best VR Immersive Story for Linear Content. For the interview, Casavecchia was joined by Mercedes Arturo, who was the installation designer responsible for all three installations.

The installation concept came as an effect of getting accepted for Sundance, where the exhibition context involved some sort of physical place. However, as Casavecchia points out, you don't have to create an artistic installation and many exhibitors choose not to. Comparing the three exhibition contexts, Arturo reflects on both practical and creative changes to the installations. Particularly, the installation design adapts according to the physical measures and restrictions of the space given at the venue. Furthermore, Arturo notes how local logistics and budgets function as very practical but real constraints to the creative process. The installations in Sundance and Venice were more tactile, including several physical props as part of the design. Both installations represented rooms that were not part of the VR experience.

In Sundance, the installation represented, in Arturo's words, "the aftermath of the whole experience", being Lupe's bedroom one year later. The installation design included poetry on the walls, a lot of pieces of vinyl, instruments, and clothes scattered across the space. The design even included an original New York Times from 1979. In Venice, the installation represented the bathroom of what looked like a punk music venue, including toilet stalls, graffiti on the wall, and trash scattered on the floor. In Tribeca, however, the team was not allowed to alter the room. Here, the solution was instead based on a special lamp construction projecting words on the walls, which required a considerable amount of research. Comparing the two types of installations, Arturo notes how the tactility of the spaces prompted people to explore the world outside of the VR experience: "(...) people wanted to be there, wanted to touch, wanted to check her books, wanted to check her vinyls, wanted to check her clothes (...)". She furthermore adds how, in her opinion, installations themselves tell stories and contribute with a second layer of experience and produce a feeling of "being properly surrounded by a change of world." Apart from adding to the overall experiential aspect of the experience, this change of world furthermore has a very functional aspect in the way it transitions the audience into and out of the experience and how it, with Arturo's words "(...) softened up the moment of getting into the headset and getting out of the headset."

In the second experience, *The Key*, the transition into the experience is similarly helped by the set-design of the installation. *The Key* is directed by Céline Tricart and produced by Lucid Dreams Production and Oculus VR For Good [26]. In Venice, the piece won the Grand Jury Prize for Best VR Immersive Work. As the only piece of the six chosen for this paper, it included a live actor in the installation, who help you into and out of the experience. The piece was initially shown in Tribeca in April 2019, and in the interview, producer Gloria Bradbury, explains how it was always intended for the work to have a physical component due to the desire to "experiment with something that was semi-theatrical". In the design process, the idea of including a live actor in the work stemmed partly from the director's attention to the onboarding and outboarding for the work to strengthen the emotional trajectory. Bradbury explains how: "Putting on the headset is this mechanical action that normally interrupts the story, so the idea was to have a person who would also be the person practically helping to put on the headset as part of the story from the beginning and the headset became a magical device that would enable the participant to continue the story." As they wanted to keep the same voice as you hear once inside the VR, the experience makes use of a voice recording and sound collars to ensure the consistency of

Fig. 3. *Battlescar: Punk was invented by girls.* Photo copyright by Nico Casavecchia.

the audio. However, the team was aware of the difficulty for the actor to engage with the audience without speaking, which meant that before both installations in Tribeca and Venice, they provided the actors with training: "(...) in New York we hired a friend who worked at Sleep No More (...) to come and do a training for the staff that we had in Tribeca because they (...) had never really done interactive theater before. She provided them tips so that they would feel confident in interacting with people and know how to put the participant at ease and adapt to different reactions (...) that's actually quite difficult (...)". In Venice, they showed the staff videos from Tribeca and thus coached them based on the previous experience. For the outboarding of the experience, the live actor similarly had an important role that included helping take off the headset and guiding viewers in how to interact with photographs that were part of the installation and story. Bradbury added that "we anticipated or hoped that the story would have an emotional impact and having the actor there helped complete the journey for the viewer (...) practically speaking, we needed the actor to give a little gift at the end to the viewer." The gift is a small key that functions as a story component but also as a way to make people remember the work: "We wanted to solicit engagement and empathy, so we came up with the idea to give each participant a key so that they remember the experience they just went through." Besides, there is a marketing component to the leave-behind object: "(...) we have seen other projects do this in the past and it becomes a talking point, creates some buzz (...) it's kind of a marketing play but more importantly for us, it was meant to symbolize that we are all part of this humanistic journey and thank the participant for being vulnerable to it." Apart from the audience experience side of the work, several other design considerations were

Fig. 4. *The Key*. Photo copyright by Gloria Bradbury.

made. One refers to the transportability of the work and its potential afterlife as it travels between festivals or other venues. As Bradbury explains: "One of the questions that went into our thinking of designing the experience is, can we design something kind of like a kit-of-parts so we can keep it, put it in a container and ship it to another venue or activation to save costs, building costs on the initial pieces." However, with *The Key*, they found that it was almost easier to recreate as shipping is a huge consideration and there are still relatively few venues to consider. Therefore, they considered "how can we design it so that we can easily recreate it?" However, even with this consideration in mind, each venue has different criteria, including space and safety considerations, and even aesthetic considerations, which pose potential alterations to the design. When comparing the installations in Tribeca and Venice, Bradbury mentions a number of changes which were made due to the above factors including lack of availability of the right type of digital Meural screens in Europe, color scheme and decoration for the outwards space to respect branding of the event and fog machines being either allowed or not (or potentially not working to the satisfaction of the team).

3.2 Designing the Attraction Window

To summarize, the "attraction window" strategy is described as a semi-open installation space that uses a window as a suspenseful interface through which the extensive set-design of the space is revealed to passing spectators.

This section similarly covers two different installations, both of which I have categorized under the name "attraction window". The first work, *Porton Down*, is directed by Callum Cooper, co-written with Don Webb, and produced by

Cooper and Constance Nuttall [24]. The work is based on the experiences of Don Webb, who in the 1950s became a military test subject and the aftereffects of the experiment. In the experience, participants similarly become test subjects both in the effect of the narrative of the VR experience but also by the design choices of the installation. In the interview, Cooper explains how the aesthetic choices of the installation design are based around photographs of Webb's original stage play from the '80s. Before entering the primary experience room, there was a waiting area designed in the same laboratory aesthetic as the installation, preparing the audience for the experience while also playing with the infrastructural aspect of the film festival itself, where everyone has to wait her turn for the experience. Cooper adds that working with the installation design, the work became more of an artistic and performative thing, more "an artwork". Upon entering the experience and the HMD, the audience member is seated in front of a red button and underneath a timer, all directly in front of a window to the general area, which allows for all passers-by to observe what is happening. This too is referred to by Cooper as belonging to the overall theatrical aspect, thus turning people into performers themselves. Originally, he wanted to have a two-way mirror but decided that it wouldn't have drawn enough attention. However, looking through the window was not intended to be an innocent act: "(...) you feel complicit in this kind of, you're seeing somebody else almost like they are in some kind of laboratory and you're the lab attendant by being outside, and on the timer at the top that kind of presents how quick people's reactions are, adds a level of voyeurism to it, which I feel is, you know, it's an odd, vulnerable experience already of being in VR because you're basically being blindfolded (...)." Upon exiting the installation, you are handed a piece of paper including your test results of the different experiments conducted while in VR. On a narrative level, this relates to the fact, that this was exactly what Webb was not given access to. He was never given any validation of the data that was mined as part of the experiment. On a bigger level, it comments on the general theme of data mining in digital platforms and hardware, including that of the VR medium itself. As part of the experience design, this takeaway paper is intended to invite for reflection after leaving the installation, and as Cooper explains: "The paper you receive in the end is kind of like punctuation to the overall experience and something that you can meditate on later and kind of evaluate (...)." The individualistic aspect of the paper furthermore allows for conversations between friends where comparisons of the results might spark bigger discussions of how to navigate in a data-mining world.

The second work, *A Life In Flowers*, is directed by Armando Kirwin and produced by RYOT and Artie [21]. The experience revolves around the work of the renowned botanical sculptor, Azuma Makoto, and the harmony between flowers and human life. Through artificial intelligence technology, the audience enters into a conversation with Azuma resulting in an individualized, virtual bouquet based on the answers of the participant. In the interview, Kirwin explains how the physical component was always something intended for the work, even being unsure if the final budget would allow it. Referring to the work of Azuma, Kirwin

Fig. 5. *A Life In Flowers*. Photo copyright by Camillo Pasquarelli.

argues: "(. . .) because all of his work is physical, everything he does is essentially an installation (. . .) and then it felt like such a shame to not have a physical component because he is an installation artist." The physical flower arrangements in the installation thus represent the work of Azuma but also connect with the narrative of the VR experience, which is only fully understood after the experience. As Kirwin explains: "(. . .) when you come out of the experience and you look around and you see all these unique arrangements, maybe some people, I don't know how successful this was, but to think, oh I'm surrounded by all these lives. All these other people's lives.". Another design consideration of the installation space had to do with the speech recognition software and the fact that people had to speak out loud to engage with the experience: "Even before the Venice layout we wanted to make it a safe, enclosed space because some people were talking about really personal things, you could say something that is 100% not for anybody else to hear." However, in addition to the audible privacy of the room, the installation furthermore had an outward-facing window similar to that of *Porton Down*. Kirwin explains how the window was both a matter of attracting audiences and to get them excited and curious about the work, but it was also a way of engaging with the urge for social experiences and a generation of social media natives: "We thought, let's make it a little easier for people to at least take a picture". However, it did get the team in a bit of trouble due to privacy issues, which made the venue apply the restriction that you had to get permission ahead of time and to know the person to take a picture. That way, the solution was simply too effective, and Kirwin further adds that: "I think people are hungry for that and even this very simple solution we had was enough to get us in trouble because it worked well and because people want that kind of thing." An additional feature of the window solution is its function as a transitional element. Kirwin argues how, even a simple thing like a window between the virtual and physical world can help transition people, which was a design consideration also applied to the installation and the VR experience itself: "Because we were hoping to get people to be emotional, in the experience, we wanted to have a transition into the world as much as possible (...) you are in the cube of flowers and then you finally go in VR and then it starts very simple, you're not in a full environment yet, it's just an abstract world (...) we're just trying to slowly onboard you and also because of the speech recognition and AI component, we wanted people to be comfortable."

After Venice, *A Life in Flowers* got acquired by the Phi Centre in Montreal, Canada. Speaking about the future of the work in this context, Kirwin explains how, from the beginning, the installation design was intended for touring and museum exhibition: "We wanted to do something that was more repeatable, something a museum could take over easily, that could pop up in other places (...) not that I'm only a practical kind of creator, but for practical reasons we wanted to make the installation easy to tour and yet still hopefully kind of cool. We have three copies of it, and we have plans for it to tour like two years."

3.3   Designing the Performance Space

Lastly, the "performance space" strategy is characterized by having several "parts" either as differing experiential qualities within the same space or as adjacent rooms with different functions. Both versions must, however, be "activated" by the audience which is thus expected to act and "perform" the space. This section similarly covers two different installations, both categorized as "performance space".

Cosmos Within Us is directed by Tupac Martir and produced by Satore Studio, aBAHN, and Satore Tech [23]. In Venice, it was nominated for the Best VR Immersive Experience for Interactive Content 2019. The piece has a duration of 45 min and the story draws us inside the mind of Aiken, a 60-year-old man suffering from Alzheimer's. The installation of the piece and the experience space is twofold, or, put with the words of the director himself, "happens in different realities". One audience member enters the room in an HMD and experiences the full piece in VR. This person is what Martir terms "the interactor". Additional four persons are allowed into the room, seated across the back of the room as audience members. They all wear headphones but no HMD. To these audience members, all parts of the "behind-the-scenes" are visible, including the entire crew that holds, among others, a live orchestra, a live voice-over narrator, the director himself as the conductor, two "shadow men" ensuring the haptics of the experience, sound designers, and more. Put bluntly, the audience members are all watching the one interactor having a VR experience. But, they are also watching the performative - and real-time - enactment around what is happening inside the headset. Therefore, even as the premise and the story are the same, the question is, with Martir's words, "in which reality are you inhibiting the story"? In the interview, Martir explains how, after Venice, the piece has scaled its exhibition format rather dramatically. From hosting four audience members in Venice, it hosted 10 people in London, 115 people in Amsterdam, and 150 people in New York. On a first note, it is interesting how this touring nature was always something intended for the work, as Martir states how the company origins from live entertainment, and therefore a touring model of distribution was natural. This has several implications for the design, as with different venues come different specifications including that of spatial dimensions and available technologies. Here, Martir stated how "The advantage of how the piece is made is actually that we adapt to the space that we are given. (. . . .) Every single time, we shift and adapt. Audience, and size of us and how we are distributed based on the space that we are given." However, not only was the design of the piece affected by adaptions to the spaces given, but it was also continuously rethought in terms of potential audience experience enhancements. Since Venice, Martir states how there was very little for them to add to what is already happening to the interactor, but there was a big potential to the experiential layer available to the audience. These changes included technical upgrades including that of bigger screens but also changes to existing experience elements and the addition of new ones. To put the audience members even more into the space, the team added an entire lighting design for the performance. Furthermore, by the time the piece went to London, the role of the shadow men was changed from functional deliverers of the haptics to performative dancers, all adding to the "volume of what the audience is experiencing". This inclusion of additional media and the physical component of the experience was similarly inherent to the original concept of the piece. Martir states how they considered several different elements to enhance the story with the first proof-of-concept including a technical engine, a dancer in a motion capture suit, two musicians, and two actors to imagine how the story would feel. With his own words, it is a performance that happens in different realities - realities that will need to be subdivided and designed for to understand what they are serving and what they give to the experience. As such, it is not an experience by proxy with a hundred "cheap ticket" audience members watching the one lucky person in the headset. It truly is a performance designed with these different layers in mind. However, met with the criticism that "why would I want to watch someone else having an experience in VR?", Martir further suggests that there might also be a generational perspective on these new types of experiences. With the explosive growth of e-sports across the globe with viewing numbers exceeding many other media, we are starting to see other configurations of entertainment experiences that might pave the road for artistic experience and distribution models such as the one employed by *Cosmos Within Us*. Martir, at least, states how he hopes that others will copy his model and that he considers it to be what he has termed "theatre for the e-sports generation".

In the second experience, *The Collider*, there is a similar use of a performance space, a space of doing, but one which discusses the problematics and body politics of having spectators watching others in VR by zooming in on these extra-experiential qualities of being in VR and providing a privately shared experience between only two people. *The Collider* is directed by May Abdalla and Amy Rose and produced by Anagram [25]. In Venice, it was included in the Best of VR section and was thus out of competition. The piece was first shown at IDFA in 2018 as a prototype and later traveled to both Tribeca and Sandbox Immersive, which made the installation in Venice its fourth. The installation consists of three consecutive rooms in which the two audience members are joined in the last two. Before entering the first room, it is decided who will wear the HMD and who will wield the controllers in the second, shared "experience" room. Each audience member thus enters the first room individually, the rooms being placed side by side, where you listen to the first part of the story through a pair of headphones while seated in armchairs. In the room, there is also a cabinet and on it is a glass cake stand that holds several little figurines. Through the audio, you are prompted to lift the lid of the cake stand and make your own scene with the figurines based on your memory. On the controller side, you are asked to remember a time in which you felt powerful or had power over somebody else. On the VR side, you are asked to remember a time where you felt under somebody else's power. In the interview, Rose explains how, in the design process, they spent a lot of time considering the beginning of the experience and "how you can get somebody into the right state of mind, get them to think about the right sort of things, in a way that's still fairly gentle (...) so that somebody has a chance to arrive, emotionally, physically, in all ways.". A big part of this transition was attributed to the physical act of making the scene with the figurines: "We wanted something where people had to kind of do something actively, not just think, but do but do something that also didn't betray too much of themselves, so there's something abstract about what they do." Furthermore, this act functioned as a way of introducing the two audience members to the overall elements of the piece that will continuously ask you to go back and forth between your memories and the experience, to highlight what the piece is about, with Rose's words: "how our experiences impact on how we relate to people (...) and how you meet somebody or you're with somebody and you respond to them in a particular way and the way you respond is a result of all of your memories and past experiences." After making the scenes in the cake stand, the VR person puts on the headset, the controller person picks up the controllers, and both audience members enter the second room. This transition into the second room and the VR part of the experience was similarly designed for along the same theme of interpersonal relationships: "One thing we were interested in is the moment of drama when the controller person opens the door and sees the person wearing the headset, and we wanted to make the most out of that moment and make it feel as dramatic as possible. And as kind of compelling as possible, like this vision of this person wearing this headset and looking like they're kind of half in another world and yet they are like still here (...) Giving people full license to really look and think about that." Even though the experience states that the controller person is in control, Rose states how, in reality, both are kind of handicapped by the imbalance of only having one half of a VR hardware set-up. This way, it was possible for the directors to explore how, with Rose's words, "(...) you could create this line of communication between two people where one person had something and the other person had something and it only really worked together." She notes how some people, who haven't tried the work, have pointed towards potential issues of risk, but in reality, she explains how her general impression after installing the piece four times is that "(...) when strangers do it together they are very careful, they are much more careful than if it's people who know each other because this thing kicks in where, like, this sense of responsibility to the other person (...)." Exiting the second room, both audience members leave their piece of VR technology and enter the last room, where they are invited to sit down and speak about their shared experience before leaving the installation and, if strangers, parting ways. When asked about considerations of increased audience put-through, Rose is very clear on the fact, that the experience was never intended for spectatorship, as it would potentially mess up the way the piece puts on the spot, with great precision, the relationship between two people, and two people only. However, she underlines how, at the moment, there is not a functioning distribution model for this type of installation-based work, where, in her opinion, galleries might be the best possible infrastructure. Festivals simply do not have the proper budget and also reach a too limited audience due to its short exhibition period.

4   Discussion

During the interviews, several design considerations became evident. Some of them were directly connected to the context of film festivals, while others point towards more general challenges for the future of location-based entertainment. Both of these are massively impacted by the current Covid-19 pandemic. While this was not directly formulated as a question in the interviews, it naturally became a topic while discussing distribution and the future of the works. Some of the experiences already had the flexibility to adapt to government regula-tions, including *Cosmos Within Us*, where Martir points out how the number of audience members can be scaled up and down and the space between audience members can be easily increased. Furthermore, there is only one person in the headset per show, which makes considerations of hygiene easier. Other experi-ences had to make additional changes to current installation contexts. Kirwin explains how, for installing *A Life in Flowers* at the Phi Centre, they had to temporarily change the installation because Canada banned VR in a museum setting: "We had to adapt it for a big screen, so you go in and you, there's a big screen in front of you and there's a microphone that's kind of coming down from the ceiling and you're from a fixed position which isn't nearly as immersive, I think, but it's still intriguing to people to kind of talk to this flower arrangement and have it reflect back to them, so, that's a temporary thing for a few months

(...)". For other designers, including Arturo, the situation had them speculate about possible future infrastructures at venues that would be safer: "(...) if the Quest becomes more economic, more affordable, maybe there's a way that, maybe if you have a Quest, you can go with your own Quest, and that would be very safe, and then maybe there's (...) a thousand Quests headsets, and then only one has it and you go through the whole festival with one of them, and in the end, it goes to a (...) dry-cleaning or something."

Apart from the Covid-19 situation, the specific exhibition context of film festivals similarly produced several design considerations. As became evident during the interviews, several of the experiences have a touring life of more festivals, where the installation in Venice was rarely the first or last one. This leads to considerations of transportability and adaptability to varying venues, which was highlighted in the individual interviews. However, with only a handful of prominent festival venues, this type of context also dictates the overall life of the project. Bradbury notes how she believes that: "(...) anything that is entering the festival circuit kind of has a natural 18-month life, from start to finish (...)". For many designers, this lack of existing venues and distribution networks is a huge issue for future work. Rose states how she believes that "(...) what would be good for audiences, is if there were more venues or opportunities for broad audiences to see this kind of work (...) And so it's like, how do we find a distribution network? Is it like a gallery network? What's the right institution? What's the right infrastructure that will enable that to happen? I think it doesn't really exist yet (...)." In her interview, Bradbury similarly notes: "(...) There are so many things that need to be created (..) it's kind of like the chicken or the egg thing, right? Without a proper distribution system, you don't have the proper financing (...)". The lack of a proper distribution system and venues pointed towards some challenges identified by the designers. The biggest issue is one both for the potential venues but also for the content creators; that of sociality. At the moment, the majority of experiences are designed and exhibited in a way, that allows for singular experiences of one person at a time. Therefore, many experiences are challenged by a low audience put-through, which in itself makes it hard to establish an economically viable venue. However, it also poses the challenge of making the venues and experiences a social destination where people go with their friends and families. Arturo notes how with cinema we have a clear social ritual and she speculates: "What is going to be our social ritual in terms of VR?" For Bradbury, the social aspect is furthermore coupled with the question of recurrence: "With cinema, you're always going to be like, "Oh, new film" and you might consider going to see it, but with location-based VR venues, how often do they have new experiences or that you hear about them? You go once, maybe twice a year?"

For some designers, this led them to think of other established distribution systems and institutions, including that of theatres. For *Cosmos Within Us*, Martir believes that "(...) the best place to perform the piece is at theatres or black boxes." For other designers, the lack of existing solutions functions as a springboard for considering individual location-based business models. For

Battlescar – Punk Was Invented by Girls, Casavecchia and Arturo are working on a full location-based experience in a customized venue. While it might solve the issues of audience put-through and sociality, it brings with it several additional challenges. Arturo sums up: "It's a complicated thing between, the number of computers you need, the number of square meters you need, and how much audience you can attract.". And with the lack of existing venues to distribute between, these challenges would return with each move to a new country and city.

For some designers, the exhibition modus of the installation is only but one out of several versions of the experience. For distribution purposes and/or for considerations regarding investment and sponsorship, several of the experiences exist also as in-headset experiences distributed on existing platforms including Steam and Oculus Store, which in some cases lead to slight alterations to the design. Concerning *Porton Down*, Cooper notes how "(...) those theatrical elements need to be reduced to, needs to be changed slightly to be fitted onto those platforms." Furthermore, he shares the plans of making a future short film version "(...) because it is an animation essentially, to try to keep this thing alive once the system's dead."

This leads to the last design consideration included in this discussion, exactly that of the preservation of installation-based experiences and VR works in general. Kirwin notes how: "The issue is that there is no aftermarket, preservation, there's no intrinsic value (...) if you work in another medium, the value can actually grow, and in VR you're basically kind of dead after two years. (...) People who are making stuff in VR, it's all about the process really, because there isn't much else right now. (...) It is process-driven, some of these things take a year to make, they go to one festival because they're an installation with live actors or something, and they are never seen again. (...) And that certainly creates a certain context for the works from the concept all the way through the, you know, last gasp of the project. (...). So, this lack of preservation and the afterlife of the works are not only tied to the lack of distribution and business models but also has massive effects on the work processes and work context of the industry professionals. While distribution and business considerations might seem unfitted for academic inquiry, these interviews have shown clearly that in emerging media, due to the lack of commercialization and institutionalization, it is not only a matter of understanding the works themselves as 'unassimilated' (Rouse, 2016) but starting to understand how these bigger forces of economy and distribution are shaping how the works are made.

5   Conclusion

This paper has investigated some trends within installation design at film festivals exemplified by a selection of six works exhibited at the Venice 2019 VR selection. These works were initially divided according to the design strategies of 'the story room', 'the attraction window' and 'the performance space'. While it can be discussed if the three design strategy categories are accurate and homogeneous enough to be sustained in future research, they did provide a helpful initial structure for considering the experiences. Through interviews with industry professionals about their retrospective thoughts on the installation design for the experiences, the paper uncovered some design considerations and strategies, including consideration of installations as a transitional element of the audience experience design, how to approach audience put-through and spectatorship, ways to ensure transportability and distribution of design, and dealing with venue specificity and adaptability of the installation, among others. These design considerations lead to bigger discussions of not only the current challenge of the Covid-19 pandemic but also the general forces of economy and distribution shaping the future for location and installation-based work. This way, the paper has contributed to the larger notion of media in 'attraction phases' (Rouse, 2016) by documenting and discussing design approaches shaped by the forces of the industry. However, this paper is only but a small contribution and underlines the continued need for documentation, preservation, research, and development within the field. It is hoped, that by contributing to this perspective on CVR design, exhibition and distribution, we might take a tiny step towards more cross-pollinated research between academia and industry so that we might solve the challenge of creating standards for location and installation-based experiences to make it easier for the works to meet a bigger audience in the future. Following this paper and its insights, future areas of investigation for this researcher includes the co-existence and co-design of physical (location-based) and virtual versions of the same work, the adaptation of location-based works for virtual distribution, and virtual onboarding practices for the transition of the audience into the experiences.

References

1. Baudry, J.-L., Williams, A.: Ideological effects of the basic cinematographic apparatus. Film Q. **28**(2), 39–47 (1974)
2. Bellour, R.: Cinema, alone/multiple cinemas. Alphaville: J. Film Screen Media **5**, 1–28 (2013)
3. Benford, S., Gabriella, G.: Temporal trajectories in shared interactive narratives. In: Proceedings of the SIGCHI Conference on Human Factors in Computing Systems (2008)
4. Benford, S., et al.: From interaction to trajectories: designing coherent journeys through user experiences. In: Proceedings of the SIGCHI Conference on Human Factors in Computing Systems (2009)
5. Benford, S., Giannachi, G.: Performing Mixed Reality. The MIT Press, Cambridge (2011)
6. Benyon, D.: Presence in blended spaces. Interact. Comput. **24**(4), 219–226 (2012)
7. Benyon, D., Mival, O.: Blended spaces for collaboration. Comput. Supported Cooperative Work (CSCW) **24**(2–3), 223–249 (2015)
8. Deleuze, G.: What is a dispositif? In: Armstrong, T.J. (ed.) Michel Foucault, Philosopher. Routledge, New York (1992)
9. Ding, N., Zhou, W., Fung, A.Y.: Emotional effect of cinematic VR compared with traditional 2D film. Telematics Inform. **35**, 1572–1579 (2018)

10. Dooley, K.: Storytelling with virtual reality in 360-degrees: a new screen grammar. Stud. Austr. Cinema **11**(3), 161–171 (2017)
11. Furht, B. (ed.): Handbook of Augmented Reality. Springer, Heidelberg (2011). https://doi.org/10.1007/978-1-4614-0064-6
12. Jaller, C., Serafin, S.: Transitioning into states of immersion: transition design of mixed reality performances and cinematic virtual reality. Digit. Creativity **31**, 1–10 (2020)
13. Mateer, J.: Directing for Cinematic Virtual Reality: how the traditional film director's craft applies to immersive environments and notions of presence. J. Media Practice **18**(1), 14–25 (2017)
14. Metz, C., Guzzetti, A.: The fiction film and its spectator: a metapsychological study. New Literary History **8**(1), 75–105 (1976)
15. Reeves, S., et al.: Designing the spectator experience. In: Proceedings of the SIGCHI Conference on Human Factors in Computing Systems (2005)
16. Rostami, A., Rossitto, C., Waern, A.: Frictional realities: enabling immersion in mixed-reality performances. In: Proceedings of the 2018 ACM International Conference on Interactive Experiences for TV and Online Video (2018)
17. Rouse, R., et al.: MRX: an interdisciplinary framework for mixed reality experience design and criticism. Digit. Creativity **26**(3–4), 175–181 (2015)
18. Rouse, R.: Media of attraction: a media archeology approach to panoramas, kinematography, mixed reality and beyond. In: Nack, F., Gordon, A.S. (eds.) ICIDS 2016. LNCS, vol. 10045, pp. 97–107. Springer, Cham (2016). https://doi.org/10.1007/978-3-319-48279-8_9
19. Rouse, R., Barba, E.: Design for emerging media: how MR designers think about storytelling, process, and defining the field. In: Nunes, N., Oakley, I., Nisi, V. (eds.) ICIDS 2017. LNCS, vol. 10690, pp. 245–258. Springer, Cham (2017). https://doi.org/10.1007/978-3-319-71027-3_20
20. Shumaker, R., Lackey, S. (eds.): VAMR 2014. LNCS, vol. 8525. Springer, Cham (2014). https://doi.org/10.1007/978-3-319-07458-0
21. Venice 2019 marketing material: A Life in Flowers. https://www.labiennale.org/en/cinema/2019/venice-virtual-reality/life-flowers. Accessed 11 Nov 2020
22. Venice 2019 marketing material: Battlescar - Punk was invented by girls. www.labiennale.org/en/cinema/2019/venice-virtual-reality/battlescar--punk-was-invented-girls. Accessed 11 Nov 2020
23. Venice 2019 marketing material: Cosmos Within Us. https://www.labiennale.org/en/cinema/2019/venice-virtual-reality/cosmos-within-us. Accessed 11 Nov 2020
24. Venice 2019 marketing material: Porton Down. https://www.labiennale.org/en/cinema/2019/venice-virtual-reality/porton-down. Accessed 11 Nov 2020
25. Venice 2019 marketing material: The Collider. https://www.labiennale.org/en/cinema/2019/venice-virtual-reality/collider. Accessed 11 Nov 2020
26. Venice 2019 marketing material: The Key. https://www.labiennale.org/en/cinema/2019/venice-virtual-reality/key. Accessed 11 Nov 2020

(AB)USE ME: A Mixed Reality Performance Installation Exploring Use of the Body as a Mediating Object

Liucija Paniuskyte[✉], Zuzana Hrubá, and Brian Bemman[iD]

Aalborg University, 9000 Aalborg, Denmark
bb@create.aau.dk

Abstract. Performance art has long been used as a means for challenging various social constructs, such as ethics and personhood, and sometimes in ways which from the outside can appear traumatic for the performer – perhaps the most famous example being Marina Abramović's *Rhythm 0* (1974). Moreover, the nature of such constructs and our experiences when they are challenged have become arguably more complex with the digital world and the ever increasing amount of our lives spent in virtual environments. In this paper, we present a mixed reality performance installation inspired by *Rhythm 0* in which the subjective experiences of both a human performer, used as an interface for mediating visual and aural outcomes in this space, and the participants interacting with the body of this performer, are gathered through a shared narrative interview following six separate performances. We evaluated the experiences of both the performer and participants through a qualitative analysis centered around the specific words and statements used with respect to performing objecthood from the perspective of the performer and cognitive absorption from the perspective of the participants. Our analysis is supplemented by methods used in information retrieval for assessing the amount of similarity in the respective transcripts of the performer's and participants' interviews.

Keywords: Performance art installation · Mixed reality · Body · Cognitive absorption · Qualitative analysis · Information retrieval

1 Introduction

Performance art works can provide spaces in which boundaries are pushed, social constructs are challenged, and artists are able to explore often deep, inner aspects of themselves and of the individuals who may take part in the performance. Moreover, such experiences can be powerfully positive or negative for all involved. Arguably, the most well-known example of such a performance art work is Marina Abramović's *Rhythm 0* (1974). In her performance, Abramović offered herself up to the audience as an object to be treated in any way they saw fit. On a table

A. Brooks et al. (Eds.): ArtsIT 2020, LNICST 367, pp. 64–84, 2021.
https://doi.org/10.1007/978-3-030-73426-8_4

in front of her she provided a variety of tools, ranging from a feather to a gun and bullet, which participants were free to use on her body. Over the course of a six-hour long performance, Abramović reportedly endured a number of rather shocking behaviors from the participants including having her clothes cut from her body, her skin pierced, and her life threatened by a loaded gun.

Rhythm 0 utilized the notion of the human body as an object to shed light on the limits to human behavior and in doing so, challenge the social constructs of what constitute ethical actions and personhood in society. Over the years, much has been written about the significance of *Rhythm 0* and its findings [1,22]. Interviews with Abramović and others closely associated with her performance have provided further insight into her experience, however, these same insights into the experiences of the participants and how these align or not with those of the performer are lacking. In recent years, the digital world and ever increasing time we spend in virtual environments, such as those found in online gaming platforms and social media, have made these limits and constructs illuminated by *Rhythm 0* perhaps more complex and difficult to navigate. Indeed, in recent research on immersive virtual gaming environments, greater perceived immersion in such spaces has been linked to greater cognitive aggression in individuals [12] and the role of anonymity and the rapid transmission of information, for example, in cyber-bullying on social media, has been explored [18]. Fortunately, this situation has provided new mediums in the form of virtual and mixed-realities as well as opportunities to explore interesting topics and questions for researchers and performance artists alike.

In this paper, we present (AB)USE ME, a mixed reality performance installation inspired by Abramović's *Rhythm 0* wherein the performer's body acts as a mediating instrument or tool through which visual and aural stimuli are produced in response to the physical movements and touch, respectively, by participants. With this work, we are seeking to better understand the subjective experiences of a performer whose body is used as an object and the participants who are asked to physically use this performer's body as an object. In particular, we are interested in exploring this dynamic in the context of a mixed-reality space in which the participant becomes fully absorbed and how this factors into the respective experiences of the performer and participant. In Sect. 2, we discuss related work pertaining to performance art with an emphasis on *Rhythm 0*, mixed reality and its use in performance art practice, and cognitive absorption. In Sect. 3, we introduce the conceptual framework used in the design of (AB)USE ME and reflect on how this framework was used to motivate the design of the interactions and outcomes of the installation. In Sect. 4, we discuss our evaluation of the experiences of both the performer and participants in six separate performances of (AB)USE ME. In particular, we provide a qualitative analysis in which the focus is on the specific words and statements used with respect to performing objecthood from the perspective of the performer and the five dimensions of cognitive absorption from the perspective of the participants. This analysis is further supported through a method frequently employed in information retrieval known as cosine similarity, which we use to assess the

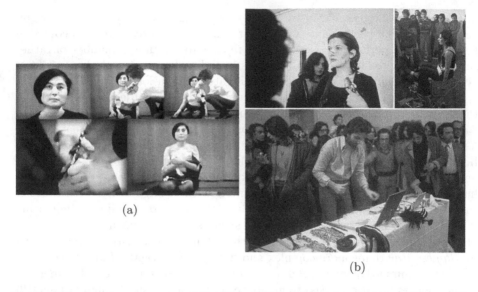

Fig. 1. Yoko Ono's performance of *Cut Piece* (1964) [17] in (a) and Marina Abramović's performance of *Rhythm 0* (1974) [2] in (b).

degree of similarity in the respective transcripts of the performer and participants' interviews. In Sect. 5, we conclude the paper and discuss some possible future work.

2   Related Work

In this section, we provide an overview of performance art practice as it relates to performing objecthood, use of mixed reality in this practice and how to design for it, as well as information concerning cognitive absorption and its relevance to experiences with digital technologies and virtual environments.

2.1   Performance Art

In the 1960s and 1970s, a new type of performance art known as *endurance art* emerged. Such performances typically involved the performer having to endure some particular experience or otherwise strenuous activity, often lasting for lengthy or unspecified periods of time in a more narrowly defined type of performance known as *durational art*. Crucial to the success of both types of performance is the performer's ability to *perform objecthood* [22] wherein the artist is required to disassociate themselves from any perceived negative experiences throughout the entirety of the performance. Consequently, an important subject emerged within these types of performance art, namely, the objectification of the human body and ethical questions concerning how we act towards others in such a performance space [22, p. 18]. Two prominent examples of performance art pieces from this time period are Yoko Ono's *Cut Piece* (1964) and Marina Abramović's *Rhythm 0* (1974) shown in Fig. 1.

Both works shown in Fig. 1 invited audience members to interact with the performers over a sustained period of time. In Ono's *Cut Piece*, she would remain seated and the audience was invited to participate in the performance by cutting away pieces of her clothing. A single performance lasted for as long as there were still clothes on her body and was performed several times over the years. Abramović's *Rhythm 0* was performed only once and in this performance, she laid out seventy-two items on a table, ranging from those that could be used in soft and caring ways, such as a feather and cake, to those intended for destruction, such as a gun and bullet. Other items included those not inherently dangerous but could be misused to cause pain, such as a rose, as well as more neutral items such as paint. "I am the object," a note on a table read, "there are 72 objects on the table that one can use on me as desired" [1]. The performance lasted for 6 h, during which she did not respond to any actions taken by any of those audience members that chose to participate.

While both performers invited their audience members to act upon them, there was no plan for how these actions should unfold. As noted in [22, pp. 44–50], the observed outcomes were the result of entirely autonomous decisions on behalf of the audience and the impulses of those individuals that arose from interacting with a "tenaciously passive female body". Importantly, however, both performances resulted in the performers having to endure sometimes shockingly aggressive responses from a number of audience members, with Abramović's life being threatened with the loaded gun [22, pp. 49–50]. Her clothes were also cut from her body, even though she did not invite the audience to do so as explicitly as Ono had done. Further still, the thorns of the rose were reportedly used to pierce her skin and one audience member cut her throat with a razor blade causing her to bleed.

In [22, p. 75], *Rhythm 0* is described as "a cautionary tale about the dangers of objectification". Abramovićs partner gave the following statement in an interview with the performance artist, Linda Montano, describing the experience of performing objecthood:

> So the whole notion of being an object became a very obvious thing in our work, in all of our performances – to make yourself an object. … If you make a mistake and fall, at that very moment you are an object. … The moment you fall unwittingly, without a choice, without choosing, in that moment you are left to be an object. … You see, it's the noninvolvement of self, of consciousness, of decision, of realization [22, p. 69].

The essence of such performances it seems lies in the performer being willing and able to let go of much of what constitutes one's sense of self including awareness, reaction, autonomy, and control. However, the degree to which performers perform objecthood can differ, as Ono in her performance can be seen in Fig. 1(a) choosing to cover herself as clothes are cut away from her body while Abramović can be seen in Fig. 1(b) remaining absolutely still. According to [22], Abramović's choice to perform objecthood in the way that she did was

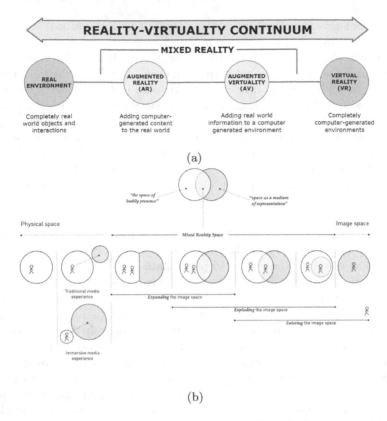

Fig. 2. The Reality-Virtuality Continuum (as described in [13]) shown in (a) and the approaches to mixing realities portrayed along this continuum (as taken from [21, p. 81]) in (b).

a significant contributing factor to the aggressive actions which ensued. Moreover, Abramović hinted at the effect these actions had on the participants at the conclusion of the performance when she stopped performing objecthood and they left without ever speaking to her [22, p. 74]. This was the pivotal moment in which the objecthood of the performer was broken for the participants and they were confronted with the realization that she was indeed a thinking, feeling person.

2.2   Mixed Reality in Performance Art

In recent years, a type of performance art known as *mixed reality performance* has emerged and involves experiences that are intended to "express both their mixing of the real and virtual as well as their combination of live performance and interactivity" [5, p. 1]. Mixed reality in this sense lies along a so-called reality-virtuality continuum, shown in Fig. 2(a), in between two, opposing spatial ends – physicality and virtuality. Mixed reality exists between these two extremes within the realms of augmented reality, where computer-generated content is added to the physical world (e.g., projecting the current weather onto the field-of-view in a pair of glasses) and augmented virtuality, where real-world information is added to a computer-generated environment (e.g., using a person's actual body rather than an avatar as the player in a virtual game) [6, p. 2].

When designing in particular for installation/media art spaces in which a mixing of realities occurs, we can look at a somewhat more nuanced view of the reality-virtuality continuum shown in Fig. 2(b). According to [21, p. 58], when designing for such a mixed reality space, one must consider the relationship between three main elements: the physical space (indicated by a clear circle), the so-called 'image' or virtual space (indicated by a shaded circle), and the viewer (indicated by one figure within the circles), where the role of the viewer can be one of an 'active user', 'participant' or 'immersant' [21, p. 58]. In a performative space, there would be an additional element of the performer to consider (indicated by a second figure within the circles). One will note in Fig. 2(b), for example, that the first diagram illustrates the space encountered by a viewer experiencing only the physical world such as when walking outdoors, while the final diagram illustrates this same viewer entirely within an image space such as when experiencing virtual reality. As one moves from a physical space to the image space (from left to right), the image space gradually becomes more prominent in the experience of the viewer – first expanding, then exploding, and finally entering [21, p. 75]. For example, the second diagram in Fig. 2(b) at top illustrates the space encountered by a viewer when consuming traditional media such as when watching television, where the viewer is situated within the dominant physical space with a wholly separate image space that is comparatively smaller in size. However, the relative importance of the image space to the experience of the viewer depends not only on how it is mixed with the physical space but how immersive this image space is for that individual. For example, the second diagram Fig. 2(b) at bottom illustrates a highly immersive image space through its relatively larger size when compared to the physical space. Of particular importance to the mixed reality space we present in this paper is the distinction between the fourth and fifth spaces illustrated in Fig. 2(b). In the fourth diagram, when one moves from an image space that is expanding to one that is exploding, the viewer and performer both exist within the physical space but with some prominent mixing of the image space as part of their experience, such as the visual presence of a hologram, However, neither individual is able to affect this projection in any way. In contrast, the fifth diagram illustrates a more exploded image space wherein the performer (or viewer) is situated within a space which is both physical and virtual and where he or she is able to affect the virtual space.

2.3 Cognitive Absorption

Exploring people's interactions with virtual environments and how to make such experiences more enriching is a wide ranging interest shared by researchers in

Table 1. The five dimensions of cognitive absorption (CA) when interacting with software and their explanations as characterized in [3].

	CA dimension	Explanation
1	Temporal dissociation	"...the inability to register the passage of time while engaged in interaction" [3, p. 673]
2	Focused immersion	"...the experience of total engagement where other attentional demands are, in essence, ignored" and "...results in amplification of perceived ease of use" [3, p. 673]
3	Heightened enjoyment	How pleasurable an experience is "contributes to perceived ease of use in that enjoyable activities are viewed as being less taxing" [3, p. 673]
4	Sense of control	A sense of being in charge and exercising control over interactions with software should reduce the perceived difficulty of interaction [3, p. 673]
5	Amplified curiosity	The extent to which an experience arouses "sensory and cognitive curiosity" and the interaction "invokes excitement about available possibilities" [3, pp. 666–673]

HCI and digital artists alike. Such endeavours necessarily require an understanding of human psychology and behavior with many terms such as immersion, cognitive flow, and enjoyment, among others, serving as relevant objects of study [3,10,15]. A multidimensional construct known as cognitive absorption (CA) is one such term encompassing many of these others that we have elected to focus on in the design and evaluation of our installation.

Cognitive absorption has been defined as "a state of deep involvement with a software" and is based largely on previous research in engagement and flow [3, p. 1]. As characterized in [3], cognitive absorption consists of the five dimensions shown in Table 1 of temporal dissociation, focused immersion, heightened enjoyment, control, and curiosity. When designing for digital technologies and interactive spaces in performance art, it is clear how artists might be concerned with many of these dimensions of cognitive absorption – from cultivating a sense of heightened enjoyment and curiosity for their participants to establishing a highly immersive setting wherein the interactions afforded by this space offer high degrees of control. As [14] notes, immersion in a skillfully designed participatory and performative digital space should encourage participants to explore the possibilities of this environment and bring joy along the way. However, highly immersive digital spaces, for example, are not without their drawbacks. As noted by [12,19], high levels of immersion and presence in such virtual environments can lead to aggressive feelings and behaviors. In particular, both perceived realism and perceived controller naturalness have been shown to have a positive effect on perceived immersion which in turn has a positive affect on cognitive aggression [12, pp. 74–75]. Designing spaces so as to avoid possibly negative outcomes from participants such as aggression may not necessarily be a great concern, however, it might be something of interest for artists to explore this boundary and balance between such immersive experiences, the participants' interactions within such a space, and the outcomes they produce.

Measuring whether or not a person is cognitively absorbed in a particular technology can be challenging due the subjective nature of such an experience and the complexity in obtaining accurate assessments of mental states [10]. However, several methods for measuring cognitive absorption as well as its related constructs of immersion, presence, and flow have been suggested, with questionnaires largely being preferred [3,10,15]. In contrast, interviews can serve as an important resource for collecting rich, qualitative data regarding not only how much a person claims to have experienced, for example, temporal dissociation or an amplified sense of curiosity, but also what words and expressions they use to describe the subjective nature of that experience. It is this latter approach that we have chosen to adopt in this paper.

3   Design of (AB)USE ME: A Mixed Reality Performance Installation

In this section, we introduce the conceptual framework for our mixed reality performance installation, (AB)USE ME, by describing our considerations when designing its physical and digital spaces. Next, we discuss our motivations for the interactions and visual and aural outcomes within this space. We conclude with an overview of its implementation details.

3.1   Conceptual Framework

(AB)USE ME is a mixed reality performance installation situated within the fifth diagram of mixing realities shown in Fig. 2(b) along the reality-virtuality continuum – containing both physical elements, in the form of a human performer, and virtual elements, in the form of a digital avatar in the likeness of the performer projected onto a screen facing the performer and participant. A participant's interactions in this mixed reality space occur through physical manipulation of the performer's body, which acts as an interface with the digital avatar, where her movements and the felt intensity of the participant's touch are presented to the participant in the form of visual and auditory feedback, respectively. The overall conceptual framework of (AB)USE ME is illustrated in Fig. 3.

As shown in Fig. 3, (AB)USE ME was designed with considerations for both the physical and digital spaces which comprise the mixed reality space of the installation. The digital space (shown on the left side) was designed with conditions supporting cognitive absorption with a particular emphasis placed on the dimension of focused immersion (shown in Table 1). These conditions were a perceived realism to the avatar and a perceived naturalness to its movements with those of the performer's body. With these conditions in mind, we might consider whether or not participants will become sufficiently immersed within this space that they ignore the nature of the interactions they are having – that is, lose sight of the awareness of and consideration for the fact they are using a

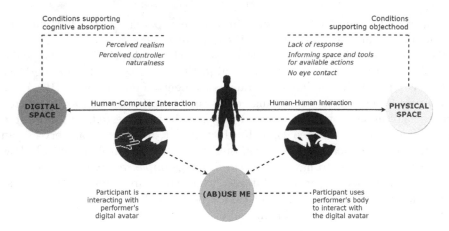

Fig. 3. Conceptual framework of the proposed mixed reality performance installation, (AB)USE ME.

living, feeling person and not merely an object. The physical space (shown on the right side), was designed with conditions inspired by those found in *Rhythm 0* that we suspect will support the ability of the performer to perform objecthood and the recognition of the performer as an object by the participants. These conditions were a complete lack response from the performer to the actions of the participants and an 'informing space' which consisted of (1) a statement, spoken aloud at the start of each performance of (AB)USE ME, clarifying that the performer is free to be interacted with, and (2) interactions of touch and movement, similar to the tools provided in *Rhythm 0*, for informing the participant of possible actions within this space. Additionally, we have designed the possible interactions with the performer to be carried out while the participant is standing directly behind the performer and behind a line on the floor that they should not cross. This ensured that both the performer and participant would remain facing the projection and that no eye contact was not possible with the performer.

3.2   Interactions and Outcomes

An important feature of the mixed reality space in (AB)USE ME is the feedback participants receive from their interactions of movement and touch with the performer's body in the form of visual and auditory stimuli, respectively. This visual stimuli consist of (1) an avatar in the likeness of the performer designed to be both realistic and exhibit movements which align naturally with those of the performer's body, and (2) a set of three different effects projected onto the avatar corresponding to three intensity levels of physical movement and touch. Figure 4 shows the six stages in designing the avatar in (a) and the final avatar with the set of three visual effects projected onto it in (b).

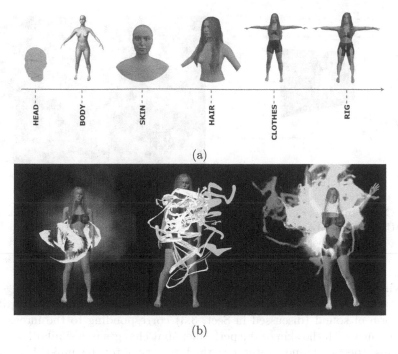

(a)

(b)

Fig. 4. The digital visual components of (AB)USE ME with the design stages of the performer's avatar in (a) and the visual outcomes corresponding to light, medium, and rough interactions with the performer's body shown projected onto the avatar (from left to right) in (b).

As shown in Fig. 4(a), the avatar situated in the virtual space was designed in six, detailed stages so as to capture as many of the characteristics of the performer as possible and in doing so, enhance the overall realism needed to facilitate immersion (as discussed in Sect. 2.3). These characteristics include accurate head and facial dimensions, approximate body proportions, realistic skin tone and texture, accurate hair length and color, clothes which match those worn by the performer, and a skeletal rig which allowed for movements mirroring those of the performer's body in line with the controller naturalness needed to further facilitate immersion (as discussed in Sect. 2.3).

As shown in Fig. 4(b), interactions with the body of the performer are illustrated visually on the avatar in one of three ways, depending on the degree of physicality. Light physical interactions with the body of the performer, such as gently caressing her arm, correspond to light, gently moving 'feathers'. Slightly more intense physical touches, such as those needed to re-position a part of her body, correspond to more harsh, faster moving lines while extremely physical touches, such as those needed to move her entire body or cause pain, correspond to fire. Such visuals were inspired by the array of pleasurable and dangerous objects Abramović provided in *Rhythm 0* and are in line with a so-called expressive strategy of designing for interaction noted in [5] where illustrating or even

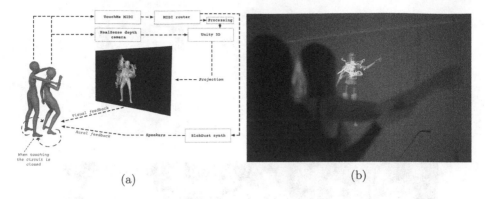

(a)   (b)

Fig. 5. Conceptual overview of the mixed-reality installation space and systems used in (AB)USE ME in (a) and an image from an actual performance showing a participant standing behind the performer in (b).

amplifying the visual effect of these physical movements is one of four suggested design strategies. In addition to these visual effects, there is further feedback in the form of sound (discussed in Sect. 3.3) corresponding to the intensity of physical touch with the skin of the performer that changes in a similar fashion to the visuals – becoming more intense as the intensity of touch similarly increases.

3.3   Implementation Overview

The conceptual overview of the mixed-reality installation space and systems used in (AB)USE ME as well as an image from an actual performance are shown in Fig. 5. The 3D modelling of the avatar was created using Blender [7] and an add-on called Facebuilder [9]. We modelled the performer's head using 6 photographs taken to form a 360 degree view. A 3D model of a body was obtained from MakeHuman [11] upon which we attached the model of our performer's head. The skin of our avatar was created by importing the model's UV map from Blender to Adobe Photoshop and applying skin texture maps from Make-Human. The avatar's hair was created with bent planes designed to resemble hair strands through the texturing node system in Blender and an additional add-on called HairTool. The clothes were created by selecting parts of the body mesh that we wanted covered and applying black material on a new, duplicated mesh at this position. The hair, clothes, and body meshes were then linked so that when the performer moved her body, the avatar's body, clothes, and hair followed suit. Lastly, rigging bones were applied to the avatar's model in Blender using armature with an automatic weights function. In order to animate the avatar, we used the Nuitrack [16] plugin for Unity which allows for skeleton tracking of up to 19 joints through a depth camera. The completed avatar was projected onto a wall approximately 2 m from the performer and participant at approximately 60% the scale of the performer's body. Visuals were produced with Unity's Mesh Effects. A TouchMe MIDI controller [23], which operates through skin conductance, is used to produce the pitch content of the sounds produced by physical contact between the participant and performer. These MIDI values are processed and received in Processing [20] and the sounds were generated through an online synth called BlokDust [8]. Three different soundscapes, corresponding to the three visual outcomes shown in Fig. 4(b), were designed so as to aurally align with intensities portrayed by their respective visual outcomes.

4 Evaluation

In this section, we explain how the procedure for performances of (AB)USE ME and the shared narrative interviews with the performer and participants which followed were carried out. We conclude with the results and discussion of our qualitative analysis of the interviews supplemented with methods from information retrieval for assessing the degree of similarity found in transcripts of these interviews. During these discussions, we compare the experiences of the performer and participants across performances as well as within individual performances with a particular emphasis on the words and statements expressed by the performer with respect to performing objecthood and by the participants with respect to the five dimensions of cognitive absorption.

4.1 Participants and Performer

We collected data from 6 volunteer participants (4 male and 2 female) with an average age of 28.2 ± 5.9 years. Five of the participants stated having extensive experience with interactive art while the remaining participant claimed to have only little experience with the same. Furthermore, four of the participants stated having extensive experience with performance and participatory art involving touch with the remaining two participants claiming little to no such experience. The performer was a female artist and co-creator of the (AB)USE ME performance installation with academic training in and several years of experience with interactive, participatory, and performance art. All participants were informed of the interactions that would be afforded to them as well as how their data would be used. Consent was obtained in accordance with the participating university's ethical guidelines for conducting experiments with human participants.

4.2 Procedure

Participants were asked to enter an empty room where the performer was standing motionless and facing away from the participant towards the wall where a projection of the performer's avatar was facing her and the participant. The experimenter then asked the participant to stand behind the performer as a conductive bracelet (already attached to the performer) for use with the TouchMe MIDI controller was fastened to the participant's ankle. The experimenter then stated aloud "The performer is an instrument. There are no boundaries, no right and wrong. The only boundary is the line marked on the floor which you cannot cross. Please feel free to explore. You can start now". With this statement, we not only wanted to pay homage to *Rhythm 0*, but we wanted the participants to understand also that the performer has given consent. As instructed, the participants were then free to begin interacting with the performer. No time limit for the performances was enforced, but participants ended their time spent with the performer after an average of 8 ± 6.1 min. After the conclusion of each performance, participants were given a five-minute break in order to facilitate reflections on their experience. Following this break, participants were asked to take part in a shared narrative interview with the performer in which an open ended question asking the interviewees to describe their experience was first posed. We believed that a shared interview of this type would allow for deeper reflections on one person's experiences by allowing for the exchange of thoughts and feeling from the other, similar to a focus group setting. More narrowly focused questions addressed to the participants pertaining to the five dimensions of cognitive absorption – such as the movements of the performer's body and those of the avatar, the alignment of the sound and visual feedback, and feelings regarding use of the performer's body as an object – comprised the semi-structured narrative follow-up. Questions pertaining to feelings of objecthood and mistreatment as well as any confrontational moments with the participants, were asked of the performer. Finally, more structured questions served to collect personal data (e.g., age and related experience) from the participants and concluded the entirety of their time with (AB)USE ME.

4.3   Results and Discussion

As a first step in our analysis, we constructed a text corpus of 12 documents corresponding to the 12 transcripts of the six shared narrative interviews conducted with the performer and participants following six performances of (AB)USE ME. Each document in this corpus contained text belonging to only the performer or participant for a given performance and was preprocessed to eliminate punctuation, make all characters lower case, remove common English stop words (e.g., 'the') as well as stem the entirety of the text (e.g., converting 'interesting' and 'interested' to their common root form of 'interest'). We will assume in our following analyses that words with similar roots express similar meanings and that use of these words (and not others) by both the performer and participant indicates at least some degree of commonality between their respective experiences. Naturally, reducing rich qualitative data to such a format will invariably lose the context and ignore semantic meaning, so further qualitative analysis is also provided.

Figure 6 shows word clouds generated from our text corpus for the performer and participants illustrating the 200 most frequent words expressed across all six performances of (AB)USE ME. Words that were expressed most frequently by the performer and participants appear towards the center of their respective word clouds and with a large font while words that were expressed less frequently appear at the edges of these clouds and with a smaller font. Additionally, words that were expressed with equal frequency are shown in the same color. One will

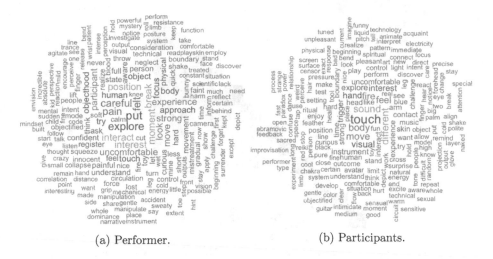

(a) Performer.   (b) Participants.

Fig. 6. Word clouds illustrating the 200 most frequent words expressed by the performer in (a) and the participants in (b) when reflecting on their respective experiences during a shared narrative interview following six performances of (AB)USE ME.

note when comparing the respective word clouds that the performer's experience is more varied, containing a greater variety of more frequently occurring words, when compared to the participants' experiences, which contain a comparatively less variety of more frequently occurring words. Some of these more frequently occurring words from the performer include (in descending order of frequency), for example, 'pain' and 'careful', 'strong' and 'uncomfortable', and 'object' and 'body'. Some of these same words from the participants include 'body' and 'move', 'sound' and 'different', and 'hand' and 'visual'. It is noticeable that words framed in the negative (e.g., 'pain' and 'uncomfortable') are used more frequently by the performer. However, both the performer and participants note the importance of the body in their experience. Perhaps not surprisingly, the participants noted the importance to their experience of the various stimuli produced by their interactions e.g., 'sound', 'visual', and 'fire'. Interestingly, the most frequently used words by both the performer and participants correspond to physical contact, however, they differ in that the performer elected to largely use the word, 'put', while the participants mostly used the word, 'touch'. This finding highlights the importance of the role physical contact played in helping to shape their respective experiences, however, the difference in how it was described suggests possibly that the nature of the participants' actions were perceived by the performer quite differently from how the participants perceived their own actions towards the performer.

These aforementioned differences between the experiences expressed by the performer and participants within each of the six performances can be explored quantitatively using a similarity measure known as *cosine similarity*. Cosine similarity is commonly employed in information retrieval to assess the extent to

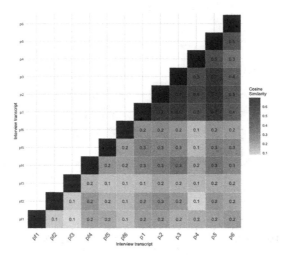

Fig. 7. Pairwise cosine similarities, c_s, for the transcripts of the shared narrative interviews conducted with the performer and participants following six performances of (AB)USE ME. Note that 'pf' denotes the performer and 'p' denotes a particular participant for a given performance number.

which two given text documents match in terms of word-for-word content [4]. Figure 7 shows the pairwise cosine similarities, c_s, between our corpus of 12 transcripts of the shared narrative interviews conducted with the performer and participants following six performances of (AB)USE ME.

As shown in Fig. 7, there is naturally a perfect similarity along the main, positive diagonal between the same documents (e.g., 'pf1' and 'pf1'). One will note, however, that there is a considerable amount of similarity between the individual documents of the participants (as indicated by darker shades of purple at the top right, $c_s = [0.3, 0.7]$) and much less similarity between the individual documents of the performer (as indicated with lighter purple at the lower left, $c_s = [0.1, 0.2]$). This observation is perhaps not so unexpected as the performer experienced interactions with six different participants while the participants experienced the same installation with the same performer acting in the same manner. Nonetheless, it does highlight that despite the apparent large number of common words participants used to describe their respective experiences, their interactions with the performer were perceived by her as being different. Within the participants' documents we can further see that participants 4 and 6 had the least similarity ($c_s = 0.3$) while several documents had the most similarity ($c_s = 0.7$). When looking at the text in their respective documents, participant 4 emphasized the visual and aural feedback as being important to his experience and participant 6 largely noted the importance of physical contact to his own.

To the extent that similarity between documents measured by cosine similarity indicates some shared or common experience, we can look at the documents of the performer and participant within a single performance (e.g., 'pf1' and 'p1').

Table 2. Select coded statements of performing objecthood from the performer during a shared narrative interview with participants following six performances of (AB)USE ME.

Perf. Obj.	Perf.	Performer experience
Objecthood	1	"It was not hard to get into the'object mode'. Although, the technical talk moments from him were encouraging my thoughts, but later on he calmed down and investigated more through physical manipulation, which brought me back into this 'object mode' once again."
	2	"I noticed the more I was asked to be the object and the more I was asked to do whatever the participant wanted to do, the less of me as a person there was."
	3	"I tried to remain as objectified as I could. Mentally it was a little hard to let go of me."
	4	"There was so much of careful consideration, I never really got fully to that state [objecthood]."
	5	"He really showed his dominance over me and full control. I absolutely lost myself in all possible ways...he made me bend on my knees and he put me in a very painful position."
	6	"I felt the need to give him a 'hint' at one point that there is a movement correlation. This moment was the biggest breaking in the objecthood I employed. For that moment I was not performing."
Perceived confrontation	1	"When I turned around and just looked at him, he had an intense reaction as if 'What? What have I done?'. He seemed a bit more uncomfortable all of a sudden."
	2	–
	3	"The participant was confident. That confidence stayed even when after interaction I looked at her."
	4	"Maybe he seemed a little uncomfortable, but that's about it."
	5	"I turned around and looked at him. At first, he said 'Hi', but then right after he asked agitated 'What? Why are you looking at me like this?'"
	6	–
Perceived mistreatment	1	"He squeezed my wrists so strong I felt the blood circulation was cut off in my hands."
	2	"I felt like a toy bunny thrown around, but it seemed more unintentional and child-like...innocent and accidental mistreatment."
	3	–
	4	–
	5	"Not much mistreated by physical force, but rather by lack of consideration. I, as a person, was not in his focus."
	6	–

Table 3. Select coded statements of cognitive absorption from participants during a shared narrative interview with the performer following six performances of (AB)USE ME.

CA Dim.	Perf.	Participant experience
Temporal dissociation	1	"I wasn't thinking about it [time] at all."
	2	"I wasn't thinking about time at all."
	3	–
	4	–
	5	"I wasn't really thinking about it [time] that much."
	6	–
Focused immersion	1	"I was focusing on, like, trigger the fire! trigger the fire!"
	2	–
	3	"Of course it's engaging [outcomes of interactions] and ... I think when you feel a bit like you have triggered what can be triggered then you're, like, 'I think I'm done'."
	4	–
	5	"It [touch] brings a very personal aspect to it. So I feel very present in it in that way."
	6	"Until the moment I stopped, I was not thinking so much."
Heightened enjoyment	1	"You get a new toy and then all of the sudden, you know you enjoyed the time. I'm sorry, you were the toy in this case."
	2	"It was interesting to see what outcomes came out from using you, but I didn't want to make it uncomfortable for you. So I felt I was put in a situation that was uncomfortable in a way. And that's also why it got exciting."
	3	"So I thought the visuals were cool."
	4	"I think it was interesting... I didn't feel that comfortable."
	5	"But I think actually the sounds were kind of more attracting to play with. Because probably in a way that felt more in control."
	6	"It was this spiritual healing process. That got me very fast and I enjoyed being there."
Sense of control	1	"When I moved up, it moved up. It was responsive in a way, it was fluent. But it wasn't...You saw it, it wasn't handling the positions very well sometimes."
	2	"I could definitely hear that when touching you in certain ways different stuff happened."
	3	"I felt a little limited in the way that I could interact with her because of the line that I was told not to cross ... Most of the time I could feel like I am in control."
	4	"The immediate feedback that I could see so that the model would move exactly like how I moved your arms and that I could hear sound instantly when I touched you."
	5	"It [avatar movements] seemed quite well tuned. Like, fine tuned...fast reacting."
	6	–
Amplified curiosity	1	"I was primarily curious to find out how you managed to make that work [responsive sound and visuals], I wanted to trigger different ones."
	2	"I also felt that when shaking you ... I was a bit curious also to see what would happen if I just slapped you, but I didn't do it because I don't want to hurt you."
	3	"It made me curious immediately, the set up, it's interesting."
	4	"There was this explorative aspect and I liked that you didn't really tell me what to do. I feel like I was exploring as much as I could."
	5	"It made me curious, like, 'what can I do?' To also see what is the relationship between your body and projection of what I interpret is your body. So then I started exploring that."
	6	"I was also testing if the strength [touch] had to do with the visuals and the sound. I see [it] more as a challenge. And making me explore this body in another way."

One will note that these documents (along a positive diagonal in the lower right quadrant) have a rather low similarity ($c_s = [0.2, 0.3]$) with performances 2 and 5 showing the highest degree of similarity between the documents of the performer and participant. In performance 2, the participant expressed of her experience that she was "careful of not ... making anything too uncomfortable", however, the performer perceived this participants' interactions differently, noting that she was "less careful than other people. ... She seemed very energetic and was challenging me in my postures and my movement". It is not immediately clear how we might interpret the similarity (or not) between a performer's experience with one participant and the experience of a different participant (e.g., 'pf4' and 'p1'), however, it might indicate some general themes common to the experience in general, irrespective of which participant took part.

In our qualitative analysis, we elected to apply a top-down approach in which the five dimensions of cognitive absorption (i.e., temporal disassociation, focused immersion, heightened enjoyment, sense of control, and amplified curiosity) served as the selective codes to which we coded the responses from the participants. We applied the same approach to the performer's responses using objecthood, perceived confrontation, and perceived mistreatment as the selective codes for performing objecthood. It was less important in this analysis the degree to which these categories factored into the experiences (as would have been measured using e.g., a rating scale) and more that we were able to capture the variety of words and statements used to communicate the subjective feelings related to these categories. Tables 2 and 3 show select coded statements expressed by the performer and participants, respectively, when reflecting on their experiences during a shared narrative interview following six performances of (AB)USE ME.

As shown in Table 2, it is clear that the performer had much to comment on with respect to her experiences with objecthood and somewhat less with how she perceived the actions of participants. If we look to the coded statements with respect to objecthood, her experiences varied with some interactions from participants greatly helping her to remain focused on her performance while others causing her to lose this focus. As the performer noted of the participant in performance 5, "He really showed his dominance over me and full control. I absolutely lost myself in all possible ways ... he made me bend on my knees and he put me in a very painful position" while of the participant in performance 6 the performer noted that she "felt the need to give him a 'hint' at one point that there is a movement correlation" and that "this was the biggest breaking in the objecthood I employed. For that moment I was not performing". Looking further to the coded statements pertaining to perceived confrontation, we can see that for a majority of the participants, the performer felt that there was indeed a moment of confrontation following the conclusion of the performance not unlike that noted by Abramović, with perceived discomfort and agitation from the participants being most common. For example, the participant in performance 1 asked in a surprised way "What? What have I done?" as if he had acted improperly after the performer looked at him while the participant in performance 5 asked in a more negative way "What? Why are you looking at me like that?". For the coded statements of perceived mistreatment we find that the performer felt her experience in this regard significant enough to comment on only half of the participants with some rather harshly perceived mistreatment from the participant in performance 1 and more innocently perceived mistreatment from the participants in performances 2 and 5.

One will note in Table 3 that the statements made by participants when reflecting on their experiences much more closely aligned with the dimensions of cognitive absorption concerning heightened enjoyment, sense of control, and amplified curiosity rather than to what could be coded as pertaining to temporal dissociation and focused immersion. With respect to heightened enjoyment, the participants' experiences varied from feeling as if they were playing with a new toy (performance 1) to being fixated on the visual and aural outcomes of their interactions (performance 5). Interestingly, two participants expressed both interest and discomfort in their respective experiences (performances 2 and 4), with one stating that this interest was actually due in part to this discomfort (performance 2). If we look to the statements pertaining to a sense of control, most of the participants felt that they had some control over the visual and aural outcomes and that the movements of the avatar in response to their movements of the performer's body were largely responsive and natural. However, the participant in performance 1 noted some issues involving the tracking of positions of the performer's body and the movements of the avatar, and the participant in performance 3 expressed a limited sense of control due to the line that she was told not to cross when interacting with the performer. With respect to amplified curiosity, a number of participants explicitly mentioned curiosity when describing their experience (performances 1, 2, 3, and 5) while the remaining participants mentioned exploratory aspects as being important (performances 4 and 6). The participants' curiosity was with respect to how the system worked (performances 1 and 3) and what the outcomes of their actions towards the performer's body would be (performances 2 and 5) with one participant going so far as to express being curious as to what would be the effect of her slapping the performer (performances 2). The exploratory aspects that participants found important involved having to figure out what could be done with the performer's body with out being told e.g., the participant in performance 4 expressed that "I liked that you didn't really tell me what to do. I feel like I was exploring as much as I could".

5   Conclusion and Future Work

In this paper, we presented a mixed-reality performance installation inspired by Abramović's *Rhythm 0* as a basis for exploring the subjective experiences of the performer and the participants in this space, where the performer acts as a mediating object through which visuals and sound are manipulated by physical interactions the participant has with this performer's body. Through a top-down qualitative analysis in conjunction with methods from information retrieval for measuring document similarity, we provided some interesting insight into these experiences with respect to the specific words and statements used regarding cognitive absorption and performing objecthood which appear to align some with Abramović's experience. The performer noted, for example, having strong feelings of being treated as an object, and with several participants, she reported confrontations when the performances ended. However, this experience did not appear congruent with how many of the participants reflected on their actions towards her – a perceptual discrepancy possibly driven by the heightened enjoyment received from their curiosity and desire to explore how the performer's body affected the space. In future work, it would be interesting to pursue a more ecologically valid approach in which an audience is present to see if the behaviors of participants or their experiences remain unchanged, consider an entirely virtual recreation, or look further into the dimensions of cognitive absorption which proved difficult to assess through our chosen qualitative method. We hope our work serves as an interesting point of departure for performance artists and researchers alike wishing to explore mixed reality spaces in artistic practice and the nature of experiences with performing objecthood in such a space.

References

1. Abramović, M.: Marina Abramović Institute (2014). https://mai.art/
2. Abramović, M.: Rhythm 0 Performance (2020). https://zeespring.wordpress.com/2013/10/20/marina-abramovic-rhythm-0/
3. Agarwal, R., Karahanna, E.: Time flies when you're having fun: cognitive absorption and beliefs about information technology usage. MIS Q. **24**, 665–694 (2000). https://doi.org/10.2307/3250951
4. Baeza-Yates, R., Ribeiro-Neto, B.: Modern Information Retrieval. Addison Wesley (2011)
5. Benford, S., Giannachi, G.: Introduction. In: Performing Mixed Reality, pp. 2–25. The MIT Press, Cambridge (2011)
6. Benford, S., Giannachi, G., Koleva, B., Rodden, T.: From interaction to trajectories: designing coherent journeys through user experiences. In: Proceedings of the SIGCHI Conference on Human Factors in Computing Systems, CHI 2009, pp. 709–718. Association for Computing Machinery, New York (2009). https://doi.org/10.1145/1518701.1518812
7. Blender: Blender Documentation (2020). https://www.blender.org/, version 2.82
8. BlokDust: Blokdust Documentation (2020). https://blokdust.com/
9. Facebuilder: Facebuilder Documentation (2020). https://keentools.io/download/facebuilder-for-blender
10. Jackson, S.A., Marsh, H.W.: Development and validation of a scale to measure optimal experience: the flow state scale. J. Sport Exerc. Psychol. **18**, 17–35 (1996)
11. MakeHuman: Makehuman Documentation (2020). http://www.makehumancommunity.org/
12. McGloin, R., Farrar, K., Krcmar, M.: Video games, immersion, and cognitive aggression: does the controller matter? Med. Psychol. **16**, 65 (2013). https://doi.org/10.1080/15213269.2012.752428
13. Milgram, P., Kishino, F.: A taxonomy of mixed reality visual displays. IEICE Trans. Inf. Syst. **E77-D**(12), 1321–1329 (1994)

14. Murray, J.: Immersion. In: Hamlet on the Holodeck: The Future of Narrative in Cyberspace, pp. 98–99. MIT Press, Cambridge (1997)
15. Novak, T.P., Hoffman, D.L.: Measuring the flow experience among web users. Vanderbilt University, Technical report (1997)
16. Nuitrack: Nuitrack SDK (2020). https://nuitrack.com/
17. Ono, Y.: Cut Piece Performance (2020). https://florica.wordpress.com/2007/09/11/yoko-ono-cut-piece/
18. Peebles, E.: Cyberbullying: hiding behind the screen. Paediatr. Child Health **19**(10), 527–528 (2014)
19. Persky, S., Blascovich, J.: Immersive virtual video game play and presence: influences on aggressive feelings and behavior. Presence **17**, 57–72 (2008). https://doi.org/10.1162/pres.17.1.57
20. Processing: Processing Documentation (2020). https://processing.org/
21. Rowe, A.: Immersion in mixed reality spaces. Ph.D. thesis, Oslo School of Architecture and Design, Norway, February 2015
22. Shalson, L.: Performing Endurance: Art and Politics since 1960. Cambridge University Press, Cambridge (2018)
23. TouchMe: TouchMe MIDI Documentation (2020). https://playtronica.com/

Acetate - Impermanence and Destruction Within Sound Art

Jimmy Eadie[✉]

Trinity College Dublin, Dublin, Ireland
eadiejj@tcd.ie

Abstract. This paper will discuss two installation pieces created for acetate vinyl and multiple turntables. The two works *Wow&Flutter* and *Collision* should be considered as spatially immersive, generative, and interactive sound sculptured objects that investigate degrading surface material and remediation as the basis for a structural composition. The turntable has been regarded as a legacy technology but has recently seen a resurgence even among emerging technologies such as 'XR' 'Network Art' and 'Live Coding'. This paper will discuss how the turntable is itself a dialogic key between mediation and materiality of sound. It's tactile and kinaesthetic nature invite interactivity in a very unique and singular manner. Firstly, I will address correlational aspects by developing the conceptual and aesthetic context in an effort to delineate and explain the term *Sound Art* before addressing the affordances of the creative use of the turntable. I will then explore how prominent artists conflated this medium's initial purpose and telos before going on to discuss the concept of *Repetition as Aesthetic*. This will be followed by an in-depth commentary of the use of acetate material in terms of investigating real-time recursive disintegration of analogue sound recording on this soft and malleable material. Intermediality and reappropriation of sonic material will also be discussed in relation to the compositional approach with a particular emphasis on *Plunderphonics*.

Keyword: Turntable art · Plunderphonics · Acetate

1 Sound Art

Sound art as a term seems to be contentious among academics and practitioners alike. Incorrectly applied, the term is nebulous and can lead to vagueness when discussing sonic arts in general. It is broad, encompassing a varied range of art and artistic practices while at times ignoring their differences. Its use can obscure associations and adherence to contrasting creative disciplines and categories. Notwithstanding these points, the term sound art can be useful in registering the fact that there does indeed exist a practice that falls between many artistic and conceptual disciplines. In my estimation, it has helped to expand the field of music theory, practice, and discourse, as well as define the boundaries between music and the visual arts. Consequently, sound art should not be considered a genre, but rather a conceptual definition that engenders a practice born out of a multitude

A. Brooks et al. (Eds.): ArtsIT 2020, LNICST 367, pp. 85–99, 2021.
https://doi.org/10.1007/978-3-030-73426-8_5

of past histories. Several areas have shaped sound art, the main influences being fine art, music, theatre, and audio technology developments. In distinguishing sound art from music, I do not take a purist stance and consider them to be mutually exclusive. However, I do believe a viable definition of sound art can exist which avoids too much confusing overlap with music. Primarily, I am looking at these fields more pluralistically, suggesting that sound art's breadth has increased somewhat to that of music and, in particular, to what is termed experimental music. Before setting aside the arguments over the terminology, I need to give some context about sound art's problematic title. I will include some current definitions from notable scholars and practitioners on the subject. These definitions are important, in that they can help in critically positioning a work within the larger field of audio culture.

Musicologist Leigh Landy claims that 'There is no single consistently used definition for sound art. Originating in the fine arts, the term is associated with sound installations, sound sculptures, public sonic artefacts and site-specific sonic art events and could further be subdivided into more specific categories' [39]. Author Seth Kim-Cohen believes that 'the language of sonic practice distinct from music is only now emerging' [35]. In his anthology of modern music, *Audio Culture Readings in Modern Music*, Christoph Cox observes that 'sound art has become a prominent field of artistic practice, presented at major museums and galleries all across the globe' [9]. Artist and author David Toop describes sound art as 'sound combined with visual art practices' [66]. Toop curated the sound art exhibition *Sonic Boom* [5] at the Haywood Gallery, London. This was considered a vital landmark exhibition for sound art practice throughout the world. But, perhaps the most significant and insightful definition, and one I consider directly applicable to my practice, comes from Alan Licht, who differentiates sound art from music principally in terms of time and duration. Licht advocates the view that:

A universal definition and definitive history of sound art may not be likely, [...] but ultimately it is better to honour sound pieces created in a non-time-based, non-programmatic way as being sound art as opposed to music than to simply shoehorn any sound work into the genre of experimental music, or to practise the lazy revisionism of blanketing any experimental sound composition, performance or recording under the rubric of sound art.

As can be seen, a definition, critique, and discussion of sound art has many difficulties. However, as Licht suggests, sound work created in a non-time and non-programmatic way should be defined as sound art, as opposed to the majority of music. Thus, we can at least begin to describe the concept of sound art, and how to apply it to a particular work. For me, the terms intermediality, art hybridity, installation, and sound art can often be interchangeable as there is overlap between them. I think it is this convergence of meaning within the stated definitions that causes much of the controversy, in terms of artists and theorists attempting to pin down exactly which work should sit where. For instance, if we take Licht's definition of sound art as 'non-time-based and non-programmatic' as a starting point and combine it with David Toop's definition of 'sound with visual art', we get closer to understanding this slippery realm of definitions. To further understand this taxonomy, artist and scholar Laura Mae created a set of useful criteria to define the 'specific characteristics and attributes' of sound art more easily.

The criteria are as follows: concept, perception, space, site-specificness, open-form, interaction, production of sound, narrativity, endurance, and visual component [41].

Professor of Media Studies Kate Lacey observes that, sound artists attempt 'to make listeners self-reflexively aware of themselves as listeners, within a particular setting and time' [38]. Don Ihde states, the 'enchantment of sound can seduce' and lead to a temporary sense of 'dissolution' of self-presence; essentially it can take you 'out of yourself' [26]. When discussing sound art, most discourse specifies only what it is not: it is not music, and it is not visual art. However, as Seth Cluett [8] observes, the visual element of sound art, although at times less apparent, can actually foreground the concept of sound by alluding to or highlighting the absence of sound. Evidence of this conceptual approach to sound art can be seen in the work of Christian Marclay [42], particularly his pieces Cube (1989), Tape Fall (1990) and Boneyard (1990). Casey O'Callaghan [48] emphasizes that hearing, compared to seeing, is considered as a secondary perceptual quality in Western philosophy, adding to the tensions between the ocular and the aural, and historically giving superiority to the visual aspect. Exploring this concept further Peter Szendy believes that 'unlike visual perception, which enables a clear separation of subject and object, sound resonates in and through the listening body' [62]. David Toop's enlightened discrimination between the visual and sonic experience demonstrates these points further: 'Seeing is now-now-now-now-now-now-now-n-n-n..., whereas hearing is then-and-now-and-then, over there at the source of the sound and then here, within the body, already gone but still dispersing into ambience' [65]. Despite these perceptual differences, and the fact that sound art is simultaneously rooted within two different discourses, that of music and visual arts, the visual component plays a significant role in many renowned works.

2   Influential Artists on Sound Art

Marcel Duchamp is a significant figure in the history of modern art who deserves to be mentioned for his conceptual use of sound and vision, which ultimately contributed to the development of sound art. It was through his ready-mades and experiments within visual art, sculpture, and music that we first see the creation of a sound-work presented within the emerging conceptual arts. I propose that the first conceptual piece of art that could be considered as a forerunner to sound art writ large is his readymade entitled With Hidden Noise (A Bruit Secret) [15]. The work was designed for interaction, audition, and vision. With Hidden Noise could be conceptually read as an infinite line that doubles back on itself, permanently fixed in this position: a solidified loop. However, the work is not activated or completed until the object is shaken to make a sound, the origin of which is hidden from view. The work creates an interesting dialogue between conceptual, visual, and auditory experience, questioning perception and meaning through chance operation. Thus, it satisfies what all sound art should achieve in my opinion. Duchamp says of this piece:

Before I finished it Arensberg put something inside the ball of twine, and never told me what it was, and I didn't want to know. It was a sort of secret between us, and it makes noise, so we called this a Ready-made with a hidden noise. Listen to it. I don't know; I will never know whether it is a diamond or a coin [16].

By creating such conceptual works, Duchamp was disrupting centuries of established thinking, that the artist must be a skilled painter or sculptor. He conceived that the skill and originality could be in the *concept,* rather than the execution. Alluding to Duchamp's importance within sound art, and drawing attention to his concept of a 'non retinal art', Seth Kim-Cohen argues that, sound art must also now become 'non-cochlear' if it is to develop. [34]. Artist Joseph Kosuth, commenting on artistic divisions and modalities, suggests that *'all art* [after Duchamp] is conceptual [in nature] because art only exists conceptually' [37]. Fifty years after Duchamp, as if to echo Kosuth's claim, artist Robert Morris created *Box with the Sound of Its Own Making* [47], an essential work of American minimalist art. Kim-Cohen contends that '[Box] is both the sound of a sculpture and a sculpture of sound. It is a very early example of a sound sculpture; of a work existing simultaneously, equally, as sculpture and as a sound art work' [35].

As well as Duchamp, seminal artists John Cage, Pierre Schaeffer, and R. Murray Schafer were each pivotal in developing concepts of sound and listening beyond the domain of music and, as such, have had a great impact on the definition of sound art. These important practitioners have been written about at length [7, 12, 49, 58, 59], so I will not go into great historical detail here. Importantly, all share the characteristic of not differentiating between 'musical sounds' and 'extra-musical sounds' which would conventionally be considered 'noise' or environmental ambient sound. This concept did have its genesis with Luigi Russolo at the turn of the 20th century [7]. However, there are pertinent differences between how Cage, Schaeffer and Schafer determine their theories.

In attempting to define sound within acousmatic music, Pierre Schaeffer, who was heavily influenced by Edmund Husserl's phenomenological principles [23, 31, 33, 54] suggested removing the sound from its original context. Through his concepts of the sonic object, reduced listening and idée fixe, Schaeffer suggested we should rely purely on the acoustic qualities of sound to gain a deeper understanding. He was concerned with the physical material of sound and how this could acquire the plasticity of compositional material. To demonstrate this phenomenon he famously removed the attack of the recording of a bell and he subsequently found it resembled the sound of an oboe [32]. Expanding the field of discussion pertinent to sound art further, R. M. Schafer introduced the concept of the soundscape and acoustic ecology. Essentially Schafer was concerned with how we experience an acoustic environment, and subsequently how to study and analyse these external sound fields, which he termed sonography [57].

Historically, one of the most influential practitioners concerning not only music but art in general is John Cage. Cage's own rhetorical character is so pervasive and entangled within his work, that objective reception and discussion of his output is quite a difficult task. But it was his theories of music composition and particularly the concept of silence that have had the greatest impact on the current debate surrounding sound art. As Cage remarked, 'Silence is all of the sound we don't intend. There is no such thing as absolute silence. Therefore silence may very well include sounds, and more and more in the twentieth century does' [36]. Essentially for silence to function as an artistic act there must be a coherent structure, a framing as it were. This frame is the filter through which we perceive the work – sound and silence. As Kyle Gann suggests, in keeping with his Zen tendency to dissolve dualities, Cage thought of 'sound and silence as merely aspects of the same continuum' [24]. Conceptually Cage's work abandoned the compositional categories of work-form, material-content, thereby questioning the necessity of an artistic work at all for the origin or creation of aesthetic experience. As Douglas Kahn comments, Cage codified silence into a 'musical' event that could be experienced anywhere and at any time, essentially arguing that all sound could be music [30].

Cage's theories represent an aesthetic ideal of listening to the sound source which does not impose an intention or will on the listener. Instead, it promotes an openness towards experiencing events simply as they are. One of Cage's greatest contributions to art was highlighting the experience of listening in the expanded auditive field. The efforts Cage made to eliminate his personal will from his work enabled him to construct aesthetic listening experiences that were free from the artefacts of traditional compositional structure, such as form, melody, harmony, etc. The absence of these structural principals goes some way to support Licht's contemporary definition of sound art, as quoted above, and in turn, help define my own practice within the wider sphere. I agree sound art has a historical attachment to experimental music. However, whereas most music could be said to be made of sound, some sound art actually omits sound completely, emphasising only silence, or referring at least to the absence of sound, through a visual medium. In summary, I believe sound art is developing a specific vernacular and approach to audible art which can be of benefit to scholars, curators and the artists themselves.

3   Impermanence and Destruction

Phonographs, gramophones, and turntables have been used throughout history not merely as a mediating device for the playback of music, but also as electronic instruments or as art objects in themselves. As such, I believe they belong in this instance within the category of sound art. The following artists and the mentioned pieces have had a particular influence on my own works involving turntables. The first known works using this medium are by Paul Hindemith and Ernst Toch in 1930, followed by John Cage's landmark work Imaginary Landscapes No. 1.

[6]. The expressive qualities and interactive nature of the turntable also had a great influence on the creation of musique concrète and were initially the primary mode of production for Pierre Schaeffer and Pierre Henry in their seminal work Symphonie pour un Homme Seul [56]. Daphne Oram, a pioneer of musique concrète in Britain, created the highly original turntable work Still Point [22] but this remained unheard for seventy years, until a contemporary turntablist, Shiva Feshareki, performed it with the London Contemporary Orchestra in 2016. Milan Knížák who was part of the Fluxus movement in eastern Europe, created loud, aggressive works during the sixties, by purposely destroying vinyl and playing the records back with homemade amplifiers. Nam June Paik also used the turntable, in his work Random Access (1963). Bauhaus artist László Moholy-Nagy advocated using vinyl as a creative, rather than reproductive tool. Christian Marclay is also an excellent example of an artist who has moved seamlessly between the disciplines of music, installation and sound art. Russell Fergusson suggests that the majority of Marclay's work is preoccupied with the concept of sound, yet the 'overwhelming majority of his output makes no sound' [21]. His work with the medium

of vinyl and record player, both as a performative instrument and as a sonic object, has direct bearing and influence on my own vinyl pieces, Wow&Flutter and Collision. With both these works I am interested in recognising the fleeting nature of the acetate medium, which is a delicate plastic that can only hold the sonic information for so long before it is eventually destroyed by the needle with which it interacts. This impermanence in relative contrast to digital technology was at the centre of both of these works. For me, the record player is simultaneously a sound-emitting object, a musical instrument, and a sound art object. Philip Jeck is a composer and multimedia artist primarily known for utilising turntables and old vinyl records, along with electronic processing devices within performance and installation settings. His Vinyl Requiem [28] sound installation in London was a remarkable large-scale installation used 180 record players creating a wall of surging an ever-changing sound. To conclude this section, my aim here has been to articulate that sound art can promote and highlight a greater sense of auditory perspective within the arts. Both music and the visual arts have influenced sound art, which, in my opinion, will remain placed between these two disciplines, though hopefully in a less contested fashion. This section is not an attempt to establish an absolute definition of sound art but should instead be read as one artist's account of a complex, sometimes contradictory area of practice. How these theories and terms apply to my work is vital in understanding my particular approach to practice.

4   Repetition as Aesthetic

Within this section, I will focus on my use of repetition, particularly in creating the installation for turntables, and more specifically, that of immediate 'phrase' repetition and the concept of 'looping' as an aesthetic device. A discussion of the related phenomenon such as mere-exposure effect from social psychology [68] and the critical theories of Theodor Adorno [2] concerning the effect of general repetition within popular music, and its subsequent effect on a societal level, is beyond the scope of this paper. Notwithstanding these arguments of high and low culture [1], repetition has been used in music for centuries as a fundamental composition device. Chris Cutler notes repetition in music is a function of memory; it is a 'creative reconstructive' process delivered through the use of the loop as a 're-iteration' of sound [29]. Many artists have used repetition in an electronic form called the 'stutter effect' producers such as Oval (94 Diskont, 1995); Pan Sonic (Endless, 1998); Tim Hecker (Haunt Me, Haunt Me Do It Again, 2001); Akufen (My Way, 2001) and Ryoji Ikeda (Dataplex, 2005). Also, minimalist works from La Monte Young, Terry Riley, and the slow generative variations of Steve Reich and Brian Eno have all used repetition extensively. Notably, Reich's concept of process music [53] and Eno's generative principles [63]. Alvin Lucier and particularly his piece I am sitting in a room [40], is a great example of the use of repetition within an installation work. I consider it to be the most elegant and simplest piece of minimalist process music that demonstrates repetition, revealing the natural acoustic phenomena of 'resonance' through audio feedback. As Edward Strickland notes, 'in its repetition, I am sitting in a room ranks with the finest achievements of minimal tape music' [60].

Repetition is a fundamental characteristic of all my work, although I do not create static loops that repeat linearly without change. Rather, I incorporate repetition of material as a type of evolving re-performance, or as Anne Danielson [13] terms it 'a changing same'. This is demonstrated in the mechanical looping of my acetate turntable works Wow&Flutter and Collision. Here the printed repetitions on each plate are independent of each other, but when experienced as a whole, they become inseparable as the work evolves through slow repeated combinatorial cycles. Sonic phenomena such as echo, delay and reverberation are all essentially time-based repeats of an original sound event, which are perceived as a type of impressionistic memory by the listener. When the transmission is of spoken word and processed in this manner, it can change the prevalent meaning, becoming almost musical, in a phenomenon known as 'semantic satiation' [27]. This simple act of repetition or 'speech-to-song' can make the most mundane spoken phrase become almost 'musicalised', as noted by psychologist Diana Deutsch [14]. As each repeat gives way to the next, we are exposed to the micro-timing, articulation and the speaker's pitch-inflections. This has the effect of making an everyday spoken-word radio broadcast acquire new contextual meaning. To illustrate the importance of repetition within music, cognitive scientist Elizabeth Hellmuth Margulis [44] carried out an extensive empirical study of the aesthetic responses to repetition, which she claims it was preferred even within what is considered complex Western art music [43, 45].

A consequence of using repetition and generative principles within my work means that the installation projects discussed in this paper are non-teleological and open artworks, the concept which is described at length by Umberto Eco in his book The Open Work [18]. I place the attribution of meaning with the participant instead of attempting to create a completed or finalised piece; in essence, the works are left open. For example, I will set up an environment where a process will begin, and the audience will essentially become a type of collaborator for the duration of their interaction with the piece. The two presented works are not built around a programmatic narrative, with a beginning, middle and end. They do not involve grand gestures or musical climatic points, but rather they durational, repetitive and non-teleological, and as such require the participant to interact actively with it.

In many ways it is a focused perceptual state I'm interested in achieving. I want the audience to experience and be aware of the sounds and how they develop. I believe that my move into this form of open and durational sonic expression came from a reaction to the practice of the finalised and fixed recording throughout my time as a musician. During this period, on listening to the material I had just committed to tape, like most musicians, I was never satisfied with what I had just performed, and even though I would continue to attempt to better the 'take', it just seemed to be always out of reach. So the idea of leaving a work open, meant that even I, as the creator of this piece, would have a new experience every time I was exposed to it. In many ways this echoes Eno's principle of generative music, where he contends, 'generative music is like trying to create a seed, as opposed to classical composition which is like trying to engineer a tree' [20].

5   Wow&Flutter (2017)

Wow&Flutter is a site-determined spatial installation consisting of eight turntables that create a 360° sound-field. As mentioned previously, I consider the record-player to be an objet d'art in its own right, particularly the older version with the built-in speaker, which is the type I chose for this installation. I designed a sculpted-stand and lighting system to accompany each turntable, which enhanced the overall visual aesthetic of the installation. The approach to designing the sonic elements was twofold. Firstly, I composed the material from the ground-up, using synthesis, recordings of acoustic instruments and voices. Secondly, I used methods of sampling to take a fully formed section of music and manipulating it to achieve the results I needed, essentially utilising the technique of plunderphonics as discussed previously (Fig. 1).

Tracklisting for Side A:

- Recording of upright piano
- Sample from the track 'things' …and after Optimism by amusement [17]
- Processed Waldorf Pulse bass synthesizer
- Sample from Collage #1(Blue Suede) by James Tenney [64]

Tracklisting for Side B:

- Children's spoken words 'wow' – 'flutter'
- Sample from 'Part 3' Metal Machine Music by Lou Reed [52]
- Sample from 'Uberfahrt' from the album 3 by Pole [4]
- Sample from 'Tjatrick' by Java the Jasmine Gamelan Music [61]

Fig. 1. Wow&Flutter, national concert hall, Dublin

Side A: There is a purposely long silent gap at the beginning of each side and also left between each track, so that the audience can experience the acetate slowly 'scratching,' 'popping', and 'crackling' – sounds which become progressively louder with each play. I included a sample of Tenney's 'plundered' version of Elvis Presley's interpretation of the original Carl Perkins track from 1955. Although I would consider it unrecognisable in this instance. The gesture is tongue-in-cheek, but also acts as a signpost to my recognition and acknowledgement to what is considered to be the first plunderphonic artwork [11].

Side B: Has more percussive and transient material; the intent here was that either side could be played and would complement the other. This side starts with children's voices saying the words 'wow' and 'flutter' and relates back to the concept of semantic satiation. The material here is self-referential, and the fact that it is two children speaking gives the work a sense of playfulness and lightness that could not be achieved with an adult voice. This slowly fades into a sample from a track by the artist Pole. This sample is again an appropriation of the artist who sampled from a dance hall reggae record, King Tubby's Herbal Dub [55]. Tonally, its inclusion pulled the work into a more rhythmic area. The final section is a percussive track of gamelan music. I cut the sample into a very rhythmic 5:4 time signature, as the development of the accents would be fascinating within the turntable octet. The rationale for choosing and working with all of these specific materials is based on wanting variation in the timbral and harmonic content. Also, somewhat humorously, I wanted my work to sit side-by-side with artists I highly respect. The fact that the majority of the sampled material is highly processed and unrecognisable is also a deliberate aesthetic choice. This could be said to be an extension of the plunderphonic

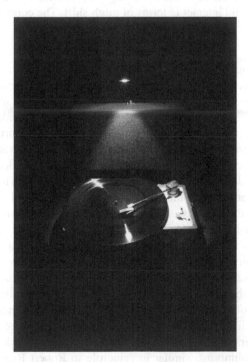

Fig. 2. Detail from Wow & Flutter, national concert hall, Dublin

principal, rather than the purest representation of the artform as illustrated by the art collective Negativland [25].

Structurally there were three overarching aesthetic principals at play within Wow&Flutter (Fig. 2):

1. Turntable as an instrument and sound art object.
2. The concept of phase-shifting as a generative compositional tool.
3. The disintegration of the surface material as an aesthetic.

Essentially, each turntable contains a duplicate acetate plate, and it is the asynchronous interaction of the record players over time that creates the generative aspect. In an attempt to eliminate the division between artist and audience, I emphasized and exploited the interactive nature of the turntable, as I believe they inherently invite tactile use. Primarily, my intention was to create a responsive and reactive environment, albeit a playful one. Acetate is a very soft plastic medium that coats a metal plate, which when held is surprisingly heavy. I wanted participants to feel, touch, and experience acetate both as a sound carrying medium, and as an object in its own right. The installation was designed with this audience interaction in mind. If a participant wanted to change the speed of a turntable from 45rpm to 33rpm, they could do so. It would pitch shift by approximately a fourth, so it would still be consonant within the overall work. I used some rudimentary mathematics[1] when designing the piece that enabled me to understand how each turntable would interact in terms of pitch shift. The equation used was:

$$n = 12 * \left(\log(f2/f1)/\log(2)\right)$$

where n is the number of semitones from original to new pitch. Importantly this meant I could better understand the interaction of each section prior to the final print. The technique of phase shifting, in which two or more identical musical patterns are played simultaneously but at slightly different speeds, was expanded upon further by using eight turntables playing asynchronously. This is similar in principle to works by Eno and Reich. However, my point of departure was in the exploitation of the inherent characteristics of acetate as the medium, which is tangible, malleable, but also very fragile, which imparted a singular uniqueness to this installation. The fact that the work is interactive, performative, and could also be viewed as a sculptural object, distinguishes my work from many other artists working with turntables. In this instance, the turntable is both a piece of visual art and a haptic instrument. It is corporeal, in the sense that the stylus, the record, and the participant are entwined into a physical relationship which engenders the discovery of new perceptual sonic experiences. Wow&Flutter exploits the innate sonic characteristics of acetate vinyl. One particular attribute of an acetate record is the fact that the sonic material is bound to the physical object, albeit in stasis, and the degeneration of the plastic occurs in real-time, as the turntable needles scratch out the groove. This disintegration of the object is at the centre of this work. Surface noise gradually appears, and the sonic quality of the original work slowly disappears, becoming almost a palimpset, similar in principle to Robert Rauschenberg's Erased

---

[1] Equation: 33.33 to 45 rpm n = 12 * (log(45/33.33)/log(2)) = 5.20 (semitones, rounded up).

de Kooning Drawing [51]. I use acetate as it disintegrates more rapidly than standard vinyl and therefore the printed material ages with each successive play until the surface noise itself has become intertwined with the printed audio. Eventually, the original recordings that were on the acetate almost disappear under the surface noise, ultimately turning the work into an accelerated aged piece. In a world in which digital accuracy and clarity is everything, I want to make people aware of these temporal idiosyncrasies and imperfections of a beautiful legacy medium such as acetate.

6 Collision (2018)

Having completed Wow&Flutter, I was commissioned to create an installation experience for the Hearsay Arts Festival in Co. Limerick, Ireland. The main diverging point from Wow&Flutter was that only three professional turntables were used. I also worked with a more limited palette of material. By constraining myself to just two audio sources – voice and piano I could explore the concepts of generative development, surface noise, and repetition in greater detail. The choice of sonic material for this piece was in some part influenced by Brian Eno's Ambient 1: Music for Airports [19], which also consisted primarily of voice and piano. Again, the rotation speed of Collision was designed to work at 33RPM or 45RPM, with tempo and pitch scaling at 73% and ±5 semitones respectively. My artistic stance is similar to that of Christian Marclay, as he aims 'to make people aware of these imperfections, and accept them' [10]. Along with these points, I further explored the turntable as an interactive and performative medium.

The standard seven-inch single disc was chosen for this composition with each side at three minutes, a nod to the maximum duration audio content on a '78' vinyl, and the length of the classic three-minute pop song. I recorded an upright piano and placed the microphones very close to the hammer felt, so you could hear the mechanical movement within the piano.

Liberal amounts of reverberation were then applied to place this close recording at a more perceptually diffuse distance. The vocalist listened to the chord progression as she improvised her performance. I instructed her only to use non-verbal utterances, as this was not a lyric-based work. The vocalist was recorded in a single take to highlight a sense of her searching for a note, which is conceptual approach similar to my piece Rehearsal. The end result is that there is no linguistic or semantic meaning within the work and, as it is based on generative principles, it is almost impossible to predict the interplay of each turntable.

Another explorative point differing from the previous installation was the principal of repetition and specifically the locked groove. Having listened to the albums RRR 500 [67], a compilation of locked grooves by Various Artists, Cycle 30 [46] by Jeff Mills and You're the Guy I Want To Share My Money With [3] by Laurie Anderson, John Giorno and William S. Burroughs, I sought to create a work that would function simultaneously as a sounding and sculptural piece of art.

The locked groove was explicitly composed for these acetates and, figuratively, the installation never ends, as it continues to play out indefinitely. The duration of the locked groove will vary with revolutions per minute; at 33rpm, the duration is 1.8 s, and at 45 rpm the duration is 1.3 s. As I was using better quality turntables and replay system, and the environment was tranquil, the three turntables' locked grooves worked very well together in creating a generative work that had a certain fragility to it as it slowly disintegrated. This installation is based on the performative aspects of turntables comparable to Wow&Flutter, but rather than using eight record players; I decided to explore a more minimal approach similar to Eliane Radique's turntable piece $\Sigma = a = b = a + b$ [50], which comprised of two independent turntables and vinyl 7" discs (Fig. 3).

Fig. 3. Collision, three turntables in exhibition space

I should point out here that in the creation of these turntable works, I never knew if the combinatorial aspects would be successful, as it was impossible to test or audition the interaction of the discs before they were cut. This uniqueness and, in many ways, an opposition to mass production furthered my interest in working with this material. The process of acetate lathe-cutting is a one-time operation, and the turnaround time is particularly long and relatively expensive (Fig. 4).

Fig. 4. Detail from collision

7 Conclusion

This paper was an exploration of the experimental use of acetate vinyl and multiple turntables using reappropriated and plundered sound as a creative material. The two pieces discussed looked at the performative and interactive qualities of the turntable within an installation setting. Overall the two works could also be considered as sculptural objects within the definition of sound art. The works spatial aspects in terms of the acoustic setting explore their sonic alterity and engender further discussion of the mediums compositional use in what could be considered a post-digital age. These two turntable pieces draw on influences from John Cage and Marcel Duchamp to demonstrate the structural ideas of experimental music within a sound art setting. By embracing the temporal nature of acetate material and the spontaneity of the interactive and generative process I believe a unique aesthetic experience was afforded by both these works.

References

1. Adorno, T., Horkheimer, M.: Dialectic of Enlightenment. Stanford University Press, California (1947)
2. Adorno, T.W.: On Popular Music. Institute of Social Research (1942)
3. Anderson, L., et al.: You're The Guy I Want To Share My Money With. Giorno Poetry Systems, New York (1981)
4. Betke, S.: 3 – Pole (2000)
5. Brown, N.: Sonic Boom (2000). https://frieze.com/article/sonic-boom-0
6. Cage, J.: Imaginary Landscape No. 1. Peters Edition EP 6716 (1939)
7. Chessa, L.: Luigi Russolo, Futurist: Noise, Visual Arts, and the Occult. University of California Press, Berkeley (2012)

8. Cluett, S.: Ephemeral, Immersive Invasive Sound as Curatorial Theme 1966–2013. In: Levent, N., Pascual-Leone, A. (eds.) The Multisensory Museum: Cross-Disciplinary Perspectives on Touch, Sound, Smell, Memory, and Space. Rowman & Littlefield Publishers, Maryland (2014)
9. Cox, C., Warner, D. (eds.) Introduction to the revised edition music and the new audio culture. In: Audio Culture Readings in Modern Music, p. 17. Continuum, New York (2004)
10. Criqui, J., Blazwick, I.: ON&BY Christian Marclay. MIT Press, Cambridge (2015)
11. Cutler, C.: Plunderphonia. In: Cox, C., Warner, D. (eds.) Audio Culture: Readings in Modern Music, pp. 138–156. Continuum, New York (2004)
12. Dallet, S.: Pierre Schaeffer: Itinéraires d'un chercheur. Ed. du Centre d'études et de recherche Pierre Schaeffer (1996)
13. Danielsen, A.: Aesthetic value, cultural significance, and canon formation in popular music. Studia Musicologica **32**, 55–72 (2006)
14. Deutsch, D., et al.: Illusory transformation from speech to song. J. Acoust. Soc. Am. **129**, 2245–2252 (2011)
15. Duchamp, M.: Object with Hidden Noise (1916)
16. Duchamp, M.: The Writings of Marcel Duchamp. Da Capo Press (1989)
17. Eadie, J.: ..and after optimism (1996)
18. Eco, U., Cancogni, A.: The Open Work. Harvard University Press, Cambridge (1989)
19. Eno, B.: Ambient 1 Music For Airports (1978)
20. Eno, B.: More Dark Than Shark. https://www.moredarkthanshark.org/eno_int_wire-may01b.html
21. Ferguson, R., Kahn, D.: Christian Marclay. Steidl, Los Angeles (2003)
22. Feshareki, S.: Still Point (1949)
23. Filimowicz, M., Stockholm, J.: Towards a phenomenology of the acoustic image. Organised Sound **15**(01), 5 (2010)
24. Gann, K.: Kyle Gann: No Such Thing as Silence: John Cage's 4'33". Yale University Press, New Haven (2010)
25. Hosler, M., Wills, D.: NEGATIVLAND Fair Use: The Story of the Letter U and the Numeral 2. Seeland-Negativland, New York (1991)
26. Ihde, D.: Listening and Voice: Phenomenologies of Sound. State University of New York Press, New York (1976)
27. James, L.: Semantic Satiation: What Happens when You Repeat A Word Over and Over Again (Doctoral Thesis). Independently published, Hawaii (2018)
28. Jeck, P.: Vinyl Requiem. https://vimeo.com/17439345
29. Julien, O., Levaux, C. (eds.): Over and Over: Exploring Repetition in Popular Music. Bloomsbury Academic, New York (2018)
30. Kahn, D.: John cage: silence and silencing. Musical Q. **81**(4), 556–598 (1997)
31. Kane, B.: L'Objet Sonore Maintenant: Pierre Schaeffer, sound objects and the phenomenological reduction. Organised Sound **12**(01), 15 (2007)
32. Kane, B.: Sound Unseen: Acousmatic Sound in Theory and Practice. Oxford University Press, Oxford (2014)
33. Kim, S.-J.: A critique on Pierre Schaeffer's phenomenological approaches: based on the acousmatic and reduced listening. In: Proceedings of the International Conference Pierre Schaeffer: mediArt, pp. 123–133 (2010)
34. Kim-Cohen, S.: In the Blink of an Ear: Toward a Non-Cochlear Sonic Art. Continuum, New York (2009)
35. Kim-Cohen, S.: Sculpture in The Reduced Field (2008)
36. Kostelanetz, R.: John Cage. Rk Editions, New York (1978)
37. Kosuth, J.: Art After Philosophy and After: Collected Writings, 1966–1990. The MIT Press, Cambridge (1993)

38. Lacy, K.: The Routledge companion to sounding art. In: Cobussen, M. et al. (eds.) The Routledge Companion to Sounding Art, Routledge (2016)
39. Landy, L.: But Is It (Also) music? In: Cobussen, M. et al. (eds.) The Routledge Companion to Sounding Art. Routledge, New York (2016)
40. Lucier, A.: I Am Sitting in a Room (1969)
41. Maes, L.: Sounding sound art : a study of its definition, origin, context and techniques of sound art. Ghent University (2013)
42. Marclay, C.: White Cube - Artists - Christian Marclay. https://whitecube.com/artists/artist/christian_marclay
43. Margulis, E.H.: Musical repetition detection across multiple exposures. Music Percept. **29**(4), 377–385 (2012)
44. Margulis, E.H.: On Repeat: How Music Plays the Mind. Oxford University Press, New York (2013)
45. Margulis, E.H., Simchy-Gross, R.: Repetition enhances the musicality of randomly generated tone sequences. Music. Percept. **33**(4), 509–514 (2016)
46. Mills, J.: Cycle 30. Axis - AX-008, Detroit (1994)
47. Morris, R.: Box with the Sound of Its Own Making (1961)
48. O'Callaghan, C.: Beyond Vision: Philosophical Essays. Oxford University Press, Oxford (2017)
49. Pritchett, J.: The Music of John Cage. Cambridge University Press, Cambridge (1993)
50. Radigue, E.: $\Sigma = a = b = a + b$ (1969)
51. Rauschenberg, R.: Erased de Kooning Drawing (1953)
52. Reed, L.: Metal Machine Music. CPL2–1101, RCA (1975)
53. Reich, S.: Writings on Music, 1965–2000. Oxford University Press, Oxford (1968)
54. Rivas, F.: What a sound object is: phenomenology of sound in Pierre Schaeffer. In: Gligo, N., Davidović, D. (eds.) Proceedings of the International Conference Pierre Schaeffer: mediArt. Museum of Modern and Contemporary Art, Croatia (2011)
55. Ruddoc, O.: Herbal Dub (King Tubby). Motion Records/Jigsaw JS 004, London (1970)
56. Schaeffer, P., Henri, P.: Symphonie pour un homme seul (1950)
57. Schafer, R.M.: The Tuning of the World. Random House Inc., New York (1977)
58. Scott, L.B.: R. Murray Schafer: A Creative Life. Rowman & Littlefield Publishers, New York (2019)
59. Silverman, K.: Begin Again: A Biography of John Cage. Northwestern University Press, Evanston (2012)
60. Strickland, E.: Minimalism: Origins. Indiana University Press, Bloomington (1993)
61. Suryabrata: Unknown Artist - The Jasmine Isle (Javanese Gamelan Music) (1969)
62. Szendy, P.: Listen A History of our Ears. Fordham University Press, New York (2008)
63. Tamm, E.: Brian Eno: His Music and The Vertical Color Of Sound. Da Capo Press, New York (1995)
64. Tenney, J.: Collage #1. Artifact Recordings, ART 1007 (1961)
65. Toop, D.: Sinister Resonance. Continuum, New York (2011)
66. Toop, D.: Sonic Boom: The Art of Sound. South Bank Centre, London (2000)
67. Various Artists: RRR 500 (Various 500 Lock-Grooves By 500 Artists). RRRecords, New York (1998)
68. Zajonc, R.B.: Attitudinal Effects of Mere Exposure (1968)

Effect of Dramatic Elements on Engagement in an Augmented Reality Experience for a Museum

André T. J. Kristensen, Casper Høgalmen, Leon Müller, Martin Kraus$^{(\boxtimes)}$, and Mohanad M. Zeitoun

Aalborg University, 9000 Aalborg, Denmark
martin@create.aau.dk

Abstract. The long-term goal of this work is to improve the experience of museum visitors with the help of Augmented Reality (AR) experiences for informing the visitors about the displayed exhibits through other means than museum labels, as these either lacked information or were placed inconveniently at the exhibitions. This paper proposes the integration of Brenda Laurel's concept of Dramatic Interaction by utilizing different non-playable characters (NPC) that serve as the users' companions during their visits to various exhibits. This approach aims to enhance the user's level of engagement which would positively influence their overall experience at the museum. The proposed solution was evaluated by comparing two versions of the developed system, one makes use of different unique NPCs in its design, while the other instead uses a single narrator. A statistical test was performed on the collected data and the results indicated that all but one aspect of engagement did not appear significantly different between the two evaluated conditions. Telling the story of artifacts through different NPCs seemed to provide a more fun experience to users, when compared to the stories being told by one narrator.

Keywords: Dramatic Interaction · Non-playable characters · Augmented Reality · Museum

1   Introduction

For more than 60 years, museums and cultural institutions have been utilizing handheld electronic technologies [30], ranging from audio or multimedia guides that usually provide additional information about exhibits [2], to digital edutainment games which can be used for children to play and have fun while learning [17]. While a museum setting can attract demographics of a wide age range, one key factor for visiting a museum is seeking new knowledge, whether it is in the field of history, culture, science, technology, art, etc. According to Packer and Ballantyne [24], one of the motivating factors for visiting a museum is to

A. Brooks et al. (Eds.): ArtsIT 2020, LNICST 367, pp. 100–118, 2021.
https://doi.org/10.1007/978-3-030-73426-8_6

expand a person's knowledge and acquire new information on various subjects. Thus, museums present an opportunity for learning which can ultimately lead to a satisfactory experience.

Lately, the aforementioned institutions have also started to incorporate the emerging technologies of Augmented Reality (AR) and Virtual Reality (VR), as these allow visitors to experience exhibitions through new ways of engagement and interaction [13]. Additionally, some museums have adapted these technologies to use virtual characters that communicate stories and information about exhibits, as well as guiding them to other exhibits that might be of interest [3,15,31]. These characters usually take the role of a traditional human guide, helping museums convey the exhibit information directly to each visitor in a more interesting way, compared to just reading about them via stands or labels placed at the exhibits. This is further enhanced by the ability to overlay supporting visuals onto the exhibits through AR.

In collaboration with Vesthimmerlands Museum, six exhibits were chosen as the ones the AR application should focus on, as the curators felt that these were lacking additional information that was not provided by the appertaining labels displayed next to them. Furthermore, some of the exhibits contained interesting characteristics or visual peculiarities that the AR could aid in identifying for visitors, considering they might not notice these when they are examining the exhibits unguided.

With the specific exhibits and basic functionality of the AR features established, we decided to further support this by focusing on achieving an engaging experience through the application. This was deemed relevant, since research suggests that designing for engaging interaction encourages and facilitates learning as well as enhances the user experience [12,32,33]. Additionally, incorporating a form a narrative into an application that attempts to facilitate learning or information, has proved to reduce the cognitive load involved when introduced to a mass of information [10,22] and offer cognitive and imaginative engagement [4,22].

In this paper, we present the results of a comparative study of user engagement where two versions of an AR application, both designed for the context of Vesthimmerlands Museum, are evaluated through a within-subjects experimental design. One version utilizes elements from the concept of Dramatic Interaction (DI), whereas the other version more closely resembles an interactive audio guide. The following section reviews work relating to the current paper and provides an overview of what entails DI. Section 3 describes the materials and methods used in the evaluation. Section 4 presents the results and a discussion of the findings, and Section 5 concludes the paper.

2   Related Work

To provide a better overview of the topics covered in this section, it was divided into three subsections. The first of these investigates general AR applications deployed in various museum contexts, the second delves deeper into the concept of DI and how it relates to engagement, and the third follows up on this by providing examples of studies that have utilized certain elements relating to the concept.

2.1   AR in Museum Contexts

There are numerous recent examples of AR applications in museums that contribute to the visitor's overall experience.

One study, carried out by Lando, E. [16], compared two different types of AR visualization systems on the learning experience in a museum. These two types were referred to as On-screen space and In-world space. The former renders the perceived virtual content from an exhibition on the screen of the mobile device, while the latter renders the virtual content directly onto the physical exhibition. Through an empirical evaluation, it was discovered that the In-world space system resulted in a more enjoyable and engaging experience when exploring the different exhibitions at the museum. Similar results were concluded by both Miyashita et al. [23], who carried out a study on AR guidance in the Louvre Museum in Paris, and Leue et al.[20], who conducted their research at Manchester Art Gallery. Lando notes that these aspects can positively influence learning, however, a larger experiment with more participants would be required to obtain more conclusive results, seeing that the experiment was only conducted with 12 participants. However, the research by Leue et al. reached the same conclusion that creating an enjoyable and engaging AR application can contribute to the user's learning outcome from a museum visit.

Chang et al. [6] developed an AR auxiliary tool for painting appreciation, and the learning performance of three groups of participants was explored. The three groups were divided into people exploring a museum with the proposed AR solution, people carrying an audio-guide, and non-guided people. When measuring the learning performance of each group, Chang et al. focused on factors such as learning effectiveness, the amount of time spent focusing on the painting, behavioral patterns, and attitude of using the guide system. Results indicated that each of the aforementioned categories showed an alleviated level for the group equipped with the AR guide, compared to the audio-guided group and the unguided group. To further underline the results of the study, Chang et al. emphasize that both teachers and students felt that AR not only promoted participation and motivation, but also created a realistic and novel environment when the real world is combined with the virtual world.

However, even though the coupling between the virtual and the physical scenes is a key element of a mobile AR-guide [14], Sparacino [28] emphasizes that such a system might cause visitors to place too much attention on the information in the guide device, thus lowering the appreciation of the physical artifact at hand. It is therefore important to find the right balance between the virtual guide information and the physical artwork when creating an AR system, to retain the advantages of a system that brings both realms together within the user's range of vision.

This is also emphasized by Marques and Costello [21] in their paper, where they investigated the different concerns and challenges that are prone to appear when AR applications are placed in the context of museums. They also argue that for AR to not just be adopted by museums because it is an eye-catching technology, it "needs to be a solution to the visitor experience by effectively weaving the virtual with the physical into the narrative, and ensuring that the interface becomes an integral layer, a storytelling tool.". Something worth considering when trying to accomplish this, is the fact that the exhibits themselves should be used to trigger the AR features rather than location based AR, as this helps avoid visitors becoming detracted from the physical museum. However, that method suffers from its own issues such as lighting conditions and line of sight. Usually proper AR activation requires higher light conditions, and some museums tend to have sections that are dimly lit due to conservation concerns. Furthermore, if a museum has peak hours with heavy crowds, there is a higher chance of a visitor losing line of sight to the exhibit with their camera, due to people being forced to walk in front of exhibits. Another unfavorable side effect of crowded spaces is the noise level. Traditional audio guides can be held against the ear, but visitors standing at objects offering augmentation, hold the device in front of their bodies to experience the visuals. This typically results in the sound being more lost to the surroundings.

These are all important matters to consider when designing an AR application to be used in the context of a museum. Sung, Chang, Hou, and Chen [29] additionally point out that a mobile guide should aim to incorporate the context of the promoted environment as much as possible, thereby including the guiding environment, their companions, the exhibits and their cultural and social implications. The interaction between the visitors and these aforementioned aspects should be fully supported when designing a mobile guide to form what Chang et al. calls "human-computer-context" . Again, the planning of the guide system is crucial to not over-exaggerate the digital part of the system, i.e. the "human-computer" guide system, whilst not neglecting the "human-situation" , i.e. the real environment at hand. Failing to balance these two factors will result in a system that is incapable of inducing a satisfying human-computer-context.

2.2   Dramatic Interaction

A concept that has been utilized to achieve a higher level of engagement is Dramatic Interaction, a term introduced by Brenda Laurel [18]. It is the concept of interactors creating their own narratives using a given system to create their own stories with personal significance. Examples of freedom within boundaries include, but are not limited to, allowing interactors to choose the order of interactions or allowing them to choose their own goals within the system. Based on the idea that things humans interact with naturally become more important to them, Laurel analyzes the relationship between player and designer as a collaborative effort towards creating an enjoyable experience. Furthermore, Laurel hypothesizes that experiences tend to spark fascination and engagement when they appear to transcend artificial structure. She therefore points to theatrics as an art form dedicated to the illusion of reality, suggesting that the use of theatrical techniques in interaction design, such as characters and dramaturgical models, can increase engagement.

These characters are usually implemented as non-playable characters (NPCs) which are defined as characters in the virtual worlds not controlled by a user. While most commonly used in video games, other applications have historically made use of NPCs for a variety of purposes. Applications including narratives often utilize NPCs as plot devices, having them help further a storyline. They can also be applied to aid the user either through helpful information or other means depending on the application type. Lastly, NPCs can be made into personified game functions such as user-interfaces or save points.

2.3 Non-playable Characters in Augmented and Virtual Reality

While the studies described in Section 2.1 indicate learning and enjoyment benefits from introducing AR in a museum context, the results from a study conducted by Jessel et al. [11] did not show a significant improvement in terms of learning. The study focused on enhancing the visitor's learning experience in museums by developing a handheld AR application called M.A.R.T.S (Mobile Augmented Reality Touring System). They compared M.A.R.T.S to two traditional and widely used museum systems: labels and audio guides. In their study, the authors implemented a virtual human guide to aid with conveying information about the works of art displayed at the Bayonne's Basque Museum. The virtual guide was utilized to provide instructions to the visitors regarding which areas of an exhibit can be explored to acquire further knowledge about it by pointing at the respective area. This approach, which was referred to as "Selection" , limited potential confusion that could be caused due to lack of obvious visual reference indicating the works of art or areas of an exhibit that are augmented by the application. The results of the study revealed that M.A.R.T.S did not perform significantly better than the labels and audio-guide in terms of learning more about the exhibits, however, on average participants scored higher using M.A.R.T.S when they had to answer questions about the works of art they had explored. Moreover, presenting information in both textual and auditory manners seemed to be redundant with participants favoring audio only. As a positive note, the "Selection" process proved advantageous when trying to identify parts of a work of art that is simultaneously referenced by the virtual guide. This means that this method can be utilized in AR to direct the visitor's attention to a particular area of an exhibit in a museum.

In 1994, Laurel, Strickland and Tow [19] attempted to utilize VR for the sake of entertainment, something that was quite a novel idea at the time, by conducting a research project they named "Placeholder". They explored new ways of narration in VR, where the environments were inspired by real life locations and users could take the form of four animated spirit critters that inhabited these environments. Doing so, would allow the user to experience the specific critter's "unique visual perception, its way of moving about, and its voice" . To enrich the DI within the virtual world, a character named "The Goddess" was added. The special trait of this character was that its personality was improvised live, usually by either Laurel herself or one of her coworkers, though occasionally, other actors would perform the role as well, including men. This resulted in the character's personality changing depending on the actor portraying it but also in relation to the participants encountering it. If the participants were children, the character would behave as a friendly helper, if they were couples it would tease them, and if the participants were acting insulting or unfriendly, so would the character. By doing this, the character would react to interactions with it, but it would also react to how it was interacted with. This is an example of how interactions with a character can be dramatized through live performance from actors that theatrically react to the specific participants that encounter it. This is not feasible in the context of the museum application; however, a scripted "performance" of an NPC could be based on such performances.

Lastly, Christopoulos et al. [7] and their paper on their VR application, 'Battle of Thermopylae', should be mentioned, as they incorporate some ideas from DI in their interactive guide approach. Based on studies confirming the importance of an actual human guide, they created a game wherein the player would walk around in historical battle camps and ask residents three questions about their relations to the world around them. According to Slater [27], this bi-directional flow of information strengthens the users' suspension of disbelief and allows them to engage more vividly with the characters. To make sure that users went through this bi-directional flow, players would have to cooperate with the characters in order to progress further into the application. With this, the group aimed for triggering Kolb's experiential learning cycle [25], wherein players would have to observe as well as directly participate in the interactive experience. During their evaluation, the research group focused on engagement and learning outcomes and found that the children evaluated had a high accuracy on the post-experience test with which they were presented. On the other hand, surveys from VR guided tours without interactive elements, showed that few individuals could answer correctly in post-experience tests. The research group concludes that interactive elements, combined with new practices in the area of games, could help facilitate learning and produce more effective learning environments.

3 Materials and Methods

One long-term aim of this study was to develop a digital platform for Vesthimmerlands Museum which they could utilize to further inform the visitors about the displayed exhibits. An AR medium offers a more engaging experience than reading text from exhibit labels which, in the case of Vesthimmerlands Museum, also suffered from a lack of information or inconvenient placements. In order to potentially further enhance the visitor experience, we wanted to measure the effects of Laurel's concept of DI on users' level of engagement.

3.1 Apparatus

The evaluated system is an AR application developed in Unity intended to detect image markers and provide information to the user in response to their inputs.

The specific exhibits that the museum saw benefit from being included in the app can be seen in Figure 1. For easier readability, the two most discussed of these exhibits, namely "Gundestrupkarret" and "Ryttergraven fra Næsby", will be referred to as the cauldron and the sword, respectively. Due to the COVID-19 pandemic, the system was not tested in the museum, but an altered version of the system was created which included 3D models of the two exhibits. This version allowed users to scan the image targets and have interactions as per the original intent.

Fig. 1. From left to right: Aars-egnens Første Bank, Petreas Skilt, Hedegårdmanden, Tatoveringsnåle fra Bronzealderen, Ryttergraven fra Næsby, Gundestrupkarret.

In order to evaluate the effects of dramatic elements on a user's experience and their level of engagement, it was necessary to create a version of the application that was devoid of any aspects of DI. Other key features of interaction were present in both variants. This allowed us to discern the difference between the two experiences by isolating that one key distinction and comparing them directly. The first variant was reminiscent of standard audio guides with a single omniscient second-person narrator where users could choose to get information about specific artifact attributes (see Figure 2). The second variant on the other hand, included a character for each supported exhibit which inferred their personalities into the interactions users would have with the system (see Figure 3).

While Laurel describes a multitude of different methods for dramatizing interaction, we chose to focus on the mix of mediated collaboration, NPCs, and a variety of theatrical writing methods. This would link to the aim of the museum of providing information about the artifacts by having NPCs historically connected to them tell stories about their origins and uses. Visitors would be able to choose questions of relevance to their own interests, thus creating mediated collaboration. Furthermore, with inspiration taken from "The Goddess" of the "Placeholder" project mentioned in Section 2.3, the characters would react to users interacting with the play, pause, or skip button. Each character would have three pre-recorded voice lines for each interaction which would be played at random when the corresponding button was pressed. Unfortunately, regarding the audio for the different characters, with no budget for hiring a professional voice actor, all the voice lines were recorded by two of the authors of this paper who were both amateurs in this field. This undoubtedly affected the quality, however, with research suggesting that audio is preferred over text, and the fact

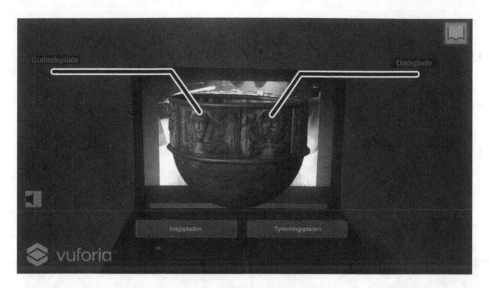

Fig. 2. Example of exhibit interaction from the application with no dramatic interaction elements

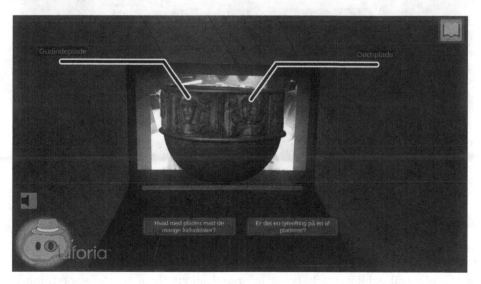

Fig. 3. Example of exhibit interaction from the application with dramatic interaction elements

that personifying a character through text, rather than audio, is more difficult, we decided to proceed with the decision.

These NPCs should also help provide some of the context incorporation that Sung, Chang, Hou, and Chen (see Section 2.1) argue for, due to the decision of making them historically connected to each specific exhibit. The interface of the application was also designed with the context of a museum in mind, while simultaneously attempting to minimize distractions and visual overload [8] by hiding most of it behind a single expandable button (see top right of Figure 2 or 3). When pressed, a panel will expand, revealing six buttons containing icons that depict each exhibit (see top right of Figure 4). These icons are semi-transparent and will remain so until an exhibit has been visited, resulting in the respective icon turning opaque (see third icon from the left in Figure 4). When any of these six buttons is pressed, a journal will show on screen that functions both as a form of guidance system, by displaying images of the exhibits supported by the application, and as a place for users to review their interactions with exhibits they have visited (see Figure 4).

Fig. 4. Example of a page in the application journal

The augmentation provided by the application was implemented in the form of highlights positioned at points of interest on the exhibit (see Figure 2 or Figure 3). These would aid the users in examining interesting or specific regions of the physical exhibit, while being informed about them by the appertaining character. Furthermore, this should prevent the users from focusing more on their device rather than the exhibit, which was emphasized by multiple authors referenced in Section 2.1.

When starting the application, a user would first be greeted with an introductory message containing instructions on how to trigger interactions. They would also be told of the journal and its functionality. Once the user had gone through the introduction, they would have to scan one of the provided image targets to activate an interaction. Here, users would be presented with three main questions each with two sub-questions, the answers to all of which, were narrated. If any of these questions contained a piece of dialogue about a specific point of interest on the exhibit, the narrator or character would instruct the user to examine the exhibit with their phone, as highlights that point towards these would be visible. Once all supported exhibits had been interacted with, a final monologue was triggered informing the user that the experience was over.

3.2 Procedure

The experiment with the altered version was conducted as a within-subject design where a participant would experience the application with and without DI. To avoid various order effects, we created four different procedures and opted for an equal number of participants going through each procedure, as a participant was instructed to follow only one of them. Two applications were created for the version containing elements from DI and likewise for the version without. These applications differed in the order of presented exhibits, as one would start with the cauldron followed by the sword and vice versa for the other. Further included in these procedures were two engagement questionnaires (see Section 3.3 Table 2), a comparative questionnaire (see Section 3.3 Table 3) and a consent form. Table 1 shows condensed examples of the four procedures, slightly altered to allow for easier readability.

Due to the restricting circumstances during the COVID-19 pandemic, testing at Vesthimmerlands Museum or setting up a dedicated space for participants to partake in the evaluation was not possible. Instead, folders containing Android Package Kits (APK) and images of the two exhibits to be used as image targets were created. Four folders were created in total, as each of them would contain different APKs depending on which category the corresponding participant was assigned (A, B, C, or D). A participant would receive an instructions file containing a link to one of these folders, a guide on how to prepare their Android phone for downloading and installing the APKs, one of the four procedures seen in Table 1, and links to the digital consent form and questionnaires.

A total of 16 participants (10 males and 6 females), aged between 22 and 32 years old, with different educational and occupational backgrounds were recruited online from various websites and platforms such as Reddit, Facebook, Microsoft Teams, and Discord. Unfortunately, it proved difficult to find participants within the limited time frame this study was carried out under due to requiring an Android phone and an advanced understanding of spoken Danish. Furthermore, the technical complexity of succeeding in installing and running the APK resulted in younger and older age groups being excluded from the evaluation due to a lack of tech familiarity. The implications of this decision are discussed in Section 4.

Table 1. Examples of participant procedures.

Participant A	Participant B	Participant C	Participant D
1. Fill out the consent form	1. Fill out the consent form	1. Fill out the consent form	1. Fill out the consent form
2. Start the application with DI containing the order of cauldron then sword	2. Start the application without DI containing the order of cauldron then sword	2. Start the application with DI containing the order of sword then cauldron	2. Start the application without DI containing the order of sword then cauldron
3. Once finished with both exhibits, answer the questionnaire (Table 2)	3. Once finished with both exhibits, answer the questionnaire (Table 2)	3. Once finished with both exhibits, answer the questionnaire (Table 2)	3. Once finished with both exhibits, answer the questionnaire (Table 2)
4. Start the application without DI containing the order of cauldron then sword	4. Start the application with DI containing the order of cauldron then sword	4. Start the application without DI containing the order of sword then cauldron	4. Start the application with DI containing the order of sword then cauldron
5. Once finished with both exhibits, answer the questionnaire (Table 2)	5. Once finished with both exhibits, answer the questionnaire (Table 2)	5. Once finished with both exhibits, answer the questionnaire (Table 2)	5. Once finished with both exhibits, answer the questionnaire (Table 2)
6. Answer the questionnaire (Table 3)	6. Answer the questionnaire (Table 3)	6. Answer the questionnaire (Table 3)	6. Answer the questionnaire (Table 3)

3.3   Hypothesis and Data Collection

Despite the fact that the developed system could not be evaluated in its intended context at Vesthimmerlands Museum, we deemed it possible to obtain similar results on the aspects of users' engagement through an evaluation of the substitute prototype.

The overall expectation of the experimental design was that the evaluated condition during which the system makes use of DI elements would achieve higher levels of engagement compared to the other condition which lacks DI. Thus, the following hypothesis was defined:

– **H1:** Introducing interactive non-playable characters in an AR museum application increases the user's feeling of engagement.

The effects of both conditions on the users' level of engagement were determined via a questionnaire that was adapted from a selection of well-established engagement questionnaires [1,5,9,26]. The questionnaire, seen in Table 2, consisted of a total of 13 questions, which were selected to measure aspects that constitute the perception of engagement or have an influence on it. These aspects form the following constructs: authenticity, curiosity, focused immersion, enjoyment and interactivity. Furthermore, a few of the questions aimed to assess the concept of narrative engagement due to its importance in the context of DI. The participants could answer the questionnaire through a 5-point Likert scale ranging from "Strongly Disagree" to "Strongly Agree".

Table 2. Engagement questionnaire

Number	Question
1	I did not find it artificial to receive information about the exhibits through the application. (You can compare it to having a human guide with you through a museum.) [9]
2	Discovering the history of the exhibits through the application gave me an authentic feeling. [9]
3	My experience with the application aroused my interest in the history of the exhibits. [1]
4	While using the application I was absorbed in what I was doing. [1]
5	While using the application I was not able to block out most distractions. [1]
6	The actual process of using the application was unpleasant. [1]
7	I find using the application to be enjoyable. [1]
8	I had fun using the application. [1]
9	Using the application provided me with an interactive experience. [26]
10	I felt I had control over my interaction with the application. [26]
11	I had a hard time recognizing the thread of the story. [5]
12	I felt like I was part of the story. [5]
13	I listened to what was said. [5]

In addition to the engagement questionnaire, a comparative questionnaire, seen in Table 3, was set up to be answered at the end of the experiment. This decision was made for the purpose of gaining more insight into the participants' favored experience, since at that point they would have tested both versions of the application, hence enabling them to make a direct comparison. A preferred procedure would have been that while the participants are answering their second questionnaire, they can go back and review their ratings from the first questionnaire, with the option of changing the ratings if they see fit. Due to the fact that the evaluation was conducted at the participants' households without the presence of a facilitator to oversee the entire process, the method of letting the participants change their ratings by themselves was deemed to be a cumbersome process that they would have to keep track of. Therefore, considering the circumstances, the comparative questionnaire was regarded as a suitable alternative to shed some light on which system version was preferred.

The comparative questionnaire had the first three questions asking the participants to choose on a Likert scale from 1 to 5, which of the two versions they perceived as more engaging, more fun and easier to use. On the scale, 1 refers to the version that does not employ the different NPCs, while 5 refers to the one that does. The last part of the comparative questionnaire had the participants explicitly state their overall preferred version during the evaluation, followed by a question encouraging them to explain the reasoning behind their choice.

Table 3. Comparative questionnaire

Number	Question
1	Which application did you find more engaging?
2	Which application provided a more fun experience?
3	Which application was easier to use?
4	Which version of the application did you prefer?
5	What is the reason for preferring one version over the other?

Questions 1, 2, and 4 in the comparative questionnaire shared the same expectation of NPCs contributing to an experience that is significantly more engaging and more fun, thereby leading participants to favoring that version of the application over the one that is guided by one narrator. As for question 3, considering that none of the functionalities that facilitate the usage of the application are any different in the two versions of the application, it was expected that there would be no perceived difference in terms of ease of use. This led to the formulation of the following hypothesis:

- **H2:** The version of the application using non-playable characters is more engaging and fun, and overall preferred, when directly compared to the version using one narrator.

3.4 Statistical Analysis

All the questions in the engagement questionnaire shared the same expected outcome as the one mentioned in Section 3.3 for the complete experience, thereby leading to the decision of treating each question as if it were an individual experiment performed independently from the rest. This is advantageous because it eliminates the necessity to carry out a correction to counteract the problem of multiple comparisons, which is a problem that has a negative impact on the reliability of the outcome. All the questions are, however, evaluated in the same questionnaire in order to save time on what would otherwise have been a lengthy process, which was not possible under the time constraints this study was carried out under.

The experimental design was a repeated measures design due the measurements of a user's level of engagement being collected under two conditions for each participant. The statistical data is ordinal, thus making it suitable to perform a non-parametric test. Moreover, the comparison process between the two conditions of the experiment is a pairwise comparison, which fits the methodology of the Wilcoxon-signed rank test, as it evaluates the significance difference between the dependent samples. The statistical analysis of the collected data was performed with a significance level of 5% ($\alpha = 0.05$), and it was done in the IBM SPSS software.

The data of each of the first three questions in the comparative questionnaire was not a pairwise measurement between two dependent variables. Therefore a set of dummy data was introduced in place of the second variable to allow for a computation of differences, thereby making it eligible for a Wilcoxon-signed rank test. The dummy data consisted of 16 entries of a rating of 3 for each of the three questions, as this rating can be considered a central point, hence a neutral response to the provided Likert scale.

The fourth question in the comparative questionnaire instead required a binomial distribution test to determine whether the participants are biased towards selecting the version with NPCs as their preferred version.

4   Results and Discussion

The p-values for the comparisons in H1 are presented in Table 4. The results for the comparisons in H2, inferred from the comparisons in the comparative questionnaire, are shown in Table 5.

Table 4. The p-values for the comparisons of questions 1 to 13 in the engagement questionnaire. Question 8 investigated the aspect of fun.

Hypothesis	Question Number	p-value	Null hypothesis
H1	1	0.998	Retained
H1	2	0.476	Retained
H1	3	0.122	Retained
H1	4	0.220	Retained
H1	5	0.056	Retained
H1	6	0.388	Retained
H1	7	0.095	Retained
H1	**8**	**0.015**	**Rejected**
H1	9	0.168	Retained
H1	10	0.340	Retained
H1	11	0.083	Retained
H1	12	0.073	Retained
H1	13	0.066	Retained

Table 5. The p-values for comparisons of question 1, 2 and 4 in the comparative questionnaire. Question 2 investigated which of the two versions was more fun.

Hypothesis	Question Number	p-value	Null hypothesis
H2	1	0.07	Retained
H2	**2**	**0.002**	**Rejected**
H2	4	0.227	Retained

The results from the Wilcoxon signed-rank test performed on H1 and H2 indicated a significant difference for 2 of the 16 comparisons. For question 4 in the comparative questionnaire, the results of the binomial distribution test did not yield a statistically significant difference, however a tendency favoring the version with NPCs could be observed.

When asked to directly compare the two versions of the application, participants did not find the version including dramatic elements in the form of NPCs significantly more engaging than the one including a single non-embodied narrator. However, comments provided during the last part of the comparative questionnaire indicated a slight bias towards the former version. Albeit, this trend did not consolidate itself statistically, it can be observed in the answers of question 4 in the comparative questionnaire.

Due to the remote nature of this evaluation, participants were gathered and approached via a multitude of online and social media platforms. Consequently, the motivation for participants to partake in this evaluation did not arise from a natural curiosity, which can normally be observed when present at the museum. This could have affected the general engagement with the application, as participants were not particularly interested in neither the exhibits nor what the narrator or characters had to say about them.

In addition to these findings, some participants negatively commented on the lack of system flexibility regarding the absence of an option to skip an exhibit mid-interaction. It is believed that the main reason for wanting to skip the interaction with an exhibit is due to a low level of interest or curiosity about the subject. Being unable to perform this action, while already experiencing a low level of curiosity, could lead to a further decrease in interest. It can therefore be concluded that the reported lack of system flexibility is a factor that can negatively impact the participant's level of engagement.

Overall, failing to reject the null hypothesis for 12 out of the 13 questions in the engagement questionnaire, indicates that deploying elements of DI does not increase engagement in this specific context. However, question 8 of the engagement questionnaire, which investigated the aspect of fun, did indicate a significant difference. This is further supported by the rejected null hypothesis H2 for question 2 in the comparative questionnaire, wherein participants were asked to directly compare which version provided a more fun experience. Furthermore, comments from the evaluation indicated that a variety of the deployed design elements can have a positive effect on AR applications seeking to induce an engaging experience. Among those elements are the highlights, which can subtly prompt users to inspect or interact with an object. Also, splitting a longer narrative into smaller parts, whilst implementing UI elements that allow users to control the flow of the narration, prevents participants from having to listen to an entire narration in one sitting. Additionally, hiding unnecessary UI elements from the user's field of view accommodates for the need of creating a balance between the physical and the virtual realms, thus preventing distractions and visual overload.

The perceived ease of use in question 3 of the comparative questionnaire (see Table 3) was evaluated through a statistical analysis to determine whether the expected outcome was realized. The test showed that our expectation of the comparison was correct, and there was no difference between the two versions of the application. Hence, it can be inferred that the deployed UI renders the same performance in both use cases. Although participants reported an equal performance regarding the ease of use of both versions, the precise level for each individual version is not recorded due to the question only being included in the comparative questionnaire.

The results of the comparison in question 4 of the comparative questionnaire (see Table 3) did not report a statistical significance regarding whether participants preferred DI over the interaction with a single narrator. It is to be noted that the authors did not have the required resources nor the artistical skills to allow for the deployment of an iterative design methodology for the development of the NPCs. Considering that NPCs reflect an integral part of the system in the form of dramatic elements, it would have been preferable to evaluate each character individually, prior to implementing it in the final system, to receive feedback regarding its conceptions. The sentiment of amateur character design in both visual and auditory appearance was voiced by some participants, thus further validating the potentially positive impact of more professionally designed NPCs. Other participants commented on the spirit-like appearance of NPCs, while wishing for a more humanoid depiction.

The deployment of an iterative design methodology could have allowed us to discover design flaws that were implemented in the final version of the prototype used for the evaluation. One of these flaws was that participants commented on not knowing when they could expect changes in what was augmented onto the exhibit. As such, some participants might have missed when highlights were shown or changed, or they would perhaps continuously have pointed their phone camera towards the image targets, even though this is not necessary. A more user-friendly design would have included indicators for the inclusion of AR content next to the relevant buttons in an exhibit interaction, thereby allowing users to aim their phone at an AR marker, only at moments when relevant content is about to be displayed.

In addition to not being in the desired context, the remote evaluation did not allow for the possibility of observing the participants' interactions and the subtleties that might have emanated from their body language. These subtleties would have had the potential to reveal further insight regarding the level of engagement. Asking participants to report these subtleties would most likely be noninformative, as participants themselves can be unaware of said actions.

Although no statistical significance can be reported, trends in the results concerning preference, and comments made by participants, facilitate the conclusion that people inherently interested in the subject conveyed by the exhibits, found the detached narrator better as facts were communicated more clearly. Participants not sharing this sentiment seemed to prefer the version including dramatic elements, as it provided a livelier approach to the potentially uninteresting subject.

Based on the conducted evaluation, it can be concluded that dramatic elements in the form of different NPCs do not necessarily evoke a greater sense of engagement when compared to a version without these elements. However, a more fun experience was reported with a statistically significant difference for the version including DI. Furthermore, data trends, though statistically insignificant, as well as comments support the claim that elements of DI have the potential to induce a greater sense of engagement for people with a low level of curiosity for the presented subject. Based on the shortcomings of the apparatus such as the inability to conduct the evaluation in its intended use-case and having a low sample size, it would be interesting to conduct a refined evaluation, which accommodates for the aforementioned flaws to conclusively report any potential enhancement of engagement in a museum context when using elements of DI.

5   Conclusion

This study was concerned with researching how engagement is affected by introducing elements of Dramatic Interaction (DI) in the form of non-playable characters (NPC) in an Augmented Reality (AR) guide application for Vesthimmerlands Museum in Aars. A within-subjects experiment was conducted, and participants were presented with two AR applications comprised of varying engaging elements. The ongoing COVID-19 pandemic, at the time of conducting the evaluation, posed the need to conduct it remotely.

Based on the deployed experimental method of this paper, it cannot be concluded that the utilized elements of DI in an AR application enhance the level of engagement. However, results indicated that a more fun inducing AR experience is created when utilizing the deployed elements of DI, when compared to the absence of these features.

The revealed increase in fun that elements of DI can have in an AR application could be considered by other AR applications such as games or edutainment software. Furthermore, while designing these applications, developers could consider some of the deployed design principles in this paper, such as the use of highlights and a visually subtle user-interface. Future work could investigate how engagement is affected by conducting the deployed evaluation of this paper in situ in its intended context, seeing that imposed restrictions prevented this. The option to improve the production quality regarding the artistical aspects of this system is worth exploring as well. Moreover, a greater sample size should be obtained to increase the robustness and meaningfulness of the reported statistical results.

References

1. Agarwal, R., Karahanna, E.: Time flies when you're having fun: cognitive absorption and beliefs about information technology usage. MIS Q.: Manag. Inf. Syst. **24**(4), 665–694 (2000)
2. Alexandri, E., Tzanavara, A.: New technologies in the service of museum education. World Trans. Eng. Technol. Educ. **12**, 2 (2014)
3. Bickmore, T.W., Vardoulakis, L.M., Schulman, D.: Tinker: a relational agent museum guide. Autonomous Agents Multi-Agent Syst. **27**(2), , 254–276 (2013)
4. Bielenberg, D.R., Carpenter-Smith, T.: Efficacy of story in multimedia training. J. Netw. Comput. Appl. **20**(2), 151–159 (1997)
5. Busselle, R., Bilandzic, H.: Measuring Narrative Engagement. Media Psychol. **12**(4), 321–347 (2009)
6. Chang, K.E., Chang, C.T., Hou, H.T., Sung, Y.T., Chao, H.L., Lee, C.M.: Development and behavioral pattern analysis of a mobile guide system with augmented reality for painting appreciation instruction in an art museum. Comput. Educ. **71**, 185–197 (2014)
7. Christopoulos, D., Mavridis, P., Andreadis, A., Karigiannis, J.: Using, environments, virtual, to tell the story: the battle of thermopylae. In: Proceedings of 3rd International Conference on Games and Virtual Worlds for Serious Applications. VS-Games, pp. 84–91 (2011)
8. Endsley, T.C., Sprehn, K.A., Brill, R.M., Ryan, K.J., Vincent, E.C., Martin, J.M.: Augmented reality design heuristics: designing for dynamic interactions. In: Proceedings of the Human Factors and Ergonomics Society (2017), vol. 2017-October, pp. 2100–2104. Human Factors an Ergonomics Society Inc. (2017)
9. Featherman, M. S., Valacich, J. S., and Wells, J. D. Is that authentic or artificial? Understanding consumer perceptions of risk in e-service encounters. Information Systems Journal 16, 2 (apr 2006), 107–134
10. Forrester, M.A.: Can narratology facilitate successful communication in hypermedia environments? Intell. Tutoring Media **7**(1), 11–20 (1996)
11. Ghouaiel, N., Garbaya, S., Cieutat, J.-M., Jessel, J.-P.: Mobile augmented reality in museums : towards enhancing visitor's learning experience. Int. J. Virtual Reality **17**(1), 21–31 (2017)
12. Jacques, R., Preece, J., Carey, T.: Engagement as a design concept for multimedia. Can. J. Learn. Technol./La revue canadienne de l'apprentissage et de la technologie **24**, 1 (1995)
13. Jung, T., tom Dieck, M.C., Lee, H., Chung, N.: Effects of virtual reality and augmented reality on visitor experiences in museum. In: Inversini, A., Schegg, R. (eds.) Information and Communication Technologies in Tourism 2016, pp. 621–635. Springer, Cham (2016). https://doi.org/10.1007/978-3-319-28231-2_45
14. Klopfer, E., Squire, K.: Environmental detectives-the development of an augmented reality platform for environmental simulations. Educ. Technol. Res. Dev. **56**(2), 203–228 (2008)
15. Kopp, S., Gesellensetter, L., Krämer, N.C., Wachsmuth, I.: A conversational agent as museum guide – design and evaluation of a real-world application. In: Panayiotopoulos, T., Gratch, J., Aylett, R., Ballin, D., Olivier, P., Rist, T. (eds.)

IVA 2005. LNCS (LNAI), vol. 3661, pp. 329–343. Springer, Heidelberg (2005). https://doi.org/10.1007/11550617_28

16. Lando, E.: How augmented reality affects the learning experience in a museum. Technical report (2017)

17. Larsen, J., Svabo, C.: The tourist gaze and "Family Treasure Trails" in museums. Tourist Stud. **14**(2), 105–125 (2014)

18. Laurel, B.: Computers as Theatre. Addison-Wesley, Boston (1993)

19. Laurel, B., Strickland, R., Tow, R.: Placeholder: landscape and narrative in virtual environments. ACM Comput. Graph. **28**, 2 (1994)

20. Leue, M.C., Jung, T., Tom Dieck, D.: Google glass augmented reality: generic learning outcomes for art galleries. In: Tussyadiah, I., Inversini, A. (eds.) Information and Communication Technologies in Tourism 2015, pp. 463–476. Springer, Cham (2015). https://doi.org/10.1007/978-3-319-14343-9_34

21. Marques, D., Costello, R.: Concerns and Challenges Developing Mobile Augmented Reality Experiences for Museum Exhibitions. Curator 61, 4 (oct 2018), 541–558

22. McLellan, H.: Hypertextual tales; story models for hypertext design. J. Educ. Multimedia Hypermedia **2**, 3 (1993)

23. Miyashita, T., et al.: An augmented reality museum guide. In: Proceedings - 7th IEEE International Symposium on Mixed and Augmented Reality 2008, ISMAR 2008, pp. 103–106 (2008)

24. Packer, J., Ballantyne, R.: Motivational factors and the visitor experience: a comparison of three sites. Curator: Museum J. **45**(3), 183–198 (2002)

25. Sims, R.R.: Kolb's experiential learning theory: a framework for assessing person-job interaction. Acad. Manag. Rev. **8**(3), 501–508 (1983)

26. Skadberg, Y.X., Kimmel, J.R.: Visitors' flow experience while browsing a Web site: its measurement, contributing factors and consequences. Comput. Hum. Behav. **20**(3), 403–422 (2004)

27. Slater, M.: Place illusion and plausibility can lead to realistic behaviour in immersive virtual environments. Philos. Trans. Roy. Soc. London Ser. B Biol. Sci. **364**(1535), 3549–3557 (2009)

28. Sparacino, F.: Accepted for publication in Proceedings The Museum Wearable: real-time sensor-driven understanding of visitors' interests for personalized visually-augmented museum experiences. Technical report (2002)

29. Sung, Y.T., Chang, K.E., Hou, H.T., Chen, P.F.: Designing an electronic guidebook for learning engagement in a museum of history. Comput. Hum. Behav. **26**(1), 74–83 (2010)

30. Tallon, L., Walker, K.: Digital Technologies and the Museum Experience: Handheld Guides and Other Media. AltaMira Press (2008)

31. Traum, D., et al.: Ada and grace: direct interaction with museum visitors. In: Nakano, Y., Neff, M., Paiva, A., Walker, M. (eds.) IVA 2012. LNCS (LNAI), vol. 7502, pp. 245–251. Springer, Heidelberg (2012). https://doi.org/10.1007/978-3-642-33197-8_25

32. Webster, J., Hackley, P.: Teaching effectiveness in technology-mediated distance learning. Acad. Manag. J. **40**(6), 1282–1309 (1997)

33. Webster, J., Ho, H.: Audience engagement in multimedia presentations. Data Base Adv. Inf. Syst. **28**(2), 63–77 (1997)

Space Pace: Method for Creating Augmented Reality Tours Based on 360 Videos

Timo Nummenmaa[1]([✉]) [iD], Oğuz Buruk[1] [iD], Mila Bujić[1]([✉]) [iD], Max Sjöblom[1] [iD], Jussi Holopainen[2] [iD], and Juho Hamari[1] [iD]

[1] Tampere University, Tampere, Finland
{timo.nummenmaa,oguz.buruk,mila.bujic,juho.hamari}@tuni.fi
[2] University of Lincoln, Lincoln, UK
jholopainen@lincoln.ac.uk

Abstract. In this paper, guidelines are presented for creating video-based guided tours that employ 360° video content and produce the feeling of augmented reality. The benefit of the approach presented in this paper is that it does not rely on heavy technological requirements but can be implemented by anyone with a consumer level camera capable of making 360° video recordings, in a variety of locations with low cost and modest technological prowess. Principle application areas are for example museum and city tours, wayfinding applications and crafted narrative experiences. The guidelines were derived via a pilot implementation of the tour experience, which was initially ideated using workshop methods. The evaluation of the pilot showed that the approach is promising as a new way to experience locations, and provides us with guidelines that can be classified as essential, recommended and needing consideration for developing and applied such technology. Our guidelines describe and specify a novel method of creating 360° video recordings using low-cost and readily available hardware. The method can be employed by a wide variety of actors to create services administering AR-like experiences in a cost and time effective manner.

Keywords: Augmented reality · 360° video · Mobile augmented reality · Guidelines · Design · Guided tour · Location-based services · Wayfinding · Navigational aids · Spatial cognition

1 Introduction

Traditionally, implementing an augmented reality application for a guided tour experience is a demanding process as it requires long implementation processes and expertise in fields such as coding or 3D modelling. It may also require specific applications, high-quality hardware and know-how by users to run the prepared content.

© ICST Institute for Computer Sciences, Social Informatics and Telecommunications Engineering 2021
Published by Springer Nature Switzerland AG 2021. All Rights Reserved
A. Brooks et al. (Eds.): ArtsIT 2020, LNICST 367, pp. 119–138, 2021.
https://doi.org/10.1007/978-3-030-73426-8_7

However, with the advent of 360° cameras, location-based sensors, and mobile devices with high quality audio-visual outputs becoming mainstream consumer devices, the possibility for anyone to produce augmented-reality 360° content has become accessible. However, while this technology now exists in the hands of consumers and non-technology centred organizations, there has still been a lack of knowledge regarding the processes and methods to undertake such productions.

Therefore, in this paper, we propose the Space Pace method which is a low-cost and practical solution that will accelerate the process for preparing augmented 360° guided tours. Space Pace is a method that includes shooting a 360° video in a specific location or along a route with a guide who will lead the user in the exhibition area. By modifying the environment during the video production, video authors can add information to the target locations which may not be possible or feasible to display in real life and at the time of experiencing the exhibition area. The Space Pace method can be used in many kinds of use cases as it is usable by anyone and allows creating content which is realistic and quite close to genuine augmented reality applications. The guiding research question in this paper is:

How can we create widely accessible, easy to produce, but also engaging and informative location-based augmented guided tours?

To answer this question, in this study we illustrate the Space Pace method, supported by our report of a preliminary evaluation on its effectiveness as a guiding experience based on the iterative process and observations, interviews and video data of 12 participants. Finally, we present *Essential, Recommended* and *To be considered* design guidelines for creating 360° guiding videos that can provide the intended user experience. An overview of the study is presented in Fig. 1.

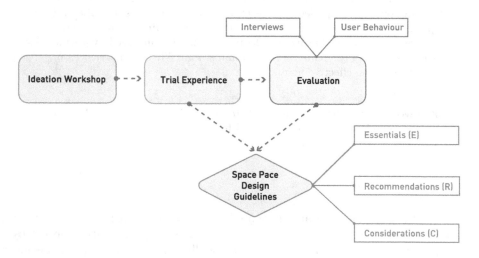

Fig. 1. Study overview

2   Related Work

The main inspiration for the project were video walks from artists Janet Cardiff and George Bures Miller [9]. In video walks, the user or users follow a video shown on a mobile phone, tablet, or other mobile device in the same location as it was shot, i.e. the users walk in the same place as if they were the camera that shot the video. The Cardiff and Miller video walks are exceptionally well produced and have high aesthetic and artistic values, providing a strikingly different *affective experience of space* [34].

Enhancing the experience of your immediate surroundings with technology has a long pre-digital history. Camera obscura, where an image is projected through small hole in a screen to a surface, can be regarded as one of the first such technologies. The principles were first mentioned in 5th century BCE in China and Ancient Greece, although the first documented uses of projecting to a screen can be traced to Al-Hazen's experiments in the 11th century [18]. Portable and more advanced versions came out in the 16th and 17th centuries culminating in magic lantern, widely attributed to Christiaan Huygens in mid-1600s. Magic lantern and other early projection techniques were used already early on to give the audience an otherworldly sense of presence through the projected images. Especially the genre of phantasmagoria with scary projections and convincing display of ghosts proved to be popular in 18th and 19th century [25].

Virtual tours have similarities to video walks as both provide a video based representation of an existing place. Virtual tours from early projects such as Movie Map [22] and Dudley Castle tour [8] to current web-based virtual tours for tourism and viewing real estate often assume that the user is stationary and somewhere else than the actual target location of the virtual tour. Video walks, however, emphasise the experience of walking [37] and how the actual bodily movement affects our sense of place [27]. Video walks aim at providing a different or reconfigured sense of the place where the user is already located.

Video walks are examples of indirect augmented reality [36], where the usual live camera view is replaced with a pre-captured panoramic view. A famous example of this approach is the augmented reality video guide for Casa Batlló in Barcelona [7,14]. Similar to many other indirect augmented reality applications the Casa Batlló video guide provides the augmented reality view from a static point of view in each of the locations in the tour. Space Pace, however, strongly encourage or even enforce movement through the place. Although one of our interests in this study is to understand how the users experience the "enforced" movement, we hope that some of the lessons learned can be applied to other indirect augmented reality use cases as well.

For wayfinding in an indoor environment, an indoor navigation solution such as SeeNav [28] provides navigation using an augmented reality application on a mobile device. Implementing an augmented reality indoor navigation application using services such as Mapbox [2] together with tools such as Unity [3] is also a possibility as demonstrated by Pavani [30] in an online tutorial. Both solutions describe different ways of obtaining the initial position of the user. In SeeNav, it is determined using an image captured by the user, with the tutorial by Pavani, special synchronization points are placed in the environment. While not specifically for on-location use, CityCompass [19] is a web technology based example of collaborative multi-user wayfinding using 360 video° worth mentioning.

Creating augmented and virtual reality guided experiences is becoming a prevalent application in the fields such as museum interaction. Those applications have a clear added value since they provide richer on-site experiences or extend the location-bound experiences to remote participants. Still, examples presented here, conventionally, require effort from both the creators and the users (i.e. downloading apps with a capable smart device that can run the them). Therefore, this study comes forward as a time and cost effective alternative to such methods by being be employed and experienced comparatively in an effortless way.

Some research that aims to guide the production 360° video has been conducted previously. However, the guidelines presented in this work differ in context from previous work that focuses on the creation of material to be experienced away from the filming location, with the user accessing the environment through various methods, such as head-mounted displays and projection technology (e.g. [20, 32, 33]).

3   Space Pace

The core idea of Space Pace is *the simple and efficient production of 360° video to be consumed using a mobile device, at the filming location, as an experience that evokes the feeling of augmented reality.* The Space Pace method was originally conceived in a design workshop and was developed further so that a trial experience could be created for testing with users.

3.1   Design Workshop

The initial aims of the workshop consisted of using a well-known cultural center (Kaapelitehdas in Helsinki, Finland) as a test bed for creating location specific augmented reality (AR) and internet of things (IoT) applications for different ways of engaging with the history and socio-cultural atmosphere of the venue. Play and playfulness were chosen as larger themes as they encourage engaging with the world and matters at hand in fundamentally liberating, engrossing, and inclusive ways [35], reflecting the values of the cultural center. The workshop lasted for three days.

The workshop was designed from start to be an intensive workshop for a small group. The final participants consisted of the two researchers mainly in charge of organizing workshop, an industry expert with previous AR app knowledge, an expert of the workshop location and a pioneer in mobile AR applications. The expert of the workshop location could not participate fully, but was able to intermittently contribute to the workshop.

The approach and aims in the workshop were closely aligned with playful design (e.g. [5,10,11,17]) both from the resulting artifact point of view and the methods and the attitude used in the workshop activities themselves. The aims of creating artifacts and interactions that elicit a playful mindset in the users are also similar to the ludic design or designing for Homo Ludens approaches [12].

The workshop was based on predetermined goals and constraints, but was designed to be dynamic and with a flexible timetable. However, a certain amount of time pressure was included in order to eventually progress from ideation to low tech prototypes. The focus of the actual workshop was on ideas, concepts and prototypes, similarly as in closely related dialogue-labs method [24].

The constraints for the workshop were based on the following factors: findings on the current state of AR applications, findings on the current state of smart space solutions, specific location related constraints, and findings from discussions with research project partners.

In addition to the authors' previous experiences with different design methods, a book named as *"Universal methods of design: 100 ways to research complex problems, develop innovative ideas, and design effective solutions"* [15] was used as a guide in the selection of suitable methods for use in the research.

The three core methods that were chosen to be used in the workshop, and which affected preparation and material selection, were body-storming, re-enactment and user experience sketching. These three methods were selected because the participants were already familiar with them and they have been proven to be effective in ideation before. In addition to these core methods, brainstorming with video stimuli and VNA (verb-noun-adjective) cards [21] and PLEX (playful experiences) cards [23] ideation techniques were used. The process of ideation was based on context awareness and the usage of ideation tools. Workshop participants were introduced to the context first through a version of the guided tour of the premises, and later through an extensive review of related work video material. Additionally, the participants discussed challenges in designing for public places, such as designing for spectators [31], barriers for collaboration [16] and playful interactions between strangers [29]. Card based ideation tools VNA [21] and PLEX [23] were used to further excite the minds of the participants.

On the second day of the workshop, one low tech prototype was created in the form of a simple video walk experience, inspired by video walks by Cardiff and Miller [9]. This prototype was created to explore the idea and test out assumptions for creating presentable prototypes on the next day. On the final day of the workshop, a further developed version, now a 360° video walk, (see Fig. 2) created with the help of an artist working within the premises, was demonstrated along three other prototypes. The prototype was made up of two parts, a simulated tour which approached the artist's studio, and a view from the inside of the studio with the artist giving a short presentation. The video was created using a Ricoh Theta 360 camera. Approaching the studio was created similarly to the video prototype from the first day, but now using a 360 camera. In the in-studio video, the camera was static. This prototype later became Space Pace.

Fig. 2. Original 360° video walk prototype

3.2   Implementation of the Trial Experience

For a trial experience, we have iterated upon the initial workshop prototype in that the experience is started from scanning a QR code at the starting location, and crafted a video-guided 360° experience in a 26 m long corridor of University of Tampere. We decided to create a short video with a sufficiently easy to use and rather low-cost hardware so as to demonstrate the accessibility of Space Pace method and its reasonably priced development requirements. For this test, the Insta360 ONE camera was used [1]. First, two videos were recorded at different candidate locations. Comparing the two videos, the width of the corridor seemed more suitable in one of the videos and in that same one the corridor included colorful pillars and construction elements that showed promise in making it easier for users to perceive their real location in relation to the location of the guide in the 360°. The selected location was also easily accessible by test participants. The selection of location does not rule out the other location as a feasible location for using Space, as the choice was made to benefit the construction and execution of the trial. After the location was chosen, two recordings were used to plan the trial, and iterate on the approach.

Tour Script and the Execution. The tour implemented for pilot testing is composed of a single video that lasts for 1 min and 40 s. For the experience, a script was drafted that would include the following content: 1) At the beginning of the video, a tour guide greets the users and invites them to walk along through the corridor. 2) Along the way, the guide introduces and points to a coffee room, whose door is closed in the real world but open in the video. 3) After passing this point, he talks about several research posters hanged on the walls. In both of those moments, the guide keeps walking while introducing the information about the environment and does not stop. 4) Following introduction of the poster, the guide stops briefly in front of a classroom of which the interior can be seen through a window. However, similar to the meeting room in the previous spot, in the real life, the blinds on the window are closed while in the video version, they are open and a gameplay video of Bioshock Infinite [1] is being played. The guide here talks about the game briefly and then continues to walk through the corridor. 4) In the last section of the video, the guide stops again and points to the wall on which the three different posters of Rapture, a fictional underwater city in the first Bioshock Game[2], are hanged in the video version but not in the real world. 5) The tour ends with the guide taking a right turn in the corridor and informs the user that the tour ended.

The script of the video was as follows:

00:03 - Hello, I will be your tour guide today in this lovely corridor of the University of Tampere. So, let's don't lose so much time and get started. Follow me!

00:14 - On your left, you can see the coffee room where our colleagues can come together and relax when they become so bored of their work.

00:24 - Of course, other than the coffee, there some other enjoyments in that room [pointing to the table on which has ample amount of LEGO parts], which you can use while relaxing.

00:33 - This corridor hosts a lot of rooms for researchers and academics of University of Tampere, and also, of course, there is some great research here of which this poster [pointing to a poster on the right] is an example.

00:49 - Other than researcher rooms, there are also classrooms on this corridor. [Guide Stops] This one is really bright, spacious and colorful classroom. And in this screen, you can see Bioschock Infinite is played which is a great game.

01:02 - Let's keep going.

01:14 - [Guide Stops Again] Here is another important part in our tour. These are the Rapture Posters. Rapture is an under water city that you can go

---

[1] https://2k.com/en-US/game/bioshock-infinite/.

[2] https://2k.com/en-US/game/bioshock/.

*and conduct your research and art, in the first game of Bioschock. So, maybe
you can visit there after. Keep going!*

    01:31 - [Guide takes a right turn in the corridor]

    01:35 - Here is the last spot of our tour.

The experience was created in such a way that with sufficient smartphone
hardware users do not need to download any software to engage with the experience. The only limitation is support for 360° video in the YouTube app, and
the ability to read QR codes. To begin the experience, a user would scan a QR
code on the wall, and then start to follow a tour guide that seems to appear in
front of the user on the screen of the mobile device, creating a feeling of AR.

Preparation Process. The workflow for the final trial experience was composed of: 1) Planning the tour, 2) recording the video, 3) exporting from the
Insta360 ONE application, 4) uploading to YouTube, 5) creating a QR code
using a QR code generator [13] and printing it on a page with the text "Scan
me for a tour!", 6) attaching the page on the wall. Recording, exporting and
uploading (phases 2–4) were all done directly on an iPhone X mobile device [4],
with no need for using a computer for any post processing or editing. The video
was recorded with the Insta360 ONE device connected to the mobile device used
for recording, enabling the cameraman to see the video being recorded. When
recording, the starting orientation of the camera was made to be such that the
video would start oriented towards the QR code and tour guide when the video
was opened. This would make the video start with the correct orientation when
a user scans the QR code to start the video (see Fig. 3).

Fig. 3. Start of the tour (for illustration purposes, not a capture of experiment participants)

Out of this process, more generic instructions for the creation of Space Pace content were derived (Fig. 4).

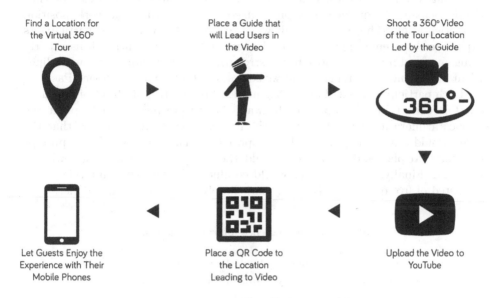

Fig. 4. Space Pace video publication process

4   User Testing and Evaluation

The pilot application of Space Pace was evaluated in a user test. This evaluation then served as grounds for developing Space Pace method guidelines.

A total of 12 participants were recruited at the scene for testing the created version of the Space Pace. It was a non-probability, convenience sample, composed of university students and employees. Participation was completely voluntary and it was explained to the participants how the collected data would be used in the research. No personal data was collected and no part of the study is directed at investigating the test subjects themselves or the test location. No video data with any identifying details of individuals was shared outside of the core researcher team and no such video is stored beyond the time-frame essential for the completion of this research. Under the guidelines of the Finnish National Board on Research Integrity, this research required no ethical approval.

Participants used an iPhone X mobile device to experience the 360° tour. The same device was used by all participants to reduce possible variability in results that would stem from factors not in the focus of the study. Additionally, it allowed us to collect the screen recordings from the tests, which we expected to provide valuable insight into how Space Pace was used. Apart from the mobile device, we also used a DSLR video camera to capture participants' behaviour during the tests. The camera was placed at the end of the corridor and was used to record each test in one take.

The data collected for this study consisted of both objective (screen and test recordings) and subjective reporting data (structured interviews). The screen recordings combined with an external camera view give us a detailed view of what the participant sees on the mobile phone in connection to their real world position and orientation. The interviews allow us to understand how the participants experienced the environment during the test and to gain additional insight. By using a mixed-method approach, we strengthened the validity of our findings when evaluating the strengths and weaknesses of this version of Space Pace.

Each participant started at the beginning of the corridor in front of a printed out QR code that was taped to the wall. They were instructed to point the phone's camera at the code, tap on the link, and turn the phone so that the video would play in full screen, landscape mode. These actions would prompt the video to play and researchers would then stay out of the sight until the very end. Finally, one researcher would conduct the structured interview that consisted of five questions (Table 1) immediately after the test was done.

Table 1. Post-experience interview questions

1. Please share two comments about the experience you just had
2. Can you remember what you saw in the coffee room?
3. Can you remember what you saw in the classroom?
4. What was the difference between the real-world classroom and the one in the mobile experience?
5. Can you remember what the posters were about and the colours they were?

4.1   Results

In the beginning of each interview, the participant was asked to share two free-form comments about the experience. The comments were predominantly positive and pertained to the novelty of Space Pace, as well as to how the experience was *fun* and *interesting* (e.g. Participant 7: "Funny and interesting. I didn't know what to expect, but it was like, well, a tour guide. Kind of like very easy to get the idea."). Two participants mentioned the possibility of "seeing behind closed doors" as a unique feature. The majority of negative comments were related to the maladjustment of participants' pacing relative to the video speed (e.g. Participant 6: "I would constantly notice that I walked too fast, and I was slightly ahead of where the video was and there was this feeling of disconnection when I could rotate the camera and see that I was a couple of meters ahead of where I was supposed to be and try to consciously slow down and pace myself more correctly").

With the structured section of the interview consisting of four questions (Table 1), we investigated participants' attention to both on-screen content and the physical surroundings. One participant's answers were discarded as they had not realized that it was a 360° video and had the mobile device pointed at the floor throughout the test. The rest of the answers were given either 1 or 0, depending on the participant's ability to recall the information. These findings are to some extent limited by the maladjusted pace speed, which prevented participants from seeing the physical location that was being described in Space Pace.

The first point of interest, the coffee room, was recalled by the least number of participants (2/11). This could perhaps be explained by the novelty of the experience and the time needed to get adjusted to the mechanics of Space Pace. On the other hand, around two thirds of participants were successful in recalling the classroom from Space Pace (7/11), as well as the difference between the real world one and that from the mobile experience (7/11). Finally, almost all of the participants recalled the posters from Space Pace (10/11), which might be contributed to the recency effect [26]. Moreover, as mentioned in the script, the guide kept walking while introducing the coffee room while he stopped in front of the classroom and posters. This difference might have also affected the results. Finally, only one participant recalled all of the points of interest.

The video data was analysed so that both the screen recording and the recording of each participant were viewed synchronously, side by side. This method ensured that both perspectives are considered at all times and in relation to each other. The analysis was conducted in such a way that occurrences of certain actions in the material were tallied. This was done by observing if an action that was previously identified to be of interest actually occurred in the recording(s) or not. The actions to examine in the videos were based on the script of the experience. This way of analysing the video proved effective and provided us with sufficient details to generate guidelines. We were especially interested in what participants do 1) at the start of the experience (turning towards the guide and starting walking) 2) regarding coffee room which has an open door in the video, but which is closed in real life 3) regarding the window which can be seen through in the video, but where the blinds are closed in real life, 4) regarding posters on the wall in the video that do not exist in the real word, 5) at the end of the tour. Additionally, we were interested in if the orientation of the participant and the device matched throughout the experience. These actions were divided into more atomic actions. The list of the final actions can be seen with the results in Table 2.

There are two specific things to note about the video analysis. Some participants walked past during the video camera in the corridor, and thus some final actions were not recorded for these participants. However, most actions that could not be seen in the video footage due to this problem took place in an area where certain actions (e.g. look at an item in the physical world) were impossible to do, and thus this is not a large issue regarding the validity of the results. Additionally, one participant did not realize that the video was a 360° recording and that it was possible to look in different directions. The participant pointed the mobile device towards the ground during the experiment.

Table 2. Aggregated data from the screen recordings and test recordings, in order of occurrence within experiment.

Observed action	% of participants
Turned away from the QR-code to face the corridor	100
Started walking as instructed by the guide	100
Was physically in front of coffee room when video showed it	100
Turned the phone to see the coffee room	50
Looked into the physical coffee room	16.7
Was physically in front of the classroom when the video showed it	50
Stopped when the guide stopped in front of the classroom	91.7
Turned the device to see inside the classroom	75
Was physically in front of the posters when the video showed them	50
Stopped when the guide stopped in front of the posters	83.3
Looked at posters	91.7
Looked at the physical wall where posters were supposed to be	58.3
Turned to see the cameraman (at any point during the experience)	50
Ended up at the correct ending point	50
Walked past the ending point	50
Orientation matched throughout the experience	100

5   Guidelines

In this section, we will present guidelines for shooting 360° guided tour videos that will successfully direct the user from one point to another while conveying the required information. Guidelines in this section are categorized in three pillars; (1) Essentials (E), (2) Recommendations (R) and (3) Considerations (C). Essential guidelines direct to points that should be applied to make the video work in the intended way. If these guidelines are not taken into consideration, there can be major problems in the user experience of the video such as disorientation or struggle to follow the conveyed information. Recommendations refer to issues that might be good to apply but can be modified according to content, context, location and users. These recommendations are created according to the user feedback and can be seen as potential solutions to some of the problems we faced. Considerations communicate points that caused or may cause obstacles according to our observations. However, we need to note that these conditions were not yet tested. Still, we see the benefit to cast light on these issues as points that need further clarification for making the Space Pace experience an optimal one. For example, we tested Space Pace in a narrow corridor and our consideration is that these guidelines may have to be modified if the video was prepared in a wider area which can be harder for users to follow visual cues in the real environment. We did not test Space Pace in a wider area, however our experience suggests that in wider environments, there might be other shortcomings that we did not observe in this test. See Tables 3, 4, 5 for the guidelines.

Table 3. Guidelines (Essentials)

Name	Guideline
Starting Orientation	The starting orientation of the user and the video should be the same. In this phase, both the video and the real environment should include similar visual cues so that the user can perceive the space easily. In our case, we used a poster with a QR code which assures the orientation of user and their device, as the user needs to point their device towards the code to read it. The same poster was also in the video that helped users to comprehend the starting orientation in the beginning. In our observations, we found that the orientation of the device and user matched for all of the participants
Guiding Orientation	In our initial tests, we tested different starting positions for the guide. It is important to render the guide visible in the first second and the guide should be present in the starting orientation of the video. If the guide is in another position, users may not be able to find her/him in case the sound or the subtitles are off. With the guide visible in the start of the video, all of the participants turned to follow the guide when the guide started to move out of the picture and along the corridor
Explicit Commands for Moving the User	A crucial point of the Space Pace experience is that the user is in the correct location and follows the guide in the right pace. The guide can stop or slow down for giving information and start walking or get faster after the information phase. In this moments, it is important to give commands such as "follow me" or express that we are in a phase of information giving. The guide should be expressive in talking and body language to make it easier for users to follow

Table 4. Guidelines (Recommendations)

Name	Guideline
Augmented content	Although having augmented content is one of the strong points of Space Pace experience, in some cases the initial need can only be having a guide in the scene. However, we observed that having content in the video that does not exist in the real world makes the experience more interesting and increases the surprise effect. It can also be confusing for some users, which should be taken into account in the design of the experience
Visible cameraman	Only half of the users pointed the mobile device at all towards the cameraman who shoots the video, and even if they did, they did not express complaints about it. Therefore, it may not be worth putting an extensive amount of effort into hiding the cameraman in the video
Size of the QR code	The starting location of the user can be influenced by changing the size of the QR code. The size of the QR code will guide the proximity of the user to the QR code. If the QR code is too small, the user will get closer and they may be confused if their starting view does not match the video. However, a sufficiently small code is not readable from afar, requiring the user to approach the code. Therefore, modifying the size of the QR code can help for orienting the user in the required location in the beginning
Instructions	We observed that users may not realize that they are looking at a 360° video and that they should be moving in the same pace as the video. A detailed instruction might work for a better experience which allows users to explore around by turning the phone in the beginning. By doing so, they can get accustomed to orientation and the required interaction style. This solution has the limitation of being an annoyance for proficient users

6   Discussion

During the iterative process from the first workshop prototype to the experience that was used for user tests, a sufficient implementation of our method was developed to produce data to confirm certain guidelines and to discover others.

One of the lessons learned already at the three-day workshop, where the initial concept of 360° video walking tours was ideated, was that the pace of

Table 5. Guidelines (Considerations)

Name	Guideline
Dynamic Pace	The pace of the video can change according to characteristic of the scene or the behaviour of the user. For example, pace is different while talking or showing an object compared to the state where the guide walks without attending anything else. Moreover, we also observe that the users who explore around with their phones were more successful to orient themselves to pace of the guide. Therefore, it might not be possible to standardize the walking pace in Space Pace videos. Instead, video authors can make sure to give required instructions in the beginning of the video to remind users to arrange their pace
Environmental Visual Cues	We chose an environment which does have different visual elements instead of a plain corridor. We wanted users to easily understand where they are when they look around. However, most of these visual elements were repetitive (such as poster boards or pillars) and half of the users who tested Space Pace faced problems to orient themselves in the environment. Therefore, it might be better to adorn the environment with visual elements which are not repetitive, standing out and existing both in video and real environment. In our tests, majority of users stopped when the guide stopped for giving information. In these phases, guide can refer to those elements to help users orient themselves according to the location in the video
Size of the Environment	In our case, the narrow corridor we used as a location helped users stay synchronized with the video, as they can only walk in one direction and it is easier to match the visual cues with the ones in the video. However, a wider space may require additional precautions to help users to stay oriented
Tutorial Requirement	As a first experience, it may not always be easy for users to arrange their pace to match it with the guide's pace, or understand how augmented content is different from the real environment. Therefore, a short separate sequence which will lead the user to a new QR code that starts the actual experience may help users to adapt to experience better. This short sequence may include some of the critical points such as exploration of an object in the environment and following the guide to adapt the pace of the video

the video must be a suitable walking pace for the person using the solution. In our solution, the speed of the tour guide was based on what is a comfortable speed to explain the surroundings, with slight pauses at certain spots. Half of the participants in the tests walked past the end point in the video, which might suggest that a faster pace should be employed. One other solution would be to set the pace to what can be observed as the walking pace of mobile phone users. Barkley and Lepp [6] have recorded the walking speed of people texting on their phone while walking, and the value from this study could be used in the design of a walking experience. However, the speed reported in the study is substantially faster than what can be considered as comfortable if one was to thoroughly absorb the surroundings, so the experience itself should then match the speed. Another way to approach the pacing issue would be to expect the users to first be unable to match their pace with the pace in the experience and to teach the users first how to pace themselves, either in the same experience or in a separate tutorial one. In some cases, cutting the video portions so that one video takes the user to a new QR code may help the user keep in sync with the surroundings, but could also prove cumbersome. We also should note that it may not be possible to reach a standardized pace for the whole experience since the speed can change according to the content (i.e. plain walking vs. information giving) or to the behaviour of the user (i.e. more exploration for the surroundings results in a slower speed). Therefore, we believe that the pace of the video should be considered and tailored according to specific use cases.

The mobile experience itself was fast to produce, only requiring two initial test videos before moving to produce the recording that would be used in our user test. The process of uploading the video was also fast, as no editing or heavy processing was required. Everything was doable directly on a mobile device up until the point when the QR code had to be created. The effort needed to produce the Space Pace experience compared to solutions where software needs to be developed, 3D models created, maps configured etc., can be considered to be significantly lower. It is also less time consuming and more affordable. However, if one would produce a heavily narrative based experience with, for example, props and costumes, the costs of this process would be affected.

There are limitations to this study that need to be addressed. The space where the tests took place was not a controlled laboratory environment. This means that the environment could change even during a test. A door could be opened by someone, a meeting could be taking palace in a space and there might be people walking in the corridor doing things like using a copy machine or just passing by. The changes in the environment state mostly affected the first stage of the experiment - the coffee room. There was a meeting taking place in this room during some of the tests. There was also some traffic in the corridor, but not so much that we would expect it to be an issue. These are also limitations that would affect real world implementations of this method, and thus may even bring a certain realism to our study.

Another limitation of the study was that due to convenience sampling, as most participants were already familiar with the corridor that was used in the study. We have to consider the possibility that this affects the way participants explored the area. While users' previous familiarity with the environment may also be the case in some implementations, it would not be the case in all possible contexts where Space Pace might be used. On the other hand, familiarity with the environment may also lead to the desire for exploration as the most of the content is known for the user. This can work towards the aims of this method since the video authors can adorn the environment for experienced users by placing other details to the outside of the centre of attraction which can be discovered in 360° video through careful exploration.

The language in the video was English and the guide was a non-native English speaker, while the majority of participants' mother tongue was Finnish. This may have slightly affected participants' experience, as understanding the content likely required additional focused attention than it would be the case with a Finnish-speaking guide. Finally, the limited number of participants, the brevity of the interview and the singular experience under study must also be taken into account. As such, the resulting guidelines, while already providing valuable insight, can be expanded and strengthened in the future.

7   Conclusions and Future Work

This study presented a novel way of creating 360° video guided tours using low-cost and readily available hardware. This method, titled Space Pace, mimics characteristics seen in augmented reality tours, using simpler hardware and more easily approachable methods that can be used by non-expert practitioners. We presented the Space Pace method through the creation process, consisting of a design workshop and iterative design that followed. We showed the method in action through a pilot user test with 12 participants and associated observations and interviews.

Based on the production and evaluation of the pilot study, we were able to construct a number of recommendations for others looking to produce similar fast and low-cost guided tours using 360° video. Along these, a number of questions were also raised that should be answered through further studies. One of the main questions still looking for an answer is the pace with which the video is filmed, and hence the pace with which the user is expected to progress. We need to explore the pace speed more thoroughly and how the environment where the 360° video walks take place should be taken into account when designing the experience. The size and shape of the space, as well as possible visual cues in the environment, are expected to be meaningful parameters that need to be taken into account in the design.

While the research has limitations, the methods and recommendations presented in this study can already be employed by a wide variety of both societal and industry actors to create services with clear added value. Examples of areas where these methods could be utilized with good results include museum tours, art exhibitions, and guided tours of large public spaces. The Space Pace method encompasses both the guidelines and procedures described in the paper, and will be expanded with future iterations.

Acknowledgements. This publication has received funding from the European Union's Horizon 2020 research and innovation programme under the Marie Sklodowska-Curie grant agreement No 833731, WEARTUAL, Academy of Finland decision 327352, and Business Finland decisions 5479/31/2017, 7488/31/2017 and 5654/31/2018.

References

1. Insta360 one - a camera crew in your hand, November 2019. https://www.insta360.com/product/insta360-one/. Accessed 7 Nov 2019
2. Mapbox, November 2019. https://www.mapbox.com/. Accessed 7 Nov 2019
3. Unity, November 2019. https://unity3d.com/. Accessed 7 Nov 2019
4. Apple: Iphone X, November 2019. https://www.apple.com/lae/iphone-x/. Accessed 7 Nov 2019
5. Arrasvuori, J., Boberg, M., Holopainen, J., Korhonen, H., Lucero, A., Montola, M.: Applying the PLEX framework in designing for playfulness. In: DPPI 2011, pp. 24:1–24:8. ACM, New York (2011). https://doi.org/10.1145/2347504.2347531. http://doi.acm.org/10.1145/2347504.2347531
6. Barkley, J.E., Lepp, A.: Cellular telephone use during free-living walking significantly reduces average walking speed. BMC Res. Notes **9**, 195 (2016). https://doi.org/10.1186/s13104-016-2001-y
7. Batlló, C.: All the information about your visit to casa Batlló, November 2019. https://www.casabatllo.es/en/visit/. Accessed 7 Nov 2019
8. Boland, P., Johnson, C.: Archaeology as computer visualization: virtual tours of Dudley Castle c. 1550. Br. Museum Occasional Pap. **114**, 227–233 (1996)
9. Cardiff, J., Miller, G.B.: Walks, November 2019. http://www.cardiffmiller.com/artworks/walks/index.html. Accessed 7 Nov 2019
10. Coulton, P.: Playful and gameful design for the internet of things. In: Nijholt, A. (ed.) More Playful User Interfaces: Interfaces that Invite Social and Physical Interaction, pp. 151–173. Gaming Media and Social Effects. Springer, Singapore (2015). https://doi.org/10.1007/978-981-287-546-4_7
11. Fernaeus, Y., Holopainen, J., Höök, K., Ivarsson, K., Karlsson, A., Lindley, S., Norlin, C. (eds.): Plei-Plei! PPP Company Ltd. (2012)
12. Gaver, W.: Homo ludens (subspecies politikos). In: Deterding, S., Walz, S.P. (eds.) The Gameful World: Approaches, Issues, Applications. MIT Press, Cambridge (2015)
13. QR Code Generator: Create your QR code for free, November 2019. https://www.qr-code-generator.com/. Accessed 7 Nov 2019
14. Gimeno, J., Portales, C., Coma, I., Fernandez, M., Martinez, B.: Combining traditional and indirect augmented reality for indoor crowded environments. A case study on the casa Batllo museum. Comput. Graph. **69**, 92–103 (2017)
15. Hanington, B., Martin, B.: Universal Methods of Design: 100 Ways to Research Complex Problems, Develop Innovative Ideas, and Design Effective Solutions. Rockport Publishers, Beverly (2012)
16. Heinemann, T., Mitchell, R.: Breaching barriers to collaboration in public spaces. In: Proceedings of the 8th International Conference on Tangible, Embedded and Embodied Interaction, TEI 2014, pp. 213–220. ACM, New York (2013). https://doi.org/10.1145/2540930.2540951. http://doi.acm.org/10.1145/2540930.2540951
17. Holopainen, J., Stain, M.: Dissecting playfulness for practical design. In: The Gameful World: Approaches, Issues, Applications. MIT Press (2015)
18. Ihde, D.: Art precedes science: or did the camera obscura invent modern science. In: Instruments in Art and Science: On the Architectonics of Cultural Boundaries in the 17th Century, vol. 2, pp. 383–393 (2008)

19. Kallioniemi, P., Sharma, S., Turunen, M.: CityCompass: a collaborative online language learning application. In: Proceedings of the 19th ACM Conference on Computer Supported Cooperative Work and Social Computing Companion, CSCW 2016 Companion, pp. 94–97. Association for Computing Machinery, New York (2016). https://doi.org/10.1145/2818052.2874334. https://doi.org/10.1145/2818052.2874334

20. Keskinen, T., et al.: The effect of camera height, actor behavior, and viewer position on the user experience of 360° videos. In: 2019 IEEE Conference on Virtual Reality and 3D User Interfaces (VR), pp. 423–430 (2019)

21. Kultima, A., Niemelä, J., Paavilainen, J., Saarenpää, H.: Designing game idea generation games. In: Proceedings of the 2008 Conference on Future Play: Research, Play, Share, pp. 137–144. ACM (2008)

22. Lippman, A.: Movie-maps: an application of the optical videodisc to computer graphics. ACM SIGGRAPH Comput. Graph. **14**(3), 32–42 (1980)

23. Lucero, A., Arrasvuori, J.: PLEX cards: a source of inspiration when designing for playfulness. In: Proceedings of the 3rd International Conference on Fun and Games, Fun and Games 2010, Leuven, Belgium, pp. 28–37. ACM, New York (2010). https://doi.org/10.1145/1823818.1823821. http://doi.acm.org/10.1145/1823818.1823821

24. Lucero, A., Vaajakallio, K., Dalsgaard, P.: The dialogue-labs method: process, space and materials as structuring elements to spark dialogue in co-design events. CoDesign **8**(1), 1–23 (2012)

25. Mannoni, L., Brewster, B.: The phantasmagoria. Film History **8**(4), 390–415 (1996)

26. Murdock Jr., B.B.: The serial position effect of free recall. J. Exp. Psychol. **64**(5), 482 (1962)

27. Nedelkopoulou, E.: Walking out on our bodies participation as Ecstasis in Janet Cardiff's walks. Perform. Res. **16**(4), 117–123 (2011)

28. Noreikis, M., Xiao, Y., Ylä-Jääski, A.: SeeNav: seamless and energy-efficient indoor navigation using augmented reality. In: Proceedings of the on Thematic Workshops of ACM Multimedia 2017 (Thematic Workshops 2017), pp. 186–193. ACM, New York (2017). https://doi.org/10.1145/3126686.3126733

29. Paasovaara, S., Lucero, A., Olsson, T.: Outlining the design space of playful interactions between nearby strangers. In: Proceedings of the 20th International Academic MINDTREK Conference, pp. 216–225. ACM (2016)

30. Pavani, A.: Indoor navigation in AR with Unity - Points of interest, November 2019. https://blog.mapbox.com/indoor-navigation-in-ar-with-unity-6078afe9d958. Accessed 7 Nov 2019

31. Reeves, S.: Designing Interfaces in Public Settings: Understanding the Role of the Spectator in Human-Computer Interaction. Springer, London (2011). https://doi.org/10.1007/978-0-85729-265-0

32. Rothe, S., Kegeles, B., Hussmann, H.: Camera heights in cinematic virtual reality: how viewers perceive mismatches between camera and eye height. In: Proceedings of the 2019 ACM International Conference on Interactive Experiences for TV and Online Video, TVX 2019, pp. 25–34. Association for Computing Machinery, New York (2019). https://doi.org/10.1145/3317697.3323362. https://doi.org/10.1145/3317697.3323362

33. Saarinen, S., Mäkelä, V., Kallioniemi, P., Hakulinen, J., Turunen, M.: Guidelines for designing interactive omnidirectional video applications. In: Bernhaupt, R., Dalvi, G., Joshi, A., K. Balkrishan, D., O'Neill, J., Winckler, M. (eds.) INTERACT 2017. LNCS, vol. 10516, pp. 263–272. Springer, Cham (2017). https://doi.org/10.1007/978-3-319-68059-0_17

34. Schaub, M.: The affective experience of space: Janet Cardiff and George Bures Miller. In: The Handbook of Sound and Image in Western Art, pp. 214–235 (2016)
35. Sicart, M.: Play Matters. MIT Press, Cambridge (2014)
36. Wither, J., Tsai, Y.T., Azuma, R.: Indirect augmented reality. Comput. Graph. **35**(4), 810–822 (2011)
37. Witmore, C.L.: Four archaeological engagements with place mediating bodily experience through peripatetic video. Vis. Anthropol. Rev. **20**(2), 57–72 (2004)

Games

The Time Machine and the Voodoo Doll: Exploring Customized Computer Game Controllers and Their Influence on the Experience of Play

Oliver Wolter Nielsen, Miriam Krebs, Jake Sølberg, Michael Holton Hovgaard, Nicolai Staal Hansen, Bjørn Dalsgaard Hansen, and Lasse Juel Larsen[✉]

University of Southern Denmark, Odense, Denmark
ljl@sdu.dk

Abstract. This paper turns attention towards an overlooked area of research: the customized computer game controller and its influence on the experience of play. Through two experimental design cases of customized game controllers, a time machine and a voodoo doll, we challenge the present theoretical assumptions inherently at play about game controllers: the Heideggerian binary paradigm where computer game controllers are either "visible" or "invisible". Moving beyond this philosophical paradigm, we propose a fresh new theoretical take where customized controllers situate themselves in a third position of being simultaneously "visible" and "invisible". This third position, we discovered, transformed the game controllers into physical game objects. Thus, the customized game controllers belonged to the game world and simultaneously acted as traditional controllers. During play the customized computer game controllers managed to draw attention to themselves without "breaking" immersion. Consequently, the customized game controllers challenged the dominant thinking about game controllers together with the theoretical backdrop on which the predominant conceptions of immersion rest. Following, we challenge the theoretical conditions upon which the present understandings of immersion are erected. Furthermore, we will advance a revitalized comprehension of the *structural pattern* and *process of interaction* between the player, the game controller, and the game world.

Keywords: Customized game controllers · Immersion · Player experience · Ludology · Theory · Design

1 Introduction

We all use game controllers when we play computer games. The setup of keyboard and mouse together with handheld game controllers for the game consoles, PlayStation and Xbox, is known to almost every computer game player on the planet. Even the simulation of joysticks and keyboards on tablets have become familiar to us. When we play games these different game controllers act in more or less the same way. They all

A. Brooks et al. (Eds.): ArtsIT 2020, LNICST 367, pp. 141–159, 2021.
https://doi.org/10.1007/978-3-030-73426-8_8

serve as interfaces and gateways to the game content. Players perceive game controllers in much the same manner: during the experience of play [1, 2], game controllers tend to become "invisible" and "disappear". When we write "invisible" and "disappear", we don't mean that game controllers by some unknown measure suddenly vanish or that their physical attributes are transformed. Instead, "invisible" and "disappear" should be understood in a Heideggerian [3] phenomenological sense. When the controller is seen from this perspective, it can occupy one of two states – either present-at-hand or ready-to-hand [4]. Present-at-hand means that players are fully aware of the controller, it is "visible". The opposite can be said about ready-to-hand. Here, players have no conscious awareness of the controller. The controller has "disappeared", so to speak. Traditionally, this "disappearance" lasts until a failure arises. Normally, such failure constitutes some sort of "break" in the interactive loop [5] between the player and the game i.e. if the keyboard, mouse or traditional console game controller somehow fails to respond during play. When that happens, players become acutely aware of the game controller. Now, the game controller has "moved" from being unseen (ready-to-hand) to being center of attention (present-at-hand). The point is that "invisibility" and "disappearance" point toward a particular process of interaction during play where players shift their attention from the game content to the controller or the other way around. This shift, normally, designate a transition between being out-of-play and in-play [6–9]. Thus, using the words "invisible" and "disappearance", are a way to describe what happens to our perception during gameplay [10, 11]. Notably, how our experience and the direction of our attention shifts during play – between focusing on the game controller and the game content.

Today, we claim, almost every game strives to "suppress" the controller and drive it into the background of the experience of play. Nonetheless, metaphorically speaking, the fictional content of computer games [12] can be said to secretly whisper "incantations" that "magically" make the game controllers disappear from the players perception during play. Players are as resilient to this spell as the stormtroopers are resistant to the Jedi mind trick in the movie *Star Wars Episode IV: A New Hope* [13]. The point being: game controllers are overlooked as venues for novel design approaches and/or as objects for research [14].

This paper attempts to ferry the controller out of its present darkness and bring it into the light of the future. Hence, we explore the computer game controller, especially the customized game controller along with its impact on the experience of play, markedly how the tailor-made game controller influences the player's experience of play – the sensation of immersion. In other words, this study scrutinizes the *structural pattern* as well as the *process of interaction* from the point of view of the custom-built game controller, notably the customized controller and its position in relation to being "out-of-play" and "in-play" [15, 16]. Of special interest, how the conditions for thinking about the concept of immersion is influenced by the presence of a customized game controller: namely a controller that concurrently act both like the traditional game controller and like a game object securely belonging to the fiction of the game. It should be noted, when we write game object, it should be understood as Fullerton defines a game object, which is by its properties, behaviors and relationships [17]. Thus, customized game controllers draw into focus the conditional underpinnings in the way the present research thinks about concept of immersion. Importantly, how the current thinking place emphasis on addressing immersion from a specific point of view: namely one that focuses on "forgetting" or "suppressing" the medium (i.e. both the game controller and the machine (computer) running the game (program)). This focus place emphasis on the experience of play through the prism of self-awareness or lack hereof. Before we move on, it deserves to be mentioned that the Nintendo Labo [18] is somewhat of an exception controller-wise. The Nintendo Labo offers players the opportunity to build their own game controller by combining sets of cardboard with the Nintendo Switch controllers to create fishing rods, pianos, or houses. However, the Nintendo Labo, in spite of Nintendo's efforts, nowhere near the experiments presented in this article.

Now, before we reach the paragraph on customized game controllers; how they influence the experience of play *and* reshape the *structural pattern* as well as the *process of interaction* between the player, the controller, and the game – not forgetting how the customized controller cast light on the conditions for thinking about immersion – a few methodological considerations are in order.

2 A Few Methodological Considerations

Our examination of how customized controllers influence the experience of play and affect the *structural pattern* as well as *process of interaction* derives from two different projects: *The Time Machine* and *The Voodoo Doll*. Each of these projects involve iterative design processes [17, 19], which created both unique customized game controllers and computer games. The purposes of these projects were to examine and scrutinize how players interacted with game controllers that diverged from the traditional generic game controller setup. Especially, how tailor-made game controllers affected the players' interaction with the computer game and impressed their experience of play. During the development processes, each project underwent numerous play and game tests, which means that our encounters with players did not follow a rigid and linear method design – qualitative questionnaires, quantitative surveys, and so on. Instead the development processes consisted, predominantly, of co-reflecting phenomenological interviews [20] together with a co-designing approach [21] to further qualify the developed artefacts. We also observed players' patterns of interactions, inquired about their experience of play, and investigated their sense of immersion.

In our project, *The Time Machine*, we discovered how an unfamiliar physical and customized game controller successfully inhabited and integrated itself into the fiction of the game world. Of special interest, how players experienced the sensation of holding and interacting with a strange physical object, which acted both as a controller and as a game object critical to the game world. Contrary to our expectations, this setup didn't break the players' sense of immersion. Actually, the opposite happened, the experience of immersion was enhanced, but even more interesting we discovered we had to rethink the condition for thinking about the concept of immersion.

In our second project, *The Voodoo Doll*, we decided to press the envelope and investigate the intricacies involving customized game controllers and their connection with the game world. Here we went even further in our effort to integrate the physical artifact (game controller) into the experience of play. In the project *Voodoo Doll*, the interaction with the game world was changed: now the customized controller became a fully integrated and active part of the fiction of the game world. In essence, project *Voodoo Doll* acted as a "natural" extension as well as a continuation of project *Time Machine*. Given how different these projects impact the structural pattern and process of interaction and how they influence the experience of play, we will walk the reader through their stories of development. This is done in order to ensure that the reader fully understand the projects, the customized game controllers, and their interesting possibilities.

The paragraphs following the descriptions of our two projects will advance reflections of how such tailor-made game controllers also act as physical game objects, and how they affect the overall interaction and influence the experience of play. Finally, we will discuss how these customized controllers challenge the conditions for thinking about the concept of immersion within the study of games.

3 Project Time Machine: An Unconventional Way to Save the World

Project *Time Machine* was inspired by the HBO tv-miniseries *Chernobyl* [22], which is a fictional interpretation portraying the nuclear meltdown in the city of Chernobyl in 1987. The idea behind the project *Time Machine* was simple: to place the player inside a nuclear power plant on the verge of a catastrophic event: nuclear meltdown. The goal of the game is, of course, to prevent the immediate nuclear catastrophe. In order to prevent the devastation from happening, the player has to solve a number of puzzles. To handle the challenges, the player is equipped with a curious device from which a mysterious voice also speaks. The cryptic device is the tailor-made game controller, which the player holds in her hands. The baffling device is also present in the game world (see Fig. 1). Now, the mysterious voice explains that the enigmatic device is indeed a time machine. Followingly the player learns how to operate the time machine.

Fig. 1. To the left, a picture of the customized controller: The Time Machine. To the right: the virtual representation of the time machine inside the game world. Notice the big red button – it activates time travel. (Color figure online)

On the top of the time machine, i.e. the customized game controller, next to the big red button is placed a much smaller black knob, which looks like something from a radio from the 1950s. The black knob can be turned into three positions: left equals yesterday, straight ahead signals the present time, but if you turn it to the right you can travel 10 years into the future. This design is aligned with the three possible time periods within the game world.

When the game begins, the player is advised to figure out how to stop the disaster from happening. The player is presented with three options: travel back in time, stay in the present time period or jump ten years into the future. If the player choices to stay in the present time, the player will have approximately 90 s before the powerplant melts down. However, if the player choices to travel one day back in time, she will find the powerplant fully operational with ample time to explore the facility. Of special interest, the solve the puzzle the player has to find a way to the top floor where the executive office is located. However, in this time period the player has limited access to important areas of the powerplant such as the executive office. If, on the other hand, the player chooses to jump 10 years into the future, a very different scenario will greet her. In this future, after the nuclear meltdown has happened, the power plant facility is completely shut down. Additionally, remains of dead bodies lie on the floors of the powerplant and the air is saturated with toxic gasses and the levels of radiation are dangerously high.

3.1 The Functionality of the Time Machine

The main feature of the customized controller is, of cause, time travel. The player configures the time travelling mechanism on the top front of the customized physical controller. When the designated date of arrival is set, the player presses the big red button to activate time travel. Instantaneously, the player is blasted through time to the desired time period.

The action of pressing the big red button triggers an embodied experience [23] of time travel. The sensation of time travel is emphasized by feedback from the game world in the form of screen shake, green circular expanding animations, and intense sound effects. This multi-layered design of feedback follows several polish metrics [24], which contributes to the player's feel of being catapulted through time. The utilized polish metrics bridge the experience of the embodied interaction with the fiction of the game world. Not only did the design of the game apply the aforementioned polish metrics [25], so did the customized game controller. For instance, the sensation of hitting the cartoonishly big red button to activate time travel, contribute to the player's experience of hurling through time. The experience was further empathized by flashing lights of different colors stemming from the game synchronized with a rumbling sound emanating directly from the game controller (see Fig. 2).

Fig. 2. The figure displays a picture of the time machine. The big red button activates time travel while smaller black rotation button is surrounded by LED lights, which indicate different time periods. (Color figure online)

Of course, the time machine also facilitates traditional game space navigation, thus assisting the player's exploration of the 3D game world. The buttons on the side of the tailor-made controller are used to maneuver the player's action inside the game world.

Additionally, the customized game controller contains and takes part in the puzzles of the game. In the last puzzle, the player encounters a broken elevator, which will take the player to the sought-after executive offices. However, in order to fix the elevator, the player needs a wire. Eventually, the player discovers that there is a secret compartment hidden inside the controller. When the player opens the compartment three colored wires are revealed. Now, the player has to pull out a wire, but, if the if the player pulls out the wrong wire not only will she fail to fix the elevator, she will also cause the time machine to break down and cease functioning (see Fig. 3).

Fig. 3. A picture of the compartment with the hidden wires. The wires are an integral part of a solution to the last in-game puzzle.

Tying the puzzles of the game world together with the player's embodied interaction with the time machine transports the customized controller into the foreground of the experience of play: now the controller becomes "visible". Nonetheless, it could be stipulated that this design run the risk of crippling the immersiveness of the entire game experience. Yet, the opposite is true. We discovered that players found the time machine intriguing; that it contributed and heightened the overall experience of the game.

The tailor-made game controller immediately transported the players into the game world. The players quickly found themselves dwelling in a novel experience where their attention oscillated between the customized game controller and the content of the game world. The time machine and the game world supplemented each other and seamlessly became part of the entire experience of play. The players' shift in focus between the customized game controller and the game content, didn't disrupt their sense of immersion. Passingly, it should be noted, the concept of immersion loosely deals with the experience of some sort of loss of self-awareness during play – this whether or not immersion is thought of as being surrounded by another reality [26]; associated with immediacy of the media [27]; thought in a continuum ranging from immersion, outmersion to meta-outmersion [28]; or resting on micro-involvement highlighting six different dimensions [29, 30], which describes moment-to-moment involvement.

In short: in the project Time Machine a customized game controller acted in direct opposition to the traditional game controller. The customized game controller is "visible", present, and bridges a strange physical object with the vibrant content of the game world. We quickly realized that the tailor-made game controller such as the time machine not only managed to insert itself as an active part of the game world, it also instantiated and elevated the player's experience of the game content.

4 Project Voodoo Doll: Finding Your Way Around Inside a Toy

Project *Voodoo Doll* is inspired by magic as it is performed in diverse religions of Voodoo. The intention of Project *Voodoo Doll* was to create a game experience that used a voodoo doll as game controller to act as an essential and integral part of the game world. The key to mastering the game runs through the player's understanding of the figurative, concrete, and abstract connection between the physical controller and the fictional events and overall design of the game content, especially, acknowledging the voodoo doll as portraying both as game controller *and* as a metaphorical map of the game world.

When the player begins the game, she is handed a physical Voodoo doll, which, initially, does not seem to share any obvious possible patterns of interaction with the game world (see Fig. 4).

Fig. 4. The voodoo doll as game controller and game object.

From a design point of view, the necessary buttons and sensors for interaction are hidden inside the voodoo doll. However, one noticeable element on the Voodoo doll manifest itself by a small light, which shines from the right arm of the doll. The player will have to figure out that the light indicates the current position of the player *inside* the Voodoo doll – inside the game world (i.e. the player has to figure out that the game takes place inside the controller).

The opening scene of the story of the game situates the player in a strange, unknown, and dark place. The player is alone except for a small spirit fragment, which is manifested as a floating blue flame on the screen. The game does not explicitly provide the player with a backstory [31], all that is revealed to the player about this dark bizarre place is that it is a peculiar universe convoluted in mystical, spiritual, and supernatural effects.

When the player progresses through this bizarre dark place, she discovers that the small spirit fragments can be infused with other spirit fragments maturing them into a glowing spirit companion. The spirit fragments also serve as navigational breadcrumbs and for solving puzzles [32].

Early on the player discovers an interesting, but unreachable cave. Followingly, the player will have to learn that squeezing the tailor-made made controller will impact the layout of the game space. For instance, if the player squeezes the doll in the room with the unreachable cave in the ceiling the cave will be lowered in conjunction with the squeezing of the Voodoo doll's limp. Thus, the up and down movement of the cave corresponds to the player's squeezing interaction with the physical voodoo doll.

Afterwards, if the player continues onward, she will arrive at a locked door. Thus, the player has to find a key to the door. Investigating the surroundings will reveal an unreachable key. The key is placed up high. Once again, the player has to explore the intriguing powers of the physical doll in order to discover an ability, which can assist the player in finding a way to get to the key. This time pressing the physical limps of the doll doesn't work it: this action will not suppress space and make the key attainable. Nonetheless, the Voodoo doll holds the solution. But, the player has to shake the physical voodoo doll, which, in turn, will make the game world shake accordingly. Thus, shaking the voodoo doll will shake lose the key from its place up high (see Fig. 5). The result of shaking the doll is that the key falls to the ground.

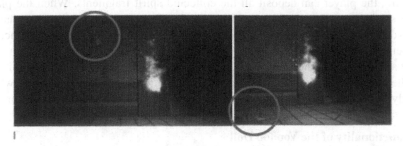

Fig. 5. The key is unreachable until the player shakes the Voodoo doll, which consequently shakes the entire room and releases the key

Likewise, the spirit companion can enact various abilities based on its present color. Changing the spirit companion's color opens up new and exciting game mechanics – defined as methods for interaction with the game state [33, 34]. The player shifts the spirit companion's color inside the game world by physically placing a colored piece of paper in front of the physical eyes of the Voodoo doll. Sensors embedded in the voodoo doll will 'read' the color of the paper and alter the spirit companion's color. The ludo-narrative aspect of this correspondence between game world and physical reality is that the voodoo doll is able to "see" the physical colored object.

Moving on. Once the player has found a solution to the puzzles, the player will find herself in a new room, which represents the heart of the physical voodoo doll. Meanwhile, the light that was previously lit up in the right arm of the physical Voodoo doll has turned off. Instead, the light in the region of heart is not ignited.

Fig. 6. The different limbs of the doll represent different rooms in the game world

The room of the voodoo doll's heart functions as a navigational hub and passageway with several doors leading to the adjacent limbs of the voodoo doll: to the head, to the left arm, to the right arm, to the left leg, and finally to the right leg (see Fig. 6).

Furthermore, at the center of the room there is a big furnace: the heart of the voodoo doll. Here, the player can deposit all the collected spirit fragments. When the player deposit spirit fragments the furnace immediately shines brighter, indicating that the voodoo doll is nearing its previous life. Thereby, the brightness of the furnace functions as a 'meter' to measure progression. Important to note, the overall goal of the game is to deposit as many spirit fragments as possible in the furnace. This effort will eventually bring the voodoo doll back to life. When the voodoo doll is awoken, the player, who is currently captured inside the doll, will simultaneously be released from her prison.

4.1 Functionality of the Voodoo Doll

The voodoo doll controller takes an active part in the way the player interacts with the game world. The multiple features and possibilities for interaction assists the player in solving the puzzles of the game. The high-level rule [24] of the game is comprised of the collection of the spirit companions in the game world. The game mechanics [33], on the other hand, are designed to metaphorically mimic the player's physical interaction [35] with the voodoo doll. The metaphorical game mechanics are intended to directly link the voodoo doll with the game world and vice versa. For example, squeezing a limb of the voodoo doll creates an immediate reaction within the game world: the room that shrinks in size when the limb is pinched. Or if the Voodoo doll is being shaken, it prompts an instantaneous reaction in terms of screen shake and the possibility of something happening inside the game world. The corresponding link between interactions with the voodoo doll and the landscape of the game world instantiate a vibrant "dialogue" between the player and content of the game: between what happens to the physical voodoo doll and the events taking place on the screen.

However, the connections between the voodoo doll and the hidden puzzle elements inside the game world needs to be discovered and interpreted in order for the player to progress the game. For example, when the furnace is lit in the room of the doll's heart, the moving mechanical gears in the game world are meant to represent the voodoo doll's heartbeats. Here the player's interpretation is helped by auditory feedback from the physical voodoo doll. For instance, the player is presented with a puzzle where she has to figure out how the varying lengths of the heart beats can be turned into Morse code.

Thus, the voodoo doll transgresses the conventional understanding of game controllers. First and foremost, due to the fact that the voodoo doll looks nothing like a game controller (it looks and feels like a doll as the previous figures have illustrated). Beyond the metaphorical link, the voodoo doll inserts itself into an unorthodox structural pattern of interaction with the game world. This happens, especially, through the said metaphorical correspondence between the player's interactions with the voodoo doll and the associated game mechanics i.e. squeeze the doll to collapse the size of the game space or shaking the doll to loosen a key inside the game world. In spite of how these links intuitively could be thought of as threatening the immersiveness of the experience of play the opposite takes place. The project *Voodoo Doll* does, like Project *Time*

Machine, propel the experience of immersion: the player finds herself intrigued by the metaphorical correspondence between the design of the physical game controller (the voodoo doll), the game mechanics, and the overall game world. The shifting of attention between game controller and game content actually accelerates the immersiveness of experience of play.

5 Towards an Understanding of the Relationship Between Customized Game Controllers, the Player, and the Game World

The traditional generic game controller in the form of keyboard, mouse or game console controller can occupy two different states of being during the experience of play: either "visible", which is what happens when the controller breaks down, cease to respond, and no longer functions or "invisible", which happens when the player's attention is solely focused on the content of the game. In other words, the game controller is inscribed a binary paradigm of being, which is directly inverted by function: either not working or fully functional – of either at the center of the player's attention or a fully "disappeared" thing operating in perfect symmetry with the content of the game (see Fig. 7).

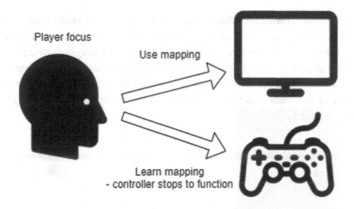

Fig. 7. Illustrates the traditional binary paradigm of the player's attention of the game controller. This model depicts how the player either looks at the controller for references to the layout of inputs (or if the controller stops to function), or fully neglects the controller and focus entirely on the visualizing the game content on the screen.

The relationship between immersion (i.e. the experience of play) within this binary paradigm of understanding game controllers follows a specific pattern. When players are either new to a game or if the controller halts the controller automatically draws attention to itself. However – when the player advances further into the game and develop familiarity with the mapping of the controller inputs in relation to game mechanics – the player's attention gradually shifts away from the controller and hatch onto the game content. So, the "visibility" of the controller decreases parallelly to the player's increased mastering of the controller (lack of attention). Within the traditional binary paradigm, the relationship between the visibility/invisibility of the controller is linearly proportional with the player's mastering of the interaction of the controller (see Fig. 8).

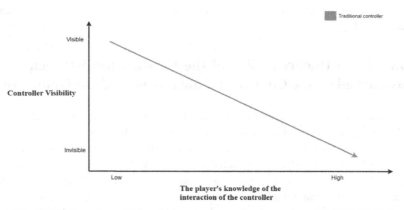

Fig. 8. This figure shows a model, which represents the decreasing "visibility" of the game controller in comparison to the player's increased familiarity with the controller during play.

Interesting, as the controller "disappears" a parallel event takes place: immersion increases. This process links the "disappearance" of the controller with the player's experience of immersion. In general terms, this process highlights, when the player's knowledge of the mapping of the controller bridges the mechanics of the game immersion has the opportunity to take hold. Stated otherwise, the player is becoming progressively more immersed in the game world as a reflection of her increased familiarity with the game controller (see Fig. 9).

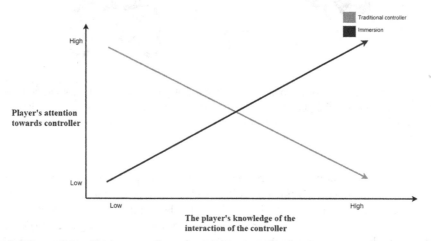

Fig. 9. The traditional binary paradigm of "visibility/invisibility or "appearance/disappearance" of the controller during play directly linked to the experience of immersion.

However, we challenged this traditional binary paradigm in the projects *Time Machine* and *Voodoo Doll*. In those projects, the controller worked in direct opposition to the traditional way of understanding controllers. Here, the customized controllers (a time machine and a voodoo doll) inserted themselves as integral parts of the whole gaming experience.

Players were, in both projects, constantly reminded of the being/status of the controllers. Beyond functioning as controllers, the tailor-made controllers also acted as game objects, which players, on the one hand was inspired to investigate, and on the other hand, strived to master. The Time Machine and the Voodoo Doll require continuous attention alongside the virtual installment of the game. Particularly, the player has to pay attention to the mapping of the inputs and the outputs of the controller and following figure out how they are referenced inside the game world (the metaphorical link between the two). All of this was, of course, presented to the player in incremental steps to mitigate an all too steep learning curve.

Additionally, the player was at no given time given complete knowledge of the game controller – hidden room or unforeseen functions could appear at any time. In spite of these possibilities immersion wasn't disturbed. Nor did the presence of the customized game controller itself and the fact that the player had to pay attention to it, to its functionality, and to learn how it worked disrupt the experience of immersion during play (see Fig. 10).

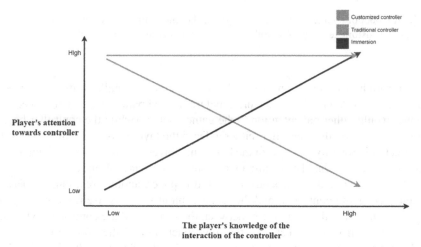

Fig. 10. Shows how immersion tracks in relation to the traditional game controller compared to the customized game controller.

Now, inserting a customized game controller/physical game object into the experience of play not only draw the traditional binary understanding of controllers into the light, it also challenges the conditional underpinnings (i.e. the framework for thinking about) in conceptualizing immersion. Moreover, when a customized controller is applied the traditional *structural pattern* of interaction changes together with the *process of interaction*. The result points towards a new paradigm of interconnectivity between the player, the game and the controller of the game, and specially, how to grasp the condition for reflecting on immersion (see Fig. 11).

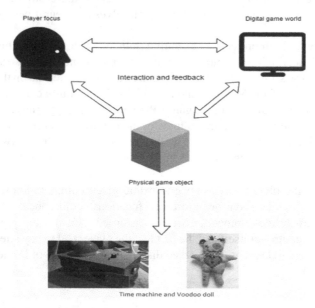

Fig. 11. A model of a tentatively new paradigm of the interconnectivity between the player, the game, and the customized game controller, acting simultaneously both as a physical game object and a controller.

In this paradigm of interconnectivity, the controller intentionally shifts between being either "visible" or "invisible". In the prior and traditional paradigm of interconnectivity, the player would either pay attention to the game content (while the controller became invisible) or focus on the controller (either to learn the layout (its mechanisms) or suffer from defect functionality). In case of the latter, the player would more or less intentional neglect the game content. The result: a languished experience of play.

Within the new paradigm, as advanced in this paper, another relationship between the player, the game controller, and the game content presents itself. Now, the player focuses and shift attention seamlessly between the screen and the controller (which can also be a physical game object, like the time machine and the voodoo doll), all the while both the screen and the object provides visual and auditory feedback to the player about the current game state. Furthermore, the game object and the game content are interconnected: they share information and data while belonging to the same universe of the fiction of the game.

Followingly, the gaming experience can be said to emerge from a tripartite formation of attention: the player, the game content and the customized game controller. Within this tripartite formation, the player *continuously* shift attention between herself, the game content, and how the customized controller works (how to operate and interact with the physical game object) (see Fig. 12).

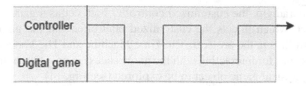

Fig. 12. Within the new paradigm of tailor-made game controllers, the *structural pattern* of interaction between the player, the game, and game controller changes along with the *process of interaction.*

Our findings regarding the difference in the *structural pattern* of interaction between the player, the game, and the controller *and* in the process of playing a game are of special interest. Before, within the old paradigm, the controller was automatically pushed into the background of the experience of play, and the further into the background the controller was positioned the better, especially in regard to the player's sense of immersion. Within this new paradigm the opposite was found to be true. Here, the structural pattern of interaction between the player, the customized controller, and the game content changes significantly. Now, the player's attention moves freely between the customized game controller and game content without disturbing the sensation of immersion during play. Actually, immersion seems to work fine within the confines of this new structural pattern of interaction and the oscillating shift of attention during the process of interaction. So, it seems, the process of interaction changes alongside the transformation in the pattern of interaction. Moreover, neither of these changes seem to negatively impact the creation of immersion or the player's sensation hereof. Instead, the opposite can and have been observed during several play sessions.

The overall consequences of these deep-rooted alterations in the player's interaction and attention, point towards a new way of conceiving the game controller *and* the conditions (i.e. the framework) for thinking about the player's sensation of immersion (see Fig. 13).

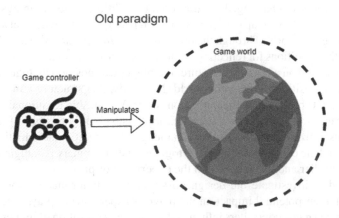

Fig. 13. The old paradigm of the interaction is binary: on the one side the player is positioned while on the other side the controller and game world are placed.

In this new paradigm, the customized controller both act as a game controller and as a game object, which injects the customized controller into the game world. The customized controllers in the projects: The Time Machine and The Voodoo Doll, simultaneously acts as sites for interacting with the game state (i.e. navigation, interaction and so on) *and* as a physical game object to be explored (see Fig. 14).

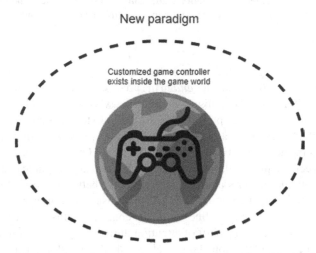

Fig. 14. This model shows how the customized controller is positioned inside the experience of play. The tailor-made controller is a device for interacting with the game state *and* establishes itself as a game object in its own right.

6   Concluding Remarks

In this paper, we have challenged the traditional conditional underpinnings for understanding immersion and the up until now structural pattern of interaction between player, controller and game world. Through the projects *Time Machine* and *Voodoo Doll* we discovered that the conditions for reflecting upon immersion as well as the traditional pattern of interaction rested on a binarily structure: the player was positioned, together with the controller, in opposition to the game world. Implicitly, this structure aims to suppress and subjugate the presence of the game controller. Within this traditional setup game controllers can occupy one of two states: either "visible" or "invisible". Our projects, with their customized game controllers, challenged the traditional formational underpinnings behind the concept of immersion together with the binary paradigm of thinking about the controller and its place within the experience of play.

We aimed to investigate the design possibilities of tailor-made game controllers together with their potential impact on the player's experience of play, especially, how these customized game controllers influenced the player's sensation of immersion during play. We found that customized controllers seamlessly integrate themselves and smoothly inhabit the experience of play. Interestingly, we discovered that the player's use of the time machine and the voodoo doll didn't disrupt immersion. On the contrary, the customized game controllers fueled the players' experience of immersion. This finding contradicts the implicit design assumptions and way of thinking about not only about controllers, but also in regard to the entire framework for thinking about immersion. Furthermore, we discovered that customized game controllers can act as game objects fully belonging to the game world *and* act as devices for interacting with the game world (i.e. solving puzzles and so on).

Taken together, these findings dispute the traditional binary paradigm of interaction between the player, the controller, and the game. Instead, customized controllers can be inserted as active "participants" in the entire experience of gaming. Moreover, we discovered that customized game controllers established new *structural pattern* of interaction between the player, the game controller, and the game world. This structure also highlighted a different *process of interaction*: now the player's attention oscillates lively between figuring out how to use the customized controller *and* interpreting metaphorical links to the game world: deciphering the mapping between the abilities of the game controller and how it corresponds to the game mechanics of the game world.

We advance the argument that the player's experience of play without difficulty can expand itself to encapsulate a physical game object in the shape of a tailor-made game controller. This argument point towards a new paradigm of thinking about the interaction between the player, the controller, and the game world, especially, the insertion of the customized game controller as an active extension of the game world and effective actor in the experience of the game.

The relationship between the experience of immersion and perception of the controller, as it is implicitly promoted in the traditional paradigm, has now undergone a significant change. Our analysis discovered that the player's sensation of immersion enhances even though the player constantly shifts attention between exploring the customized controller and solving the puzzles of the game world. Followingly, we have highlighted the conditions or underpinnings in the current way of thinking about the concept of immersion, especially, how reflections inherently are tied to the levels of presence of the game controller. Thus, we propose new paradigm of thinking about the concept of immersion *and* the interaction between the player, the controller, and the game world. Within this new paradigm different *structural patterns* of interaction together with varied *processes* of playing intersect with the player's attention and how it seamlessly can oscillate between investigating the customized controller and solving the puzzles of the computer game (see Fig. 15).

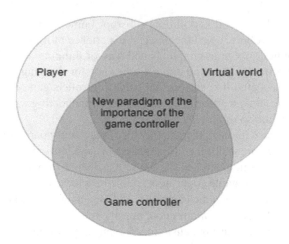

Fig. 15. The insertion of the customized game controller (controller and physical game object) in the center of the experience of play.

Finally, future research could further elaborate on the relationship between the player, the controller, and the game world, and how this tripartite structure impacts the experience of play. The future research could draw attention to another under investigated aspect of computer game play [2], namely, the aspect of rhythm and its influence on the experience of play. A natural point of departure would be to focus on how the rhythm of the player's oscillating attention resonates the rhythm of the design of the game and possibly with the experience of play.

References

1. Isbister, K.: How Games Move Us – Emotion by Design Playful Thinking Series. The MIT Press, Cambridge (2017)
2. X and Author Books (2019)
3. Heidegger, M.: Being and Time. Suny Press, Albany (2010)
4. Nardi, B.A., Kaptelinin, V.: Acting with Technology – Activity Theory and Interaction Design. The MIT Press, Cambridge (2009)
5. Crawford, C.: The Art of Computer Game Design (1982). https://www.digitpress.com/lib rary/books/book_art_of_computer_game_design.pdf
6. Elias, S.G., Garfield, R., Gutschera, K.R.: Characteristics of Games. The MIT Press, Cambridge (2012)
7. Author (2020)
8. Montola, M.: The invisible rules of role-playing: the social framework of roleplaying process. Int. J. Role-Playing **1**, 22–36 (2009)
9. Fine, G.A.: Shared Fantasy - Role-Playing Games as Social Worlds. The University of Chicago Press. Chicago and London (2002)
10. Author and X (2019)
11. Costikyan, G.: I have no words & I must design: toward a critical vocabulary for games. In: Proceedings of Computer Games and Digital Conference. Tampere University Press (2002). https://www.digra.org/digital-library/publications/i-have-no-wordsi-must-des ign-toward-a-critical-vocabulary-for-games/

12. Juul, J.: Half-Real - Video Games between Real Rules and Fictional Worlds. The MIT Press. Cambridge, London and New York (2005)
13. Star Wars Episode IV: A New Hope, Lucas (1977)
14. Kirkpatrick, G.: Aesthetic Theory and The Video Game. Manchester University Press, Manchester and New York (2011)
15. Huizinga, J.: Homo Ludens - A Study of the Play-Element in Culture. Martino Publishing, Eastford (2014)
16. Montola, M., Stenros, J., Waern, A.: Theory and Design of Pervasive Games - Experiences on the Boundary Between Life and Play. Morgan Kaufmann Publishers, Burlington (2009)
17. Fullerton, T.: Game Design Workshop: A Playcentric Approach to Creating Innovative Games, 2nd edn. Morgan Kaufmann, Amsterdam, Netherlands and Boston (2008)
18. Nintendo Labo, Nintendo (2018)
19. Macklin, C., Sharp, J.: Games, Design and Play – A Detailed Approach to Iterative Game Design. Addison-Wesley, Boston (2016)
20. Bevan, M.T.: A Method of Phenomenological Interviewing in Qualitative Health Research, vol. 24, no. 1, pp. 136–144. Sage Publications, Inc. Thousand Oaks (2014)
21. Druin, A.: The role of children in the design of new technology. Behav. Inf. Technol. (BIT) **21**(1), 1–25 (2002)
22. Chernobyl, Mazin (2019)
23. Dourish, P.: Where the Action Is: The Foundations of Embodied Interaction. A Bradford Book. The MIT Press, Cambridge (2004)
24. Swink, S.: Game Feel - A Game Designer's Guide to Virtual Sensation. CRC Press. Taylor & Francis Group, Boca Raton (2009)
25. Author (2018)
26. Murray, J.: Hamlet on the Holodeck. MIT Press, Cambridge (1997)
27. Bolter, J.D., Grusin, R.: Remediation - Understanding New Media. The MIT Press Cambridge (2000)
28. Frasca, G.: Immersion, outmersion & critical thinking (2008). https://www.dream.dk/uploads/files/Gonzalo%20Frasca.pdf
29. Calleja, G.: In-Game – From Immersion to Incorporation. The MIT Press, Cambridge (2011)
30. Calleja, G.: Revising immersion: a conceptual model for the analysis of digital game involvement. In: Situated Play, Proceedings of DiGRA, 21 May 2019. https://www.digra.org/digital-library/publications/revising-immersion-a-conceptual-model-forthe-analysis-of-digital-game-involvement/ (2007)
31. Truby, J.: The Anatomy of Story. Farrar Straus and Giroux, New York (2008)
32. Schell, J.: The Art of Game Design: A Book of Lenses, 2nd edn. CRC Press, Boca Raton (2008)
33. Sicart, M.: Defining game mechanics. In: Game Studies, vol. 8 (2008). https://gamestudies.org/0802/articles/sicart
34. Burgun, K.: Clockwork Game Design, 1st edn. Focal Press, Burlington (2015)
35. Verplank, W.: Interaction Design Sketchbook Frameworks for designing interactive products and systems (2009). https://www.billverplank.com/IxDSketchBook.pdf. 21 July 2020

The World Is Your Playground: A Bibliometric and Text Mining Analysis of Location-Based Game Research

Chien Lu$^{(\boxtimes)}$ (ID), Elina Koskinen (ID), Dale Leorke (ID), Timo Nummenmaa (ID), and Jaakko Peltonen (ID)

Tampere University, Tampere, Finland
{chien.lu,elina.m.kostinen,dale.leorke,
timo.nummenmaa,jaakko.peltonen}@tuni.fi

Abstract. Location-based games have become mainstream and have been increasingly emphasized in the academic community. However, so far, to our knowledge, no bibliometric analysis of location-based games research literature has been undertaken. We carry out an analysis of 606 publications using bibliometric analysis and text mining. The results reveal prominent researchers, institutions, and countries, as well as the most common research topics and their prevalence over time. The results are useful both to understand the current state of location-based research and for designing future research.

Keywords: Location-based games · Bibliometric analysis · Text mining · Topic Modeling

1 Introduction

Location-based games emerged in the early 2000s as a result of artistic, academic and commercial experimentation with Global Positioning System (GPS) and location-based media (LBM, or locative media) technologies [31]. These types of games incorporate physical locations into the gaming experience, with early games employing technologies like text messages and primitive mobile Java [46,50]. Other, mixed-reality location-based games blended physical and virtual environments to create large-scale, immersive experiences in public space [24,30]. More recently, commercial location-based game apps like *Pokémon GO*, *Harry Potter: Wizards Unite* and *Minecraft Earth* feature augmented reality built on smartphone cameras and sensors, and utilize their ecosystem features including cellular data and the app distribution model to reach potentially millions of simultaneous players [31,42]. With *Pokémon GO*, location-based games reached a mainstream audience through combination of a casual play style with a recognisable franchise, although no games to date have matched its success [27].

Due to this significant growth, the importance of location-based games has been increasingly emphasized in the academic community. Location-based game

A. Brooks et al. (Eds.): ArtsIT 2020, LNICST 367, pp. 160–179, 2021.
https://doi.org/10.1007/978-3-030-73426-8_9

research and design has a strong connection to academia, dating back to its emergence. One major research effort occurred with the IPerG research project (2004–2008) [1,56], even though consumer hardware was limited at the time. Other early research employed participant observation of specific experimental games, often by designers themselves or with their involvement [6,19,43]. Subsequent research focused on interviews with small samples of players to understand their everyday experiences playing location-based games [32,33,36]. Since the advent of smartphones with app stores, location-based games can reach millions of players simultaneously in countless locations around the world [31, p. 101]. This also affords researchers the opportunity to study player experiences on a larger scale. Quantitative and qualitative surveys that compare and contrast players' experiences in international and local contexts have become common – although a majority focus only on *Pokémon GO* [21,28,41,49,53]. In-depth interviews with players remain the most common method for media and cultural studies research on location-based games [24,51,55].

Despite this body of research dating back two decades to the emergence of location-based games, no bibliometric analysis of it has been undertaken. While some critical literature reviews do exist [31,39,47], these are either dated or limited to discourse analysis of a selection of publications. This article provides a bibliometric analysis that sheds light on trends in location-based game research. Our research questions are: RQ1 - How has the amount of research grown over time, and what are the countries and institutions contributing the research? RQ2 - What are the main themes of the research, and how do they vary over time?

Using bibliometric analysis and text mining techniques on 606 publications from 1995–2019 sourced from Scopus we provide insight into the frequency of publications on location-based games and the institutions and countries from which these publications most frequently appear, answering RQ1; and the most common keywords and phrases that appear in these publications, co-occurring groups of the keywords, and their prevalence over time, answering RQ2. This research will provide insights into present and previous research on location-based games, as well as providing a framework for further, qualitative research that explores more in depth the approaches used to study these games.

2 Background

Location-based games gained widespread attention after pinpoint GPS technology was made publicly available in 2000. Artists, academics, game designers and amateurs began to experiment with the potential for devices that could trace their users' location to bring play into public, primarily urban, spaces. Practices like geocaching and Alternate Reality Games like *The Beast* (2001) can be seen as precursors to location-based games, as can a whole range of practices and movements aimed at reclaiming urban space for playful behavior - including the Situationist International, New Games Movement, Gutai group, live-action role playing games and parkour [18,39]. But location-based games more specifically emerged simultaneously as a form of artistic experimentation with "locative" media technologies, exemplified by the games of artist group Blast Theory [17] and commercial games like *Botfighters* (2001)[31, p. 29]. As a result, location-based games blend a wide range of practices and influences, combining and reconfiguring new media art, locative media, mobile gaming and urban play.

One consequence of location-based gaming's heterogeneity is that no universal definition of location-based games exists. "Location-based game" most commonly refers to a game that uses mobile and/or networked technologies to incorporate their players' location into the game. One way to categorise these games is based on how they track and incorporate their players' location. "Urban games" use city streets as the game's playground or 'board', e.g. in *PacManhattan* (2004), in which players wear costumes of *Pac-Man* characters and chase each other through the streets of Manhattan communicating via "voice chat" on mobile phones. "Location-based mobile games" similarly use the city's streets and public spaces as the game space, but with the added element that player locations are tracked and incorporated into the game through GPS-enabled devices, e.g. Blast Theory's, *Can You See Me Now?* (2001) and *Botfighters*. Lastly, "hybrid reality games" include elements of the previous two types of games, combining them with a 3D visualisation of the city to produce games that blend online and offline play, such as in the treasure hunt game *Mogi, Item Hunt*. [47]

In addition to these genres of location-based games, many other terms have been employed by scholars to describe similar and related games over their near-20-year history. "Mixed-reality game" commonly refers to games that blend the virtual and physical environment, taking place in both simultaneously. "Locative game" is similar to "location-based game", but more specifically connects them to the "locative media movement" of artistic experimentation with location-ware technologies [17,18]. "Pervasive game" refers to any type of game or playful practices that extends the boundaries of play out into the physical environment, and location-based games are one type of pervasive game [39]. In turn, "augmented reality game" refers specifically to games that use augmented reality (AR) technology. Each of these terms refers to a specific, nuanced form of these types of games but they are often synonymous with, or strongly overlap, with location-based games. Other terms - like "mobile urban game", "massively multiplayer mobile game" and "hybrid reality game" - further complicate attempts to clearly delineate research on location-based games and related phenomena [31, p. 36–38].

This definitional elusiveness poses a clear dilemma for a bibliometric analysis of the literature on location-based games, since many publication may be relevant to scholarly work on this topic but employ a different term to describe them. Further, publications may use the term "location-based" and "game" but not in combination, meaning irrelevant combinations would be picked up on a broad search using these terms. As described below, we have used these two broad terms to select our sample for this initial, exploratory study, followed by a curation stage to exclude the irrelevant results. However, future research will be needed to cast a wider net that extracts publications using different terms, with curation needed again to exclude results that may not be relevant to the topic.

3   Method

We use bibliometric and text mining approaches. Bibliometric analysis uses quantitative and statistical techniques to analyze volume, growth and distribution of research literature. To better understand the content of the research works, we also employ a text mining technique called topic modeling. It enables researchers to perform a qualitative analysis in a computational manner [16, 40].

3.1   Data Collection

The Scopus database was chosen because it has indexed a wide variety of significant scientific literature and has been one of the most used sources for game studies [4]. We retrieved the data from the Scopus with the following query:

TITLE-ABS-KEY ("game*" AND "location based") AND (LIMIT-TO (DOCTYPE, "cp") OR LIMIT-TO (DOCTYPE, "ar") OR LIMIT-TO (DOCTYPE, "ch"))

where "game*" is set to cover both game and games and the results are limited to conference papers ("cp"), journal articles ("ar") and book chapters ("ch"). The search was executed in November 2019 and 778 items were collected.

3.2   Data Curation

In an initial topic analysis of our sample, topics were skewed due to publications using "location-based" and "game" separately without referring to location-based games. These separate search terms yielded relevant works using variant terms for location-based games, for example, "location-based mobile game", or a "pervasive game" that is location-based, but also yielded irrelevant publications.

To exclude irrelevant publications without excluding relevant ones, a curation stage was done where all publications were inspected. The work was divided equally among 5 co-authors of the present manuscript: each inspected about 155 articles in a spreadsheet, labeling them relevant, irrelevant (i.e. to be excluded), or unsure based on the title, abstract, and keywords; the full article was checked if needed. Articles marked unsure were discussed among co-authors, who then double-checked their exclusions and listed reasons for exclusions. Each co-author then cross-checked 5–10 articles marked for exclusion by another co-author, to ensure agreement and consistent reasoning for exclusions across the full sample. Co-authors then discussed and resolved disagreements on exclusions or reasons. Excluded articles were coded based on the reasons and the consensus reached.

This process excluded 172 (22%) out of the original 778 publications. The most common reasons for exclusion were: 1. Articles applying game theory concepts to analyze a problem involving e.g. "location-based" sensors but without discussion of actual games or related phenomena. 2. Articles on privacy or security in location-based technologies or social networks, with "game" only as an example application or coincidental word. 3. Articles on location-based and location-aware technologies, with "game" only as an example application or in another context. 4. Articles that were not about a location-based game: these included game projects and interactive art, some using AR and VR, which mentioned "location-based" in the abstract or full paper, but the game itself was not location-based. This broad term was sometimes hard to define; simply tracking participant motion through sensors, similar to Microsoft Kinect, was not deemed location-based, but if the project tracked people's movement through a physical location, including one room or building, we included it. If the distinction was not clear from the full paper, we opted to include it.

The least common exclusion reasons, with only a few examples in total, were: 5. Publications that were not research articles, for example a workshop proposal or news article. 6. Otherwise unrelated articles using "location-based" and "game" separately. 7. Articles that appeared in the search, but were not found during the coding process and seemed irrelevant based on the title.

3.3   Bibliometric Analysis

Bibliometric analysis has been widely used in different disciplines including game studies [8, 14, 35]. It has proven a useful technique to explore impact and popularity of researchers, institutions and also countries in specific research fields. We use the metadata and impact metrics (mainly citations) collected from Scopus to conduct a quantitative analysis of the publications. The analysis puts the emphasis on the temporal trend of publications, and on importance of researchers, keywords, institutions and countries in terms of publications and citations.

3.4   Text Mining

We use topic modeling to explore contents of the collected publications. A topic model finds groups (distributions) of frequently co-occurring words as topics, so that content of documents is represented as mixtures of these topics; the resulting topics often have clear semantic meaning which we can then analyze.

A topic model represents the probability $p(w|d)$ of word w in document d as

$$p(w|d) = \sum_k p(k|d)p(w|k)$$

where $p(k|d)$ is the probability a word is generated from topic k out of K possible topics, and $p(w|k)$ is the probability topic k generates word w out of the vocabulary. This can be seen as a multi-step generative process: each document is first generated a distribution of topics and each topic is generated a distribution of words, words are then generated by picking a topic and picking a word from the topic. The model is fitted by maximizing the probability of the observed words in documents, with respect to the underlying probability distributions, by iterative training algorithms. The resulting probabilities $p(k|d)$ describe which topics are most prevalent in each document, and the $p(w|k)$ describe which words are most prevalent in each topic. Unlike e.g. principal component analysis, topic modeling takes into account that documents consist of discrete words from a vocabulary.

Several topic modeling methods have been proposed. In this work a recently developed topic model called Structural Topic Model (STM, [45]) is used to analyze the collected text. Compared to methods such as Latent Dirichlet Allocation (LDA, [7]) and Dynamic Topic Model (DTM, [7]), STM is a more advanced model that is able to take available document-level covariates into account when modeling the text. For each document d, STM models the topic probabilities $p(k|d)$ of all topics $k = 1, \ldots, K$ as a vector $\boldsymbol{\theta}_d = [p(1|d), \ldots, p(K|d)]^\top$ arising from a Logistic Normal distribution,

$$\boldsymbol{\theta}_d \sim LogisticNormal_{K-1}(\boldsymbol{\Gamma}^\top \mathbf{x}_d, \boldsymbol{\Sigma}) \tag{1}$$

so that the expected topic probabilities are a linear transformation of the covariate vector $\mathbf{x}_d$ of the document, followed by logistic (softmax) normalization. The weight matrix $\boldsymbol{\Gamma}$ models interaction of covariates and topics and the covariance matrix $\boldsymbol{\Sigma}$ models variation of topic probabilities around the expected values.

We use the STM model to evaluate the association between the text content of a publication and the citations it has received. In order not to overemphasize older content merely due to accumulation of citations over time, we adjusted the number of citations according to the year of publication, so that

$$adjusted\ citations = \frac{citations}{(2020 - publication\ year) + 1} \tag{2}$$

the adjusted citation count was specified as the covariate in the model.

For each document the abstract, title, and author keywords were concatenated and considered as the document content. 8 publications without abstract were ruled out. Format-related words in the abstract (e.g. purpose, methodology, etc.), copyright text, numbers, punctuation and stop words were removed; the term "location-based" was also considered as a stop word since it appears in almost every document so that it doesn't contain meaningful semantic information. The pruned text was further lemmatized before the model building.

We select the number of topics using the held-out likelihood criterion, where a proportion of the documents is left out and the remaining part is used as the training data; the trained model is then used to predict the content of the "held-out" documents and their probability is computed as the held-out likelihood. This held-out likelihood value shows the predictive ability of the model, and we choose the number of topics that yields the best held-out likelihood. We further trained models with the selected number of topics from 20 different initializations with the full data set, and the model with the best averaged semantic coherence [38] value is taken as the final model. In brief, the semantic coherence value measures how strongly the top words in each topic co-occur over documents, thus, it can be employed to evaluate the performance of topic models and to choose the best-performing model among several models.

After topic model training, extracted topics were labeled and analyzed. Labeling was done by a common practice similar to Thematic analysis [15] but without reading through all the collected text. The labels were decided with authors of this paper examining the semantics of the top words and the example documents (documents containing high prevalence of the topic) of each topic.

4   Results

We first display the bibliometric analysis results and then the topics extracted
by text mining, their prevalence over time, and their citation impact.

4.1   Bibliometric Analysis Results

Number of Publications. The distribution of publications of in terms of publication types can be found in Fig. 1 (left). The majority type, Conference Paper,
contains 421 publications, followed by Journal Article with 158 publications and
Book Chapter with 27 publications. Figure 1 (right) shows the number of publications for each year and the proportion of each type of publication. A clearly
rising trend can be observed which reached its peak in 2017 with 90 publications
and a drop happened next year. This is likely because the game *Pokémon GO*
was published in the summer of 2016. Note though that the smaller number of
publications in 2019 can be influenced by the delay of publication and processing
time of Scopus indexing. Note also that there are 2 publications indexed with a
publication date in 2020 which is after the time of our data collection; they are
indexed from early released conference proceedings and a book.

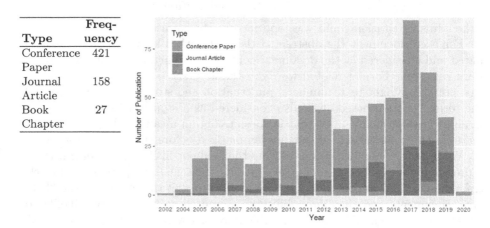

Type	Freq-uency
Conference Paper	421
Journal Article	158
Book Chapter	27

Fig. 1. Publication types. Left: overall counts, Right: counts per year/type.

Researchers. There are 1480 identified authors in the data. Table 1 (left) lists the
10 researchers with highest number of publications in which Christoph Schlieder
(head of the Cultural Informatics Research Group at University of Bamberg,
Germany) is the most productive researcher with 15 publications. Figure 2 (left)
shows the percentage of number of publications for researchers, showing that
the majority of researchers have few publications on location-based games so far:
around 80% of researchers have only 1 publication and around 91% of researchers
have less or equal to 2 publications. We further calculated the ratio of overall

citations to number of publications for researchers having at least 2 publications to identify researchers whose publications are highly cited on average. Table 1 (right) shows the 10 researchers with highest calculated ratio values. The researcher Sanne Floor Akkerman (currently Professor of Educational Sciences at Utrecht University) has the highest ratio, followed by Matt Adams (co-founder of Blast Theory) and Rob Anastasi (member of the Mixed Reality Laboratory at University of Nottingham at the time of the publications). Note that the researchers in Table 1 (right) have at most 3 publications on location-based games in our data but each publication has over 100 citations.

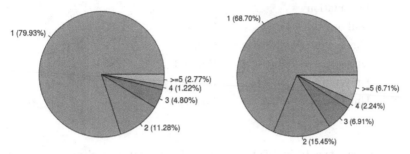

Fig. 2. Left: Number of publications for researchers. **Right**: Number of publications for research institutions.

Table 1. Researchers. Left: Researchers with highest number of publications. Right: Researchers with highest ratio of citations to publications

Researcher	Public-ations	Researcher	Public-ations	Cites	Ratio
Schlieder, Christoph	15	Akkerman, Sanne Floor	2	338	169.00
Coulton, Paul	14	Adams, Matt	2	267	133.50
Goh, Dion H.	13	Anastasi, Rob	2	267	133.50
Benford, Steve D.	12	Ten Dam, Geert T.M.	2	258	129.0
Oppermann, Leif	11	Crabtree, Andy	2	247	123.50
Avouris, Nikolaos M.	11	Huizenga, Jantina C.	3	339	113.00
Kiefer, Peter	11	Admiraal, Wilfried F.	3	339	113.00
Yiannoutsou, Nikoleta	11	Paxton, Mark	2	214	107.00
Matyas, Sebastian	10	Rowland, Duncan A.	3	302	100.67
Sintoris, Christos	9	Hampshire, Alastair	2	197	98.5

Research Institutions. In total there are 492 institutions from 57 countries among the publications. Table 2 lists the 10 institutions with the most publications, showing that University of Nottingham holds the largest count of 28 publications. As shown in Fig. 2 (right), most institutions have contributed few publications to location-based game research so far: around 69% of institutions have only 1 publication, around 84% of institutions have 2 or less.

Table 2. Top institutions based on number of publications

Institution	Country	Publications
University of Nottingham	United Kingdom	28
University of Bamberg	Germany	18
Lancaster University	United Kingdom	15
University of Patras	Greece	13
Wee Kim Wee School of Communication and Information	Singapore	13
Aalborg University	Denmark	11
Simon Fraser University	Canada	11
University of Oulu	Finland	10
University of Tampere	Finland	10
University of Porto	Portugal	9

Table 3 shows the 10 institutions with highest ratio of citations to publications, where Utrecht University has the highest value. Note that there are two institutions in the list (HP lab, Bristol and Nokia Corporation) that are not under universities but belong to technology companies. Figure 3 (left) shows the top 10 countries (based on where the institutions are located) according to the number of publications; the top two countries are United Kingdom having 133 publications and Germany having 106 publications. Figure 3 (right) provides a heat map presentation according to the number of publication of each country.

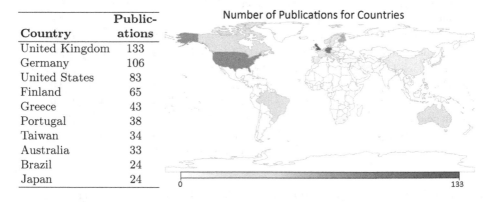

Country	Publications
United Kingdom	133
Germany	106
United States	83
Finland	65
Greece	43
Portugal	38
Taiwan	34
Australia	33
Brazil	24
Japan	24

Fig. 3. Countries by number of publications. Left: top countries. Right: heat map.

Author Specified Keywords. The top 10 author-specified keywords that have occurred the most in the collected publications can be found in Fig. 4 (left).

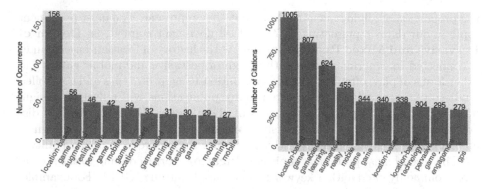

Fig. 4. Left: Top 10 author specified keywords. **Right**: Top 10 cited author specified keywords.

The term "location-based game" has occurred 156 times, followed by game genre related terms such as "augmented reality", "pervasive game" and "mobile game" that have occurred 56, 46, and 42 times respectively. When the terms are ranked by number of citations to the publications, as shown in Fig. 4 (right), the term "location-based game" still holds the first place (1005 citations), however, the term "game-based learning" has risen to the second place (807 citations), whereas "pervasive game" has dropped to 8th place.

Table 3. Top institutions based on ratio of citations to publications

Institution	Country	Publications	Cites	Ratio
Utrecht University	Netherlands	8	383	47.88
North Carolina State University	United States	5	155	31.00
University of Nottingham	United Kingdom	28	779	28.54
Hewlett Packard Laboratories, Bristol	United Kingdom	6	169	28.17
Nokia Corporation	Finland	7	166	23.71
Interactive Institute, Kista	Sweden	6	94	15.67
Nottingham Trent University	United Kingdom	6	92	15.33
University of Oulu	Finland	10	134	13.40
RMIT University	Australia	5	62	14.40
Tampere University of Technology	Finland	5	60	12.00

4.2 Extracted Topics

The STM topic model with 10 topics was the best fitting one according to the held-out likelihood criterion and was selected for analysis. The top word list of each topic can be found in Table 4, and the topics in the table are ordered by the proportion of all document content that they represent. The most prominent topic in our data, representing 16.71% of all document content, is **Design of Pervasive and Mixed Reality Games**. As the history of location-based games is connected to experimentation with design of pervasive and mobile games and other forms of play, often in an academic context using prototypes and controlled studies of games, it is to be expected many publications will reflect on design, implementation and player experiences of these games. For example, [57] discusses design of immersion in pervasive games whereas [13] uses sound design as an element of augmented reality, which is under the umbrella of mixed-reality.

The second most prominent topic is **Education**, corresponding to the second most commonly cited author keyword game-based learning (GBL). For example, [37] discusses how teachers can be involved in designing these type of games.

The third most common topic is **Mobile Application** which relates more specifically to the technologies employed by location-based games and services. For example, [2] introduces "mobile Real-time Kinematics", a refined solution related to GPS (Global Positioning System).

The topic **Urban Space** further focuses on where location-based games are played - primarily (although not always) the urban environment. For example, [23] has introduced a game called *Placemaking* to facilitate participatory urban planning. Often location-based games are framed by researchers and their designers as encouraging social interaction and bringing communities together.

Since location-based games are still relatively new to mainstream audiences, there is a lot of discussion on game production. **Design and Development** is related to, for example, the authoring tools that support making location-based mobile experiences[9]. **Player Studies** is about how users perceive and experience location-based games and media, and their impact on players. One example is [25] which probes the impact of the gamification design called "user score" of the mobile app *Foursquare*.

Pokémon GO is the only specific game within the topics. No other location-based mobile game has attracted such a large audience of players to date, so it makes sense that it would be prominent in academic scholarship even though it is relatively recent (released in 2016). Articles where this topic was prominent studied *Pokémon GO* from perspectives such as: how it affects players' place attachment [41], social behavior [26], and how players experience the game [5]. **Physical Activity** is an essential component of location-based games, since they usually encourage players to walk and explore the environment around them to accomplish their goal. For example,[52] investigates the exercise and health benefits of playing location-based games and [22] discusses how simulations can be used in exploring the available design options for location-based games.

The topic of **Gamification of Cultural Experiences** relates to how different cultural experiences can be gamified through location-based mobile technology. For example, [11,12] enhance museum experiences with location-based games; [29] has developed an authoring platform in order to deliver unique experiences to cultural heritage visitors, and [48] discusses the gamification of tourism through geocaching. The topic **Spatial Data Processing** reflects the technical aspect of how the information (e.g. player's position and movement, data curation) related to location-based games is dealt with. Some works are about platforms used to process this data, from GIS (Geographic Information System) software to crowdsourced mapping platforms like MapQuest[44] or OpenStreetMap[10]. Other works focused on the exploitation of geographic data within the game itself, such as "location" spoofing' in *Pokémon GO*[10].

Table 4. Extracted topics. "Pr(%)" is the proportion of document content represented by a topic, and "Top Words" are its most common words.

Topic	Pr(%)	Top words
Design of Pervasive and Mixed Reality Games	16.71	Game, player, reality, mobile, pervasive, augment, design, play, experience, virtual
Education	13.14	Learn, game, design, mobile, student, educational, use, education, technology, teacher
Mobile Application	13.05	Mobile, application, user, system, use, game, service, information, device, paper
Urban Space	8.80	Game, urban, city, gaming, mobile, technology, social, community, use, new
Design and Development	8.78	Design, tool, author, mobile, support, present, compute, new, will, development
Player Studies	8.69	Study, game, social, geocaching, result, share, user, perceive, group, effect
Pokémon GO	8.32	Pokémon, place, mobile, player, play, medium, social, model, game, experience
Physical Activity	8.28	Game, activity, design, player, physical, use, simulation, child, time, walk
Gamification of Cultural Experiences	7.62	Cultural, experience, mobile, museum, tourism, design, technology, game, narrative, heritage
Spatial Data Processing	6.61	data, game, map, use, lbgs, information, spatial, position, movement, object

4.3   Topic Prevalence over Time

Figure 5 shows the sum of prevalence of topics over time and Fig. 6 shows the average prevalence of topics over time. In a topic model, each topic has a proportion (zero to 100%) of prevalence in each document, and the figures are yearly summaries of the prevalences. The sum of prevalence is the sum of a topic's prevalence over all documents of the year, and can represent the overall volume of content published about the topic, thus its change over time reveals the trend of absolute volume of discussion about the topic. On the other hand, the average prevalence of a topic is the average of document-wise prevalences over publications of the year, and reflects the relative popularity of topics among publications. The average prevalence can be seen as an adjusted topic popularity of the year according to the total number of publications of the year.

The topic **Education** had been popular since 2014 as seen in its average prevalence, the sum of the prevalence had grown and reached a peak in 2017, although due to growing popularity of **Pokémon GO** and other topics, the average prevalence in 2017 is not as high as in some previous years. The average and sum of prevalence of **Education** has a clear decreasing trend since 2017.

Pokémon GO had a growing trend from 2016 and reached a peak in 2017 both in sum of prevalence and average prevalence, likely because *Pokémon GO* was launched in 2016. Even though it probably wasn't discussed in articles before that, other topic words of this category have come up already before 2016.

Design and Development remains present in all years by average prevalence, indicating design of location-based games is not settled and there is continuing need for new design research, in part this may be due to new technologies.

Likewise, **Physical Activity** also has stable average prevalence over time but with a slight increasing trend. The sum of prevalence reaches its peak on 2017 which is corresponding to the trend of total publication volume.

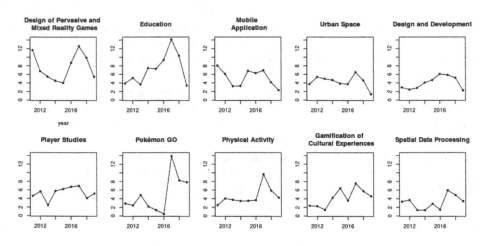

Fig. 5. Sum of topic prevalence over time

4.4 Relationship Between Topics and Citations

Figure 7 shows how the adjusted citation count (according to Eq. 2) interacts with topic prevalence, as extracted from the trained topic model. The STM topic model uses adjusted citation count as a covariate when modeling the text content of documents, and the figure depicts this interaction: the horizontal axis displays how much the topic prevalence of a publication increases or decreases when the publication has one more adjusted citation. Thus, compared to an average

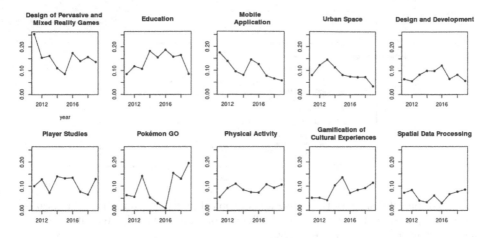

Fig. 6. Average topic prevalence over time

publication, an increase of one adjusted citation tends to happen for publications having around 1% more content of **Pokémon GO**, 1.1% less content of **Mobile Application** and correspondingly for the other topics.

Topics **Urban Space, Education, Spatial Data Processing** and **Design of Pervasive and Mixed Reality Games** lean to higher adjusted citations but not **significantly**. The 95% confidence interval of topics **Gamification of Cultural Experiences, Design and Development, Physical Activity** and **Player Studies** covers the middle but lean to lower adjusted citations.

Education has a positive but not significant effect although the game-based learning (see Fig. 4, right) is the second most cited keyword. The reason might be the accumulation of citations over time, as shown in Fig. 5 there were a considerable amount of publications after 2014, and the citations of the keyword "game-based learning" have then accumulated. The Eq. 2 mitigated this influence, therefore, the effect on adjusted citations is not significant.

5 Discussion

The frequency, prevalence and geographical dispersion of publications in our sample shows the number of publications has been growing over time and it is not only a regional phenomenon. Publications peaked in 2017, although the drop in 2018 might be partly due to delayed indexing as our search was conducted before the end of 2019. The 2017 peak can be partially attributed to the surge of interest in these games following *Pokémon GO*'s release, but there is no clear correlation between this and prevalence of individual topics. Publications in our sample are from a variety of institutions (universities and companies) in different countries, although the U.K. and Germany have a higher proportion of publications than others (and this proportion would likely be higher if weighted by population).

Most topics concern practical aspects of location-based games, such as their design; evaluation of players' experiences; the technologies and data they employ;

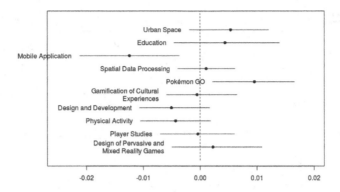

Fig. 7. Graphical display of the differences of topical prevalence on adjusted citations. For each topic the dot shows the mean influence of adding one adjusted citation, and the bars show a 95% confidence interval.

and their application to real-world situations. This reflects that location-based games have been a highly experimental genre as mentioned in Sect. 2 [31, p. 29], many early, seminal location-based games, such as *PacManhattan, Can You See Me Now?* and *Insectopia*, were developed by or in collaboration with research centres: NYU's Big Urban Games program, Nottingham University's Mixed Reality Lab and the E.U.-funded IPerG project, respectively. Similarly, commercial games like *Botfighters* and *Mogi, Item Hunt* were the subject of numerous player studies and have long been noted for groundbreaking design that inspired future location-based games [37,38]. This long-standing association between location-based games, research and design and humanities and social sciences research is particularly evident in the position of **Design of Pervasive and Mixed-Reality Games**, **Design and Development**, **Urban Space**, **Mobile Application** and **Player Studies** among the extracted topics. "Pervasive game", a term developed and popularised in an academic context [46], also ranks highly in both top author-specified and cited keywords. Academic interest in the practical application of location-based games and location-based gamification to other fields is evidenced by the presence of **Education** and **Gamification of Cultural Experiences** in the extracted topics; and keywords like "game-based learning", "mobile learning" and "engagement" that appear in top author-specified and cited keywords. Nevertheless, as gamification has been applied to a wider domain (e.g. healthcare, marketing), we expect that a wider-ranged application can be further explored in the future.

Despite the history of location-based games dating back to the early 2000s, *Pokémon GO* is the only topic about a specific game. This may be unsurprising given its unprecedented popularity, but it does indicate a disproportionate number of publications about the game relative to its brief history. *Can You See Me Now?*, *Botfighters* and *Mogi, Item Hunt* were all released by 2003 and have consistently been cited as canonical location-based games [31,47,50]. *Pokémon GO* is also not the first commercially successful location-based game on a global scale. It was preceded by *Parallel Kingdom* (2008), *Shadow Cities* (2011) and *Ingress* (2012) which, although far less successful, attracted media attention at their release [31, p. 106–112]. *Pokémon GO*'s presence in the top 10 topics indicates that even though these games had between 4–15 years longer to accumulate mentions in articles, the ubiquity of *Pokémon GO* since its release enabled it to surpass them. This underscores the impact of the game in industries and academia, as well as how quickly the research community has responded to the phenomenon of the game - something existing research has already highlighted [42].

Pokémon GO's prominence be due to interest from fields outside the arts, humanities and social sciences (especially game and media studies) and computer science, where most previous location-based game research was situated, such as interest from health and medicine fields [34]. Some publications do not discuss *Pokémon GO* in most of the full text but use it as an example location-based game in the abstract or introduction [3,54]. The popularity of *Pokémon GO* in can enhance the visibility and opportunity of receiving citations.

Conversely, when comparing **Mobile Application** and **Design and Development** to other topics, we note their effect on citation is more negative. This can be attributed to more interest being on other aspects of games than design and development processes. Due to the limitations and constraints in creation of early location-based games and the rapidly changing technologies that support them, technical discussions in early papers are unlikely to remain relevant to the wider community. Also, many papers may discuss game development but refer to it as "game design", reducing prevalence of the "game development" topic. Intriguingly, the topic **Urban Space** has decreased in prevalence (both sum and average) over time, trending downwards since 2017. This coincides with the release of *Pokémon GO*, but we could speculate that as location-based games have become more popular and accessible through smartphone apps, and thus able to be played virtually anywhere with cellular data, discussions about them have become less tethered to "the urban". Although commercial location-based games still often privilege densely populated urban locations, they are less restricted to cities compared with pre-smartphone location-based games, which relied on bespoke technologies and were often limited to specific cities, countries or regions, rather than available to potentially billions of players globally [31, p. 102–106].

6   Conclusions, Limitations and Opportunities

In this research, bibliometric and text analysis were conducted. We found that "location-based games" as a term has been broadening in the research community and entangling with different notions from different fields. This yields a wide-ranged result of keywords and extracted topics. The analysis answered our research questions: for RQ1, the analysis revealed a rising trend of publications up to 2017, and differing contributions in terms of number of publications and citations across researchers, institutions and countries. For RQ2, the text analysis extracted topics from the collected text content across the publications, and revealed clear themes, their temporal trends, as well as their interactions with citations, which were further analyzed and discussed. This research provides an overview of the current state of development and can help researchers gain a general understanding and identify potential future research directions.

We used the Scopus indexing system to gather the articles. We chose Scopus as it allows detailed Boolean queries and assures results represent peer-reviewed work and not for example technical reports. However, there might be some relevant research works not available through Scopus search and not analyzed in this article. This can be solved for instance by combining with other digital libraries such as Google Scholar to expand the result set; however, as this would greatly expand the workload at our data curation stage, we focus here on Scopus and consider an expanded search future work. It is possible to extend the corpus also by using additional search terms such as "mixed-reality game," "locative game, or "augmented-reality game" and merging these with our existing data. Besides, our sample focuses only on English-language publications. We acknowledge that there is an abundance of relevant research works in other languages. The inclusion of literature in other languages is considered a future direction.

The qualitative analysis of text content was assisted by a computational technique (topic modeling). The results were both interesting on their own and supported human interpretation and efficient reading of the documents. We expect such computational methods will become ever more crucial in similar studies.

Our results and discussion illuminated and revealed trends in location-based game research, focusing on quantitative findings. Further qualitative research, such as coding for common themes and terms, could be conducted to reveal other trends: such as the top-mentioned specific games, genres and types of games, technologies they employ and disciplines where they are discussed. An even richer discourse analysis could examine how the discourse around these games has evolved over time and the balance of positive versus negative framing about their impact. This type of analysis is beyond the scope of this paper, however, given the aforementioned resource constraints. Instead, we signal it here as an avenue for future research building on the findings of this paper.

Acknowledgment. This work was supported by Academy of Finland decisions 312395, 313748 and 327352.

References

1. Iperg. http://web.archive.org/web/20141028144114/www.pervasive-gaming.org/index.php. Accessed 29 Nov 2019
2. Alanen, K., Wirola, L., Kappi, J., Syrjarinne, J.: Inertial sensor enhanced mobile RTK solution using low-cost assisted GPS receivers and internet-enabled cellular phones. In: 2006 IEEE/ION Position, Location, And Navigation Symposium, pp. 920–926. IEEE (2006)
3. Alavesa, P., et al.: City knights: spatial realism and memorability of virtual game scenes in pervasive gameplay. In: 2017 9th International Conference on Virtual Worlds and Games for Serious Applications (VS-Games), pp. 71–78. IEEE (2017)

4. Alha, K.: The imbalanced state of free-to-play game research: a literature review. In: DiGRA Conference (2019)
5. Alha, K., Koskinen, E., Paavilainen, J., Hamari, J.: Why do people play location-based augmented reality games: a study on Pokémon GO. Comput. Hum. Behav. **93**, 114–122 (2019)
6. Benford, S., et al.: Coping with uncertainty in a location-based game. IEEE Pervasive Comput. **2**(3), 34–41 (2003)
7. Blei, D.M., Ng, A.Y., Jordan, M.I.: Latent Dirichlet allocation. J. Mach. Learn. Res. **3**(Jan), 993–1022 (2003)
8. Bragge, J., Storgårds, J.: Profiling academic research on digital games using text mining tools. In: DiGRA Conference (2007)
9. Brundell, P., Koleva, B., Wetzel, R.: Supporting the design of location-based experiences by creative individuals. In: 11th International Workshop on Semantic and Social Media Adaptation and Personalization (SMAP), pp. 112–116. IEEE (2016)
10. Celino, I.: Geospatial dataset curation through a location-based game. Semant. Web **6**(2), 121–130 (2015)
11. Cesário, V., Coelho, A., Nisi, V.: Enhancing museums' experiences through games and stories for young audiences. In: Nunes, N., Oakley, I., Nisi, V. (eds.) ICIDS 2017. LNCS, vol. 10690, pp. 351–354. Springer, Cham (2017). https://doi.org/10. 1007/978-3-319-71027-3_41
12. Cesário, V., Trindade, R., Olim, S., Nisi, V.: Memories of Carvalhal's palace: haunted encounters, a museum experience to engage teenagers. In: Lamas, D., Loizides, F., Nacke, L., Petrie, H., Winckler, M., Zaphiris, P. (eds.) INTERACT 2019. LNCS, vol. 11749, pp. 554–557. Springer, Cham (2019). https://doi.org/10. 1007/978-3-030-29390-1_36
13. Chatzidimitris, T., Gavalas, D., Michael, D.: SoundPacman: audio augmented reality in location-based games. In: 2016 18th Mediterranean Electrotechnical Conference (MELECON), pp. 1–6. IEEE (2016)
14. Çiftci, S.: Trends of serious games research from 2007 to 2017: a bibliometric analysis. J. Educ. Train. Stud. **6**(2), 18–27 (2018)
15. Cooper, H.E., Camic, P.M., Long, D.L., Panter, A., Rindskopf, D.E., Sher, K.J.: APA Handbook of Research Methods in Psychology, Vol 1: Foundations, Planning, Measures, and Psychometrics. American Psychological Association, Washington, D.C. (2012)
16. Evans, M.S.: A computational approach to qualitative analysis in large textual datasets. PloS One **9**(2), e87908 (2014)
17. Farman, J.: Mobile Interface Theory: Embodied Space and Locative Media. Routledge, Abingdon (2013)
18. Flanagan, M.: Critical Play: Radical Game Design. MIT Press, Cambridge (2009)
19. Flintham, M., et al.: Where on-line meets on the streets: experiences with mobile mixed reality games. In: Proceedings of the SIGCHI Conference on Human Factors in Computing Systems, pp. 569–576. ACM (2003)
20. Foursquare: Foursquare City Guide (2009)
21. Fragoso, S., Reis, B.M.S.: Ludic re-enchantment and the power of locative games: a case study of the game ingress. In: Abdelnour-Nocera, J., Strano, M., Ess, C., Van der Velden, M., Hrachovec, H. (eds.) CaTaC 2016. IAICT, vol. 490, pp. 131–148. Springer, Cham (2016). https://doi.org/10.1007/978-3-319-50109-3_9
22. Heinz, T., Schlieder, C.: Addressing spatio-temporal geogame relocation issues using design evaluation heuristics and agent-based simulation. In: 2019 11th International Conference on Virtual Worlds and Games for Serious Applications (VS-Games), pp. 1–4. IEEE (2019)

23. Innocent, T.: Play about place: placemaking in location-based game design. In: Proceedings of the 4th Media Architecture Biennale Conference, pp. 137–143 (2018)
24. Innocent, T., Leorke, D.: Heightened intensity: reflecting on player experiences in Wayfinder live. Convergence **25**(1), 18–39 (2019)
25. Jin, L., Zhang, K., Lu, J., Lin, Y.R.: Towards understanding the gamification upon users' scores in a location-based social network. Multimedia Tools Appl. **75**(15), 8895–8919 (2016). https://doi.org/10.1007/s11042-014-2317-3
26. Kari, T., Arjoranta, J., Salo, M.: Behavior change types with Pokémon GO. In: Proceedings of the 12th International Conference on the Foundations of Digital Games, pp. 1–10 (2017)
27. Keogh, B.: Pokémon Go, the novelty of nostalgia, and the ubiquity of the smartphone. Mobile Media Commun. **5**(1), 38–41 (2017)
28. Koskinen, E., Leorke, D., Alha, K., Paavilainen, J.: Player experiences in location-based games: memorable moments with Pokémon GO. In: Geroimenko, V. (ed.) Augmented Reality Games I, pp. 95–116. Springer, Cham (2019). https://doi.org/10.1007/978-3-030-15616-9_7
29. Kotsopoulos, K.I., Chourdaki, P., Tsolis, D., Antoniadis, R., Pavlidis, G., Assimakopoulos, N.: An authoring platform for developing smart apps which elevate cultural heritage experiences: a system dynamics approach in gamification. J. Ambient Intell. Human. Comput. 1–17 (2019). https://doi.org/10.1007/s12652-019-01505-w
30. Lantz, F.: Big urban game. In: Space Time Play, pp. 390–391 (2007)
31. Leorke, D.: Location-Based Gaming: Play in Public Space. Springer, Singapore (2019). https://doi.org/10.1007/978-981-13-0683-9
32. Licoppe, C., Inada, Y.: Emergent uses of a multiplayer location-aware mobile game: the interactional consequences of mediated encounters. Mobilities **1**(1), 39–61 (2006)
33. Licoppe, C., Inada, Y.: Geolocalized technologies, location-aware communities, and personal territories: the Mogi case. J. Urban Technol. **15**(3), 5–24 (2008)
34. Ma, B.D., et al.: Pokémon GO and physical activity in Asia: multilevel study. J. Med. Internet Res. **20**(6), e217 (2018)
35. Martí-Parreño, J., Méndez-Ibáñez, E., Alonso-Arroyo, A.: The use of gamification in education: a bibliometric and text mining analysis. J. Comput. Assist. Learn. **32**(6), 663–676 (2016)
36. McGonigal, J.E.: This might be a game: ubiquitous play and performance at the turn of the twenty-first century. Ph.D. thesis, University of California, Berkeley (2006)
37. Melero, J., Hernández-Leo, D., Blat, J.: Teachers can be involved in the design of location-based learning games. In: Proceedings of the 6th International Conference on Computer Supported Education, vol. 3, pp. 179–186 (2014)
38. Mimno, D., Wallach, H.M., Talley, E., Leenders, M., McCallum, A.: Optimizing semantic coherence in topic models. In: Proceedings of the Conference on Empirical Methods in Natural Language Processing, pp. 262–272. Association for Computational Linguistics (2011)
39. Montola, M., Stenros, J., Waern, A.: Pervasive Games: Theory and Design. CRC Press, Boca Raton (2009)
40. Nikolenko, S.I., Koltcov, S., Koltsova, O.: Topic modelling for qualitative studies. J. Inf. Sci. **43**(1), 88–102 (2017)
41. Oleksy, T., Wnuk, A.: Catch them all and increase your place attachment! the role of location-based augmented reality games in changing people-place relations. Comput. Hum. Behav. **76**, 3–8 (2017)

42. Paavilainen, J., Korhonen, H., Alha, K., Stenros, J., Koskinen, E., Mayra, F.: The Pokémon GO experience: a location-based augmented reality mobile game goes mainstream. In: Proceedings of the 2017 CHI Conference on Human Factors in Computing Systems, pp. 2493–2498. ACM (2017)
43. Palmer, S., Popat, S.: Dancing in the streets-a design case study. Interactions (New York) **15**(3), 55–59 (2008)
44. Pulsifer, P.L., Caquard, S., Taylor, D.R.F.: Toward a new generation of community atlases-the cybercartographic atlas of Antarctica. In: Cartwright, W., Peterson, M.P., Gartner, G. (eds.) Multimedia Cartography, pp. 195–216. Springer, Berlin (2007). https://doi.org/10.1007/978-3-540-36651-5_14
45. Roberts, M.E., Stewart, B.M., Airoldi, E.M.: A model of text for experimentation in the social sciences. J. Am. Stat. Assoc. **111**(515), 988–1003 (2016)
46. de Souza e Silva, A.: Alien revolt (2005–2007): a case study of the first location-based mobile game in brazil. IEEE Technol. Soc. Mag. **27**(1), 18–28 (2008)
47. de Souza e Silva, A., Hjorth, L.: Playful urban spaces: a historical approach to mobile games. Simul. Gaming **40**(5), 602–625 (2009)
48. Skinner, H., Sarpong, D., White, G.R.: Meeting the needs of the millennials and generation Z: gamification in tourism through geocaching. J. Tour. Futures **4**, 93–104 (2018)
49. Sobel, K., Bhattacharya, A., Hiniker, A., Lee, J.H., Kientz, J.A., Yip, J.C.: It wasn't really about the Pokémon: parents' perspectives on a location-based mobile game. In: Proceedings of the 2017 CHI Conference on Human Factors in Computing Systems, pp. 1483–1496. ACM (2017)
50. Sotamaa, O.: All the world's a botfighter stage: notes on location-based multi-user gaming. In: CGDC Conference. Citeseer (2002)
51. Spallazzo, D., Mariani, I.: Location-Based Mobile Games. SAST. Springer, Cham (2018). https://doi.org/10.1007/978-3-319-75256-3
52. Stanley, K.G., Livingston, I., Bandurka, A., Kapiszka, R., Mandryk, R.L.: Pinizoro: a GPS-based exercise game for families. In: Proceedings of the International Academic Conference on the Future of Game Design and Technology, pp. 243–246 (2010)
53. Stokes, B., Dols, S., Hill, A.: Cities remix a playful platform: prominent experiments to embed Pokémon GO, from open streets to neighborhood libraries. American University, Washington, DC (2018)
54. Tregel, T., Raymann, L., Göbel, S., Steinmetz, R.: Geodata classification for automatic content creation in location-based games. In: Alcañiz, M., Göbel, S., Ma, M., Fradinho Oliveira, M., Baalsrud Hauge, J., Marsh, T. (eds.) JCSG 2017. LNCS, vol. 10622, pp. 212–223. Springer, Cham (2017). https://doi.org/10.1007/978-3-319-70111-0_20
55. Vella, K., Johnson, D., Peever, N., Cheng, V.W.S., Davenport, T., Mitchell, J.: Motivating engagement with a wellbeing app using video games and gamification (2017)
56. Waern, A., et al.: IPerG position paper. In: Workshop on Gaming Applications in Pervasive Computing Environments, Second International Conference on Pervasive Computing: Pervasive 2004, April 2004
57. Waern, A., Montola, M., Stenros, J.: The three-sixty illusion: designing for immersion in pervasive games. In: Proceedings of the SIGCHI Conference on Human Factors in Computing Systems, pp. 1549–1558 (2009)

A Matrix for Gamifying Development Workshops

Kristina Maria Madsen[(✉)] [ID] and Mette Hjorth Rasmussen [ID]

Aalborg University Business School, Fibigerstræde 2, 9000 Aalborg, Denmark
{krma,mhl}@business.aau.dk

Abstract. The interest in potentials of gamification for innovating businesses through collaboration and innovative development in businesses has been an ongoing topic in gamification research for the last decade. This based on the theoretical notion of gamification's potential to facilitate "third space communication" and games capability to improve user engagement in non-game settings by transforming this space into a "magic circle" of gameplay for innovative thinking. In this paper an initial matrix is presented for discussing the parameters of gamifying development sessions or workshops conducted throughout innovation and development processes. The purpose of the matrix is to visualize the parameters involved in deciding the level of gamification for a workshop setting. Thus, a tool for identifying a balance in implementing game mechanics, one that can serve to support and facilitate innovative processes rather than purely creating and playing a game for its own sake. Therefore, through this paper the parameters of the matrix and gamifying facilitation of innovative development processes through gameplay, is discussed and presented. This is followed by the exemplification of use and application of the gamification matrix through four gamified workshops.

Keywords: Gamification · Innovation · Workshop design

1 Games as a Workshop Facilitation Approach

The interest in the potentials of gamification for innovating businesses through participant innovation [1–3] or for collaborative and innovative development in businesses [4, 5] has been an ongoing topic in gamification or "games with a purpose" [6] research for the last decade. Fundamentally, this approach demonstrates the potential of game mechanics and associated structures to enhance the motivational affordances of collaborative work [6, 7], which can facilitate innovation. Thus, when discussing development workshops in this paper, we are broadly referring development sessions conducted throughout innovation and development processes in businesses, it being design of a business or concept or products within a business.

Facilitating innovative development processes can be complex. There are many ways to approach development processes because, as Brown [8] describes, innovative design is a product of interdisciplinary team efforts, where *"all of us are smarter than any of*

A. Brooks et al. (Eds.): ArtsIT 2020, LNICST 367, pp. 180–197, 2021.
https://doi.org/10.1007/978-3-030-73426-8_10

us" which is key to unlocking the creative power of any organization. Cross [9] points to the fact that the participants of interdisciplinary collaborations assume different roles in development processes rather than just representing their profession. They assume a social role in the group dynamic as e.g. a facilitator, one who takes charge, etc. As Brown [8] describes it, it is through group dynamics that we can distinguish between the terms multidisciplinary and interdisciplinary. Interdisciplinarity occurs when multiple professions collectively take ownership of ideas rather than advocating for their own respective domains.

Sanders and Stappers [10] propose generative tools as an approach to creating a shared language for the participating stakeholders to communicate and discuss ideas, requirements, potentials, limitations, and dreams. Sanders and Stappers describe generative design methods and research as a way to provide this shared language: *"Generative design research gives people a language with which they can imagine and express their ideas and dreams for future experiences. These ideas and dreams can, in turn, inform and inspire other stakeholders in the design and development process"* [10]. By approaching a collaborative development process through generative workshops, stakeholders can be supported in developing a common interdisciplinary language, one which can make their different ways of seeing, thinking, and doing come together in agreement – from multidisciplinary to interdisciplinary. Gudiksen and Inlove [4] approach the generative toolbox idea through the relevance of gamification and game design as a facilitating method for collaborative and innovative development in businesses. Gudiksen and Inlove [4] propose that games and game-based design can facilitate better communication, break down silos and engage staff. Thus, games can be used as a method for facilitating development processes and initiating shared language between participants.

The logic of using games, or more specifically, gamification, for facilitating innovative development processes is based on multiple perspectives. First of all this paper builds on Deterding et al.'s [6] definition of gamification as being an "umbrella term for the use of video game elements (rather than full-fledged games) to improve user experience and user engagement in non-game services and applications". Furthermore, the logic of using gamification is based on how games can act as a space between spaces through the concept of "third space communication" [4, 11] and "the magic circle" of games [12]. The "Third Space" can be described as the space that exists between two or more participants with different professional domains, as visualized below in Fig. 1.

Each participant is unique in their knowledge and background, and in their history and specialized language, which they bring into a development process. With these different backgrounds, confusion and misunderstandings can arise between the participants in a development process. The argument is therefore that the third space offers a way to facilitate and mediate between participants through the use of generative tools, by which participants can work toward a common goal.

"The Magic Circle" is a core concept in game design that can be explained as the space in which a game takes place [12]. The magic circle formalizes the game space, as you can see visualized in Fig. 2 below, in which game rules create a special set of meanings for the players in the game setting and guide the game. In the magic circle, the players accept the boundaries of the game rules in order to experience the pleasure a game can afford.

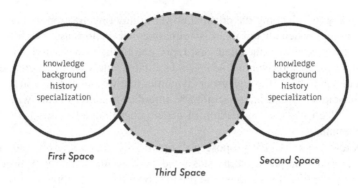

First Space

Second Space

Third Space

Fig. 1. The figure shows first, second, and third spaces. The "Third Space" is the space that exists between two or more participants, e.g., the first and second spaces, which have different professional domains. The figure was redrawn based on [4] and its third space figure (p. 8).

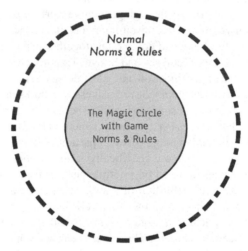

Fig. 2. The Magic Circle is the circle with the solid line, indicating a game situation with norms and rules that work to create a separate space from that of the norms and rules of everyday lives, which is visualized as the dotted circle.

The purpose of presenting the concept of both the third space and the magic circle is to start exploring the potentials of games and gamification as the facilitator of the third space. This is based on the argument that bringing participants together in a workshop setting may be insufficient when striving for an innovative development process; a structure is required to engage in an innovative process whereby participants can be supported into engaging in a process that will enable the transition from multidisciplinary to interdisciplinary [8]. In other words, the argument is that a collaborative setting that includes the gamification of tools, methods and techniques can support stakeholders in developing a common interdisciplinary language [4, 10] and heighten the potential for innovation.

The idea of defining the use of games and game elements for facilitating collaborative development processes is not a new notion but rather builds on past research. As mentioned in the introduction, Gudiksen and Inlove [4] have published an extensive work on the "Gamification for Business,". Thus, games can be used as a method for facilitating development processes and initiating a shared language between participants. In a non-game workshop context, Sanders and Stappers [10] have compiled an explicit introduction and guidelines for conducting generative workshops that aim at innovating through the front end of design processes. Even though Sanders and Stappers [10] do not talk about gamification or games in regard to development workshops, they present foundational knowledge on how to use generative workshops as a research method to unlock creativity and innovation, which is a relevant framing for both game and non-game workshops. Both Gudiksen and Inlove [4] and Sanders and Stappers [10] focus on the collaborative aspect of creating a shared language through a third space. The difference lies in Gudiksen and Inlove [4] referencing gamification and games, and in Sanders and Stappers [10] mentioning generative tools as an approach to creating this third space and a shared language.

Gudiksen and Inlove [4] have compiled a wide range of gamification types for business games, discussing their potentials and game mechanics and structures, which they base on [4] the framed challenges and structures of gamification for business. Games as drivers for innovation is not limited to the previous examples. Patricio [2], presents a study on the game IdeaChef as an approach to address innovation challenges; or Madsen and Krishnasamy [13], who present a game as a dialogue tool for designing museum experiences. Lastly, Thomsen, Sort, and Kristiansen [14] have developed a set of booster cards as an inspirational and ideate tool to innovate business model configurations. These games have different contexts, purposes, levels of gamification, and facilitation, described in different ways. Nevertheless, the discussion of why which level of gamification and facilitation is chosen for the level of innovation is not clear.

There are examples of frameworks for understanding and creating gamified processes, but the connection between the level of gamification and facilitation chosen for the level of innovation is rather vague. Patrício, Moreira, and Zurlo [15] present a study exploring the relationship between gamification and the early stage of innovation in which they categorize the dimensions of gamification into early innovation, environment, game elements, and motivation; and further, through a range of case studies, they explore these dimensions based on the game elements, tools, challenges, and outcomes.

This goes in line with Gudiksen and Inlove's [4] presentation of the challenges and structures of business games. Roth, Schneckenberg, and Tsai [16] even conclude that research on gamification needs to balance the differing expectations of innovation while not losing coherence as a theoretical reference point. They also question the dark side of gamification for innovation and ask whether there is currently too much use of gamification.

Therefore, what we propose in this paper is how we can balance the gamification of third spaces so that the purpose of the game mechanics is to facilitate an innovative process rather than playing a game for its own sake. Thus, the question is asked: Which parameters are essential in balancing the level of gamification, and how can these parameters be transformed into a tool for defining and creating gamified innovative processes?

The purpose here being to create a matrix, that can support decision making in workshop planning for innovative development and for designing the right game fidelity for a given setting.

2 Gamification Fidelity of Workshops

When we discuss appropriate levels of gamification to support the facilitation of workshops, the discussion is built on the understanding that types of workshops can be defined based on a scale from dialogue to gamification, as visualized below in Fig. 3, depicting the gamification fidelity of workshops. Thus, different types of workshops are defined depending on the desired participant interaction in the workshop situation.

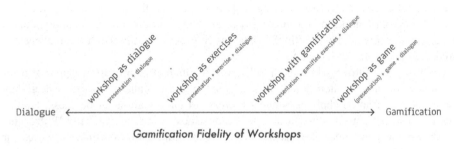

Gamification Fidelity of Workshops

Fig. 3. Gamification fidelity in workshops from dialogue to gamification.

The first type of workshop is *workshop as dialogue*, which is placed closest to the *dialogue* end of the fidelity scale since it is characterized by being mainly founded in a dialogue, perhaps as a round table discussion based on a presentation. These types of workshops are highly dependent on the facilitator to take charge of the dialogue and to ensure that the setting is fruitful, depending on the desired outcome. This type of workshop often will not have any specific methods planned, and therefore it will not be relevant to introduce game elements on this level.

Moving a step further on the fidelity scale to *workshop as exercises*, an element of exercises is added to the workshop, but is not gamified. Here Sanders and Stappers' [10] generative toolbox approach can be rather relevant to facilitating the workshop. The addition of exercises requires a higher level of engagement and interaction from the participants, and the facilitator's role changes because, compared to the first type of workshop, the facilitator is now able to activate the planned exercises instead of controlling the dialogue, let the method support the participants' creativity and dialogue.

The third type of workshop, *workshop with gamification*, is characterized by the exercise element being gamified through the application of game mechanics as a facilitating approach for driving engagement and interaction between participants. As with *workshop as exercises*, the facilitator's role is to frame, guide, and activate the planned exercises and let the gamified method "do its magic". This allow the participants' creativity and dialogue to evolve. It is on this and the next workshop level that Gudiksen and Inlove's [4] approach to gamification for business is grounded; namely using gamified sessions to break down challenges in businesses.

The final type of workshop on the fidelity scale is *workshop as game,* which is characterized by the entire workshop being designed as a game. At this level of gamification, the workshop becomes a full *magic circle* [12]. The workshop or game session is a tight ruleset and guides the participants through the content of the workshop in the process of generating the desired outcome through designed challenges and quests. At this level, a facilitator and the introductory presentation should become irrelevant because the game rules, as with a regular game, should be self-explanatory and allow the participants or players to create the magic circle of a game session through the rule book.

It is important to stress that this list can be further developed and nuanced, but the purpose here is to outline where and which types of workshops we are focusing on for this paper, as well as to make clear that it is not in all situations that it is relevant to apply gamification or create a full game. To be able to make an informed decision on which type of workshop is relevant for a given situation, it is evident that when initiating a design process for a gamified workshop, some basic parameters need to be clarified before deciding on which level of gamification is relevant for a given situation to achieve the desired outcome. This is not just a decision on whether or not a gamified workshop is desired, but also on whether or not it is appropriate for a given purpose. Therefore, with this paper, we strive to create a matrix that will help avoid falling into "the dark side of gamification" [16].

3 The Parameters of a Gamification Matrix

In this section, we highlight parameters that are important to consider when using gamification as an approach for facilitating innovative development processes while, at the same time, recognizing that games are highly complex, multilayered systems. We have extracted the core parameters of designing/planning a workshop setting that are facilitated through different levels of game mechanics. These are converted into a matrix, presented at the end of this section, consisting of three parameters: *purpose and outcome, framing context and process,* and lastly, *game fidelity.* The matrix is intended as a framing tool for designing workshops, providing the workshop designer with a frame to make deliberate decisions on the level of gamification depending on context, purpose, and requirements.

3.1 Purpose and Outcome

Purpose and outcome, which is closely connected to the identification of challenges, such as those presented by Gudiksen and Inlove [4] and Patrício, Moreira, and Zurlo [15]. In all generative processes lies a purpose and intended outcome, which are often based on a challenge that is intended to be explored and solved through various processes. The desired outcome of a process or workshop is essential for deciding how and if gamification can be relevant. The axis for *purpose and outcome* differentiates between *mapping* and *innovation* (Fig. 4). This is because the workshop setting (gamified or not) that we are discussing in this paper is gamification's effect in innovative development processes for businesses.

Fig. 4. The Purpose and Outcome axis spanning from *innovation* to *mapping*.

Mapping in this context is understood as defining or visualizing a current state – the *"as is"* situation – in a given organization. This is often researched and mapped in the early stages of a design process, such as empathizing [8, 17]. Thus, mapping is a process of defining and agreeing on what the current state is for the participants and what the challenges and potentials are for the organization. Mapping is part of the empathizing stage of the design process and an important part of understanding on what foundation to innovate. Therefore, a gamified workshop can be just as relevant to, for instance, uncover a business' potentials and flaws, as it can be for exploring innovative endeavors.

The counterpart to mapping in this matrix is *innovation*, understood as developing or changing the existing *"as is"* situation of the company to a new *"to be"* situation depending on the purpose of the development processes. If innovation is the desired outcome, the workshop setting will often be determined later in the design process, such as in the ideation stage of the process [8, 17]. Innovation can take many shapes and assume different levels, from incremental to radical [18, 19], which is why it is important to be aware of the desired outcome before deciding on the level of gamification, since there is a difference in the way that we approach a workshop situation when striving for incremental or radical innovation. If we strive for incremental innovation, knowing the *as is* might need to be incorporated into the workshop game; whereas if the goal is radical innovation, the workshop game should be more focused on exploring out-of-the-box ideas. But the different shapes and levels of innovation is also why the axes between innovation and mapping need to be dynamic, since they should be able to incorporate all levels of innovation.

Thus, there are multiple levels of purpose and outcome, when talking about gamifying a workshop, but this axis is meant for discussing the desired outcome when using gamification as a driver for the workshop session as part of achieving the larger purpose of the development process. Therefore, the workshop designer needs to ask: What is the purpose of using gamification as an approach for this workshop session? What is the desired outcome? Are we striving to use game elements to encourage creativity and push participants out of their comfort zone to explore innovative perspectives? Or is it rather an approach to helping along a specific mapping process, one for which we need to unlock some specific knowledge and create this magic circle that needs to be realized before we can start innovating?

3.2 Framing Context and Process

The second parameter and axis; *Framing Context and Process,* is closely connected to the type of workshop that is desired for a given situation, as discussed in Sect. 2. This parameter requires a discussion on the context and process intended for the gamified workshop in order to determine which level of facilitation is desired for the workshop, since this is unequivocally connected to the level of gamification needed. If we want a workshop that is non-facilitated, it needs a strong set of rules and mechanics for the participants to be able to play. Whereas if the game is highly dependent on facilitation, then game mechanics can be more dynamic and simple because there is a facilitator to help the process along. Therefore, this framing context and process axis differentiate between facilitated gameplay and non-facilitated gameplay (Fig. 5). Since this paper is based on Sanders and Stappers' [10] and Gudiksen and Inlove's [4] framing of generative tools, workshop approaches, and gamification for business, it is assumed that whenever the purpose of a workshop is innovation some level of facilitation is required to achieve a co-creative space for creativity between participants holding multible professions to achieve the desired interdiciplinary outcome.

Fig. 5. Framing Context and Process axis spanning from *facilitated* to *non-facilitated gameplay*.

At facilitated gameplay the facilitators role is not control the dialogue but to frame, guide, and activate the planned gamified exercises and let the gamified method facilitate the participants' creativity and allow the dialogue to evolve. The facilitator can help if there are misunderstandings, the progression slows, or disagreements occur. As a gamemaster, the facilitator can keep an objective position and let the participants unfold their creativity. With non-facilitated gameplay, a facilitator and introductory presentation become irrelevant, because the game rules, as with a regular game, should be self-explanatory. Thus, a workshop session at this extremity should be solely facilitated through the game rules which guides the participants through the content of the workshop in the process of generating the desired outcome through specific challenges and quests. Apart from the extremities of the axis, it can be argued that somewhere in the middle is a level of co-creation. Here the designer/researcher/facilitator becomes an active participant in the development workshop and not a mediator [10].

There are multiple levels of framing context and process, when talking about gamifying a workshop, but this axis is meant for discussing what role the workshop designer needs to assume in the workshop session and is based here on to what extent gamification is necessary as a driver or facilitator for the workshop session. Therefore, the workshop designer needs to ask: What is the context in which the workshop session is intended? Where in a development process is it intended to be played? Who are the participants? What are the roles of the different stakeholders? Is it necessary to have a facilitator, or can a game facilitate the desired outcome?

3.3 Game Fidelity

This leads us to the last axis and, for this paper, the most central one, *Game Fidelity*. The game fidelity axis is highly connected to the gamification fidelity of workshops as presented in Sect. 2 with Fig. 3. Here, the presented game fidelity axis represents the second half of the gamification fidelity of workshops (Fig. 3), which contains the two levels of workshops that entail levels of gamification. Apart from this, the axis is based on Deterding et al.'s [6, 7] definitions of gamification versus games. In *From Game*

Design Elements to Gamefulness: Defining "Gamification" [7], they present a figure (p. 13) that entails a vertical axis from *game* to *play* and a horizontal axis from *whole* to *parts*. In the top *game* part of the figure, they differentiate between a *whole* game as being *(serious) games* and a design with game *parts* as *gameful design (gamification)*. Therefore, based on Deterding et al. [7] and our gamification fidelity figure, this *Game Fidelity* axis differentiates between *gamification* and *game* (Fig. 6).

Gamification ←――――――――――――――――――――――――――――――→ Game

Fig. 6. The Game Fidelity axis spanning from *gamification* to *game*.

The right extremity of the *game fidelity* scale is *game,* which is characterized by an entire workshop being designed as a whole game. With this level of game mechanics, the workshop is no longer just a workshop using game mechanics but also becomes a full *magic circle* [12] of a game, one that facilitates the workshop or game session through a tight ruleset and guides the participants through the content of the workshop in the process of generating the desired outcome through specific challenges and quests. These types of games are what Deterding et al. [7] describe as (serious) games, because when using games in a business or development process, the game's purpose is no longer just for the sake of the game but also to achieve the goal of creating or getting something out of the gameplay. Furthermore, as described earlier, at this level of game fidelity, facilitation should become irrelevant.

At the other end of the scale we have *gamification,* which is characterized by a workshop session possessing various gamified elements through the application of game mechanics as a facilitating approach for driving engagement and interaction between participants. This level is also called *gameful play* in Deterding et al. [7], and it is defined by a design incorporating game parts. Thus, this level mimics a magic circle [12] to take advantage of the gamified method and let it "do its magic" by breaking down barriers [4] between participants and encouraging creativity and dialogue. Furthermore, as described earlier, at this level of game fidelity, a facilitator's role becomes to frame, guide, and activate the planned gamified exercises and not to control the dialogue.

Thus, there are multiple levels of game fidelity that need to be considered when talking about gamifying a workshop. This axis is meant for discussing which level of game fidelity is relevant when the workshop designers have decided on the other parameters of the gamified workshop.

Therefore, the workshop designer needs to ask; Which level of gamification is necessary to achieve the desired level of facilitation and outcome? What game mechanics [12] are relevant? What game mechanics are necessary to create the desired magic circle [12] around this third space [4]? Furthermore, it is relevant to consider whether the level of desired facilitation is unequivocally connected to the level of gamification needed in a workshop setting. The thought here is that the more unfacilitated a workshop can be, the more game-like the workshop game should be, with well-defined rules, mechanics, and artifacts that create a strong magic circle around the workshop and thereby make the process clear and approachable. This is in contrast to a highly facilitated workshop setting, in which game mechanics can be used as creativity drivers in the workshop setting.

3.4 The Gamification Matrix

With the three axes and parameters presented and described, this section will present the gamification matrix (Fig. 7) for innovative development workshops.

The matrix thus summarizes the parameters that should be considered when designing gamified workshops and consists of the three axes visualized in the above three sections (Figs. 4–6). The gamification matrix is intended to provide a frame and tool for workshop designers to discuss the combination of the three axes. It is based on the desired game fidelity, outcome, and level of facilitation provided for a workshop with a customer, participants, or company that want a gameful design for their development process.

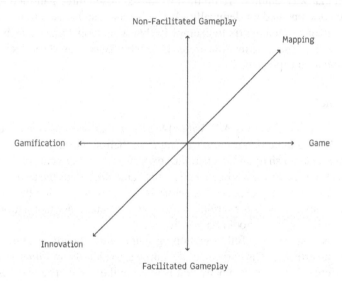

Fig. 7. The full matrix composed of the three axes: *game fidelity, purpose and outcome,* and *framing context and process.*

It is essential to find a balance between these three parameters, as discussed earlier in this paper, to avoid ending up on "the dark side of gamification" [16]. We argue that it is important for workshop designers to ask the overarching questions: What is the desired outcome of the innovation workshop? Why is gamification or a whole game the right approach for this specific development process? Where in the development process is gamification relevant based on the desired outcome – is it for mapping or innovation? It is also necessary to go into depth about each parameter with the questions described for each axis before gamifying a workshop.

In this section, we have outlined the gamification matrix and described the foundation of the different parameters that are relevant to consider before designing a gamified workshop. This might be novel for experienced workshop designers, but with the continued interest in using gamification for innovation and development processes in business [1–6], it is crucial to have a framework to explain and discuss the parameters, limitations, and potentials of gamification with a business that wants to embark on a gamification adventure so that it can create a gameful design that fits with the desired outcome and avoids using gamification for the sake of gamification.

4 Game Cases

In this section, we will exemplify the use of the gamification matrix through the analysis of three existing games that are placed into the matrix and, lastly, a use case for which the matrix has already been used for framing a workshop game design. By looking at already existing games for innovation development processes, it is possible to place them in the matrix by looking at their purpose, the game mechanics they used, and the level of facilitation that was required. To do this, we have chosen three gamified approaches that have been documented academically [4, 13, 14] and can be used to visualize three different placements in the matrix to exemplify that workshop games vary between the parameters. Lastly, a use case that illustrates how the matrix is used for deciding on the level of gamification is presented.

4.1 Add Value

The first game presented here is *Add Value* [4, 20], which is a customer journey tool. Companies rely on unique opportunities to improve their services to customers. Therefore, the game seeks to sharpen the customer experience – where can value be gained, and where can time and resources be saved? At the same time, does the customers get the experience and service they expect? The game is designed to provide the players with insight into customers' needs for service, an overview of customer interactions with the company, and where efforts should be prioritized.

The game is designed as a fully functioning game with a board, a set of clear rules, steps to take, and artifacts. The purpose of the game is to identify, or rather *map*, the customer's experience of a given company that is playing the game. The game is designed so that it can be replayed multiple times to test different customer segments and can be repeated throughout the development process. The game is offered as both a facilitated and a non-facilitated game. Since it takes shape as a fully functioning game to buy, the exemplification used in the following matrix is the game without facilitation. This combination of elements places the *Add Value* game in the top right corner of the gamification matrix (Fig. 8).

Mapping: This game is placed at the furthest extremity of the purpose axis by mapping, since the *Add Value* game seeks to map customer journeys for a business segments. *Non-facilitated*: On the context and process axis, the game is placed high up close to non-facilitation, since the game is a fully functioning game that is facilitated by a rulebook rather than a facilitator (person).. This leads us to the last axis: game fidelity. *Add Value* is placed at the right extremity of the axis, since it is a fully functioning game that can be played for mapping customer journeys without facilitation.

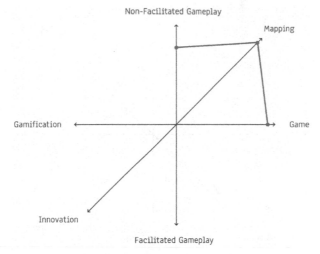

Fig. 8. The matrix with *Add Value* placed mainly in the top right corner, as a *non-facilitated mapping game.*

4.2 Our Museum Game

The *Our Museum Game* [13] is designed as a game for the innovation of interactive museum communication. The game is intended as a user-centered collaborative dialogue game, one that brings together different professions around the game to discuss new ways to communicate to their users based on the users' challenges. The *Our Museum Game* [13] uses game mechanics to drive and facilitate the progression and ideation throughout the game while being supported by questions to drive dialogue.

The game consists of a game board, a clear set of rules, and multiple game mechanics, such as time constraints, tokens, and roles [13]. The *Our Museum Game* uses these mechanics to guide participants through three design stages: *define, design,* and *evaluate,* thereby facilitating and visualizing a process of ideas, discussions, and choices rather than being an actual game. The game requires a facilitator with design knowledge to introduce the purpose and foundation of the game while being able to support the participants through the processes by answering questions, since the time constraints are tight compared to the complexity of the game. There is a ruleset and instructions for the game, which to some extent can be facilitated by the game or by an appointed gamemaster. But to achieve the full extent of the game, it needs facilitation. The game can be played multiple times or at different stages of the design process, either with specific challenges or just to explore potentials. This means that the *Our Museum Game* is placed in the far bottom of the purpose axis but closer to the middle on both the context and fidelity scales, as can be seen below in Fig. 9.

Innovation: This game is placed at the furthest extremity of the purpose axis by innovation, since the *Our Museum Game* seeks to explore new ways of communicating to museum users and not mapping museum practices as is. *Facilitated*: On the context and process axis, the game is placed between middle and full facilitation, since the game needs facilitation for framing and guiding throughout the game as an objective support

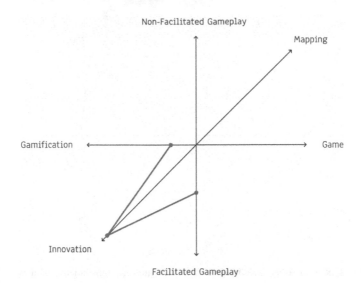

Fig. 9. The matrix with the *Our Museum Game,* which is mainly placed in the bottom left part of the matrix, as a mainly *facilitated innovative gamified workshop tool.*

to ensure that the game does not stagnate or end in frustration. *Gamification*: Lastly is the game fidelity axis, where the *Our Museum Game* is placed closely to the middle of the axis. As described above, the game does have quite a few game mechanics but is not a full-on game; rather, it uses game mechanics to drive the creative process and progression. Therefore, the game is placed close to the middle on the game fidelity axis.

4.3 Booster Cards

Booster Cards [14] is a deck of cards that consists of 71 business model configurations. The booster cards are used as a practical and generative tool in workshop settings to create a foundation for unlocking business model innovation (BMI). These booster cards offer hands-on experimentation with BMI through inspirational analogies and conceptual combinations to break down barriers, capture value potential, and generate new ideas. The cards in themselves are a game artifact and, through the descriptive paper [14], act as a guide for how to conduct a workshop with booster cards. The guide presents a workshop session that contains an *element of chance*, which can be defined as a game mechanic. Thus, *Booster Cards* can be defined as being at the border between a generative workshop with exercises and a gamification workshop. This is further underlined by the presented guide [14], which is made for facilitators and cannot be claimed to be a set of game rules. The authors also claim that *Booster Cards* cannot be a stand-alone solution. As such, *Booster Cards* is placed in the bottom left of the matrix, as can be seen in Fig. 10.

Innovation: This game is placed at the furthest extremity of the purpose axis by innovation, since *Booster Cards* seeks to generate BMI through inspirational analogies and conceptual combinations. *Facilitated*: On the context and process axis, the game is placed

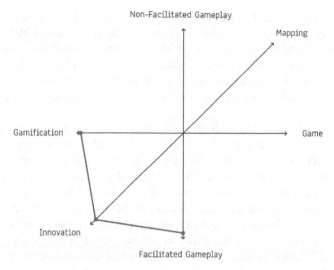

Fig. 10. The matrix with *Booster Cards,* which is placed in the furthest bottom left part of the matrix, as a *facilitated innovative gamified workshop.*

at the full facilitation extremity, since the game cannot stand alone and needs facilitation for framing and guiding of the workshop session and perhaps even a set of rules or constraints for the session. *Gamification*: Lastly is the game fidelity axis, where *Booster Cards* is placed at the gamification extremity. As described above, the game borders on being a generative tool rather than a gamified workshop approach. Since they are a deck of cards and thereby a game artifact that relies on an element of chance, *Booster Cards* is placed as close to gamification as possible.

4.4 Use Case - Cards for IoT

We have now presented three games and their placements in the gamification matrix to exemplify how they can visualize the construction and game fidelity of games. In this section, we will present how the matrix has been used in the development process to discuss and define an appropriate level of gamification based on the axes defined in this paper.

The gamification matrix's relevance and construction was tested when designing a game for IoT development and innovation in relation to business perspectives. This was done in collaboration with Force Technology that helps customers develop and implement new technological solutions. The task was broad and undefined in regard to the relevance of designing a game for solving the company's problem. Thus, using the parameters of the matrix to map and discuss the company's expected outcome of the game, its desired level of facilitation around the game, and at what stage of the development process the game was intended. The level of game fidelity relevant for this type of workshop session was identified.

Furthermore, the matrix functioned as a tool to visualize and discuss the level of game fidelity with the company to help them understand that we cannot just make a game for the game's sake, but we must instead be mindful to avoid the dark side of gamification. By exploring the parameters of the gamification matrix with the company, it could be identified at which process stages the company intended to use the game with their customers, what the purpose of the game was, and what level of facilitation was desired, thus making it possible to design a game meeting the company's requirements while informing them of the importance of finding a balance when using gamification for innovation.

Thus, the initial discussion with the company framed the purpose for a workshop game as needing a game that can function as an icebreaker in the very beginning of an innovation process to make the company's customers aware of the possibilities with IoT and to familiarize themselves with the associated technologies and terminologies. This places this workshop session at the innovation end of the purpose axis (Fig. 11). In addition, the company would like its customers to think about how these technologies could affect the current business model and potentially innovate based on this, preferably in a facilitated setting in which the game would be played at the initial workshop in continuation of a short introduction to IoT and a whole development process. This places the workshop session at the facilitated gameplay end of the context and process axis (Fig. 11). This left us to identify and discuss the game fidelity placement. Another wish from the company was that the workshop game could be dynamic in such a way that it potentially could be played in two iterations and sent out to the customers beforehand to familiarize themselves with it and IoT. In this way, when they played the game with the company, they would already have some understanding of the game. This is partly what we saw with the *Add Value* game (Sect. 4.1), which can be played with or without facilitation. Therefore, we decided that we should aim at a full game, because then we could make dynamic rulesets depending on in which setting the company desired the game to be played. Thus, the game artifacts and content will be constant, and the rules or game mechanics can be differentiated depending on the situation. This places the workshop session at the game end of the game fidelity axis while also adding a dotted line to the middle of the matrix's purpose axis and the non-facilitated gameplay to the context and process axis (Fig. 11).

What this use case shows, is the matrix potential in being a supportive tool in discussing the purpose, context and relevant game fidelity for development workshops, to insure that the right gamified approach is being used for the given purpose of a workshop setting. Thus, insuring a more constructive workshop setting, that is optimized for its purpose and taking full advantage of the game mechanics applied. Whether it being fully fledge game or gamification.

As this use case and the three game examples show, it is evident that there are no straight answers to the gamification of workshops. What is relevant can always be discussed. Nonetheless, the matrix's axes provided a valuable tool for clarifying the motivation behind applying gamification and engaging in an informed dialogue with a company that wants to use this approach in innovative development processes. It can be discussed whether this is too novel for workshop designers, but these gamified workshops are not always created by designers who have a deeper understanding of gamification; therefore, it is crucial to have some kind of guideline or tool to help the assessment of

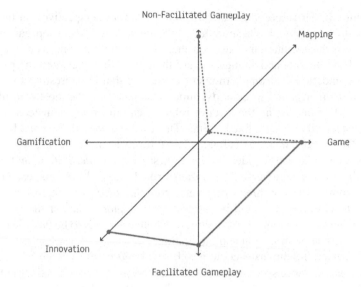

Fig. 11. The matrix with the *Cards for IoT*, which is placed in the bottom right of the matrix with a solid line and primarily in the top right with a dotted line, indicating the dynamic characteristics of the game design.

the level of gamification along to avoid the dark side and the overuse of a gamification approach in businesses.

5 Process and Discussion

Through this paper we have described and argued for the workshop session as a third space facilitated through games' magic circle based on different theories [4, 10], which leads to the definition of the matrix. In the process of using the matrix, in analyzing both the three existing games and the use case presented above, we learned that it is important to know the purpose of the game and the desired outcome before deciding on the level of facilitation, and that these two parameters combined give an indication of where to place the game on the game fidelity scale. This is because the nature of the workshop game is dependent on the level of facilitation, the purpose, and the outcome. We argue that a full game with a defined set of rules used for mapping will require no or less facilitation than a workshop with gamified additions to the exercises. The precise correlation between the parameters in the matrix is a matter for further research.

Therefore, it can be summarized that one of the lessons learned from the application of the gamification matrix is that the axes in the matrix should be addressed in the following order: (1) Purpose and Outcome, (2) Level of Facilitation, and lastly (3) Game Fidelity. Thus, the intent of the workshop and the relevance of gamification must be determined before deciding on the level of gamification.

Furthermore, the matrix provides a frame for discussing the needs for the game, thus providing a foundation for relevant game design. This paper only outlines the matrix and the idea behind it. Therefore, there are still many relevant perspectives on this matrix that remains to be explored. These include the dynamics of workshop games: if one game moves on the facilitation scale, can that change the outcome from mapping to innovation? How flexible and changeable are the connections between the parameters if the game foundation is strong? Another perspective that is interesting to explore is the realms of the matrix and whether dynamic visualization is the most fruitful type of visualization when discussing the level of relevant gamification, or instead whether it could be transformed into more fixed realms. This can be seen with Pine and Korn's [21] *multiverse*. The *multiverse* matrix is founded on three axes: *time, space,* and *matter.* The gamification matrix is also founded on three axes: *purpose, facilitation,* and *gamification.* Nevertheless, the multiverse [21] is transformed into eight realms, each of which represents a combination of three extremities from the three axes, representing realms from reality to virtuality. It would be interesting to explore whether the gamification matrix could define some more fixed realms, or whether it needs to be flexible to support the varying levels of gamification and facilitation.

Lastly, the game fidelity axes could also be explored in more depth by researching whether they can be more specific about when a workshop is gamification and when it is a game. Can the number of game mechanics be a factor in determining what needs to be present for a workshop to be one or the other?

6   Conclusion

There are many interesting and thorough examples of how to work with gamification and games in business, for either creating innovation or mapping [2, 4, 13–15]. Nevertheless, there is a tendency to overuse gamification, and it therefore loses coherence as a theoretical reference point [16]. Therefore, the purpose of creating this gamification matrix is to help avoid falling into "the dark side of gamification" while giving workshop designers a tool to discuss why it is relevant to apply game elements to the workshop, as well as at which level it is relevant to gamify a workshop. The matrix thus represents a framework that is relevant to discuss early in the workshop design process to ensure that we are not using gamification for the sake of using gamification, but rather to help us achieve the intended outcome. Thus, optimizing the potentials for creating an innovative development session, which can help to unlock creative processes and ideation at the right level. In this paper, we have presented the different levels of gamification fidelity in workshops, followed by a presentation of the parameters that are essential to discussing the balance of the level of gamification in a workshop, depending on the level of facilitation and the desired outcome, from mapping to innovation. These parameters were then transformed into a matrix for defining/creating gamified innovative processes, before we exemplified the use of the matrix through a use case and analysis of three workshop games. The matrix gives workshop designers a dynamic tool to visualize and discuss the relevant levels of gamification.

References

1. Jipa, G., Marin, I.: Enterprise gamification in business to consumer (B2C) engagement model. In: Proceedings of the 8th International Management Conference Management Challenges for Sustainable Development, pp. 489–496 (2014)
2. Patricio, R.: A gamified approach for engaging teams in corporate innovation and entrepreneurship. World J. Sci. Technol. Sustainable Dev. **14**, 254-262 (2017)
3. Paravizo, E., Chaim, O.C., Braatz, D., Muschard, B., Rozenfeld, H.: Exploring gamification to support manufacturing education on industry 4.0 as an enabler for innovation and sustainability. Procedia Manuf. **21**, 438–445 (2018)
4. Gudiksen, S.K., Inlove, J.: Gamification for Business: Why Innovators Changemakers Use Games to Break Down Silos, Drive Engagement and Build Trust. Kogan Page, London (2018)
5. Gudiksen, S.: Business model design games: rules and procedures to challenge assumptions and elicit surprises. Creativity Innov. Manag. **24**(2), 307–322 (2015)
6. Deterding, S., Sicart, M., Nacke, L., O'Hara, K., Dixon, D.: Gamification: using game-design elements in non-gaming contexts. In: CHI 2011 Extended Abstracts on Human Factors in Computing Systems, pp. 2425–2428 (2011)
7. Deterding, S., Dixon, D., Khaled, R., Nacke, L.: From game design elements to gamefulness: defining "gamification". In: Proceedings of the 15th International Academic MindTrek Conference: Envisioning Future Media Environments, pp. 9–15 (2011)
8. Brown, T.: Change by Design - How Design Thinking Transforms Organizations and Inspires Innovation. Harper Collins Publishers, New York (2009)
9. Nigel, C.: Design Thinking - Understanding How Designers Think and Work. Berg Publishers, Oxford (2011)
10. Sanders, L., Stappers, P.J.: Convivial Toolbox: Generative Research for the Front End of Design. BIS Publishers, Amsterdam (2013)
11. Muller, M.J., Druin, A.: Participatory Design: The Third Space in HCI. 70 (2007)
12. Salen, K., Tekinbaş, K.S., Zimmerman, E.: Rules of Play: Game Design Fundamentals. MIT Press, Cambridge (2004)
13. Madsen, K.M., Krishnasamy, R.: Our museum game: a collaborative game for user-centered exhibition design. In: Brooks, A., Brooks, E. (eds.) ArtsIT 2019: Interactivity & Game Creation, vol. 328, pp. 427–435. Springer, Heidelberg (2020). https://doi.org/10.1007/978-3-030-53294-9_31
14. Thomsen, P., Sort, J.C., Kristiansen, K.B.: Booster cards: a practical tool for unlocking business model innovation. J. Bus. Models **7**(3), 131–142 (2019)
15. Patrício, R., Moreira, A.C., Zurlo, F.: Gamification approaches to the early stage of innovation. Creativity Innov. Manag. **27**(4), 499–511 (2018)
16. Roth, S., Schneckenberg, D., Tsai, C.W.: The ludic drive as innovation driver: introduction to the gamification of innovation. Creativity Innov. Manag. **24**(2), 300–306 (2015)
17. Interaction Design Foundation. https://www.interaction-design.org/literature/article/5-stages-in-the-design-thinking-process. Accessed 13 June 2020
18. Norman, D.A., Verganti, R.: Incremental and radical innovation: design research vs. technology and meaning change. Des. Issues **30**(1), 78–96 (2014)
19. Souto, J.E.: Business model innovation and business concept innovation as the context of incremental innovation and radical innovation. Tour. Manag. **51**, 142–155 (2015)
20. Add Value. https://www.ucn.dk/kurser-og-videreuddannelser/skr%C3%A6ddersyet-forl%C3%B8b/teknologi-og-produktion/add-value. Accessed 11 July 2020
21. Pine, B.J., II., Korn, K.C.: Infinite Possibility: Creating Customer Value on the Digital Frontier. Berrett-Koehler Publishers, San Francisco (2011)

Creative Process of Pre-production of Video Games
Multidisciplinary Model Approach of Historical Imaginary that Contributes to Generate Engagement

Raquel Echeandía Sánchez[1,2]([✉]) [iD], Nelson Zagalo[2] [iD], and Sara Cortés Gómez[1,2] [iD]

[1] Philology, Communication and Documentation, University of Alcalá, Alcalá de Henares, Madrid, Spain
`raquel.echeandia@edu.uah.es, sara.cortesg@uah.es`
[2] Comunicação e Arte, University of Aveiro, Aveiro, Portugal
`nzagalo@ua.pt`

Abstract. Video games are one of the mainstays of audiovisual production and entertainment activities for society. Every year many games are released on the market, which means an evolution for this industry in constant growth and adaptation. This article is part of a research, development and innovation project (R&D&I) that aims to document the process of pre-production, production and distribution of a video game, focused on helping independent developers who are starting out in the sector as well as researchers and teachers who want to apply this content in their own studies. In this article the main objective is to establish a creative and artistic model approach of multidisciplinary references that contributes to generate engagement through the historical imaginary.

Keywords: Videogames · Creative process · Visual references · Aesthetic

1 Introduction

Video games have become one of the most successful, massive and ubiquitous forms of entertainment in society. Thanks to free development engines and modeling and animation programs, independent video games are established as an exponential power of content on the Internet. Since they can't compete with the same resources available to AAA productions that invest in special effects or large marketing campaigns, they must win the support and diffusion of the public by making more original and creative bets (Pratten 2015). As a highly innovative sector, R + D + I play a crucial role in the development of video games today. In 2009, video games were officially recognized by the Spanish government as a cultural product and the creators were qualified as protagonists of the Spanish cultural scene (IX Legislature No. 235, 2009). The plasticity of the video game makes it a medium capable of uniting other arts without losing its essence. Furthermore, the video game has a unique language: the rhetoric of the game, carried out through mechanics and the system. Being a cultural product means recognizing its

A. Brooks et al. (Eds.): ArtsIT 2020, LNICST 367, pp. 198–211, 2021.
https://doi.org/10.1007/978-3-030-73426-8_11

value as an audiovisual product for society and valuing the work of designers, artists, musicians and computer scientists, as well as highlighting the application of video games in a didactic way, contributing values to society, encouraging group work, perseverance and creativity, above all, recognizing and supporting the activity of a growing industry.

Serious video games can improve academic results, offer environments more conducive to the acquisition of knowledge, or even increase student motivation. However, serious or educational video games are far from commercial and very focused on the educational goal and therefore tend to be less attractive to the audience. The main objective of this current research project is to generate a video game that simulates an escape room that will allow us to make known the narrative, culture, patrimony and history that the University of Alcalá teaches. However, the main contribution does not consist of the product, but rather in analyzing the entire development and distribution process, generating a methodology that facilitates the creation of independent video games with an educational or moral approach based on culture and history.

We base this theoretical framework on the consideration of video games as a cultural product, a form of communication and artistic expression. By this we consider that the content of a game is a visual, sound and interactive language that generates an experience linked to certain objectives, within a socio-cultural context. Thinking about games from the intersection of culture, communication and art allows them to be framed as systems that build behavior through interaction with multidisciplinary theoretical references. It allows a clearer choice and analysis of the design at all levels of study and development.

The framework developed in this article focuses on pre-production, because it is a process in which innovation and recognition of creative ideas arise from a thorough investigation of the concepts and correlations that arise from the observation of multi-disciplinary reference areas. As the purpose of this research is not only focused on the area of video games, and we hope that it will serve as an approach for other disciplines, we have supported the theoretical framework in applied studies of areas of social and artistic sciences that have investigated the processes of generation of creative ideas and psychological models of how they generate engagement in the audience through the association of ideas.

It is a theoretical framework in process that serves as a starting point to establish the project. Once it has been completed and a post-mortem analysis will be carried out, complemented by interviews with the students and the audience of players, we will check whether the hypotheses that have been established throughout the process have made a significant difference and can be taken into consideration as a framework for future video game developments.

1.1 State of the Art Game Studies

The remainder of this state of art is a discussion of this conceptualization and how it is an improvement on our inherited ideas about games. Video games and virtual worlds generate their own culture, with their own languages and symbols, but they are also part of a global digital culture, representing a technological evolution, which promotes a construction of meanings and exchange. Therefore, what is important about video games is their inherent capacity to universalize, generate and share knowledge through digital methods. From an analytical point of view, Aarseth (2003) establishes three dimensions of the video game: gameplay, game-structure and game-world. The first one refers to the player's gaming experience, that is, the focus of this dimension is centred on strategies, motives, social relations and the knowledge of video players. The second dimension refers to the structure of the game, in which the mechanics, dynamics, rules and flow's theory that sets the balance between difficulty and ease (Csikszentmihalyi 1990, Chen, 2007). Finally, the third dimension covers the game world from the elements that integrate it. We consider relevant the creative processes, established by developers and users, redefining the discourses and participation (Cortés et al. 2016). Henry Jenkins describes this work as narrative architecture: "Examining games less as stories than as spaces ripe with narrative possibility." (Jenkins 2004). References to literary or cinematographic genres are of great importance for game design because it is a more suitable context to generate immersion and spatial narration, from a more truthful representation of fictional worlds. The environmental narrative generated by the environments and the soundtrack allows the story to be evoked through the atmosphere, reinforcing the concept to be communicated through the experience. Jenkins states that there are four forms of immersive environmental narrative experiences:

In this research we start by analyzing two types of categorizations, in relation to narratives designed by the development team. On the one hand, explicit embedded narrative, in close relationship with traditional linear media narrative, especially with cinematic language, such as kinematics, dialogues or camera movements that go beyond the player's control to focus on forced sequences. They often decrease the playability to focus the player's attention on a narrative element, although the evolution of the design has made it possible to reach intermediate points. The video game has its own language and its plasticity allows it to make use of all kinds of audiovisual material. This type of narrative has been subject to debate, since from the position of ludology, the non-interactive character, generates that during this type of moments the player becomes a passive spectator. However, its value exists in finding a balance with the game and reserving that content for playable material. On the other hand, while explicit embedded narrative used the techniques of other media, ambient narrative is a form of narration almost exclusive to the video game. It is also known to be used in the context of amusement parks, comic book fairs or escape rooms. The structure of the environment can guide the player to his destination without the need of guidelines or maps. It favors the visual path to create a narration. By placing certain elements in the playable environment, the developer can create a narrative tone, explain elements of the fictional world, detail the atmosphere of the game, and even provoke sensations, alert, inform or create expectation in the player. Jenkins distinguished four possible ways in which narration created the preconditions for an immersive narrative experience. The first and second categories proposed by Jenkins are related: "Spatial stories can evoke pre-existing narrative associations and they can provide a staging ground where narrative events are enacted" (Jenkins 2004). In this case, the environmental narrative can recreate spaces already known from other media, which can be adaptations of books, films or other narrative media. For example, the video game The Witcher (CDProjekt 2007) is an RPG where it recreates the settings of "Saga or wiedźminie", a series of heroic fantasy novels, in the same way that The Lord of the Rings: The Return of the King (EA Redwood Shores 2003) recreates the settings of the 2002 film by Peter Jackson. In this way, the player can virtually enter spaces that previously could only be recreated in their fantasy. The creator can also use this previous knowledge to subvert it, as Alice: Madness Returns (Spicy Horse 2011) does with Lewis' original work.

The last two categories are: "They may embed narrative information within their mise-en-scene; or they provide resources for emergent narratives" (Jenkins 2004). With this, it is proposed that within the environmental narrative, it is possible to find elements that generate a narrative previously established by the developers, or an emergent narrative, which arises from the interaction during the game. According to Jenkins, the emergent narrative is made up of those design choices (in this case, environmental promote the emergence of this type of narrative. In these cases, he often refers to The Sims (Maxis 2000). It was described by Salen and Zimmerman (2004) and by Jenkins. The latter says about Will Wright, the designer of games like SimCity (1989), The Sims (2000) or Spore (2008): "Wright has created a world ripe with narrative possibilities, where each design decision has been made with an eye towards increasing the prospects of interpersonal romance or conflict." (Jenkins 2004).

In Jenkins' theoretical proposal of embedded narrative, although the elements embedded in the environmental narrative are of great importance, they are only information, "signals and textual clues" from which the player "assembles and formulates hypotheses about probable narrative developments" (Jenkins 2004). Comparing this process to a detective story: the game is the story of the investigation and the embedded information; the clues of the case being tried to solve. Certainly, this type of narrative works especially well in thrillers or horror stories, such as Amnesia: The Dark Descent (Frictional Games, 2010), post-apocalyptic world, to learn about the society before, as in The Last of Us (Naughty Dog 2013) and in detective stories and psychological thrillers, such as Heavy Rain (Quantic Dream 2010).

The narrations of video games emerge from the consumer's experience, making the player more committed to the product, since he or she must decipher the story in order to continue interacting satisfactorily with the world (Nitsche 2008). It is connected to the proposal of (Cardero et al. 2014) in relation to the abductive thinking generated by the player during a game, exposing the differences between video games as a narrative medium and the narrations of other audiovisual media such as film, beyond the formal construction. Considering video games as cultural products and a means of communication, we highlight the contribution of Malaby (2007) who presents video games from the perspective of social processes, as a response to the debate generated on the issue of if games are just enjoyment, fun or entertaining: "Games are generators of these new practices, new tactics, which always carry the potential to fundamentally alter the game itself". As Malaby explains, reducing them to the emotion of fun devalues the complex and varied characteristics that make them interesting to the public. As Calleja explains in the digital video game immersion research (2011), video games encompass a set of emotional states conditioned by the player and the socio-cultural context. If we analyze the concept of fun, it is a not very concrete conceptualization and difficult to analyze for researchers and designers. For this reason, game studies and research in this field seek to specify what it is that generates commitment and participation on the part of the public. Calleja (2011) analyses the concept of immersion by proposing a more precise and concrete model of player participation that more accurately reflects the relationship and commitment that exists between the player and the game. His model consists of two temporal phases. The first, the player's involvement in the very moment of interaction with the game, and the second, the player's participation in spaces and times outside the direct relationship with the game, his or her long-term involvement. The combination between the temporal phases and the involvement in the six dimensions proposed by Calleja determines the level of immersion or, as the author proposes, "incorporation" of the player. With this model, Calleja opts for an approach to pleasure and immersion in digital gaming that takes into consideration the characteristics of the video game itself.

1.2 A Visual-Cultural History of the Artistic Image

What can art history contribute to the communicative processes applied to the new branches of digital culture? Iconography is the branch of art history that deals with meaning (Panofsky 1989). It constitutes a classification and description of images. It only describes the elements that make it possible, unlike iconology, which is the method of interpretation that comes from an analysis. For this purpose, it is necessary to understand the allegories and stories that precede it and to investigate if a previous representation of this artistic object took place (Panofsky 1955). Our practical experience must then be corrected by an investigation that comes from asking ourselves: how did historical conditions, objects and social events affect the form? In this way we obtain Heinrich Wölfflin's "history of style" (Wolfflin 1986), presenting itself as an autonomous form of evolution of artistic forms. This historian, who studied with Burckhardt (Aby Warburg's mentor), supported "a history of art without names". It implies a conception of artistic creation in which the role of the singular creators are the protagonists of the art of their time. In the book Fundamental Concepts of Art History, he made a taxonomy of the European artistic styles, chronologically and geographically categorizing the different European pictorial and sculptural schools between the 15th and 18th centuries using strictly formal approaches (Didi-Huberman and Calatrava 2009).

Aby Warburg constitutes for art history the equivalent of what Sigmunt Freud, his contemporary, contributed to psychology: he incorporated radically new questions for the compression of art. Through his Bilderatlas or image atlas, composed between 1924 and 1929 and left unfinished, Warburg managed to transform the way we understand the process of creating images. He called it Mnemosyne, as a way of expressing that his questioning referred to the memory of images, including unconscious memory, theorized at the same time by Freud on the psychological plane (Warburg 2010). The Mnemosyne atlas shows the survival of symbols and archetypes that have migrated since antiquity, presenting itself as a methodological reference for historians and artists, since it is a game of association. With it, it modifies the way of conceiving the relations of the works among them and of all together in front of the historical cultural evolution. It constitutes a movement of inexhaustible thought on ideas. Before the works as a finished product, a work process is shown, constituting a new way of telling stories of the visual arts far from the historical and stylistic schemes of the academy. Works that dialogue with each other in search of a visual and sound thought drawn by resonance, alteration and juxtaposition. In short, the image cannot be dissociated from the current global of the members of a society:

"(...) one of the real tasks of art history (Kunstgeschichte) is to bring into the framework of an in-depth study those creations that emerged in the most enlightened regions of literature (...) it is the only way to understand in its full extent one of the most important questions of scientific research on civilizations and styles (kulturwissenschaft)" (Didi-Huberman and Calatrava 2009).

That is why this contribution is so significant, because it develops from art history to culture science. In this way, it does not consider the work of art as a closed object about its own history, but as a dynamic meeting point for the history of social culture. Each period of history is woven with its own knot of antiquities, anachronisms, presents and propensities for the future.

2 The Model Approach

From the theoretical argumentation, which was based on proposals from communication and culture (Jenkins, Malaby), history of art (Arheim, Munari, Didi-Huberman, Hockney), psychology (Boden, Sautoy) and game research (Aarseth, Salen & Zimmerman, Juul, Schell, Adams, Calleja), we reached a set of concepts on experience aligned with current interaction design tripartite proposal, but aimed specifically at creative process. For that we propose a global iterative process of creation of cooperative creative intelligence, from the interaction between the production of video games, developers and players, promoting the creative memory of society and a creative behavior by the entire digital community. The question that arises is: What is a creative idea? Is a creative product the same as a well-executed product? When we consider something creative on a personal level, is it also creative for the whole society?

2.1 References of Models

As Margaret Boden explained in her book Creativity and art, we are creative within a socio-cultural context and within a frame of reference (Boden 2010). Thanks to this theoretical model approach, we want to demystify the process of ideas, understanding that artistic and cultural processes do not depend on a genius or a muse, but on a process of interaction of references in which new connections are generated when they leave the pre-established zone.

Therefore, first delimiting when we consider something creative, linked to culture and society, allows us to establish different types of processes to generate new ideas and connections. Understanding at the same time the narrative capabilities of video games, the more creative proposals are made, the more creative intelligence will be generated and shared by developers and players. We consider it an iterative process since it is constantly being contributed by both sides, since the language and culture that is generated, is expanding thanks to the developers and the public. As Brian Eno, musician and developer of the multidisciplinary creative process Oblique Strategies (Eno and Schmidt 1979), explained that the figure of genius, refers to an individual creative intelligence, while the term scenius is the result of a community creative intelligence that generates society in cooperation. Therefore, new creative proposals favour the creation of creative scenarios where to share and make new cultural relations, generating a creative behaviour.

We take as a reference the contributions of Jesse Schell in relation to the skills involved in the creative processes of video game design. For Schell, videogames are not just about creativity (Schell 2014). Designing a video game implies critical and logical thinking and communicative skills, but above all, the ability to listen actively, since it is the first thing to know how to communicate. Listening is not just hearing. It is understanding what your team, audience, self or the game is saying. Listening and developing communication skills allows you to generate knowledge references, and that drives creativity. The need to develop increasingly refined skills is what is behind the evolution of culture. It motivates both individuals and cultures to change in more complex experiences. The optimal state of experience can be experienced by all people regardless of age, gender, culture and economic status. The flow state, applied to generate audience engagement in video games, was first theorized by Csikszentmihalyi (1990) as a psychological process in pursuit of an optimal experience. Applied to our model, we consider that the creative experience of pre-production of video games should be characterized by the fusion of knowledge and action, concentration and a high sense of control, generating a sensation of immersion in the process in search of an innovative and unexpected idea.

Research has been published that analyzes how to generate a flow sensation in players during the game of a video game, characterized by high levels of full concentration, forgetting about themselves and their problems, and losing, at times, the notion of time. During this state, the person feels that he or she has control over his or her skills and activity, as well as a feeling of effortless performance. All of this results in an inherently rewarding experience, which leads the person to repeat the activity often in order to relive this experience again and again (Reeve 1994). According to Csikszentmihalyi (1990) the appearance of these states depends on the activity, the person and the socio-cultural environment in which it is carried out. For this reason, we consider that this model of creative processes in the ideation of new video game proposals would facilitate the expansion of the audience of players and developers, by making proposals that are differentiated from those commercialized by the AAA videogame companies.

Our proposal of approach to creativity pre-production in videogames is presented as the intersection between the individual imaginary of the players and the developers, understanding that it is included in a historical human imaginary marked by the socio-cultural context and the artistic and cultural production. As we proposed from the beginning, it is a process of communication between developers and spectators, being considered creative when it is original and strangeness.

We categorize an idea as original when it surprises with unusual characteristics. This factor is framed in relation to personal experience. Thus, we should differentiate between being original at an individual level and being original at a historical level in a socio-cultural context. As Bruno Munary explained in the book Fantasia: Invenzione, creatività e immaginazione nelle comunicazioni visive (Fig. 1):

"Thus, fantasy will be more alive the more possibilities the individual has to establish relationships. An individual of very limited culture cannot have a great fantasy; he must always use the means at his disposal, the means he knows; and if

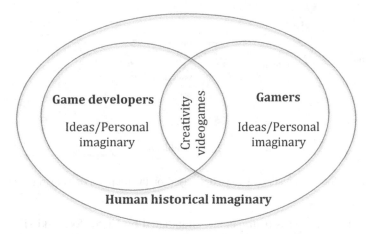

Fig. 1. Model of intersection between the individual imaginary of the players and the developers.

he knows few things, at most he can imagine a sheep covered with leaves instead of wool. That is enough, from the point of view of suggestion. But instead of continuing to establish new relationships with other things, at a certain point he will have to stop." (Munari 1977).

Munari (1977) related the creative processes to references by means of the deconstruction of thought and memory. To this end, he linked the resolution of divergent problem solutions to imagination, fantasy or play, because there are no restrictions. He explains an associative model of ideas that takes as a reference database (memory) to fantasize or associate ideas with the imagination. In this sense, Munari argues that the larger this database is, the more diverse knowledge you have, the easier it is to develop creativity. In this sense, in relation to the production of video games, we believe that this process would not only be applicable at the individual level of the developers. If we understand video games as generators of iterative communicative processes, an increase in the production of game proposals would increase the historical imaginary, facilitating tools and contexts for the development of divergent, creative and associative intelligence.

Therefore, based on Munari's proposal for creativity, we conceptualize that all sociocultural information to which we are exposed at an individual level, at the moment we perceive and experience it, goes through a process of personal development that favours divergent and associative intelligence, by generating memories from significant experiences, resulting in new relationships that are knowledge.

This approach proposes that the creative idea represents strangeness, being capable of deautomatizing perception and forcing the mind to make a reconstructive effort to form a unit from information that at first seems disjointed. From the perspective of strangeness, inspiration is no longer considered a mythical and ambiguous notion, but a fundamental piece for the successful development of creation, compatible with the application of artistic techniques. Therefore, strangeness, generally seen as an effect on the reader, is now revealed as an imperative creative need, as well as a useful concept to explain the role that each phase of creation -inspiration, technical- plays for the artist.

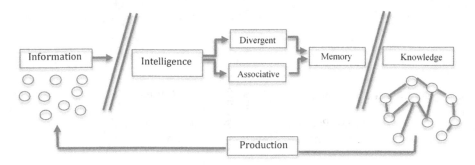

Fig. 2. Model of creativity knowledge based on the proposal of Munari (1977).

The concept of strangeness (ostranenie), enunciated by Victor Sklovski since his first works, has generally been associated with the aesthetical-receptive field. Perhaps his most remembered formulation is that of his 1917 manifesto article, "Art as an artifice" (Fig. 2):

> *"To give a sensation of life, to feel the objects, to perceive that stone is stone, there exists that which is called art. The purpose of art is to give a sensation of the object as vision and not as recognition; the procedures of art are that of the singularization of objects, and that which consists in obscuring the form, in increasing the difficulty and duration of perception. The act of perception is in art an end and must be prolonged. Art is a means of experiencing the becoming of the object: what has already been done is of no interest to art"* (Sklovski 1970).

We take as a reference point the reflections of Paul Valéry, a modern poet whose conception of the process of creation presents parallels with Russian Formalism. From Valéry's perspective, artistic works are, on the one hand, the end of a process (from the designer's and developer's perspective), and on the other hand, the origin of another experience (what the public generates by interacting with it). The author's activity consists of two aspects: first, the author researches to find an inspiration, and then works with that state to produce a certain effect on the audience, analogous to the state of inspiration and immersion experienced by him/her. Thanks to this state of immersion in the creative process that alienates the author, he/she can go beyond the usual schemes of reality and connect with his/her most original and primary empirical background. Valéry described this state as a moment in which a harmonic communication between reality and the internal world was produced, being the result of this absence of conventional restriction.

Having delimited when we consider a creative idea, we have categorized the parts that make up a video game, based on the MDA theoretical framework. In 2004, at the conference of Video Game Developers in San José, Robin Hunicke, Marc LeBlanc and Robert Zubek, presented a new conception of taxonomy related to videogames that includes a formal approach, trying to bring design and development closer: "What makes a game fun? How do we know a specific type of fun when we see it? (Hunicke et al. 2004). They develop a framework through the acronym MDA that encompasses Mechanics,

Dynamics and Aesthetics, proposing a methodology that strengthens the iterative processes of developers, academics and researchers. They suggest that while designers build the game from mechanics to aesthetics, the player experiences it from the end of aesthetics to mechanics, understanding aesthetics as the sensory experience that emerges from the video game. In this way, for our proposal of model we understand that there are some elements that facilitate the actions, that conform the environmental narrative. Schemes that allow interaction and measure the degree of playability. Finally, the player has experienced a sensation linked to the aesthetic of the videogame, encompassing the narrative, the genre and the final moral (Fig. 3).

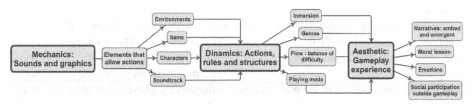

Fig. 3. Elements of a videogame.

2.2 The Model Approach of Creativity Process

We are creative within a culture and framework of references. Applying creativity to development processes implies generating new connections from established knowledge by going outside the comfort zone. To do so, our proposal is based on the following tripartite model of creative processes (Fig. 4).

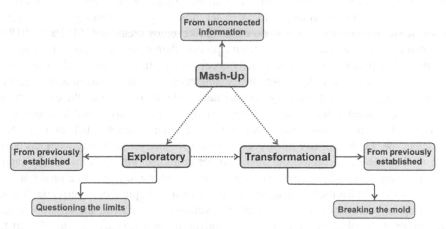

Fig. 4. The model approach of creativity process.

Based on ideas and concepts with which we are familiar, it is a matter of seeking novelty. **The mash-up creative process** includes the dynamic capacity to integrate previously unconnected information. It involves a mixture or fusion of disparate elements with the idea of generating strangeness but from familiarization. This process emphasizes the number of ideas, which can be every day and ridiculous concepts. It generates surprises that statistically would have been improbable otherwise, since this psychological process stands out for establishing random connections between previously undone information. Examples of mush-up creativity include visual collage, poetic imagery; analogies (verbal, visual or musical); and unexpected juxtapositions of ideas. It is the creative process characteristic of the production of audiovisual content generated by the audience on social networks, since it is fluid, encompasses historical and personal novelty, and serves as a means of expressing and communicating ideas in a direct way. It facilitates virality by being previously impossible proposals of easily recognizable elements.

The Deconstructeam studio prepared an unusual combination of three different game dynamics: the use of pottery to create cybernetic implants, cocktail making and voice impersonation on the phone. The thread of the narrative was a story with a cyberpunk setting that spoke of a corporation that sought to eliminate the most intense emotions of human beings, awakening in the players moral emotions by questioning their own decisions. The working method of Deconstructeam is to create ideas in Game jams. In a talk at Fun and Serious Game Festival in 2018, Jordi de Paco (Deconstructeam's developer) explained that designing a video game that works is difficult for the independent sector. He explains that it is easier to recover from a two-week project, that's why they take the ideas coming from Game Jams as a focus of ideas. The first game that Deconstructeam marketed was Gods Will Be Watching, and after the success of the studio (it sold more than 300,000 units) they decided to develop something bigger, expanding the team and renting an office. A year later the money had run out and they decided to cancel the project. They decided to go through the dozen games they had created on the Game Jams and choose the ideas they liked best and see how they could combine them into a single game. This spanish's studio learned from their previous experience and they have dedicated themselves to prototype ideas to see how they work "without commercial ballast, we have dedicated a year to do what we like: enjoy creativity" (de Paco 2018).

Exploratory creativity is more intuitive process than mash-up. It consists of investigating and fully understanding a socially accepted structure or rules and questioning them. In exploratory creativity, it uses the existing rules or stylistic conventions to generate new concepts, whose possibility may not have been realized before the exploration. This process applied to the ideation of new videogame proposals would be applied by analyzing all the proposals made in relation to the same structure, such as a genre, a character type, an objective or rules. It is interesting to analyses not only what has been done in the videogame sector, but also in other multidisciplinary areas. Understanding the archetypes that have developed throughout a culture in a socio-cultural context allows us to test the limits. It can be approached from a conceptual or experiential break, depending on whether the elements that are exchanged are part of the environmental narrative or in the objective that serves as motivation. In this process, it is relevant to make a timeline and see the references, since in this way relationships with other concepts are encouraged. It is also important to raise questions, since the aim is to break with the pre-established. It allows to surprise by questioning socio-culturally accepted models. The figure below shows a timeline of video games that work based on Flow's concept. It highlights that they have many factors in common based on socially accepted mechanics, dynamics and experience. It serves to exemplify this creative process by asking which limits they have in common and what would happen if these limits were changed (Fig. 5).

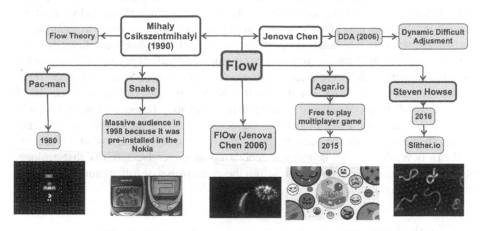

Fig. 5. Exploratory creativity process of concept "*Flow*"

Finally, we consider the strategy of creative **transformational processes**. Like exploratory processes, they arise from something previously established and socially accepted. However, instead of seeking the limits and questioning them, it seeks to surprise through the surprise of including the impossible. It is difficult for it to be socially accepted because it abruptly breaks the pattern. We take Marcel Duchamp as our main reference. Pioneer Dada, he questioned what art should be and how it should be done. Through a selection of objects produced in mass, he gave them the title of "*Readymades*" as works of art, questioning the figure of the artist as creator of objects. The theory behind the readymade was explained in an anonymous editorial published in the May 1917 issue of avant-garde magazine The Blind Man run by Duchamp and two friends:

> "*Whether Mr Mutt with his own hands made the fountain or has no importance. He chose it. He took an ordinary article of life and placed it so that its useful significance disappeared under the new title and point of view - created a new thought for that object.*"

We understand that as a process three phases stand out: the choice of the object is a creative act. Secondly, that by cancelling the 'useful' function of an object it becomes art. Thirdly, that the presentation and the addition of a title to the object has given it a new thought, a new meaning. Duchamp's readymades also affirmed the principle that the artist defines what is art (Kamien-Kazhdan 2018). In art, where aesthetic judgments presuppose the recognition of the relevant cultural style, there will also be aesthetic continuities and discontinuities, which may or may not be considered valuable. After the transformation has occurred, the artist can add new rules, defining and exploring the new style more fully.

To exemplify this creative process of transformation, we analyzed the video game launched in 2019 by the Spanish studio The Game Kitchen. When they launched the crowfunding campaign for their video game Blasphemous, they had no idea of the repercussions it would have. Of the $50,000 they asked for to develop the title, they got $333,246. In Blasphemous, they took as their starting point such dark fantasy references as Dark Souls, The Witcher, Hollow Knight. However, the transformational value of the game is that the user puts himself in the skin of The Penitent, a man who must atone for his sins and wants to free humanity from the curse in which it has been plunged. To do this, the character will have to travel through a universe full of religious iconography, dark and monstrous, full of references to the culture of southern Spain, to Easter. There are not only tributes to Goya, but also to other authors such as Velázquez, since one of the enemies of the game is based on the menina Margarita Teresa of Austria who was turned into a fearsome giant. In a classic Castlevania, you see the Gothic aesthetic, but in Blasphemous you are the penitent giving the opportunity to learn what a Nazarene is, the Holy Week, how it is celebrated, generating an immersive narrative that explores beyond the game. Blasphemous starts from the controversy of folk culture to generate an intergenerational product.

3 Conclusions

In the scenario of communitarian creative processes, we understand that creative intelligence is inherent to society, within an environment that is both cooperative and individual, which allows for interdisciplinary connections to be established and for new and valuable proposals to be made for the development of a culture with a great creative and imaginative capacity. The game's rhetoric is capable of transmitting sensations, narrating events, establishing relationships between characters, constituting metaphors and altering the discourse of the story. The creative freedom of the independent sector creates an environment where a community can grow, make mistakes and then learn from them. This in turn fosters talent and offers more to the gaming industry. Videogames are part of a socio-cultural context and are a form of creative communication between digital creators and users. We are creative within our frame of reference and cultural environment; therefore, the more productions are made, the greater the social and individual creative intelligence will be. Independent video game developers can take more risks when it comes to doing something different, increasing players' interest in generating new content.

References

Aarseth, E.: Playing Research: Methodological Approaches to Game Analysis (2003)

Boden, M.A.: Creativity and Art: Three Roads to Surprise. Oxford University Press (2010)

Calleja, G.: In-Game: From Immersion to Incorporation (1 edition). MIT Press (2011)

Cardero, J.L.N., Rufí, J.P.P., Pérez, F.J.G.: El pensamiento abductivo como fundamento ontológico de los videojuegos 12(2), 416–440 (2014). https://doi.org/10.7195/ri14.v12i2.670

Chen, J.: Flow in games (and everything else). Commun. ACM 50(4). https://doi.org/10.1145/123 2743.1232769

IX Legislatura Núm. 235, 235, 10 (2009). https://www.congreso.es/portal/page/portal/Congreso/PopUpCGI?CMD=VERLST&BASE=puw9&DOCS=1-1&QUERY=(CDC200903250235. CODI.)

Cortés, S., Mendez, L., Lacasa, P.: Ipads, Apps and Social Networks. Creating multimodal narratives in classrooms. Digit. Educ. Rev. **0**(30), 53–75 (2016). https://doi.org/10.1344/der.2016. 30.53-75

Csikszentmihalyi, M.: Flow: The Psychology of Optimal Experience (1990)

de Paco, J.: VIT Talks 2018: The Red Strings Club: Postmortem – Oro parece, platano es (2018). https://www.youtube.com/watch?v=o4BKruFGQt4&t=1229s

Didi-Huberman, G., Calatrava, J.A.: La imagen superviviente: Historia del arte y tiempo de los fantasmas según Aby Warburg. Abada (2009)

Eno, B., Schmidt, P.: Oblique strategies: Over one hundred worthwhile dilemmas. [The Authors] (1979)

Hunicke, R., Leblanc, M., Zubek, R.: MDA: A Formal Approach to Game Design and Game Research. AAAI Workshop - Technical Report, 1 (2004)

Jenkins, H.: Game design as narrative architecture. In: Harrigan, P., Wardrip-Fruin, N.: First Person, pp. 118–130. Massachusetts: MIT Press (2004)

Kamien-Kazhdan, A.: Remaking the Readymade: Duchamp, Man Ray, and the Conundrum of the Replica. Routledge (2018)

Malaby, T.M.: Beyond Play: A New Approach to Games **2**(2), 95–113 (2007)

Munari, B.: Fantasía: Invención, creatividad e imaginación en las comunicaciones visuales (B. M. Carrillo, Trans.; Edición: 1). Editorial Gustavo Gili S.L. (2018)

Nitsche, M.: Video Game Spaces: Image, Play, and Structure in 3D Worlds. The MIT Press (2008). https://doi.org/10.7551/mitpress/9780262141017.001.0001

Panofsky, E.: Meaning in the Visual Arts. Doubleday & Company, Inc., Garden City (1955). https://gen.lib.rus.ec/book/index.php?md5=d50a026e9a5d54c1a3d4b490c45a3e07

Panofsky, E.: Idea. Gallimard (1989). https://gen.lib.rus.ec/book/index.php?md5=5a117efcb48f7d75277dcd005a6450b2

Pratten, R.: Getting Started in Transmedia Storytelling: A Practical Guide for Beginners. CreateSpace Independent Publishing Platform (2011)

Reeve, J.M.: Motivación y emoción (Edición: 5). McGraw-Hill Interamericana de España S.L. (2010)

Schell, J. (2014). The Art of Game Design: A Book of Lenses, Second Edition (Edición: 2). A K Peters/CRC Press.

Sklovski, V.: La disimilitud de lo similar: Los origenes del formalismo. Alberto Corazon Editor (1970)

Warburg, A.: Atlas Mnemosyne (J. C. Mielke, Trans.; Edición: 1). Ediciones Akal, S.A. (2010)

Wolfflin, H.: Principles of Art History: The Problem of the Development of Style in Later Art (Edición: DOVER). Dover Publications Inc. (1986)

Video Game Development Processes that Generate Engagement in the Players: A Case Study of Don't Starve

Raquel Echeandía Sánchez[(⊠)] [iD] and Sara Cortés Gómez[iD]

Philology, Communication and Documentation, University of Alcalá, Alcalá de Henares, Madrid, Spain
raquel.echeandia@edu.uah.es, sara.cortesg@uah.es

Abstract. The digital distribution of video games presents more options than ever, where multiplatform accessibility means a change in philosophy. The aim of this article is to analyse the strategies that allow games to stand out in the market through different aesthetics, the appearance of new characters in a periodic way or the synergy of social media. We have analysed the case of the independent video game series Don't Starve, developed by Klei Entertainment and available on Steam. In this context, reporting mechanisms allow us to extract information on the impact of the video game from the launch and during the use of the product. As a result, through the analysis of data from the Steam digital distribution platform, we have extracted quantitative information about players and gaming sessions, establishing correlations with other games and behaviours linked to the player experience. This has been combined with a qualitative study of the media synergy they have implemented to generate audience participation through their characters and multiplayer mode, narrative and aesthetics, resulting in players identifying with the content and taking an active role as producers and consumers.

Keywords: Indie games · Development · Engagement · Audience · Aesthetic

1 Introduction

According to data from the White Paper of the Spanish Video Game Development 2018, the video game is the main engine of global entertainment and represents an industry that has been able to generate 134.9 billion dollars in 2018, growing by 10.9%, according to company data Newzoo (DEV 2018). The computer market has also grown more than expected, thanks to the explosion of the Battle Royale genre games led by the *Fortnite*, title of Epic Games. In relation to computer games, Steam, the digital video game distributor of the developer Valve, had a relatively monopoly without opposition, since 2003 he practices this business model successfully.

The launch at the end of 2018 of the online store of Epic Games, the developer and editor of *Fortnite*, has generated a more competitive environment in digital distribution, resulting in a decentralization of the market. Epic Games has taken advantage of the

© ICST Institute for Computer Sciences, Social Informatics and Telecommunications Engineering 2021
Published by Springer Nature Switzerland AG 2021. All Rights Reserved
A. Brooks et al. (Eds.): ArtsIT 2020, LNICST 367, pp. 212–227, 2021.
https://doi.org/10.1007/978-3-030-73426-8_12

Fortnite audience to attract consumers to the new Epic Games store, while also offering exclusive games and a better revenue division for developers (Gómez 2018). Another of the key strategies is to offer a new free computer game every two weeks, especially indie games.

In a market dominated by large producers, the rise of independent companies is notable, achieving recognition by considering Indie games (Lisanne and James 2011) as its own category in multiple distribution media. Indie video games are characterized by being designed and developed by small teams without financial help. Having a limited budget, these games cannot compete with large productions that invest in special effects or motion capture. For this reason, they have to gain the support and dissemination of the public by making more original and creative bets (Pratten 2015) and involve them in the development of the games through early access.

We will go deeper into the challenges and opportunities that arise from the digital distribution of independent videogames, from the social practices organized around the *Don't Starve Together* game, from Klei Entertainment.

We will start from this indie game to analyze how iterative development methodologies, indie aesthetic proposals, game modes and network distribution influence the consolidation of a community around it, comparing with other indie games and AAA games.

2   Literature Review

2.1   Frameworks Theories for the Development of Video Games

In 2004, at the conference of Video Game Developers in San José, Robin Hunicke, Marc LeBlanc and Robert Zubek, presented a new conception of taxonomy related to videogames that includes a formal approach, trying to bring design and development closer: "What makes a game fun? How do we know a specific type of fun when we see it? Talking about games and play is hard because the vocabulary we use is relatively limited. In describing the aesthetics of a game, we want to move away from words like fun and gameplay towards a more directed vocabulary" (Hunicke et al. 2004). Starting from the idea of specifying the factors that make a video game fun, they develop a framework through the acronym MDA that encompasses Mechanics, Dynamics and Aesthetics, proposing a methodology that strengthens the iterative processes of developers, academics and researchers. They suggest that while designers build the game from mechanics to aesthetics, the player experiences it from the end of aesthetics to mechanics, understanding aesthetics as the sensory experience that emerges from the video game. The classification by aesthetics establishes an approach to the experience and emotions of the player. The authors of the MDA explain that any design change that alters the rules and mechanics affects the game decisively, since they expose that video games generate behavior and are not mere audiovisual media: "*Fundamental to this framework is the idea that games are more like artifacts than media. By this we mean that the content of a game is its behavior - not the media that streams out of it towards the player*" (Hunicke et al. 2004).

Johan Huizinga, Dutch philosopher and historian recognized for his studies and publications in relation to the game and its social and cultural factor, such as the book Homo

Ludens, was the first to introduce one of the key concepts of video game development, the circle magical, that is, the virtual world built by the video game and its limits, different from those outlined by the real world (Huizinga 1938). Eric Zimmerman and Katie Salen adopted the term and made reference in their book Rules of Play: Game Design Fundamentals, explaining that it is necessary to differentiate between the virtual and the real world since, when players voluntarily accept the rules of a game, there are certain actions that we do not consider adequate in the real world, such as killing, but are essential for the gameplay (Salen and Zimmerman 2003). Another fundamental proposal was put forward by Roger Caillois in his Game Theory, in which he considers the game as a voluntary activity, uncertain, unproductive and capable of creating fictions. Caillois also orders the games based on two antagonistic poles, paidia and ludus. While the first is defined by fun, unbridled and uncontrolled imagination, in the second the exuberance of the game is channeled through rules and conventions that establish a series of objectives to reach the goal (Caillois 1958). In this way the dichotomy between whether video games should be considered from ludology or narratology is established. Since the beginning, video games have served as a means to tell stories, although not always explicitly. We consider relevant the creative processes that both users and developers establish, redefining discourses and participation (Cortés et al. 2016). The proposal of Navarrete et al. (2014a, b) in relation to the abductive thinking generated by the player during a game, exposes the differences between videogames as a narrative medium and the narratives of other audiovisual media such as cinema, beyond formal construction (Navarrete et al. 2014a, b).

2.2 Aesthetics and Graphic of Video Games

Video games represent an emerging mode of animated art, adaptable to the digital resources of the 21st century, new aesthetic experiments, which transform the screens into a medium for very accessible innovation, which offers emotional experiences to the player. As Henry Jenkins puts it: "The category of aesthetics has considerable power in our culture, helping to define not only cultural hierarchies but also social, economic, and political ones as well." (Jenkins 2005). Gilbert Seldes explained the arts and aesthetics through his ability and immediate affective power (Seldes 2003).

Often, there is a tendency in the video game industry to consider graphics and aesthetics the same. There is a dichotomy that becomes evident when we compare an AAA game to an indie game. The graphics that the first one can offer, whose general tendency is realism with the latest movement recognition technologies, cannot be matched by an indie title, whose financing is very limited and are small development teams. However, the aesthetics of indie games, even with the limitations, are more likely to last over time by making more intimate, creative and evocative proposals. The graphic power allows an infinite number of details, but it must be taken into account that the graphic quality alone does not build a good video game. The aesthetic includes the interaction between different aspects such as style, soundtrack, movement architecture, characters, environments and artistic techniques, being as a whole. Gordon Calleja analyzes and exposes the concept of immersion by proposing a more concrete player participation model that reflects the relationship and commitment that exists between the gamer and the game, consisting of two phases. The first, the involvement of the player in the same moment of interaction during the gameplay, and the second, the player's participation in spaces and times outside the direct relationship with the game, its long-term involvement, through other platforms (Calleja 2011). Eriz Zimmerman, game designer and co-founder and CEO of the independent game development studio Gamelab, argued in 2002 that video games should return to aesthetics in essence and remove the cinematic effects, which subtracted gameplay. He exposed that independent video games they would really work when network distribution was a reality (Zimmerman 2002). Even large companies, seeing that the audience demanded more creative and evocative proposals, and criticized the commercial trend, although it stood out for implementing the best graphics and technological options, began to make more intimate proposals taking as reference the indie experimentation, such as the company French Ubisoft, developer and distributor, with titles such as *Child of light* (Ubisoft 2014) and *Valiant Hearts: The Great War* ™ / *Soldats Inconnus: Mémoires de la Grande Guerre*™ (Ubisoft 2014), which stand out for their aesthetics, with graphics simulating illustration, watercolor and comic techniques, unlike the titles they usually make of realistic 3D graphics.

The art of video games can't be a mere reproduction, since it is a medium rich in resources to surprise and innovate, especially in the indie games sector, as Steve Pool explains: *"Whereas film - at least naturalistic, 'live-action' film - is tied down to real spaces, the special virtue of videogames is precisely their limitless plasticity. And only when that virtue is exploited more fully will video games become a truly unprecedented art - when their level of world-building competence is matched with a comparable level of pure invention. We want to be shocked by novelty. We want to lose ourselves in a space that is utterly different. We want environments that have never been seen, never been imagined before"* (Poole 2000).

2.3   Characteristics of Digital Video Games that Involve the Public

In this section we will analyze some aspects that make it possible for a videogame to generate engagement in the audience:

Early Acess Games: It is a way to develop videogames with the participation of the audience. It facilitates the consolidation of a community. It is an iterative process that allows developers to get quick feedback from the direct audience of the game. The audience takes an active role, ceasing to be passive consumers and being prosumers of their own experience (Olin-Scheller and Wikström 2010), emphasizing literacy (Zagalo 2010). In this way, games in development grow and evolve in parallel to the community. That the video game is available in the initial stages of development implies involving users and building engagement towards developers and their products.

Crafting Games: This game mode is within the action and survival games, but not to be confused with the current Battle Royale phenomenon, which is characterized by very fast and short games in which you have to find weapons and eliminate the opponent. Crafting games stand out for extending to infinity, gradually increasing the difficulty of survival. One of the main handicaps of indie games is the short duration, so this game mode, in which the gameplay extends a lot in time because each game is different, is an interesting factor for indie developers. They are active video games, if you don't act and look for a strategy, you die. The environments are wide and provided with useful items for survival: Map, clock, tools for cutting, building or cooking, etc. Another feature is that by combining resources, the player can create a new element, useful for more productions. It is common that developers do not explicitly give the player how to achieve these elaborations, since the idea is that it be learned through experimentation, which generates player forums and values the community. Salen and Zimmerman analyze the emerging narrative as the narrative that emerges from the interaction, being characteristic of this modality. The narrative experience changes from one player to another and each game is different. The term *"emerging"* has given rise to many debates. Jesper Juul, at the Computer Games and Digital Cultures Conference Proceedings conference in 2002, explained that there are two basic structures of game modes, emersion and progression. In his opinion, improvisation and the variety of opportunity that facilitates emersion, which is not predesigned, and the infinite combinations of play are preferable (Juul 2002). According to Henry Jenkins, the emerging narrative encompasses implicit environmental elements, such as items, characters or soundtrack that generate a narrative when the player interacts with the video game: *"Wright has created a world ripe with narrative possibilities, where each design decision has been made with an eye towards increasing the prospects of interpersonal romance or conflict"* (Jenkins 2004a, b).

Multiplayer: This mode stands out for allowing a large number of users to play in the same virtual world. They are characterized by having a cooperation theme, being able to establish alliances. They stand out for being real players whose performance is not marked by a narrative, which determines that each game is different. It encourages sharing experiences as environments in which strategy and action predominate. It is a success factor because it helps the public to try and share it. It allows greater dissemination by users on streaming platforms and social networks, which increases the number of players. It is also a resource to compensate the level of frustration when losing a game, since competitiveness facilitates the recovery of the level of flow of the game, as Mihaly Csikszentmihalyi explained that success is in maintaining a balance between boredom for ease and the frustration for the difficulty (Csikszentmihalyi 1990).

Based on these areas we can conclude that they provide a gateway to the world of video games that expands their access possibilities, the versatility of their game modes with other players and cooperation. These factors guarantee the success in the market that is reflected in the distribution platforms.

3   Research Methodology and Objectives

As we have indicated at the beginning of this work, the main objective is to analyze from different perspectives the social phenomenon of Don't Starve Together, the independent game available on the Steam platform, and the factors that have favored audience participation before a market full of titles that offer similar content. This objective is complemented by the following specific objectives:

- Analyze how horror survival aesthetics and character design with narratives generate audience engagement through media synergy.

- Analyze and compare some of the main competitions and establish what preferences the public has when the games are in equal accessibility (free weekend).
- Study the role of users as active players and critics of video games, trying to discover how they continue and participate in the development of the game.

Taking as a starting point specific situations to explore how indie games can be significant, we focus on the Steam digital distribution platform of the developer Valve, since although decentralization has begun with the appearance of other distribution companies, so far it is the most complete platform in the industry. On the one hand we adopt a point of quantitative and qualitative inestigation (Sampieri 2018; Denzin and Lincoln 2012) which we understand as a situated activity that places the observer in the world and immersed in meaning construction processes, on the other hand, we use a virtual ethnographic research (Boellstorff et al. 2012) method to conduct ethnographic studies of communities and cultures created through social interaction in digital ecosystems.

Digital distribution platforms such as Steam allow you to monitor player audience data through Big Data (Kitchin 2014), which becomes a fundamental analysis tool. Statistics can be generated that measure how often a title is played and compared to others, what times of day are most popular demographically, and the impact of complementary actions such as additional discounts, the launch of new DLCs or the inclusion of new characters or elements in the game.

We will analyze the data of a monitoring generated by a selection of indie games on the SteamDB platform, obtaining data since the moment they were published. The chosen video games have leaked from the platform's "Indie" tag. There has been an increase of 9163 titles in one year (36490 registered on July 30, 2019 compared to 45653 on July 24, 2020). In this sense, it highlights the need for this type of monitoring from the launch of a video game and over time, as it allows to understand patterns of behavior of players and how they react to changes and as reflected in the scope of the video game. It has also been filtered by average user score, number of players online at the time of analysis and the highest peak of registered players. This analysis can provide information to the developers of the selected video games, address their content from the platform and implement new strategies to capture the attention of the public. SteamDB provides markers in relation to changes in the number of users, which allows to locate the impact of the strategies carried out. After identifying behavioral patterns in the global top charts of the most demanded indie games to date, we have deepened in the process of creative development and the strategy to generate engagement in the audience, of the game Don't Starve Together, since it experienced an increase 461% of online players, going from 12182 to 68418 in four days in the month of May 2019, being very remarkable figures in the indie game sector.

4 Analysis of Research Results

4.1 Steam Global Top Charts

The idea of approaching the game from various platforms and the multiplayer possibility that allows you to connect with friends and family, remains a key value for the players. Within SteamDB, which allows you to order under the label "*Indie*" the titles in relation to the number of players online at the moment and the highest peaks of players online since its launch, Stardew Valley and *Don't Starve Together* have similar figures in these aspects and also in relation to the average user rating, as shown in Table 1, and both independent titles being among the top 10 in the ranking of the highest peak parameter of online players on the Steam platform.

Table 1. SteamDB platform data on Steam users. Last update of the registration data on July 29, 2019, own source.

Game	Rating	Player count right now	Player count all time
Stardew Valle	95.98%	10.559	64.427
Donít Starve To-	94.96%	10,180	68.418

Stardew Valley is a rural role-playing game (RPG) that stands out for its 8-bit and 16-bit style aesthetics. As recorded by the SteamDB platform, the average total game time is 53.7 h. Following the start icon of "Developed by ConcernerApe" is Eric Banore, who has written the story, designed art and sound and programmed the entire video game, in a four-year process, and launched on the market on February 26, 2016. Tom Coxon collaborated with the multiplayer version that is available since 2018 for PC and Nintendo Switch. As the creator explains, he had as main reference a video game that marked his childhood, Harvest Moon, from Nintendo launched in 1996 (Grathwohl and Lachausse 2016). When starting we will be in an attractive place in the middle of nature, without the burden of the city. We will hardly see people at the beginning, in fact the stores restrict their activity to business hours. You have some tools that serve to break stones, cut down or remove grass. It is also a crafty title with Don't Starve Together. Eric Barone refused to use Steam's Early Access program to be available in beta, and only released the game when it was complete. After that, he continues to work on the game, enriching it with more content, such as the multiplayer option, and correcting technical failures.

As shown in Fig. 1, the results of the market launch and diffusion strategies of both Stardew Valley and Don't Starve are reflected in the number of players since the games were launched. In comparison to the high public expectation for the Stardew Valley launch, Don't Starve gets the player peaks not at the beginning but years later.

Under a very careful Pixel Art aesthetic and thanks to having shared the entire development process in his blog, he has stood out since its launch. In a month at Steam he had accumulated a total of 1,246,837 in the player counter, with a peak of 64,427 on March 7, 2016. It is also worth noting, alliances with Humbble Bundle, charity games packages frequently developed by independent studies, which resulted in an

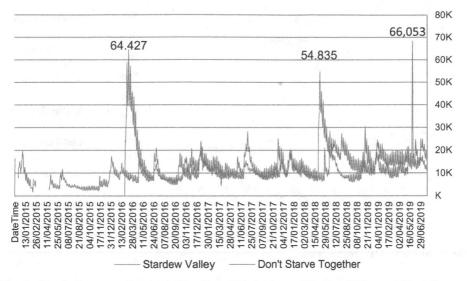

Fig. 1. Graph of comparative data of the SteamDB platform of Stardew Valley and *Don't Starve Together* users on Steam, own source.

increase in players, as reflected in graph 1 in the marking. But the biggest increase experienced on the Steam platform by the game, since its launch, was on April 30, 2018, when the publication of the multiplayer beta phase was announced in the game blob and social networks, reaching a peak of 54,835 in a single day (ConcernedApe 2018). In comparison, Don't Starve Togeter did not generate great expectation in the player community as it was a game in development, and progress was gradual as they had an iterative methodology. When analyzing its figures, it oscillated with a trend of between 5,000 and 20,000 registered players on Steam presenting peaks of periodic increases of around 10,000 players during that time.

However, the most representative for the statistics of *Don't Starve Together* happened in the month of May 2019 when it has experienced an increase 461% of online players, going from 12182 to 68418 in four days, accumulating a total of 308,005 in nine days, following the Free Weekend - May 2019 by Steam, which made available to users 7 free games from May 24 to 28. *Don't Starve Together* excelled the second after *Dead by Daylight* as shown in Fig. 2. It is not the first game to experience a tremendous increase in the participation of major players PC when its price is reduced. Epic Games Store, is key to attracting new PC strategy gamers, offering a free game every fortnight. The first game was Subnautica, an indie game developed by the Unknown Worlds Entertainment company. According to Newzoo data, after two free weeks in Epic Games Store, it increased its numbers of PC players worldwide from 0.4% to 2.9%, *"obtaining a monthly growth of + 625%"* (Weustink 2019). However, the relevance of the exponential increase that *Don't Starve Together* experienced during the Free-weekend-May 2019, lies in the opponents of that weekend. It was under the same conditions with 6 most popular multiplayer games of the moment, three of them indie game too (Table 2).

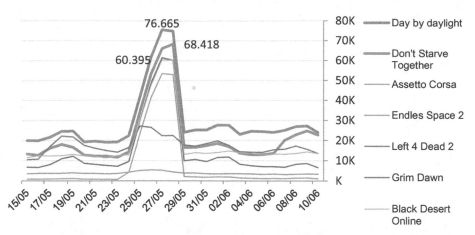

Fig. 2. Graph of comparative data of the SteamDB platform of users on Steam during Free Weekend - May 2019, own source.

Table 2. SteamDB platform data on Steam users. Last update of the registration data on July 28, 2019, own source.

	Game	Rating	Player count register 28/07/19	Player count all time
	Dead by daylight	76,90%	**18.290**	**76.655** (Free-Weekend)
	Left 4 Dead 2	**95,77%**	**14.869**	162.399 (23/12/2003)
	Black Desert online	65,65%	10.810	60.395
# Indie	*Donít Starve Together*	**94,96 %**	**15.337**	**68.418** (Free-Weekend)
	Assetto Corsa	85,02%	3.158	7.067
	Grimm Dawn	**89,58%**	6.981	61.435
	Endless Space 2	79,13%	1.377	53.435

Left 4 dead 2 of the company Valve, whose highest peak was in 2013, is the only AAA video game that achieves better user ratings than *Don't Starve Together*. In relation to the number of online players, Dead by Daylight developed by Behavior Interactive, has similar values to *Don't Starve Together* during the Free Weekend of May 2019. It should be noted that the indie games on this list were developed in access anticipated, being *Don't Starve Together* again the one with the best rating and the most played online.

In order to analyze the impact, it had on the game rankings, we have analyzed the average number of players before and after the free weekend. During the previous three months, the average was 13457 online players. After the peak of 68,418 players, the next three months reflected an increase of 17.52%, 15815 gamers. We have continued to monitor throughout 2020 until it was higher again on free weekend, in order to see if there were any more player fructions. The average increased by 33% over the previous year, with 15815 players on average.

4.2 Don't Starve: Single and Multiplayer Modes

Since 2012, Klei Entertainment has used Early Access as a tool to gather feedback and build our games in collaboration with their community, producing games like *Don't Starve* and the spin-off *Don't Starve Together*. Jamie Cheng and Jeffrey Agala, the founders of Klei Entertainment, set out as an experiment to do something really economical, in short time, and that could be self-published. They took as a methodology the cyclic iterative design of the game. In the development of independent video games, the processes tend to change very frequently, so this methodology allows them to have some flexibility under a low risk. In the case of Klei Entertainment, they took as a starting point a concept of a survival game that emerged in a Game Jam that they had done as experimentation. A production timeline of 2012 was established in which they would carry out the prototype during spring, stealth launch in Chrome Store in summer for free, in autumn commercial launch in Chrome Store doing a two for one, in winter the pre-launch to Steam also two for one and in the spring of 2013 the complete one. They established some pillars of the game to specify the style on which to develop the video game. They were interested in dark humor and took LucasArt video games as a reference source. They were not interested in the heroic of *"the more you have the better"* and leave becoming more powerful. They were captivated by the idea of how a character with a strange personality would interact through the stories of his past. Similarly, they decided that the game structures in which the player must explore, worked very well, such as the Roguelike games, which they used to play. Finally, the last factor would be the mystery, since it is the best way to create expectation, and people comment on the lore and spread the video game better. Also, they started from the theory that the early access could improve QOL (Quality of life): if you can change the game every two weeks and include updates, and adapt it to events, you expand the narrative and the gameplay. During the experimentation phase of the prototype production, they followed a video game aesthetic that condensed the general tastes of a casual audience, with warm and friendly colors. However, for the type of levels and category of game they had in mind, it did not follow the same aesthetic. After the experience of production in their previous games, as Kevin Forbes indicated in the Game Developers Conference® (GDC) of 2016, they aimed to make a style less polished, faster and more efficient. In this way, it evolved from a friendly and colorful concept to a raw graphics of dark and mysterious sketch, reminiscent of the style of Tim Burton, the Quay brothers or the *steampunk* style (Fig. 3).

They started with C++ code that they already had from their previous games, Shank (2010) and Sugar Rush (unreleased). They were also clear that they didn't want a Head-Up Display (HUD) loaded with items that could generate software error or bugs. They decided that the funniest story would be to not starve and survive, so they chose the crafting mode in the survival category. Don't starve consists of many items in the same environment, very easy to understand and implement. The loops always occur, being

Fig. 3. On the left, the first concept of *Don't Starve*, on the right, the final aesthetic of the video game (Agala 2012).

interesting as the player establishes the sequential of the items that are found, and the combinations and new resources that are obtained.

4.3 Engagement Custom Audience

The evolution that has experienced since 2013 with the expansions has been decisive thanks to listening to the demand of the public and making an iterative title. The most significant was *Don't Starve Together*, the multiplayer game that allows players to socialize, build, and strategize throughout the gameplay, maintaining the aesthetic and genre of the game. The cooperative multiplayer opportunity provides the option to enjoy an estimated total of 26.1 h of playability according to Steam DB. It is presented as a multiplayer strategy crafting game where every action player makes can affect the player's future. The player enters a strange and unexplored world full of strange creatures, dangers and surprises, with a style art unique from other games. The player must gather resources to make objects and structures that adapt to his survival style. Dying implies losing everything obtained and having to start over, with the only background of our experience. Although a priori it was a great defect to start from scratch without save points, it is presented as an incentive in multiplayer mode. It has three game modes: The first, survival. It is intended to be the most difficult in cooperative mode and is the default mode. It is designed for dead characters to become ghosts that persecute the live players. Each death will have an impact on health, unless an amulet is used, which brings life back. When all players have died, a two-minute countdown starts and if no player is revived, the game is restarted. The second mode is Desert, in which random players are generated throughout the map. When the character dies, it reappears in a random section like another character, characteristic only in this mode. There are no resurrection items and the world is not restored as in survival mode. Finally, the endless mode, proposes a more relaxed gameplay that does not require cooperation, the world will never restart and revive as many times as they want. However, if the mechanics of death and revival are used repeatedly, it will affect the maximum health, as was the case in survival. No one map is alike, thus making players explore until they can no longer go anywhere further. The story is meticulously hidden so that the player becomes more immersed in the action of the game itself. Progressing through the game to piece together the story, makes *Don't Starve Together* interesting and rewarding to play.

It should be noted that the game has evolved from its beginnings to its multiplayer expansion. There was in the first version a boss who appeared in the winter season of the game, and with two attacks you beat him. Subsequently, more bosses were added but with similar mechanics. In the cooperative version, there are seven new rare bosses with high health performance and more ability to harm and a great aura of madness. They are the biggest threats to players in the virtual world *Don't Starve Together* (Fig. 4).

Fig. 4. Own composition of the seven rare bosses of *Don't Starve Together*.

Developers and the community of players explore and build the tradition of the game. The support of mod is also very important for Klei Entertainment, so they made available to the players the Steam workshop option, so that they continue creating once the early access has finished (Fig. 5).

Fig. 5. On the left, a played mod of Shaggy Rogers from Scooby-Doo for Don't Starve Together made by a gamer, on the right, video game and movie characters with Don't Stave Together style by the artist Jeff Agala (Agala 2012).

One of the strengths of Klei Enterteinment's video games is media synergy. The story of Don't Starve Together characters is shown by animation shorts clips in Klei Entertainment's YouTube channel and Steam's profile. The first cinematic they used to introduce the video game was presenting the main character, Wilson, in 2013. From then on, they made more movies but using gameplays and captures from the video game itself. However, since March 7, 2019, they have made a total of 10 cinematics with new characters that have been introduced in the game modes (Fig. 6).

Fig. 6. Character cinematics of Don't Starve Together

In this way, it not only generates extra content that makes it easier to reach new players in other ways, but also makes the characters known beyond the game's skills and mechanics: they acquire entities such as characters with history and past, and justify how they appear in the game environment.

5 Conclusions

The decentralization of network distribution is breaking the uniqueness of PC games when only Steam existed. The future of videogame distribution presents more options than ever, where cross-platform accessibility means a change of philosophy with respect to current game modes. With the definitive implementation of the Internet for general use, digital purchases became popular, and in this way the concept of independent video games was consolidated. They were not designed to market millions of physical copies, but to enter many computers through digital stores. It reflects the reality of an increasingly less traditional digital ecosystem. The personality, the aesthetic indie, and the innovation of the lore, have been shown to be differentiating and successful factors that facilitate highlighting in a sector collapsed by titles.

Early access is an increasingly used strategy in the indie gaming sector. Indie developers who have limited budgets, can't always afford the method of AAA developers to invest in large specialized teams to test the video game before its launch. Titles recognized as Minecraft or PlayerUnknown's Battlegrounds were consolidated as social phenomena thanks to early access, both with full version today.

Together with social networks, videogames and the Internet facilitate the creation of social groups that become communities, that is, spaces of affinity where to interact and share with other players the concerns, experiences and curiosities about the game (Gee 2004; Jenkins 2005; Knobel and Lankshear 2010). The active role of the audience in the development of the industry, especially the indie, and the feeling of community, is key to the evolution of the sector.

Together with social networks, videogames and the Internet facilitate the creation of social groups that become communities, that is, spaces of affinity where to interact and share with other players the concerns, experiences and curiosities about the game (Gee 2004; Jenkins 2005; Knobel and Lankshear 2010). The active role of the audience in the development of the industry, especially the indie, and the feeling of community, is key to the evolution of the sector.

Steam, although with more competitors than ever, has consolidated resources that favor public participation. Labels, comments from players on the platform, workshop modes and early access are some of the keys offered to the player community and independent developers. In the case of *Don't Starve Together*, those resources implemented from the beginning, have facilitated that years after its launch, they continue to stand out against other titles. Klei Entertainment is one of the many studios that started on Steam and is now beginning to diversify, having put the option of early access to Oxygen Not Included, in the Epic Games Store. The full title has been published recently, on 30th July of 2019, after being in development since 2017. The player reviews section is very important in Steam at the moment of launch, since during two years the users of early acess have seen its evolution and once it has been launched, they make very exhaustive and positive reviews, which facilitates that new players trust and pay for the game, unlike the Epic games Store, which has not developed the ability to make reviews so far.

A convergence between effective modes of development and engagement of the audience that goes beyond the multiplatform, gives rise to a new meaning of the indie games that are distributed digitally.

References

Agala, J.: tumblr de Jeff Agala, director creativo de Klei Entertainment (2012). https://jeffagala.tumblr.com/page/5

Boellstorff, T., Nardi, B., Pearce, C., Taylor, T.L.: Ethnography and Virtual Worlds: A Handbook of Method (2012)

Caillois, R.: Los juegos y los hombres: la máscara y el vértigo. Fondo de Cultura Económica (1958)

Calleja, G.: In-game: From Immersion to Incorporation. MIT Press, Cambridge (2011)

ConcernedApe: ConcernedApe on Twitter: 'Stardew Valley 1.3 update beta is now available for testing on Steam! Instructions here (2018). https://t.co/zz4EGwGuHm. https://twitter.com/ConcernedApe/status/990987892091580417?s=20

Cortés, S., Lacasa, P., Méndez, L.: Ipads, Apps y Redes Sociales: Construyendo narrativas multimodales en las aulas. Digit. Educ. Rev. 53–75 (2016)

Csikszentmihalyi, M.: Flow: The Psychology of Optimal Experience. Harper & Row (1990)

DEV: Libro Blanco del Desarrollo Español de Videojuegos 2018. España (2018)

Dezuanni, M., Hernandez, A.M.: «Prosumidores interculturales»: La creación de medios digitales globales entre los jóvenes - «Prosuming» across cultures: youth creating and discussing digital media across borders. Revista Comunicar 19, 59–66 (2012). https://doi.org/10.3916/C38-2012-02-06

Gee, J.P.: Lo que nos enseñan los videojuegos sobre el aprendizaje y el alfabetismo. Aljibe (2004)

Gómez, S.M.: Discord responde a los incentivos que ofrecen Steam y Epic Games Store (2018). https://www.zonared.com/noticias/discord-responde-a-los-incentivos-que-ofrecen-steam-y-epic-games-store/

Grathwohl, M., Lachausse, J.: Eric Barone- Stardew Valley (2016). https://www.matadorreview.com/eric-barone

Huizinga, J.: Homo ludens. Alianza, Madrid, España (2010)

Hunicke, R., Leblanc, M., Zubek, R.: MDA: a formal approach to game design and game research. Presented at the Game Developers Conference (2004)

Jenkins, H.: Game Design as Narrative Architecture (2004a)

Jenkins, H.: Games, the New Lively Art (2005). https://web.mit.edu/~21fms/People/henry3/GamesNewLively.html

Jenkins, R.: Social Identity. Routledge (2004b)

Juul, J.: The open and the closed: games of emergence and games of progression. Presented at the Computer Games and Digital Cultures Conference Proceedings, Tampere University Press June (2002)

Kitchin, R.: Big Data, new epistemologies and paradigm shifts (2014). https://doi.org/10.1177/2053951714528481

Knobel, M., Lankshear, C.: Remix digital: la nueva escritura global como hibridación sin límites. In: El Valor de la Palabra. Alfabetizaciones, liberaciones y ciudadanías planetarias, pp. 19–43. Ediciones de Centre de Recursos I Educació Continuá, Valencia, Spain (2010)

Lisanne, P., James, S.: Indie Game: The Movie (2011)

Navarrete, J.L., Gómez, F.J., Pérez, J.P.: An approach to the paradigms of Game Theory (2014a)

Navarrete, J.L., Pérez, J.P., Gómez, F.J.: El pensamiento abductivo como fundamento ontológico de los videojuegos. 1. 12, 416–440 (2014b). https://doi.org/10.7195/ri14.v12i2.670

Olin-Scheller, C., Wikstrom, P.: Literary Prosumers: Young People's Reading and Writing. Education Inquiry (2010). https://doi.org/10.3402/edui.v1i1.21931

Pink, S.: Doing Visual Ethnography. SAGE (2013)

Poole, S.: Trigger Happy: Videogames and the Entertainment Revolution. Arcade, New York (2000)

Pratten, R.: Getting Started in Transmedia Storytelling: A Practical Guide for Beginners, 2nd edn. Createspace Independent Pub. (2015)

Salen, K., Zimmerman, E.: Rules of Play: Game Design Fundamentals. MIT Press, Cambridge (2003)

Sampieri, R.H.: Metodología de la Investigación: Las Rutas Cuantitativa, Cualitativa y Mixta. McGraw Hill Mexico (2018)

Seldes, G.: The 7 Lively Arts. Dover Publications Inc., Mineola (2003)

Weustink, J.: Free Games on Epic Games Store Enjoy Huge Spike in Player Share among Core PC Gamers (2019). https://newzoo.com/insights/articles/free-games-on-epic-games-store-enjoy-huge-spike-in-player-share-among-core-pc-gamers/

Zagalo, N.: Alfabetización creativa en los videojuegos: comunicación interactiva y alfabetización cinematográfica - Creative Game Literacy. A Study of Interactive Media Based on Film Literacy. Revista Comunicar **18**, 61–68 (2010). https://doi.org/10.3916/C35-2010-02-06

Zimmerman, E.: Do Independent Games Exist? (2002). https://www.ericzimmerman.com/publications

Collaborative Game Design for Learning: The Challenges of Adaptive Game-Based Learning for the Flipped Classroom

Muriel Algayres[1]([⊠]), Evangelia Triantafyllou[1], Lena Werthmann[2], Maria Zotou[3], Tambouris Efthimios[3], Christos Malliarakis[4], Eleni Dermentzi[5], Roberto Lopez[6], Eirik Jatten[7], and Konstantinos Tarabanis[3]

[1] Aalborg University, Copenhagen, Denmark
mgal@create.aau.dk
[2] Nurogames, Cologne, Germany
[3] University of Macedonia, Thessaloniki, Greece
[4] Mandoulides School, Thessaloniki, Greece
[5] Northumbria University, London, UK
[6] Artelnics, Barcelona, Spain
[7] Revheim Skole, Stavanger, Norway

Abstract. In recent years, game-based learning and gamification have increasingly been used within flipped classroom approaches. Many research showed that both approaches were efficient in conjunction in an active learning perspective. However, we observe that few games have been designed with use in the flipped classroom in mind, and there is therefore potential to improve the flipped classroom experience by approaching the development and integration of games with a more holistic and adaptive experience in mind. For that purpose, a focus group of educators was assembled for a pilot project and their educational practices, objectives and gaming experience analyzed. Following this investigation, co-constructed game design choices were made to try and develop a game that could support a variety of subjects and learning experience in the FC. Although the focus group answers showed that a fully adaptive gaming experience needed, for reasons of flexibility, to lean towards a gamified platform, the final design solution can have the potential to support fully the flipped classroom experience for any subject or class desired.

Keywords: Game design · Gamification · Learning game applications · Flipped classroom

1 Introduction

Interest for learning games has increased since the early 2000s and the discourse regarding the benefits of playful education has become more and more pervasive. While early interest in the educational value of games spawns back decade, in more recent years

A. Brooks et al. (Eds.): ArtsIT 2020, LNICST 367, pp. 228–242, 2021.
https://doi.org/10.1007/978-3-030-73426-8_13

constructivist approaches and more focus into the articulation between playing, learning and engagement has built learning games as an active research field [1].

In this context, research into game-based learning (GBL) has become a cornerstone of the field of active learning (AL). Active learning, according to Frey [2], "shifts the focus of learning from passively receiving content information to diligently participating in learning activities", and allow students to develop and nurture important skills such as "critical thinking, creativity, communication, and collaboration" and "promotes social interactions, allowing students to work collaboratively with their peers and teachers". A solid example of active learning approaches is the considerable of the flipped classroom (FC), which is a set of pedagogical approaches that (1) move most information-transmission teaching out of class, (2) use class time for learning activities that are active and social and (3) require students to complete pre- and/or post-class activities to fully benefit from in-class work." [3].

Research into the potential of integrating educational games in the FC is a more recent development that dates back to the past five years. Many studies have shown the potential of using gamification and games in the FC to support students' preparation for class or engage in collaborative in-class activities.

However, although there is a great diversity of approaches in integrating serious games in the FC, few were designed with FC usage in mind. Some common approaches consist in using commercial games for engagement purpose [4], gamifying the pre-class preparation using tools from the virtual learning environment (VLEs) [5], or using serious games as a strictly in-class activity bound by the class temporality and rather detached from the general FC process [6]. A rare outlier could be the example of the game the Protégé [7], designed with the idea of scalable access to learning material in mind, which is a staple of the FC pre-class process.

There is therefore a dearth in FC focused games and our research project, FLIP2G, aims at filling in this gap by developing a gaming system that could be used as a tool for FC implementation. In this research, a focus group of five participants representing both secondary and higher education was gathered, and an open-ended qualitative questionnaire used to determine what were the needs of educators using the FC and wanting to expand the integration of game-based learning in their methodology. From this collaborative design process, the bespoke model for a gaming platform dedicated to the FC and capable of providing an adaptive learning experience was developed and implemented.

2   Related Works

2.1   Serious Games and Gamification

There is extensive research in the potential of games in an educational context. Educational research especially is a domain in which game studies have strayed away from the notion of studying game as an object or system to the study of play as an ensemble of attitudes and activities [10]. The expanding field of playful learning research has covered a wide range of activities introduced as learning tools: digital game-based learning, non-digital games, gamified learning systems, simulation games, and escape rooms to name only a few [11]. For this study, however, we focused on two essential categories: serious games and gamification. A serious game is defined as a game in which education (in its various forms) is the primary goal, rather than entertainment" [12]. While the original definition concerned the field of digital game studies, the term can also apply to non-digital forms of games such as board games and role-playing games. Gamification is an "umbrella term for the use of video game elements to improve user experience and user engagement in non-game services and applications" [13]. Those two wide definitions allow covering and describing a variety of playful learning experiences.

The game app Kahoot is a solid example of gamification used to great efficiency. Based on a simple quiz system with a timed answer competitive mode, it boasts millions of active users in the world. Several studies have highlighted the game's efficiency in supporting students' engagement in learning. For example, O'Donnell and Gabriel [14] tested the gamified version - through Kahoot - of science course on climate protection for high school students, against a non-gamified version of the same program taught in the control group. Although the gamified version of the curriculum failed to improve the performance of the whole cohort, students in the gamified class presented a more positive feedback on the course and improved knowledge of environmental issues. Similarly, the game platform MaTHiSiS, developed with support from the European Union, provided a mobile platform with several game modules developed to support math education in primary and secondary schools [15].

Research has thus widely underscored the benefits of playful learning and gamification. The meta-study examination carried by Sauve [8] pointed to the effectiveness of games for cognitive, affective and psychomotor learning. Muntean [16] similarly covers how gamification in e-learning can trigger better engagement in participants by involving students in social play and interactions. The efficiency of playful learning has also been connected to improved intrinsic motivation: Bowman [17] through a constructivist approach thus underlines how cognitive, affective and behavioral benefits of educational games trigger better intrinsic motivation and engagement in students. Therefore, the integration of game studies in education has a solid foundation, and this research aims at furthering use of playful learning within the specific context of the FC.

2.2 Serious Games in the FC

The FC is a very significant model developed to support active learning and students' autonomy in the past decade. Many reviews of the FC reveal the interest for the method in the scientific and educational discourse. Former reviews make a compelling argument to the efficiency of the FC: student perceptions and engagement toward FC approaches are generally positive, the FC helps to improve students' communication skills and independent learning, and allows teachers to spend more time with students individually (e.g. [18–20]). However, the main limitations of the FC are also well documented, especially the challenge of getting students prepared for class, in a way that supports the learning process in a continuous manner that include personal work and scalable engagement with the learning material [21].

While research into the FC has expanded during the past decade, investigation into the integration of gamification and serious games in the FC is a most recent subject of exploration. Studies of the educational benefits of the FC accelerated in the 2010s following its popularization in the secondary education in the United States [22], and research into the integration of game-based learning in the FC developed in the past five years.

Our own scoping literature review [23] allows us to show an exponential increase of publication on the subject in the years 2017–2019. It also shows that this theme of research has so far being extremely disjointed, covering a wide variety of approaches and initiatives. For example, almost half of the literature was concerned by gamification applied in the FC, a sign of early experimentations mostly relying on VLE traces. Furthermore, we also observe in this study that, in the minority of studies using an actual GBL approach, one out of five studies covered non-digital games, and a similar proportion on the other hand focused on simulation games. Finally, three out of five articles focused on serious games with, again, a huge diversity of approaches ranging from commercial games, curriculum based serious games, coding games, or digital roleplaying games used for contextual practice. We finally observe that different types of games or gamification are used outside of class and in the classroom, showing the versatility of the GBL practice in the FC (Fig. 1).

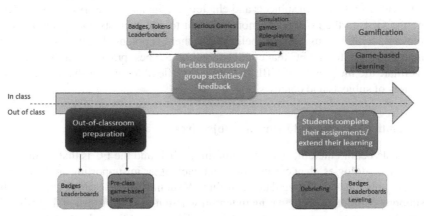

Fig. 1. Synthetic representation of GBL and gamification in the FC (based on Algayres & Triantafyllou [23])

Although games used in the FC cover a large spectrum, they usually focus on specific issues and usually fall in one of the following categories.

- Subject-driven curriculum-dependent games that support a very specific curriculum, usually through targeted in-class activities. For example, Lin et al. [24] studied the impact of a game developed on RPG maker targeted towards business university students. The game would pit students against a variety of scenarios meant to reflect real life business challenges and practices.
- Flexible gaming structures or gamification that allow playful learning in a variety of subject, usually used off-class or at the beginning of the class. The purpose of this approach is to support students' preparation for class by scaling the interaction with the learning material, and engage them in an active manner. The game The Protégé, studied by Ling [7], as mentioned before, offers perhaps one of the most elaborate

examples, inviting students to engage with the learning material as they are trying to solve the mystery of a teacher's disappearance. This is an example of meaningful gamification [25], a new approach to the concept of gamification that puts greater focus on user-based experience and engagement beyond simple game mechanics. Similarly, Hung [26] ran a study on the positive impact of a digitally-enhanced board game with QR codes and gamified quizzes to test the preparation of the students at the beginning of each class, and research carried by Estriegana et al. [27] presented the dual integration of gamification for pre-class preparation and in-glass GBL activities.

Studies into the integration of GBL in the FC showed positive learning outcomes for students, who presented better learning performances and less anxiety towards the studied subject [26]. The combination of GBL and the FC also yielded better learning outcomes in terms of performance and engagement than other structures to deliver the curriculum, both against standard non-gamified FC (e.g. [26, 28, 29]), and non-flipped game-based learning [24].

Due to our specific constraints, of a European project involving a great number of partners with each their own subjects and challenges, the latter, ore specific approach to integrating GBL in the FC seemed more relevant to our interests. Our examination of the relevant literature thus led us to believe that there is potential to develop a bespoke gaming experience for the FC that could expand on the best practices already observed and facilitate the integration of GBL in the FC in a flexible manner that could be used in a variety of subjects and contexts.

2.3 Cognitive Benefits and Learning Objectives

The rationale behind the efficiency of combining GBL and the FC is that, being active learning methodologies, they can complement each other in supporting students' motivation, engagement and self-regulated learning. We define active learning as any method that supports "diligently participating in learning activities" [2] instead of a passive attitude in class. For that purpose, Abeysekera and Dawson [3] used self-determination theory (SDT) to examine the FC in terms of student motivation. They theorized that the FC encourages self-determined forms of intrinsic and integrated extrinsic motivation, by supporting students' sense of competence, autonomy, and relatedness.

Similarly, several studies dealing with the integration of GBL and gamification in the FC quoted self-determination theory as one of the factors that can explain sustained engagement and motivation in students (e.g. [5, 7, 30]). In this context, the gaming elements in the program allow for trial and error, thus enabling both a greater sense of autonomy and competence in the students.

Our project therefore aims also at determining the tools and structure through which we can use GBL in the FC in such a way that the motivational and educational benefits of both methodologies could reinforce each other. For that purpose, we aimed at developing a collaborative gaming design that would allow the creation of an adaptive gaming system that could be adapted to any curriculum requirement within the FC.

3 Methodology

3.1 Focus Group Investigation

The objective of the FLIP2G project is to build a dedicated gaming platform for the FC, that could provide an adaptive experience to a variety of users. The choice of a collaborative co-design made therefore sense in the development stage. Design Participation, or the action of involving end users in the design process, has a long history dating back to the 1970s [9]. According to Lee [9], one benefit of Design Participation is allowing collaboration between scientific design research and creative design research, and bridging the abstract space of design with the concrete space of users.

To that end, our approach to the development of the gaming platform was to work with a specific focus group, comprised of the partners who volunteered to be part of the project and active participants in the pilot tests of the game. The result of the focus group investigation was then the basis for implementation by the game designers. There is a long practice of using focus groups as a tool for educational design research. Focus groups provide a qualitative approach to such purposes as generating ideas among staff for purposes of curriculum development [31], or getting specific understanding of social issues for a certain group [32]. For our purpose, we follow the steps suggested in Morgan et al. [33]: research design, data collection, analysis and reporting of results.

3.2 Research Design and Data Collection

As stated above, the focus group was comprised of the project partners enrolled to be stakeholders in the pilot projects ($n = 5$), representing four different nationalities and two types of educational institutions (secondary and higher education). The purpose of the group was to determine the needs for a gaming platform developed to fit a FC model.

A questionnaire was built which focused on the following themes:

– Subjects and levels that would be taught using the platform
– Conventional learning activities carried out in class
– Objectives pursued in using GBL in the FC

The questionnaire was comprised of six open questions. The participants could write their own detailed answers. Due to the extreme dispersion of participants in the European territory, the questionnaire was conducted online, with a timeframe of two weeks to answer the questions (Table 1 and Fig. 2).

The data was synthesized in a thematic table based on the keywords used by each participant.

Table 1. Description of participants

Participant code	Country	Institution	Main subjects taught	Student age	Class size
#1	UK	University	Digital business, Mathematics	18–25	10–50
#2	Greece	University	Project management	18–30	20–60
#3	Denmark	University	Programming	18–25	60–70
#4	Norway	Secondary	Social sciences, English	12–16	20–30
#5	Greece	Secondary	Mathematics, History, Geography, Computer	9–15	20–30

Please fill out and return this questionnaire until the 31.10.2019

Which is/are the main subject(s) that you want to teach with Flip2G?

Which is the main age group that you want to teach with Flip2G?

Which traditional learning activities do you like to use in class?

Do you play any "analogue" learning games in class? If so, which?

Which features are missing in traditional learning activities that gaming can help with?

How long are your classes on average and how often do they take place during the week (in one subject)? How much of that time would you use for any gamified content?

Fig. 2. Screen capture of questionnaire

4 Results

4.1 Analysis and Results: The Challenges of Collaborative Design

The result of the focus group questionnaires showed a few points of convergence, but many points of divergence.

The main similarities resided in the objectives pursued in wanting to introduce a game-based learning approach in the classroom. The main motivation for using the game is to give students better engagement or motivation in their studies and facilitate the understanding of the learning material (three occurrences each). Secondary elements regarding the objectives of the game related to the learning experience of the students: to facilitate the integration and use of assignment and quizzes (two occurrences), and to support the use of game in a way that would feel more organic and less time consuming (one occurrence) (Fig. 3).

A majority of respondents (three out of five) had previous experience using games in their classroom in different forms: gamification via Kahoot, use of commercial games for educational purpose, and finally use of a cybersecurity simulation game online. While this is cohesive with the fact that partners were volunteers for the project, it also

Subjects Taught	Age	Class Size	Academical BG	Session Length (h)	Sessions	Total hours	Traditional Learning Activities	Games used	Objective of the Game
Digital Business, Linear Programming, Mathematics	18-25	10 to 50	Business Students	3	6	18	Group Discussions, Reading Assignments, Exercises (e.g. SWOT), Internet Research (e.g. Analytical)	Online games (cybersecurity simulation game)	More engaging/fun, Engaging to students who already know the topics
Project Mgmt, Open Data, E-Government	18-30	20-60	Applied Informatics	1 to 2	13	26	Assignments, Quizzes, PBL		Integrate assignments & quizzes to the game, Understanding of the learning
OOP with Java, Android Programming	18-25	60-70	Undergraudates (CS)	1	10	10	Quizzes, Programming Exercises, Q&A Rounds, Lectures with Slides, Demonstrations		Better understanding, Higher Motivation
Social Sciences, English	12 to 16	20-30	High Schoolers	1	40	40	Reading Assignments, Group Work, Presentations, Frontal Teaching, Videos, Class Discussions	D&D (tentative), OTS digital games (Frostpunk, AC)	Audio-visual output, tactile input, Easy to engage games that is [?]
Mathematics, Physics, History, Geography, Informatics	9 to 15	20-30	Middle Schoolers	1 to 2	40	40	Exercises, Multiple Choice Quizzes, True / False Quizzes, Assignments, Open Quizzes	Riddles, Kahoot	Understanding of material, Adding assignments & quizzes, Increased Motivation

Fig. 3. Screen capture of response table

underlined the necessity of developing a game that would be accessible to educators without a prior gaming experience.

All respondents however had various different needs in terms of classes and curriculum. Due to integrating participants of both secondary and higher education, a huge variety of potential subjects was covered, nine in STEM subjects ranging from mathematics to programming, two in economics, and four in Humanities. Similarly, class sizes and session length were of a diverse range, ranging from 20 to 60 students to sessions ranging from one to three hours, with an average length of 1.6 h.

This diversity of responses showed that a truly adaptive game should be able to adapt to a variety of circumstances, although participants' objectives were aligned with the objectives of the FC and active learning. In that, the participants in our study reflected the main challenges regarding the implementation of game-based learning, previously identified in other studies such as Meletiou-Mavrotheris and Prodromou [34]: the teacher's gaming literacy and training, the curriculum constraints in space and time, and the resources, both financial and technical.

These challenges and the need to cater to a diverse audience led the design team to choose a gamified structure and develop a platform that would allow scalable access to learning resources and games while allowing for full personalization from the teachers.

4.2 Design Choices and Elaboration of the Game Platform

The final design of the gaming platform aimed at providing an adaptable gaming experience. Owing to the constraints in target groups and course structure, the final design ending up leaning towards a gamified experience. The game was developed for use on personal computer via Unity. The initial data structure aimed at structuring the game around the course requirements, translated in the form of quizzes and learning material. Interactions with the game and the platform would then provide analytics for both students and teachers (Fig. 4).

A very light framing device provides a scenario, in which the student play as spy with an animal avatar, designed to be appealing to younger audiences while still relatable

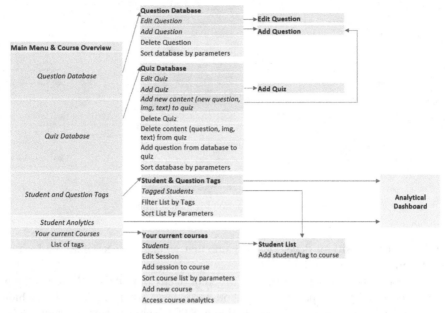

Fig. 4. Data model for FLIP2G (source: Nurogames)

to older groups. Each course is presented as a mission, during which the student must go through a series of quiz-based quests and to defeat final bosses (Fig. 5).

Fig. 5. Screenshot of student menu screen (source: FLIP2G platform, Nurogames)

In the main menu, students can access information regarding their progress and performance during each connection to the game, which allow them to monitor their progression and support self-directed learning.

The game possesses a solo mode and a collaborative mode to cover the different forms of engagement in the FC (both solo preparation at home and collaborative activities in class). In solo mode, the player has to answers questions correctly to defeat a final boss. In collaborative mode, each participant gets only part of the questionnaire (questions or answers), and participants must team up to connect the correct questions and answers (Fig. 6 and Fig. 7).

Fig. 6. Screenshot of student quiz in solo mode (source: FLIP2G platform, Nurogames)

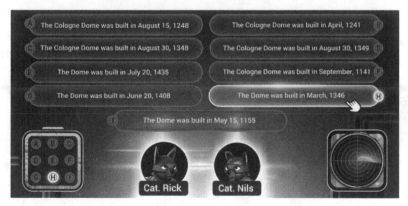

Fig. 7. Screenshot of the student screen in cooperative mode (source: FLIP2G platform, Nurogames)

Before and during the game, participants can access the learning material to prepare for the class or to help them go through the questions (Fig. 8).

Fig. 8. Course material access (source: FLIP2G platform, Nurogames)

Finally, the students can access a dashboard page that presents dedicated analytics regarding their progression and engagement over the course of the game. They can also access a list of their wrong answers to correct themselves if they want to take a test several times, to support a trial-and-error progression (Fig. 9 and Fig. 10).

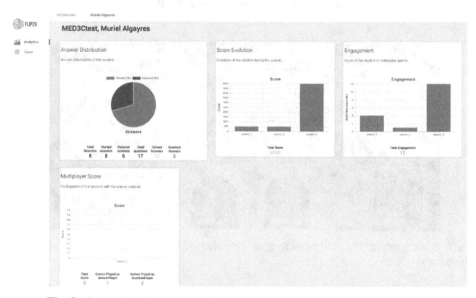

Fig. 9. Screenshot of student dashboard (source: FLIP2G platform, Nurogames)

The content of the games (questions and answers) is plugged in through the teacher interface. The teacher interface is web-based, and its structure is similar to that of other VLEs, including Moodle, to facilitate implementation and adaptation of the game to any time of curriculum or student. The teacher's dashboard also includes information

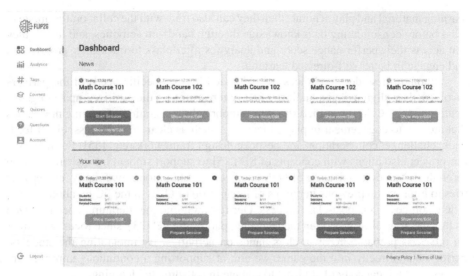

Fig. 10. Teacher's dashboard (source: FLIP2G platform, Nurogames)

regarding the performance of each student and allows adaption of the curriculum and intervention to prevent risk of student dropout.

Therefore, the requirements for an adaptive gaming experience and for wide flexibility got us to lean towards a gamified experience. The students benefit from a dedicated gaming platform and access to their own analytics, and the teachers can follow the evolution of their own cohorts with the possibility to identify which parts of the curriculum need revision for better engagement and which students might be at risk of dropout.

5 Discussion

Our project started with the objective of expanding and improving the FC learning experience by using the best practices of game-based learning and developing a dedicated, adaptive gaming platform.

Our literary reviews showed us that previous research had established the validity of using games in the FC, but that there was some untapped potential in trying to develop a platform that could support more closely to the needs of active learning methodologies.

During investigation into educators' needs and expectations for this game, however, we faced the challenge of needing a game that could fit the needs of a huge variety of subjects, curriculum and learning environments. This leads us to conclude that there is currently a tension between higher flexibility and adaptability of usage and more specialized gaming content. In the former case, adaptability imposes the use of gamification and/or more flexible games, whereas the latter case allows for more tailored content and game narratives, but limit its transmissibility and adaptation to other learning circumstances.

However, the final design for our gaming platform allow to cover for the wide range of experiences that structure the FC learning process. First, the student can access the learning material and play at home, then they can also train with the collaborative mode in class before consolidating their knowledge through hands-on activities, and finally they can access their performance score and analytics after class to track their progression and engage in better self-directed learning.

Although these design choices were dictated by the specific needs of the partners involved, they align with the findings of current research on the positive impact of gamification in the FC. The gamified structure supports the integration of gaming mechanics that are key to engagement in playful learning, such as clear goals, access, direct feedback, challenge, collaboration, and bespoke design framework (e.g. [35]) Furthermore, our project also aligns with concepts of SDT [5] to support student intrinsic motivation through stimulation and sense of both competence and autonomy. Finally, our project tries to improve on previous iterations of integration of GBL in the FC by allotting specific resources to the post-class process. Our research into the literature indeed showed us that the after-class was often the neglected part of the FC [23], since focus was either on pre-class preparation, or in-class hands-on activities. By integrating the students' performance directly into the game, we aim at supporting a continuous improvement process and the capacity of students to engage in self-directed learning.

Our study into collaborative game design came yet with several limitations. The size of the focus group was limited and the participants decided by being the partners engaged in the FLIP2G project for the following pilot study into the implementation of the game. Therefore, their positioning was both as practitioners and stakeholders in the implementation process, which conditioned and biased their choices and answers.

Our design choices ended up being severely constrained by the diversity of profiles that we ended up with, and forced us to choose a gamified solution that appears more limited from a narrative perspective. As the game reaches its final stages of development, validity to its use in classroom situations remains to be evaluated in pilot trials. The model however has the potential to offer a new perspective on the integration of GBL in the FC by putting a greater attention to the analytics and analysis of the engagement process both by students and teachers. Furthermore, it might also be improve in future iterations of the game or new platforms by the incorporation of games other than simple quizzes (e.g. collaborative games, word games, crosswords, etc.). This project aims at building up and improving our understanding of the efficiency of GBL in the FC through best practices, with its full impact to be evaluated in the future through wide implementation in full cohorts of students.

6 Conclusion

The FC and GBL have been consequent developments in active learning, and recent educational developments promoting integration of 21st century skills and self-directed learning in secondary and higher education. As those two approaches are used more and more in conjunction, new challenges arise regarding the most efficient way to integrate games in the FC. Our projects aimed at designing a bespoke gaming platform that could support the whole of the FC learning experience. To that purpose, we organized a focus group of the participants in the project pilot trial. However, faced with a huge diversity of profiles and needs, we concluded that we needed a flexible structure that could adapt to these requirements, and our final design choice was to develop a gamified learning experience that prioritized scalable access to the learning material and easy implementation of quizzes, both in solo and cooperative mode. Further research perspective will aim at testing this playful learning approach over the duration of a full curriculum.

References

1. Egenfeldt-Nielsen, S., Smith, J., Tosca, S.: Understanding Video Games: The Essential Introduction. Routledge, Abingdon (2012). https://doi.org/10.4324/9780203116777
2. Frey, B.B.: The SAGE Encyclopedia of Educational Research, Measurement, and Evaluation. SAGE Publications, Inc., Thousand Oaks (2018). https://doi.org/10.4135/9781506326139
3. Abeysekera, L., Dawson, P.: Motivation and cognitive load in the flipped classroom: Definition, rationale and a call for research. High. Educ. Res. Dev. 34(1), 1–14 (2015)
4. Ye, S.H., Hsiao, T.Y., Sun, C.T.: Using commercial video games in flipped classrooms to support physical concept construction. J. Comput. Assist. Learn. 34(5), 602–614 (2018)
5. Tsay, C.H.H., Kofinas, A., Luo, J.: Enhancing student learning experience with technology-mediated gamification: an empirical study. Comput. Educ. 121, 1–17 (2018)
6. Tao, S.Y., Huang, Y.H., Tsai, M.J.: Applying the flipped classroom with game-based learning in elementary school students' English learning. In: 2016 International Conference on Educational Innovation through Technology (EITT), pp. 59–63. IEEE (2016)
7. Ling, L.T.Y.: Meaningful gamification and students' motivation: a strategy for scaffolding reading material. Online Learn. 22(2), 141–155 (2018)
8. Sauvé, L.: Effective educational games. In: Kaufman, D., Sauvé, L. (eds.) Educational Gameplay and Simulation Environments: Case studies and Lessons learned, pp. 27–50. IGI Global: Information Science Reference (2010)
9. Lee, Y.: Design participation tactics: the challenges and new roles for designers in the co-design process. Co-design 4(1), 31–50 (2008)
10. Triclot, M.: Game studies ou études du play ?, Sciences du jeu [En ligne], 1 | 2013, mis en ligne le 01 octobre 2013, consulté le 01 juillet (2020). https://doi.org/10.4000/sdj.223, https://journals.openedition.org/sdj/223
11. Whitton, N.: Playful learning: tools, techniques, and tactics. Res. Learn. Technol. 26 (2018)
12. Michael, D.R., Chen, S.L.: Serious Games: Games That Educate, Train, and Inform. Muska & Lipman/Premier-Trade Thomson Course Technology, Boston (2005)
13. Deterding, S., Sicart, M., Nacke, L., O'Hara, K., Dixon, D.: Gamification: using game-design elements in non-gaming contexts. In: CHI 2011 Extended Abstracts on Human Factors in Computing Systems, pp. 2425–2428. ACM (2011)
14. O'Donnell, B., Gabriel, F.: Gamifying graph reading. In: European Conference on Games Based Learning, pp. 926–932. Academic Conferences International Limited (2017)
15. Spyrou, E., Vretos, N., Pomazanskyi, A., Asteriadis, S., Leligou, H.C.: Exploiting IoT technologies for personalized learning. In: 2018 IEEE Conference on Computational Intelligence and Games (CIG), pp. 1–8. IEEE. (2018)
16. Muntean, C.I.: Raising engagement in e-learning through gamification. In: Proceedings of the 6th International Conference on Virtual Learning ICVL, (ressource en ligne) (2011). Accédé le 19 July 2019
17. Bowman, S., Standiford, A.: educational larp in the middle school classroom: a mixed method case study. Int. J. Role-Playing 5(1), 4–25 (2015)
18. Bishop, J.L., Verleger, M.A.: The flipped classroom: a survey of the research. In: ASEE National Conference Proceedings, Atlanta, GA, vol. 30, no. 9, p. 18 (2013)

19. O'Flaherty, J., Phillips, C.: The use of flipped classrooms in higher education: a scoping review. Internet High. Educ. **25**, 85–95 (2015)
20. Zainuddin, Z., Halili, S.H.: Flipped classroom research and trends from different fields of study. Int. Rev. Res. Open Distrib. Learn. **17**(3), 313–340 (2016)
21. Herreid, C.F., Schiller, N.A.: Case studies and the flipped classroom. J. Coll. Sci. Teach. **42**(5), 62–66 (2013)
22. Bergmann, J., Sams, A.: Remixing chemistry class: two Colorado teachers make vodcasts of their lectures to free up class time for hands-on activities. Learn. Lead. Technol. **36**(4), 22–27 (2009)
23. Algayres, M., Triantafyllou, E.: Combining game-based learning and the flipped classroom: a scoping review. In: European Conference on Games Based Learning. Academic Conferences International Limited, pp. 823-XII (2019)
24. Lin, C.-J., Hwang, G.-J., Fu, Q.-K., Chen, J.-F.: A flipped contextual game-based learning approach to enhancing EFL students' English business writing performance and reflective behaviors. Educ. Technol. Soc. **21**(3), 117–131 (2018)
25. Nicholson, S.: A user-centered theoretical framework for meaningful gamification. Paper presented at Games+Learning+Society 8.0, Madison, WI (2012)
26. Hung, H.T.: Gamifying the flipped classroom using game-based learning materials. ELT J. **72**(3), 296–308 (2018)
27. Estriegana, R., Medina-Merodio, J.A., Barchino, R.: Analysis of competence acquisition in a flipped classroom approach. Comput. Appl. Eng. Educ. **27**(1), 49–64 (2019)
28. Hsu, W.C., Lin, H.C.K.: Impact of applying WebGL technology to develop a web digital game-based learning system for computer programming course in flipped classroom. In: 2016 International Conference on Educational Innovation through Technology (EITT), pp. 64–69. IEEE (2016)
29. Wang, Y.H.: Exploring the effectiveness of adopting anchor-based game learning materials to support flipped classroom activities for senior high school students. Interact. Learn. Environ., 1–20 (2019)
30. Liao, C.W., Chen, C.H., Shih, S.J.: The interactivity of video and collaboration for learning achievement, intrinsic motivation, cognitive load, and behavior patterns in a digital game-based learning environment. Comput. Educ. **133**, 43–55 (2019)
31. Breen, R.L.: A Practical guide to focus-group research. J. Geogr. High. Educ. **30**(3), 463–475 (2006). https://doi.org/10.1080/03098260600927575
32. Nyumba, O., Wilson, K., Derrick, C.J., Mukherjee, N.: The use of focus group discussion methodology: Insights from two decades of application in conservation. Methods Ecol. Evol. **9**(1), 20–32 (2018)
33. Morgan, D.L., Krueger, R.A., King, J.A.: The Focus Group Kit, vols. 1–6. Sage Publications Inc., Thousand Oaks (1998)
34. Meletiou-Mavrotheris, M., Prodromou, T.: Pre-service teacher training on game-enhanced mathematics teaching and learning. Technol. Knowl. Learn. **21**(3), 379–399 (2016). https://doi.org/10.1007/s10758-016-9275-y
35. Huang, B., Hew, K.F., Warning, P.: Engaging learners in a flipped information science course with gamification: a quasi-experimental study. In: Cheung, S.K.S., Lam, J., Li, K.C., Au, O., Ma, W.W.K., Ho, W.S. (eds.) ICTE 2018. CCIS, vol. 843, pp. 130–141. Springer, Singapore (2018). https://doi.org/10.1007/978-981-13-0008-0_13

Enhancing the Educational Value of Tangible and Intangible Dimensions of Traditional Crafts Through Role-Play Gaming

Nikolaos Partarakis[1(✉)], Nikolaos Patsiouras[1], Thodoris Evdemon[1],
Paraskevi Doulgeraki[1], Effie Karuzaki[1], Evropi Stefanidi[1], Stavroula Ntoa[1],
Carlo Meghini[2], Danai Kaplanidi[3], Maria Fasoula[3], and Xenophon Zabulis[1]

[1] Foundation for Research and Technology Hellas, 100 N. Plastira Street, 70013 Heraklion,
Crete, Greece
`{partarak,patsiouras,evdemon,vdoulger,karuzaki,evropi,stant,`
`zabulis}@ics.forth.gr`
[2] Istituto Di Scienza e Tecnologie della Informazione (ISTI), Consiglio Nazionale delle
Ricerche (CNR), Area della Ricerca CNR, via G. Moruzzi 1, 56124 Pisa, Italy
`carlo.meghini@isti.cnr.it`
[3] Piraeus Bank Group Cultural Foundation, 6 Ang. Gerontas Street, 105 58 Athens, Greece
`FasoulaM@piraeusbank.gr`

Abstract. Advances in Cultural Heritage (CH) representation and presentation technologies are explored concerning new potentials brought by the gaming industry. These include the use of digitisation technologies for the creation of realistic digital assets, educational gaming concepts, and immersive technologies. In this context, it is shown how the creative sector can exploit these potentials in novel educational and gaming experiences, inspired by CH. The aim is to enhance the way that cultural content is experienced in the digital world, to present, and to valorise intangible dimensions and, ultimately, exploit technological advances to enhance our understanding, appreciation, and preservation of tangible and intangible heritage.

Keywords: Culture · Cultural heritage · Heritage crafts · 3D reconstruction · Digitisation · Semantic knowledge representation · Role play gaming · Virtual reality · Education · Training

1 Introduction

Traditional Crafts (TCs) exhibit tangible and intangible dimensions. Tangible dimensions regard craft articles and products, materials and tools, as well as natural resources, built workshops, and workplaces. The tangible, or material, aspect of TCs is evident in their practice, where materials are transformed with the use of tools. At the same time, intangible dimensions as skill and technical knowledge are intimately involved in this process, evidencing that "crafts are probably the most tangible of intangible heritage"

A. Brooks et al. (Eds.): ArtsIT 2020, LNICST 367, pp. 243–254, 2021.
https://doi.org/10.1007/978-3-030-73426-8_14

[39]. Moreover, craft artefacts reflect the socio-historical content of the communities, times, and places within which they were developed, reflecting their history, values, collective memories, and oral traditions. TCs are part of the history and economic life of the regions and communities in which they flourish. As Kurin points out, long-standing market or exchange economy systems have an impact on geographical regions and networks [17] and reveal the way for sustainable development.

In the Mingei project [24], we focus on representing tangible and intangible content due to TCs [44], to enhance the appreciation and value of a cultural visit. This is strategized by providing educational content and engaging experience for uses prior, during, and after a visit. These facilitate engagement with local culture, using modern, intuitive, and attractive presentations that impact a wide range of audiences, including younger ages.

In this work, we propose an approach towards the presentation of both tangible and intangible CH dimensions, through an informal gaming context. This context offers learning potentials through immersion in a virtual setting that enables exploration of the past, the inspection of tangible artefacts, and the engagement in activities that transmit intangible dimensions.

2 Related Work

2.1 Representation and Digitisation for CH Preservation

In the past decades, the evolution of technologies for CH preservation and presentation regarded mainly Semantic Web technologies for preserving knowledge and digitisation technologies for preserving material dimensions. Semantic technologies and ontologies, in particular, are nowadays standard tools in CH. There is a significant history of pertinent approaches in CH, since the pioneering work of Europeana [13], which triggered the model of CH with semantic technologies in 2007 [10]. We distinguish three phases of the adoption of semantic technologies in the CH sector. During the first phase (2000–2010), projects relied mostly on existing approaches to knowledge classification, stemming from the library and archival science. During the second phase (2010–2015), the focus shifted towards richer, event-centric representations, in response to the realization of the drawbacks and scarce utility of object-centric representations (the class Event is one of the basic classes that the Europeana Data Model [10]). Finally, during the third phase (2015, today), we are observing significant changes supported by the development of new representations of CH artefacts, based on new digitization techniques, able to exploit the above-mentioned technological advances [8].

2.2 Digitization Approaches for Tangible CH

Approaches towards the digitisation of CH components initially focused on artefacts and monuments of material heritage. With the evolution of digitisation technologies, in the CH sector, efforts have been made to standardize the digitization process, providing guidelines on how to digitize books and documents as well as objects and monuments of CH [1, 4, 7, 12, 18]. Guidelines regarding file management, digital preservation, online publication, and Intellectual Property Rights (IPR) management can be found through the MINERVA EU funded Thematic Network (IST-2001-35461), whose Website and handbook [23] comprise a valuable starting point for these matters, as well as, the foundation of online heritage repositories, such as Europeana [13]. Digitisation guides and good practice guidelines [4, 11] are now the norm in photographic documentation.

Among digitisation technologies, the most relevant to this work is the 3D reconstruction, defined as the process of capturing the shape and appearance of a physical object. The proliferation of surface digitisation technologies streamlined the 3D digitisation of artefacts and monuments. Digital 3D models of artefacts have a wide range of uses, from conservation and preservation to reunification of dispersed heritage [1]. The capabilities of the individual technologies vary in terms of several criteria that must be considered and balanced when deciding on the digitization strategy [1]. The 3D reconstruction of physical objects has been improved with laser scanning and photogrammetry, which enable digitizing tangible artefacts for cultural heritage and archaeological sites. Each methodology proposes a different approach to face the challenge of digitization for visualization or preservation purposes.

2.3 Advances in the Gaming Industry

The gaming industry has proposed game genres for creating types of gameplay that could increase the engagement of players with the game scenario. The ultimate goal is the illusion of natural immersion in a way that avails a "sense of place" [19] and provides the context of the targeted experience. One of the most relevant game genres is fantasy role-playing games, which are leisure activities that entail a unique form of play. The game is not competitive, has no time limits, has no score-keeping, and, has no finite definitions of winning or losing. Fantasy role-playing games are not merely for players to play well nor to "win". Instead, the goals are survival, knowledge, skill acquisition, and character development [42]. In the context of role-playing games, the creation of 3D models of real-world scenes has always been an attractive topic in the game industry. According to [28] building virtual 3D scenes has always required talented people with artistic sense, specialized and expensive software, strong computational resources for photorealistic visualization, and significant manual effort. This process includes the acquisition and usage of several visual references such as concept art and photographs [34]. Realistic productions rely heavily on photographs, with higher budget games investing in field trips during the preproduction phase to capture authentic photographs on location [31, 35]. Until recently photogrammetry was only used sporadically in game development as the dense millions of polygons meshes generated by these processes are highly unsuitable for real-time rendering.

The announcement of EA DICE in May 2015 that its new flagship title "Star Wars: Battlefront" would **rely heavily on photogrammetry** to capture the franchise's acclaimed settings [33] was a **radical change to game development**. Faced with the challenge of capturing the well-established visual style of Star Wars, the team opted for photogrammetry to recreate not only props and outfits previously used in the movies but also the epic locations that are familiar to Star Wars fans [5]. The creation of realistic photogrammetry scans is still computationally demanding, requiring high-end computers and many hours of processing time. Thus, as demonstrated by [2], populating extensive game worlds with photogrammetry assets demands larger-scale solutions. Another consideration is the need to manually post-process photogrammetry reconstructions, including cleaning, re-texturing, etc. [3]. It is foreseen that photogrammetry will be extensively used for creating realistic assets, due to reconstruction realism and reduction of production costs [29]. Furthermore, it is conceivable that 3D art will follow the evolution of painting. In painting, the primary goal of the artists of the past centuries was to create a visually convincing replication of the real world. Then with the evolution of photography, it was made apparent that in the future the work of the painter will be replaced by one of the photographers. This fact resulted in an evolution in art mainly because artists were relieved by the burden of realism and allowed to explore their creativity to create novel forms of artistic expression resulting in the modern art revolution [21].

2.4 This Work

In this work, an attempt is made to merge different worlds, the world of scientific representation of CH and the world of the gaming industry. We assert, that the third phase of knowledge representation technologies and 3D digitisation strategies combined with the advances of the gaming industry (new Game Development Engines, usage of 3D reconstructions for gaming, new gaming genres, etc.) can support a new form of CH powered innovation. This could support the creation of appealing demonstrations through an informal gaming context, where entertainment and knowledge join forces to increase our understanding of our cultural heritage. The workflow presented in this research work is rooted in the requirements set by the Mingei Project [27] and follows the defined approach for knowledge representation and presentation [43].

3 The Island of Chios Game Concept and Implementation

The game provides information regarding the historic period of the medieval occupation of Chios and more specifically regarding the socio-historic context of mastic cultivation and the creation of the first settlements resulted in the formulation of the so-called mastic villages. The game is based on the third-person action principles (a third-person game is a game in which the player character is visible on-screen during gaming [45]), and navigation in an open 3D environment where only the restrictions of the sea around the island exist, together with limitations related to the angle of the terrain surface. The proposed, by this work, implementation approach contains the following activities: (a) study of history and definition of a scenario for the game, (b) basic knowledge acquisition & 3D reconstructions of heritage sites, (c) knowledge representation, (d) semantic export and creation of game assets, (e) terrain implementation and (f) implementation of the main game concept and mini-game scenarios.

3.1 Game Scenario and Objective

The game scenario is built on top of the history of Chios a small island on the northeast side of the Aegean Sea. According to [32], among others, mastic was always a great asset of trading for the rulers of Chios. During the Byzantine Empire (4th–13th century) mastic monopoly was under the emperor's rule. From 1349 to 1566, Chios was under the rule of the Republic of Genoa. At that time, a trading company was founded, which was called Maona. Mastic was a monopoly of Maona and as a company, it had a very strict program regarding the production of mastic. Maona kept contracts of three, six, eight, and ten years with companies from Genoa, Armenia, Cyprus, Istanbul, Alexandria, Greece, and Syria. The transportation of the product was taking place using vessels that transported crates with mastic that were called 'mastic boats' and they could transfer fifteen to thirty crates. From the 16th to the 20th century, Chios was under Ottoman rule. The Ottomans had also the monopoly of the mastic trade but they allowed some facilitations for the mastic communities. Based on this order, various settlements were created, houses were built to a specific architecture, while the social life of mastic growers was adapted to it as well. First, the "castra", the square towers in the centre of fortified rectangular courtyards, were created. Later, probably within the framework of a wider defensive plan, it was decided that settlements would be fortified with a surrounding wall equipped with round towers in the corners and with gates at the points where the wall met the basic roads. Most probably, the walls also enclosed undeveloped land, which was built later [16].

The main storyline of the game starts with the appearance of the player to an unknown world in the middle of the forest. The game involves exploration of the Chios landscape to access historic information regarding the medieval occupation of the island and through exploration learn about the cultivation of mastic and the significance of this product for the local population. Furthermore, the game scenario includes exploration of mastic villages each of which reveals its unique architecture, decorative patterns, house structures, etc. In this journey, the main ports of the island are presented, the transfer and export of mastic, the mastic field as the dominant cultivation of the island, etc. The storyline of the game is not linear and relies on the exploration decisions that the player is making following the principles of open-world gaming. In video games, an open world is a game mechanic of using a virtual world that the player can explore and approach objectives freely, as opposed to a world with more linear and structured gameplay [3].

3.2 Knowledge Acquisition and 3D Reconstructions

PIOP is a cultural heritage stakeholder that has created a museum dedicated to Chios mastic with the cooperation of the Chios Gum Mastic Growers Association. Extensive historical, environmental, social, and craft knowledge was collected for the creation of the museum and is now part of PIOP's archive. Knowledge acquisition for the specific game was carried out through PIOP's archive which also includes the Chios Gum Mastic Growers Association archive on the trade and industrialization of mastic. Archival material included scientific essays, audio recordings of local oral traditions, audio-visual documentation of craft and industrial processes, as well as digitized historical books. For the collection of new assets audio-visual material was produced, as well as 3D scans of the museum's items, the mastic tree, and open spaces such as the Chios Mastic Museum and mastic villages.

The 3D reconstructions of the villages are part of the game assets and were acquired through on-site aerial 3D reconstruction. Their characteristic structure reveals fortification against pirates and storage buildings at the centre of the village to guard mastic (see

Fig. 1, Sect. 1). To do so, a dataset was created containing aerial images acquired via a UAV overlooking a village. In the results (see Fig. 1, Sect. 2), building structures are reconstructed with fidelity and alleys, streets, and village squares are clearly outlined (see Fig. 1, Sect. 3). Furthermore, reconstructions of additional rural environment elements and mastic cultivation tools were made, including 3D modelling of some of the tools and were further post-processed to be converted to 3D assets (Fig. 2).

Fig. 1. Aerial photograph of a village (1), 3D reconstruction results (2) map view of the same village (3) (street map retrieved from [30]).

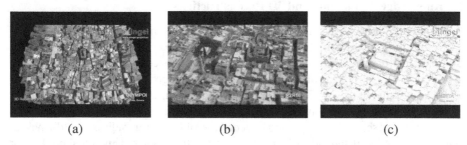

(a)   (b)   (c)

Fig. 2. Videos showing the 3D reconstruction of three mastic villages. a) https://youtu.be/adP DVx7RGVc. b) https://youtu.be/15NcRlg3360. c) https://youtu.be/9xNlrGSBfIE

3.3 Knowledge Representation and Authoring

The representation of knowledge was facilitated by the Mingei Online Platform (MOP), which has been developed based on the Research Space (RS) [26] platform, enriched with features for representation, digital preservation, and dissemination of this content. MOP offers seamless treatment of heterogeneous data and implements a repository of content created in the project, inherited as a legacy from archives, as well as links to knowledge and assets created by third parties, and are available online. The Mingei Crafts Ontology (CrO) [22] was used to represent the collected knowledge on mastic cultivation and the relevant socio-historic context (Fig. 3).

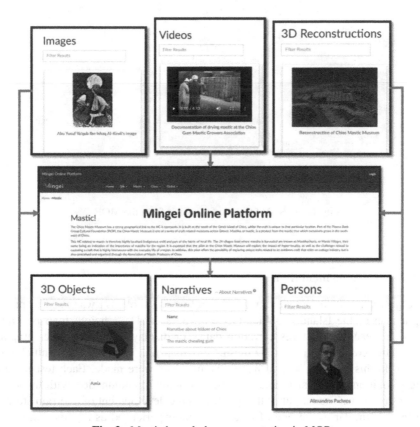

Fig. 3. Mastic knowledge representation in MOP.

To provide **access to the authored knowledge**, two routes were explored (a) runtime access to and (b) offline access. The first route poses several limitations mainly because all assets used in Unity3D should be precompiled and, thus, creating a runtime compilation feature for Web-based URIs could pose extra development effort. In this work, the second solution was preferred. In this solution, digital assets were exported from the MOP in a structure JSON based format. The JSON file includes metadata of assets and the URIs, where assets are located on the Mingei Online Repository (see Fig. 4). Furthermore, it provides the relations between digital assets for the needs of the game and allows the game to reference digital assets from the Asset Bundle. An Asset Bundle is an archive file that contains platform-specific non-code Assets (such as models, textures, prefabs, audio clips, and scenes) that Unity can load at run time (see Fig. 5). Asset Bundles can express dependencies between each other; for example, a material in one Asset Bundle can reference a texture in another Asset Bundle [41]. From the export, game assets were collected and pre-compiled in the form of Asset Bundle files imported to the Unity3D project. Grouping was used to organise assets in bundles e.g. textures and layout data for a User-Interface screen, game scenario and texts, textures and models for pieces of the scenery, etc.

```
 1  ⊟{
 2  ⊟    "head" : {
 3  ⊟      "vars" : [
 4            "subject",
 5            "name",
 6            "source"
 7          ]
 8        },
 9  ⊟    "results" : {
10  ⊟      "bindings" : [
11            {
12  ⊟          "subject" : {
13              "type" : "uri",
14              "value" : "http://www.mingei-project.eu/resource/be3dfc7b-d4af-4328-ab25-46003800445d"
15            },
16  ⊟          "name" : {
17              "type" : "literal",
18              "value" : "Reconstruction of Chios Mastic Museum"
19            },
20  ⊟          "source" : {
21              "type" : "literal",
22              "value" : "http://139.91.186.146/media/recon-viewer/index.html#53"
23            }
24          },
```

Fig. 4. A JSON formatted response from the MOP.

3.4 3D Game Implementation

For the generation of the game terrain, a terraforming tool [37] was used to prepare a height map of the Island of Chios (see Fig. 5, Sect. 1). A height map is a raster image where each pixel stores elevation data, for display in 3D computer graphics, typically after conversion into a 3D mesh. This map was imported into Unity3D as a 3D mesh. In this process, several iterations and tests were made. Each test included editing resolution, terrain size, and maximum altitude in conjunction with the size of the reconstructions. The output of this process is the development of a terrain structure that although similar to the one of Chios, can be experienced as a game terrain (see Fig 5, Sect. 2). To this end, the final terrain is scaled down in terms of dimensions to be played "on foot" by a single player and at the same time have a logical distance between action points that can be easily covered by the player either "on foot" or using several portals that transfer the player in several places of the terrain. Furthermore, the game terrain and the player avatar are deviated from reality to enhance the "play" characteristics (e.g. less gravity or zero gravity areas, increased player speed, increased climbing capabilities, etc.). Other post-processing activities include the creation of game planes such as roads, hills, harbours, etc. Then, the 3D reconstructions of the villages were integrated into the terrain considering the dimensions of the terrain, player, and reconstructions. Fig 5, Sect. 3, presents the placement of the Olympoi reconstruction in the terrain. The placement included terraforming of the surrounding to the reconstruction areas to eliminate any overlapping between the terrain and the reconstruction.

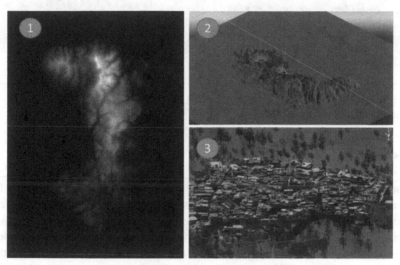

Fig. 5. A height map (image source [15]) for the Island of Chios (1), 3D Chios game terrain (2), Placement of Olympoi in the game terrain (3).

3.5 Gameplay Implementation

Gameplay implementation was based on "The Explorer: 3D Game Kit" which is a collection of mechanics, tools, systems, and assets for third-person action games [38]. Based on this framework several components of the kit related to character animation and rendering, terrain navigation through teleports (see Fig. 6 left), areas unlock, etc. were reused. The implementation was initiated through the formulation of the main game environment and routes within the environments and then moved to the 3D modelling of specific areas of the landscape. These areas were created with imaginary scenery build with assets from the Unity3D asset store [40] and reconstructions of (a) mastic villages, (b) rural sceneries, (c) mastic trees, and (d) mastic tools. In the case of 3D reconstructions, Level of Detail (LOD) post-processing [20] was performed to ensure that game assets do not pose extremely high GPU rendering prerequisites.

For demonstration purposes, a scenario was created and recorded following the path of a user from game start until the discovery of two main points of interest (a) the mastic field and (b) the village of Olympoi to experience its architecture (see Fig. 6 right).

Fig. 6. Setting transition points through teleports (left), mini video from the main game plot (right) https://youtu.be/fsEgKhMydJw.

4   Discussion and Future Work

In this work, we provided evidence regarding the exploration of the third era of knowledge representation technologies and 3D digitisation strategies combined with the advances of the gaming industry to support a novel form of gaming experiences powered by tangible and intangible CH. To this end, the creation of the Chios exploration game was presented which is a fantasy role-playing game situated at the medieval island of Chios infused with 3D reconstructions of CH sites, validated and semantically represented knowledge and enhanced immersive experiences. During game creation, state of the art technologies from the CH sector and Gaming Industry were used and thus the game heavily relies on 3D game platforms and game building tools, 3D reconstruction technologies for content regarding places of historical significance and traditional terrain building and gameplay concepts. At the same time, the semantic representation of knowledge provided ready to use structured knowledge representations that made easier the integration of knowledge in the form of precompiled asset bundles thus enhancing traditional approaches considering that content authoring is happening in an external platform accessed by anyone including scientists and curators.

Regarding future work, the prototype will be first evaluated by experts employing not only traditional usability evaluation guidelines, such as Nielsen's heuristics [25] but also domain-specific guidelines for games [6, 14]. The expert-based evaluation will be followed by user testing, aiming to assess not only usability but the entire user experience, thus studying issues about game enjoyment and flow [36], as well as the overall learning experience an aspect of particular importance in serious games [9]. This game is a technology exploration created in the context of the Mingei H2020 project and it is a candidate for its inclusion in the pilot setup of the project in the Chios Mastic Museum. An additional research direction that could be pursued would certainly include the concept of a multiplayer online role-playing game, which are video games that combines aspects of role-playing video games and multiplayer online games. In such a game context, multiple users could be spawned in different parts of the island and competitive collaborative learning experiences could take place. This, of course, requires further development and effort but it is foreseen that will contribute to the educational value and exploitation potential of the presented concept.

Acknowledgements. This work has been conducted in the context of the Mingei project that has received funding from the European Union's Horizon 2020 research and innovation programme under grant agreement No 822336.

References

1. 3D-ICONS project: Guidelines & Case Studies (2014)
2. Azzam, J.: Porting a real-life castle into your game when you're broke. In: GDC 2017 (2017). https://www.gdcvault.com/play/1023997/Porting-a-Real-Life-Castle. Accessed 16 Jan 2020
3. Bishop, L., Chris, C., Michal, J.: Photogrammetry for games: art, technology and pipeline integration for amazing worlds. In: GDC 2017 (2017)
4. Brosseau, K., Choquette, M., Renaud, L.: Digitization standards for the Canadian museum of civilization corporation (2006). https://museumsassn.bc.ca/wp-content/uploads/2015/01/smcc_numerisation-cmcc_digitization-eng.pdf. Accessed 16 Jan 2020
5. Brown, K., Hamilton, A.: Photogrammetry and star wars battlefront. In: GDC 2016: Game Developer Conference (2016)
6. Brown, M.: Evaluating computer game usability: developing heuristics based on user experience. In: Proceedings of IHCI Conference, pp. 16–21 (2008)
7. CARLI Digital Collections Users' Group: Guidelines for the creation of digital collections, Consortium of Academic and Research Libraries at the University of Illinois (2017). Accessed 16 Jan 2020
8. D'Andrea, A., Niccolucci, F., Bassett, S., Fernie, K.: 3D-ICONS: world heritage sites for Europeana: making complex 3D models available to everyone. In: 2012 IEEE International Conference on Virtual Systems and Multimedia, pp. 517–520, September 2012
9. De Freitas, S., Oliver, M.: How can exploratory learning with games and simulations within the curriculum be most effectively evaluated? Comput. Educ. **46**(3), 249–264 (2006)
10. Doerr, M., Gradmann, S., Hennicke, S., Isaac, A., Meghini, C., Van de Sompel, H.: The Europeana data model (EDM). In: World Library and Information Congress: 76th IFLA General Conference and Assembly, vol. 10, p. 15, August 2010
11. ETH Library's Best Practices in Digitization (DATE). https://www.library.ethz.ch/en/ms/DigiCenter/Best-Practices-in-Digitization. Accessed 16 Jan 2020
12. ETH-Bibliothek: Best Practices Digitization, Version 1.1 (2016)
13. Europeana. https://www.europeana.eu/en
14. Federoff, M.A.: Heuristics and usability guidelines for the creation and evaluation of fun in video games, Doctoral dissertation, Indiana University (2002)
15. Height Mapper. https://tangrams.github.io/heightmapper/
16. Kallinikidou, A.: Chios Mastiha Museum. Athens: Piraeus Bank Group Cultural Foundation (2017)
17. Kurin, R.: A conversation with Richard Kurin. In: Stefano, M.L., Davis, P. (eds.) The Routledge Companion to Intangible Cultural Heritage, pp. 40–45, Routledge, UK (2017)
18. Donkin, L.: Crafts and Conservation, Synthesis Report for ICCROM (2001)
19. Puhol-Tost, L., Champion, E.: Evaluating presence in cultural heritage projects. IJHS J. **18**, 83–102 (2012)
20. Luebke, D., Reddy, M., Cohen, J.D., Varshney, A., Watson, B., Huebner, R.: Level of Detail for 3D Graphics. Morgan Kaufmann, Burlington (2003)
21. Maximov, A.: Future of art production in games. In: GDC 2017: Game Developer Conference. UBM Tech., San Francisco (2017)
22. Meghini, C., Bartalesi, V., Metilli, D., Partarakis, N., Zabulis, X.: Mingei Ontology (Version 1.0), Zenodo (2020). https://doi.org/10.5281/zenodo.3742829

23. MINERVA: Ministerial Network for Valorising Activities in digitisation. D6.2. Good Practice Handbook (2003)
24. Mingei-project. https://www.mingei-project.eu
25. Nielsen, J.: Heuristic evaluation. In: Nielsen, J., Mack, R.L. (eds.) Usability Inspection Methods, pp. 25-63 (1994)
26. Oldman, D., Tanase, D.: Reshaping the knowledge graph by connecting researchers, data and practices in researchspace. In: Vrandečić, D., et al. (eds.) ISWC 2018. LNCS, vol. 11137, pp. 325–340. Springer, Cham (2018). https://doi.org/10.1007/978-3-030-00668-6_20
27. Partarakis, N., Zabulis, X., Antona, M., Stephanidis, C.: Transforming Heritage Crafts to engaging digital experiences. In: Liarokapis, F., Voulodimos, A., Doulamis, N., Doulamis, A. (eds.) Visual Computing for Cultural Heritage. SSCC, pp. 245–262. Springer, Cham (2020). https://doi.org/10.1007/978-3-030-37191-3_13
28. Parys, R., Schilling, A.: Incremental large-scale 3D reconstruction. In: IEEE International Conference on 3D Imaging, Modeling, Processing, Visualization & Transmission, pp. 416–423. IEEE, October 2012
29. Photomodeler Technologies, How is Photogrammetry Used in Video Games? (2020). https://www.photomodeler.com/how-is-photogrammetry-used-in-video-games/. Accessed July 2020
30. Purgi village on Open Street Map. https://www.openstreetmap.org/directions?from=38.247 0313%2C%2025.9422563#map=15/38.2395/25.9452. Accessed 17 July 2020
31. Ryckman, M.: Exploring the graffiti of the division. Ubiblog, 15 April 2016. https://blog.ubi.com/exploring-the-graffiti-of-the-division-interview-with-amr-din
32. Savvidis, D.: Chios Mastic Tree. Kyriakidis Bros S.A. Publications, Thessaloniki (2000)
33. Starwars, E.A.: How we used photogrammetry to capture every last detail for Star Wars Battlefront. StarWars EA, 19 May 2015. https://starwars.ea.com/starwars/battlefront/news/how-we-used-photogrammetry
34. Statham, N.: Use of photogrammetry in video games: a historical overview. Games Cult. 15(3), 289–307 (2020)
35. Steinman, G.: Far Cry 4—Vice Dev Diary & Quest for Everest.UbiBlog (2014). https://blog.ubi.com/far-cry-4-vice-developer-diary-quest-for-everest. Accessed 16 Jan 2020
36. Sweetser, P., Wyeth, P.: GameFlow: A model for evaluating player enjoyment in games. Comput. Entertain. (CIE) 3(3), 3 (2005)
37. Tangram Heightmapper. https://tangrams.github.io/heightmapper/. Accessed 16 Jan 2020
38. The Explorer: 3D Game Kit. https://learn.unity.com/project/3d-game-kit. Accessed 16 Jan 2020
39. UNESCO. Traditional craftsmanship. https://ich.unesco.org/en/traditional-craftsmanship-00057. Accessed 16 Jan 2020
40. Unity3D asset store. https://assetstore.unity.com/. Accessed 16 Jan 2020
41. Unity3D manual, Asset Bundle definition. https://docs.unity3d.com/Manual/AssetBundles Intro.html. Accessed 16 Jan 2020
42. Waskul, D.D.: The role-playing game and the game of role-playing. In: Gaming as Culture: Essays on Reality, Identity and Experience in Fantasy Games, pp. 19–38 (2006)
43. Zabulis, X., et al.: Representation and preservation of heritage crafts. Sustainability 12(4), 1461 (2020). https://doi.org/10.3390/su12041461
44. Zabulis, X., et al.: What is needed to digitise knowledge on heritage crafts? Memoriamedia Rev. 4(1), 1–25 (2019). ISSN 2183-3753
45. Know Your Genres: Third-Person Shooters - Xbox Wire. news.xbox.com. Accessed 17 July 2020

Design

Context-Based Visual Design Language
for Shape Generation

Arus Kunkhet[(✉)]

College of Arts, Media and Technology, Chiang Mai University,
Su Thep 50200, Chiang Mai, Thailand
arus.k@cmu.ac.th

Abstract. Design development is an expensive process and time consuming. A
design language system assists design development. The system is highly used
to investigate design characteristics in many design studies. The high volume of
research interprets it as design elements and principles analysis to deliver consistent visual aesthetics. The absences of meaning and context significantly impact
the quality of visual design communication and create design ambiguities. To fulfil
the mentioned issues, this research extends harmonised shape grammar (HSG) to
develop a context-based visual design language (CVD). The proposed framework
provides semantics and pragmatics levels of analysis to bring meaning and context
to a visual design communication. Visual communication and language communication share the similarity in fundamental concepts. A context-based visual design
language adopts grammatical design and natural language processing approaches
to analyse visual communication requirements. Grammatical design provides generative design development when natural language processing analyses levels of
language communication. In linguistics, morphological units (morphemes) form
a vocabulary. Vocabularies construct a sentence following a grammar structure. A
semantically well-formed sentence provides meaning. Meaningful sentences combine pragmatically to achieve a successful communication. In the design aspect,
one must speak a language of design. However, speaking does not guarantee a successful communication. This research aims at defining a framework to create a set
of meaningful visual design language in order to achieve a visual communication
correspondingly to the way natural language can in linguistics.

Keywords: Visual design language · Harmonised shape grammar · Natural
language processing

1 Introduction

Language is a system of communication consisting of sound, words, and grammar [1].
It can be used to communicate by people in a particular country or a specific group of
individuals and tasks. Learning one language requires an understanding in its meaning
and structure [2]. Linguistics is a scientific study of language and its structure [3]. The
study includes morphology, syntax, phonetics, and semantics [4, 5]. Morphology studies

A. Brooks et al. (Eds.): ArtsIT 2020, LNICST 367, pp. 257–270, 2021.
https://doi.org/10.1007/978-3-030-73426-8_15

the forms of words. Syntax deals with a language structure and phrasing. Phonetics classifies speech sounds. Semantics concerns meaning [6]. In a natural language processing (NLP), the study aims at using artificial intelligence (AI) to understand and be able to communicate between computers and humans [7]. The study develops knowledge in both natural language and AI fields [8]. In the natural language aspect, it includes lexicon, syntax, semantics, and pragmatics studies. Lexicon deals with vocabulary when pragmatics deals with context. Design language refers to a scheme or a style that guides the design. The aim is to create a consistency in design. It focuses on design elements and principles by describing aspects of design such as shapes, colour schemes, materials, patterns, and layouts [9]. It is used in many design processes such as product design, architectural design, and industrial design [10].

To communicate in one language, one must understand its vocabularies and grammar. Design can speak similarly to the way natural language does. The cognitive abilities that people apply in order to speak and understand a language are similar to those applied to other cognitive tasks, such as visual perception or reasoning activity [11]. To communicate in one design, the design must carry a form of coherence structure. A design language speaks with design elements and principles to create a consistent visual aesthetic [12]. However, the absences in design meaning and design context bring serious issues in communication ambiguities. A meaningful design requires further analysis in semantics and pragmatics levels. The design vocabulary and structure must be defined in morphology, lexicon, and syntax levels to achieve a successful communication.

This research aims at adopting knowledge of linguistic concepts, natural language processing, and design language system to provide a visual design framework namely a context-based visual design language. The proposed framework aims at creating a consistency in design and visual communication the way people communicate in natural language. The proposed framework consists of five levels of analysis including shape morphology, design lexicon, design syntax, design semantics, and design pragmatics.

2   Overview of Natural Language Processing and Design Language

This section describes the uses of linguistics and visual design that are adopted in this research by following the fundamental concept to identify a context-based visual design language.

2.1   Natural Language Processing

Natural language processing is a computational linguistics that studies the engineering of computational models [13]. It aims at creating a cognitive process to understand human language. Natural language consists of emotional expressions and spoken languages [14]. People use natural language to communicate to each other. Natural language processing, on the other hand, is a knowledge-based approach to analyse human language to communicate between humans and machines [5]. Natural language processing involves levels of analysis including morphology, lexicon, syntax, semantics, and pragmatics [4, 5]. The first level of analysis is morphology which focuses on word morphemes. A word is constructed from a series of morphemes so-called morphological units in terms of a word structure. The second level of analysis is lexicon which concerns word meaning. For example, this word is a noun or a verb and what meaning it is carried. The third level of analysis is syntax which determines the grammar structure of a language. Grammar is a structural dependency relationship used to put words together syntactically to form a sentence [15]. The fourth level of analysis is semantics which considers the meaning of a sentence. The interactions among word-level meaning have to be considered to avoid ambiguities in language [16]. The fifth level of analysis is pragmatics which focuses on the overall context of conversations. A sentence can carry more than one meaning depending on its surrounding sentences. In order to define a correct meaning, a completed context of the communication must be considered together. Ambiguities in language processing can be found at many levels of language analysis and types of communication [17]. The overall context is required to be defined.

2.2 Design Language System

Design is defined as the process of creating new structures characterised by new parameters, aimed at satisfying specific requirements [18]. Design elements and design principles are the fundamental structure of design. Design elements consist of point or mark, line, shape, form, space, colour, and texture [19]. The artist uses these basic elements as design building blocks. Design principles consist of balance, proportion, emphasis, movement, pattern, repetition, rhythm, variety, harmony, and unity [20]. These principles are used as laws and guidelines for design considerations. Design elements are combined to create components when design principles are applied to create design direction [21]. It is similar to the way music is composed. Notes and tones are components put together to identify a form of patterns. These patterns follow a constructive direction to create harmony. Design language is a design scheme describing choices of design aspects [22]. The aim is to achieve aesthetics and consistency in the design development the way harmony is achieved in music composition. A language of design must speak through design characteristics. By applying design elements and principles, any design can speak. However, the absences in design meaning and context lead significantly to design ambiguities. A successful visual communication must be meaningful. To communicate effectively, two more levels of analysis are required; design semantics and design pragmatics. Speaking a design language meaningfully requires design morphology at semantics level and design context at the pragmatics level.

2.3 Perception in Design

Design aesthetics can be quite a subjective issue. This research applies a processing of human perception development as a guideline to analyse the human perception in design. A design aesthetics is appreciated when humans experience an art form [23]. There are three levels of processing including visceral, behavioural, and reflective [24]. The first level of analysis is visceral which focuses on the human first impression of design appearance. It is a reaction toward the look of an object. The second level of analysis is behavioural which concerns design function. Human brain processes the passing pf the point on how it looks to how it works and the information it carries [25]. Function that is suitable with user requirements raises the level of user appreciation toward the design. The third level of analysis is reflective which involves the personal satisfaction. Each person can have a different feeling toward one design. The feeling depends on that person's self-image, self-satisfaction, and memories [24]. In order to achieve a satisfaction perception in design, the three levels of analysis must be fulfilled. To accomplish a meaningful and consistent visual aesthetics, the design must not only speak its design language but must communicate without design ambiguities and clarifies its morphology and functionality through the design meaning and context.

3 Context-Based Visual Design Language

This research proposes a context-based visual design language (CVD) to provide a successful design communication. The proposed framework adopts the approaches of natural language processing and design language system by extending three levels of analysis; shape morphology, design semantics, and design pragmatics. Natural language processing is a subarea of research in linguistics. It concerns analysing and studying the natural language data. Design language system uses design principles to create a design scheme. This design scheme can be used as a guideline to create design style. Grammatical design generates a design using design syntax and semantics without any concerns of design morphology, contexts, and ambiguities. A context-based visual design language consists of five levels of analysis; shape morphology, design lexicon, design syntax, design semantics, and design pragmatics. They are interpreted as compatible to semantics and pragmatics in natural language. The extensions of design semantics and design pragmatics provide meaningful and contextual design outcomes. They also prevent design ambiguities in visual communication (Fig. 1).

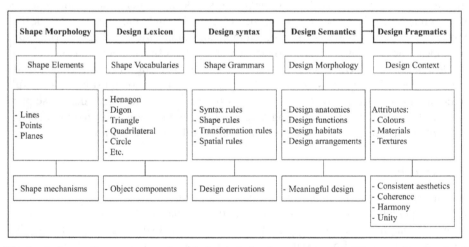

Fig. 1. A figure shows a context-based visual design language model. There are five levels of analysis starting from left to right. Shape morphology creates shape vocabularies. Design syntax brings design structure to generate design derivations. Design semantics develops those derivations with design morphology consideration. Design pragmatics provides context of design.

3.1   Shape Morphology Level of Analysis

In linguistics, morphology focuses on word morphemes. In terms of a word structure, a word is constructed from a series of morphemes called morphological units. Alphabet is the smallest component of a word. Alphabets build a set of morphemes conceptually the way a series of points build a line in design. A combination of lines creates a shape component the way words are created with a group of morphemes.

In a context-based visual design language, shape morphology investigates design elements. Design elements analyse shape componentry. Shape componentry is a fundamental component of shape. It consists of point(s), line(s), and plane(s). A point is the smallest unit of shape componentry. Multiple points form a single line. Connecting multiple lines together is to create a plane. Any shape or form must consist of at least one of these components. A set of rules can be applied to design elements in order to create a set of shape morphologies. The created shape morphologies can be used to develop a shape vocabulary at the next level of a design analysis. To define consistent morpheme rules is the key to achieve a set of useful shape components. The developed shape components can create a design coherence. It is similar to morphology rules in natural language. One can apply a language morphology rule as a guideline to create a number of new words using the same rule. This is a significant step forward to start a design development process where new shape elements are difficult to create with consistency and coherence in a visual communication. Shape morphology works as a design assistance providing such a guideline to generate new shape elements (Fig. 2).

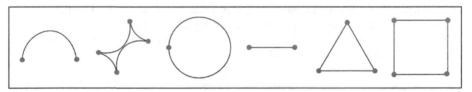

Fig. 2. A figure shows shape morphologies, from left to right; a parabola curve (1-side-2-vertex), a hyperbola shape (4-side-4-vertex), a henagon (1-side-1-vertex), a line (1-side-2-vertex), a triangle (3-side-3-vertex), and a quadrilateral (4-side-4-vertex). Morphology level operates design elements mathematically to create shape components.

3.2   Design Lexicon Level of Analysis

In linguistics, lexicon concerns the meaning of words and their part(s) of speech. Lexicon determines types of words such as a noun and a verb. Each type plays their own roles in language structure. Ambiguities occur when a word has more than one meaning. For example, a word "bar" carries multiple meanings in both noun or verb forms. This issue must be dealt with at the further analysis levels; syntax, semantics, and pragmatics levels.

In a context-based visual design language, design lexicon includes design vocabulary analysis. Design vocabulary is a container of shapes. It consists of 2D shapes and 3D forms developed from the same shape morphology rule(s). Polygons can be created by combining a set of vertices (points) and sides (lines) together geometrically. Polygon types are divided by their specific number of sides. For example, a 1-side-1-vertex component forms a henagon; a 2-side-2-vertex component forms a digon; a 3-side-3-vertex component forms a triangle; a 4-side-4-vertex component forms a quadrilateral, a 5-side-5-vertex forms a pentagon, and 4-side-4-vertex curved lines form a hyperbola shape. Design lexicon creates shape vocabularies from shape morphology. Morphologically well-formed shapes themselves can be meaningless or meaningful depending on the design purpose. Sets of selected shape morphologies are stored at the morphology level. At lexicon level, those shape morphologies are developed in such a way to create a shape vocabulary (a lexically well-formed shape) to use as design materials. By applying a set of rules repeatedly, a number of new shape vocabularies can be achieved. All shape members are developed sharing the same design direction (Fig. 3).

Fig. 3. A figure shows two sets of shape vocabularies. The left picture shows a set that is developed by a quadrilateral, 4-side-4-vertex, shape morphology. The right picture shows a set that is developed by a henagon, 1-side-1-vertex shape morphology. Lexicon rules analyse the two shape elements to generate sets of shape vocabularies.

3.3 Design Syntax Level of Analysis

In linguistics, to form a sentence, a type of language structure is required. Grammar is a set of rules to construct a sentence. Syntax level of analysis determines word types; noun phrase and verb phrase. In general, a sentence is created by applying grammar rules to these word types. Language grammar uses these word types to create a sentence following the defined sentence structures. A syntactically well-formed sentence can be used for communication without any guarantee of language ambiguities.

In a context-based visual design language, design syntax provides a grammar of design. Design grammar defines a shape rule which is similar to the grammar rule in natural language. Grammatical design is used in many design fields such as architectural, engineering, and product designs. Shape rule offers a structure to develop design vocabulary following one direction. It consists of spatial relation rules and transformation rules. The rules develop syntactically well-formed design choices. By applying a shape rule repeatedly to one shape vocabulary, a number of design derivations are generated. All design derivations in one particular set share the same conceptual design structure. Harmony and unity in shape development are achieved as a result. This level adopts a concept of grammatical design approach by developing syntax rules. A generated shape, called design derivation, is created by applying a set of well-formed syntax rules to shape vocabularies. Defining effective but simple and repeatable syntax rules is an important factor. It requires an in-depth understanding in mathematics and shape geometry. A grammatical design generates random derivations but still lacks meaningful structure to develop those vocabularies. A context-based visual design language tackles the mentioned issue by applying another two levels of analysis (Fig. 4).

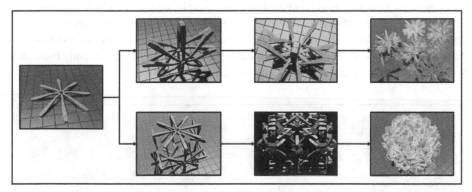

Fig. 4. A figure shows design developments at the syntax level. A quadrilateral shape is developed to form a fan shape at lexicon level. Multiple syntax rules are applied to the fan shape to generate two sets of design. Different spatial and transformation rules, such as rotation and translation, are applied repeatedly. A number of complex design derivations are generated as the result.

3.4 Design Semantics Level of Analysis

In linguistics, semantics considers the meaning of a sentence. Words that have multiple meanings lead to language ambiguities. The interactions among word-level meanings have to be considered to avoid ambiguities in language. To understand which is the correct meaning, one must understand the overall denotation of each word individually and as a sentence. A meaningful sentence must be clear and meaningful without any language ambiguities.

In a context-based visual design language, design semantics concerns design morphology. The term morphology is interpreted differently to the term used in linguistics. Design morphology deals with meaning of design. A grammar-based design language does not guarantee the design to be meaningful. The same problem occurs in both design and linguistics studies. For example, in linguistics, a sentence "hat eats table" is grammatically correct. However, it is not semantically well-formed because the sentence makes no sense and meaningless. Design syntax creates random design derivations which mostly lead to an ambiguity in design. Design semantics controls design development by applying design morphology to make it meaningful. The design morphology consists of design anatomy, design function, design environment, and design arrangement. Design anatomy defines bodily structure of objects or character requirements. For example, a car anatomy requires the car body, seats, steering wheels, control system, engine, and wheels. Design function concerns activities and purposes of each part of that anatomy. For example, a car body is to hold car components together; driver and passengers' seats are to give a driver and passengers spaces to operate inside; a steering wheel and controls are to govern direction and movement; a car engine is to provide its power; and wheels are to mobilise a car when rotated simultaneously. Design environment analyses object surroundings that affect the behaviours of design. For example, a terrestrial, aquatic, or atmospheric environments affect design approach of the car. Design arrangement considers the design components composition. For example, wheels should be attached one part to the car body and one part touches the ground; driver seat should be next to the steering wheel, and seats should be inside the car body. Design derivations are developed to follow design morphology to achieve meaningful design which significantly increases design quality and reduces the time-consuming issue (Fig. 5).

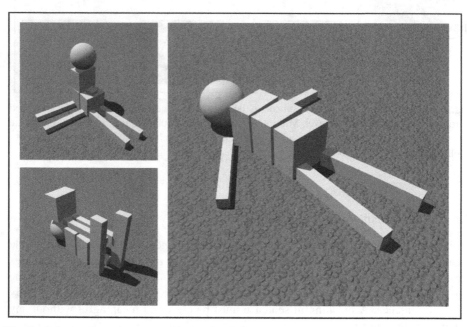

Fig. 5. A figure shows three sets of design developments. Each set has exactly the same derivation structure. Applying different syntax rules creates diversity in design. The two on the left are generated by syntax rules without design semantics. The one on the right is developed with design semantics consideration. Providing design morphology, design anatomy, function, environment, and arrangement, a meaningful humanoid character is created.

3.5 Design Pragmatics Level of Analysis

In linguistics, a conversation consists of a series of sentences. In order to avoid language ambiguities, it is not an individual sentence but the overall context of a conversation must be considered. All sentences must communicate with the same purpose and direction. It is similar to music composing. A sequence of notes and tunes are combined to create melody harmoniously. A level of satisfaction is achieved when listening to the whole composition as a piece of music not as an individual note and tone.

In a context-based visual design language, design pragmatics provides the context of design. Design semantics focuses on the meaning of an individual design. Design pragmatics considers the context of a set of design as a whole. An absence of context consideration leads significantly to an inefficient visual communication. At the first four levels of design analysis, an individual design speaks its own language separately. Design pragmatics aims at offering contexts to those designs in a specific direction harmoniously. Design context consists of design attributes; colours, materials, and textures. Design attributes define characteristics of a design surface in terms of a colour scheme. This colour scheme is applied to create a set of materials and textures that share the same characteristic and behaviour. These attributes are applied to all objects to create a consistent visual aesthetic. This analysis can be applied for both 2D and 3D designs. All design objects are developed to share the same design morphology and context. In the design perception, each shape vocabulary has its own meaning. For example, round shape gives friendly and unstable feelings; a triangle shape gives dangerous and dynamic feelings; a square shape gives static and stable feelings; and a straight horizontal line makes people feel calm and stable. A context-based visual design language analyses the design perception to bring meaning to compound shapes. Design syntax creates a set of derivations that share the same design characteristics. Design semantics combines them in such a way that is meaningful. Design pragmatics provides the overall context as a design theme. Harmony and unity in design can be achieved when all designs in one set speak in the same design as morphology and context.

4   Implementation of the Framework

The proposed framework can be applied to generate many types of design. To implement the framework, this research uses game environment design as a case study. The aim is to generate a set of game assets, a terrestrial habitat game environment. All generated assets must carry consistent visual aesthetics and design coherence. This design development process follows the five levels of analysis of context-based visual design language; shape morphology, design lexicon, design syntax, design semantics, and design pragmatics.

The process begins with defining shape morphology. A henagon (1-side-1-vertex) and a curve line (1-side-2-vertex) are used as shape elements. Henagons and Curved lines are basic shape elements found in many organic forms. They give the feelings of smoothness and movement. Shape morphology defines these shape elements to be developed as shape vocabularies.

At a design lexicon level, the spatial and transformation rules are applied to the defined shape vocabularies. Rotation rules are applied to henagon to create a sphere. Translation rules are applied to curved line to move 360° along henagon radios to create a cylinder.

At a design syntax level, syntax rules, emergent rules, spatial rules, and transformation rules are applied to develop those shape vocabularies using shape algebra. The rules define a henagon-sphere as a starting vocabulary. A curved-line-cylinder emerges from the starting vocabulary to any direction to form a new shape vocabulary. The rules are reapplied limitlessly and are terminated when the design derivation meets the level of satisfaction.

At a design semantics level, the syntax shapes are further developed to create design morphology which consists of design anatomy, design function, design environment, and design arrangement. This process divides design morphology into three specific sub-morphologies including building, character, and vehicle. The developments of each sub-morphology are as follows;

1) The building anatomy requires a building to have a building body and a roof. The building function creates interior spaces, doors, and windows. The interior spaces are for habitation purposes. The door is to connect an interior space with outside spaces. The windows for air ventilation provide interior lighting. The building environment defines surrounding factors that affect building morphology. In this case, the morphology focuses on a terrestrial habitat. The building arrangement deals with placing building components in the right order. For example, the roof is on top of the building body; the door is placed on a ground level; and the windows are attached to the building body not the roof. This implementation uses henagon-spheres to offer an interior space. Emerged curve-line-cylinder shapes are used to develop exterior structures such as roofs and terraces (Fig. 6).

2) Character anatomy requires head, body, and limbs to be created. A henagon-sphere shape is used to create the head part with emerging curved-line-cylinders as body and limbs. The head function is to carry facial components. Each component carries its own specific function; eye to see, ear to hear, or nose to breathe. The body is for limbs to be attached to. The upper limbs functions are to grasp and hold, and the lower limbs are for standing and moving. Terrestrial morphology is required to fulfil the character environment. Character arrangement follows the function and environment. Head and limbs are attached to the body. Upper and lower limbs must be placed according to their functions. Upper limbs are attached to the upper body. Lower limbs are placed at the bottom to carry the body and to move.

3) Vehicle anatomy requires vehicle body and wheels. A henagon-sphere is used as a starting vocabulary. Curved-line-cylinders emerge from this henagon-sphere to create the vehicle of the body and wheels. Vehicle function requires driving or riding spaces. Vehicle handles are created to fulfil control system function. A vehicle requires a mechanism to move effectively. Instead of wheels, this implementation mimics caterpillar movement functions to suit the terrestrial environment. Vehicle arrangement places caterpillar legs at the bottommost position and driving or riding spaces on the vehicle body next to its control system.

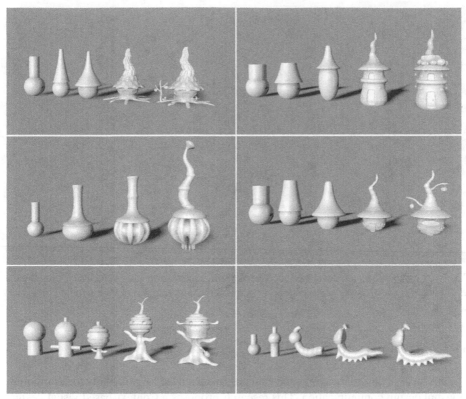

Fig. 6. A figure shows design developments of buildings, character, and vehicle. The process starts, from left to right, with two shape vocabularies; a henagon-sphere and a curved-line-cylinder. Syntax, semantics, and pragmatics rules are applied to develop the design with consideration of design morphology and context.

At the design pragmatics level, the contexts of design are applied. The three sub-morphologies; building, character, and vehicle, are developed individually at the previous four levels. The shape morphology, design lexicon, design syntax, design semantics processes develop designs that share identical forms. This level interprets design contexts through design attributes. The design context provides a design theme to achieve a consistent visual aesthetic, coherence, harmony, and unity in design. This implementation focuses on colour and material. Black and white based colours are applied to create a grayscale colour scheme. A low specular value is used to create environment materials when a high specular value is applied to asset materials (Fig. 7).

Fig. 7. A figure shows the developed models; buildings, characters, and vehicles, at pragmatics level of analysis. All assets are expressed with the same conceptual morphology and context of designs.

5   Conclusions and Future Work

The absences of design meanings and contexts in design lead significantly to ambiguities in visual design communication. This research proposes a Context-based visual design language to tackle the mentioned issues. Design meanings and contexts are achieved through semantics and pragmatics levels of analysis. The proposed framework extends harmonised shape grammar to provide an alternative successful visual communication framework. The proposed framework adopts natural language processing and design language system approaches. A context-based visual design language consists of five levels of analysis; shape morphology, design lexicon, design syntax, design semantics, and design pragmatics. Shape morphology deals with defining shape element; point, line, and plane. Design lexicon offers transformation, and spatial rules to create shape vocabulary from shape morphology. Design syntax analyses the syntax rules to develop shape vocabulary following its shape grammar structure. Design semantics delivers meaningful shapes following the design morphology; design anatomy, function, environment, and arrangement. Design pragmatics considers the overall context of design to communicate in the same representative determination and to avoid ambiguities in design. This research applies the context-based design language to produce the game environment design as a case study to implement the framework. The result shows a significant improvement in design quality and reduction of time-consuming issues. A set of game environment design is generated as a case study for the research implementation. The generated assets consist of three types of design; building, character, and vehicle. The design results are checked up against design elements and design principles to evaluate the quality of design. The design analysis follows design criteria of harmonised shape grammar and the three levels of design perception which provides a platform to evaluate design qualities. The evaluation yields a successful and harmonious result with a very little time consuming in term of design development. The context-based visual design language can be used as an alternative design development approach when a huge number of designs is required with a time limitation.

This research addresses serious issues in the absences of design meaning and context. The proposed framework introduces an alternative generative design development framework. This research focuses on visual design and its development. There are a number of important areas for further improvement. Firstly, this framework has not focused on motion graphics and movements. Directions, velocities, patterns, and behaviours of a motion provide their meanings. These factors significantly affect design decisions and should be considered. Secondly, the semantics and pragmatics rules require an in-depth understanding in 2D and 3D shape algebra, and geometry transformation. In order to operate the rules effectively, a guideline in semantics and pragmatics rules are advised to be analysed and studied further.

References

1. McIntosh, C.: Cambridge Advanced Learner's Dictionary, 4th edn. Cambridge University Press, Cambridge (2013). ISBN 978-1107035157
2. Yule, G.: The Study of Language, 7th edn. Cambridge University Press, Cambridge (2020). https://doi.org/10.1017/9781108582889
3. Kaplan, J.P.: Linguistics and Law: Routledge Guides to Linguistics, 1st edn. Routledge, Abingdon (2019). ISBN-13 978-1138326132
4. Lea, D., Bradbery, J.: Oxford Advanced Learner's Dictionary, 8th edn. OUP, Oxford (2020). ISBN 978-0194799003
5. Bender, E. M.: Linguistic Fundamentals for Natural Language Processing: 100 Essentials from Morphology and Syntax. Synthesis Lecture on Human Language Technologies. Morgan and Claypool Publishers (2013). ISBN 9781627050111
6. Nilsen, D.L.F.: The Language of Human. Cambridge University Press, Cambridge (2018). ISBN 9781108241403
7. Baties, M., Weischedel, R.: Challenges in Natural Language Processing. Studies in Natural Language Processing. Cambridge University Press, Cambridge (1993). https://doi.org/10.1017/CBO9780511659478
8. Indurkhya, N., Damerau, F.J. (eds.): Handbook of Natural Language Processing, vol. 2. CRC Press, Boco Raton (2010)
9. Brommer, G.F.: Illustrated Elements of Art and Principles of Design, Special edn. Crystal Productions (2011)
10. Brunner, R., Emery, S., Hall, R.: Do you Matter?: How Great Design Will People Love Your Company, pp. 157–172. Pearson Education, London (2009)
11. Croft, W., Alan Cruse, D.: Cognitive Linguistics. Cambridge University Press, Cambridge (2004)
12. Kunkhet, A., Sharp, B., Noriega, L.: Natural language processing based shape grammar. In: International Workshop on Natural Language Processing and Cognitive Science, vol. 2, pp. 15–23. SCITEPRESS (2012)
13. Otter, D.W., Medina, J.R., Kalita, J.K.: A survey of the usages of deep learning for natural language processing. IEEE Trans. Neural Netw. Learn. Syst. (2020). https://doi.org/10.1109/TNNLS.2020.2979670

14. Baynton, D.C.: Forbidden Signs: American Culture and the Campaign Against Sign Language. The University of Chicago Press, Chicago (1996)
15. Ghosh, S., Gunning, D.: Natural Language Processing Fundamentals: Building Intelligent Applications that can Interpret the Human Language to Deliver Impactful Result. Packt Publishing, Birmingham (2019). ISBN-13 9781789954043
16. Chowdhary, K.R.: Natural language processing. In: Chowdhary, K.R. (ed.) Fundamentals of Artificial Intelligence, pp. 603–649. Springer, New Delhi (2020). https://doi.org/10.1007/978-81-322-3972-7_19
17. Hirst, G.: Semantic Interpretation and the Resolution of Ambiguity, 1st edn. Studies in Natural Language Processing, Cambridge University Press, Cambridge (1987)
18. Renner, G., Ekrárt, A.: Genetic algorithms in computer aided design. Comput.-Aided Des. **35**, 709–726 (2003)
19. Samara, T.: Design Elements: Understanding the Rules and Knowing When to Break Them, 2nd edn. Rockport Publishers, Beverly (2014). ISBN-13 9781592539277
20. Tondreau, B.: Layout Essentials Revised and Updated: 100 Design Principles for Using Grids, Reprint Rockport Publishers, Beverly (2019). ISBN-13 9781631596315
21. Badley, K.: Curriculum Planning with Design Language, 1st edn. Routledge Publishers, Abingdon (2018). ISBN-13 9781138504721
22. Poulin, R.: The Language of Graphic Design Revised and Updated: An Illustrated Handbook for Understanding Fundamental Design Principles, Revised Rockport Publishers, Beverly (2018). ISBN-13 9781631596179
23. Argenton, A.: Art and Expression: Studies in the Psychology of Art. Studies and Research in the Psychology of Art. Routledge, Abingdon (2019). ISBN-13 9781138604100
24. Norman, D.A.: Emotional Design: Why We Love (or Hate) Everyday Things. Basic Books, New York (2004)
25. Mijksenaar, P.: Visual Function: AN Introduction to Information Design. Princeton Architectural Press, New York (1997). ISBN-13 9781568981185

Synergia: A Multimodal Virtual Reality System for Creative Expression and Positive Change Through Cognitive Flow

Oana Camelia Burca, Maros Pekarik, and Brian Bemman$^{(\boxtimes)}$ (iD)

Aalborg University, 9000 Aalborg, Denmark
maros.pekarik@pm.me, bb@create.aau.dk

Abstract. In recent years, virtual reality (VR) technologies for positive change have emerged as a way to combat various physical and mental issues, such as anxiety and depression, which have been linked to an increased use of digital technologies. Moreover, a state of *cognitive flow* in VR has been shown to have positive effects on human well-being. When designing for such VR technologies that can support positive change, feedback through aural and visual stimuli as well as interaction through movement have been suggested. However, evaluations of cognitive flow when using such technologies and with those designed for creative and artistic expression are lacking. In this paper, we present the multimodal VR system, *Synergia*, which encourages creative and artistic expression through bodily movement that is used to generate aural and visual feedback. In particular, participants' experiences with Synergia were evaluated using the Flow State Scale (FSS) in conjunction with semi-structured interviews. Our results indicate that Synergia shows promising potential for inducing aspects of cognitive flow related to increased concentration and an autotelic experience. Furthermore, these findings highlight the importance of multi-modalities to the flow experience but suggest also that visual-sound mappings may present a problem when designing for similar systems in the future.

Keywords: Interactive art · Positive technology · Virtual reality · Cognitive flow · Cross-modality · Movement

1 Introduction

As technology has become an increasingly more integral part of what makes a person's life both productive and fulfilling, a growing interest from researchers in human-computer interaction (HCI) and artists alike in designing technologies for improving mental and physical well-being has emerged [16]. Studies across a variety of disciplines have shown that virtual reality (VR), in particular, can have a positive impact on human flourishing, such as improving mental wellness [30], supporting mindfulness [32], improving physical and psycho-social well-being [18]

© ICST Institute for Computer Sciences, Social Informatics and Telecommunications Engineering 2021
Published by Springer Nature Switzerland AG 2021. All Rights Reserved
A. Brooks et al. (Eds.): ArtsIT 2020, LNICST 367, pp. 271–290, 2021.
https://doi.org/10.1007/978-3-030-73426-8_16

as well as inducing a state of cognitive flow – a mental state largely characterized by an increased focus desirable in many physical and creative activities [5,6]. Designing effective VR technologies for achieving these ends, however, remains challenging. Moreover, evaluations of existing systems designed for both cognitive flow and creative pursuits (as opposed to e.g., computer gaming) are limited [27].

In this paper, we present the multimodal VR system, Synergia, which was designed to allow for creative expression and to elicit positive mental change in users through cognitive flow. Concretely, a user's experience with Synergia involves 'painting' with free-flowing particles in a virtual environment and creating sound using the movement of their arms. We evaluate how well our system brings about cognitive flow using a standard questionnaire known as the Flow State Scale (FSS) with two experiments intended to (1) establish which modalities of the system – sound, visuals, or a combination of both – contribute most to cognitive flow and (2) determine for the result from (1) which of two possible design elements – a visual response to sound or not – factor most significantly. In Sect. 2, we provide an overview of cognitive flow, strategies for designing immersive, interactive technologies for positive change, as well as those that have been employed in mapping the modalities of sound and visuals in multimodal systems. In Sect. 3, we explain the conceptual design of Synergia, how this design was improved through usability testing, and provide insight into the implementation of the system. In Sect. 4, we present the two aforementioned experiments and discuss our findings as they relate to cognitive flow and the design of our system. In Sect. 5, we conclude with a discussion of possible future work.

2   Related Work

In this section, we discuss the nine dimensions which characterize cognitive flow and their importance to creative expression and practice. We conclude with an overview of design considerations for immersive, interactive technologies for positive change. In particular, we discuss such systems for VR and cognitive flow as well as various mapping strategies that have been employed in designing multimodal systems.

2.1   Cognitive Flow

Cognitive flow is a multidimensional mental state largely characterized by the feeling of being fully immersed in and focused on an activity which is intrinsically rewarding [9]. Situations in which a person may experience being in a state of cognitive flow include being particularly 'locked in' during a physical activity, sport, computer game, or meditation [7,9]. The flow experience has often been described as 'optimal' as one feels an accompanying profound sense of enjoyment which has the potential for long-lasting effects on a person's well-being [9]. The markers of cognitive flow have been categorized along nine dimensions in [9] and three categories in [7], shown in Table 1.

Table 1. The nine dimensions of cognitive flow and their respective explanations divided into the three categories, "Antecedents", "Characteristics", and "Consequences", of being in a state of flow, as described in [7,9].

Category		Flow Dimension	Explanation
Antecedents	1.	A challenging activity that requires skill	Accomplishing a physical or mental activity while being challenged enough by its requirements
	2.	Clear goals	The objectives of the activity are clear
	3.	Immediate feedback	Straightforward and immediate feedback allows for understanding how well one is doing
Characteristics	4.	Concentration on the task at hand	Worries and concerns from everyday life disappear from consciousness
	5.	The merging of action and awareness	Attention is completely absorbed by the activity which becomes spontaneous, almost automatic
	6.	A sense of control	Taking control over a novel, unpredictable situation without conscious control
Consequences	7.	Loss of self-consciousness	The concern for the self disappears allowing for immersion and unity with the environment
	8.	Transformation of time	Perception of time is altered – time seems to pass slower or faster
	9.	Autotelic experience	The activity is an end in itself, self-contained and intrinsically rewarding

As shown in Table 1, the nine dimensions of cognitive flow according to [7,9] consist of three antecedents, three characteristics, and three consequences. These antecedents involve the difficulty of an activity being in alignment with a person's skill level, clear goals for completing this activity, and immediate feedback on this person's progress. The characteristics of cognitive flow are full concentration, a merging of action and awareness, and an increased sense of control. The consequences of being in a state of cognitive flow are a loss of self-consciousness, a transformation of time, and a sense that this activity is intrinsically rewarding.

Importantly, cognitive flow has been noted as being a significant facet of creativity and artistic expression [6]. Creativity has been defined as an "interaction among aptitude, process, and environment by which an individual produces a perceptible product that is both novel and useful as defined within a social construct" [29, p. 90]. In [6], semi-structured interviews with artists demonstrated that the creative process often depends in part on the activation of flow states, with artists intentionally striving to foster the conditions and preconditions of flow. When asked to describe their creative process, respondents explicitly mentioned flow and associated this process with being in a meditative state or having a profound sense of concentration and calmness. Further analysis of their responses revealed significant overlap between the creative process and the nine dimensions of cognitive flow such as having a sense of purpose in creating an artwork which serves to clarify one's goals, receiving immediate feedback as this artwork takes shape, requiring a balance between challenge and skill when working with their chosen medium, as well as being an intrinsically rewarding pursuit, among others [6].

Measuring Cognitive Flow. Assessing whether or not a person is in a state of flow is not a straightforward process due to the complexity and subjective nature of such an experience. Nonetheless, several methods for measuring cognitive flow in individuals have been suggested, such as interviews, questionnaires, experience sampling (e.g., through diary studies), and various physiological measures (e.g., heart rate and eye tracking) [25–27, 33]. Interviews were particularly useful to researchers in the early stages of developing theories around the construct of cognitive flow as these can often provide a rich understanding of a person's subjective experience [24]. However, questionnaires presently comprise the bulk of methods employed in research on this phenomenon – whether it be cognitive flow in physical activity [15], media use [35], work settings [31], computer games [8], or task absorption [20]. Perhaps the most widely used of these questionnaires is the Flow State Scale (FSS) which was designed to measure the extent to which a person experiences a state of cognitive flow during physical activity shortly after having completed it [15]. The FSS questionnaire consists of 36 Likert items using a 5-point rating scale (ranging from 1 being 'strongly disagree' to 5 being 'strongly agree') grouped into sets of four items according to the nine dimensions of cognitive flow described in [9] and shown previously in Table 1. Examples of these items include "I felt I was competent enough to meet the high demands of the situation", "I performed automatically", "I knew what I wanted to achieve", "I found the experience extremely rewarding", and "Time seemed to alter (either slowed down or sped up)". Due to the difficulty of measuring cognitive flow, it has been suggested that combining multiple methods consisting of both qualitative and quantitative data can provide a more valid measure and understanding for researchers [15, 33]. Further still, in many situations such as user testing of various systems designed for cognitive flow, large numbers of participants are not always possible. Even with a sufficient number of participants, multiple measures and lengthy questionnaires are not often practical in terms of time. For these reasons, other approaches such as surveys have been employed [12], or such systems are not fully evaluated at all [27].

2.2 Designing Immersive Interactive Technologies for Positive Change

Artists and researchers, working in HCI-related endeavours and who are interested in developing immersive, interactive systems that have a positive impact on the well-being of the people who use them, are tasked with determining how exactly to design such technologies. This design process can often be quite complex and involve, for example, guiding theories of interaction from the fields of psychology or persuasive technology as well as methods intended to prioritize the user's needs. Moreover, with complex multimodal systems such as those found, for example, in VR or when creating new musical interfaces, knowledge concern-

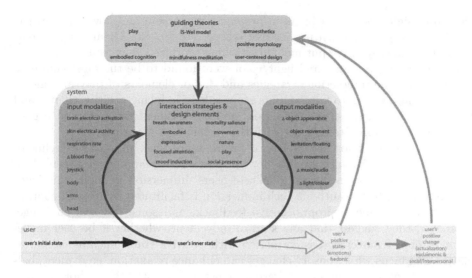

Fig. 1. A framework for designing immersive, interactive systems which elicit positive states and produce experiences which support positive change in users (as taken from [16]).

ing appropriate mapping strategies of these various modalities and their effects is crucial.

With these points in mind, in work by [16], the authors constructed a suggested framework shown in Fig. 1, based on observations from existing literature and systems of the various design elements, interaction strategies, input-output modalities, and the positive effects these had on users, for designing immersive, interactive technologies that promote positive states. The researcher begins using this framework in Fig. 1 by identifying a certain positive change for the user that he or she wishes to design for. This change is grounded in one or more possible theories or models (purple box at top), which, in turn, influence the choice of design elements and interaction strategies (green box at middle). These elements and strategies include, for example, breath awareness, expression, and play, among others, and collectively, these form a feedback loop in connection with the input and output modalities (blue box at left and red box at right, respectively). When the user interacts with the system, input data is collected through various possible modalities such as physiological measures, bodily movement, or the use of controllers, and transformed by the system into one or more possible output modalities such as object movement or changes in sound or visuals. These output modalities are intended to influence the user's inner state which, in turn, affects his or her interaction with the system, and thereby leading to the intended positive change [16].

As noted in [16], there is a relatively low number of such technologies for positive change that use controllers as input modalities – further stating that "traditional controllers do not map well to eliciting positive states" and that their use might "lead to a break in presence, immersion and flow ... distracting from the goal of eliciting positive states" [16, p. 13]. Of all the systems the authors surveyed, output modalities which produced changes to an object's appearance, music/audio, and light/color were found to be the most common. Furthermore, the interaction strategies and design elements of play and movement were also shown to have an important role in inducing positive change and led to a sense of curiosity, imagination, and embodiment for users which gave them the opportunity to interact with the system in a natural way.

As a framework for the design of future immersive, interactive technologies such as VR, the authors note how, in particular, mappings between physical and virtual movements can facilitate users' immersion in their experience [16]. According to the authors, such immersion is facilitated by natural control, mimicry of movement, proprioceptive feedback, and some physical challenge. Moreover, they suggest that any kind of movement, whether it be user movement or object movement, is correlated with positive states such as calmness, clarity, and focus while sensory changes can enhance relaxation, enjoyment, balance, and harmony for users [16]. Perhaps most importantly, the authors address the need for further investigation and empirical evidence for determining how exactly immersive, interactive technologies can elicit positive states and support positive change.

Cognitive Flow in Creative Applications of Virtual Reality. Cognitive flow and its related constructs of presence and immersion have been extensively studied subjects in computer gaming and VR largely also in the context of gaming [5,22,36]. Far less research, however, has explored cognitive flow in the context of creative and artistic applications of VR – despite their strong connection – and of these efforts, many lack formal evaluations [27]. Nonetheless, researchers have noted several criteria for designing explicitly for cognitive flow in virtual environments with creative applications in mind, such as those used in the creation of *Flow Zone* [27], a cross-modal VR system for music creation and visual exploration through movement. Moreover, these design criteria overlap significantly with several of the dimensions of cognitive flow (shown in Table 1). According to [27], such virtual environments must (1) maintain a challenge-skill balance, (2) present clear goals, (3) facilitate concentration on the present moment, (4) encourage strong interactions for inducing a sense of control, and (5) offer a space for inward motivation. Moreover, the rich environments provided by VR and cross-modal stimuli, deep embodiment through music and movement, and the intrinsically rewarding experience of creative expression are further noted design elements for cognitive flow [27].

2.3 Mapping Strategies for Sound, Visuals, and Movement in Interactive Systems

Simply knowing which of the possible input and output modalities (as shown e.g., in Fig. 1) one wishes to use in the design of a system is insufficient, as how these modalities can be mapped to one another can vary significantly. Moreover, the choice of one particular mapping over another affects the expressiveness afforded to the user and ultimately, the overall effectiveness of the system. There are several variations of possible mappings whether one is working with mapping sound to movement when creating, for example, new musical interfaces, or mapping visuals to movement as is often required in interactive art installations.

In addition to a many-to-one or *convergent* mapping, in which several controls affect a single parameter, and its inverse – a *divergent* one-to-many mapping, other variations such as one-to-one and the more complex many-to-many are possible [13]. It has been suggested in [13], however, that when working with sound and movement, mappings which are not one-to-one are generally more engaging and less frustrating for users. Such strategies encourage a certain level of effort in which "the output sound energy should be in some way proportional to the amount of movement, momentum, or acceleration" [11, p. 157]. On the other hand, having too many mappings can unnecessarily increase the complexity of interaction in a way which is confusing for users, so a proper balance must be found.

When tasked with determining effective mappings of visuals to movement, artists who design interactive art installations have employed a number of compelling strategies with various goals in mind e.g., amplifying the expressiveness of gestures [3], enhancing the 'liveness' of performative movement [4], establishing a sense of presence [28], extending body awareness [19], and stimulating creative expression [2]. Many of the same considerations when mapping sound to movement, are relevant to mapping visuals to movement as well as to visuals to sound, such as the visual perceptual correlates to one's movements (e.g., what constitutes a 'calm' looking visual in response to 'calm' movements) and the phenomenological effects of cross-modal stimuli.

3   Design of Synergia: A VR System for Creative Expression and Positive Change

In this section, we provide an overview of how Synergia was designed according to an adaptation of the aforementioned framework for designing immersive, interactive technologies for positive change [16] (shown in Fig. 1) that includes design elements from [27] for inducing cognitive flow in virtual environments (discussed in Sect. 2.2). Next, we discuss how this framework informed the mapping of sound and visual components found in Synergia to arm movements and provide the results of our usability testing of this design. We conclude with an overview of the implementation details of the final design of the system.

Figure 2 shows the framework from [16], adapted to include the design elements suggested in [27], used in guiding the design elements, interaction strategies, and input/output modalities in Synergia. As noted in Fig. 2, Synergia is a multimodal VR system which makes use of the arms as input modalities (blue box at left) that, through creative and expressive movements (green box at middle), produce output modalities of changes in sound, light appearance, and

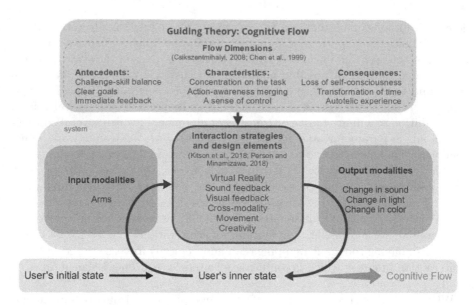

Fig. 2. Proposed design framework for Synergia – an adaptation of a framework in [16] for designing immersive, interactive technologies for positive change which includes design elements suggested in [27] for inducing cognitive flow in virtual environments. (Color figure online)

color (red box at right). These output modalities, in turn, serve as aural and visual feedback for the user. In line with the original framework [16], this aural and visual feedback can be used to stimulate concentration and focused attention, inform the users about their performance, facilitate emotional expression, and support feelings of contentment and harmony. Where our proposed design framework in Fig. 2 differs considerably from the suggestions presented in [16] is in its guiding theory (purple box at top). With Synergia, we have chosen to use the dimensions of cognitive flow [9] as well as its preconditions [17,27] as criteria for guiding the design of the system's sound and visual feedback (discussed further in Sect. 3.1). Furthermore, our choice to use VR as an interaction strategy and design element (green box at middle) was motivated by its potential to provide several preconditions of cognitive flow, as discussed in Sect. 2.2, through an immersive, rich environment as well as to possibly facilitate further dimensions of flow such as an increase in concentration and a transformation of time. Moreover, a cross-modal interaction between sound and visuals (green box at middle) was incorporated as a means for increasing the complexity of the VR environment and in doing so, potentially provide a more appropriate challenge-skill balance for the user.

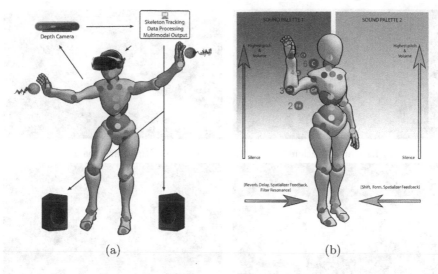

(a)   (b)

Fig. 3. Conceptual design of the Synergia system in (a) and its mapping of various parameters of sound to movements of the arms in (b).

3.1   Mapping Sound and Visuals to Arm Movements

Synergia was designed to allow users the ability to creatively 'paint' with free-flowing particles in a virtual environment and create sound using the movement of their arms. This sound, in turn, affects the visual appearance of the particles and adds to the complexity of the interaction in a way which we suggest will enrich the experience. The conceptual design of the system and mapping of sound to arm movements is illustrated in Fig. 3(a) and (b), respectively.

As indicated in Fig. 3(b), the right and left arms of the user control separate sound palettes, chosen so as to be distinguishable but consonant to the ear. The pitch of each sound palette is generated through a one-to-one mapping with one of six possible positions of the user's elbows relative to his or her torso (as indicated by the six blue dots circling the figure's shoulder). A divergent, one-to-many mapping utilized the position of the wrists to control several additional parameters of sound such as reverb, and delay, among others. As a means for facilitating an effort-based mapping strategy (discussed in Sect. 2.3), high and low positions of the wrists were further mapped to the amplitude of each sound palette (as indicated by the vertical arrows).

Detailed images of the left and right hand particle systems controlled by the movements of a user's arms (as depicted in Fig. 3(a)), are shown in Fig. 4(a) and (b), respectively. Each particle system consists of a source, responsible for emitting the actual particles (circled in red), a trail (circled in yellow) that slowly disappears over the lifetime of the particles, and an associated attraction source (circled in orange) which invisibly encapsulates the body of the user and provides a direction in which the particle's trail can float towards. The left and right hand particle systems differ in their size, visual appearance, and gradient of

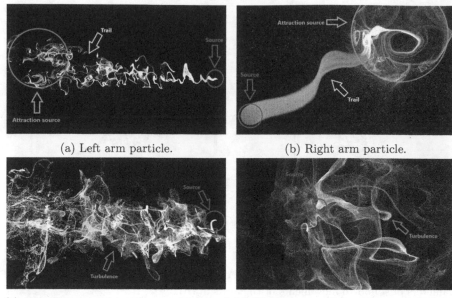

(a) Left arm particle.

(b) Right arm particle.

(c) Left arm particle with sound-induced turbulence.

(d) Right arm particle with sound-induced turbulence.

Fig. 4. Two example particles created with Synergia using a person's moving left hand in (a) and moving right hand in (b), shown in gradients of turquoise and pink, respectively. These same particles are shown in (c) and (d) with a turbulence effect after having been perturbed by certain frequencies of sound produced by movement. (Color figure online)

color so that they are easily distinguished in the same way as their corresponding sounds described above. With the preconditions of flow discussed in Sect. 2.2 in mind, we introduced an additional element of complexity to the interaction by making the visuals reactive to certain frequencies of sound. As shown in Fig. 4(c) and (d), the particles can be perturbed with a turbulence effect in which their respective color gradients are changed and their visual appearances are made more disparate.

Prototype Testing. Usability tests were conducted with nine participants who were asked to complete a set of tasks using their right and left hands separately while interacting with three versions – sound alone, visuals alone, and sound and visuals – of a prototype design of Synergia. Participants were asked to think aloud as they attempted each task and upon completion of all tasks, we conducted a brief semi-structured interview for further clarification on their experience when interacting with the system. The goal of these tests was to assess (1) how aware participants were of what they could and could not control, (2) how intuitive the various mappings (i.e., sound-movement, visuals-movement, and sound-visuals) were, and (3) how immediate the feedback in the form of visuals and sound

Table 2. Usability tasks participants were asked to complete while interacting with three versions – sound alone, visuals alone, and sound with visuals – of Synergia. Note that each task for a given version was completed for each arm except for the version with both sound and visuals.

	Version	Arms	Tasks
1.	Sound	Both	1. Produce a high pitched sound
			2. Choose an interesting sound and repeat it
2.	Visuals	Both	1. Draw a rectangle
			2. Bring the particles closer to the body
3.	Sound and Visuals	Single	1. Right arm only: Create a 'smoky' visual effect
			2. Left arm only: Create a 'chaotic' visual effect

was. Table 2 shows the set of usability tasks carried out in the design testing of Synergia.

The participants' successful completion (or not) of the usability tasks, their thoughts while attempting them, and their feedback expressed during the following interviews demonstrated that (1) the sound-movement mapping could be made more intuitive, and (2) the visual-movement mapping lacked full control. With respect to (1), we reduced the number of one-to-many sound parameters manipulated by the movements of each arm and incorporated a velocity component to the movements such that more energy and effort would be required to produce sound. The problem in (2) appeared to be caused by the inherent latency of the system, but several participants noted that not being fully in control proved to be a motivating challenge so we opted not to make any adjustments. Another participant expressed that the attraction speed of the particles was too fast, so we connected their speed to the overall amplitude of sound so that the attraction occurred more slowly. While all participants were able to successfully complete the tasks associated with the sound-visual mapping, they expressed that they found it challenging to determine what aspects of their actions contributed to their experience. For example, some participants correctly attributed the turbulence effect of the visuals to sound, while others misattributed this effect to rapid arm movements or nothing at all. Based on the challenging nature of this mapping and the importance to cognitive flow of having such an antecedent, we decided against making any adjustments to the sound-visual mapping.

3.2 Implementation Overview

The hardware used in Synergia is a single Intel RealSense D415 depth camera [14], an HTC VIVE head-mounted-display (HMD), and a set of floor-mounted Magnat speakers. The software for running Synergia consists of a real-time, machine learning skeleton tracking SDK from Cubemos [10], a 3D virtual environment created in Unity [34], sound processing through Ableton Live [1], and

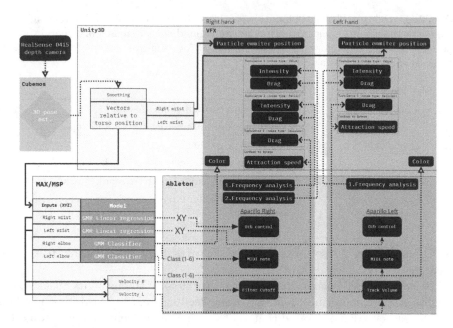

Fig. 5. Overview of the implementation details of the Synergia system using Cubemos, Unity3D, Max/MSP, and Ableton Live.

a Max/MSP [21] patch available in the MuBu toolbox [23] for interactive sound and motion applications using machine learning. All communication between programs is handled through a network using the Open Sound Control (OSC) protocol. Figure 5 shows the overall technical diagram of the final design of the Synergia system[1].

As shown in the upper left corner of Fig. 5, Synergia first uses Cubemos to detect the coordinates in 3D space corresponding to the 18 skeletal joints of a user. These coordinates and corresponding confidence levels for each joint are then sent to Unity (yellow box) where the positions of the wrist and elbow joints for each arm are computed relative to the coordinates of the torso. Subsequently, these positions are used to generate locations in virtual space for the sources that produce the particles which have been set to emanate at a slight offset from the left and right wrist joints using Unity VFX (grey overlays). Determining the positions of the joints in this way addresses the problem of individuals with different body sizes by ensuring that their arm movements are independent from their body position relative to the location of the depth camera. The positions of these joints are then sent from Unity to a Max/MSP patch (grey box at lower left) which uses MuBu to handle their respective mappings to the sound palettes. The actual sound generation is carried out in Ableton Live (blue box)

---

[1] The complete code for the Synergia system can be found in the following repository: https://github.com/marospekarik/synergia.

and the mapping of the particles to color and any turbulence effects is handled by Unity VFX. In VFX (grey overlay on yellow box), the 'color' parameter is assigned a 'sample gradient' operator that returns a color value depending on the particular pitch produced by the locations of the user's elbows while the 'attraction speed' parameter is connected to the amplitude of the sound. Two parameters, 'intensity' and 'drag', are then used by the 'Turbulence 1' block to modify the appearance of the particles for both hands based on their respective pitch frequencies. These same parameters in the 'Turbulence 2' block further modify the appearance of the particles for the right hand based on the range of frequencies present. Finally, the 'drag' parameter in the 'Turbulence 3' block is modified by the amplitude of the sounds for both hands.

4   Evaluation

In this section, we discuss two experiments carried out with Synergia. The first of these experiments was intended to discover which of the three design versions (discussed in Sect. 3.1) of our system – sound alone, visuals alone, and both —- contributed most to cognitive flow. The second of these experiments was carried out in order to establish for the version of our system which most contributed to cognitive flow, as determined by the first experiment, which of two design elements had the greatest influence along the nine dimensions of cognitive flow. In analyzing the participants' ratings from the FSS questionnaire, we have elected to consider the data as interval (as opposed to ordinal), as has been commonly done in previous work [7,25]. In our case, this data were the mean participant ratings in the aforementioned two experiments both across the entire FSS questionnaire and along the nine dimensions of cognitive flow. All participants were informed of what actions would take place during both experiments as well as how their data would be used. Consent was obtained in accordance with the participating university's ethical guidelines for conducting experiments with human participants.

4.1   Experiment 1

In our first experiment, we constructed a repeated measures design in which each participant interacted with Synergia in three conditions: (1) sound alone, (2) visuals alone, and (3) both sound and visuals. Conditions were completely counter-balanced so that any observed order effects were minimized. Following each respective condition, participants were asked to complete the Flow State Scale (FSS) and after having completed the third questionnaire, participants took part in a follow-up semi-structured interview designed to collect qualitative data concerning the nature of their experience with the system and any perceived positive change to their physical or mental well-being.

Participants. We collected data from seven, volunteer participants (six male and one female) of largely university students with an average age of 25.3 ± 3.8

years. Of these participants, three claimed to have 10 or more years of experience in art, while three others noted less than 10 years of experience and one stated no such experience at all. Four of the participants stated having more than 10 years of experience with music while the remaining three stated having no such experience. Furthermore, six participants stated having previous experience with VR with only one having no such prior experience.

Procedure. Participants were asked one at a time to enter the room in which the Synergia system had been set up and two experimenters were present. They were then asked to respond to a few questions concerning their age, gender, and prior experience with art, music, and VR. Afterwards, they were informed that they would be experiencing a VR system a total of three separate times and that with each time, their arms should be used to interact with this system. Participants were fitted with the VR head-mounted display (HMD) and situated in a standing position at the center of an approximately 2.5 by 2.5 m square area facing the depth-camera. Each condition was stopped by an experimenter after 10 min and the participant was given 5 min of resting time without the HMD followed by time to complete the FSS questionnaire. Following the third condition and the completion of the third FSS questionnaire, participants were asked to take part in an interview with both experimenters, where further information was gathered regarding their experience such as "Which experience had a stronger impact on you and why?", "How natural was it for you to control the environment through movement?", and "Were you able to anticipate what would happen next in response to your actions?". Following the completion of this interview, the test was concluded and participants were thanked for their time.

Results and Discussion. The mean ratings from each of the three conditions met the assumptions for a repeated measures ANOVA. However, the mean rating of cognitive flow proved statistically insignificantly different across the three conditions (F(1.15,6.93) = 1.315, $p > 0.2$, ges = 0.113). It is worth noting that treating the actual participant ratings as ordinal data (rather than considering the mean rankings as interval data) in which each individual item on the FSS is a separate observation, the differences between the three conditions proves significant when using a Friedman ranked sum test ($F_r = 23.2$, $p < 0.001$), where the assumptions for this test have similarly been met. Nonetheless, some interesting trends can be observed in the mean ratings. Figure 6 shows box plots of the mean ratings from the FSS for our participants interacting with Synergia across the three conditions in (a) and along the nine dimensions of cognitive flow for these same conditions in (b).

As shown in Fig. 6(a), the mean rating (noted with a diamond symbol) in the condition with both sound and visuals was highest of all, followed by the second condition with only visuals, and lastly, the third condition with only sound. When looking at Fig. 6(b), one will note this trend persists across a majority of the dimensions of cognitive flow (i.e., CHAL, GOAL, FDBK, ACT, TRAN, and

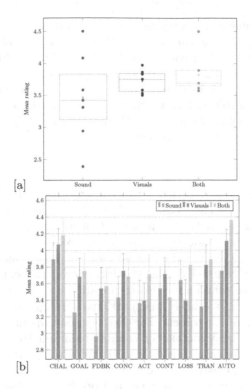

Fig. 6. Mean participant ratings from the Flow State Scale (FSS) questionnaire after interacting with Synergia across each of the three conditions, sound alone, visuals alone, and sound and visuals, in (a) and along the nine dimensions of cognitive flow for these same conditions in (b).

AUTO) except for those concerning concentration, a sense of control, and loss of self (i.e., CONC, CONT, and LOSS), however, these differences in mean ratings between conditions within all dimensions proved insignificant ($p > 0.1$). Were we to again consider the actual ratings (as opposed to their means), the difference between conditions observed in the dimensions concerning clear feedback and a sense of a transformation of time (i.e., FDBK and TRAN) proved significant ($p < 0.05$).

The fact that for the majority of dimensions, the sound and visual condition resulted in an overall greater mean rating than the others suggests that having both modalities is an important component of what may constitute a flow experience with Synergia. Concerning the dimensions of concentration and a sense of control, the visual only condition was rated higher than the other two conditions likely because users are in general more acutely attuned to visual stimuli rather than sound (as indicated by the lowest overall rating for feedback in the sound only condition) and the visual particles were designed to have fewer adjustable parameters in comparison to the sound. Moreover, the mapping of movement-generated sound to affect the visual appearance of particles possibly proved difficult for participants trying to understand the effects of their actions which might explain the comparative lack of perceived control in the sound and visual condition. This lack of control in the third condition likely factored into the greater perceived challenge-skill balance as well. However, participants found the perceived goals and feedback more or less equally as clear in the second and third conditions, possibly indicating that any perceived lack of control in the third condition was not overly negative. More promising still is that participants found the sound and visual condition more intrinsically rewarding (i.e., AUTO).

4.2   Experiment 2

Our second experiment was carried out in response to the finding from our first experiment that the sound and visual version of Synergia appeared to contribute most to cognitive flow but that some aspect of its design elements seemed to result in a reduced sense of concentration and control for these participants when compared to the other versions (i.e., sound alone or visuals alone). Based on the qualitative feedback received during the interviews, the nature of how these visuals reacted to the sound appeared responsible for this response from these participants. Moreover, it is likely that participant fatigue was a negative factor in the design of the first experiment. For these reasons, in our second experiment, we adopted a paired and completely counter-balanced two samples design in which participants interacted with a sound and visual version of Synergia (as was done in the third condition of experiment 1) where the appearance of the visuals was changed in response to the sound produced by the participants' arm movements (as shown e.g., by the turbulence effect added to the particles in Fig. 4(c) and (d)), and a version where the appearance of visuals did not react to the sound produced by the participants' arm movements (as shown e.g., in Fig. 4(a) and (b)).

Participants. We collected data from 13, volunteer participants (seven male and six female) with an average age of 28.4 ± 4.7 years. Of these participants, four claimed to have 10 or more years of experience in art, while four others noted less than 10 years of experience and five stated no such experience at all. Five of the participants stated having more than 10 years of experience with music while two others noted less than 10 years of experience with music and the remaining six stated having no such experience. Furthermore, six participants stated having previous experience with VR while seven others reported having no such prior experience.

Procedure. The procedure for the second experiment followed that of the first experiment with only minor adjustments made. First, participants were asked to fill out the FSS questionnaire only twice – once after each of their two respective conditions. Second, participants were given up to 20 min to interact with the system instead of 10 min. Finally, the area in which participants were free to explore in the physical space was blocked from view by the experimenters so that the users might feel less inhibited in their interactions with the system.

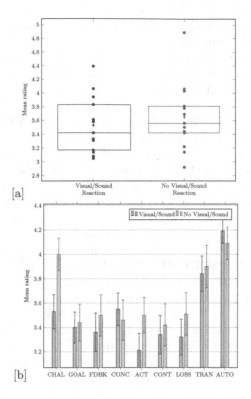

Fig. 7. Mean participant ratings from the Flow State Scale (FSS) questionnaire after interacting with a sound and visual version of Synergia across each of the two conditions, visuals reacting to sound and visuals not reacting to sound in (a) and along the nine dimensions of cognitive flow for these same conditions in (b).

Results and Discussion. The mean ratings from each of the two conditions met the assumptions for a two-tailed dependent (paired) samples Student's t-test. However, the mean rating of cognitive flow proved statistically insignificantly different across the two conditions (t $= -1.4842$, $p > 0.1$). It is worth noting that, as with the first experiment, treating the participant ratings here as ordinal data in which each individual item on the FSS is a separate observation, the differences between the two conditions proves significant when using a Wilcoxon signed-rank test ($W = 10670$, $p < 0.05$), where the assumptions for this test have also been met. Nonetheless, as with the first experiment, some interesting trends can be observed in the mean ratings.

As shown in Fig. 7(a), the mean rating in the condition with visual particles reacting to sound is marginally lower than in the condition with no such reaction. When looking at Fig. 7(b), this difference holds across most of the dimensions of cognitive flow (i.e., CHAL, GOAL, FDBK, ACT, CONT, LOSS, and TRAN) with the notable exceptions being concentration and an autotelic experience (i.e., CONC and AUTO). Of the nine dimensions, however, only the difference in mean ratings for a challenge-skill balance proved significant ($p < 0.05$) with all other dimensions proving insignificantly different ($p > 0.5$). Were we to again consider the actual ratings (as opposed to their means), the difference between conditions observed in the dimensions concerning both a challenge-skill balance and merging of action and awareness (i.e., CHAL and ACT) proved significant ($p < 0.05$).

Recall that our motivation for having visuals which react to sound was to increase the perceived complexity of the experience in compliance with the dimension of cognitive flow concerning a challenge-skill balance. Surprisingly, however, our results indicate that the mean rating in this dimension (i.e., CHAL) is significantly lower in the first condition with visuals reacting to sound than in the second condition without this reaction. If we look then to the dimension of increased control (i.e., CONT), the lower mean rating in the first condition when compared to the second condition suggests perhaps that participants found the added complexity prohibitively large, resulting in a perceived challenge that exceeded their perceived skill (rather than the reverse). We might interpret also that the lower mean ratings in the first condition when compared to the second condition for the dimensions concerning immediate feedback and merging of action and awareness (i.e., FDBK and ACT), indicate for the participants a sense of confusion or frustration with respect to this added complexity. Regardless, our finding with respect to the dimension of autotelic experience (i.e., AUTO), suggests that interestingly, participants still found their experience with visuals reacting to sound more intrinsically rewarding than not having this reaction.

5   Conclusion and Future Work

In this paper, we presented a multimodal VR system called Synergia for creative expression and positive change which allows users to 'paint' with particles in a virtual environment and create sound through movements of the arms. We evaluated this system through two experiments which demonstrated that (1) the use of both sound and visuals contributes most to cognitive flow over sound or visuals alone, and (2) when using sound and visuals, a cross-modal design element, which uses sound to further modify the appearance of visuals produced by arm movements, factored negatively into the overall contribution of cognitive flow. In particular, this cross-modal design element resulted in rather lower levels of perceived challenge-skill balance and feedback but contributed to an increased sense of concentration and greater autotelic experience for our participants. In future work, it would be necessary to look further into what exact parameters of the sound and visuals in Synergia contribute to the users' experiences along the nine dimensions of cognitive flow. Furthermore, it would be worthwhile to consider additional measures of cognitive flow beyond the FSS. With the work presented here, we hope that we have provided some ways forward for artists and researchers in HCI interested in positive uses of technology and looking to design VR systems for creative expression and cognitive flow.

References

1. Ableton: Ableton (2020). https://www.ableton.com/
2. Akten, M.: Body paint (2009). http://www.memo.tv/works/bodypaint/
3. Alaoui, S.F., Bevilacqua, F., Pascual, B.B., Jacquemin, C.: Dance interaction with physical model visuals based on movement qualities. Arts Technol. **6**(4) (2013)
4. Almena, M.: Transcendence: can live performance art in combination with interactive technology induce altered states of consciousness. Electronic Visualisation and the Arts (EVA) (2018). https://doi.org/10.14236/ewic/EVA2018.38
5. Bian, Y., et al.: A framework for physiological indicators of flow in VR games: construction and preliminary evaluation. Pers. Ubiquit. Comput. **20**(5), 1–12 (2016)
6. Chemi, T.: The experience of flow in artistic creation. In: Harmat, L., Ørsted Andersen, F., Ullén, F., Wright, J., Sadlo, G. (eds.) Flow Experience, pp. 37–50. Springer, Cham (2016). https://doi.org/10.1007/978-3-319-28634-1_3
7. Chen, H., Wigand, R., Nilan, M.: Optimal experience of web activities. Comput. Hum. Behav. **15**, 585–608 (1999). https://doi.org/10.1016/S0747-5632(99)00038-2
8. Choi, D., Kim, J.: Why people continue to play online games: In search of critical design factors to increase customer loyalty to online contents. Cyberpsychol. Behav. **7**(1), 11–24 (2004). The Impact of the Internet, Multimedia and Virtual Reality on Behavior and Society
9. Csikszentmihalyi, M.: Flow: The Psychology of Optimal Experience. HarperCollins (2008)
10. Cubemos: Skeleton Tracking SDK for Intel RealSense Depth Cameras (2020). https://www.intelrealsense.com/skeleton-tracking/
11. Dahlstedt, P., Dahlstedt, A.S.: Otokin: mapping for sound space exploration through dance improvisation. In: Queiroz, M., Sedó, A.X. (eds.) Proceedings of the International Conference on New Interfaces for Musical Expression, Porto Alegre, Brazil, pp. 156–161. UFRGS, June 2019. http://www.nime.org/proceedings/2019/nime2019_paper031.pdf
12. Hassan, L., Jylhä, H., Sjöblom, M., Hamari, J.: Flow in VR: a study on the relationships between preconditions, experience and continued use. In: Proceedings of the 53rd Hawaii International Conference on System Sciences, pp. 1196–1205 (2020). https://doi.org/10.24251/HICSS.2020.149
13. Hunt, A., Kirk, R.: Mapping strategies for musical performance. Trends in Gestural Control of Music (2000)
14. Intel: Intel RealSense Depth Camera D415 (2020). https://www.intelrealsense.com/depth-camera-d415/
15. Jackson, S.A., Marsh, H.W.: Development and validation of a scale to measure optimal experience: the flow state scale. J. Sport Exerc. Psychol. **18**, 17–35 (1996)
16. Kitson, A., Prpa, M., Riecke, B.E.: Immersive interactive technologies for positive change: a scoping review and design considerations. Front. Psychol. **9**(1354) (2018). https://doi.org/10.3389/fpsyg.2018.01354
17. Kotler, S.: The Rise of Superman: Decoding the Science of Ultimate Human Performance. Amazon Publishing (2014)
18. Lee, L.N., Kim, M.J., Hwang, W.J.: Potential of augmented reality and virtual reality technologies to promote wellbeing in older adults. Appl. Sci. **9**(17) (2019)
19. Legarnisson, E.: (un)balance (2018). http://www.interactivearchitecture.org/lab-projects/unbalance
20. Martin, A.J., Jackson, S.A.: Brief approaches to assessing task absorption and enhanced subjective experience: examining 'short' and 'core' flow in diverse performance domains. Motiv. Emot. **32**(3), 141–157 (2008)

21. Max: Max (2020). https://cycling74.com/
22. Michailidis, L., Balaguer-Ballesterand, E., He, X.: Flow and immersion in video games: the aftermath of a conceptual challenge. Front. Psychol. **9**, 16–82 (2018). https://doi.org/10.3389/fpsyg.2018.01682
23. MuBu: Mubu for Max (2008). http://ismm.ircam.fr/mubu/
24. Nakamura, J., Csikszentmihalyi, M.: The concept of flow. Flow and the Foundations of Positive Psychology, pp. 239–263. Springer, Dordrecht (2014). https://doi.org/10.1007/978-94-017-9088-8_16
25. Nijs, L., Coussement, P., Moens, B., Amelinck, D., Lesaffre, M., Leman, M.: Interacting with the music paint machine: relating the constructs of flow experience and presence. Interact. Comput. **24**(4), 237–250 (2012)
26. Novak, T.P., Hoffman, D.L.: Measuring the flow experience among web users. Technical report, Vanderbilt University (1997)
27. Person, T., Minamizawa, K.: Flow zone: inducing flow to improve subjective well-being by creating a cross-modal music creation experience in virtual reality. In: SIGGRAPH Asia 2018 Virtual & Augmented Reality (2018)
28. Plant, N.: Sentient flux (2015). http://nicolaplant.co.uk/sentientflux.html
29. Plucker, J.A., Beghetto, R.A., Dow, G.T.: Why isn't creativity more important to educational psychologists? Potentials, pitfalls, and future directions in creativity research. Educ. Psychol. **39**(2), 83–96 (2004). https://doi.org/10.1207/s15326985ep3902_1
30. Roche, K., Liu, S., Siegel, S.: The effects of virtual reality on mental wellness: a literature review. Ment Health Fam Med. **14**, 811–818 (2019)
31. Schaufeli, W., Bakker, A.: Utrecht work engagement scale: preliminary manual. Occupational Health Psychology Unit, Utrecht (2003)
32. Seabrook, E., et al.: Understanding how virtual reality can support mindfulnesspractice: mixed methods study. J. Med. Internet Res. **22**(3) (2020)
33. Tian, Y., Bian, Y., Han, P., Wang, P., Gao, F., Chen, Y.: Physiological signal analysis for evaluating flow during playing of computer games of varying difficulty. Front. Psychol. **8**, 1–10 (2017)
34. Unity: Unity 3D (2020). https://www.unity.com
35. Witmer, B.G., Singer, M.J.: Measuring presence in virtual environments: a presence questionnaire. Presence: Teleoper. Virtual Environ. **7**, 225–240 (1998)
36. Yao, S., Kim, G.: The effects of immersion in a virtual reality game: presence and physical activity. In: Fang, X. (ed.) HCII 2019. LNCS, vol. 11595, pp. 234–242. Springer, Cham (2019). https://doi.org/10.1007/978-3-030-22602-2_18

Evaluating Consumer Interaction Interfaces for 3D Sketching in Virtual Reality

Alberto Cannavò[1] , Davide Calandra[1(✉)] , Aidan Kehoe[2] ,
and Fabrizio Lamberti[1]

[1] Dipartimento di Automatica e Informatica, Politecnico di Torino, Turin, Italy
{alberto.cannavo,davide.calandra,fabrizio.lamberti}@polito.it
[2] Logitech Design Lab, Cork, Republic of Ireland
akehoe@logitech.com

Abstract. Since its introduction, 3D mid-air sketching in immersive Virtual Reality (VR) proved to be a very powerful tool for many creative applications. However, common VR sketching suites rely on the standard hand controllers bundled with home VR systems, which are non-optimal for this kind of tasks. To deal with this issue, some research works proposed to use dedicated pen-shaped interfaces tracked with external motion-capture systems. Regrettably, these solutions are generally rather expensive, cumbersome and unsuitable for many potential end-users. Hence, lots of challenges regarding interfaces for 3D sketching in VR still exist. In this paper, a newly proposed sketching-oriented input device (namely, a VR stylus) compatible with the tracking technology of a consumer-grade VR system is compared with a standard hand controller from the same system. In particular, the paper reports the results of a user study whose aim was to evaluate, in both objective and subjective terms, aspects like, among others, sketching accuracy, ease of use, efficiency, comfort, control and naturalness.

Keywords: Virtual Reality · Human-computer interaction · 3D sketching · VR stylus

1 Introduction

Thanks to the recent developments in the consumer market, Virtual Reality (VR) technology is increasingly widening its areas of application. One of the most prominent fields in which VR can have a huge impact is the creation of digital contents. Tasks such as painting [17], modelling [4], sculpting [18], and animation [12] greatly benefit from the possibility for the user to visualize and interact with the actual workpiece in an immersive virtual environment [2].

This work has been partially supported by VR@POLITO.

A. Brooks et al. (Eds.): ArtsIT 2020, LNICST 367, pp. 291–306, 2021.
https://doi.org/10.1007/978-3-030-73426-8_17

In particular, sketching, which is a fast and intuitive method for communicating and conceptualizing ideas by hand drawing [14], is a basic requirement for many of the above tasks. According to [9], sketches are quick, inexpensive, disposable and plentiful. They have a clear vocabulary offering minimal detail: thus, they are open to different interpretations, which make them capable to suggest new solutions to a given problem, rather than just confirm existing ones.

Although sketching is generally considered a 2D activity, many sketch-based interfaces for creating 3D contents have been proposed already [4,5,20,26]. Usually designed for 3D modeling tasks, these solutions generate the final 3D sketch by combining multiple 2D sketches iteratively drawn by the user from different point of views inside the 3D environment. However, as reported in [14], this approach can be an obstacle for inexperienced users. To overcome this limitation, sketching can be easily moved from 2D to mid-air 3D by exploiting an external 6-DOF tracking technology [13]. However, the visualization of the output of a 6-DOF interface on a classical 2D display can be a source of inaccuracies due to the lack of depth perception. This latter issue can be solved by exploiting an immersive technology, like VR. Some commercial sketching tools targeting a broad creative audience, such as TiltBrush [17] and PaintLab VR [24], are specifically designed for being used in VR. Recent years have also seen the emergence of commercial software applications aimed at business users enabling both sketching and some modelling activities in VR, e.g., Gravity Sketch [18], flyingshapes° [16], Alias CreateVR [3]. The user, wearing a Head-Mounted Display (HMD), visualizes (and moves within) a virtual environment that serves as a 3D canvas. Sketches can be drawn by using one of the two 6-DOF hand controllers (or both) typically bundled with the VR system. This approach appears to be fast and highly intuitive, but it is characterized by a low level of accuracy, stability and control over what is being drawn [32].

To deal with the lack of accuracy and control introduced by the adoption of VR, works in the literature investigated the contribution of various forms of guidance (visual or physical [2,32]) that can be provided to the user while sketching in order to mitigate the said issues. Although these works showed that any kind of guidance can reduce the inaccuracy penalty introduced by the mid-air sketching in VR, most of them relied on complex, poorly feasible and non-generalizable approaches which are not representative of the typical usage of the previously mentioned commercial VR sketching tools. In [2], for instance, the user input for sketching is not captured by the VR system itself, but is managed through an external (and expensive) tracking system. The sketching is then performed by handling a tracked physical prop resembling a pen, which is also visualized in VR. Since the pen is a passive device, the drawing input is obtained by pressing a button on a VR controller held in the non-dominant hand. Although the work addressed the problem of mitigating inaccuracies by means of various forms of guidance, the selected configuration still appeared to suffer from some inaccuracies, because the reference systems may not always remain properly aligned, as well as because having the input button on a hand different than the drawing one may introduce unwanted stokes in case of imperfect coordination between the two hands [2]. In [32], the hand controller of a home VR system is directly used as input device, solving the issue of having a second tracking system, but in a way that cannot be considered as natural, efficient or ergonomic; this is due to the fact that the sketch is generated from the tail of the controller, which is held in an unconventional way.

As evidence, all the commercial VR sketching tools support the hand controllers as per any other interactive VR application. The user holds the controller the way it was designed, and he or she uses the trigger button to generate the sketches from the controller's tip. This approach minimizes the need for additional hardware, but it does not solve the problem of non-optimal performance of the standard hand controllers for sketching. Thus, it is not surprising that, recently, a new type of pen-shaped hand controller named VR Ink [28] appeared on the market. This device can be seamlessly integrated with the tracking technology of common VR systems and replace standard VR controllers, promising to be very accurate and ergonomic without requiring external expensive tracking systems.

The aim of this work is to investigate the possible contribution brought to the considered domain by devices like the one above. Thus, a user study was carried out, by following an experimental protocol mainly based on the approach adopted in [2] for the objective measurements, and in [32] for the subjective part. The evaluation compared the VR Ink device with a standard VR controller on a set of sketching tasks under a number of representative conditions, considering a large set of aspects including accuracy, usability, enjoyability, ease of use, efficiency, comfort, control and naturalness.

2   Related Work

Numerous works investigated the advantages of 3D over traditional 2D sketching [4,5,22,26]. However most of them focused on the use of 2D sketching interfaces for generating the 3D sketches, whose output was visualized on classical 2D displays. This being an obstacle for inexperienced users [13], literature moved towards the use of externally tracked 6-DOF sketching interfaces (i.e. pens and styluses) that allow user to directly draw mid-air in 3D.

For instance, the authors of [21] conducted a study, involving expert designers, aimed to compare traditional 2D and mid-air 3D sketching performed in an immersive Cave Automatic Virtual Environment (CAVE). Both the user and the input device (a pen) were tracked by an Ascension MotionStar magnetic tracking system. Although no quantitative measures were collected, results of the qualitative evaluation showed a high interest and a positive attitude of the focus group, indicating the existence of possible benefits coming from the adoption of 3D sketching in the design process.

In [2], the factors affecting human ability to freely sketch in 3D within an immersive VR environment were investigated. The study was preceded by a preliminary observational activity. This activity involved five expert designers who participated in a design session using a popular VR sketching tool. Designers appreciated the freedom of mid-air 3D sketching, but they also observed that more precision and control are often required for obtaining meaningful results. Then, a first experiment was aimed to compare traditional non-VR sketching on a physical surface to sketching performed in VR, with and without a physical surface. A second experiment studied how much the presence of visual guidance in VR could mitigate the loss of accuracy caused by VR itself. Both experiments used a passive 6-DOF pen tracked by an OptiTrack motion capture system (which also tracked the physical surface, when available), whereas the drawing input was triggered by pressing a button on a regular hand controller held with the other hand. Results showed that the presence/lack of a physical surface, the position/orientation/shape of the drawing surface, the size of the stroke and the presence/absence of a visual guidance are all factors affecting the drawing performance. Physical surface increased the accuracy by 20% if compared to unguided mid-air drawing, whereas a virtual representation of the surface could increase it by 15%. Moreover, in applications where the shape to be drawn is known in advance, showing it could boost accuracy even more. Regarding physical guidance, sketching on a virtual surface was 50% worse than sketching on its real counterpart in terms of accuracy, whereas maintaining the physical surface aligned with the virtual one worsened it only by 20%. Although the work provides a useful quantitative analysis of the multiple factors affecting accuracy of 3D sketching in VR, the uncommon input metaphor (triggering the sketching with a hand different than the one holding the pen) and the expensive additional hardware are not exactly representative of the common usage scenarios for VR sketching. Researchers have also explored the usage of a stylus form factor in VR [27,29]. However, these studies were limited to point-and-click and scroll tasks, and did not consider sketching.

An alternative approach presented in [23] exploited a hand-held mobile Augmented Reality (AR) device for drawing and visualizing 3D sketches. The work addressed issues of mobile AR sketching compared with VR-based alternatives, such as the lack of a stereo visualization, the narrow field of view, and the coupling of 2D and 3D input. The result of the pilot study showed that the use of various expedients used in the work like relative drawing, various forms of snapping, and planar/curved surface proxies can mitigate the mentioned issues. The robustness of the solution was showed to be highly dependent on the inside-out motion tracking algorithm available on the device, which is often unstable and influenced by environmental factors. Although this solution may be acceptable when the cost of a VR system is not acceptable, the huge difference in performance (especially in terms of tracking accuracy) showed that VR is actually way more suitable than AR for 3D sketching.

In [1], a hybrid sketching system is proposed, combining mid-air 3D drawing with 2D surface drawing to create 3D designs in AR. In this case, the AR device is a Microsoft HoloLens HMD, which guarantees a more precise inside-out tracking with respect to mobile AR devices. The system combines the use of a 6-DOF passive pen (tracked via a Vicon motion capture system) and a Microsoft Surface Book tablet. Drawing input is triggered through a standard mouse magnetically tightened on the back of the tablet. Authors performed an evaluation which showed that the solution is useful, effective and able to support a variety of design tasks. Nevertheless, the proposed system suffers from many limitations characterizing the previously cited works, in particular the cost of the hardware setup and the decoupling between the drawing hand and the button used to trigger the sketching.

Finally, the combination of 2D and 3D input while using a 6-DOF pen (again tracked with a OptiTrack system) in VR were investigated in [15]. The presented VR sketching tool takes advantage of a 6-DOF tracked pen for mid-air 3D interaction, complemented by a 6-DOF tracked tablet to support 2D surface-based sketching. A user study explored all the possible combinations of the input devices (pen, tablet, and pen plus tablet), for both the 2D and 3D input dimensions, showing that the 2D and 3D sketching metaphors were each suitable for different tasks. Moreover, authors argued that the current VR input devices (the standard hand controllers) are not optimized for sketching in immersive environments; hence, the inclusion of traditional devices (like a pen) could bring benefits and opportunities to the end-user.

Starting from these considerations, the current work focuses on the evaluation of the performance of a sketching-oriented VR stylus directly compatible with the tracking technology (LightHouse 1.0 [19]) of a well-known consumer-level VR kit, which is compared with the standard hand controller bundled with the kit. The tasks selected for the experimental protocol, as well as the objective and subjective metrics used in the evaluation, were derived from existing literature, and will be discussed in detail in the following section.

3   Methodology

As previously mentioned, the experimental protocol developed for the testing activity was for the most part inspired to the first experiment presented in [2]. The aim was to investigate the impact of physical guidance on the stroke accuracy, by comparing mid-air drawing of planar curves (which play a fundamental role in 3D design processes [2]) with drawing the same curves on physical flat surfaces. Three configurations were explored, *traditional*, in which the users had to draw planar curves on a physical surface without being in VR, *VR*, in which they wore a VR HMD and drawn directly mid-air in a 3D space, and *hybrid*, in which drawing was performed on a physical surface aligned with its digital representation in the virtual environment. The VR system used for the evaluation was the HTC Vive.

In our case, the main comparison is related to the sketching device; hence, only two of the above configurations, namely *VR* and *hybrid*, were considered (hereafter referred to as *modalities*). The same VR system was used. The software adopted for the experimental activity was developed starting from the VR tool presented in [12] as a Blender 2.79 [30] add-on. This tool was previously used in other research works like, e.g., [10,11], and [25].

The two main configurations, *controller* and *pen*, will be referred to as *interfaces* for sake of clarity. With the *controller* interface, the study participants

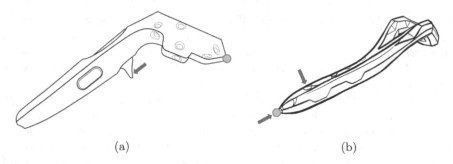

(a)   (b)

Fig. 1. The yellow points indicate where the stroke is generated from with a) *controller* and b) *pen*. The buttons used to initiate the sketching are indicated with a red arrow (for the *pen*, pressing the tip on a physical surface acts as a trigger too). (Color figure online)

performed the tasks by using the controller bundled with the HTC Vive and acted on its trigger to start sketching. The controller generates the sketch from its tip (Fig. 1a), so that it can be placed on physical surfaces to draw on them. With the *pen* interface, the Vive controller is replaced by a VR Ink stylus, which is tracked by the LightHouse system already used for the HTC Vive system. The pen has an analog, force-sensitive control on its tip which automatically triggers the drawing when pressed on a surface (Fig. 1b). Moreover, in case of mid-air sketching, a further force-sensitive control on the stylus's side can be operated with the index finger. Other inputs (grip and touch-pad, present in both the controller and the pen) were not used.

The experiment was designed as a $2 \times 2 \times 3 \times 3 \times 3$ within-subjects study, with *interface (controller, pen)*, *modality (hybrid, VR)*, *drawing plane orientation (horizontal, vertical, sideways)*, *stroke shape (horizontal line, vertical line, circle)* and *stroke size (small 10 cm, medium 30 cm, large 60 cm)* as independent variables. *Horizontal line, vertical line* (in the following referred to as *u-line* and *v-line*) and *circular* shapes are illustrated in Fig. 2a, whereas the three *drawing plane orientations* and the two *modalities* are illustrated in Fig. 3.

Similarly to [2], a Latin square order was used, except for the shape dimension that was randomized; for each shape, three set of trials were performed (each one being a random permutation of the stroke sizes), resulting in a total of 324 strokes per participant. In case of sampled points more than 20 cm farther from the target, the trial was rejected and the participant asked to repeat it. The *horizontal* drawing plane was placed at 0.75m from the floor, whereas the other orientations were chosen so that the center of the stroke was at 1. 5m.

Regarding the experimental procedure and the data preparation steps, most of indications and precautions reported in [2] were implemented and followed. Participants were shown both the target stroke and its starting point until they started drawing, and were told to draw circles in clockwise direction, horizontal lines from left to right or far to near, and vertical lines from top to bottom. They were also asked to draw as quickly and accurately as possible. In the

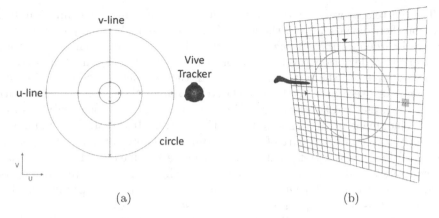

Fig. 2. Representations of a) the three *stroke shapes* (light blue 60 cm, green 30 cm, magenta 10 cm), and b) the grid provided as visual guidance during the experiment. (Color figure online)

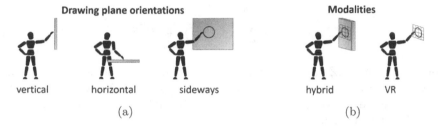

Fig. 3. Representations of a) the three *drawing plane orientations* and b) the two *modalities*.

hybrid modality, the surface was tracked by attaching a HTC Vive Tracker to it. In both *modalities*, a grid was displayed as visual guidance modality (Fig. 2b), aligned with the physical surface in the *hybrid* modality. When using the pen, participants were able to exploit the sensorized tip to draw automatically when pressing it on the surface (in *hybrid* modality), or by using the second force sensitive control when drawing mid-air (in *VR* modality).

Strokes were sampled 60 Hz, and samples were represented in local coordinates relative to the target. A median filter with a window size of 6 was applied to the sampled points; afterwards, a piecewise linear approximation was exploited to resample strokes to a set of 100 equidistant points in order to facilitate the mean stroke calculation over the three trials. Similarly to what done in [2], some of the strokes performed with the *VR* modality were characterized by small tails drifting apart from the drawing plane, either at the start and at the end of the drawing; these artefacts were due to the slight delay between the time the participant decided to start/stop drawing and the time he or she actually pressed/released the trigger.

These artefacts were removed by discarding all the initial and final samples based on their deviation from the local Z axis; in particular, samples were iteratively discarded until a sample characterized by a deviation from Z lower than the average Z deviation (over the whole stroke) was found, and that became the first sample (or the last, when removing the artefact at the end). Finally, all the strokes were processed ("translated") to align their starting point with that of the target stroke, thus mitigating the impact of positional errors caused by a misjudgment of the displayed target's position. If the starting point was previously filtered out as part of a tail, a dummy point, obtained by replacing the Z coordinate of the first point with the average Z value over the whole stroke was generated, and used as a reference for the alignment phase (and then discarded, in order to avoid deleterious translations due to particularly bad starts). As result of this, a resampled and translated stroke S is obtained, defined as a sequence of points $P_1, P_2, ..., P_{100}$ where each point is represented by a 3D vector $P_i = (X, Y, Z)$.

For the objective evaluation, two metrics were used. The first one is the *Mean Overall Deviation* that, for lines, is defined as:

$$MOD_L = \frac{1}{n} \sum_{i=0}^{n-1} \sqrt{(P_i.Y)^2 + (P_i.Z)^2} \tag{1}$$

where $P_i.Y$ and $P_i.Z$ are respectively the Y and Z components of the local position of the i-th point of the stroke, and n is the number of points on the stroke. It basically corresponds to the average deviation from the local X axis. For circles, it is defined as:

$$MOD_C = \frac{1}{n} \sum_{i=0}^{n-1} \sqrt{(\sqrt{(P_i.X)^2 + (P_i.Y)^2} - l/2)^2 + (P_i.Z)^2} \tag{2}$$

where $P_i.X$, $P_i.Y$ and $P_i.Z$ are the three components of the local position of the i-th point of the stroke, n is the number of points on the stroke, and l is the diameter of the target circle. It corresponds to the average deviation from the target circle.

A further metric was introduced to evaluate the deviation from the target shape for the *VR* modality. This metric, named *Mean Projected Deviation*, is obtained by settings the Z term to zero in the previous equations:

$$MPD_L = \frac{1}{n} \sum_{i=0}^{n-1} |P_i.Y| \tag{3}$$

$$MPD_C = \frac{1}{n} \sum_{i=0}^{n-1} |\sqrt{(P_i.X)^2 + (P_i.Y)^2} - l/2| \tag{4}$$

For the *hybrid* modality, *MOD* and *MPD* are expected to be equivalent, since the projection plane coincides with the drawing one, net of eventual tracking issues.

For what it concerns the subjective evaluation, after the experiment the participants were asked to fill in a post-test questionnaire (available for download at http://tiny.cc/ld7msz) including two sections. The first section was aimed to evaluate the usability of the two input interfaces by means of questions in the standard System Usability Scale (SUS) [8]. In the second section, participants were requested to rank the input interfaces based on a number of criteria (1 for best, 2 for worst) and to provide comments on their experience, similarly to what done in [32]. The list of ranking criteria is reported in Table 2.

4 Discussion

Results obtained by applying the evaluation criteria described in the previous section were used to compare the two input interfaces. For the testing activity, 11 participants were involved, 6 males and 5 females, aged between 20 to 61 years ($\mu = 27.91$, $\sigma = 11.55$). For what it concerns familiarity with VR sketching tools, participants would be considered as amateurs, since they reported limited to no prior experience with it.

4.1 Objective Results

The overall MOD and MPD averaged among participants, strokes types, stroke shapes, and drawing orientations are reported in Fig. 4. Wilcoxon signed-rank tests for paired samples ($p < 0.05$) were used to compare *controller* and *pen*. Before applying the statistical test, outliers were detected and removed in pairs of controller-pen strokes from the same user. For example, if a controller stroke with a given modality, orientation, shape and size is detected as outlier, it is removed along with the same stroke drawn with the pen by the same user, in order to preserve the equality of the two sample sizes and guarantee applicability of the paired statistical tests. In the plots, statistically significant results are marked with the * symbol.

It can be observed that, overall, the *pen* allowed participants to obtain more accurate strokes as confirmed by the lower values achieved with this interfaces with respect to the *controller* for both the MOD (0.52 vs 0.47, $p = 0.0027$) and MPD (0.44 vs 0.39, $p = 0.0035$) metrics. It should be noted that MPD, being basically the MOD without the depth (local Z) deviation, can be helpful to spot whether the inaccuracy is simply caused by an erroneous depth perception (in such a case, MPD would be low, whereas MOD would be high).

In order to deepen the analysis, it is possible to study the two metrics aggregating their values by considering different sets of conditions. Data averaged considering the *modality* (*hybrid* or *VR*) will be presented first. Then the analysis will consider the *drawing plane orientation* (*vertical*, *horizontal*, and *sideways*) perspective. Finally results categorized by *stroke shape* and *stroke size* will be reported.

Focusing on the *modality* (Fig. 5), with the pen participants were significantly more accurate than with the controller in the *VR* modality both in terms of MOD

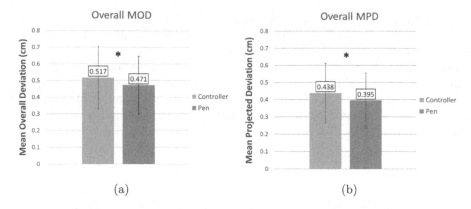

Fig. 4. Mean Overall (a) and Projected (b) Deviation for *controller* and *pen*. The lower the score, the better the result. Standard deviation is expressed via error bars. Statistical significance is indicated by the * symbol.

(0.67 vs 0.58, $p = 0.0019$) and MPD (0.54 vs 0.47, $p = 0.0059$). This result was not observed for the *hybrid* modality, probably because of the presence of the physical surface, which acted as a guide for the drawing and mitigated the inaccuracies of the controller, as shown in Fig. 5 (and as already observed in [2]). The improved accuracy brought by the physical surface reduced the differences between the two interfaces, leading to more comparable performance.

An interesting result comes up when analysing results aggregated by *drawing plane orientation* (Fig. 6), where the *pen* showed its superiority with respect to the *controller* for drawing *sideways*. In fact, results obtained in [2] indicated that drawing sideways was the worst condition, with the highest values of MOD and MPD. The results of our experiments suggest that the *pen* allows participants to improve their accuracy under this condition, letting them obtain lower values of MOD (0.55 vs 0.48, $p = 0.0096$). As revealed in the comments collected after the experiment, this result could be related to the possibility to grip the pen in a more comfortable and natural way compared to the controller while drawing in this "critical" situation. The differences were not statistically significant in terms of MPD, even though the p-value ($p = 0.0554$) is close to the chosen threshold; hence, a significant difference might be found by increasing the group size.

For what it concerns the *stroke shape* (Figs. 7 and 8), it can be observed that, except for the MPD in the *hybrid* modality where the p-value was slightly greater than the threshold, participants were significantly more accurate when operating with the *pen* to draw *v-lines* in terms of both MOD (*hybrid* 0.28 vs 0.23, $p = 0.0323$, *VR* 0.54 vs 0.44, $p = 0.0112$) and MPD (*hybrid* 0.23 vs 0.19, $p = 0.0694$, *VR* 0.45 vs 0.36, $p = 0.0162$). This result could be related to how the hand controller has to be handled. In fact, as can be seen from Fig. 1 the actual shape of the controller was a source of occlusion by itself (because the tip hid the stroke origin), whereas with the pen the user were able to slightly rotate it to disalign the pen body from the stroke. When users were requested to

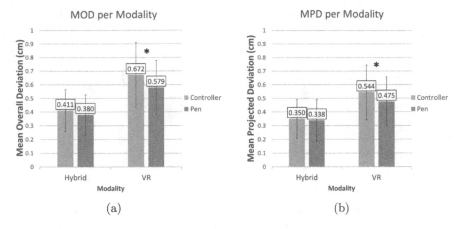

Fig. 5. Mean Overall (a) and Projected (b) Deviation per *modality*. The lower the score, the better the result. Standard deviation is expressed via error bars. Statistical significance is indicated by the * symbol.

draw a *v-line*, the controller handle contributes to such occlusion too, possibly reducing the sketch accuracy.

Finally, regarding *stroke size*, no statistical difference was observed between the two *interfaces* for any of the three size values although, as found in [2], both MOD and MPD increased with the target stroke size.

4.2 Subjective Results

For the subjective analysis, statistical significance was tested with the same methodology adopted for objective measures.

Starting from results concerning the SUS [8] that are reported in Table 1, it can be noticed that participants perceived both the input interfaces as characterized by a high usability, with scores that were greater than 80.3 (threshold for *Excellent*). No statistically significant difference was observed between the two interfaces although, according to the categorization in [6], the *controller* was rated as grade A, whereas the *pen* obtained a grade equals to A+.

Table 1. Subjective results about overall usability according to SUS [8].

Interface	Score	Grade	Adj. Rating
Controller	82.04	A	Good
Pen	85.68	A+	Good

Regarding the preferences expressed by the participants for the ranking criteria proposed in [32], focusing only on statistically significant results it can be observed that the superiority of the *pen* already observed above was confirmed.

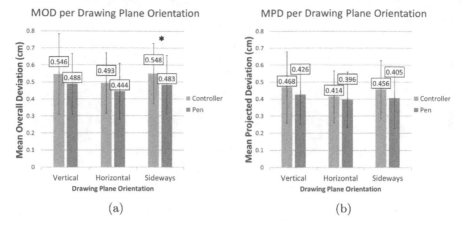

(a)   (b)

Fig. 6. Mean Overall (a) and Projected (b) Deviation per *drawing plane orientation*. The lower the score, the better the result. Standard deviation is expressed via error bars. Statistical significance is indicated by the * symbol.

In fact, participants judged the VR Ink as easier to use for drawing (90.90% vs 9.09%, $p = 0.0163$), more comfortable (90.90% vs 9.09%, $p = 0.0163$) and natural (100.00% vs 0.00%, $p = 0.0163$) compared to the controller.

Comments provided by the participants at the end of the experiment could explain the reported results. In fact, the participants highly appreciated the possibility offered by the *pen* to automatically trigger the drawing when the tip touches the drawing surface. Moreover, the pose assumed by the hand to handle

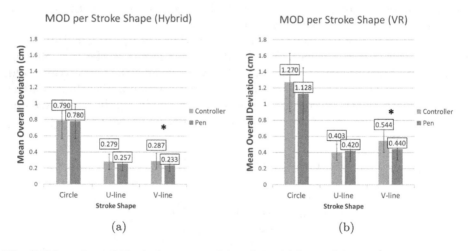

(a)   (b)

Fig. 7. Mean Overall Deviation per *modality, hybrid* (a), *VR* (b), per *stroke shape*. The lower the score, the better the result. Standard deviation is expressed via error bars. Statistical significance is indicated by the * symbol.

Table 2. Results for the ranking criteria derived from [32], expressed as a preference between *controller* and *pen*. Statistical significance is indicated by the * symbol.

Ranking criteria	Contr.	Pen	p-value
Which interface helped to **enjoy** the sketching task best	36.36%	63.64%	0.4235
Which interface was the **easiest** for drawing*	9.09%	90.91%	0.0163
Which interface could improve the task **efficiency** best	27.27%	72.73%	0.1823
Which interface was the most **comfortable** to operate*	9.09%	91.91%	0.0163
Which interface helped you **feel** most **in control of** the stroke trajectory	45.45%	54.55%	0.7896
Which interface was the most **natural** to operate*	0.00%	100.00%	0.0033

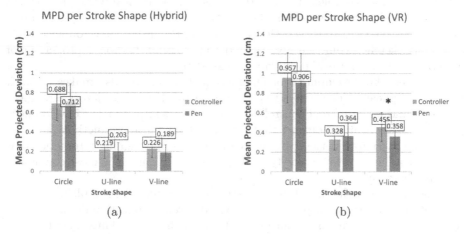

(a)   (b)

Fig. 8. Mean Projected Deviation per *modality*, *hybrid* (a), *VR* (b) per *stroke shape*. The lower the score, the better the result. Standard deviation is expressed via error bars. Statistical significance is indicated by the * symbol.

the stylus while drawing was considered much more similar to that adopted in real drawing and, hence, more natural and comfortable for long lasting sketching. There is no physical click associated with activating the VR Ink trigger for mid-air drawing. This mitigates some of the potential accuracy issues associated with the Heisenberg effect of spatial interaction [7,33]. However, the lack of this feature was lamented by a small number of participants. VR Ink includes a haptic module and in future we could imaging creating a haptic effect to provide such feedback to the participants. Regarding the *controller*, apart from an initial astonishment phase for participants who never tried the VR before, it was perceived as more cumbersome and unpractical when compared with the stylus, especially in the most critical configurations.

5   Conclusions and Future Work

In this paper, a new consumer-grade pen-shape interface for 3D mid-air sketching in VR is compared with the standard hand controller bundled with the commercial VR system the said interface was designed to be integrated with.

The experiment carried out in this work showed the superiority of the pen interface with respect to the controller from several viewpoints. In particular, the pen interface allows the users to improve the final accuracy of the sketching output in a number of conditions, in particular when no physical guidance is available (which is a common situation in VR). Moreover, participants judged the pen as the most natural, comfortable and easy to use interface.

Future works will be devoted to deepen the analysis by including in the experiments more complex drawing tasks, as well as by involving professional artists and designers in order to make the experimental conditions closer to real application scenarios. Moreover, the adherence of the user's intention with what is actually sketched could be investigated too, possibly finding a proper set of objective measures for evaluating any stroke shape.

Moreover, the development of OpenXR [31] standards also makes it much easier for application developers to create software that works across a range of platforms and with different controllers. Recent years have seen the development of a range of application software that attempts to enhance productivity and creativity in VR. However, there are many differences in designing interactions for use with a stylus grip versus the typical "pistol grip" controllers most commonly used in VR today.

Finally, as said, the use of mid-air sketching started to be applied not only for creative and artistic purposes, but also in different application domains ranging from virtual character animation to 3D modelling, etc. Thus, new tasks as well as a different set of metrics could be considered in order to investigate the effectiveness of using the pen interface in such scenarios, e.g., to create poses for virtual characters or controlling 3D modeling tools (like, for instance, sculpting and prototyping).

References

1. Arora, R., Habib Kazi, R., Grossman, T., Fitzmaurice, G., Singh, K.: SymbiosisSketch: combining 2D & 3D sketching for designing detailed 3D objects in situ. In: Proceedings of the 2018 CHI Conference on Human Factors in Computing Systems, pp. 1–15 (2018)
2. Arora, R., Kazi, R.H., Anderson, F., Grossman, T., Singh, K., Fitzmaurice, G.: Experimental evaluation of sketching on surfaces in VR. In: Proceedings of the 2017 CHI Conference on Human Factors in Computing Systems, pp. 5643–5654 (2017)
3. Autodesk® Alias CreateVR. https://www.autodesk.it/products/alias-products. Accessed 3 Aug 2020
4. Bae, S.H., Balakrishnan, R., Singh, K.: ILoveSketch: as-natural-as-possible sketching system for creating 3D curve models. In: Proceedings of the 21st Annual ACM Symposium on User Interface Software and Technology, pp. 151–160 (2008)

5. Bae, S.H., Balakrishnan, R., Singh, K.: EverybodyLovesSketch: 3D sketching for a broader audience. In: Proceedings of the 22nd Annual ACM Symposium on User Interface Software and Technology, pp. 59–68 (2009)
6. Bangor, A., Kortum, P., Miller, J.: Determining what individual SUS scores mean: adding an adjective rating scale. J. Usability Stud. **4**, 114–123 (2009)
7. Bowman, D., Wingrave, C., Campbell, J., Ly, V.Q.: Using Pinch Gloves[TM] for both natural and abstract interaction techniques in virtual environments. In: Proceedings of HCI International, pp. 629–633 (2001)
8. Brooke, J., et al.: SUS - a quick and dirty usability scale. Usability Eval. Ind. **189**, 4–7 (1996)
9. Buxton, B.: Sketching User Experiences: Getting the Design Right and the Right Design. Morgan Kaufmann Publishers Inc. (2007)
10. Cannavò, A., Demartini, C., Morra, L., Lamberti, F.: Immersive virtual reality-based interfaces for character animation. IEEE Access **7**, 125463–125480 (2019)
11. Cannavò, A., Lamberti, F.: A virtual character posing system based on reconfigurable tangible user interfaces and immersive virtual reality. In: Livesu, M., Pintore, G., Signoroni, A. (eds.) Smart Tools and Apps for Graphics - Eurographics Italian Chapter Conference, pp. 45–55 (2018)
12. Cannavò, A., Zhang, C., Wang, W., Lamberti, F.: Posing 3D characters in virtual reality through in-the-air sketches. In: Tian, F., et al. (eds.) CASA 2020. CCIS, vol. 1300, pp. 51–61. Springer, Cham (2020). https://doi.org/10.1007/978-3-030-63426-1_6
13. Celozzi, C., Paravati, G., Sanna, A., Lamberti, F.: A 6-DOF ARTag-based tracking system. IEEE Trans. Consum. Electron. **56**(1), 203–210 (2010)
14. Do, E.Y.L.: Create instant 3D worlds by sketching on a transparent window. Proc. CAAD Futures **2001**, 161–172 (2001)
15. Drey, T., Gugenheimer, J., Karlbauer, J., Milo, M., Rukzio, E.: VRSketchIn: exploring the design space of pen and tablet interaction for 3D sketching in virtual reality. In: Proceedings of the 2020 CHI Conference on Human Factors in Computing Systems, p. 114 (2020)
16. flyingshapes GmbH: flyingshapes°. https://www.flyingshapes.com/. Accessed 3 Aug 2020
17. Google: TiltBrush. https://www.tiltbrush.com/. Accessed 3 Aug 2020
18. Gravity Sketch: Gravity Sketch. https://www.gravitysketch.com/. Accessed 3 Aug 2020
19. HTC: Vive LightHouse 1.0 - Base Station. https://bit.ly/3gqovlQ. Accessed 3 Aug 2020
20. Igarashi, T., Matsuoka, S., Tanaka, H.: Teddy: a sketching interface for 3D freeform design. In: Proceedings of the 26th Annual Conference on Computer Graphics and Interactive Techniques, pp. 409–416 (1999)
21. Israel, J., Wiese, E., Mateescu, M., Zöllner, C., Stark, R.: Investigating three-dimensional sketching for early conceptual design-results from expert discussions and user studies. Comput. Graph. **33**, 462–473 (2009)
22. Kim, Y., An, S.G., Lee, J.H., Bae, S.H.: Agile 3D sketching with air scaffolding. In: Proceedings of the 2018 CHI Conference on Human Factors in Computing Systems, pp. 1–12 (2018)
23. Kwan, K.C., Fu, H.: Mobi3DSketch: 3D sketching in mobile AR. In: Proceedings of the 2019 CHI Conference on Human Factors in Computing Systems, p. 1–11 (2019)
24. LAB4242: PaintLab VR. http://paintlabvr.com/. Accessed 3 Aug 2020

25. Lamberti, F., Cannavò, A., Montuschi, P.: Is immersive virtual reality the ultimate interface for 3D animators? Computer **53**, 36–45 (2020)
26. Lee, J.H., Ham, H.G., Bae, S.H.: 3D sketching for multi-pose products. In: Extended Abstracts of the 2020 CHI Conference on Human Factors in Computing Systems, pp. 1–8 (2020)
27. Li, N., et al.: Get a grip: evaluating grip gestures for VR input using a lightweight pen. In: Proceedings of the 2020 CHI Conference on Human Factors in Computing Systems, pp. 1–13 (2020)
28. Logitech: VR Ink Pilot Edition. https://www.logitech.com/en-us/promo/vr-ink.html. Accessed 3 Aug 2020
29. Pham, D.M., Stuerzlinger, W.: Is the pen mightier than the controller? A comparison of input devices for selection in virtual and augmented reality. In: 25th ACM Symposium on Virtual Reality Software and Technology (2019)
30. The Blender Foundation: Blender. https://www.blender.org/. Accessed 3 Aug 2020
31. The Khronos Group Inc.: The OpenXR Specification. https://bit.ly/33nFdiq. Accessed 3 Aug 2020
32. Wang, S., et al.: Holding virtual objects using a tablet for tangible 3D sketching in VR. In: 2019 IEEE International Symposium on Mixed and Augmented Reality Adjunct (ISMAR-Adjunct), pp. 156–157 (2019)
33. Wolf, D., Gugenheimer, J., Combosch, M., Rukzio, E.: Understanding the Heisenberg effect of spatial interaction: a selection induced error for spatially tracked input devices. In: Proceedings of the 2020 CHI Conference on Human Factors in Computing Systems, pp. 1–10 (2020)

3D Localisation of Sound Sources in Virtual Reality

Edvinas Danevičius$^{(\boxtimes)}$, Frederik Stief, Konrad Matynia,
Morten Læburgh Larsen, and Martin Kraus

Department of Architecture, Design, and Media Technology, Aalborg University,
Fredrik Bajers Vej 7K, 9220 Aalborg Øst, Denmark
{edanev19,fstief14,kmatyn16,molars15}@student.aau.dk,
martin@create.aau.dk

Abstract. This paper presents a comparison of 3D localisation of sound sources using various 3D audio engines for Virtual Reality (VR) environments. An experiment was created with the Oculus Spatializer, Unity Default engine, Unity Reverb engine and the AM3D Spatializer. These four engines were tested against each other in a Virtual Reality setting, where the tester was tasked with the localisation of invisible audio sources present in the virtual room. The evaluation of the experiment showed that there were statistically significant differences between the four engines under specific circumstances.

Keywords: 3D audio · Virtual reality · Sound localisation · Audio experiment · Spatializer plugin

1 Introduction

Immersive audio effects, ambience and music in virtual applications comes from panning audio from side and rear of the listener. This is used to widen the perceived dimensions of the scene, by extending what is being seen on a display. The ability to work in an environment where audio can be relayed from any direction around the listener greatly expands the acoustic space in which audio engineers can work [11].

3D Audio is an essential aspect of most Virtual Reality (VR) applications. It is used to enhance the experience, and sometimes even serves as a key gameplay element that guides the progression of video games. However, the three dimensional aspect of audio usually has been implemented as simple stereo panning. Audio is fed to either one of the headphones' speakers to represent the position of the source in the virtual environment and guides the attention of the player. A realistic 3D audio implementation involves the tracking of the audio source and simulating the environment surrounding it. Mainly, they improve the player's immersion and, in addition, enhance the localisation of audio objects [3].

In order to test this localisation of audio objects, a simulation comparing four 3D audio engines was created. This includes the AM3D Spatializer, Oculus

© ICST Institute for Computer Sciences, Social Informatics and Telecommunications Engineering 2021
Published by Springer Nature Switzerland AG 2021. All Rights Reserved
A. Brooks et al. (Eds.): ArtsIT 2020, LNICST 367, pp. 307–319, 2021.
https://doi.org/10.1007/978-3-030-73426-8_18

Spatializer, Unity Default engine and Unity Reverb. Unity Default being Unity's built-in audio engine and Unity Reverb a different configuration of the same engine, enabling the Reverb feature. The simulation is a VR experience, which is based on sound localisation using the four different engines. The results of each test and engine are analysed based on the accuracy, which is represented by the distance from the tester's selection to the actual position of the audio source. With this in mind, the following hypothesis was created:

There is a difference in accuracy when locating 3D audio between the four investigated engines.

To test this hypothesis, relevant research was conducted, the simulation designed, implemented, evaluated and analysed.

The research began as a collaboration agreement between the authors and the company Goertek Europe. As the interest of the authors was to investigate the importance and impact of 3D audio in games and virtual environments, Goertek Europe suggested testing and evaluating using their engine AM3D Spatializer, which they supplied for the test. We signed a Non-Disclosure Agreement (NDA) form, which prevents us from describing the details of the engine, thus it will not be explained in detail in the later chapters.

2   Background

2.1   Sound Localisation

Sound localisation is the process of identifying sounds' actual or perceived positions in terms of direction and distance relative to the listener [15]. People can identify sounds all around them, but are less accurate when the sounds are coming from the sides or behind their head. Binaural cues are used to localise sounds and while many accumulative factors impact a sound before it reaches the ear, the factors can be simplified and represented as a filtering operation based on the difference between the signal received by the left and right ear [3,11]. This can be utilised by using Head-Related Transfer Functions (HRTFs), which are functions that describe how the ears receive a sound after it interacted with objects. The result is a binaural sound that contains localisation information, which is used to pin point the origin of the sound [15].

2.2   Reverb

The height dimension contains useful acoustic data for enhancing the experience. Reverb is useful when trying to access height information [11]. Reverberation, or reverb, is an acoustic phenomena that occurs in enclosed spaces. When sound is produced in these spaces, it does not disappear immediately but will gradually decrease in loudness while bouncing off surfaces [8]. The time it takes for the sound to go from audible to silent depends on the sound's characteristics as well as the size and material of the space [14]. The reverb can be examined with an impulse response. The impulse response of a space can be divided into three parts: the direct sound, early reflections and the reverberation.

The first sound to reach the ears is the direct sound. Afterwards, the early reflections will reach the ears after being reflected once or twice from surfaces like walls, ceilings or floors. The last part to reach the ears is the reverb tail or late reflections. The early reflections can also be described as echoes. Since early reflections are loud and arrive only 50 ms after the direct sound it tends to create an echo environment [3].

2.3 Related Work

Multiple ways of detecting the location of sound sources have been investigated in the past. For example, evaluation in audio localisation has been done by placing participants in virtual MCRoomSim scenes. Movement sampling was done by sampling the participants head positions and orientations using Vicon camera tracking system [12].

Other studies about localising sound sources in a virtual environment include the "The Binaural Navigation Game". This game was made for both normal sighted and visually impaired individuals. The objective was to test and train the user's ability to localise sounds. This is done by utilising how 3D binaural sounds are perceived and implementing HRTFs [2].

Some of the findings include the listener not being very good at determining the distance to the audio source. Other findings include a slight increase in accuracy when the test participant points towards the audio source and is able to turn their head [10].

3   Test Environment Design

To compare the aforementioned engines, a VR simulation was created. In the simulation, the tester is placed in the middle of an empty, light-grey room. Sounds from different engines are played in different positions of the room, one after another. The tester is then supposed to pinpoint the exact position they believe the sound is playing from by using a virtual laser pointer device. The audio sources are invisible, so the tester has no visual aid. Furthermore, the room is kept as minimalistic as possible, to not distract from the task. The only details added are an ambient occlusion effect to darken corners and a tile pattern for the floor, to ease the estimation of the depth of the room. This helps pinpointing the sources and also alleviates problems with motion sickness.

3.1 Audio Source

Localisation of sound becomes easier for people if it is a familiar sound. A typical example for this is the sound of a telephone ringing. Telephone ringtones are easily recognisable and also in the real world the sound cue signalises a person to find the source, in order to answer it [9]. Therefore, the iPhone Marimba ringtone has been chosen. The audio is played omnidirectional to enable the production of as many reflections as possible, opposed to a limited degree emitting source.

3.2 Room Setup

The simulation is comprised of two rooms. The first room acts as a tutorial room to familiarise the tester with the surroundings and controls. It contains a button in the middle, which loads the second room and starts the test. This allows the tester to start the test whenever they are ready. Both of the rooms have the same dimensions of $10 \times 10 \times 3\,\mathrm{m}$ (width, depth, height). In both of the rooms, the tester is placed in the middle and can move around in a small area indicated by a blue square on the floor. Apart from the button in the tutorial room they are identical.

The ability to move as well as tilting the head enables the person to pinpoint the audio source more precisely by listening to and analysing how the sound changes in different head positions. In addition to that, a $45°$ turn can be executed by tilting the left thumb-stick left or right. The tutorial room can be seen in Fig. 1a.

The wall properties of the room that alter the intensity of the reflections and reverb have been kept to default or slightly adjusted to even out the differences in the engines as much as possible.

3.3 Laser Pointer

Both of the rooms allow the tester to use a virtual laser pointer, which is emitted from the right controller. The laser pointer is activated by clicking and holding down the right grip button. Additionally, while the laser is activated, the right thumb-stick can be used to change the length of the laser by tilting it forwards or backwards. In order to confirm the position of the laser, the right trigger button must be pressed while the right grip is held. Once the position is confirmed, haptic feedback is relayed to the right controller. In addition to haptic feedback, an audible click sound is played, to inform the tester that the confirmation action was executed successfully.

The selection is visualised by intersecting coloured lines for the x, y and z-axis. The purpose is to help the user pinpoint the location of the audio source as precisely as possible in a 3D virtual environment.

3.4 Audio Source Positions

We defined in total 216 scattered positions where audio can play. These positions are split into three groups; near field, mid field and far field, which are based on the distance from the centre. Each field consists of 24 positions on 3 different height settings, totalling 72 positions per field. The layout of these positions can be seen in Fig. 1b.

The positions have been scattered as evenly as possible to have sounds playing all over the room, while still having varying distances to the walls as to experiment with different distances for early reflections. Furthermore, all positions get randomly moved up to 0.45 m upon start of each testing session.

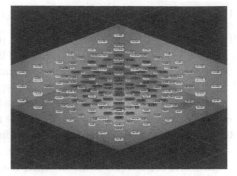

(a) The tutorial room.

(b) Audio positions. Red - near field, orange - mid field and yellow - far field.

Fig. 1. Tutorial room and testing room with visible audio source positions.

3.5   Experimental Procedure

The testing was performed by one of the authors. For each test, no time limit is set for locating each audio source as the focus was on accuracy. After the test session, the tutorial room is loaded once more, where the tester starts the next test when ready.

Multiple tests were conducted in a row with breaks in-between. The testing sessions were spread out throughout the week, each day consisting of 15 sessions at most. In total, 54 test runs were carried out, consisting of 24 selections each.

4   Experimental Setup

The simulation was created using Unity 2019.3 [13] and made use of the Oculus Integration 15.0 [4] asset for Head Mounted Display (HMD) tracking. In addition to that, the Oculus Audio Spatializer 15.0 [6] and AM3D Spatializer 1.1.9.0.0 [7] plugins were used for relaying 3D audio. The simulation can run without a VR headset in desktop mode, which can be used for internal testing.

In terms of hardware, Oculus Rift [5] with two base stations and Oculus Touch controllers were used. For audio, SONY MDR-7506 [1] professional headphones were utilised.

4.1   Scenes and Data Collection

The tutorial and testing rooms were implemented using Unity's scene feature. Each scene acts as a container for said room. The most important room however is the second room, where the tester is required to use the laser pointer in order to locate audio sources. If the laser pointer's position is confirmed while an audio source is playing in the room, information is collected, aggregated and saved in a in-memory buffer. The parameters which are being saved are: distance to the audio source, time taken to find the audio source, linear and angular movement of the HMD.

4.2   Engine Setup

The two audio sources that were set up to work without a spatializer plugin were UnityReverbAudioSource and UnityAudioSource. The UnityReverb-AudioSource was configured to use Unity's built-in reverb functionality while UnityAudioSource is set to use no reverberation. This was achieved by adjusting the Reverb Zone Mix value between 0.0 (minimum) and 1.0 (maximum). In addition to that, the Output value was set to different mixer groups: (Unity-Reverb for UnityReverbAudioSource and Unity for UnityAudioSource). Other settings for both audio sources were the same.

In order for reverb to work when using UnityReverbAudioSource, a Game-Object (centred at world origin) with AudioReverbZone component was added. AudioReverbZone component's min and max distances were configured so that they cover the entire testing room. In addition to that, the Room reverb preset was used.

The remaining two audio sources AM3DAudioSource and OculusAudioSource require the additional components AM3DAudioSourceSettings and Oculus Spatializer Unity. Settings of AudioSource component are the same as in UnityAudioSource, except different mixer groups were assigned: Oculus for OculusAudioSource and AM3D for AM3DAudioSource.

Since these audio sources are linked to different mixer groups, the attenuation of mixer groups was adjusted so that the loudness of each audio source was similar. All groups except Oculus have been tuned -13 dB. In addition to that, Oculus and AM3D require mixer effects to fully utilise spatialization features: OculusSpatializerReflection for Oculus and AM3D Spatializer Room Processor for AM3D.

The OculusSpatializerReflection effect allows to configure the reflectivity and reverb settings of each wall in the room. The value 0.7 was chosen for each surface, which was recommended by Goertek for surfaces made out of concrete. Room dimensions are only specified for consistency, as OculusSpatializer determines the size of the room dynamically. The AM3D Spatializer Room Processor mixer effect only allows to adjust gain of direct sound and reverberations, which were set to 1.00 as volume is attenuated via the Attenuation mixer effect.

In order to configure reflectivity settings of AM3D Spatializer further, a GameObject (centred at world origin) with AM3DAudioRoom component was added. The AM3DAudioRoom component was configured to have the same room dimensions as the testing room and uses the same reflectivity settings as Oculus-SpatializerReflection mixer effect.

4.3   Engine Selection

When the testing room is loaded, 24 positions are randomly picked from the NearField, MidField and FarField groups (8 from each) and displaced on x, y and z coordinates by a random offset within $[-0.45, 0.45]$ range. Each position is then randomly assigned an audio source so that each engine appears twice in each group, which results in each engine being used exactly 6 times throughout the test. For randomisation, the C# class `Random` is used, which is initialised using a `Guid` value. This ensures that each test run is unique.

The sounds to be played appear in the aforementioned 24 positions. As the order of the pool is randomised, positions are picked incrementally starting from index 0. Once a position is chosen, the appropriate engine is enabled and the audio is played using the assigned audio source. Engine switching is performed at run-time, right before playing each audio source. This is achieved by leveraging Unity's `AudioSettings.SetSpatializerPluginName(string)` function. However, one downside to this is that the project cannot be built and must be used within the Unity editor.

5 Results

The tester performed 50 test runs and 1200 data points were collected in total.

5.1 Means

In Fig. 2 the data is visualised as histograms. Only small differences in accuracy are visible for each engine.

To gain an understanding of the data and make it easier to compare, the mean of the distances from the participant's selections to the actual position of the sound sources for all engines is calculated.

Examining the means of the four engines in Table 1 show that the participant was marginally more precise with the Oculus Spatializer engine, with a mean distance of 1.51 m. This was closely followed by the Unity Default and AM3D Spatializer engines with scores of 1.52 m and 1.55 m respectively. The Unity Reverb engine had the highest distance mean of 1.63 m.

Table 1. Distance means for each engine.

Engine	Mean
Oculus Spatializer	1.51 m
Unity Default	1.52 m
AM3D Spatializer	1.55 m
Unity Reverb	1.63 m

5.2 Scatter Plots

A trend is showing when presenting the data of the participant's selections as well as the actual locations of the sounds in all engines combined in 3D scatter

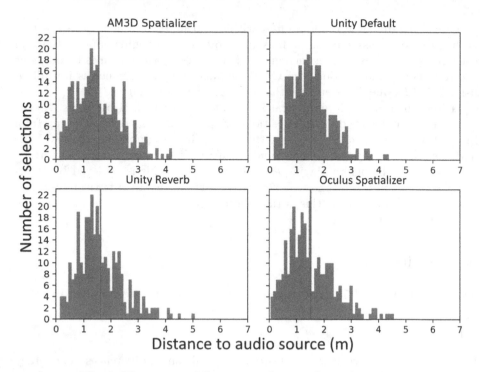

Fig. 2. Histograms of distances and means for each engine.

plots. An example of this can be seen in Fig. 3a. The x-axis is the width of the room and the y-axis the height. The participant's selections are displayed as red dots and the actual positions as blue dots.

The Unity Default engine gives a very good idea of the general direction of the sound, which is proven by the means, but no good indication of the height. This can be seen when looking at Fig. 3b, showing only the distributions of the Unity Default engine, compared to the sum of all engines in Fig. 3a.

In terms of distance to the sound, there are no definitive trends, as the participant tended to put selections further away than the actual positions. This can be seen in Fig. 4.

5.3   Friedman Test

To detect statistically significant differences between the engines, the Friedman test was used, which is a non-parametric statistical test. A p-value below 0.05 obtained this way is expected to reject the null hypothesis. The p-value for the internal participant's data was 0.44. This shows that there are no statistically significant differences when comparing the engines against each other using all the data.

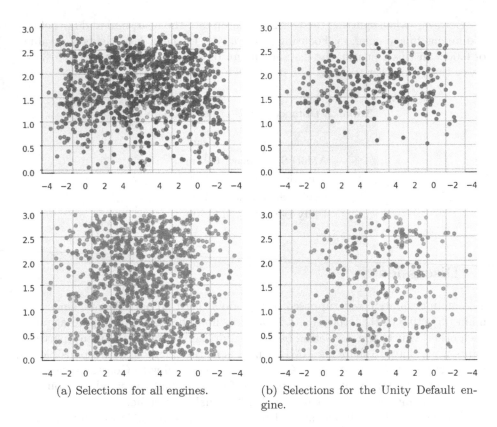

(a) Selections for all engines.

(b) Selections for the Unity Default engine.

Fig. 3. Side view of internal tester's selections (red) and actual positions (blue). (Color figure online)

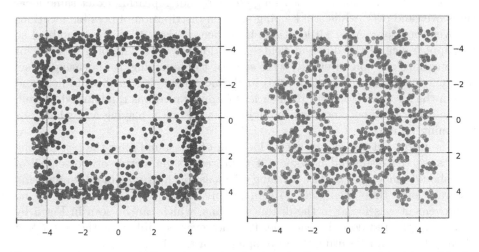

Fig. 4. Top down view of all participant's selections (red) versus actual positions (blue). (Color figure online)

However, when splitting the testing data up into the near, mid and far fields, a different image emerges. Focusing only on the far field data yields a p-value of 0.002. In this scenario, the distance mean of AM3D Spatializer was 25–35% lower than the other engines. The means can be seen in Table 2.

Table 2. Distance means of far field data.

Engine	Mean
AM3D Spatializer	0.93 m
Unity Reverb	1.17 m
Oculus Spatializer	1.19 m
Unity Default	1.25 m

6   Discussion

The main evaluation was supposed to include at least 50 participants, since the main objective of this study was to evaluate how the engines compare against each other. Due to the simulation being in a virtual reality environment, participants would have to share one HMD, which is neither possible nor responsible in the current COVID-19 situation. Given the NDA signed with Goertek regarding the use of their plugin, it was not possible for us to send the simulation out to test participants who have their own HMD available at home.

Evaluating with only an internal tester was made possible by randomising most aspects of the test. The audio positions are randomly picked from a large pool of predefined locations and displaced by the earlier specified margin. The goal of this was to hinder the learning effect by not repeating exact same locations over and over, while still keeping an even distribution of possible locations all over the room. After all locations have been picked, they are scrambled so the appearance of the different fields is random as well. The plugins used for the locations are spread evenly, with each of the four plugins appearing in six different locations each test run: two in the near field, two in the mid field and two in the far field. However, their order of appearance was randomised as well, so the tester does not know which engine was currently playing and which one is coming up next.

The tester did not see the actual location of the sound after the test nor the results, so the tester did not know if their results get better or worse. All of this should hinder the tester's learning effect as much as possible. By analysing accuracy over time there was no sign of any learning effect occurring as no improvement was found in the distance means, which can be seen in Fig. 5 by looking at the red dotted trend line. It is however possible that the tester had already been primed during the development of the simulation.

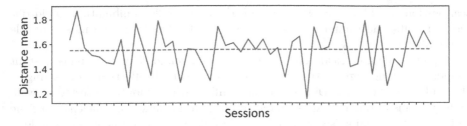

Fig. 5. The learning curve for the tester. (Color figure online)

All of the design choices regarding the room and sounds are as simple and minimalistic as possible, to make this test easily repeatable and achieve a higher reliability. The focus was on functionality, instead of distracting the users with aesthetics. Having no time limit during the tests means that the tester had the opportunity to fine-tune his selections on the audio sources. This could result in increased accuracy, compared to a time limited approach.

The choice of an instrument based marimba sound bears a lot of overtones and harmonic content in the sound, which could have impacted the perception of sound, compared to simpler sound sources, such as a white noise.

The tests were conducted with the headphones provided by Goertek (SONY MDR-7506), which they also recommended. Each headphones' frequency response is different, which could result in the sound being perceived differently. Four different headphones were tested internally prior to the evaluation and SONY's chosen as subjectively best.

The main study comparing the four engines in all three fields did not result in a statistically significant difference, although the outcome might have differed if the study was conducted with more than one tester.

Lastly, it is also important to note that hearing is subjective and differs from person to person. This has an influence on how we hear and perceive sound volume, distance and direction, amongst other things. This means that the origin of the sound will be perceived differently by each tester with individual differences becoming less apparent in a bigger sample size.

7 Future Work

During internal testing it was noticed that HMD tracking malfunctions when facing away from the base stations. Due to this, additional controls had to be added in order to facilitate all angles. This issue could be alleviated by using more base stations or a HMD that supports hand tracking via mounted cameras. For example, an Oculus Rift S would be suited better for such a test.

When analysing collected session data, most selections are directed towards the ceiling. This could be the result of improperly chosen reflectivity coefficients for each engine. In addition to that, the audio file that was played during the test sessions could be changed, to see if different audio combinations yield different results. More internal testing is needed to determine the most suitable configuration.

Having a symmetrical room increases the likelihood of perceiving distant sounds as having higher attenuation due to the sound reflections converging in the middle of the room. Different room configurations should be tested as well, having rooms of different sizes and asymmetrical layouts. The placement of the tester could be randomised as well instead of always placing them in the middle. This changes the way the sounds would reflect and when the tester perceives it, but also increases the complexity of the test, since it introduces more variables.

Increasing the test participant's freedom of movement could impact the results. Should the tester be allowed to move further within a perimeter or even freely, another variable would have to be taken into account. The attenuation of sound while approaching the source in the VR setting would increase, so the importance of reverb and early reflections might become less apparent.

8   Conclusion

Overall the four engines only showed significant differences in performance when investigating the far field data. The initial interest in early reflections and reverb as key components to reproduce realistic 3D audio sensation was then analysed and interpreted. Reverb has made the biggest impact on the tester in the aspect of localising the sounds' altitude. When analysing the results of the Unity Default engine for example, the issue with the attenuation of sound when moving one's head around in the VR environment becomes apparent. The difference in volume in the left and right channels seems more important than the effects of reverb, as the gain changes alone serve as a good basis for localising the sound sources' general direction.

As for the early reflections, which were the main point of interest with Goertek's AM3D Spatializer plugin, the results from the analysis of the far field sources portion of the test indicate an advantage. From our observations, the task of localising the sound sources in the far field was more accurate with AM3D's early reflections the closer the sources are to walls. This is likely caused by the principle of how early reflections are calculated. The reflections of sound are simulated, thus the surfaces closest to the source are taken into account. This also impacts the decision of restricting the testers from moving around to a minimum during the experiment.

While the experiment as a whole only showed significant differences when investigating the far field, given different circumstances and more participants to test with, the results might have shown more differences.

Acknowledgements. We would like to thank Goertek Europe for supplying us with their AM3D spatializer plugin for Unity, an Oculus VR HMD and Sony MDR-7506 as well as suggestions for this study.

References

1. Sony Electronics Inc.: SONY MDR-7506. https://pro.sony/ue_US/products/headphones/mdr-7506. Accessed 22 Apr 2020
2. Balan, O., Moldoveanu, F., Moldoveanu, A., Butean, A.: Developing a navigational 3D audio game with hierarchical levels of difficulty for the visually impaired players. In: RoCHI, pp. 49–59 (2015)
3. Cervera, A.S.: Effects of room acoustics on players' perceptions in audio games. B.S. thesis, Universitat Politècnica de Catalunya (2017)
4. Facebook Technologies, LLC: Oculus Integration 15.0. https://developer.oculus.com/downloads/package/unity-integration. Accessed 22 Apr 2020
5. Facebook Technologies, LLC: Oculus Rift. https://www.oculus.com/rift. Accessed 22 Apr 2020
6. Facebook Technologies, LLC: Oculus Spatializer 15.0. https://developer.oculus.com/downloads/package/oculus-spatializer-unity. Accessed 22 Apr 2020
7. Goertek Europe ApS: AM3D Spatializer. http://goertek.eu/solutions/am3d-software-suite/spatial-audio. Accessed 22 Apr 2020
8. Kuttruff, H.: Room Acoustics. CRC Press, Boco Raton (2016)
9. Mendoza, M.L.D.: Towards measuring and improving human sound localization and physical response to perceived sound through auditory conditioning (2016)
10. Middlebrooks, J., Green, D.: Sound localization by human listeners. Ann. Rev. Psychol. **42**, 135–159 (1991). https://doi.org/10.1146/annurev.ps.42.020191.001031
11. Roginska, A., Geluso, P.: Immersive Sound: The Art and Science of Binaural and Multi-channel Audio. Taylor & Francis, Milton Park (2017)
12. Rudrich, D., Zotter, F., Frank, M.: Evaluation of interactive localization in virtual acoustic scenes. 43. Jahrestagung für Akustik (DAGA 2017), pp. 279–282 (2017)
13. Unity Technologies: Unity 2019.3. https://unity.com/releases/2019-3. Accessed 22 Apr 2020
14. Vorländer, M.: Auralization: Fundamentals of Acoustics, Modelling, Simulation, Algorithms and Acoustic Virtual Reality. Springer, Heidelberg (2007). https://doi.org/10.1007/978-3-540-48830-9
15. Zhong, X., Xie, B., Glotin, H.: Head-related transfer functions and virtual auditory display. In: Soundscape Semiotics-Localization and Categorization, vol. 1 (2014). https://doi.org/10.5772/56907

Optimizations of VR360 Animation Production Process

Wei-Chih Liao$^{(\boxtimes)}$, Chun-Tsai Wu, and Szu-Ming Chung

Department of Digital Content Design, Ling Tung University, 1 Ling Tung Road, Taichung 408, Taiwan, ROC

Abstract. The conventional 3D animation production process often takes place through a design stage, including modeling, mapping, animating, and rendering. A frame of movie quality 3D animation can take tens of minutes or even hours to compute and render. In these cases, a large-scale render farm is often utilized to perform rendering and save time and money. Owing to advances in technology, virtual reality (VR) has become a current trend in animation film production. Whether with a 360° panoramic camera recording or 3D technology, many artists and software developers are continually researching more creative forms of expression in this field. Compared with panel-view 3D animation, those in VR animation production must deal with the spherical images of a virtual space in 360°. Details are intensively emphasized. An 8-K or even 4-K rendering resolution provides substantially enhanced viewing quality, but the rendering workload increases substantially. Recently, game engines have developed progressively. Real-time rendering GPU performance, compared with nonreal CPU clusters, has effectively improved the production process, especially regarding instantaneous preview and editable features. Through a creative production of VR360 animation, we optimized the process for a small team. The optimization of the VR360 animation production process comprises seven stages: initial modeling, 3D concept design, and details, texture drawing, rigging, motion capture, motion adjusting, and final integration.

Keywords: VR animation production process · Real-time rendering · Unreal game engine

1 Introduction

Conventionally, a 3D computer-based key-frame animation is based on hand-drawn animation. It remains the main method by which to create 3D animation today. Virtual reality (VR) animation and video is a new, expressive form for media artists to present their creative artworks. The recent prosperity of the gaming industry has led to prolific VR games and game animation products. To take advantage of the real-time rendering capabilities of a game engine, without sacrificing the fidelity of live performance and by saving time and money, in the present study, a team of technology artists examined and improved animation workflow by creating a VR360-based animated short film. This paper presents an optimized VR animation short film production process. First, the

A. Brooks et al. (Eds.): ArtsIT 2020, LNICST 367, pp. 320–330, 2021.
https://doi.org/10.1007/978-3-030-73426-8_19

relevant literature is reviewed. Second, the process of creating a VR360 animation short film is detailed, and many fundamental concepts and procedures are discussed. Finally, the results of an interview with a team leader and three technology artists to discuss technical problems and solutions to optimize the production process are presented.

2 Literature Review

2.1 VR Animation Production Process

Many influential animated films and their characters, such as Pixar's *Toy Story* (1995), *Finding Nemo* (2003), *Up* (2009), *Toy Story 3* (2010), and *Monsters University* (2013); George Lucas and Industrial Light & Magic's *Star Wars* (1999–2005); and *Lord of the Rings'* iconic Gollum character (2001) all took a considerable length of time to render and thousands of computers to complete final production [1]. Many small production studios are wary of investing such an abundant amount of assets and time to create 3D animations. The most popular game engines, such as Unity 5 and Unreal 4.2, can now be used for VR game and animation creations. They possess substantial graphical technologies and real-time rendering capabilities. Unreal game engines can be supported by many animation production tools and are compatible with Maya, a 3D software program. Unreal engines with the capabilities of VR360's motion capture and real-time photorealistic rendering are ideal tools for integrating 3D animation software and, for the first time, enable animation artists to create short artistic VR animation films at a low cost and within a reasonable time frame.

2.2 Real-Time Rendering

Although real-time rendering is mostly used in interactive gaming, it also allows artists to instantly preview the final results throughout the entire working pipeline. Using a physically based rendering (PBR) shader in an unreal game engine, artists can obtain high-quality rendering results and avoid programming in Unity, which lowers resolution geometry and textures, has less complex rigs, and reduces the requirement for expensive calculations from the rendering engine [2].

2.3 Motion Capture and Live Performance

Motion capturing can produce realistic animation. This process uses cameras to record live performances and map them onto rig characters. Applying such a procedure to drive animation is referred to as performance animation. A computer puppetry system must capture the live performance, accurately interpret and map a performer's motion onto the target digital character, and finally, make the digital character mimic the performance. Such processing can lead to low fidelity [3] and a lack of similarity between the performer and digital character. Even overcoming a seemingly minor obstacle, such as a character disconnectedly interacting with objects in a scene, and the subsequent retargeting that is required is a nontrivial task [4]. Shin et al. [5] proposed an approach that maps input based on an analysis of the root position of the character, joint angles, end effector positions, and the distance of the character to an object in the scene.

3   Design Content

3.1   VR360 Animation Short Film

The Abandoned Deity is a VR360 Animation Short Film. The story brings the audience back to the 1980s to early 1990s. For the first time, the viewers can wear a VR device and watch the old time with the gods' perspectives. We as gods witness humans' fallen religious belief and realize it is human to be abandoned by gods.

The protagonist of the film, Xiaolun, is the son of a famous master of local Buddha idol maker shop. The main scene of this short film occurs in a traditional craftsmanship family making Buddha idols.

3.2   Art Design

The Abandoned Deity was filmed in the Sanmin and Yancheng Districts of Kaohsiung in South Taiwan. The art design was based on the documentary and graphical data of the late 1980s and early 1990s. The characters' appearances and costumes were developed by referencing photographs and works of art from that period. For example, the game room in the work is designed with reference to the 80s style of the movie 'Rebels of the Neon God' (Fig. 1) [6].

Fig. 1. Game room in 1980s, image retrieved from "Rebels of the Neon God"

3.3   Modeling and Materializing

Maya is the most popular 3D animation software program. Conventional 3D animation production uses Maya for modeling, materializing, binding, animating, lighting, and rendering. Its technology is highly developed with advanced processing techniques and controllability. Although it is occasionally insufficient, requiring additional software to accelerate the animation process and improve quality, Maya was adopted here to construct the preliminary modeling for our production. ZBRUSH was used to assist with 3D concept design and detail processing, and Substance Painter was used to creating PBR material texture. Finally, the converted FBX file was imported to Unreal for integration (Fig. 2, 3 and 4).

Fig. 2. Maya-topology and UV disassembly

Fig. 3. ZBRUSH-digital model sculpture design

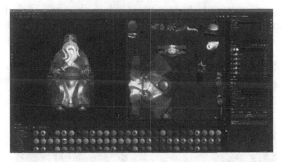

Fig. 4. SubstancePainter-material texture drawing

The inter-software conversion uses the common model format FBX. FBX files can contain lights, cameras, textures, animation, skeletal animation, material properties, polygons, curves, surfaces, normal maps, texture coordinates, and point group materials. The major 3D software is completely compatible with the Unreal game engine.

3.4 Motion Capture

For motion capturing, we adopted "Shōgun," a new motion capture software program that has been recreated by Oxford's Vicon Company in the United Kingdom. It improves the quality of real-time motion capturing and also considerably shortens the postproduction processing time. After a 3D character model was constructed, the rigging was performed in Maya. We then used a free third-party software program, Advanced Skeleton, which is a fully functional rigging tool that has been continuously developed to support Maya updates. The Advanced Skeleton system can also retarget motion capture and facial expression capture data (Fig. 5).

Fig. 5. Free third-party software (Advance Skeleton)

We hired a professional actor to engage in performance and used motion capture to record his performance as digital data. Next, we optimized the data using a post-animator and polished the performance (e.g., corrected action data generated by the recording). We also enhanced the subtle expressions and delicate muscle changes of the characters' fingers—particularly important when showing idol craftsmanship—to authentically present fine animation and dramatic acting (Fig. 6).

Fig. 6. Hand motion and finger gesture

3.5 Faceware

In the past, we had to manually adjust the facial expressions of animated characters, which can produce stiff and unnatural results. Here, we used Faceware to accurately capture facial performance and preserve subtle expressions. During his performance, the actor wore a homemade helmet with a camera attached to the front to fully capture and record his facial performance. Subsequently, we used Faceware Analyzer to analyze the recorded video, set the tracking point, and save the data as an FWT file. After the 3D character digital data were imported by rigging into Maya, Faceware specified the corresponding end, effectors. An initial animated version of the character's facial expressions and movements was created, which was later optimized and finalized by the animator (Fig. 7).

Fig. 7. Faceware effects

3.6 Integration in Unreal Game Engine

Construction of Virtual Space. We measured the 3D scene space in advance. According to our measurements, we limited the sensing area and placed furniture purposefully to avoid the use of oversized objects so as not to block the camera or cause mistakes. The more accurately virtual space is matched with real space, the more accurate action data are, which can considerably reduce adjustment time (Fig. 8 and 9).

Fig. 8. Scene space measurement

To unify the size of the Maya and Unreal environments, we first constructed all scene objects and imported them into Unreal as a blueprint. All the models were mapped

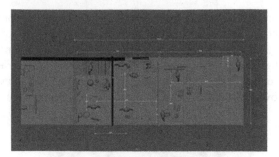

Fig. 9. Virtual space measurement

and completed in Substance Painter and then imported into Unreal (Fig. 10). All the texture files exported by Substance Painter were divided into BaseColor, Normal Map, and OcclusionRoughnessMetallic. OcclusionRoughnessMetallic is channeled in RGB, which are Occlusion, Roughness, and Metallic. These properties are synthesized as one texture to save memory space. Unreal, like Substance Painter, utilizes PBR. As long as the channel is matched, the display will be the same as in Substance Painter.

Next, we positioned the processed model material with Asset according to the blueprint. Pre-calculating the lighting effects into LightMap can considerably reduce the lighting-related computing resources required, although instant rendering also allows the animator to easily adjust the lighting in the Unreal environment. With this GUI functioning of the WYSIWYG process, the animator can focus on aesthetic design to improve the graphics quality without waiting for rendering.

Pistage Application. Maya has always been better than Unreal in the operation of action design and action capture data, so we usually process animation characters in Maya and then test the converted FBX files in Unreal. Any problematic files are transferred back to Maya for correction. However, this is not efficient at all. Therefore, the plugin tool Pistage in Maya helps connect Maya and Unreal. While specified files are being edited in Pistage, the adjusted and modified motions are instantly transferred to the file in Unreal. In other words, the final results of lighting and parameter configuration can be instantaneously previewed, which greatly shortens the conversing time.

To ensure that digital characters accurately interact with desired objects, we built the scene and set a camera in Unreal and then imported the converted FBX files to Maya. The characters were constructed as 3D models in a 3D environment. At this stage, we adjusted the characters according to scene planning and lens arrangement and also polished action details and modified their interactions with scene objects.

The animation of a character's emotions and facial expressions was tested in Unreal to determine if an adjustment of the lighting would be required. The animation was then modified using the Unreal particle system and reinforced and embellished with special effects.

VR360 Sequence Rendering. Unreal is a game engine wherein it is common to view ambient objects in 360°. The program is efficient at capturing 360° continuous images through a camera with instantaneous rendering. The rendering of an image with 3840

× 1920 resolution on a display card (GTX1080) takes an average of 1 s. A cube is photographed by an Unreal internal camera with a 360° planar acquisition system. Each facet of six sides of the cube is captured at the 2-K resolution, after which all the facets are tied together and projected onto a sphere and then deformed and converged to obtain the final full image (Fig. 10).

Fig. 10. Final result of VR360

4 Methodology

To optimize our production process, we interviewed the production team leader and three technology artists. The following interview questions were asked:

1. Regarding the production process and technical aspects, please compare the differences between VR360 animation production and conventional animation production.
2. What software and hardware are used in the production process and what are their respective functions?
3. How do you seamlessly integrate different software programs?
4. Please state the problems you face and the solutions you employ regarding your job content and tasks (such as concerning animation, lighting, and motion capture).
5. How do you operate a computer effectively in case of memory space and performance issues? For example, do you have a backup of material texture files?
6. Are there different requirements for VR animation and conventional animation in terms of resolution?

Our interviews included discussions of the establishment of a VR360 animation production process, the integration of different software programs, and problem-solving.

4.1 VR360 Animation Production Process

To obtain the best final product, we experimented, solved problems, and optimized the production process (see the flowchart in Fig. 11). An optimal VR360 production process

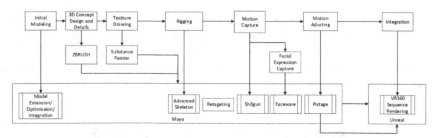

Fig. 11. Optimization of VR360 animation production process

contains seven stages, namely initial modeling, 3D concept design and details, texture drawing, rigging, motion capture, motion adjusting, and final integration.

The fundamental difference between conventional 2D/3D animation and VR360 animation is narrative techniques. Conventional animation uses the 2D shot as a basic unit, after which a series of frames on a single timeline is converted into a linear film. The audience views such a film and can understand its metaphor of a created story. The development of VR360 animation vastly supersedes this production. The immersive power is unique, with the audience being able to fully enter a scene as a protagonist and experience the story in a virtual environment. VR360 provides an innovative expression form that allows artists to explore and experiment with their narrative abilities.

Due to the advances in 3D and photographic technologies, VR360 animation framing is remarkably different from conventional animation with its single-plane composition. To depict a scene, no dead angle should be included. Such a concept is borrowed from conventional animation. For VR360 animation, the distortion projection must be calculated by a computer and captured by a 3D camera. Based on human knowledge related to reality, 3D scenes and characters must be constructed in a 3D environment and realistic VR360 images, which is a technical threshold that cannot be met by the techniques of hand-drawn 2D animation.

4.2   Integration of Different Software Programs

Maya, Substance Painter, and Unreal were the main software used in this production. Maya was supported by third party plugins such as Faceware and Pistage. The primary advantage of Unreal was the instantaneous rendering, which enabled images to be previewed instantly. Unreal is also adequate for editing and adjusting. Its fast calculations work effectively and shorten overall production time. Regarding resolution, due to the 360° rendering technology demanding a better result, we increased the resolution from 4K to 8K and conducted several tests to achieve the optimal effect and efficiency.

Faceware (Face Dynamic Capture System) can capture the live performance of facial expressions. The captured motion is vivid and makes it easy to synch a live speaking mouth to an animated character.

Substance Painter provides a more intuitive method of drawing material textures than does Photoshop or 3Dcoat. Through the material process and instant preview, artists can create new material textures in a short time with a few simple configurations.

We are a small team of Maya users. In terms of interacting with interfaces, Unreal was new to us all. It was not efficient to make everyone learn to use Unreal, but Unreal results can be previewed in real-time and we were able to create animations more intuitively. Pistage connects traditional and modern animators, allowing us to preserve old production habits while also familiarizing ourselves with new techniques. This enabled us to focus on aesthetic effects and artistic expressions.

4.3 Problem Solving

Problems occurring in the production process were largely technical issues, such as motion capture, lighting, and memory space. We created a cartoon-like character and needed to track motions repeatedly to ensure that this character stylishly would not inconsistent with other characters, as well as optimize its artistic style matched with the entire film.

Though motion capture systems performed most of the work for us, the results were heavily modified. Certain motions could not be captured by the motion capture system, such as minute finger motions; thus, we were required to create an entirely new animation that mimicked the actor's performance as best as possible. This was time-consuming.

The game engine does not produce better lighting. To increase efficiency, we pre-calculated and stored lighting information at the preproduction stage. It took more time than we expected; however, the advantage was that the action and material could be previewed instantaneously. Eventually, the rendering effect became more intuitive.

Generally, we used PBR rendering, but there are many channel textures (e.g., Base color, Roughness, Metallic, Normal, Op, and AO). Unreal integrates the channels of Roughness, Metallic, and AO into one material texture and controls these channels simultaneously. This allowed us to export the BaseColor, Normal, and three-channel textures from Substance Painter to Unreal. This advantage directly reduced the number of material texture files we had. In short, we were able to use memory space effectively. Unreal also greatly reduced the complexity of processing and shortened production time.

5 Conclusion

VR 3D animation technology is a suitable solution for dealing with the production of VR360 animation. Currently, advances in the development of production tools induce mature productions. The public's pursuit of high-quality images has promoted the progression of computing technology. Conventional full HD picture quality is insufficient to display spherical VR360 films. Although a 4-K quality picture is still considered above standard, to pursue a better movie experience, 8K or even 16K will undoubtedly become the future trend. Such a pursuit also aims to increase the threshold and restrictions on creative and experimental productions. Therefore, by borrowing technology from 3D game engines, using their real-time display rendering power, and instantly modifying WYSIWYG features, we considerably improved the VR360 production process and the final animated film result.

Unreal Engine 4 is the game engine released by Epic Games. It is the world's best-known and most widely licensed top-level game engine, accounting for 80% of the global commercial game engine market. Many VR games are developed using this game engine. This is because Unreal has particular advantages in rendering effects and operational efficiency that are crucial for the VR experience. Recently, it has become more actively used in film and television productions. Unreal's excellent VR function and expansion capabilities make it easy to integrate 3D software, which has the advantages of plugin tools, to obtain high-quality VR360 images.

This was our first VR360 animation production, finalized by the Unreal game engine and aided by several types of 3D mainstream software. By using FBX files and PBR materials, we faced relatively few technical issues integrating these software programs. The instant preview feature of Unreal also made the error review process smoother. With high-speed rendering, it was effective at correcting errors, solving problems, and rerendering quickly. With 4K resolution, continuous images can be quickly captured and image presentation is satisfactory while the static or mirror movement is indivisible. However, for light or material details displayed in a large screen scene, it is easy to see flickers and jagged images. To solve these problems, we used 8K resolution for our highly animated scenes. The quality was improved, the jagged images could be completely dissolved. Due to the limitations of our hardware equipment, the final resolution was 3840×1920, with a single-eye resolution of 1440×1600 pixels (two eyes: 2880×1600 pixels). However, the final result viewed in the VR device is satisfactory. (The 47th International Conference and Exhibition on Computer Graphics & Interactive Techniques/SIGGRAPH, Computer Animation Festival Electronic Theater: Official Selection: https://s2020.siggraph.org/presenter/?uid=2082287891416180395).

Acknowledgement. This project is funded by the Kaohsiung Film Archive in Taiwan, ROC.

References

1. Ramos, L.A.G.T.: Production of 3D animated short films in Unity 5: Can game engines replace the traditional methods? Dissertation, Portuguese Catholic University, Lisbon, Portugal (2017)
2. Beane, A.: 3D Animation Essentials. Wiley, Indianapolis (2012)
3. Menache, A.: Understanding Motion Capture for Computer Animation. Morgan Kaufmann, Burlington (2011)
4. Gleicher, M.: Animation from observation: motion capture and motion editing. SIGGRAPH Comput. Graph. **33**(4), 51–54 (1999)
5. Shin, H.J., Lee, J., Shin, S.Y., Gleicher, M.: Computer puppetry: an importance-based approach. ACM Trans. Graph. **20**(2), 67–94 (2001)
6. Derakhshani, T.: Film Review - 'Rebels of the Neon God'. Philadelphia inquirer. World Wide Web (2015). https://www.inquirer.com/philly/entertainment/movies/20150703_Film_R eview_-__Rebels_of_the_Neon_God_.html. Accessed 05 Aug 2020

TeMoG – An Accessible Tool for Creating Custom Soft Robotics Parts

Jonas Jørgensen[✉] [iD]

SDU Biorobotics, University of Southern Denmark, Campusvej 55, 5230 Odense, Denmark
jonj@sdu.dk

Abstract. Soft robotics research aims to create robots made of elastic and pliable materials such as silicone rubber. Soft robotics components are endowed with a singular biomorphic aesthetic and have recently made their way into art, design, and architecture projects. However, the design and fabrication of soft robotic parts presents a substantial challenge to most beginners. A number of resources containing instructions for how to fabricate soft robotic parts currently exists, yet they focus on reproducing existing soft robotic designs. This sets a limitation on the number of soft robotics components that a creative practitioner, who is not an experienced user of the technology, might utilize in their work. To address this lack, we developed a tool that allows the user to easily fabricate custom soft robotic parts. This tool, called the Tentacle Mold Generator (TeMoG), can be used by someone with no prior experience in soft robotics. It generates STL files for 3D printing a mold to cast a custom soft robotic tentacle in silicone. In this paper, we describe the TeMoG tool and how to use it. We demonstrate the tool's versatility and usefulness by presenting examples of its previous use in creative projects. TeMoG is distributed under a Creative Commons license and a link to download the tool with a detailed instructions manual is provided.

Keywords: Soft robotics · Fabrication · Design · Interactive art · Interaction design

1 Introduction

Soft robotics has within the past decade become a fast growing research field [1]. Soft robots can be defined as systems capable of autonomous behavior that are composed of materials with an elastic modulus in the range of that of soft biological materials [2]. Albeit still only commercially available as soft grippers for industrial automation [3–5], soft robotics technology has been proposed for several applications, including assistive technology, wearable technology, emergency relief, and collaborative robots (cobots). Soft robotics technology has a radically different appearance and behavior than conventional mechatronics and is endowed with a singular biomorphic aesthetic. Hence, soft robotics technology has also recently been appropriated in a number of art, design, and architecture projects [6].

© ICST Institute for Computer Sciences, Social Informatics and Telecommunications Engineering 2021
Published by Springer Nature Switzerland AG 2021. All Rights Reserved
A. Brooks et al. (Eds.): ArtsIT 2020, LNICST 367, pp. 331–342, 2021.
https://doi.org/10.1007/978-3-030-73426-8_20

The design and fabrication of soft robotic parts, however, still presents a substantial challenge to most beginners that want to explore and utilize the technology. A number of accessible resources containing instructions for fabricating soft robotic parts currently exists, notably the *Soft Robotics Toolkit* (https://softroboticstoolkit.com/), instruction sets found on DIY websites including *Instructables, MAKE*, and *Adafruit*, and a recently published introductory DIY book [7]. These entry-level introductions to the area, however, only provide access to a limited number of existing soft robotic designs that can be replicated (excepting [8]). This sets an unfortunate limitation on the types of soft robotic components that an artist, designer, or architect who is not experienced in working with the technology might incorporate into their work.

To address this lack, we developed a tool that makes it easy to fabricate custom soft robotic parts. The tool can be used by someone with no prior experience in soft robotics. It generates files for 3D printing a mold to cast custom soft robotic parts, more specifically variations of a soft tentacle morphology. In this paper, we describe this tool, dubbed *Tentacle Mold Generator (TeMoG)*, and how to use it. We also provide suggestions for how to power, alter, and augment soft robotic tentacles created with it. Lastly, we demonstrate the tool's versatility and usefulness for creative practice projects by describing select examples of its previous usage. TeMoG is distributed under a Creative Commons license and a link is included to download the tool and a detailed instructions manual. By sharing TeMoG with practitioners outside the soft robotics community and showcasing examples of its use in creative projects, we aim to make soft robotics more accessible to creative practitioners and to encourage novel usages of the technology within interactive art, interaction design, and related fields.

2   Soft Robotic Tentacles

Tentacle-inspired soft actuators are a basic and versatile component class used for many types of soft robotic systems and tasks including manipulation, locomotion, and positioning [9]. The first soft tentacles were developed in the early 1990s, by the Suzumori lab at Okoyama University, where researchers constructed small tri-cellular elastomer units, and demonstrated that different designs for manipulators and walkers could be assembled from them [10, 11]. Since then, pneumatically actuated tentacle structures have frequently served as both dexterous legs and cylindrical manipulator modules in soft robot designs [12, 13]. A soft robotic tentacle works similarly to a biological muscular hydrostat, as it realizes movement by expanding different sides of the overall structure, to create bending in the opposite direction. This expansion is realized by inflating internal chambers with pressurized air coming from electrical pumps or a compressor. A tentacle with just three internal chambers can thus realize a three-dimensional movement range.

Existing projects within art, design, and architecture that incorporate soft robotics technology have mainly used bending actuators with *pneumatic networks* (*pneunets*) or simple inflatable pouches [6]. However, a tentacle design has been used in media artist Paul Carlo Esposito's piece *Symbiont* (2018), a performance installation that sees the artist enveloped by a suspended tubular structure featuring protruding tentacles (Fig. 1).

Fig. 1. Paul Carlo Esposito, *Symbiont* (2018). Images courtesy of the artist.

3 Tentacle Mold Generator (TeMoG) – Tool Overview

TeMoG enables a user to easily generate 3D printable molds to cast custom soft robotic tentacles. The tool consists of parametric files that are executed in OpenSCAD, an open-source geometric CAD software program that can be downloaded for free (https://www.openscad.org/). With the OpenSCAD files, the user can generate STL files of the mold parts needed to fabricate a tentacle and subsequently 3D print them (Fig. 2).

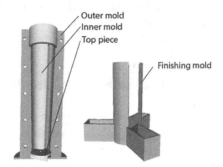

Fig. 2. Mold parts (only one out of two identical outer mold parts is shown).

The CAD modeling of the parts is done by parametric programming, hence all dimensions of the tentacle (e.g. maximum- and minimum diameter, length etc.) can easily be altered by simply changing variable values listed at the top of the script (see Fig. 3 and examples in Table 1).

4 Fabrication Procedure

Below we describe the steps involved in fabricating a soft robotic tentacle with TeMoG. A detailed description of each step can be found in the instruction manual included as a PDF file with the tool.

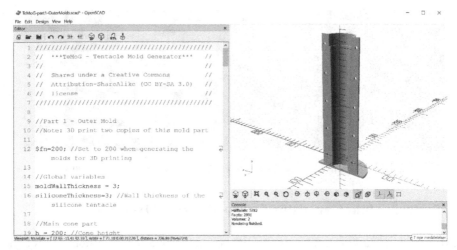

Fig. 3. Screenshot from OpenSCAD showing the variable list in the script (left) and the CAD rendering of one side of the outer mold (right).

4.1 Designing the Mold

- The "ResultingCast" file is loaded in OpenSCAD. This file is not a mold file, but instead gives a rendering of the complete tentacle.
- Variables are adjusted to achieve the desired tentacle morphology (see Table 1 for an overview of the main variables).
- The variable list is marked and copied.
- The first mold file is opened and the variable list inserted. The mold part is rendered and exported as an STL file.
- Similarly, the variable list is copied to the other parametric files and the remaining mold parts generated.

4.2 3D Printing Mold Parts

The mold parts can be printed on a consumer grade 3D printer in PLA or another rigid material.

- The STL file for the mold part is imported in the slicing software (e.g. Cura or Simplify3D) and oriented correctly for printing.
- Appropriate print settings are chosen, we recommend printing in solid to increase strength and durability. Adding a brim to prevent curling and improve adhesion during printing helps to obtain a successful print.

4.3 Fabricating the Tentacle

We have used Ecoflex 00-30 and 00-50 silicones to cast tentacles, but other high stretch rubbers can also be used. Only requirement for the fabrication technique described here

Table 1. CAD renderings of a tentacle with different values chosen for the main variables of the tool.

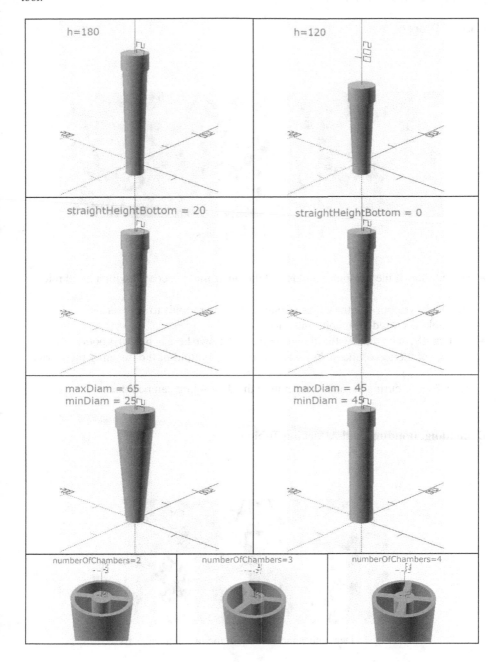

to work is that the mixed liquid rubber should be able to act as a glue between the cured rubber pieces, like Ecoflex silicones will.

Casting Process

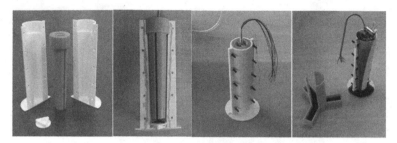

Fig. 4. The casting process.

- The interior of the two outer molds and the inner mold is coated with a mold release agent
- Play-Doh is applied to the edges of one of the outer molds to act as a seal
- The mold is closed with bolts and nuts
- Ecoflex silicone mixed with silicone pigments (shown here in black) is poured through the hole at the top of the inner mold and into the bottom of the finishing mold (right image Fig. 4)
- After 24 h of curing at room temperature the demolding can be done

Demolding, Bonding, and Attaching Tubing

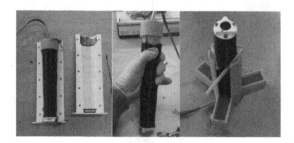

Fig. 5. Demolding and bonding of the two tentacle parts

- The mold is opened (Fig. 5)
- The inner mold is pulled out of the tentacle

- Liquid Ecoflex is brushed on the contact surfaces between the tentacle and the bottom part of the tentacle that has been cast in the finishing mold
- Ecoflex is poured into the finishing mold and the tentacle is placed standing upright in the finishing mold (right image)
- After 24 h, the tentacle is removed from the finishing mold
- The air chambers are perforated individually from below and tubing for inflation inserted and glued in place

5 Additions

Once finished, the tentacle can be actuated by hand with a syringe or with an electro-pneumatic control setup consisting of a microcontroller with a motor shield, an electrical pump, and solenoid valves. Detailed instructions for assembling a low-cost setup are available online [14]. Pneumatically actuated soft robots have also previously been powered by more exotic means such as controlled explosions [15–18] and chemical reactions [19].

For uses in aesthetic practice projects, a limitation of TeMoG would appear to be, that tentacles made with the tool are limited to being either conical or tubular and having a flat surface. However, this apparent limitation is easily circumvented, as tentacles made with the tool can be modified to obtain other design aesthetics. They can also be augmented with sensors to gain interactive capabilities. Here we describe three easy ways for getting started with this.

5.1 Fiber Reinforcements

Fiber reinforcements can be added to the tentacle to prevent radial expansion. This will create a more focused movement, as the tentacle will not expand, but only extend when inflated (see Fig. 6).

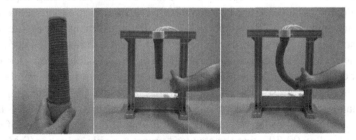

Fig. 6. Fiber reinforcements are added to the cast tentacle before a second layer of silicone is added (left). The finished tentacle in uninflated (middle) and inflated (right) state.

When the tentacle has been removed from the outer mold, braided fishing line is wrapped around the tentacle from the bottom to the top and back again in the opposite direction (Fig. 6, left image). A second layer of silicone is cast on top of it to conceal the windings (detailed instructions for doing this are included in the instruction manual).

5.2 Surface Texture

Surface texture can be added to the tentacle by casting another layer of soft silicone on top of the finished tentacle. However, it is important that the tentacle is completely clean to obtain good adhesion when casting a second layer, and mold release agent should not be used on the outer mold, when casting the tentacle. A mold for casting surface texture can be created in clay or alginate by depressing objects into these substrates before allowing them to harden. Texture molds can be made after human skin, for instance, to give the tentacle an uncanny look (Fig. 7, left). Or with deep thin channels to create small polyps or tentacles on the surface like e.g. sea anemones have (Fig. 7, right).

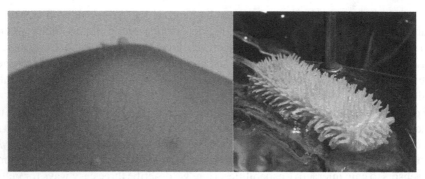

Fig. 7. Skin texture cast in silicone using a mold made from alginate by depressing an elbow into it (left). Small tentacles cast in silicone onto a soft robotic actuator using a mold made from clay (right). Right image courtesy of Studio ThinkingHand, detail from their work *INTERTIDAL SYNTHESIS* (2020), 3 channel video and sculpture installation.

5.3 Sensing

To make the tentacle interactive, sensors can be added to it. With sensing implemented, a tentacle could, for instance, be used for an interactive game, as an experimental interface, or become autonomous and have feedback-controlled movements. Soft silicone robots can be sensorized via the addition of channels of liquid metal (e.g. eutectic gallium-indium) to detect touch and deformation [20]. Two more accessible options for a tentacle, are to either cast a resistive flex sensor inside in the middle (if it is two-chambered) or to use one or more pressure sensors connected to the tentacle's pneumatic supply tubing. To test the latter idea, we attached a cheap barometric pressure sensor (GY68 BMP180) to an Arduino microcontroller. We connected it to one of the supply tubes of a tentacle fabricated in Ecoflex 00-30 using the standard preset variable values in TeMoG. When the tentacle was inflated, we noted an increase in pressure detected by the sensor upon compressing the tentacle chamber by hand.

6 Example Projects

Soft robotic parts made with the tool have already been used for several projects, both within creative practice and in a research context. These include robotic art installations, a plant-inspired light-seeking robot prototype [21], a platform to conduct human-robot interaction experiments [22–24], and an embodied neuromorphic computing experiment [25]. Two additional examples are described below to showcase the designs that the tool can produce and different ways they might be used within creative projects.

6.1 LARPing AI

Larping AI is a series of live action role-plays (LARPs) and workshops by artist Susan Ploetz that interrogate emergent relations surrounding AI algorithms and robotics through somatic practices and embodied simulation. When *Larping AI* was exhibited in Tokyo in late-2019, a soft robotic three-chambered tentacle fabricated with TeMoG was integrated into the live action role-plays (Figs. 8, 9). The semitranslucent uncolored tentacle was equipped with a temperature sensor and the tentacle would respond with movement when held in the hands and exposed to body heat [26].

Fig. 8. Photos taken during one of the runs of the live action role-play showing the soft tentacle and participants. Images courtesy of the artist. Photo: Yuki Maniwa.

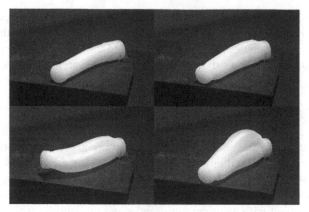

Fig. 9. Example of the soft tentacle's movements. Video available at: https://youtu.be/Rq_-geG 6N-s

6.2 Tales of C

Tales of C (2017–2018) (Fig. 10) is a soft robotic artwork by the author featuring a cephalopod-inspired soft robot, whose upper body was created with TeMoG [27]. The artificial creature moves in a tank by inflating and deflating its body and swaying its arms. It emits light and a speak performed by a synthetic voice narrates the installation. *Tales of C* explores the cultural imaginary of cephalopods (the molluscan class that counts the squid, cuttlefish, octopus, and nautilus). It weaves an unstable narrative that occasionally unmasks uncanny overlaps between cultural perceptions of cephalopods and fears voiced about computational media technologies.

Fig. 10. Installation view of *Tales of C* (left). CAD rendering of the cephalopod robot (right). A video showing the installation is available at: https://youtu.be/B4S0E5D4zck

7   Conclusion and Further Work

In this paper, we presented the TeMoG tool. By doing so, we sought to contribute to democratizing soft robotics technology by enabling creative practitioners to easily fabricate custom soft robotic parts. Our paper described how to use the tool and we shared an instruction manual detailing this use written for people with no experience in soft robotics. Lastly, we presented ways to power, augment, and sensorize tentacles made with the tool and described two arts-led projects that have used them. The TeMoG tool can be used as it is but given that the code is distributed under a Creative Commons Attribution-ShareAlike (CC BY-SA 3.0) license, it easily lends itself to further modifications. Any user can in principle fork the repository and start adding additional features and more detailed functionalities to the tool, in order for it to support the fabrication of even more types of morphologies. The option to make tentacles with a single inner pneumatic chamber placed asymmetrically (as in [28]), for instance, could be implemented as well as the choice to have a round instead of a flat tip on the tentacle. We encourage such modifications and hope to see the community of creative practitioners use the tool for novel exciting projects. With any luck, this will accelerate the recently initiated aesthetic explorations of soft robotics in arts-based experiments that, as we have argued extensively in prior work [6], can contribute to developing a transdisciplinary perspective on soft robotics, that is more adequate to their full range of relational capacities.

Download

TeMoG and the instruction manual can be downloaded from:
    https://github.com/RobotisMollis/TeMoG

References

1. Bao, G., et al.: Soft robotics: academic insights and perspectives through bibliometric analysis. Soft Robot. **5**, 229–241 (2018). https://doi.org/10.1089/soro.2017.0135
2. Rus, D., Tolley, M.T.: Design, fabrication and control of soft robots. Nature **521**, 467–475 (2015). https://doi.org/10.1038/nature14543
3. Empire Robotics – Agile Robotics Grippers. https://www.empirerobotics.com/. Accessed 10 Nov 2020
4. OnRobot. https://onrobot.com/da. Accessed 10 Nov 2020
5. Soft Robotics Inc. https://www.softroboticsinc.com/. Accessed 10 Nov 2020
6. Jørgensen, J.: Constructing Soft Robot Aesthetics: Art, Sensation, and Materiality in Practice (2019)
7. Borgatti, M., Love, K.: Soft Robotics: A DIY Introduction to Squishy, Stretchy, and Flexible Robots. Make Community, LLC (2018)
8. Jørgensen, J.: Parametric Tool to Generate 3D Printable PneuNet Bending Actuator Molds. https://softroboticstoolkit.com/parametric-tool-3d-printed-molds. Accessed 10 Nov 2020
9. Martinez, R.V., et al.: Robotic Tentacles with Three-Dimensional Mobility Based on Flexible Elastomers (2013)
10. Suzumori, K., Iikura, S., Tanaka, H.: Flexible microactuator for miniature robots. In: 1991 IEEE Micro Electro Mechanical Systems, MEMS 1991, Proceedings. An Investigation of Micro Structures, Sensors, Actuators, Machines and Robots, pp. 204–209 (1991). https://doi.org/10.1109/MEMSYS.1991.114797
11. Suzumori, K., Iikura, S., Tanaka, H.: Development of flexible microactuator and its applications to robotic mechanisms. In: Proceedings of the 1991 IEEE International Conference on Robotics and Automation, vol. 2, pp. 1622–1627 (1991). https://doi.org/10.1109/ROBOT.1991.131850

12. Marchese, A.D., Rus, D.: Design, kinematics, and control of a soft spatial fluidic elastomer manipulator. Int. J. Robot. Res. **35**, 840–869 (2016). https://doi.org/10.1177/027836491558 7925

13. Cianchetti, M., Ranzani, T., Gerboni, G., De Falco, I., Laschi, C., Menciassi, A.: STIFF-FLOP surgical manipulator: mechanical design and experimental characterization of the single module. Presented at the Proceedings of the IEEE/RSJ International Conference on Intelligent Robots and Systems, 1 November 2013. https://doi.org/10.1109/IROS.2013.6696866

14. Jørgensen, J.: Laser Cut Molds for PneuNet Bending Actuators. https://softroboticstoolkit. com/laser-cut-molds. Accessed 10 Nov 2020

15. Shepherd, R.F., et al.: Using explosions to power a soft robot. Angew. Chem. **125**, 2964–2968 (2013). https://doi.org/10.1002/ange.201209540

16. Stergiopulos, C., et al.: A Soft Combustion-Driven Pump for Soft Robots. V002T04A011 (2014). https://doi.org/10.1115/SMASIS2014-7536

17. Bartlett, N.W., et al.: A 3D-printed, functionally graded soft robot powered by combustion. Science **349**, 161–165 (2015)

18. Loepfe, M., Schumacher, C.M., Lustenberger, U.B., Stark, W.J.: An untethered, jumping roly-poly soft robot driven by combustion. Soft Robot. **2**, 33–41 (2015). https://doi.org/10. 1089/soro.2014.0021

19. Wehner, M., et al.: An integrated design and fabrication strategy for entirely soft, autonomous robots. Nature **536**, 451–455 (2016). https://doi.org/10.1038/nature19100

20. Farrow, N., Correll, N.: A soft pneumatic actuator that can sense grasp and touch. In: 2015 IEEE/RSJ International Conference on Intelligent Robots and Systems (IROS), pp. 2317–2323 (2015). https://doi.org/10.1109/IROS.2015.7353689

21. Jørgensen, J.: Prolegomena for a transdisciplinary investigation into the materialities of soft systems. In: ISEA 2017 Manizales: Bio-Creation and Peace: Proceedings of the 23rd International Symposium on Electronic Art, pp. 153–160. Department of Visual Design, Universidad de Caldas, and ISEA International, University of Caldas, Manizales, Colombia (2017)

22. Jørgensen, J.: Interaction with soft robotic tentacles. In: Companion of the 2018 ACM/IEEE International Conference on Human-Robot Interaction, p. 38. ACM, New York (2018). https:// doi.org/10.1145/3173386.3177838

23. Jørgensen, J.: Appeal and perceived naturalness of a soft robotic tentacle. In: Companion of the 2018 ACM/IEEE International Conference on Human-Robot Interaction, pp. 139–140. ACM (2018)

24. Jørgensen, J., Bojesen, K.B., Jochum, E.: Is a soft robot more "natural"? Exploring the perception of soft robotics in human–robot interaction. Int. J. Soc. Robot. (2021). https://doi.org/ 10.1007/s12369-021-00761-1

25. Jeppesen, M.H., Jørgensen, J., Manoonpong, P.: Adaptive neural CPG-based control for a soft robotic tentacle. In: Yang, H., Pasupa, K., Leung, A.-S., Kwok, J.T., Chan, J.H., King, I. (eds.) ICONIP 2020. LNCS, vol. 12533, pp. 762–774. Springer, Cham (2020). https://doi. org/10.1007/978-3-030-63833-7_64

26. Jørgensen, J., Ploetz, S.: LARPing human-robot interaction. In: HRI 2020 Workshop on Exploring Creative Content in Social Robotics (2020)

27. Jørgensen, J.: Leveraging morphological computation for expressive movement generation in a soft robotic artwork. In: Proceedings of the 4th International Conference on Movement Computing, pp. 20:1–20:4. ACM, New York (2017). https://doi.org/10.1145/3077981.307 8029

28. Xie, Z., et al.: Octopus arm-inspired tapered soft actuators with suckers for improved grasping. Soft Robot. (2020). https://doi.org/10.1089/soro.2019.0082

Evolutionary Typesetting: An Automatic Approach Towards the Generation of Typographic Posters from Tweets

Sérgio M. Rebelo^(✉), João Bicker, and Penousal Machado

Centre for Informatics and Systems of the University of Coimbra,
Department of Informatics Engineering, University of Coimbra, Coimbra, Portugal
{srebelo,bicker,machado}@dei.uc.pt

Abstract. The recent developments on Artificial Intelligence are expanding the tools, methods, media, and production processes on Graphic Design. Poster designs are no exception. In this paper, we present a web system that generates letterpress-inspired typographic posters using, as content, tweets posted online. The proposed system employs Natural Language Understanding approaches to recognise the emotions, the sentiments, and the colours associated with the content. Also, the system employs an Evolutionary Computation approach to generate and evolve a population of poster designs. The outputs are evaluated according to their legibility, aesthetics, and semantics, throughout an automatic fitness assignment hybrid scheme that combines a hard-wired fitness function part with a multi-objective optimisation approach part. We experimented with the system to perceive its behaviour and its ability to evolve posters from contents with distinct textual purposes and lengths.

Keywords: Evolutionary computation · Generative design · Poster design · Natural language understating · Twitter

1 Introduction

Posters have a ubiquitous presence in our everyday lives. They were already present in ancient societies and, throughout the centuries, have adapted to new social and technological contexts, changing their formats and purposes [4,34]. The recent developments on Artificial Intelligence (AI) are also reflected in Graphic Design (GD) and Visual Communication, expanding their tools, methods, media, and production processes [2,50]. In posters design, we observed the exploration of new digital media and computational techniques to create customised, distinct and interactive experiences for their viewers.

In this paper, we presented a system that generates, from scratch, typographic poster designs, similar to letterpress posters, using content posted online on Twitter. Letterpress is a printing technique that emerged on the follow-up of

A. Brooks et al. (Eds.): ArtsIT 2020, LNICST 367, pp. 343–362, 2021.
https://doi.org/10.1007/978-3-030-73426-8_21

the Industrial Revolution (*c.* early 19th century) driven by developments of new printing technologies and the necessity of mass communication. At the time, it became popular because it allowed a cheaper, easier and faster printing of commercial posters [17,34].

Nevertheless, the design of letterpress posters was a process slightly different from the present-day one. At the time, designers composed the visual elements to carry out a matrix, often in collaboration with the client. The visual elements were selected from an extensive set of standard typefaces, fillets, ornaments and engravings and the philosophy of work, at the time, was to use the maximum of them [34]. The design decisions were very pragmatic: longer words and text were composed in more condensed typefaces and shorter words were composed in wider fonts. The most important parts of the content were emphasised through the use of bigger typefaces. Thus, designers needed to hold the elements firmly and strongly, imposing vertical and horizontal tension between the elements.

The present system generates outputs replicating this workflow. Briefly, the system (*i.e.* the designer) composes the content, divided into text boxes to fulfil, as much as possible, the posters' canvas (*i.e.* the matrix). The content is dynamically gathered from the Twitter API using a textual input given by the user (*i.e.* the client). In this process, an Natural Language Understanding (NLU) classifier and lexicon-based approaches recognise sentiments and emotions in the gathered content, and a Evolutionary Computation (EC) approach automatically generates and evolves the outputs. Each generated poster is evaluated according to its (I) legibility, *i.e.* how much content it is possible to read in the poster, (II) aesthetics, *i.e.* how much the design of the poster satisfies a set of aesthetics measures for typographic poster design, and (III) semantics *i.e.* how much the visual characteristics of the poster convey the semantic meaning of its content. The merit of each poster is assigned by a hybrid fitness scheme that combines a hardwired fitness function technique with a multi-objective optimisation approach. The users may communicate their preferences to the system throughout a design guidelines sheet. This system, which is available online at http://pf.dei.uc.pt/et/, is aligned with our previous experiments with hardwired fitness assignment methods (see [47] and [46]).

The outputs generated by the system fully communicate their content while achieving high levels of visual balance and expressiveness. The system addresses the contemporary phenomenon of posting, exploring the usage of posters as a canvas for personal and ephemeral expression. A relatively unexplored subject that goes against the common public and informative nature of posters [4]. Also, the system unveils how computational design techniques may expand the tools and automate some processes in GD, creating novel ways to communicate with people.

The key technical contributions presented in this paper include (I) a generative system capable of automatically designing typographic posters, regardless the length and purpose of the content, (II) a method to recognise sentiments, emotions and colours associated with tweets that combines an NLU network with lexicon-based approaches, (III) an evolutionary framework to generate typographic poster designs, and (IV) a method to evaluate typographic poster designs, combining a hardwired fitness assignment method with a multi-objective optimisation approach.

The remainder of this paper is organised as follows. Section 2 summarises the related work. Section 3 comprehensively describes the system. Section 4 reports the experiments conducted to analyse the behaviour of the system and presents some results. Finally, Sect. 5 draws the conclusions and points the directions for future work.

2 Related Work

The use of computational processes to generate visuals already existed in the earlier times of the second half of the 20th century [23]. However, the introduction of the personal computer approximated graphic designers from these processes. From then on, a growing number of designers began to use computer programming as a tool to generate visual artefacts that solve problems in a flexible and customised way. Muriel Cooper, and her Visible Language Workshop, at MIT, and John Maeda were pioneers that explored on poster generation, using presenting tailor-made software (*e.g.* [7] and [31]).

Several graphic designers explored, afterwards, the use of these technologies. Most of these designers were focused on the generation of visuals to be used on their designs (*e.g.* [39] or [16]). Nevertheless, as far as we know, some automatic approaches were developed. LUST, in 2008, employed a generative system to generate posters using content gathered from multiple internet sources in the installation *Poster Wall for the 21st Century* featured in Graphic Design Museum in Breda (Netherlands) [29]. Between 2008 and 2019, Stephan and Haag [53] generated parametric posters optimised for cheap reproduction, using Bash scripts. In 2010, Cleveland [6] proposed a method for generating style-based design layouts that explores the inter-relationships between text and graphics. Also, he presented a system to generate layouts employing these principles. Damera-Venkata et al. [9] presented, in 2011, a template-based probabilistic framework for generating document layouts for variable content. In 2014, LUST presented the interactive installation *Camera Postura* that creates posters using movies' frames where the actors' gestures are similar to the viewers' gestures [30]. In the same year, O'Donovan [40] presented an energy-based approach for designing single-page layouts. In 2016, Bleser [10] developed the *Pita Style Generator* that designs posters according to a specific style using the interactive design tool *Logic Layout*. In 2017, Zhang [55] developed a system that automatically generates banners of varied sizes using a style parameter learned from a set of training examples. More recently, in 2019, Rodenbröker [51] lectured the workshop *Programming Posters*, where the attendants designed posters using computer programming. Rebelo et al. [48] presented, in the same year, an installation that designs posters according to the state of the physical surroundings around them and, simultaneously, learns how to design successful posters for the place where it is placed. Moreover, there is an increasing interest in the employment of deep learning approaches to solve and study layout generation problems (*e.g.* [27] or [56]).

EC has been used with success in several creative domains related to GD, such as the generation of pictorial symbols (*e.g.* [8,11]), type designs (*e.g.* [25,32]) or web designs (*e.g.* [41]), *etc.* Lewis [26] presents a good overview of the field. Although few, some related work exists in the context of document and poster design. In 2002, Gatarski [14] developed a system to evolve automatically digital banners using the user's click-through as fitness metric. In the same year, Goldenberg [15] employed an EC to automatically generate page layouts minimising the waste of space on the page. Purvis et al. [44] presented, in 2003, a multi-objective optimisation approach to automatically generate document layouts that satisfies certain content and layout constraints, as well as certain desired design aesthetics. Quiroz et al. [45] developed, in 2009, an evolutionary approach to generate brochure documents where the user guides the system assessing only a small subset of the results. In 2010, Morcilllo et al. [38] created *GAUDII*, an evolutionary system that generates single-page designs using Interactive Evolutionary Computation (IEC) to define the design properties. Önduygu [42] developed, soon thereafter, *Gráphagos*, an IEC system that generates design compositions through the evolution of position, scale and rotation of a set of visual elements. In 2011, Kitamura and Kanoh [20] evolved poster designs using IEC to assess visual features on the generated posters (such as the size or colour). In 2012, Denis Klein developed *Crossing, Mixing, Mutating* [21], a tool to generate variations of a template using genetic operators. Subsequently, in 2016, he and Lisa Reimann updated the tool and released it as an Adobe InDesign plug-in named *Evolving Layout* [24].

3 The System

The presented system is a web application that generates letterpress-inspired typographic posters, displaying content posted online on Twitter. The system generates posters by organising a certain content, divided into text boxes, to fulfil the available space on a canvas. It performs this task through the employment of 3 modules: (I) Input Processing; (II) Evolution; and (III) Evaluation.

The system dynamically gathers the content using Twitter API, based on a textual input given by the user. The Input Processing module is responsible to gather the content, processing it, and recognising its most important parts. Thus, it recognises the sentiments, emotions and colours associated with the content, employing an NLU classifier and lexicon-based approaches. The Evolution module randomly initialises a new population of candidate solutions and uses a Genetic Algorithm (GA) to evolve this population. In this work, a candidate solution, or an individual, consists of a poster design. The evolution is performed by the iterative employment of variation operators (*i.e.* mutation and recombination) on the most promising poster designs. These posters are selected by tournament based on their fitness. This method practices elitism, persevering the best individual of each generation to the next generation. The fitness of each poster is assigned by the Evaluation module through a hybrid method that blends characteristics from hardwired and multi-objective optimisation assignments. The fitness calculation is based on 3 objectives: (I) legibility; (II) aesthetics; and (III) semantics. The legibility objective assesses how much content it is possible to read on the poster. The aesthetics objective assesses how much the individuals fulfil a set of aesthetics measures for typographic poster designs. The semantics objective assesses how much the individuals' visual characteristics convey the semantic meaning of its content.

The users of the system can communicate their preferences to the system by fulfilling the design guidelines sheet. In this sheet, users can define a set of core variables for the functioning of the system. These variables are the weights of the evaluation of each objective, the GA setup parameters, the available typefaces and their scores of pairing, as well as their emotional scores. The system will take into consideration these variables in its generation and evaluation processes. A schematic of the system is overviewed in Fig. 1.

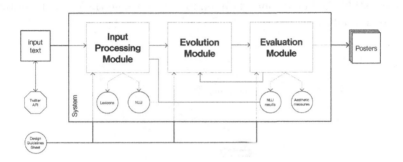

Fig. 1. Schematic of the system's architecture.

3.1 Input Processing Module

The Input Processing module dynamically gathers and processes the content to be placed on poster. The content is gathered using Twitter API based on a textual input given by users throughout a specific form (see Fig. 2). This way, when a user inputs a text string, a standard search in Twitter API is performed and the tweet that better meets the query is returned. In this form, the users can select what type of search they prefer and define the search's specifications. The system performs 3 types of searches: (I) general search, *i.e.* to search by tweets that contain the inputted text; (II) username search, *i.e.* to search by tweets of a specific Twitter user; and (III) hashtag search, *i.e.* to search by tweets with a specific hashtag. Also, users may select if the tweet returned will be selected based on its popularity, newness, or both.

The present module analysis the gathered content to recognise sentiments and emotions. It performs this analysis on global and local levels. The global analysis recognises sentiments and emotions transmitted by the text as a whole.

We achieve this by implementing a Bayes NLU classifier that recognises sentiments and the intensity of certain emotions in the tweets. The sentiment analysis
is performed in multiple languages and on the positive-negative axis. Furthermore, this network was trained to identify the intensity of certain emotions on
text using a manually annotated data set of tweets, in the English language,
collected by Mohammad and Bravo-Marquez [36]. Currently, this model can
recognise 4 emotions (anger, fear, joy, and sadness) and their intensity on the
text. The NLU classifier was implemented and trained using the tools available
at NLP.JS library [3]. The local analysis recognises emotions and sentiments
in every word on the text. Thus, after tokenising and lemmatising the text,
each word is searched in a word-emotion association lexicon. The used lexicon,
developed by Mohammad and Turney [37], enables to recognise 8 basic and
prototypical emotions (*i.e.* anger, anticipation, disgust, fear, joy, sadness and
surprise) [43] and 2 sentiments (*i.e.* positive and negative). The local analysis,
therefore, perceives what are the more emotional parts of the text and, so, the
parts that should be emphasised in the outputs. Currently, this analysis also
uses more established emotional data, enabling to bridge the current limitations
of the global analysis.

Fig. 2. Screenshot of the interaction form. The users can input a text string in the text
area on the top. In the drop-down selector, below at left, the user may select the type
of search. In the buttons, at the right, the user may define the way how the tweet is
selected.

The module also analyses the content to recognise colours associated with
it. Similarly to the local analysis, this analysis is performed using a word-colour
association lexicon by Mohammad [35]. The used lexicon relates several words
with 11 colours: black, blue, brown, green, grey, orange, purple, pink, red, white,
and yellow. In the end, this analysis creates an annotated map that describes the

intensity of the relation between the colours and the content. The intensity of each colour is the sum of its scores of association with the words of the content.

At the end of the analysis, the present module splits the text into lines as follows. First, it performs a Sentence Boundary Detection [49] method to divide the content into sentences. After, it subdivides into lines the sentences that are lengthier than a predefined maximum characters threshold. In this subdivision, an optimal characters length threshold defines the probability of breaking the sentences. This probability increases when the sentence's length approaches a maximum characters threshold. The optimal threshold is randomly defined in each subdivision based on a predefined range, creating, therefore, more organic subdivisions of the content. The maximum threshold and the optimal range are defined in the design guidelines sheet.

3.2   Evolution Module

The Evolution module implements a GA to create a population of poster designs at random and, subsequently, evolve them using variation operators, *i.e.* crossover and mutation (*e.g.* see [12] for further information about GAs). Also, this module provides the necessary methods to render and export the outputs.

Each poster is a set of arranged text boxes. The text boxes are encoded as a sequence of numeric arrays (*i.e.* the genotype). The first array in the sequence encodes the poster's background colour (*i.e.* the colour configuration gene). The following arrays encode the text boxes (*i.e.* the text boxes genes). Figure 3 schemes the genotype of the individuals. The colour configuration gene is a two-position length array, where the first position encodes the base colour and the second encodes percentage of the tint. The text boxes genes are four-position length arrays that encode the typeface, the font's weight, the height, and the font size in percentages of the height, respectively. Since posters' contents may have different lengths, the number of text boxes and, consequently, the size of genotype may vary.

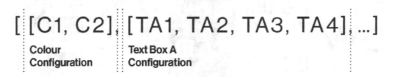

Fig. 3. The genotype is encoded as a sequence of numeric arrays. The first array (the colour configuration gene) encodes the background colour of the output, *i.e.* the base colour (C1) and the percentage of tint (C2). The following arrays (text boxes configuration genes) encode the properties of the text boxes, *i.e.* the typeface (TA1), the font's weight (TA2), the height (TA3) and the font size (TA4).

The posters' canvas is subdivided in a one-column grid with multiple rows. This grid constraints the text boxes position and sizes. The canvas has, by default, the dimension ratio of the $\sqrt{2}$ by 1 (*i.e.* the format of the standard paper size ISO 216 A series). Perceptible poster designs (*i.e.* phenotypes) are generated through the definition of its background with the colour defined by the colour configuration gene and the draw of the text boxes defined by the text box configuration genes. The method that renders the phenotype is implemented using p5.JS library [33]. The margins, grid density (*i.e.* the number of rows) and the size/format of the outputs are defined in the design guidelines sheet.

Initialisation. The initialisation method generates the first population of poster designs at random. This implies the random definition of the colour configuration gene and the text boxes genes of each individual. The colour configuration gene is defined through the random selection of a base colour and its percentage of tint according to the possibilities available for the selected base colour. The percentages of tint are defined in increments of 20%. Black and white are the only colours that do not support tints. The typography's colour is defined based on the colour selected. The number of text boxes is determined based on the lines resulting from the content split process. This way, for each line, it generates a text box and sets its proprieties. The typeface is selected at random from the set of available typefaces. The font's weight is also randomly selected from the options available for the selected typeface. The height of the text boxes, although selected at random, is defined by ensuring that the text boxes fulfil all the available space on the canvas. We ensured this by randomly generate a sequence of numbers. This sequence has the same length that the number of text boxes and its sum is equal to the number of rows in the grid. Next, this sequence is shuffled and each value on sequence is assigned to a text box. Finally, the font size is defined at always at 100% of the height. Figure 4 presents the phenotypes of an initial population. The available base colours and their percentage of tint, as well as the typefaces and their weights, are defined in the design guidelines sheet.

Fig. 4. An initial population of 10 individuals generated, at random, by the system.

Variation. Poster designs are evolved iteratively through the employment of crossover and mutation operators. Both operators are designed to preserve the validity of the generated individuals.

The crossover operator exchanges genes between two parents to generate new posters designs. Thus, it randomly selects two parents regarding their fitness and, after, employs a uniform crossover method, *i.e.* it randomly selects, for each gene, what will be the parent that will give the gene to the children [54]. This operator does not crossover the genes related to the height of the text boxes, ensuring that the generated individuals are always valid (*i.e.* posters where the text boxes fill all the available canvas space).

The mutator operators perform random modifications in several parts of the individuals' genotype. We designed these operators ensuring that they cover all the search space. This resulted in 3 operators: (I) independent; (II) specialised and (III) swap. The mutations are performed based on a certain probability. Thus, the system for each candidate solution, in the new offspring, randomly defines if it will be mutated and, subsequently, selects the mutation operator. Each operator has the same probability of being employed.

The independent mutation operator random selects a gene and, subsequently, a parameter inside of the gene and mutates it. The only exception is the font-size parameter, which can not be selected by this operator. Each parameter has its own range of values. Thus, a customised method is employed depending on the parameter that is selected. If the base colour or the typeface parameter are selected, *i.e.* an unsubordinated parameter, the new value is changed at random according to the options available. The modification of these parameters may also require the change of their subordinated parameters (*i.e.* the percentage of tint or the font's weight). Thus, if the resulting mutated unsubordinated parameter value does not support the value of the subordinated parameter, a new value is defined at random. On the other hand, if a subordinated parameter is selected, the value is randomly modified according to the possibilities available for the unsubordinated parameter. If the text box height parameter is selected, two genes are randomly selected, having one, at least, its value bigger than 1. After, the module decides what will be the gene that will decrease the height and the one that will increase. This selection is made at random, unless one of the selected genes has a value of 1. In this case, the gene with a value of 1 will increase its height and the other will decrease.

The specialised mutation operator is a custom implementation of the independent mutation method. This operator mutates the highest text box on the individual and the font size parameter. We empirically observed that the evolution of the posters often was slow and easily stabilised in specific designs. This was mostly because a text box was much bigger than the average and/or some content was too long for text box and, so, it was not fully displayed, even when it was composed in the most condensed typeface. This way, we designed bespoke methods to perform regular modifications on these parameters, allowing a faster and more diverse evolution. When this mutator is selected one method is randomly chosen and performed in the individual. The mutator of the highest text box decreases the height of the highest text box and increase the height of another randomly selected text box in the individual. The mutation of the font size randomly selects a text box gene and decreases, or increases, the value of its font size parameter in 1%. The direction of the mutation is defined at random unless the parameter value is the maximum, *i.e.* 100%, (the value will only be decreased) or the minimum, *i.e.* 30% (the value will only be increased).

The swap mutation operator, as the name indicates, randomly selects two text boxes, in the same individual, and swaps the value of their genes.

Export. The presented module also provides the necessary means to export the outputs, when necessary. The users may export one or multiple outputs at any time during the evolutionary process. When the user exports an output, 4 files are downloaded: the vector (SVG file) and raster (PNG file) versions of the phenotype, the genotype of the output (JSON file) and the content (text file).

3.3   Evaluation Module

The Evaluation module assesses the generated outputs according to 3 objectives: (I) legibility, *i.e.* how much content it is possible to read on the poster; (II) aesthetics, *i.e.* how much of the poster design satisfies a set of aesthetics measures for typographic poster design; and (III) semantics, *i.e.* how much of the poster's visual characteristics convey the semantic meaning of its content. Each objective has its own evaluation method.

The present module implements an automatic fitness assignment hybrid scheme that combines a hardwired fitness function part with a multi-objective optimisation approach part. The fitness of each poster is calculated by a weighted arithmetic mean of legibility (the hardwired part) with the relation between the semantics and aesthetics objectives (the multi-objective part). This way, it values fully legible posters while, simultaneously, searches by different relations between the aesthetics and semantics objectives. This relation can be a balance or the optimisation of one objective over another. The overall fitness value ranges from 0 (bad) to 1 (good).

The relation between the aesthetics and the semantics objectives is calculated in the following way. First, the module sorts the entire population based on the non-domination of each individual (see [52]). A solution dominates others if it is better in at least one objective and same as, or better, in another objective. A non-dominated solution is, therefore, a solution that is not dominated by any other solution in the population. Next, the population is organised in fronts. The first front is populated by the non-dominant set, the second front by the solutions dominated by the ones only in the first front and the fronts goes so on. The value of this relation for an individual is the rank of the front where it is placed, normalised according to the number of fronts.

This evaluation process is in accordance with the discussions about how we should measure the quality in GD. Posters' evaluation is a subjective task influenced by multiple factors such as the purpose, the *zeitgeist,* the context, the target people, *etc.* (see [34] and [17]). In this sense, the present module evaluates the outputs, considering that a poster should communicate its content above all. Besides that, there is no direct way to evaluate the quality of a poster and it (like other GD's artefacts) should not only be evaluated by its aesthetics [13]. This way, like graphic designers, the system designs posters by trying to balance the pure aesthetics with the semantics meaning of the content, valuing one characteristic over the other to understand where the borderline is, when the overall quality of a poster begins to decrease.

Legibility. The legibility objective measures how much of the content is legible on the poster. The overall legibility value of a poster is related to the legibility of its text boxes. The legibility of a text box is the difference between its target width (*i.e.* the available width of the poster) and the width of its content when rendered. This difference is calculated considering that the content should be always rendered inside of the poster and the negative space inside of the text box (*i.e.* the space coloured with the background colour) should, as much as possible, be minimised. Thus, the legibility of a text box is this difference mapped to assign a poor assessment when the rendered text exceeds the width of the poster and, simultaneously, to prejudice progressively the assessment as soon as the amount of negative space inside text box surpasses a certain threshold. The overall legibility value of a poster is the weighted arithmetic mean of the value of text boxes. The weight of each text box in the mean is given according to its height. In the end, the value is normalised between 0 (bad) and 1 (good).

Aesthetics. The aesthetics objective measures how much the poster design satisfies a set of aesthetic measures for typographic posters' design. We defined these measures based on the work of Harrington et al. [18]. However, we decided not to measure the white-space free-flow, the proportion, and the uniform separation because these measures are not applicable to the generated outputs since they are composed in a one-column grid. The outputs are typographic posters and a good pairing of the typefaces is a key factor to create harmonious layouts [5,28]. In this sense, we also added a font pairing measure. The aesthetics of a poster is, then, evaluated according to (I) the alignment, (II) the regularity, (III) the balance, (IV) the negative-space fraction, (V) the composition security, and (VI) the font pairing. The overall aesthetics measure is the weighted arithmetic mean of these attributes ranged from 0 (bad) to 1 (good). The weight of each measure, as well as the optimal thresholds and offsets of certain measures, are defined in the design guidelines sheet.

The alignment measures how much the edges of the content share similar horizontal positions on a poster. This measure depends on the distance between neighbouring text boxes. Thus, the module creates a histogram with the current positions of the left edges of the text boxes and after compares the distance between the values on adjacent positions. The closer the distance values are, the higher is the alignment score. The overall alignment measure is the arithmetic mean of all distances.

The regularity measures how much regular is the placement of text boxes in vertical on a poster, *i.e.* if the heights of text boxes are similar. The calculation of the regularity is a process similar to the calculation of alignment. However, it uses a histogram with the positions of the top edges instead of the left edges.

The balance measures how much the posters are centrally balanced. The centre balance measure of a composition is the difference between the centre of the visual weight and the visual centre. The centre of the visual weight is calculated based on the visual weights and centres of the text boxes. The visual weight of a text box is defined by its area times its optical density. The optical density of a text box is the 10 logarithm of the average normalised of its Luminance (Y). The Y is calculated through the weighted average formula of $Y = 0.2125R + 0.7152G + 0.0722B$ where R, G, B are the red, green, and blue channels from the average pixel, respectively. The position of the visual centre of a text box is the horizontal geometric centre and the vertical geometric centre with a small offset towards the top of the page. The poster's centre of the visual weight and the overall measure of balance is calculated according to the method presented by Harrington et al. [18].

The negative-space fraction measures if the space coloured with the background colour is balanced in the poster. This measure is the distance of the current percentage of pixels coloured with the background colour to a certain optimal percentage threshold.

The composition security measures if the text boxes positioned near the edges of the poster are secure, *i.e.* small text boxes when placed near the composition edges appear to fall off. The security of each text box is the minimum between the top edge and bottom edge. The overall value is the minimum between the values of all text boxes.

The font pairing measures if the employed typefaces pair well between them. The pairing value of each text box is the arithmetic mean of pairing scores between its typeface with other typefaces used on the poster. The overall value is the arithmetic mean of the value of all text boxes.

Semantics. The semantics objective measures how much the posters' visual characteristics convey the semantic meaning of its content. This way, the most important parts of a poster's content should be emphasised over the less important ones, *i.e.* they should be composed on higher text boxes. Also, the background colour and the typography on the poster should transmit the semantic meaning of the content. The semantics are evaluated, then, according to (I) the background colour, (II) the layout of the text boxes, and (III) the typefaces employed. The overall semantic measure is the weighted arithmetic mean of these attributes ranged from 0 (bad) to 1 (good). The weight of each measure in the mean is defined in the design guidelines sheet.

The background colour of a poster conveys the semantic meaning of its content when it is aligned with the annotated map that describes the relationship between the colours and the content defined before. As before mentioned, the colours in this map are sorted by intensity. This way, the more intense is the relation of one colour with the content, the fewer should be the percentage of tint employed and *vice versa*. Every colour in the map obtains a good assignment when used on output with the proper tint value. The optimal tint value of a colour is the quotient of the number of available percentages of the tint of this colour by the intensity of the relationship with the content (*i.e.* the position of the colour on the map). The overall measure of the appropriateness of the background colour is the normalised distance of the optimal tint value to the current value.

The layout of a poster should emphasise the most important parts of the content by assigning higher text boxes to them. We consider that the more important text boxes are those with a higher amount of emotions recognised in the local sentimental and emotional analysis performed before. Each recognised emotion has a certain weight on the layout. This weight is the division of the total number of emotions recognised in all text boxes by the number of rows on the grid. The optimal text box height is the product of the number of emotion present in its content by the weight of each emotion. The appropriateness of each text box's layout is the normalised distance between its current height and its optimal height. The overall value is the normalised arithmetic mean of all distances.

The typefaces employed on a poster convey the semantic meaning of its content when their shape and weight reflects the sentiments and emotions present in the content. This measure is the arithmetic mean of the other 3 measures: (i) global appropriateness; (ii) local appropriateness; and (iii) font's weight appropriateness. The global appropriateness measures if the typefaces employed on poster convey the results of the global sentimental and emotional analysis performed before. Thus, the global appropriateness of a typeface in a poster is the arithmetic mean of the differences between the intensities of the emotions and sentiments present on the content and the intensities that this typeface conveys these emotions and sentiments. The overall value is the arithmetic mean of the value of all typefaces used on the poster.

The local appropriateness measures if the typefaces employed on the poster convey the results of the local sentimental and emotional analysis performed before. The calculation of this measure is similar to the global measure, however, performed at the text boxes level. Thus, the local appropriateness of a typeface in a text box is the arithmetic mean of the difference of the intensities that this typeface conveys the emotions and sentiments present on the text box. The overall value is the arithmetic mean of the value of all text boxes. The font's weight appropriateness measures how the weight of the typeface employed in a text box conveys the results of the local sentimental and emotional analysis. This measure was created because certain emotions are easier conveyed by the typeface weight than by typeface design [19,22]. The font's weight appropriateness of a text box is the distance between the current font's weight and an optimal range. The optimal range is the average of the optimal ranges of all emotions present on the text box. The overall value is the arithmetic mean of the values of all text boxes.

4   Experiments

We conducted experiments to study and analyse the possibilities of the system, by evolving posters for contents with different lengths and textual purposes. The experimental parameters used in these experiments are defined by empirical exploration and are summarised in Table 1. The weights of the parameters on the fitness assignment and on the evaluation of the aesthetics and semantics objectives were also defined by empirical exploration and are summarised in Table 2.

Table 1. Experimental parameters.

Parameter	Value
Generations	500
Population size	30
Elite size	1
Selection	Tournament
Tournament size	2
Mutation probability	0.7
Phenotype size	298 × 420
Margin size	15px
Grid	26 × 1
Maximum line length (in characters)	40
Optimal line length (in characters)	[10–30]
Visual centre vertical offset	1/12
Optimal percent of negative space	50%

Table 2. Experimental weights on evaluation components.

Evaluation	Parameter	Weight
Fitness	Legibility	90%
	Aesthetics/Semantics	10%
Semantics	Background Colour	25%
	Layout	25%
	Typographic choices	50%
Aesthetics	Alignment	10%
	Regularity	10%
	Balance	15%
	Negative-Space Fraction	10%
	Page Security	05%
	Font pairing	50%

The experiments were conducted using 15 typographic families. The typefaces, their pairing scores as well as their emotional and sentimental score, were empirically defined by us in the design guidelines sheet. The typographic families were dynamically loaded using the Adobe Typekit Webfonts service [1]. All the typefaces in the typographic family are loaded, except the italic and slanted ones. We defined the emotional and sentimental score of each typeface based on the work of Koch [22] and Hyndman [19]. The pairing scores were defined based on the guidelines presented by Bringhurst [5] and Lupton [28]. One may analyse the scores of each typeface in the design guidelines sheet example used on these experiments and available for download at https://cdv.dei.uc.pt/evoposter/. The typeface families selected are the following: (I) *LTC Globe Gothic* designed by Colin Kahn, Frederic W. Goudy, and Morris Fuller Benton (Lanston Type, 1897); (II) *News Gothic* designed by Morris Fuller Benton (Adobe, 2007); (III) *Futura PT* designed by Isabella Chaeva, Paul Renner, Vladimir Andrich, and Vladimir Yefimov (ParaType, 2007); (IV) *Century Old Style* designed by Morris Fuller Benton (Adobe, 2007); (V) *Azo Sans* designed by Rui Abreu (R-Typography, 2013); (VI) *Franklin Gothic* designed by Morris Fuller Benton (URW, 2002); (VII) *Clone Rounded* designed by Lasko Dzurovski (Rosetta Type Foundry, 2016); (VIII) *Bureau Grot* designed by David Berlow (Font Bureau, 1989); (VII) *Titling Gothic FB* designed by David Berlow (Font Bureau, 2005); (IX) *Benton Modern Display* designed by David Berlow, Dyana Weissman, Richard Lipton and Tobias Frere-Jones (Font Bureau, 2008); (X) *Miller Display* designed by Matthew Carter (Carter & Cone, 1997); (XI) *Whitman Display* designed by Kent Lew (Font Bureau, 2008); (XII) *Bodoni FB* by Richard Lipton (Font Bureau, 1989); (XIII) *Trade Gothic Next* designed by Akira Kobayashi, Tom Grace and Jackson Burke (Linotype, 2008); (XIV) *Zeitung Pro* designed by Underware (2017); and (XV) *Zeitung Mono* designed by Underware (2017).

Fig. 5. Typical outputs generated by the system using contents gathered from tweets posted online between 14/04 and 29/04/2020 by the users @elporrote, @jessphillips, @joy, @latimes, @mypaws, @realDonaldTrump and @RealKunalMC. More example outputs are accessible at https://cdv.dei.uc.pt/evoposter/.

Figure 5 display several obtained results. One may see more examples of the system outputs and demo video of the system in https://cdv.dei.uc.pt/evoposter/. Visually observing the results, one can conclude that the system often prefers to use typefaces from the same typographic family. This way, more extensive typographic families, such as *Bureau Grot* or *Titling Gothic FB*, are more observable in the results. The reason is simple: the extension of these typographic families ensures that often exists a proper typeface for each text box size as well as achieving good scores of pairing by using them together, since they are part of the same family and share common traits. Concerning the background colours, it is possible to see that for some contents, the system tends to select always the same set of colours over different runs. Also, we observed that the system evolves well-evaluated outputs faster when the content is lengthier, since the number of possible solutions is minor and, so, it needs to perform less operations to achieve a good result. Nevertheless, the lengthier the content, the more similar will the achieved outputs be over different runs.

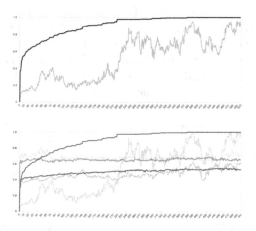

Fig. 6. Evolution of the posters' fitness (top) and objectives evaluation (bottom) over the generations. In the figure above, the solid line displays the fitness' best individual. The semi-transparent line displays the average fitness of the population. In the figure below, the blue, green, and purple lines display the legibility, aesthetics, and semantics objectives, respectively. The solid lines display the fitness' best individual. The semi-transparent lines display the average fitness of the population. The visualised data is the average of 30 runs. (Color figure online)

Figure 6 displays the evolution of the fitness, the evolution of the objectives of the best individual and the average of the population, over the generations. The displayed data is the average of 30 runs, using 6 different contents with an average of 83 characters by content. The fitness of the individuals (the top of Fig. 6) is a qualitative value since the relation between the aesthetics and semantics objectives is not a quantitative value, *i.e.* it corresponds to the front that the individual belongs. This way, to study the system's behaviour, this value should be observed in conjunction with the evaluation of the objectives on the population (the bottom of Fig. 6). This way, one can observe that high fitness values are attained in a few generations and this value is strictly related to the evaluation of the legibility objective. It is also observable that, in the early stages, the evolution is faster than in the later stages. This occurs because, in the earliest stages, the evolution is mostly focused on generating a good layout and in the later ones it is mostly focused on performing minor adjustments to increase the fitness of the best individual and, so, of the entire population.

One can also observe that in the earlier stages of evolution, the evaluation of aesthetics and semantics achieves higher values than in the later ones and, often, these values decrease over the generations. Also, it is observable that in these stages the average evaluation of these objectives in the population is often above to their evaluation of the best individual. This occurs because the legibility acts like a constraint and in the earlier stages of evolution, posters have poor legibility evaluations. Nevertheless, the values of the evaluation of aesthetics and semantics objectives are always directly related to the characteristics of the content.

5   Conclusions and Future Work

We have described a system that generates letterpress-inspired posters, using tweets posted online as content. The content is dynamically gathered based on a textual input given by the user. Outputs are generated through 3 modules: (I) Input Processing; (II) Evolution; and (III) Evaluation. In the Input Processing module, sentiments, emotions and colours are recognised on the content using an NLU classifier and lexicon-based approaches. The Evolution module employs a GA to generate and evolve a population of posters. The Evaluation module assesses the outputs according to 3 objectives: (I) legibility; (II) aesthetics; and (III) semantics. The merit of each poster is assigned by a hybrid fitness scheme that combines a hardwired fitness function part (the legibility) with a multi-objective optimisation part (relation between the aesthetics and semantics). We experimented with the system to perceive its behaviour and its ability to evolve posters. The system outputs achieves high levels of legibility and diversity. Also, we observed that the legibility objective works as a constraint, allowing the system to balance the relation between aesthetics and semantics to find the best relationship between these two objectives, without decreasing the legibility.

Future work will focus on (I) to explore different fitness assignment schemes (which may promote diversity and visual novelty in the generated outputs), (II) to design and to develop an interface that allows a parametric definition of several system's variables and to lock several visual properties of the outputs during the evolution, (III) to automate the gathering of the typefaces and the definition of their pairing, emotional and sentimental scores (using *e.g.* Adobe Typekit Webfonts or Google Fonts APIs), (IV) to include images and illustrations in the posters, and (V) to create real letterpress posters, based on the outputs generated by the system.

Acknowledgments. This work is partially supported by national funds through the Foundation for Science and Technology (FCT), Portugal, within the scope of the project UID/CEC/00326/2019. The first author is funded by FCT under the grant SFRH/BD/132728/2017.

References

1. Adobe: Adobe typekit web fonts (2020). https://fonts.adobe.com/typekit/
2. Armstrong, H., Stojmirovic, Z.: Participate: Designing with User-Generated Content. Princeton Architectural Press, New York (2011)
3. AXA Group Operations Spain S.A.: Nlp.js (2020). https://github.com/axa-group/nlp.js/
4. Blauvelt, A.: The persistence of posters. In: Blauvelt, A., Lupton, E. (eds.) Graphic Design: Now in Production, chap. 11, pp. 92–111. Walker Art Center, Minneapolis (2011)
5. Bringhurst, R.: The Elements of Typographic Style, 3rd edn. Hartley & Marks, Vancouver (2005)
6. Cleveland, P.: Style based automated graphic layouts. Des. Stud. **31**(1), 3–25 (2010)
7. Cooper, M.: Computers and design. Des. Q. **1**(142), 1–31 (1989)
8. Cunha, J.M., Lourenço, N., Correia, J., Martins, P., Machado, P.: *Emojinating*: evolving emoji blends. In: Ekárt, A., Liapis, A., Castro Pena, M.L. (eds.) EvoMUSART 2019. LNCS, vol. 11453, pp. 110–126. Springer, Cham (2019). https://doi.org/10.1007/978-3-030-16667-0_8
9. Damera-Venkata, N., Bento, J., O'Brien-Strain, E.: Probabilistic document model for automated document composition. In: Proceedings of the 11th ACM Symposium on Document Engineering, September 2011, pp. 3–12. ACM, Mountain View (2011)
10. De Bleser, F.: Generative design: the nodebox perpective. Ph.D. thesis, University of Antwerp, Antwerp, Belgium (2016)
11. Dorris, N., Carnahan, B., Orsini, L., Kuntz, L.A.: Interactive evolutionary design of anthropomorphic symbols. In: Proceedings of the 2004 Congress on Evolutionary Computation, 19–23 June 2004, pp. 433–440. IEEE, Portland (2004)
12. Eiben, A.E., Smith, J.E.: Introduction to Evolutionary Computing, 2nd edn. Springer, Heidelberg (2015). https://doi.org/10.1007/978-3-662-44874-8
13. Frascara, J.: Graphic design: fine art or social science? Des. Issues **5**(1), 18–29 (1988)
14. Gatarski, R.: Breed better banners: design automation through on-line interaction. J. Interact. Mark. **16**(1), 2–13 (2002)
15. Goldenberg, E.: Automatic layout of variable-content print data. Master's thesis, University of Sussex, Brighton, United Kingdom (2002)
16. Groß, B., Laub, J.: Diploma - generative systeme posters (2007). https://benedikt-gross.de/projects/diploma-generative-systeme-posters/
17. Guffey, E.E.: Posters: A Global History. Reaktion Books, London (2014)
18. Harrington, S.J., Naveda, J.F., Jones, R.P., Roetling, P., Thakkar, N.: Aesthetic measures for automated document layout. In: Proceedings of the 2004 ACM Symposium on Document Engineering, October 2004, pp. 109–111. ACM, Milwaukee (2004)
19. Hyndman, S.: Why Fonts Matter. Virgin Books, London (2016)

20. Kitamura, S., Kanoh, H.: Developing support system for making posters with interactive evolutionary computation. In: 2011 Fourth International Symposium on Computational Intelligence and Design, 28–30 October 2011, pp. 48–51. IEEE, Hangzhou (2011)
21. Klein, D.: Crossing, mixing, mutation (2012). http://www.gutenberg-intermedia. de/wissenschaft-gestaltung/denis-klein-crossing-mixing-mutation/
22. Koch, B.E.: Emotion in typographic design: an empirical examination. Visible Lang. **46**(3), 206–227 (2012)
23. Leavitt, R.: Artist and Computer. Harmony Books, New York (1976)
24. LESS: Evolving layout (2016). http://www.evolvinglayout.com/
25. Levin, G., Feinberg, J., Curtis, C.: Alphabet synthesis machine (2002). http://web. archive.org/web/20080513044335/www.alphabetsynthesis.com/
26. Lewis, M.: Evolutionary visual art and design. In: Romero, J., Machado, P. (eds.) The Art of Artificial Evolution: A Handbook on Evolutionary Art and Music, pp. 3–37. Springer, Heidelberg (2008). https://doi.org/10.1007/978-3-540-72877-1_1. chap. 1
27. Li, J., Yang, J., Hertzmann, A., Zhang, J., Xu, T.: LayoutGAN: synthesizing graphic layouts with vector-wireframe adversarial networks. IEEE Trans. Pattern Anal. Mach. Intell., 1 (2020). https://doi.org/10.1109/TPAMI.2019.2963663
28. Lupton, E.: Thinking With Type: A Critical Guide for Designers, Writers, Editors, & Students, 2nd edn. Princeton Architectural Press, New York (2010)
29. LUST: Graphic design museum: Poster wall for the 21st century (2008). https:// lust.nl/#projects-3041/
30. LUST: Camera postura (2014). http://lust.nl/#projects-5939/
31. Maeda, J.: Maeda@Media. Thames & Hudson, London (2000)
32. Martins, T., Correia, J., Costa, E., Machado, P.: Evolving stencils for typefaces: combining machine learning, user's preferences and novelty. Complexity, **2019** (2019)
33. McCarthy, L.: Processing Foundation, NYU ITP: P5.js (2020). https://p5js.org/
34. Meggs, P.B., Purvis, A.W.: Meggs' History of Graphic Design, 6th edn. Wiley, New York (2016)
35. Mohammad, S.M.: Colourful language: measuring word-colour associations. In: Proceedings of the Second Workshop on Cognitive Modeling and Computational Linguistics, June 2011, pp. 97–106. ACL, Portland (2011)
36. Mohammad, S.M., Bravo-Marquez, F.: Emotion intensities in tweets. In: Proceedings of the Sixth Joint Conference on Lexical and Computational Semantics (*Sem), August 2017, pp. 65–77. ACL, Vancouver (2017)
37. Mohammad, S.M., Turney, P.D.: Crowdsourcing a word-emotion association lexicon. Comput. Intell. **29**(3), 436–465 (2012)
38. Morcilllo, C.G., Martin, V.J., Fernandez, D.V., Sanchez, J.J.C., Albusac, J.A.: Gaudii: an automated graphic design expert system. In: Proceedings of the Twenty-Second Conference on Innovative Applications of Artificial Intelligence, 11–15 July 2010, pp. 1775–1780. AAAI, Atlanta (2010)
39. Müller, B.: Poetry on the road 2002–2013 (2002). https://www.esono.com/boris/ projects/poetry02/
40. O'Donovan, P., Agarwala, A., Hertzmann, A.: Learning layouts for single-page graphic designs. IEEE Trans. Vis. Comput. Graph. **20**(8), 1200–1213 (2014)
41. Oliver, A., Monmarché, N., Venturini, G.: Interactive design of web sites with a genetic algorithm. In: Isaías, P. (ed.) Proceedings of the IADIS International Conference WWW/INTERNET, 13–15 November 2002, pp. 355–362. Lisbon, Portugal (2002)

42. Önduygu, D.C.: Graphagos: evolutionary algorithm as a model for the creative process and as a tool to create graphic design products. Master's thesis, Sabancı University (2010)

43. Plutchik, R.: A general psychoevolutionary theory of emotion. In: Plutchik, R., Kellerman, H. (eds.) Theories of Emotion, chap. 1, pp. 3–33. Academic Press, Cambridge (1980)

44. Purvis, L., Harrington, S., O'Sullivan, B., Freuder, E.C.: Creating personalized documents: an optimization approach. In: Proceedings of the 2003 ACM Symposium on Document Engineering, 29 September–2 October 2003, pp. 68–77. ACM, San Jose (2003)

45. Quiroz, J.C., Banerjee, A., Louis, S.J., Dascalu, S.M.: Document design with interactive evolution, chap. 29. In: Damiani, E., Jeong, J., Howlett, R.J., Jain, L.C. (eds.) New Directions in Intelligent Interactive Multimedia Systems and Services. Studies in Computational Intelligence, vol. 226, pp. 309–319. Springer, Heidelberg (2009). https://doi.org/10.1007/978-3-642-02937-0_28

46. Rebelo, S., Bicker, J., Machado, P.: Evolutionary experiments in typesetting of letterpress-inspired posters. In: Cardoso, F.A., Machado, P., Veale, T., Cunha, J.M. (eds.) Proceedings of the Eleventh International Conference on Computational Creativity, Coimbra, Portugal, 7–11 September 2020, pp. 110–114 (2020)

47. Rebelo, S., Fonseca, C.M., Bicker, J., Machado, P.: Evolutionary experiments in the development of typographical posters. In: Rangel, A., Ribas, L., Verdicchio, M., Carvalhais, M. (eds.) 6th Conference on Computation, Communication, Aesthetics & X (xCoAx 2018), pp. 65–75. Universidade do Porto, Madrid (2018)

48. Rebelo, S., Pires, C., Martins, P., Bicker, J., Machado, P.: Designing posters towards a seamless integration in urban surroundings: a computational approach. In: ARTECH 2019: Proceedings of the Ninth International Conference on Digital and Interactive Arts, Article 54. ACM, Braga (2019)

49. Reynar, J.C., Ratnaparkhi, A.: A maximum entropy approach to identifying sentence boundaries. In: Proceedings of the Fifth Conference on Applied Natural Language Processing, March 1997, pp. 16–19. ACL, Washington, DC (1997)

50. Richardson, A.: Data-Driven Graphic Design: Creative Coding for Visual Communication. Bloomsbury Publishing, London (2016)

51. Rodenbröker, T.: Programming posters (2018). https://timrodenbroeker.de/projects/programming-posters/

52. Srinivas, N., Deb, K.: Muiltiobjective optimization using nondominated sorting in genetic algorithms. Evol. Comput. 2(3), 221–248 (1994)

53. Stephan, B., Haag, C.: Bash scripts for generative posters. Libre Graph. Mag. 3(1), 30–34 (2011)

54. Syswerda, G.: Uniform crossover in genetic algorithms. In: Proceedings of the Third International Conference on Genetic Algorithms, June 1989, pp. 2–9. Morgan Kaufmann Publishers Inc., Fairfax (1989)

55. Zhang, Y., Hu, K., Ren, P., Yang, C., Xu, W., Hua, X.S.: Layout style modeling for automating banner design. In: Proceedings of the on Thematic Workshops of ACM Multimedia 2017, October 2017, pp. 451–459. ACM, Mountain View (2017)

56. Zheng, X., Qiao, X., Cao, Y., Lau, R.W.H.: Content-aware generative modeling of graphic design layouts. ACM Trans. Graph. 38(4), Article 133 (2019)

Intelligence and Creativity in
Healthcare, Wellbeing and Aging

Data City: Leveraging Data Embodiment Towards Building the Sense of Data Ownership

Allen Xie, Jeffrey C. F. Ho, and Stephen Jia Wang[✉]

School of Design, The Hong Kong Polytechnic University, Hung Hom, Kowloon, Hong Kong
allen.xie@connect.polyu.hk, stephen.j.wang@polyu.edu.hk

Abstract. Human-Data Interaction (HDI) is an emerging area of research as personal data are being increasingly collected, analyzed and traded. We conducted a small-scale qualitative research to explore people's perception, behaviour and attitude towards data via survey, interview and workshop. The results revealed that the vagueness of data ownership is the main concern. To form a better understanding, also help the novice users to have an enhanced awareness on their data privacy, together with the findings, we leverage embodied interaction aiming at enhancing the sense of data ownership through providing augmented physical representations. Following this approach, we propose an Augmented Reality installation 'DataCity' as a sample application, that connects the user's smartphone application data to physical objects. Through physical manipulation and augmented reality control, our design provides evidence on how to clear the boundaries of users' personal data, building their senses of ownership and eventually develop a better privacy literacy.

Keywords: Data embodiment · Data ownership · Human-Data Interaction

1 Introduction

We are living in an era in which ubiquitous computing via mobile and IoT device is emerging, and normal and novice users are yet to have a sufficient understanding of the digital information generated by them [12].

With the development of Big Data technology, personal data, as one of the richest class of data [20], becomes extremely valuable, in particular in targeted advertising, because of its capability in performing users' behavior profiling [22]. Yet from the users' point of view, such information may be considered private and sensitive [9]. Over the years, researchers, regulatory bodies and activists have articulated the power imbalance in personal data between individuals and third-party entities that collect, analyze and distribute their data [5, 22, 27]. Regular users must gain awareness for their data and develop better privacy literacy [23].

However, according to recent studies, users normally have a complex attitude towards the privacy issues of their data, and sometimes contradictory [24]. When asked explicitly about their attitudes on privacy, users generally show a high awareness towards their data

A. Brooks et al. (Eds.): ArtsIT 2020, LNICST 367, pp. 365–378, 2021.
https://doi.org/10.1007/978-3-030-73426-8_22

privacy, but it does not reflect on their daily behavior [2]. In the meantime, while there are people who are enthusiastic to keep track on their data (e.g. the Quantified Self movement [3]), the rest of them may not always feel interested or motivated to engage with their data [4]. Such complexity makes it challenging to address the issue of personal data awareness.

Under this context, we proposed a novel method to tackle the data privacy dilemma, to bridge users' concern and distrust in their interaction with data and to increase their awareness and understanding of personal data, that is, leveraging embodiment to build the sense of data ownership.

As a constantly discussed topic, different attempts from different aspects have been made to enhance people's understanding and awareness of data privacy. However, legal systems are not sufficiently agile to respond to the situation, and self-initiated proposals have been ineffective in stopping the practice of data tracking and analysis from users [5]. In the design field, current studies have been focusing on personal data management and curation [13, 20, 21], which are solely based on screen-based devices and virtual environment. There is little research that focuses on using physical objects and tangible interaction to increase the understanding and awareness for data, while some prior study has found out that the physicalization of data can be very effective in helping people reflect on their data [18] and increase their engagement with the data [16].

Therefore, we explore how people perceive and interact with data, as well as the concerns and find challenges [25], and physicalize such understandings and interactions into an interactive installation [11].

We propose a conceptual installation 'DataCity', which presents personal data embodiments using the metaphor of building one's own city to leverage the physicality. We have been focusing on the following criteria:

1. Increase the sense of owning one's own data through data physicalization
2. Facilitate users to understand better about their personal data through a boundary
3. Provide playful and reminding signal to foster the engagement with data

The following sections describe the details of this paper: Sect. 2 presents the related work of this study. Section 3 describes the research methodology as well as the key insights, explains the design and system structure, and demonstrates the user testing results. Section 4 illustrates four different interaction modes. Section 5 and 6 give a detailed discussion and conclusion about the project concerning possible future work.

2 Related Work

The trend of collecting and analyzing digital information has brought to a new discussion of the interaction between human and data. Human-Data Interaction (HDI) aims at investigating how people interact with data as an analogy with how Human-Computer Interaction investigates the relationship between people and computers [6]. Recently, to address the challenges in HDI, Mortier et al. [12] have proposed three key aspects for meaningful interaction with data – legibility, agency and negotiability. Legibility concerns making data and analytics algorithms both transparent and comprehensible to the people who care about their own data and how they are being processed. Agency concerns giving people the capacity to act within these data systems, to opt-in or to opt-out, to control, inform and correct data and inferences, and so on. Negotiability concerns the many dynamic relationships that arise around data and data processing.

To help people explore, understand and manage digital information, embodied interaction is emerging as a research topic. In this aspect, different applied scenarios are discussed, such as using embodied interaction for exploring and learning datasets at a museum [1] or for urban planning with augmented reality [15]. The Shape-Changing Interfaces [14], as a proof-of-concept prototype, also provides a physical experience to feel and manipulate data. These studies have proven the effectiveness of exploring and understanding data with immersive and physical experience. However, most of the existing studies focused on understanding open or public data. There is still limited study on designing embodied interaction for personal data, with particular concerns on privacy awareness.

Data embodiment is tightly related to data physicalization, which is defined as using a physical artifact to encode and represent data. Although data physicalization is closely connected to data visualization and tangible user interfaces, it focuses on data analysis in a physical form [8]. Prior studies have investigated the effect on how data physicalization can help people reflect on data by building personalized artifacts [18]. Moreover, there are a lot of different projects that turn data into physical artifacts, such as the use of LEGO bricks, 3D printed data sculpture or even handicrafts. Such physicalization can address on the non-visual senses and make data analysis more accessible [8].

Besides making data accessible, ensuring data, especially personal data, safe and private is another well-discussed topic in HDI. Begin with the privacy by design framework, most of the studies in data protection focus on the system structure or the data life cycle framework. In system design, DataBox [13] by Haddadi et al. and Virtual Walls [10] by Kapadia et al. both leveraged the metaphor of containment, which can be considered as the common physical encapsulation of data. Meanwhile, Hornung et al. [6] proposed a semiotic framework for data life cycle, and Romansky [17] provided a similar framework for data life cycle in personal data protection.

Previous studies of personal data management have been focusing on virtual and screen-based interaction. Vitale et al. designed Data Dashboard [21] for personal data curation which focused on centralization and customization. My Data Store [20] by Vescovi et al. is another example that enables individuals to gain awareness and control on personal data. These applications provided meaningful ways to categorize and manage personal data, but the virtual representation is yet to have a sufficient impact on gaining awareness.

3 Design Rationale

In order to design a meaningful interaction for personal data, a qualitative research approach was applied, including an online survey, a semi-structured interview and a participatory workshop. The idea of data ownership was raised in the survey and interview. It was also consolidated during the workshop and refined after the user testing. Eventually, the findings led to the design of DataCity.

3.1 Survey and Interview

We conducted an online survey ($N = 93$) and a number of semi-structured interviews with individuals ($N = 10$) who is concerned with their own data. The survey and interview aimed at investigating the general understanding of people's interaction with personal data.

The survey included 14 questions about an individual's daily habit of using digital devices and their attitude towards personal data collection, while the interviews were more detailed with follow-up questions. Each interview took roughly 45 min and was audio-recorded. The interview participants were from different professional backgrounds with an average age of 28 years old.

The findings from the survey and the interview revealed people's perception, behaviour and attitude towards personal data. To be more specific, we conclude that instead of data privacy awareness, the most significant issue in people's daily interaction with data is the lack of the sense of ownership, which is mainly caused by following factors:

- **The difficulty in understanding data or the process behind it.** Data and its backend process (life cycle) are always abstract and opaque. They require a high level of expertise to understand.
- **The passiveness in engaging with personal data.** Novice users tend to act passively in the interaction with data, which on the one hand, is because of their limited capability to manage and control data, and on the other hand, since the operations given by third-party service providers is also limited.
- **The lack of meaningful insights provided by the system.** Although a huge amount of data about the user is generated, there is no sufficient way for users to gain insight from the data, which also makes users lose the sense of owning it.

3.2 Participatory Workshop

Following the survey and interview, a participatory workshop, also based on the concept of data ownership, was conducted. The workshop aimed at finding the suitable physical form of data that can address the awareness of ownership. Four participants were recruited to the workshop, among whom there are three designers and one engineer. During the workshop, participants were asked to create a physical representation of their personal data out of clay and other materials that they prefer. A discussion on the interaction with the physical object as well as the way to protect it was followed. Eventually, the participants were divided into two groups and groups designed two unique artefacts separately (Fig. 1).

Figure 1 left shows a design of a data bookshelf, which contains different partitions used for a different purpose, like displaying memorable personal images or containing locked and hidden secret information. Figure 1 right shows a data eraser and a data message-in-a-bottle, both of which are used to delete the unwanted or secret data, such as browser history.

The workshop has provided useful insights into building a sense of data ownership. First, the physical boundary and relationship of containment help users to gain the understanding and sense of control of their own data. Second, the sections which serve different functions also add to the sense of data ownership. Third, allowing physical manipulation such as re-arranging, keeping and discarding data can also contribute to the sense of ownership.

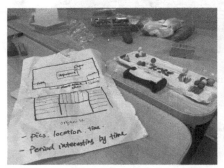

Fig. 1. The artifacts on data ownership workshop

3.3   Design of DataCity

Based on the findings above, we create an embodied interaction design, DataCity. DataCity (see Fig. 2) is an integrated system including a physical installation and a mobile application. The application is an entry point of the system which is connected to other mobile applications on the user's phone, and the installation is where the user performs interaction with data (see Fig. 3). The concept of DataCity is to use city building as an approach to physicalize user's personal data on their mobile devices, encourage the user to watch over and perform physical manipulation to the city she builds, and eventually gain the sense of data ownership. The interaction can be divided into two parts, one is the digital interaction via augmented reality on the mobile application, the other is the physical interaction via tangible manipulation.

The features of DataCity are designed according to the design insights obtained from the qualitative user research, which are:

– Provide physical representation using a series of metaphors for users to gain a better understanding of their data

- Encourage users to explore their data by themselves by building their own cities in a gradual process, which helps to build the proactiveness in the interaction with data
- Provide useful insights (e.g. notifying data breach) in a novel and interactive way.

Fig. 2. The mobile application and the installation of DataCity

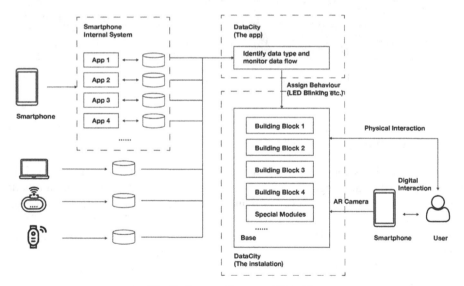

Fig. 3. System diagram of DataCity

To increase the user's sense of data ownership, designing an intuitive and natural interaction is crucial. A city building metaphor is chosen because it is a common form in business simulation games, and some mobile applications use city building to perform certain kinds of behaviour change such as spending management. The proper linkage between the city blocks and the data it represents has to be intuitive. At first, we have different ideas of linking the mobile personal data to the buildings. After user testing,

Table 1. Components and their representations in DataCity.

Component	Physical Object	Virtual Representation / Usage
DataBlock		The eight different types of personal data on mobile apps The type is represented by LED
DataBuilding		The mobile applications on the user's smartphone It consists of multiple DataBlocks which depend on the application
Fences		Sensitive data protection It is a special module that is used to protect certain the sensitive data of certain DataBuilding
Incinerator		Data deleting It is a special module that is used to delete the data contained within a certain DataBlock
Fountain		Data displaying It is a special module that is used to display the data the user wants to showcase (such as memorable images) which would be seen in the AR view
Home		Data backup It is a special module that is used to copy or move the target data to an external storage

one of the ideas is chosen and further developed, which is shown in Table 1. This representation has a clear boundary and a containment relationship.

The eight types of data are defined as follows: media (photo, video, audio etc.), text (message, email, SNS post etc.), location (GPS location), health (Biometrics, health tracking data etc.), finance (banking information, credit cards etc.), social (contact, connections), log and cache (browser history, use logs), account (profile, demographics etc.). It is worth mentioning that there are a lot of different categorizations regarding personal data, for example, Haddadi et al. [5] analyzed one of the researchers entire digital footprint, and concluded with 5 data types: communication (email, instant messaging etc.), financial (bank statement, credit card statement etc.), family (photographs, trips, etc.), individual (personal location traces, personal calendar etc.) and online social networks (Twitter, Facebook, Google+ etc.). However, this categorization is relatively personal. Other categorizations might focus on the semiotic meaning of personal data [19] or the sensitivity of data [7], which is too concise for personal use. Therefore, we decide to use our own categorization which mainly comes from one of the questions from the user research that asked about *"what kinds of data do you check and track in your daily life"*.

3.4 User Testing

To ensure the design concept matches the criteria of our design goal, we conducted two rounds of user testing. The first round focused on the form of the linkage be-tween mobile the personal data and the DataBlocks and was tested before finalizing the design of DataCity, while the second round was conducted with the AR application and mainly focused on testing the interactivity of the overall system.

During the first-round testing, different ideas of linking the data and the city blocks were considered: a) each block represents one mobile app and the colour of LED shows the types of data access in real-time; b) each block shape represents one type of applications, the LED shows the data access and each building represents one mobile app; c) each block shape represents one type of data, the colour of LED shows the types of the mobile applications and each building represents a cluster of the same type of data access in real-time. We invited test users to build a DataCity using these three forms and asked them to rate the intuitiveness, effectiveness and clarity of the ideas and to leave comments. According to the feedbacks, keeping each building as one shape and using the number of blocks to indicate the level of data access is more user friendly and has a clear containing hierarchy and boundary. Eventually, we have chosen b) as our design.

In the second-round testing, we asked participants to build the blocks together with the DataCity mobile application using the think-aloud protocol. As they performed the tasks, we collected useful insights that helped refine the design. First, according to the participants, more clear instructions and call-to-actions of the flow is preferred. Second, as they enjoyed the process of building the city, customization and more interactivity on the screen is desired. Moreover, they also indicated small details of improvement such as the unclear visual effect or the position of the LEDs. We collected these results and finalized the overall design and interactivity of DataCity.

The ways of how to interact with DataCity will be introduced in the next section.

4 Interactivity

With the mobile application and the installation set up, the user can start to interact with DataCity. Synthesizing the results from the user research, we define four key functionalities for meaningful interaction:

1. Giving Consent
2. Monitoring
3. Protecting
4. Managing

The functionalities above reflect users' needs for data ownership. Giving consent and monitoring are two main functions related to the users' concerns from the survey and interviews which aims at increasing the proactiveness and sense of control of the users' personal data. The remaining two functionalities, protecting and managing, are tightly connected to the workshop insights, allowing users to curate, save and discard their data in physical form.

Each of these functionalities requires the physical interaction with DataBlocks, and some of them require digital interaction via augmented reality on the user's phone. The detailed description is listed in Table 2.

Giving Consent. Every application on the smartphone would ask for permission to access data, and there are already a lot of discussions on how to design for consent. In DataCity, we propose an interaction that allows users to give consent to a certain type of data only by layering blocks and eventually form a DataBuilding. When a new app is installed, DataCity intercepts its request for data access, showing how many different types of data are being requested and asks the user to put on blocks to build the building. The building consists of at least a base which represents the user account, and other data if any, and shows the data type by blinking the LED inside. It adds friction in giving the consent which we believe is a way to increase the sense of data ownership.

Monitoring. Monitoring is another function that leverages the physical objects and their attributes. Once the DataCity is built, users can check the status of their city both physically or via smartphone AR view. Physically, the user would see the data flow indicated by the blinking LED. When the data traffic is huge, the brightness of the LED will be higher accordingly. When checking via smartphone AR view, the user can see three different special effects indicating three different situations. When there is ivy on the building, it means the data is not accessed for a while. When thick clouds are surrounding the building, it means the related app is constantly sending huge data to the cloud. If the user sees water leaking on the building, it means the data might be exposed to malicious third-parties and needed to be repaired (Fig. 4).

Fig. 4. Three special effects on the AR view

Protecting. Once the user spotted the abnormal behaviour of the data, she can protect the DataBuilding by putting a Fences module under it. The Fences module acts as a

Table 2. Key functionalities of DataCity.

	Description	Demonstration
1	**Giving Consent** User is asked to build a new building when a new application is installed. DataCity shows the request for data access from the application, and the user gives consent by putting blocks on the building.	
2	**Monitoring** User uses the AR camera to scan DataCity, spot the animated special effects shown on the AR view and check the abnormal data behaviours from each application.	
3	**Protecting** User puts the Fences module under the building she wants to protect and set the sensitivity setting. The sensitive data that are uploading would be blocked and waiting for approval.	
4	**Managing** User uses three modules to perform delete, display(decorate) and backup using physical manipulation.	

filter. It blocks the data type which is set sensitive by the user from uploading and waits for the user to check and approve. For example, the user sets location data as sensitive data, and the protected app is a social media platform. Once the user posts something accidentally with the location information, the post would be blocked and wait for the user to confirm to send. Meanwhile, the red LED on the Fences would blink to warn the user.

Managing. Besides the functionalities above, the user can manage their data use three special modules. The incinerator is a metaphor of the city's refuse destructor plant. The user can throw a DataBlock inside, and the sensor detects the object and send a confirmation message on the phone, the user confirms the deleting process, and the data within the DataBlock will be deleted. The Fountain is a metaphor of the city square, which is a place for the user to decorate and display the information they want to show on AR view. For example, a memorable photo can be shown, and the user can take a screenshot or video of their own city and share to others. The Home module is similar to the incinerator; however, it is mainly used to store or backup the data. User can put the DataBlock inside the Home module, and similarly, a notification will be sent to the user's phone, and the user confirms to copy, move or cancel. After that, the data will be stored in an external hard drive.

5   Discussion

We propose a novel embodied interaction design to increase novice users' sense of data ownership, and we are envisioning that this can be the first step to a better understanding of personal data. We hope that, eventually, it will enhance people's privacy literacy and promote a better human-data interaction. Despite the fact that this prototype is unique and interesting, there is still a lot of space for discussion and improvement.

5.1   The Effectiveness of the Prototype

DataCiy is a sample application to demonstrate our idea of building users' sense of data ownership, and the prototype was tested with participants during user testing. Through the think-aloud protocol and observation, we found that users need better guidance besides the tutorial on the mobile screen, which indicates the improvements of design of the blocks. In addition to this, some of the participants also reported that they have an unclear understanding of some of the visual metaphors such as the cloud effect on the AR view. It implies that these metaphors should be more carefully defined as people have different perceptions towards it. Apart from these, participants enjoyed playing with the prototype and have no doubts about its functionalities, including building, monitoring and performing tasks using the special blocks. The participants all reported the increase in the interests of engaging with their personal data, as well as the sense of owning them, which helped prove the initial effectiveness of the prototype. However, further observations and discussion should be included and the trust and acceptance of DataCity should be tested after the prototype is able to connect to the data in a real scenario.

5.2 The Pros and Cons of Tangible User Interface

Although studies have proven that a physical manifestation of data is very powerful in helping people understand the complexity of it, there is still limitations of the tangible user interface (TUI). First of all, it is hard to install, store or display physical installations, especially within the home context. Though assembling and disassembling blocks is effectively effective to foster users' engagement, but it could also be burdensome. DataCity could further be developed into a demonstrative installation in public spaces such as museums, as to increase the awareness of the public. Another possible form of development of DataCity is a home-use lego-like toolkit that is easier to assemble or disassemble. Second, there is a significant limitation for physical objects. Unlike Graphical User Interface (GUI), objects with a tangible interface cannot change its shape or colour etc. It could be useful to represent more diverse information of the data. In DataCity, we used LED lights to represent the data type. To leverage more physical attributes, we may need to rely on new technologies such as shape-changing interfaces. In order to address these issues, a lighter and refined design of the tangible component should be considered as a further development direction.

5.3 The Need for Long-Term Development

From survey and interviews, participants have expressed the need to understand data better and to know how to protect their data. We understand that as a part of the privacy literacy, this needs long-term development and improvement. Although during user testing, DataCity has been reported to be fun to play with, however, we could not test the long-term effect of it. In fact, further investigation is needed to explore whether the design can nurture people's understanding and sense of control of their personal data within a longer period of time, and incentives should be considered to maintain the user engagement.

5.4 Further Improvement of Data Aggregation and Categorization

One of the main efforts in developing the concept of DataCity is about how to convert personal data on a smartphone into tangible objects. Although the smartphone is the biggest source of personal data, with the development of Internet of Things and various kinds of wearables devices, data from other sources will become more and more important in the future. Including data from different personal devices, perform proper categorization of them has become another direction for further development. As there is still limited research in the aggregation and categorization in personal data from different sources, it relies on the development of edge computing to perform the aggregation and categorization. Therefore, it is a future challenge that needs researchers from different backgrounds to tackle.

6 Conclusion

To conclude, we build a physical embodied interaction to help people understand data and have a better sense of control of it. We believe it would contribute to building a sense of data ownership and develop people's privacy literacy. The data-driven paradigm has just begun, and there is still a lot of space for design to either improve the awareness or to improve the human-data interaction. All in all, we believe that the most important principle in developing future digital products and applications is to put the user in the centre of the interaction among all the devices. DataCity is an attempt to practice this principle, and more interactive experience is needed to push this concept further and further.

Acknowledgements. The authors would like to acknowledge and thanks to the funding support from Project P0032185, the Hong Kong Polytechnic University. We would also like to thank the reviewers for their relevant and detailed feedback on the initial draft of this paper.

References

1. Cafaro, F., et al.: Framed guessability: using embodied allegories to increase user agreement on gesture sets. In: Proceedings of the 8th International Conference on Tangible, Embedded and Embodied Interaction - TEI 2014, Munich, Germany, pp. 197–204. ACM Press (2013). https://doi.org/10.1145/2540930.2540944
2. Callanan, C., et al.: User awareness and tolerance of privacy abuse on mobile Internet: an exploratory study. Telemat. Inform. **33**(1), 109–128 (2016). https://doi.org/10.1016/j.tele.2015.04.009
3. Choe, E.K., et al.: Understanding quantified-selfers' practices in collecting and exploring personal data. In: Proceedings of the 32nd Annual ACM Conference on Human Factors in Computing Systems - CHI 2014, Toronto, Ontario, Canada, pp. 1143–1152. ACM Press (2014). https://doi.org/10.1145/2556288.2557372
4. Gulotta, R., et al.: Fostering engagement with personal informatics systems. In: Proceedings of the 2016 ACM Conference on Designing Interactive Systems - DIS 2016, Brisbane, QLD, Australia, pp. 286–300. ACM Press (2016). https://doi.org/10.1145/2901790.2901803
5. Haddadi, H., et al.: Personal Data: Thinking Inside the Box. arXiv:1501.04737 [cs]. (2015)
6. Hornung, H., Pereira, R., Baranauskas, M.C.C., Liu, K.: Challenges for human-data interaction – a semiotic perspective. In: Kurosu, M. (ed.) HCI 2015. LNCS, vol. 9169, pp. 37–48. Springer, Cham (2015). https://doi.org/10.1007/978-3-319-20901-2_4
7. Islam, M.B.: Privacy by Design for Social Networks, 377 (2014)
8. Jansen, Y., et al.: Opportunities and challenges for data physicalization. In: Proceedings of the 33rd Annual ACM Conference on Human Factors in Computing Systems - CHI 2015, Seoul, Republic of Korea, pp. 3227–3236. ACM Press (2015). https://doi.org/10.1145/2702123.2702180
9. Kamleitner, B., et al.: Information bazaar: a contextual evaluation. In: Proceedings of the 5th ACM Workshop on HotPlanet - HotPlanet 2013, Hong Kong, China, p. 57. ACM Press (2013). https://doi.org/10.1145/2491159.2491161
10. Kapadia, A., Henderson, T., Fielding, J.J., Kotz, D.: Virtual walls: protecting digital privacy in pervasive environments. In: LaMarca, A., Langheinrich, M., Truong, K.N. (eds.) Pervasive 2007. LNCS, vol. 4480, pp. 162–179. Springer, Heidelberg (2007). https://doi.org/10.1007/978-3-540-72037-9_10
11. Lee, C.H., et al.: Synaesthetic-translation tool: synaesthesia as an interactive material for ideation. In: Extended Abstracts of the 2019 CHI Conference on Human Factors in Computing Systems, pp. 1–6 (2019)

12. Mortier, R., et al.: Human-Data Interaction: The Human Face of the Data-Driven Society. SSRN Journal (2014). https://doi.org/10.2139/ssrn.2508051
13. Mortier, R., et al.: Personal data management with the databox: what's inside the box? In: Proceedings of the 2016 ACM Workshop on Cloud-Assisted Networking - CAN 2016, Irvine, California, USA, pp. 49–54. ACM Press (2016). https://doi.org/10.1145/3010079.3010082
14. Nakagaki, K., et al.: Materiable: rendering dynamic material properties in response to direct physical touch with shape changing interfaces. In: Proceedings of the 2016 CHI Conference on Human Factors in Computing Systems, San Jose, California, USA, pp. 2764–2772. ACM (2016). https://doi.org/10.1145/2858036.2858104
15. Narazani, M., et al.: Extending AR interaction through 3D printed tangible interfaces in an urban planning context. In: The Adjunct Publication of the 32nd Annual ACM Symposium on User Interface Software and Technology, New Orleans, LA, USA, pp. 116–118. ACM (2019). https://doi.org/10.1145/3332167.3356891
16. Rapp, A., Cena, F.: Personal informatics for everyday life: how users without prior self-tracking experience engage with personal data. Int. J. Hum. Comput. Stud. **94**, 1–7 (2016). https://doi.org/10.1016/j.ijhcs.2016.05.006
17. Romansky, R.: Social Media and Personal Data Protection 17 (2014)
18. Thudt, A., et al.: Self-reflection and personal physicalization construction. In: Proceedings of the 2018 CHI Conference on Human Factors in Computing Systems - CHI 2018, Montreal, QC, Canada, p. 13. ACM Press (2018). https://doi.org/10.1145/3173574.3173728
19. Veghes, C., et al.: Privacy literacy: what is and how it can be measured?. JASO **14**(2), 704–711 (2012). https://doi.org/10.29302/oeconomica.2012.14.2.36
20. Vescovi, M., et al.: My data store: toward user awareness and control on personal data. In: Proceedings of the 2014 ACM International Joint Conference on Pervasive and Ubiquitous Computing Adjunct Publication - UbiComp 2014 Adjunct, Seattle, Washington, pp. 179–182. ACM Press (2014). https://doi.org/10.1145/2638728.2638745
21. Vitale, F., et al.: Data dashboard: exploring centralization and customization in personal data curation. In: Proceedings of the 2020 ACM Designing Interactive Systems Conference, Eindhoven, Netherlands, pp. 311–326. ACM (2020). https://doi.org/10.1145/3357236.3395457
22. Wang, S.J.: Fields Interaction Design (FID): the answer to ubiquitous computing supported environments in the post-information age. Homa & Sekey Books (2013)
23. Wang, S., Moriarty, P.: Big data for a future world. In: Wang, S., Moriarty, P. (eds.) Big Data for Urban Sustainability, pp. 141–155. Springer, Cham (2018). https://doi.org/10.1007/978-3-319-73610-5_8
24. Wang, S.J., Moriarty, P.: Big Data for Urban Sustainability. Springer, Heidelberg (2018). https://doi.org/10.1007/978-3-319-73610-5
25. Zuboff, S.: Big other: surveillance capitalism and the prospects of an information civilization. J. Inf. Technol. **30**(1), 75–89 (2015). https://doi.org/10.1057/jit.2015.5

Bio-related Design Genres: A Survey on Familiarity and Potential Applications

Nurul 'Ayn Ahmad Sayuti[1,2]([✉]), Bjorn Sommer[1], and Saeema Ahmed-Kristensen[3]

[1] School of Design, Royal College of Art, London, UK
ayn.sayuti@network.rca.ac.uk
[2] Faculty of Art and Design, Universiti Teknologi MARA, Shah Alam, Malaysia
[3] University of Exeter, London, UK

Abstract. Biophilia, biophilic design, bio-inspired and bio-design are design genres that adopted nature and biological elements as part of design processes. With the spread use of natural elements in design nowadays, from the analogical approach to the application of the biological materials in design brought up a different connotation towards the diverse use of nature in everyday life. This paper discusses the background knowledge of Biophilia, biophilic design, bio-inspired and bio-design and the application of biological materials in urban environments, especially for home. As part of a larger project on the application of biological materials in everyday products, this study investigates the emotional design and perception, while identifying the purposes of biological materials which incorporated into designs or systems. Data from 158 potential consumers were collected in an online survey specifically designed for this study, differentiating between design and non-design participants. Interesting findings are that more than 65% of non-design respondents are not aware of the terms biophilia and biophilic design, but they are familiar with the terms *bio-inspired* and *bio-design*. On the other hand, the potential consumers which are from non-design and design background as well agreed that having biological materials indoors, can a) help to release stress, b) create awareness of nature and ecological impact, c) can foster a sense of care, and d) can be educational.

Keywords: Biophilia · Biophilic design · Bio-inspired · Bio-design

1 Introduction

1.1 The Background of Biophilia, Biophilic Design, Bio-inspired and Bio-design

Referring to the Dictionary of Environment and Ecology (Colin 2004), the prefix "bio" means "referring to living organisms" and the suffix "philia" means "attraction towards or liking for something". As such, biophilia describes the innate feeling of human beings to be associated with nature and living organisms. Introduced by Fromm in 1973, and mentioned by Eckardt (1996), biophilia proposes benefits to human vitality and well-being as nature offers a conducive environment for human development and growth.

A. Brooks et al. (Eds.): ArtsIT 2020, LNICST 367, pp. 379–393, 2021.
https://doi.org/10.1007/978-3-030-73426-8_23

Moreover, Wilson (1984, page 1) developed the biophilia theory and defined it as "the innate tendency to focus on life and lifelike processes." Arvay (2018) supports Wilson by suggesting the effect of biophilia through the exploration and reconnection of scientific and spiritual process with nature in the wilderness and from the comfort of home.

Biophilia theory has evolved into practical applications of biophilic design, by Kellert et al. in 2008. Kellert et al. (2008, page 3) defined biophilic design as:

"The deliberate attempt to translate an understanding of the inherent human affinity to affiliate with natural systems and processes – known as biophilia, into the design of the built environment."

Biophilic design are divided into six design elements based on Kellert et al. (2008, page 7–15), which are (1) *Environmental features* which involve colour, water, air, sunlight, plants, animals, natural materials, views and vistas, facade greening, geology and landscape, habitats and ecosystems and fire in nature, (2) *Natural shapes and forms in man-made designs* that include the natural traits, motifs, forms or structures, (3) *Natural patterns and processes* which comprise the integration of natural elements and cycles that are compatible to be adapted to the built environment, (4) *Light and space*, involving the function of lights and spaces outdoors and indoors of built environments, (5) *Place-based relationship*, as the merging of ecology into culture, and finally (6) *Evolved human-nature relationships*, where the affiliation between human beings and nature is elaborated and the way nature has influenced human beings.

Studies which addressed the benefits of natural elements to human nearby or indoors include Mehrabian and Russell (1974), Ulrich (1981), Balling and Falk (1982), Kaplan (1995), Frumkin (2001), Huelat et al. (2008), Hoffman et al. (2009), Grinde and Patil (2009), O'haire (2010), Simaika and Samways (2010), Howell et al. (2011), Bartczak et. al. (2013), Johnson (2014), as well as Terrapin Bright Green (2012 and 2014). Recent studies on biophilic designs have been published by Sayuti et al. (2015 and 2018), Gunawardena and Steemers (2018), Rosenbaum et al. (2018), Yin et al. (2018), Parsaee et al. (2019), among others. These studies were conducted in the disciplines of the built environment, health, employees' productivity, and employee well-being among others.

Bio-inspired design approaches adapt or mimic the natural elements and incorporate them into designs or technologies to solve problems (Thorpe 2007; Montana-Hoyos 2010; Gruber et al. 2011). Bio-inspired design was proposed by Massimo et al. (2017) as: (1) Nature as inspiration where designs are inspired by a systematic ecological or natural process, and (2) Nature as a design constraint; as nature is very resourceful, many aspects can be learned in terms of new designs and applications.

Myers (2018) defined bio-design as the incorporation of living biological materials or ecosystems that enable the systems designed to be more renewable and sustainable. The use of living biological elements are no longer restricted to the scientific field, but it has gone beyond engineering and design with the incorporation of these living materials into structures, objects and processes (Myers 2018). Myers (2018) also provided examples of developed bio-design products, such as *Local River* by Matthieu Lehanneur, *Moss Table* by Alex Driver and Carlos Peralta, *Bacterioptica* by the MADLAB, among others. Moreover, Magnan (2018) emphasized on the bio-design thinking through the use on visual images towards the perception and cognitive psychology to elevate creative thinking abilities in order to help enhancing scientific and technical innovations. This literature review shows parallels to our study, as a series of biological images was used to gain feedback on emotional reactions, perceptions, and opinions on the use of biological materials in everyday designs.

This publication is part of a larger study on emotional design and perception (Sayuti and Ahmed-Kristensen 2020) which were executed to gain feedback on positive and negative emotions, purposes and the application of biological materials in everyday design, as well as the ownership of designs that incorporate biological materials.

1.2 Research Aim

This study investigates the emotional responses and perception of users with design and non-design background towards biological materials. The emotional responses and perceptions which affected the consumers when the materials are embedded in a product are also reviewed. Moreover, the sense of ownership towards this type of product is also analysed. In this way, this paper focuses on the clarification of user perception and knowledge regarding biophilia, biophilic design, bio-inspired and bio-design.

1.3 Structure

This paper is divided into four sections which are: 1) the introduction of the bio-related design theories involved in this study – this section, 2) the methodology used to perform the research followed by 3) the results and discussion of the selected section from the survey, and finally 4) conclusions and outlook.

2 Methodology

2.1 Research Project Structure

This research project was developed in eight stages, namely: 1) structuring the question-naire by identifying the online platform to be used and subdividing the questionnaire into six sections, 2) an initial compilation and classification of biological materials and related products, 3) setting up the online survey in correspondence to the chosen online survey platform, 4) testing the online survey, 5) obtaining ethical approval for the survey from the ethic commission of the Royal College of Art 6) dissemination of the online survey through social media and emails, 7) further development of the conceptual model based on results of a previous study (Sayuti et al. 2015 and 2018) and finally 8) analysis and discussion of the results gathered from the survey to understand the emotional responses and perception of potential consumers towards the biological elements.

This paper addresses theoretical aspects of this study in stage 8, as well as the questionnaire design as part of stage 3. It mainly focuses on those results of the overarching research project related to the theory, knowledge, and familiarity of bio-related design genres, as well as the application of biological materials in everyday designs and indoor spaces. As previously mentioned, the publication of this project will be divided into sections because it covers different topics and would be wise to discuss in sequences.

2.2 Questionnaire Design

A survey was designed to gather the respondent's perceptions and their emotions towards biological elements. As previously mentioned in the research aims, this survey gathered data on how potential consumers perceived biological elements in existing products, and also might experience it in future product designs. The study also surveys consumer's emotional response through the purpose of materials, functionality, sense of ownership and also the general knowledge on Biophilia, biophilic design, bio-inspired and bio-design.

The online questionnaire was designed using SurveyGizmo.com consisted of six main sections which are: A) respondent background, B) artificial and real biological materials, C) emotional design: biological materials, D) the purpose of biological elements, E) existing Biophilic Design/Bio-design by designer (product designs which currently available in the market or still in the conceptual development stage), and F) Biophilia, biophilic design, bio-inspired design and bio-design. The SurveyGizmo.com was chosen as the platform for this project because of its specific feature allowing to use images and custom designed buttons with the 'logic' connection of each question (question within question feature with ratings – which was used for section C, D and E to rate the emotions). The questionnaire was designed by providing illustrative images of biological materials in each section. A total of 234 responses were collected and analysed for this project. However, this paper only discusses Section F – Biophilia, biophilic design, bio-inspired design and bio-design – which was only completed by 158 participants, because they were allowed to withdraw at any point during the survey. This project received an ethical clearance from the ethical committee of the Royal College of Art before the online survey circulated for six months. Participants were recruited through social media and the survey was also disseminated through emails.

In Section F, 13 questions, as shown in Table 1, were asked to investigate the understanding of respondents' and their personal preferences with nature and biological materials/elements in terms of their interaction, awareness and behaviour. This section was designed using a 5-point Likert scale (Matell and Jacoby 1972; Albaum 1997; Johns 2010), Yes/No and finally an open-ended format. A mean score uses the scale of (-)2; Strongly Disagree, (-)1; Disagree, 0; Neither Agree or Disagree, 1; Agree and 2; Strongly Agree. The findings from this section were analysed using SPSS.

Table 1. The list of questions for Section F: biophilia, biophilic design, bio-inspired and bio-design

The list of questions	Format
Q1: I like to have biological elements (such as plants or animals) inside my house	Likert scale
Q2: It is important to have biological elements indoors?	Likert scale
Q3: Having natural and biological elements indoor can: A. release stress/calm	Likert scale
Q4: Having natural and biological elements indoor can: B. create awareness of nature and ecological impact	Likert scale
Q5: Having natural and biological elements indoor can: C. foster a sense of care (as living organisms need to be watered or fed)	Likert scale
Q6: Having natural and biological elements indoor can: D. be educational (especially for children)	Likert scale
Q7: Having natural and biological elements indoor can: E. be dangerous and inconvenient, as in the case of allergies	Likert scale
Q8: Having natural and biological elements indoor can: F. Not desirable, as they are usually messy, dirty, or require much of my time	Likert scale
Q9: Do you know what is Biophilia?	Yes/No format
Q10: Do you know what Biophilic design is?	Yes/No format
Q11: Do you know what Bio-inspired design is?	Yes/No format
Q12: Do you know what Bio-design is?	Yes/No format
Q13: Your opinion on biological materials embedded in product design	Open-ended format

3 Results and Discussion

3.1 Respondents Background

A total of 158 responses were received and analysed for this section. Background data were collected on gender (67.1% of female, 32.3% of male while 0.6% preferred not to answer), age (ranging from 18 to 25 with 12.1%, 26 to 30 with 12.1%, 31 to 40 with 42.0%, 41 to 50 with, 51 to 60 with 7.0%, and 61 or older with 1.9%. The respondents are from design and non-design background with 39.2% (62 respondents) and 60.8% (96 respondents) respectively. Their Cultural Background (88.6% Asian, 7.6% White, 1.7% Mixed, 1.3% Other, 1.9% preferred not to answer and 0% Black/African - American).

Almost all respondents have access to nature with 89.9%. Fifty-five-point-seven percent (55.7%) of the respondents prefer to experience nature outdoor while 42.4% preferred to experience both (outdoor and indoor) and only 1.9% preferred to experience it indoor. 24.1% of the respondents preferred to spend time in nature 2–3 times a week. Another 24.1% also preferred to spend once a month in nature, followed by 20.3% on daily basis, 19.6% experience nature once a week, only 10.1% spend twice a month in nature and 1.9% has no access to nature at all.

The results can be seen in Table 2 until Table 6 below. They are presented with the mean value and a nonparametric (Mann-Whitney U Test) analysis from the SPSS test. A mean score uses the scale of (-)2; Strongly Disagree, (-)1; Disagree, 0; Neither Agree or Disagree, 1; Agree and 2; Strongly Agree. The mean value and Mann-Whitney U Test was used to analysed Questions 1 to 8. The value used for Question 9 to 12 is 0 for No and 1 for Yes. Question 13 is using an open-ended format which allow the respondents to answer according to their opinion and it is recorded in a categorization table.

3.2 The Knowledge on Biophilia, Biophilic Design, Bio-inspired and Bio-design was Analysed

The Table 2 below shows the mean for responses regarding the level of agreement on having the natural and biological elements indoor. Responses close to a mean value more than 1.000 would indicate the level of agreement by respondents. Question 1 to 6 is designed to have an agreement response while 7 and 8 a disagreement response. Question 1 to 6 shown a level of agreement as the mean value is more than 1.000 respectively. However, Question 7 indicates of 0.500 to 1.000 value which is close to neither Agree nor Disagree. Also, the disagreement level tends towards the negative side for the opinion that having natural/biological elements indoors might be dangerous and inconvenient. The respondents disagree with Question 8 on having the natural biologicals indoor is dirty or time consuming with a -0.100 Mean value.

Table 2. The analysis of Mean value on the level of agreement on having the natural and biological elements indoor

Working Background		Q1	Q2	Q3	Q4	Q5	Q6	Q7	Q8
Non design	Mean	1.1915	1.2447	1.3750	1.2421	1.2000	1.2917	0.6526	−0.1667
	N	94	94	96	95	95	96	95	96
	Std. Dev	0.85856	0.71371	0.66886	0.72517	0.76631	0.76663	0.93135	1.13013
Design	Mean	1.0806	1.2787	1.5082	1.1639	1.1613	1.2258	0.3226	−0.1774
	N	62	61	61	61	62	62	62	62
	Std. Dev	1.10585	0.91526	0.53613	0.77847	0.70580	0.66331	0.86412	1.01665
Total	Mean	1.1474	1.2581	1.4268	1.2115	1.1847	1.2658	0.5223	−0.1709
	N	156	155	157	156	157	158	157	158
	Std. Dev	0.96255	0.79641	0.62228	0.74496	0.74094	0.72637	0.91698	1.08371

The Mann-Whitney test has verified the significance value Question 7 (Having natural and biological elements indoor can: E. be dangerous and inconvenient, as in the case of allergies) which has significantly different responses, i.e. Sig. Value (below 0.05) with 0.015Asymp. Sig. (2-tailed) value as highlighted in yellow in Table 3 below.

Table 3. The Non-Parametric test for the level of agreement on having the natural and biological elements indoor

	Q1	Q2	Q3	Q4	Q5	Q6	Q7	Q8
Mann-Whitney U	2908.00 0	2617.00 0	2655.50 0	2752.50 0	2807.00 0	2737.50 0	2309.50 0	2966.50 0
Wilcoxon W	4861.00 0	7082.00 0	7311.50 0	4643.50 0	4760.00 0	4690.50 0	4262.50 0	4919.50 0
Z	-0.024	-1.014	-1.120	-0.591	-0.561	-0.947	-2.444	-0.035
Asymp. Sig. (2-tailed)	0.981	0.311	0.263	0.555	0.575	0.344	0.015	0.972
a. Grouping Variable: Working Background								

Relating to the question in the respondent background section on nature experience, 42.4% of participants preferred to experience both – outdoor and indoor – and this information can be used to support these findings on how natural elements or biological materials affected them in daily life. Moreover, the connections of the Q1 to Q8 with the preferences of respondents regarding spending their time in nature, shows the ANNOVA test has a significant value for *Question 6. Having natural and biological elements indoor can: D. be educational (especially for children)* with 0.022 Sig. Value (below 0.05) in Table 4 below.

Table 4. The analysis of ANNOVA relating to experience nature (outdoor and indoor) with preferences of biological elements indoor.

ANOVA

		Sum of Squares	df	Mean square	F	Sig.
Q6. Having natural and biological elements indoor can: D. be educational (especially for children)	Between Groups	3.977	2	1.988	3.908	.022
	Within Groups	78.859	155	.509		
	Total	82.835	157			

The Mann-Whitney test was done for the preferences on nature experience (comparing outdoor and both – indoor and outdoor – experiences), to see the connection of having the biological elements indoors. The test has verified the significance value for *Question 2 (It is important to have biological elements indoors?), Question 3 (Having natural and biological elements indoor can: A. release stress/calm), Question 4 (Having natural and biological elements indoor can: B. create awareness of nature and ecological impact), Question 5 (Having natural and biological elements indoor can: C. foster a sense of care (as living organisms need to be watered or fed)), and Question 6 (Having natural and biological elements indoor can: D. be educational (especially for children))* which have significant responses, i.e. Sig. Value (below 0.05) with 0.041, 0,017, 0.005, 0.47 and 0.007, asymp. Sig. (2-tailed) value respectively, as highlighted in yellow in Table 5 below.

Table 5. The Non-Parametric test for the level of agreement on having the natural and biological elements indoor within the preferences on nature experience

	Q1	Q2	Q3	Q4	Q5	Q6	Q7	Q8
	Test Statistics[a]							
Mann-Whitney U	2763.500	2333.000	2342.000	2193.500	2423.500	2276.000	2846.500	2485.500
Wilcoxon W	6504.500	6161.000	6170.000	6021.500	6339.500	6192.000	6674.500	4763.500
Z	-.471	-2.042	-2.380	-2.797	-1.990	-2.703	-.265	-1.730
Asymp. Sig. (2-tailed)	.638	.041	.017	.005	.047	.007	.791	.084
a. Grouping Variable: Experience nature								

This part of the question is using a Yes/No format represented by the values 1/0. Table 6 below shows the mean values regarding the knowledge on biophilia, biophilic design, bio-inspired and bio-design. The overall responses for biophilia, biophilic design are ranging around a value of 0.4 which is closer to No, whereas the overall responses for Bio-inspired and Bio-design are around 0.7 which is closer to Yes. In this way, Question 9 and 8 indicate that half of the respondents may not have any knowledge on biophila and biophilic design.

Table 6. The analysis of Mean value on the knowledge on biophilia, biophilic design, bio-inspired and bio-design

Working background		Q9: Do you know what Biophilia is?	Q10: Do you know what Biophilic design is?	Q11: Do you know what Bio-inspired design is?	Q12: Do you know what Bio-design is?
Non design	Mean	0.3438	0.3333	0.6979	0.6170
	N	96	96	96	94
	Std. Dev	0.47745	0.47388	0.46157	0.48872
Design	Mean	0.5484	0.6129	0.7903	0.7581
	N	62	62	62	62
	Std. Dev	0.50172	0.49106	0.41040	0.43175
Total	Mean	0.4241	0.4430	0.7342	0.6731
	N	158	158	158	156
	Std. Dev	0.49577	0.49832	0.44318	0.47060

Table 7 below shows the descriptive and frequency analysis. The non-design group has negated the question on biophilia and biophilic design with a percentage of 65.5% and 66.7%. However, the design group seems to be familiar with the terms biophilia and biophilic design where 54.8% and 61.3% answered with Yes. Both groups confirmed the questions on bio-inspired design and bio-design with a minimal percentage of more than 61%.

Table 7. The descriptive and frequency analysis of the knowledge on biophilia, biophilic design, bio-inspired and bio-design

Working background			Q9: Do you know what Biophilia is?		Q10: Do you know what Biophilic design is?		Q11: Do you know what Bio-inspired design is?		Q12: Do you know what Bio-design is?	
			Freq	Valid %	Freq	Valid %	Freq	Valid %	Freq	Valid %
Non design	Valid	No	63	65.6	64	66.7	29	30.2	36	38.3
		Yes	33	34.4	32	33.3	67	69.8	58	61.7
		Total	96	100.0	96	100.0	96	100.0	94	100.0
Design	Valid	No	28	45.2	24	38.7	13	21.0	15	24.2
		Yes	34	54.8	38	61.3	49	79.0	47	75.8
		Total	62	100.0	62	100.0	62	100.0	62	100.0

The Mann-Whitney test has verified the significance value of the questions regarding knowledge on biophilia and biophilic design with a Sig. Value (below 0.05) with 0.011 and 0.001 Asymp. Sig. (2-tailed) value as highlighted in yellow in Table 8 below.

Table 8. The Non-Parametric test for the knowledge of on biophilia, biophilic design, bio-inspired and bio-design

	Q9: Do you know what Bi-ophilia is?	Q10: Do you know what Bi-ophilic design is?	Q11: Do you know what Bio-inspired design is?	Q12: Do you know what Bio-design is?
Mann-Whitney U	2367.000	2144.000	2701.000	2503.000
Wilcoxon W	7023.000	6800.000	7357.000	6968.000
Z	-2.533	-3.443	-1.280	-1.832
Asymp. Sig. (2-tailed)	0.011	0.001	0.201	0.067
a. Grouping Variable: Working Background				

Finally, Question 13 was designed in open-ended format, allowing respondents to share their opinion on biological materials embedded in product design. Listed in Table 9 are the corresponding answers. The comments received by the potential consumers were divided into four sections which are a) Positive responses, b) Neutral responses, c) Negative responses, and d) Other selected responses. Positive responses are relating to the potential consumer emotions concerning products embedding biological materials. Obviously, positive reactions are associated with terms such as 'love', 'good', 'really

Table 9. The opinion on biological materials embedded in product design

Q13: Your opinion on biological materials embedded in product design	
Positive responses – relating to emotions etc.	
• I love it	• Good
• Really good	• Excellent
• Good	• Fantastic!
• Good idea	• Good
• Ok	• Interesting
• Interesting	
Neutral responses	
• No preference	• Neutral but I won't buy it
Negative responses	
• No	
Other selected responses – relating to products etc.	
I think it's the future	
It is good for people nowadays living in an apartment or for indoor worker Good innovation where the natures and lifestyle meet	
Very artistic like Batik design	
I think using biological materials embedded in product design shows creativity, gives value-added to the product and as a symbol of therapy	
I'd only purchase them if it were valuable to the product	
I love the idea; nature knows a lot more than we do. But it makes me nervous	
I think the most important aspect is context of the product that we design for. If it suits the space aesthetic, yea why not. Like indoor garden office or restaurant. But product for common home seems impractical	
They are usually aesthetically appealing and have the ability to biodegrade without use of any external energy	
(I) hope that sharing your experience will help teachers and senior researchers disseminate useful concepts and real examples of biomimetic principles and tools for the development of new materials, new/improved design and fabrication strategies, and innovation methodologies	
A positive way to utilise and research on other purposes of the vast biological materials available in nature. A very interesting subject particularly involving the material properties in finished products	
Desirable as nowadays more and more people living in a small place and yet still need for biological material which are convenient and easy to be taken care of inside their house/room- to balance their emotion/stress & to relax	
It can be one way of creating awareness of nature conservation and its benefits to our living	
Needs to be more commonplace, without being intrusive	
I think it's important to explore the intersection of the natural world with the man-made world and how we can live a more environmentally conscious life to be more connected with ourselves and with nature. It is important for humans physical and mental health, as well as being important for the preservation of our natural world	
Sense of connection with the nature	
An excellent way to appreciate nature and reduce stress at home and the work place	
The incorporation of biological materials in product design is for environmentally-conscious people. It has appeal to educated people, but not for people who prioritize practicality over aesthetic functions	

good', 'ok,' 'excellent', 'fantastic!', and 'interesting'. The neutral responses consist of reactions such as 'No preference' and 'Neutral but I won't buy it'. Negative responses tend towards the 'No' answer.

Other selected responses are relating to products which are associated with positive opinions regarding products embedded with biological materials. Related opinions are for example, that those products are positive in terms of lifestyle, supporting creativity and sustainability, for therapeutic purposes and stress reduction, improving the atmosphere in an apartment (also in terms of limited space availability) or office environments. An interesting opinion is also that these approaches might be primary appealing to educated people, but not for people who prioritize practicality over aesthetic functions.

An appropriate conclusion of this section are the following two comments:

- '(I) hope that sharing your experience will help teachers and senior researchers disseminate useful concepts and real examples of biomimetic principles and tools for the development of new materials, new/improved design and fabrication strategies, and innovation methodologies.'
- 'A positive way to utilise and research on other purposes of the vast biological materials available in nature.'

The respondent feedback on the incorporation of biological materials with their knowledge on the bio-related design genres was identified and a cross-comparison analysis was performed. Table 10 below shows the analysis of the findings gathered based on the working background (design and non-design). The results have shown that some of the respondents know at least one bio-related design genre. For positive design responses, two respondents do not know any of the bio-related design genres. Others at least responded to one genre, for example, bio-inspired design. For neutral responses, one respondent knows all bio-related topics, and the other one does not know any of these terms. Respondents with negative response only knew about bio-inspired design. Other selected responses – relating to products etc. – also responded to at least one design genre. These findings show that – although some people are not familiar with bio-related design genres – they can relate to the advantages of incorporating biological elements into everyday products or merely integrating biological elements into indoor living spaces. These results also show a strong, affecting outcome in terms of those who were aware of biophilia and also the acceptance of having biological elements as standard part to be included in everyday living. It is also interesting to find that some respondents from design background do not have any knowledge on the bio-related design genre, and people from non-design are more aware of the "environmental" topic.

Table 10. The Cross-comparison analysis on the opinion on biological materials embedded in product design with the knowledge on bio-related design genres

Cross-comparison analysis between the opinion and knowledge on bio-related design genres					
Responses or opinion received	Q9	Q10	Q11	Q12	Working background
Positive responses – relating to emotions etc.					
I love it	Yes	Yes	Yes	Yes	Design
Really good	No	No	Yes	No	Non-design
Good	No	No	No	No	Design
Ok	Yes	Yes	Yes	Yes	Non-design
Good	No	No	Yes	Yes	Non-design
Excellent	Yes	Yes	Yes	Yes	Non-design
Fantastic!	No	No	Yes	Yes	Design
Good idea	No	No	Yes	Yes	Non-design
Good	No	No	No	No	Non-design
Interesting	Yes	Yes	Yes	Yes	Design
Interesting	No	No	No	No	Non-design
Neutral responses					
No preference	Yes	Yes	Yes	Yes	Non-design
Neutral but I won't buy it	No	No	No	No	Non-design
Negative responses					
No	No	No	Yes	No	Non-design
Other selected responses – relating to products etc.					
I think it's the future	No	Yes	Yes	Yes	Design
It is good for people nowadays living in an apartment or for indoor worker	Yes	No	Yes	Yes	Design
Good innovation where the natures and lifestyle meet	Yes	Yes	Yes	Yes	Non-design
Very artistic like Batik design	No	No	Yes	Yes	Non-design
I think using biological materials embedded in product design shows creativity, gives value-added to the product and as a symbol of therapy	Yes	Yes	Yes	Yes	Non-design
I'd only purchase them if it were valuable to the product	No	Yes	Yes	Yes	Design
I love the idea, nature knows a lot more than we do, but it makes me nervous	No	No	Yes	No	Design
I think the most important aspect is context of the product that we design for. If it suits the space aesthetic, yea why not. Like indoor garden office or restaurant. But product for common home seems impractical	Yes	Yes	Yes	Yes	Design
They are usually aesthetically appealing and have the ability to biodegrade without use of any external energy	Yes	Yes	Yes	Yes	Design
(I) hope that sharing your experience will help teachers and senior researchers disseminate useful concepts and real examples of biomimetic principles and tools for the development of new materials, new/improved design and fabrication strategies, and innovation methodologies	Yes	Yes	No	No	Design
A positive way to utilise and research on other purposes of the vast biological materials available in nature. A very interesting subject particularly involving the material properties in finished products	Yes	No	Yes	Yes	Non-design
Desirable as nowadays more and more people living in a small place and yet still need for biological material which are convenient and easy to be taken care of inside their house/room- to balance their emotion/stress & to relax	Yes	Yes	Yes	Yes	Non-design
It can be one way of creating awareness of nature conservation and its benefits to our living	Yes	Yes	Yes	Yes	Design
Needs to be more commonplace, without being intrusive	Yes	No	Yes	No	Non-design

(continued)

Table 10. (*continued*)

Cross-comparison analysis between the opinion and knowledge on bio-related design genres					
Responses or opinion received	Q9	Q10	Q11	Q12	Working background
I think it's important to explore the intersection of the natural world with the man-made world and how we can live a more environmentally conscious life to be more connected with ourselves and with nature. It is important for humans physical and mental health, as well as being important for the preservation of our natural world	No	No	No	Yes	Design
Sense of connection with the nature	Yes	Yes	Yes	Yes	Non-design
An excellent way to appreciate nature and reduce stress at home and the work place	No	Yes	Yes	Yes	Design
The incorporation of biological materials in product design is for environmentally-conscious people. It has appeal to educated people, but not for people who prioritize practicality over aesthetic functions	Yes	Yes	Yes	Yes	Non-design

4   Conclusions and Outlook

The exploration and usage of biological materials allow the consumers to understand the basic needs regarding the interaction with/emotions and behaviour towards natural surroundings and their elements. The study was conducted using an online survey to investigate the knowledge towards biophilia, biophilic design, bio-inspired and bio-design.

From the findings, the background of the participants was analysed to investigate the difference between design or non-design background. Thirteen question were asked for this section. The respondents agreed with Question 1 to 6 which means that they like to have biological materials in the house, they think it is important to have biological elements indoors, that natural elements can release stress/calm, create awareness of nature and ecological impact, can foster a sense of care, and can be educational (especially for children). However, Question 7 – if it is dangerous and inconvenient to have biological elements in the house – could not be decided. The respondents disagree to Question 8 asking if natural and biological elements indoor are dirty or time-consuming. Moreover, the connection of the preferences of experiencing nature (whether outdoor or both, indoor and outdoor) towards the preferences on having the biological elements indoor was proven to be significant based on our survey. This could be the reason why participants seem to favour or agree in integrating biological materials into indoor environments.

For the knowledge on biophilia, biophilic design, bio-inspired and bio-design questions, the non-design group has knowledge on biophilia and biophilic design with a percentage of 65.5% and 66.7% respectively, whereas most of the design and non-design group claim to be familiar with the term bio-inspired and bio-design. Based on the cross-comparison analysis, there is also an interesting finding that participants (with design as well as non-design background) are widely affirmative regarding incorporating biological elements in everyday products and living spaces.

This study is part of an ongoing larger research project on emotional design and perception toward biological materials in everyday products (Sayuti and Ahmed-Kristensen 2020). Therefore, future work on, e.g., the study of emotional responses, identification of purposes, as well as ownership regarding biological products will be presented in upcoming publications (Sayuti et al. 2020). This project can also be explored further with the use of real living biological materials and embedded into existing products to investigate the direct experience of living materials to gather results that provide more emotional layers while also enhancing the consumers' experience. The application of natural or biological elements in everyday products shows strong potential to be further explored in design disciplines, such as industrial design and product design engineering. These disciplines can help to develop and open up new market opportunities for more innovative and productive bio- or nature-inspired designs which promote and encourage interaction, communication, empathy, emotional connection and awareness towards the importance of human-nature-symbiotic relationship for future nature preservation.

Moreover, the significant threats of the vast usage and overconsumption of natural resources are encouraging the growing awareness to alleviate the problems of non-renewable resources exhaustion by incorporating biological materials as alternate options.

References

Albaum, G.: The Likert scale revisited: an alternate version. J. Mark. Res. Soc. **39**(2), 331–332 (1997)

Arvay, C.G.: The biophilia effect: a scientific and spiritual exploration of the healing bond between humans and nature. Sounds True, Canada (2018)

Balling, J.D., Falk, J.H.: Development of visual preference for natural environments. Environ. Behav. **14**(1), 5–28 (1982)

Bartczak, C., Dunbar, B., Bohren, L.: Incorporating biophilic design through living walls: the decision-making process. Construct. Green. Soc. Struct. Sustain. **307** (2013)

Collin, P.: Dictionary of Environment & Ecology, 5th edn. Bloomsbury Publishing Plc (2004)

Eckardt, M.H.: Fromm's humanistic ethics and the role of the prophet. A Prophetic Analyst: Erich Fromm's Contributions to Psychoanalysis, pp. 151–165 (1996)

Frumkin, H.: Beyond toxicity: human health and the natural environment. Am. J. Prev. Med. **20**(3), 234–240 (2001)

Grinde, B., Patil, G.G.: Biophilia: does visual contact with nature impact on health and well-being? Int. J. Environ. Res. Public Health **6**(9), 2332–2343 (2009)

Gunawardena, K., Steemers, K.: Living walls in indoor environments. Building and Environment (2018)

Gruber, P., Bruckner, D., Hellmich, C., Schmiedmayer, H.-B., Stachelberger, H., Gebeshuber, I.C.: Biomimetics- Materials, Structures and Processes: Examples. Ideas and Case Studies. Springer, Heidelberg (2011)

Hoffmann, A.O., et al.: Dog-assisted intervention significantly reduces anxiety in hospitalized patients with major depression. Eur. J. Integr. Med. **1**(3), 145–148 (2009)

Howell, A., Dopko, R., Passmore, Holli-Anne., Buro, K.: Nature connectedness: associations with well-being and mindfulness. Pers. Ind. Differ. **51**(2), 166–171 (2011). https://doi.org/10.1016/j.paid.2011.03.037

Huelat, B.J.: The wisdom of biophilia-nature in healing environments. J. Green Build. **3**(3), 23–35 (2008)

Johns, R.: Likert items and scales. Survey question bank: methods fact sheet **1** (2010)

Johnson, N.: Biophilic design benefits (2014). https://www.architectureanddesign.com.au/features/features-articles/why-biophilic-architecture-works-five-reasons-and?mid=7603c8 1e3d&utm_source=Cirrus+Media+Newsletters&utm_campaign=9a3dbdbe88-Architecture+ and+Design+Newsletter+-+201&utm_medium=email&utm_term=0_fe913f1856-9a3dbd be88-59078485. Accessed 2014

Kaplan, S.: The restorative benefits of nature: toward an integrative framework. J. Environ. Psychol. **15**(3), 169–182 (1995)

Kellert, S.R., Heerwagen, J., Mador, M.: Biophilic Design: The Theory. Science and Practice of Bringing Buildings to Life. Wiley, Hoboken (2008)

Magnan, R.A.: Discover Bio-design Thinking: Adopting Visual Images to Transform Our Information Processing Abilities. Xlibris Corporation (2018)

Matell, M.S., Jacoby, J.: Is there an optimal number of alternatives for Likert-Scale items? Effects of testing time and scale properties. J. Appl. Psychol. **56**(6), 506 (1972)

Montana-Hoyos, C.: BIO-ID4S: Biomimicry in industrial design for sustainability. VDM-Germany (2010)

Mehrabian, A., Russell, J.A.: The basic emotional impact of environments. Percept. Mot. Skills **38**(1), 283–301 (1974)

Myers, W.: Bio design: nature, science creativity. Revised and expanded version. Thames and Hudson (2018)

O'Haire, M.: Companion animals and human health: benefits, challenges, and the road ahead. J. Vet. Behav. Clin. Appl. Res. **5**(5), 226–234 (2010)

Parsaee, M., Demers, C.M., Hébert, M., Lalonde, J.F., Potvin, A.: A photobiological approach to biophilic design in extreme climates. Build. Environ. **154**, 211–226 (2019)

Rosenbaum, M.S., Ramirez, G.C., Camino, J.R.: A dose of nature and shopping: the restorative potential of biophilic lifestyle center designs. J. Retail. Consum. Serv. **40**, 66–73 (2018)

Sayuti, N.A.A., Montana-Hoyos, C., Bonollo, E.: A study of furniture design incorporating living organisms with particular reference to biophilic and emotional design criteria. Acad. J. Sci. **4**(1), 75–106 (2015)

Sayuti, N.A.A., Ahmed-Kristensen, S.: Understanding emotional responses and perception within new creative practices of biological materials. In: Conference proceeding, the Sixth International Conference on Design Creativity (ICDC2020). University of Oulu, Finland (2020)

Sayuti, N.A.A., Sommer, B., Ahmed-Kristensen, S.: Identifying the purposes of biological materials in everyday designs. Environ.-Behav. Proc. J. **5**(15). Accepted. Conference on AMEABRA International Virtual Conference on Environment-Behaviour Studies, 2nd Series (2020). https://amerabra.org/aivce-bs-2-2020shahalam/

Sayuti, N.A.A., Montana-Hoyos, C., Bonollo, E.: Biophilic design: why do designers incorporate living organisms in furniture design? In: Conference Proceeding, the Fifth International Conference on Design Creativity (ICDC2018). University of Bath, UK (2018)

Simaika, J.P., Samways, M.J.: Biophilia as a universal ethic for conserving biodiversity. Conserv. Biol. **24**(3), 903–906 (2010)

Terrapin Bright Green: 14 Patterns of biophilic design: Improving health & well-being in the built environment. New York, USA (2012)

Terrapin Bright Green: The Economic of biophilia: why designing with nature in mind makes financial sense. New York, USA (2014)

Thorpe, A.: The Designer's Atlas of Sustainability. Island Press (2007)

Ulrich, R.S.: Natural versus urban scenes some psychophysiological effects. Environ. Behav. **13**(5), 523–556 (1981)

Wilson, E.O.: Biophilia. Harvard University Press (1984)

Yin, J., Zhu, S., MacNaughton, P., Allen, J.G., Spengler, J.D.: Physiological and cognitive performance of exposure to biophilic indoor environment. Build. Environ. **132**, 255–262 (2018)

IoT Product Pleasurability - Investigating the Pleasurable User Experiences Between Conventional Products and IoT Products Through Watches

Zidong Lin[1]([✉]) [iD], Bjorn Sommer[1] [iD], and Saeema Ahmed-Kristensen[2] [iD]

[1] Royal College of Art, London SW7 2EU, UK
zidong.lin@network.rca.ac.uk
[2] Business School, University of Exeter, London SE1 8ND, UK

Abstract. The arrival of Internet of Things (IoT) overcomes limitations of time and space by providing ubiquitous accessibility of its products. Design and HCI research are challenged by an increasingly complex network of diverse types of interaction. To design pleasurable user experiences (UXs), new models need to be developed for emerging IoT products as previous models for conventional products might not be applicable anymore. From a human-centred perspective, this project investigates how the pleasurable UXs will change after a product develops into an IoT product. The project aims at understanding the attributes of IoT products that might contribute to understand the future relationship between users and IoT objects. The project applies UX theories by Jordan (a hierarchy of consumer needs, 2003) and Hassenzahl (top-ten psychological needs, 2010) as theoretical guidelines. These theories classified the contribution of human factors to design pleasurable products and agreed that the enjoyments from the psychological level are at the top of UX. The project uses two online questionnaires to collect data on 1) the UX of Smartwatches and 2) conventional Wristwatches (digital and analogue), in order to reflect on the influence of IoT products on the pleasurable UXs. The results show that the UXs of IoT Watches and conventional watches were not significantly different in terms of the four kinds of pleasure as proposed by Jordan; however, IoT products and conventional products did appear to influence some items in top-ten psychological needs differently.

Keywords: IoT · User experience · Smartwatch

1 Emerging of IoT Products

The *Internet of Things (IoT)* appeared with the development of ubiquitous computing [1] and pervasive computing [2]. In the system of the Internet of Things, the Internet connects products to form a relationship network that is more complex than ever, including *human-to-human (H2H), human-to-thing (H2T)* and *thing-to-thing (T2T)* interaction [3]. A multitude of goods have been developed that are connected to the Internet, and

A. Brooks et al. (Eds.): ArtsIT 2020, LNICST 367, pp. 394–408, 2021.
https://doi.org/10.1007/978-3-030-73426-8_24

have powerful and complicated functions for improving our lives and enhancing our abilities. The physical objects people interact with everyday are now different from the things (objects) humans previously encountered in their history. In his design fiction, Bruce Sterling catalogued the development of objects into six types [4]: artefacts, machines, products, gizmos, SPIMEs and Biots. He defined SPIMEs as, "manufactured objects whose informational support is so overwhelmingly extensive and rich that they are regarded as material instantiations of an immaterial system", and biots as, "the logical intermeshing, the blurring of the boundary" between human beings and SPIMEs. Some existing IoT objects are already close to his notion of Spimes, such as smart home appliances are interconnected in a complex network and exchange large amounts of data with each other. It could be speculated that Biot will be the future form of IoT products. Redström and Wiltse named the new type of object, one that is unfolding, assembled and dynamic, "fluid assemblages" [5]. "Assemblages", because they are made out of a diverse range of material and immaterial resources, both contained within the object as it appears in front of us and located elsewhere in the network; "fluid", because their precise forms are assembled dynamically and thus change continuously. Redström and Wiltse summarised five attributes of fluid assemblages that make them different from traditional objects: present-as-particular, multi-instability, multi-intentionality, tuning formations and the aesthetics of immanence, which reveal why and how IoT products are unique and make the design methods for IoT products different from that of conventional products.

The increasingly complex interactions between users and products brought challenges to designers to deliver stable and instrumental user experiences. HCI researchers had two main orientations to consider products in IoT systems, 1) looking at their relationship to human activity, or 2) look at looking at the things in themselves [6]. Studies explored the implications of IoT products from an object-oriented ontological perspective and revealed that IoT products have more agency and are found to influence human's behaviours more easy than ever before [7–9].

Marenko and van Allen used an animistic design method to make IoT objects anthropomorphic and reimagine digital interactions between the human and the networked object [7]. The project of Larrisa et al. used a coffee machine "Bitbarista" to explore users' perceptions of data processes in the Internet of Things [8]. Taylln et al. designed a chatbot called 'Ethnobot' to do an ethnographic study which revealed benefits and drawbacks using IoT devices to collect data regarding the UX [9]. However, none of these projects reflects how UXs of IoT products differentiate from conventional products.

As the theories above revealed, the relationship between human and non-human became increasingly blurry after the emerging of IoT products, it is vital to understand how this change can influence users gaining pleasurability when they use these products. Thus, this research is focusing on pleasurable user experiences which are especially relevant in the context of human-centred design. By knowing how "pleasurable" IoT products can be developed, designers will be able to create positively-connotated UXs for users and design more pleasurable interactions. From a human-centred design perspective, this publication presents a study investigating differences in UX's pleasurability between an IoT product and its original (non-IoT) product.

2 User Experience Theory of Designing Products

There is a variety of frameworks discussing the user experiences of products. Jordan introduced a framework of three levels of consumer needs indicating how to design pleasurable products [10]. Norman proposed a framework for positive emotional design with three corresponding levels of design: visceral, behavioural and reflective based on human brain processing [11]. Desmet and Hekkert created a general framework for product experience that applies to all affective responses that can be experienced in human-product interaction [12]. McCarthy and Wright presented a framework considering the emotional, intellectual, and sensual aspects of human experience with technology [13]. Hassenzahl illustrated a holistic goal-directed system with a hierarchy which includes three levels; 'motor-goals', 'do-goals' and 'be-goals' (from low to high level) [14]. This study uses UX Theories by Jordan (a hierarchy of consumer needs) [10] and Hassenzahl (top-ten psychological needs) [14] as theoretical guidelines as both of these theories emphasised designing pleasurable products.

In Jordan's hierarchy, the three levels of consumer needs (from low to high) are functionality, usability and pleasure (Fig. 1). Following Maslow's Hierarchy of Needs [15], in Jordan's model, the lower level needs must also be met before the fulfilment of higher-level needs. For Jordan, functionality indicates the application area of a product, as well as the context and environment in which the product will be used. Usability represents the extent to which a product is easy to use. Pleasure means the emotional benefits provided by a product, regarding pleasure as a factor that provides users with emotional benefits, in addition to the functional ones. Jordan borrowed four types of pleasure – physical, social, psychological and ideological – from the framework in Lionel Tiger's book "The Pursuit of Pleasure" [16], which might be relevant in the context of products. Table 1 shows their descriptions. Jordan believed that designers could design pleasurable products by following the three levels in his framework to fulfil consumer needs. Hassenzahl proposed top-ten psychological needs to identify the most important phycological needs for satisfying UXs based on Sheldon et al.'s work [17]. The descriptions of Hassenzahl's top-ten psychological needs are shown in Table 2. These psychological needs can be seen as components that influence psycho-pleasure in Jordan's model.

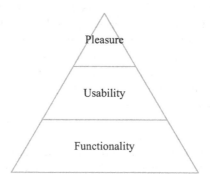

Fig. 1. A hierarchy of consumer needs redrawn based on Jordan [10]

Table 1. Four types of pleasure by Jordan [10]

Pleasures	Description
Physio-pleasure	Relates to the body and pleasures derived from the sensory organs. They include pleasures connected with touch, taste and smell, as well as feelings of sensual pleasure
Socio-pleasure	Enjoyment derived from relationships with others, e.g. relationships with friends and loved ones, with colleagues or with like-minded people
Psycho-pleasure	Psycho-pleasure pertains to people's cognitive and emotional reactions
Ideo-pleasure	Ideo-pleasure pertains to people's values

Table 2. Top-ten psychological needs by Hassenzahl [14]

Items	Description
Relatedness	Feeling that you have regular intimate contact with people who care about you rather than feeling lonely and uncared of
Meaning	Feeling that you are developing your best potentials and making life meaningful rather than feeling stagnant and that life does not have much meaning
Stimulation	Feeling that you get plenty of novelty and stimulation rather than feeling bored and under-stimulated by life
Competence	Feeling that you are capable and effective in your actions rather than feeling incompetent or ineffective
Security	Feeling safe and in control of your life rather than feeling uncertain and threatened by your circumstances
Popularity	Feeling that you are liked, respected, and have influence over others rather than feeling like a person whose advice or opinion nobody is interested in
Luxury	Feeling that you have plenty of money to buy most of what you want rather than feeling like a poor person who has no satisfying possessions
Bodily	Feeling like your body is healthy and well-taken care of rather than feeling out of shape and unhealthy
Independence	Feeling like you are the cause of your own actions rather than feeling that external forces or pressure are the cause of your action
Self-respect	Feeling like you are a worthy person who is as good as anyone else rather than feeling like a "loser"

There is a lack of evidence that these frameworks of conventional product design can be used to assess the pleasurability of new emerging IoT products. Therefore, this study investigated how the pleasurable user experiences (UXs) will change after a product develops into an Internet of Things (IoT) product. The research aims and methodology are discussed in the following sections.

3 Research Aims

The long term aims of this research are to understand the attributes of IoT products and generating a new framework for IoT products that contributes to the future relationship between human beings and IoT objects. The specific aim of the research is comparing user response for a specific non-IoT and an IoT product to facilitate generating new insights for pleasurable user experiences of IoT products. More specifically, this research aims to reflect the differences regarding pleasures delivered by IoT and non-IoT products to users by conducting a survey related to conventional watches and Smartwatches.

According to Collins English Dictionary, a *Smartwatch* is defined as [18]:

"A Smartwatch is an electronic Wristwatch that is able to perform many of the functions of a smartphone or tablet computer."

Based on this definition of a Smartwatch, we are using the following definition for an *IoT Watch* (short for IoT Smartwatch) in the context of this work:

"An IoT Watch is a Smartwatch which provides Internet-connected functionality."

And for *Wristwatches*, we are using the extended definition based on Collins English Dictionary [19]:

"A traditional watch worn strapped around the wrist including analogue or digital quartz watches which neither belong to Smartwatches or IoT Watches."

Smartwatches and Wristwatches were selected as the product to investigate for the following reasons:

- The Smartwatch is a typical product that, in recent years, has evolved into a networked object.
- Smartwatches are popular so it is easier to find sample users than for most other IoT objects.
- The development of Smartwatches represents market demands and customer needs.
- The significant differences in functions might result in different experiences.

4 Methodology

The study chose a questionnaire as the research method because this survey is a preliminary study to identify areas that need further investigation, where other data collection methods will be employed at a later stage. As a method used in the early stage of research projects, questionnaires are quick to administer; they can be sent out to a large number of participants at relatively low time and monetary costs [20]. Compared to interviews, questionnaires are more convenient for respondents to answer and formulate their responses and are not influenced by the interviewer's bias [21]. Online questionnaires changed the ways how researchers undertake their research and they are used commonly by manufacturers on their websites to collect feedback from customers [22]. To effectively collect feedback from users of a conventional product and an IoT product, we designed questionnaires in digital form and distributed them online to collect data.

5   The Questionnaires

Each questionnaire was separated into four sections based on Jordan's hierarchy model. At the beginning of each questionnaire, there was a consent letter to introduce the research background and inform the participants' that their information would be kept confidential. The participants needed to answer the first question of each questionnaire (asking if they had a Smartwatch or a Wristwatch) to check whether their questionnaire would be valid. The study also secured Ethics Approval from the Research Ethics Committee of the Royal College of Art.

In the first part, users were asked to provide basic information about themselves and their product (including their age, gender, nationality, country of residence, product model, etc.), as this might influence their perceptions of their UXs. The questions in Sect. 1 were closed questions. The second section asked questions concerning their watches' functionality, including the used functions, the frequency of functional usage, as well as the environments they used their watches in. The third section contained questions related to usability and ease of use. In the fourth section, users were asked to evaluate the four types of pleasure in Jordan's theory in relation to the UX their watches provided. The participants were also asked about the six specific items selected from Hassenzahl's top-ten psychological needs that are relevant to watches. The six items selected in the context of this work were relatedness, meaning, stimulation, competence, security and popularity (descriptions see Table 2).

The questions in part 2 and 3 are mainly rating-scale questions. As the aim of this research is measuring and comparing the pleasurability of two kinds of watches, UX metrics which present some aspect of the UX in a numeric format naturally became the appropriate tool. UX metrics are an efficient, engaging and easy to use tool to be used, but they also need to use the same set of measurements each time to be comparable and produce results that are directly or indirectly observable and quantifiable [23]. The scale used for these questions in part 2 and part 3 was the semantic differential (SD) scale. Osgood developed the semantic differential scale to measure the affective and cognitive components of respondents' attributions to words or concepts [24]. The questionnaires in this study used the original SD scale which is a seven-point scale (-3; 0; $+3$) between bipolar, contrasting adjectives (e.g., infrequent–frequent, unpleasurable–pleasurable) and a neutral zero point. There were also some open-questions in part 2 and 3 which enable respondents to provide further opinions and feedback.

6   Data Analysis

6.1   Sample Size and Analyse Method

The questionnaires were posted on the online forum Reddit and also sent to students at the Royal College of Art through email by the college's School of Design Administration Office. The survey collected 171 responses in total. There were 87 individuals who answered the Wristwatch questionnaire and 84 individuals who answered the Smartwatch questionnaire. Of those, 80 participants of each questionnaire were deemed valid and selected as the final sample to analyse. Statistical analysis was applied to the sample data; ANOVA tests and t-tests were conducted to determine if there is a significant difference between the means of two groups. In order to compare a conventional product and an IoT product in terms of their UXs, it needs to distinguish IoT Watches from Smartwatches in the context of this study. (In Sect. 3, it has been classified that not all Smartwatches belong to the class of IoT Watches.) We checked the models of participants' Smartwatches (they answered this question in part 1 of the questionnaire) and selected models with Internet functions as IoT Watch. After the selection, there were 67 IoT Watch users of 80 Smartwatch users.

6.2 Background of Participants

For both Smartwatches and Wristwatches, there were more male users than female users in the sample. There were 76% male users and 21% female users of Smartwatches, and 85% male users and 13% female users of conventional Wristwatches. In this survey, Wristwatch users were slightly younger than Smartwatch users: 38% of Wristwatch users were aged 18 to 24 and 40% of Wristwatch users were aged 25 to 39, compared to 23% of Smartwatch users aged 18 to 24 and 55% of Smartwatch users aged 25 to 39. The majority of the participants were living in the UK and the US (40% of users in the US and 20% of users in the UK for Wristwatches, 48% of users in the US and 18% of users in the UK for Smartwatches). For the Wristwatch users, the top three brands owned were Seiko (16%), Omega (11%) and Timex (9%). 83.75% of the Smartwatch users' models had an Internet feature (the remaining 16.25% had normal Smartwatch features like health tracker (usually track how many steps users walk and how many calories users burn in one day) and 68% of these were Apple brands. 50% Smartwatch users had used their models for between 1 and 3 years and only 3% Smartwatch users had been using their models over 3 years. 38% of the Wristwatch users had been using their models from 1 to 3 years, and 29% of Wristwatch users had been using their models over 3 years.

7 Findings

7.1 Functionality and Usability

Firstly, we looked at the functionality level and usability level in Jordan's theory. The function most often used by both groups of users was checking time. Obviously, Smartwatch users had more functions available to them than Wristwatch users; however, it was noticeable that 72% of the Smartwatch users believed the feature, "surfing Internet" to be unimportant (8% "slightly unimportant", 23% "very unimportant", 41% "extremely unimportant") and 63% Smartwatch users believed the feature, "using social media" unimportant (13% "slightly unimportant, 16% "very unimportant, 34% "extremely unimportant"). It seems that these Smartwatch users did not value the IoT features of their watches; however, they considered the health and sleep trackers more important as 84% participants believed "health tracker" and 72% participants believed "sleep tracker" to be important. Most of participants in both groups believed that their watches basic functions were easy to learn to use (92% for Wristwatches and 88% for

Smartwatches) and easy to use after they became familiar with them (97% for Wrist-watches and 92% for Smartwatches). 48% of Smartwatch users claimed the, "surfing Internet" feature was difficult to use; 29% of Smartwatch users had a neutral attitude about it while only 24% of Smartwatch user found it easy to browse webpages with their devices. 32% of Smartwatch users thought "using social media" was difficult to use; 29% of Smartwatch users had a neutral attitude about it and 30% of Smartwatch users found this function easy to use. The data presented that all IoT features on Smartwatches got negative or neutral overall feedback in terms of their usability. After we have checked the participants' Smartwatch models, it might be that two reasons caused this result. 1) Some non-IoT Smartwatches lacked internet functionality. 2) A number of IoT Watch producers did not install a browser application on their products; although these IoT Watches are able to connect to the internet, users cannot use them to browse webpages and social media. The internet connection on these watches was mostly used to transfer data to servers or other devices.

7.2 Pleasure

By comparing the means of four types of pleasure (Table 3), it can be seen that watches were experienced as most pleasurable in terms of their physical aspects no matter what kind of watches the participants were using. By comparing the mean of four types of pleasure, it can be seen that ideo-pleasure was associated with minimal gain, regardless of the sort of watch they used. The differences between the means of the same type of pleasure were all below 0.15, which means the means of different kinds of watch in the same type of pleasure were close. Figure 2 represents the means of four types of pleasure in a bar chart; it shows that the four types of emotional experience that users gained from IoT watches, Smartwatches and Wristwatches were approximately at the level of "slightly pleasurable".

Table 3. The means of four types of pleasures of wristwatches, smartwatches and IoT watches

	Physio-pleasure (touch)	Socio-pleasure	Psycho-pleasure	Ideo-pleasure
Wristwatch (n = 80)	1.613	1.238	1.113	0.850
Smartwatch (n = 80)	1.613	1.100	0.938	0.888
IoT Watch (n = 67)	1.761	1.149	1.000	0.955
Non-IoT Smartwatch (n = 7)	0.429	0.143	0.714	0.286

By applying ANOVA tests (Table 4) and t-test (Table 5) between IoT Watches and Wristwatches, we can see that the p-values are all above the threshold (0.05) chosen for statistical significance, suggesting there is no statistical significance between the four types of pleasures from using Wristwatches and IoT Watches.

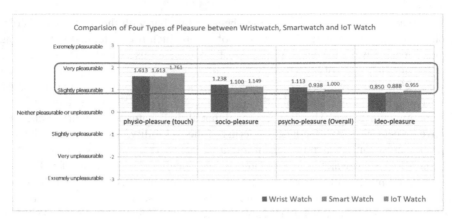

Fig. 2. Comparison of four types of pleasure between Wristwatch, Smartwatch and IoT Watch

Table 4. ANOVA of four types of pleasure between wristwatches (n = 80) and IoT watches (n = 67)

	Physio-pleasure (touch)	Socio-pleasure	Psycho-pleasure	Ideo-pleasure
F	0.570	0.175	0.360	0.316
P-value	0.452	0.676	0.550	0.575

Table 5. T-test of four types of pleasure between wristwatches (n = 80) and IoT watches (n = 67)

	Physio-pleasure (touch)	Socio-pleasure	Psycho-pleasure	Ideo-pleasure
P-value	0.447	0.674	0.543	0.571

Looking at the means of the six items in psycho-pleasure (Table 6), popularity was the item that had much more obvious influence on the psycho-pleasure of Wristwatches than that of Smartwatches and IoT Watches, while stimulation the item influencing the psycho-pleasure of Smartwatches and IoT Watches more obvious than the psycho-pleasure of Wristwatches. Interestingly, the user experience of non-IoT Smartwatches was always the most unsatisfying in the six psychological needs comparing to Smartwatches, Wristwatches and IoT Watches.

Figure 3 demonstrates that the psycho-pleasure influenced by six items gained by using Wristwatches was rated by participants as being below the slightly pleasurable level. For Smartwatches, only psycho-pleasure influenced by stimulation was higher than the "slightly pleasurable" level, while for IoT Watches, psycho-pleasures influenced by stimulation, competence, meaning and security were all above or at the slightly pleasurable level. It is noticeable that in this survey for all of the six phycological needs except popularity, the means of the pleasurable level of IoT Watches were higher

Table 6. The means of six items in psycho-pleasure of wristwatches, smartwatches and IoT watches

	Relatedness	Stimulation	Popularity	Competence	Meaning	Security
Wristwatch (n = 80)	0.563	0.738	0.625	0.838	0.738	0.938
Smartwatch (n = 80)	0.763	1.150	0.263	0.975	0.875	0.938
IoT Watch (n = 67)	0.851	1.224	0.269	1.060	1.000	1.000
Non-IoT Smartwatch (n = 7)	0.000	0.429	0.429	0.286	0.429	0.429

than those of Smartwatches, which were, in turn, higher than those of Wristwatches. It reveals that IoT Watches might provide more pleasurable user experience in terms of psychological aspects than Wristwatches.

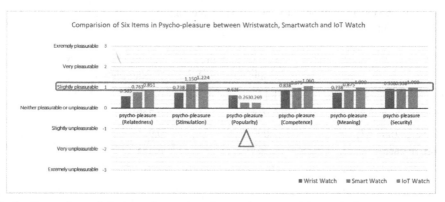

Fig. 3. Comparison of six items in psycho-pleasure between Wristwatch, Smartwatch and IoT Watch

By applying ANOVA tests (Table 7) and t-tests (Table 8) for IoT Watches and Wristwatches, it showed that the p-values of stimulation were below the threshold (0.05) chosen for statistical significance. Thus, it can be seen that stimulation had significantly different influence on psycho-pleasure of Wristwatches and that of IoT Watches, and also significantly differed from that of IoT Watches. It also emerged that the p-values of popularity were close to the threshold (0.05) chosen for statistical significance which means that popularity also had obviously different influence on psycho-pleasure of Wristwatches and that of IoT Watches. Calculating the average means of six items influencing psycho-pleasure enabled a comparison with means of overall psycho-pleasures in order to find out how these components influenced the psycho-pleasure overall (Table

9). For Wristwatches, Smartwatches and IoT Watches, the average means of six items influencing psycho-pleasure were all lower than the means of overall psycho-pleasure.

Table 7. ANOVA of six items in psycho-pleasure between wristwatches (n = 80) and smartwatches (n = 80)

	Relatedness	Stimulation	Popularity	Competence	Meaning	Security
F	2.286	6.097	3.260	0.994	1.521	0.085
P-value	0.133	0.015	0.073	0.320	0.219	0.771

Table 8. T-test of six items in psycho-pleasure between wristwatches (n = 80) and IoT watches (n = 67)

	Relatedness	Stimulation	Popularity	Competence	Meaning	Security
P-value	0.132	0.014	0.073	0.332	0.217	0.771

Table 9. Comparison of means of overall psycho-pleasure and average mean of six items in psycho-pleasure

	Psycho-pleasure (explicit overall)	Average mean of six items in psycho-pleasure
Wristwatch (n = 80)	1.113	0.827
Smartwatch (n = 80)	0.938	0.740
IoT Watch (n = 67)	1.000	0.921
Non-IoT Smartwatch (n = 7)	0.286	0.333

8   Discussion

8.1   Improved Functionality and Uncertain Usability of IoT Products

Functionality and usability are the bases of pleasurable user experience in Jordan's model. Obviously, IoT Watches have more functions than non-IoT Smartwatches and conventional watches. The findings (Sect. 7.1) showed that there are several functions, like using social media and surfing the Internet, which were only available on a smart device that is able to connect to the Internet. From this finding, we might speculate that users can only notice the value of functional extension of an IoT product when they use its internet feature and it can be seen that all the smart features of a product which make it more powerful than its conventional form benefit from IoT. Moreover, an increase of functions related to IoT does not mean they are all easy to use and this would influence the pleasurability of an IoT product. In this study, respondents claimed that functions like using social media and surfing the Internet were more difficult to use than non-IoT features like health trackers and reminders, which are provided by all Smartwatches. This finding also reflected the multi-instability and the multi-intentionality in attributes of fluid assemblages [5] (mentioned in Sect. 1). The final question in the functionality part of the survey asked participants to fill in any special reason of using a Smartwatch. 13 (of 80) participants mentioned they felt convenient to receive notifications by Smartwatches in a scenario they cannot look at their mobile phone. This finding revealed that a new way of interaction generated by IoT products' thing-to-thing interactions that conventional products hardly ever had. Thus, the usability has high potential to be improved when a conventional product evolves into IoT form but this improvement strongly depends on the UX designer's ability to implement an appropriate user-device interaction. This result also reflected the features of Spime in Sterling's theory [4] – the Smartwatches are not only material products but also part of a notification system involving multiple devices. Comparing to the disappointing IoT functions like using social-media and surfing the Internet, notification received more positive feedback. The implication of IoT product might should emphasise how different devices work together in a social network rather than a single piece of product. Therefore, when UX designers design the functionality and usability of IoT, they should have a societal perspective to consider the devices network and the service holistically to shape pleasurable user experiences.

8.2 No Obvious Differences in Four Kinds of Pleasure Between Conventional & IoT Products from Data

Comparing the means (Table 3) and the p-values (Table 4, Table 5), the four types of pleasure did not reveal significant statistical differences between Smartwatch/IoT Watches and conventional watches (Sect. 7.2). This finding suggests that the extended functionality of IoT products do not enhance UXs on the level of pleasure. The four types of pleasure the user experienced from IoT, non-IoT Smartwatches and Wristwatches all reached a pleasure level of "slightly pleasurable" (Sect. 7.2, Fig. 2). As these watches were user-centred design-products and designed to be instrumental, the designers might have considered four types of pleasures when they designed these watches and their interventions were successfully reflected in the UXs. If, however, all IoT and non-IoT products all achieved the same UX pleasure-level, it could imply that the advantages of IoT in pleasurable UXs cannot be seen from Jordan's model (2003). It might be that a higher level of consumer needs (beyond the level of pleasure) could be delivered by IoT products or some kinds of pleasure are missing in Jordan's model, and this would be worth exploring in future studies.

However, the means of and the p-values from ANOVA and T-test only can represent statistical differences but not all of the differences in pleasurability can be presented by data. In the opening question at the end of the questionnaire which asked their additional opinion about watches, two Smartwatch users and seven Wristwatch users stated that a watch is only a tool for them and they cannot connect it to any emotional feelings. Even the results did not differentiate regarding the four terms of pleasure in Jordan's model but they showed differences in the six psychological needs (which are introduced in the next section). Socio-pleasure and ideo-pleasure need a deeper investigation using different components that might influence them just like the psycho-pleasure.

8.3 The Different Psycho-Pleasures Between Conventional and IoT Products

From the exploration of the six items (Sect. 7.3) in psycho-pleasures (Table 6 and Table 9), the aspect that has the most significantly-different influence on psycho-pleasures between IoT Watches and Wristwatches is stimulation. The reason for this could be that IoT Watches allow users to set their goals through a health tracker, sleep tracker and reminders, and this stimulates users to achieve their goals (based on the opening questions in the questionnaire). The aspect that has the second-most significantly-different influence on the psycho-pleasures between IoT Watches and Wristwatches is popularity. This might be due to the fact that watches tend to have a similar appearance, but Wristwatches are often designed to users' status, 'identity' and tastes through their appearance (and marketing). This finding reflects the aesthetics of immanence in attributes of fluid assemblages (mentioned in Sect. 2). In this way, this study might also have revealed the high potential for traditional watch brands to enter the Smartwatch market, as well as to improve the design of existing Smartwatches. Comparison of means of overall psycho-pleasure and the average mean of the six items in psycho-pleasure (Table 9) showed that the selected six items influenced the psycho-pleasure of IoT Watches more than Wristwatches. There might be other elements that influence the psycho-pleasure of Wristwatches and IoT Watches that have not been explored in this study.

8.4 Limitations of the Study

The study had several limitations in terms of its development. Firstly, watches were chosen as the type of product to investigate, but watches may not represent all the features of a product that are relevant for the transformation of a traditional to an IoT product. IoT products vary enormously, so it is impossible for a single product to be representative for all IoT products. Some IoT products, like Wi-Fi routers, did not have a form before becoming an IoT product; they were invented as IoT products. Secondly, the sample size of each questionnaire was 80 and all the questionnaires were sent out online, meaning that the current group of study participants might not have been representative for all characteristics of the target group. Also, most of the participants were English-speakers, from or living in an English-speaking country, so their response may not be representative for other cultures, and UXs in HCI are highly culturally-determined. Thirdly, the data analysis used a quantitative method, and the figures may not fully represent the subjective opinions of each user. The closed questions did not give participants the opportunity to explain how they evaluated their pleasurable experience of using watches. For a more detailed and in-depth investigation of the pleasurability of IoT products; they should be investigated qualitatively, by observing and interviewing. In addition, the two questionnaires used in the context of this study ignored the experiences of users who are using Smartwatches and Wristwatches in parallel. We are currently undertaking a follow-up survey addressing this user group.

9   Conclusions

This research project compared and discussed the pleasurable UXs of IoT Watches and conventional Wristwatches using a quantifying UX method. The aim of this study with 160 participants was to reflect the differences in pleasures that IoT and non-IoT products provide to users, as well as to create a new pleasurable user experience framework in further studies. The three key findings are:

1. The functionality of IoT Watches is more advanced than non-IoT Watches, but unique features of IoT products are not always easy to use. Thing-to-thing interactions of IoT products could bring convenience and new ways of interactions to users. UX designers should consider how IoT Watches work with other devices in a network when they design their usability and functionality to enhance pleasurable user experiences.
2. In this study, IoT Watches and non-IoT Watches provides the same level of pleasurability to users did not show a statistical difference. Also, UXs of IoT Watches and non-IoT Watches did not show significant statistical differences in four kinds of pleasures in Jordan's framework.
3. In terms of the six items associated with IoT Watches in the top-ten psychological needs, stimulation and popularity showed significant differences in their influences on the psycho-pleasures of IoT Watches and conventional watches. There is a high potential for traditional Wristwatch brands to launch Smartwatches. Moreover, Smartwatch developers might also benefit from learning design languages from Wristwatches.
4. When investigating pleasurable UXs of two different product types, it might be more effective to collect feedback from users who used them in parallel.

The key contribution of this paper is to provide new insights for designing pleasurable UXs for IoT products. The testing of existing UX theories on Wristwatches and Smartwatches could help researchers to address the shortage of current UX frameworks and develop new ones for IoT products specifically. Designers could benefit from this research by better understanding the differences in UXs between IoT and conventional products and the shortages of existing IoT Watches in order to design more-instrumental IoT products. Traditional Wristwatch and Smartwatch companies might also benefit from this study by identifying new design opportunities for increasing the pleasurability of their products. Further work should gain feedback from users who have used both Smartwatches and Wristwatches. In the future, we are going to use experimental methods to explore the specific reasons for the differences in the perception of pleasurability between IoT products and conventional products.

References

1. Weiser, M.: The computer for the 21st century. Sci. Am. **265**, 94–104 (1991). https://doi.org/10.1038/scientificamerican0991-94
2. Satyanarayanan, M.: Pervasive computing: vision and challenges. IEEE Pers. Commun. **8**, 10–17 (2001). https://doi.org/10.1109/98.943998

3. International Telecommunication Union: The Internet of Things - Executive Summary. 28 (2005).
4. Sterling, B.: Shaping Things. MIT Press, Cambridge. (2005)
5. Redström, J., Wiltse, H.: Changing things: the future of objects in a digital world (2018)
6. Rowland, C., Goodman, E., Charlier, M., Light, A., Lui, A.: Designing connected products. O'Reilly Media, Inc., Newton (2015)
7. Marenko, B., van Allen, P.: Animistic design: how to reimagine digital interaction between the human and the nonhuman. Digit. Creat. **27**, 52–70 (2016). https://doi.org/10.1080/146 26268.2016.1145127
8. Pschetz, L., Tallyn, E., Gianni, R., Speed, C.: Bitbarista: exploring perceptions of data transactions in the internet of Things. In: Proceedings of the 2017 CHI Conference on Human Factors in Computing Systems, pp. 2964–2975. Association for Computing Machinery, New York (2017). https://doi.org/10.1145/3025453.3025878
9. Tallyn, E., Fried, H., Gianni, R., Isard, A., Speed, C.: The Ethnobot: gathering ethnographies in the age of IoT. In: Proceedings of the 2018 CHI Conference on Human Factors in Computing Systems. pp. 1–13. Association for Computing Machinery, New York (2018)
10. Jordan, P.W.: Designing Pleasurable Products: An Introduction to the New Human Factors. Taylor & Francis e-Library (2003)
11. Norman, D.A.: Emotional Design: Why We Love (or Hate) Everyday Things. Basic Books, New York (2005)
12. Desmet, P.M.A., Hekkert, P.: Framework of product experience (2007)
13. McCarthy, J., Wright, P.: Technology as experience. Interactions **11**, 42–43 (2004). https://doi.org/10.1145/1015530.1015549
14. Hassenzahl, M.: Experience design: technology for all the right reasons. Synth. Lect. Hum.-Centered Inf. **3**, 1–95 (2010). https://doi.org/10.2200/s00261ed1v01y201003hci008
15. Maslow, A.H.: A theory of human motivation. Psychol. Rev. **50**, 370–396 (1943). https://doi.org/10.1037/h0054346
16. Tiger, L.: The Pursuit of Pleasure. Transaction Publishers, Piscataway (2000)
17. Sheldon, K.M., Elliot, A.J., Kim, Y., Kasser, T.: What is satisfying about satisfying events? Testing 10 candidate psychological needs. J. Pers. Soc. Psychol. **80**, 325–339 (2001). https://doi.org/10.1037/0022-3514.80.2.325
18. "smartwatch": Collins English Dictionary – Complete and Unabridged, 12th Edition 2014 (2014). https://www.thefreedictionary.com/smartwatch
19. "wristwatch": Collins English Dictionary – Complete and Unabridged, 12th Edition 2014 (2014). https://www.thefreedictionary.com/wristwatch
20. Bryman, A.: Social Research Methods. Oxford University Press, Oxford (2012)
21. Collins, H.: Creative research: the theory and practice of research for the creative industries. AVA Academia; Distributed in the USA & Canada by Ingram Publisher Services, Lausanne: La. Vergne, Tenn. (2010)
22. Milton, A.: Research Methods for Product Design. Laurence King Pub., London (2013)
23. Tullis, T., Albert, B.: Measuring the User Experience: Collecting, Analyzing, and Presenting Usability Metrics, 2nd edn. Elsevier Inc. (2013). https://doi.org/10.1016/C2011-0-00016-9
24. Osgood, C.E.: The Measurement of Meaning. University of Illinois Press, Urbana (1957)

A Budget Setting Design Intervention for Reducing Personal Expenses for Chinese Young Generation

Yuxiang Yan[(⊠)], Huaxin Wei, Jeffrey C. F. Ho, and Analyn Yap

School of Design, The Hong Kong Polytechnic University, Hung Hom,
Kowloon, Hong Kong SAR
yuxiang.yan@connect.polyu.hk, {huaxin.wei,
jeffrey.cf.ho}@polyu.edu.hk

Abstract. In China, the young generation faces the problem of low savings, partially due to their lack of self-control in monetary spending. This paper would like to provide a design solution to reduce this demographic's spending based on a literature review covering such behavioral economics theories as mental accounting and prospect theory. A quantitative research method consisting of surveys and experiments were conducted to collect design insights from users. Our proposed design is a budget setting and spending tracking system in the form of a mobile application and a smartphone case. This system uses a relational display of value and cost to primarily help users reduce spending by setting up a limited budget and facilitate the recording of transactions. Based on user evaluation of the initial prototype, we reflect and summarize a set of strategies for future design for personal finance .

Keywords: Spending control · Behavioral economics · Personal finance · Interaction design

1 Background

With rapid development of the Internet, China has witnessed an expansion of the consumer market and digital payment systems. However, many cases about Chinese young adults' excessive consumption relying on personal loan and mortgage products and ending up with unaffordable liabilities have revealed some negative consequences of the development. As young adults' living expenses keep increasing, and due to the one-child policy in China, the current young generation may need to be responsible for the expenses – in whole or in part – of all four grandparents and possibly, children in the future, they will face severe challenges in their financial situations.

According to the report from Zhaopin.com in 2018 [1], 21.89% of the surveyed white-collar workers are in debt and 15.57% of white collars have savings less than ten thousand Yuan. Another survey conducted by Zhenai.com in 2019 [2] revealed that, among those among the so-called post-90s generation who are single in China, about

30% of them do not have savings. Financial pressure is the second top (44.84%) concern of the 2019 survey respondents. On the other hand, another report from Alipay [3] shows different numbers, 92% of the post-90s generation have a surplus every month and 90% will save money every month. It is hard to verify which report is more accurate. The Alipay report did not disclose the exact amount of subjects' saving, the figure of small amount savings can be deduced from the first two survey reports mentioned above. While Chinese young generation has a high awareness of saving money, they are not able to save much. There is a gap between their motivations in saving and their actual capabilities.

To fill the gap, this work aims to improve the financial situation of members of the young generation in China, using design intervention in people's everyday spending habits. Due to the limitation of the regional access and context of our study, all of our study subjects are Chinese; no insight was collected from individuals from other cultural backgrounds. As Chinese people have different attitudes towards wealth, we do not claim our design strategies working for people not from the Chinese culture. Nevertheless, since the theories referenced are universally applicable, we do believe that our strategies provide a good starting point for design for other demographics with a similar goal.

2 Related Work

2.1 Natural Mental Bias

Many researchers have found that humans make financial decisions which does not align with economic principles. Experiments from Chen et al. [4] support that humans have a natural mental bias when making economy-related decisions. These biases are often rigid, but they also provide design opportunities for improving personal financial habits.

Non-fungibility of Mental Accounting. In 1980, Thaler introduced the term "Psychic Accounting," and later this concept was developed into "mental accounting" [5], which refers to people's mental processing in making financial decisions and evaluating the outcomes. People will build and label different accounts mentally for their income and spending. Thaler defined this phenomenon as "non-fungibility" [6]. People will cognitively build different accounts that have their respective operating rules and may interpret different transactions depending on the account where it is applicable.

For example, a person will consider a luxury perfume expensive if he plans to use it for work, but when he is dating a girl and wants to give her a gift, he will consider a perfume at same cost worth the price. It is because the spending on perfume for work can be regarded as a commodity expense, but a gift for a girl will be considered as a relation expense, of which one may have a higher willingness to pay. Although the product and the price are the same, the mental feeling will be different. This is the same for savings accounts - if a person saves some money for further education, he will likely take a mortgage to pay for a car rather than using the savings for education. Although extra interests will be needed to pay, it would be more painful if he used the money which is originally set for education.

Ratio Bias: Relatively Larger Number Feels More Concrete. Experiments [7, 8] have suggested that people have difficulties in processing ratio as opposed to absolute numbers. When buying expensive products, for example, a $100,000 backpack with a discount shown as $1,000 off or 1% off, although the absolute discount is the same, people feel that the number "1,000" is a larger discount. The effect is the opposite when the spending reference number is small, for a $10 pen, a discount as $2 off and as 20% off, "20%" feels a larger discount.

Loss Causes Stronger Feelings than Gain. In Kahneman's perspective theories [9], the degree that people feel and perceive loss is more pronounced than how they feel and perceive gain. For the same amount of loss and gain, people tend to have stronger feelings towards the loss.

2.2   The Affecting Factors for Consumption Choice After Getting the Consumption Needs

The Particular Resource Account Consumers Cognitively Access will Affect Their Consumption Decisions. In 2007, Morwedge and his colleagues [10] found if people cognitively access a larger financial account before shopping, they will spend more compared to a mental access to a small account. They set two groups of people, one group was asked to indicate how many accounts (checking, savings, bonds, stocks, and certificates) they possessed, another group was asked to check their wallet. As a result, the account group spent 36% more than the wallet group. Morwedge et al. consider that there is a fraction that describes consumption choices. The objective cost of an item is the numerator, the account people consider consuming is the denominator. The larger the account is, the smaller the fraction is, and the same item will seem cheaper, thus it is more possible for people to consume.

People Need Help in Relating to Their Own Future. Benartzi and his colleagues [11] found most Americans failed to join the government's retirement plan. Although people have a high awareness of saving for the future, when it comes to action, it is more painful for people to reduce their current assets on hand, than reduce their future prospective assets. So instead of directly asking people to hand over part of income for the retirement plan, they set the choice to "Save More Tomorrow," and part of the salary they ought to receive will be redirected to the retirement plan beforehand. This helps many people to join the plan and therefore have savings. Goldstein, Hal and Allianz investigated saving behaviors in relation to how people viewed their future self and referenced the philosopher, Derek Parfit, who mentioned that people tend to neglect the future self, due to a lack of imagination [12].

The Wealth Used for Consumption: Current Income has a Higher Marginal Propensity to Consume. Shefrin and Thaler raises the theory that people will construct three mental accounts for their economic resources: *current income*, *current assets*, and *future income*. *Current income* is associated with the highest marginal propensity to consume, while *future income* is associated with a lowest one (cf. [13]). Thus, people tend to spend *current income* more easily. When the income resource remains the same, but a person puts more money into the *current assets* account, less money will be put into *current income*, therefore there would be less spending.

The Feeling of Paying and Consumption: The Closer Timings in Between Payment and Consumption, the More Pain. Many observations have supported the double-entry mental accounting theory raised by Prelec and Loewenstein: time is an important factor to consider in the consumption process; the closer the consumption happens around the payment timing, the more painful the consumption will feel [14]. People tend to spend more when the consumption feels less painful.

These related works of behavioral economics and the theories they have put forth heavily inform the design direction of our work.

3 Research Design

In searching for strategies for creating interventions to enable young adults to improve their savings, we first took a broad look at the current design solutions in the mobile application market as it is one the most concentrated areas for personal finance products, especially in China. We investigated a range of 12 different mobile applications from the Chinese market and a few from international market (i.e., listed in app stores across multiple countries). The majority of these products are bookkeeping applications, such as Shark Keeping, Alipay Bookkeeping; a few of them have other functions such as selling financial products, bookkeeping through conversations. We can rarely see in these products application or usage of any of the above highly relevant behavioral economic theories. They appeared to us to be tedious to use and difficult to persist the usage for a long time.

This observation prompted us to come up with a two-phase iterative research design. In the first phase, we collected responses on user experiences and issues with current solutions through surveys and identified the key problems and gaps. We then in the second phase to target at these key issues with a set of iterative experiments, each embedded with varied solutions, and tested their efficacies in an experimental study. In the following we will introduce each study with the details of study design and its results, with each study design built on top of the knowledge gained from the previous study.

4 Study 1: Surveys of People's Financial Habits and Experiences with Current Solutions

In the first phase of our research, surveys were chosen in order to understand people's habits, rationales and attitudes towards spending. Open-ended questions were designed to get more qualitative insights.

4.1 First Survey: Current Accounting Tools Are not Efficient in Helping Self-finance-Management

It is commonly considered that, to accumulate assets, it is important to track one's income and spending and reach a balance between them, usually with the help of accounting tools. To have a basic understanding of people's self-financial-management behaviors, we conducted a short survey about accounting tools. This survey was initially posted on a personal WeChat Moments (i.e., timeline posts) entry and was reposted by personal connections.

The survey first asked participants about their existing sources of income and financial resources for later analysis. In the second part we asked if they have experience with accounting tools. For people who have the experience, they were asked to write down the reasons for using the tools. If they have stopped using the tools, they were also asked for the reasons behind the decision. The survey also wanted to see if the degree of financial resources had a relation with accounting tool usage.

The survey collected 70 effective responses through snowball sampling, with 48 participants having their own incomes, and 22 participants not. They have shown similar financial awareness: both groups have about 60% of people who have used accounting tools before (62.5% and 59.09% respectively) and both have the same top reasons for using the tools. The answers to the question of asking why they use accounting tools were theme-coded, "know where the money goes" is the top reason with 42.86% of people mentioned and "want to control own spending" is the second reason with 28.57% people mentioned (see Fig. 1).

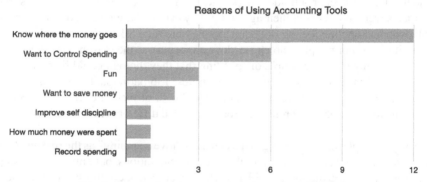

Fig. 1. Respondents' reasons for using accounting tools

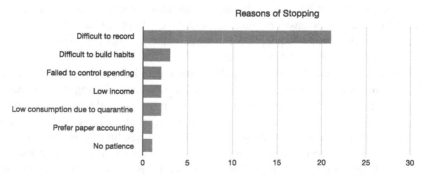

Fig. 2. Respondents' reasons for stopping using accounting tools

Among the participants who have used accounting tools, 67.44% of people (29 samples) have stopped using them. 75.86% of them mentioned the difficulties of using the tools ("too lazy to book each spending", "always forget to book", "the process is too complicated", "It is too troublesome and difficult to keep on recording each spending" etc.). 9% of people considered that the accounting tools cannot help with control their spending (see Fig. 2). Following a short interview with these participants, an interesting insight was drawn: even they successfully recorded the spending, they felt that most of their spending is rational and so they still consumed in the same way.

One possible interpretation of the survey data is that many participants considered accounting tools useful for improving spending and saving habits, but they failed to continuously use the tools due to the usability issues and their effectiveness. Some participants found only *tracking* the spending alone is not effective in helping to control their spending. To help people build a healthy financial habit, therefore, new approaches rather than merely tracking should be considered. Our first survey shows that it is challenging for many to control spending as people tend to self-rationalize their purchases.

4.2 Second Survey: The Type of Spending that People Are Willing to Reduce

After a refocusing from the broad first survey results, we conducted a second survey to understand the deeper attitudes of people towards their spending. In this survey, participants were asked about their age and if they ever had the feeling of "being poor." People who had had the feeling of "being poor" were then asked to choose the reasons for this situation. For people who chose "love spending" as the reason, they were asked to write down any type or example of spending that they thought could be reduced.

The survey has collected 160 effective samples. 136 participants have had feelings of "being poor", 66 of them are aged from 20 to 25, 40 of them are from 25 to 35, and 30 of them are above 35. Different age groups revealed different choices patterns for the reason.

30.3% of people aged 20 to 25 groups consider "love spending" as the reason, 27.5% of participants aged from 25 to 35 have the same considerations, but only 6.7% of people who are above 35 have the same problems. This supports that controlled spending tends to be more effective in helping younger people to achieve saving assets. While for older people, probably due to the fact that they have a more mature financial awareness and self-control, they do not have much trouble in spending. For the portion of spending which can be reduced, the answers were theme-coded, "shopping" and "eating" are the top two choices with 15 and 13 people choosing separately. Other mentioned types were "game", "entertainment", and "social" (see Fig. 3).

According to the study from Li et al. [15], Chinese people build four mental accounts for determining their spending: commodity expense account (referring to the necessary daily spending: clothing, transportation, telephone bills, etc.), development expense account (referring to family and development sending: real estate, car, etc.), relation expense account (referring to donating, gift and another spending for maintaining relationships with others) and hedonic expense account (the spending for relaxation and entertainment, which improves their living quality). It can be seen that the boundary between commodity expense and hedonic spending is blurry and dependent on the situation. When people buy clothes, if they are the cheap ones for basic wearing, it will be

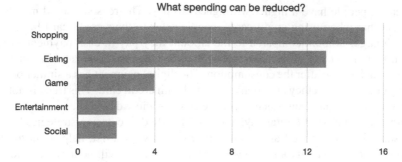

Fig. 3. What spending respondents think can be reduced

the commodity expense, but if they are fancier clothes for a stylish look, the clothing will be a hedonic expense. From the results of the survey, among the spending most participants choose to reduce, "shopping", "game", "entertainment" can all be grouped as hedonic expense, "eating" can both be commodity and hedonic, so the spending worth controlling will be a hedonic expense and hedonic related commodity expense.

4.3 Limitations of the Survey

Given the online mode of survey distribution, we could not encourage participants to write in more detail, so most of them have written only a few words in the answer. Thus, the result cannot cover the participants' deep value on certain behaviors, which limits us in drawing strong conclusions.

The wording "love spending" in the second survey cannot be fully interpreted as people's failure to control their own spending. It cannot directly prove that younger people have less control in self-control, but possibly only show that they may be more willing to reduce the amount of their spending to maintain a better financial situation.

5 Study 2: Design-Oriented Experiments

In the second phase of our research, we focus on generating promising strategies as design intervention, by drawing insights from both our survey results and relevant behavioral economics theories we reviewed previously. Given the rapidly growing and dominating trend of digital payments in China and other Asian countries like South Korea, we consider digital payment is the design space where we could effectively place our intervention. In this phase, we first identify a set of key design considerations based on the survey results. We then conduct an iterative experiment-based study to verify and fine-tune a number of key strategies derived from those design considerations.

5.1 Design Considerations

Replacing cash payment with digital is now the trend. What comes with this is that people now tend to spend more money. Prelec and Simster [16] argued that when using credit cards, people have a higher willingness to pay. The reason behind may be due to the fact that when using credit cards, people refer to their credit card limit, which is a much larger amount compared to the amount they pay in cash payment. Another reason is that the feeling of paying happens in repayment, the moment when one has to pay the credit balance after the consumption. The digital payment has a similar problem, probably due to the fact they are often associated with credit card. This trend is not likely to be reverted as it may cause inconvenience as the society develops.

Within the context of digital payment, we identified five design strategies based on the existing theories as well as findings from the surveys. First, help users *to plan a rational spending account and a saving account*, so people will be less likely to spend too much (exceed the numbers set in the spending account). Second, *give consumption consequence hints both in absolute numbers and proportions*, with adjustment of the showing mode according to the spending behaviors. Third, help people to build *a financial plan related to their future*. Fourth, *build accounts with smaller relative amounts* for people to refer to when purchasing. Lastly, the intervention ought to focus on *only hedonic and hedonic-related commodity expense*.

5.2   Experiment 1: A Pre-test and Post-test Activity with an Attempted Intervention In-Between

Drawing from the above considerations and findings of Morewedge et al. [9], the design intervention should focus on suggesting users to *use a small number as a spending reference mental account* so they will spend less on daily consumptions. To test the effectiveness of this key strategy, we conducted two experiments. The first one is a daily budget with a future plan. It serves as a mental restriction for people's spending. This first experiment only displays the budget for daily expenses, so the amount of the mental account is small.

16 architects were recruited for the experiment. They were all based in Shanghai and Shenzhen as these two cities have similar income and consumption levels. The same working industry was chosen to minimize the effect caused by participants' different income and work-life modes. The experiment consists of three parts. Due to the pandemic and geographical restriction, the experiment was conducted online. To save time, participants were gathered in WeChat groups. A link with a survey form which included the contents of the experiment were sent in the group.

Part 1: The Auction (Pre-test).   This part of experiment design followed the experiment conducted by Prelec and Simester [16]. At the beginning, all our participants were asked to offer a price for three things (Pre-test):

1.   Uncertain market price (higher value) – A redemption ticket for a VIP concert ticket;
2.   Uncertain market price (lower value) – A redemption ticket for a celebrity signed album;
3.   Certain market price – A 100 CNY Alibaba Group product coupon.

The uncertain market price items were auctioned with the Second Price Sealed Bid Auction-participants do not know each other's offering. The highest offering price wins the auction, but only need to pay for the second-highest offering price. The certain market price item was auctioned with the Becker-DeGroot procedure – while participants do not know each other's offering, a random participant will be chosen and the system will generate a number from zero to the face value of the auction item. If the chosen participant offers a higher price than that generated number, he wins and pays his offering price. Otherwise, this process will be repeated until a winner is found. Both auction rules are considered effective to measure people's willingness to pay.

Part 2: Survey Embedded with Attempted Intervention. After participants offered the price of the three items first (Pre-test), they were invited to fill out a survey. The survey started off with basic information, such as the salary increasing level in their industries in the cities, the cost of real estate, and so on. They were then asked to set a savings goal for themselves when they reach 35 years old. According to the saving goal, participants were asked to calculate and set a daily spending budget for now.

Part 3: Auction Again (Post-test). After setting the two financial numbers in part 2, participants were asked to go for the price for the same items in the second round (Post-test). The financial calculation process was considered as financial education for the participants, and people would offer a lower price in the second round in reference to the daily budget. If the second-round auction price is lower, it can support that the "daily budget" strategy is effective to control people's willingness to pay thus reducing the amount of spending.

Results. All participants offered the same price for concert tickets (higher value uncertain market price) and coupon (certain market price) in both rounds. Only very few offered lower prices for the album (lower value uncertain market price). After the test, we did short interviews with some the participants, trying to understand why they did not seem to be affected by our "attempted intervention." We asked about their feelings about the education process. The saving goal and budget setting did make participants reflect on their current spending habits. However, the auction items do not belong to daily spending in their mind, so they did not use the daily budget as the reference when deciding the price. They came up with a price based on their understanding of the value of the items and their overall financial situations (mainly income). This result showed us the need to emphasize "daily budget" more with additional elements to augment the perceived impact. We thus adjusted our strategy to include both daily budget and monthly hedonic budget. It is further tested in the second experiment.

5.3   Experiment 2: Controlled Experiment

40 participants, from different industries this time, were recruited, all of whom were, again, based in Shanghai and Shenzhen. For the purpose of a controlled experiment, they were manually separated into two groups so people with the same background will not be in the same group. Participants were asked for their current monthly spending before being exposed to the experiment.

The experiment group was supported with a suggested spending budget form, which suggests different spending budgets for different income levels. We claimed that the

suggested budgets were calculated based on the average salary increase rate of the participants' respective industries in their living areas, by following the spending suggestions,
they can obtain a good financial savings for future demands. On the other hand, the
reference group had no suggested form (i.e., no intervention). Both groups were asked
to determine the daily budget and monthly hedonic budget (related with the suggested
form or not) according to their own situation. After setting the budget plans, they were
asked for consumption choices under different scenarios:

1. It is a lunch break of the day. You want to order food delivery for yourself. What
   price range will you choose? (Commodity scenario)
2. You finished a big project today. You would like to celebrate it with your
   friends/partners. You want to have dinner and have some them. What price range
   (per person) of a restaurant will you choose? (Hedonic scenario)

The results showed no clear pattern for the two groups (see Fig. 4, 5, 6). No pattern
showed that people who have a higher income will spend more, but people in different
industries show different spending habits. For instance, the participants who work in the
art industry spend more than others despite having lower income.

Short interviews were conducted with four participants in the experiment group to
understand the mental process of dealing with the budget. A participant thought that the
budget was higher than his current spending habits, so for commodity spending, he did
not make any difference as it was already his routine habit. However, for the hedonic
scenario, he raised the amount of his spending compared to his usual habits. One revealed
that as the experiment was conducted in a survey format of which he does not feels
serious about it, so he just finished the survey quickly with his current habits without
much consideration about being given a budget. Another two participants indicated that
the budget had affected their spending choices. They combined the suggested number
with their current spending habits and came up with the average choice. The interview
results gave us many explanations that the statistic results could not tell us.

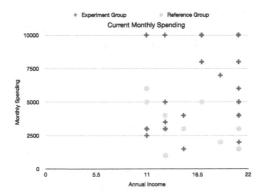

Fig. 4. Respondents' current monthly spending with their income (numbered in thousands)

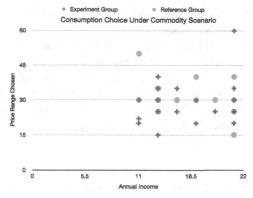

Fig. 5. Respondents' consumption choice under commodity scenario with their income

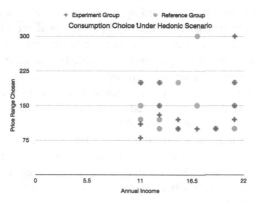

Fig. 6. Respondents' consumption choice under the hedonic scenario with their income

5.4 Lesson Learned

According to the findings from the experiment, income and spending habit are not always directly proportional. Thus, when help to build a rational spending account, each individual's habit should be considered. Otherwise, the suggesting plan may be too difficult to follow, the users will easily be frustrated and give up.

6 Design Concept *BUDG* and Its Initial Feedback

Although both experiments did not show promising results, some insights were taken. Drawing from insights and considerations built from both literature review and our empirical studies, we incorporate the key strategies into a design concept called *BUDG* that includes a mobile application and a smart phone case. We then implemented the concept in a low-fi prototype. The app will help the user to create a budget plan (daily budget and monthly hedonic budget) and record the user's spending. The phone case aims to provide a strong visual hint of the balance situation of the budget. As the mobile phone is usually the most frequently used item in people's lives, and will become an increasingly important platform for payment, a phone case can be a reminder for spending control since it is always with the user.

The phone case uses lightning to connect with the phone, they will work together to auto-track user's consumption. For other payments not conducted by phone, the user can manually record the expense. A "Quick Record" feature helps the user to quickly record routine spending without going through the complete recording process. There are two light strips on the sides of the case to serve as a visual reminder. One stands for daily budget balance, another for hedonic budget balance (see Fig. 7).

6.1 Budget Planning

The first time the user logs in BUDG, the system will collect the user's income, working city, daily spending habits, other fixed spending items, and ask the user to set a future saving goal and their expected time to achieve. The user's total wealth accumulation during this time will be estimated according to the salary level of the industry in the city that the user lives in. The daily budget will be suggested according to the average consumption level or remain the same as the user's current habits (depending on which one is lower). After deducting the target saving amount, daily routine spending, and fixed spending, the rest amount will be set as the Monthly Hedonic Budget. Users can still edit the suggested budgets according to their situations. When the user changes one budget item, the other budget items will be changed automatically by the system in accordance in order to keep the saving goal still achievable.

For example, a user may set a goal of buying a 100 thousand dollars car in 5 years, and the system suggests a daily budget of 100 dollars and a hedonic budget of 6,000 dollars for every three months. The user may consider 100 is not enough for spending and changed the number as 120 dollars, then the system will adjust the hedonic budget accordingly to 4,800 dollars, so the 100 thousand dollars saving can still be saved in 5 years.

The budget setting is mainly to help the user build a rather small mental account for daily and hedonic expense before the consumption. People will refer to this account when buying in-situ, rather than referencing to their current income, digital account (which usually saves a large proportion of total wealth) or a fuzzy wealth impression coming from the credit card limit. Relating to the future saving goal helps users better prepare for the future.

6.2 Budget Balance

The money spent will be highlighted on the homepage of BUDG to keep users aware of each spending. It attempts to cause a lasting painful experience of spending in the users and to urge them to spend less in the future. The amounts of spending display in two modes: absolute numbers and a balanced proportion in percentage (see Fig. 7).

The threshold of the changing effects of absolute number and proportion in ratio bias effect has not been discovered. So currently, in the design, the consumption of hedonic budget which usually is a higher absolute cost will be shown as an absolute number. Spending in the daily budget which is usually a relatively lower absolute number will be shown in percentage. When half of the budget is spent, an exclamation mark will reveal to remind the user to be thoughtful for the next consumption. If there is a surplus in the budget, the user can choose to set a "reward account" for himself or move the surplus to next month's budget.

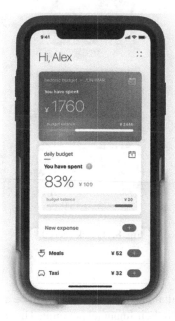

Fig. 7. The phone case and the app homepage which reveals the budget balance

6.3 Spending Recording

Users can record their spending manually. To simplify the recording steps, the user only needs to choose first-level spending categories and the amount of spending. They can add more details by unfolding the menu to choose the second-level category and add some notes. According to Chinese people's expense mental account, the four first-level categories are: commodity, relation, development, and hedonic. Commodity expenses are divided into the high-frequency "daily expense" and low-frequency "commodity expense."

Users can choose to set a record as "quick record." The quick record will be listed on the homepage. By clicking add and confirm, the same record will be made. Only the consumed amount can be changed in the quick record pop-up. For frequently repeated spending like routine transportation costs, users do not need to go through the whole record process (Fig. 8).

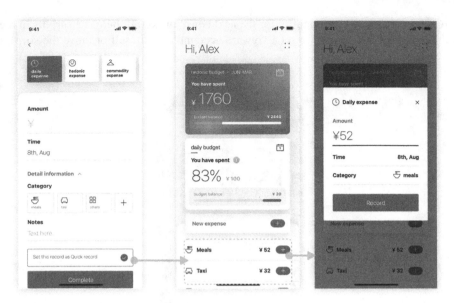

Fig. 8. Quick record

6.4 Auto Recording

All the spending through digital and bank accounts will be automatically recorded after the user connects the app with their financial account. There will be notification pop-up every time when a consumption is detected. A permanent reminder will stay on BUDG's notification page, together with the light strips on the phone case to remind users of the budget balance situation and increase the feeling of losing their wealth. If no expense is detected during the day and no manually expressed record is added, the app will push a notification to the user, reminding them to record today's expense at night. If till midnight there is still no record, the system will automatically eliminate a full day daily budget amount in the record. User can change this record later.

6.5 Initial User Testing

Three people were invited separately to participate in the initial user testing that are done under the COVID-19 pandemic situation - remotely via screen sharing of the UI prototype with the researcher acting on users' behalf. Participants are highly attracted by the colorful light strip phone case which they consider "cool", "give a sense of science." They consider this will attract them to use the system. They think auto-tracking and "Quick Record" are effort-saving which can help them to keep using the product finally achieve the saving goals. One participant did question the technical feasibility of incorporating a person's other financial accounts into the app, which will be a concern for our next stage development. Some modifications in the UI are made after the testing:

1. The original hedonic budget is only set for one month. One participant suggests he does not spend in hedonic expense monthly but two or three months. So, the suggested

hedonic budget in the system can be set manually to calculate as "monthly" "every three months" or "half a year."

2. The saving goal set in the beginning is only for urging users to spend less, but not strictly a wealth accumulation system. So, the progress of how much users have achieved in the saving goal is not displayed. The participants think even the process is not strictly accurate, it is still encouraging to keep on controlling the spending if they have a feeling of saving money toward a target. Thus, the display of the process of money been saved is added (estimated saving calculated from user's estimated income and spending recorded).

3. The item in the manual record page is simplified. The manual record used to have a "merchants" column, but participants reveal they do not care about the merchants, or they can add this content in the "Note" area. So, this item is removed.

7 Conclusion and Future Work

In this paper, we argued that design intervention is needed for the Chinese young generation to control their spending to improve their financial situations, as they have the motivations to reduce certain types of their expenses but lack the capability in practice. Hence, our proposed design solution is focused on controlling the willingness to pay. The design to control spending relates to the users' saving goals and future plan. The key strategies carried into the BUDG design concept are to make users feel more on their expense and to foreground and highlight their spending mental account with visual hint and UI design in the app.

Although our design-oriented research showed promise in applying behavioral economics principles in personal finance design, our empirical studies reveal a real challenge in seeking a universal strategy that works for everyone. Our study findings suggested that an effective solution needs to be versatile and intelligently catered to each individual's situation. Nevertheless, our study results critically paved the way to the formation of a more sophisticated, personalized solution, as we found the individual differences tend to come from detailed threshold figure setting and the priority of different budget items.

In our future work, a more functional and higher-fidelity prototype for BUDG will be developed with refinements in personalization. We plan to conduct longitudinal user study on our target audiences; namely, people who do not have savings due to difficulties in controlling their spending. They will be invited to use the prototype in longer terms while the behavioral data, real saving amounts and cognitive feedback will be recorded after different period of time: a week, a month, three months and half a year. The results will be compared with their spending habits before and are expected to support the effectiveness of the budget intervention. Moreover, additional design features such as goal setting and habits building will also be considered to reinforce the original concept and make the design suitable for long-term use.

References

1. Zhaopin.com: 2018 Bai ling man yi du zhi shu diao yan bao gao [Intervention for Reducing Personal Expenses for Chinese Young Generation]. 199IT (2019). https://www.199it.com/arc hives/818240.html

2. Zhenai.com: 2019 90 hou dan shen ren qun bai pi shu [2019 White Book for single after 90s]. 199IT (2019). https://www.199it.com/archives/989643.html

3. Chao Hui: Zhi fu bao fa bu shou fen 90 hou zan qian bao gao: 90 hou chu ci li cai bi fu mu zao le shi nian [Alipay published the first money saving report of after 90s: there first investment is 10 years earlier than their parents] (2019). https://news.mydrivers.com/1/638/638499.html

4. Chen, M.K., Lakshminarayanan, V., Santos, L.R.: How basic are behavioral biases? Evidence from capuchin monkey trading behavior. J. Polit. Econ. **114**, 517–537 (2006). https://doi.org/10.1086/503550

5. Li, A., Ling, W.: Mental accounting: theory and the application inspiration. Adv. Psychol. Sci. **15**, 727–734 (2007)

6. Thaler, R.H.: Mental accounting and consumer choice. Mark Sci. **27**, 15–25 (2008)

7. Kirkpatrick, L.A., Epstein, S.: Cognitive-experiential self-theory and subjective probability: further evidence for two conceptual systems. J. Pers. Soc. Psychol. **63**(4), 534 (1992)

8. Burson, K.A., Larrick, R.P., Lynch, J.G.: Six of one, half dozen of the other: expanding and contracting numerical dimensions produces preference reversals. Psychol. Sci. **20**, 1074–1078 (2009). https://doi.org/10.1111/j.1467-9280.2009.02394.x

9. Tversky, A., Kahneman, D.: The framing of decisions and the psychology of choice. Sci. Am. Assoc. Adv. Sci. **211**, 453–458 (1981). https://doi.org/10.1126/science.7455683

10. Morewedge, C.K., Holtzman, L., Epley, N.: Unfixed resources: perceived costs, consumption, and the accessible account effect. J. Consum. Res. **34**, 459–467 (2007). https://doi.org/10.1086/518540

11. Thaler, R.H., Benartzi, S.: Save more tomorrow^{TM}: using behavioral economics to increase employee saving. J. Polit. Econ. **112**, S164–S187 (2004). https://doi.org/10.1086/380085

12. Hershfield, H.E., Goldstein, D.G., Sharpe, W.F., et al.: Increasing saving behavior through age-progressed renderings of the future self. J Mark Res **48**, S23–S37 (2011). https://doi.org/10.1509/jmkr.48.SPL.S23

13. Antonides, G., Ranyard, R.: Mental accounting and economic behaviour. In: Ranyard, R. (ed.) Economic Psychology, pp. 123–138. Wiley, Chichester (2017)

14. Li, A., Hao, M., Li, L., Ling, W.: A new perspective on consumer decision: double-entry mental accounting theory: a new perspective on consumer decision: double-entry mental accounting theory. Adv. Psychol. Sci. **20**, 1709–1717 (2013). https://doi.org/10.3724/SP.J.1042.2012.01709

15. Li, A., Ling, W.: The implicit structure of mental accounting among Chinese people. Acta Psychol. Sin. **39**, 706–714 (2007)

16. Prelec, D., Simester, D.: Always leave home without it: a further investigation of the credit-card effect on willingness to pay. Mark. Lett. **12**, 5–12 (2001). https://doi.org/10.1023/A:1008196717017

Bukas: Material Messages for Filipino Migrant Workers and Their Transnational Families

Analyn Yap(✉), Huaxin Wei, and Kenny K. N. Chow

School of Design, The Hong Kong Polytechnic University, Kowloon, Hong Kong
{huaxin.wei,ka.nin.chow}@polyu.edu.hk

Abstract. This paper presents findings from a design research project that looks into the phenomenon of communication and expression in the diasporic family relationship, particularly between Filipino domestic workers and their kin. The research also looks into material culture and the meaning of the *"balikbayan box"* metaphor as a design prompt, leading to the creation of design guidelines and a concept development for *Bukas*, a tangible product linked with a mobile interface that facilitates meaningful daily communication for migrant Filipina workers and their families through a material artifact. The design inquiry consists of immersive human-centered qualitative methods including semi-structured field interviews, cultural probes, and participatory workshops to deepen the understanding of the stakeholders' mindsets, behaviors, and expressive needs. These methods reveal migrant workers' latent needs for self-identity expression and communication. The research endeavors to explore migrant workers' self-identity and results in a coexisting spectrum of values consisting of positive achievements and negative feelings of sadness, from which we posit a set of criteria and develop a design concept that tests these guidelines .

Keywords: Migrant worker · Domestic intimacy · Family communication · Augmented reality · Tangible interaction · Physical artifacts · Routines · Materiality · Overseas Filipino Workers (OFW)

1 Introduction

The Philippines has a long and storied history of labor export in Hong Kong. As early as 1988, former President Corazon C. Aquino had already been using the term "Bagong Bayani" (modern heroes) to refer to the remarkably large group of Overseas Filipino Workers (OFW) working in Hong Kong. According to the Hong Kong Immigration Department's official data, there are around 219,073 Filipino migrant domestic helpers, comprising around 54% of the population of foreign workers in Hong Kong [1]. Transnational labor is widely accepted as an alternative strategy for social and economic mobility among low to middle-class Filipino households, especially for families living in lower-income provinces in the Philippines. Filipina migrant workers in Hong Kong are typically domestic helpers aiding Hong Kong families in their daily home life, cleaning the house, buying necessities, cooking, and taking care of children, pets, and the elderly. They are

© ICST Institute for Computer Sciences, Social Informatics and Telecommunications Engineering 2021
Published by Springer Nature Switzerland AG 2021. All Rights Reserved
A. Brooks et al. (Eds.): ArtsIT 2020, LNICST 367, pp. 425–445, 2021.
https://doi.org/10.1007/978-3-030-73426-8_26

officially engaged in these routine activities for six days and are given the Sunday of every week as a day-off. Since the early 1980s, migrant domestic workers have congregated in Hong Kong's public spaces every Sunday and for public holidays [2]. The Statue Square in the Central district of Hong Kong, for example, can be seen every Sunday populated by Filipina migrant workers gathering and relaxing. Another noticeable activity held in these public spaces is the frantic packing of goods inside large cardboard boxes, commonly known as the '*balikbayan box*'—a package of items sent back home to the Philippines containing gifts and various household items. The *balikbayan* box is embedded in the socio-cultural psyche of the modern Filipino family and is one of the most recognizable artifacts of the Filipino diaspora and the transnational worker's life. In an ethnographic study by Clement Camposano, he argues that the preparation of a *balikbayan* box "is a performance of intimacy, a way for migrant women to bridge the Hong Kong and Philippine segments of their diasporic and fragmented lives, which enables them to sustain coherent narratives of the self" [3].

In the design space, not many projects and studies have been made to address the relationship between migrant workers and their families. However, many anthropological studies have already studied the negative effects of an extended absence in the relationship on the elder workers and the children left behind. On the side of the migrant worker, there is psychological stress, depression, anxiety [4], loneliness, and feelings of inadequacy leading to overcompensation. As for the children left behind, this absence of a parent has been known to breed miscommunication, materialism [5], and a sense of dependency leading to a loss of initiative to work [6].

The nature of the design problem deals heavily with the performance of intimacy and the preservation of the domestic relationship in a transnational context. The economic circumstances of the migrant Filipina worker create a situation of physical and emotional distance that causes her many complex and conflicting feelings. She must juggle multiple roles as she is relegated from being a homemaker and caring mother in her home in the Philippines to the role of a breadwinner, separated in a foreign land. The problems of distance in relationships have been widely studied in HCI (human-computer interaction) and tangible interaction design, but most of the literature and design products produced address romantic intimacy [10] and even sexual intimacy, not familial relationships. This research aims to address the gap in design and HCI literature that pertains to the specific context and relationships of the migrant worker and her transnational family that go beyond the expected value of intimacy and domesticity.

2   Related Work

While there is a large number of studies dealing with computer-mediated communication and design for relationships and connectedness, this research project particularly shares its domain knowledge with several earlier endeavors in HCI that look into technology mediation in the context of the family and distance relationships. In this section, we will briefly discuss three related research projects and a framework for the critique of family phatic communication technologies.

2.1 Habitat

Habitat is a project consisting of a series of networked furniture (coffee tables) that studies awareness of Life Rhythms over a distance. The goal of the research was to see if the usage of this technologically-enabled furniture could simulate between distanced people the same rhythms – conveying the same reassurance and intimacy as physical proximity. The study notes the importance of the following considerations: maintaining continuity, seamlessness with the original function of the furniture, and the ability to access past states of the product. Habitat shares a similar premise to our work in the sense of connecting distanced people with the goal of supplanting physical presence through shared items [7].

2.2 FamilyPortals

The researchers of Family Portals (FP) deployed an always-on multifamily media space among six families for a period of eight weeks. The media space consists of a targeted portal for sharing of live videos of the remote family, and a shared portal for common information and to be displayed to all remote families connected by the portal. These portals have different features such as writing on shared whiteboards, enabling "blinds", etc. The study discusses how domestic awareness systems such as FP perform when there is a visual medium that affords an explicit sharing of daily moments through writing. This work makes the case for the importance of writing, verbal and written communication in familial spaces [8].

2.3 MemoryReel

MemoryReel deals with the special moments of online social interactions. It is intended to nurture connectedness for people with long-distance relationships through positive reminiscence. It enables people to capture, select these special moments and restore them as memory cues, which potentially will invoke reminiscence later. These memory cues include three modes of contents: text, audio, and animated images, which correspond to text messages, audio messages, and moments of video calls respectively. The design and study of MemoryReel provide design implications and strategies regarding designing for reminiscing, scaffolding relationships at a distance, as well as designing meaningful interactions [9].

2.4 Strategies for Designing Technology for Intimate Relationships

Hassenzahl et al. provide a useful set of guidelines in designing for the mediation of intimacy. They have outlined six particular strategies: awareness, physicalness, expressivity, gift-giving, joint action, and memory collection. Awareness is when ambient information about the individuals involved is shared among users of the product, creating a sensation of continuous presence. Physicality is the simulation and transmission of gestures or physiological effects among users. Expressivity is when partners can articulate their feelings and emotions to each other through words, symbols, language, or any other mode of communication. Gift-giving is self-explanatory as intimate experiences enable partners and individuals to express appreciation and value in the form of a given artifact or experience. Joint action is the strategy that allows partners to fulfill tasks and actions together through a product or service. Lastly, memory collection is a strategy that fosters intimacy by keeping a record of past moments that partners can fondly look back on. These strategies provide a helpful basis, design inspiration, and cross-reference for the design criteria formed for this work later on [10].

3   Theoretical Framework

Three main theoretical frameworks have significantly informed the research and concept development of Bukas. Firstly, the ethnographic study by sociologist Clement Camposano has provided an added depth and understanding of the phenomenon, given the limited timeframe of this research. In our online interview with Dr. Camposano, he discusses in great detail how he has tapped into Daniel Miller's theories of materiality in investigating the role of physical objects in meaning-making in social, cultural, and political relationships. He further pushes the inquiry by studying the box-sending behavior of OFW's and frames it as a manner of self-making. This particular insight was further reinforced by this research's qualitative study to be discussed in the next sections. Camposano's interpretation of how through the box, the traffic of goods in this material culture "gives form" to the migrant worker's identity coherence and meaning-making [11].

Our intention with this research is to directly draw an extension of Camposano's discourse on the role of the *balikbayan* box in material culture by studying it through the lens of interaction design and HCI. As an interaction artifact, the box is an interesting medium that carries a myriad of meanings, co-constructed by both the senders and the receivers, imbibing a relational and social meaning symbolically when they are collaboratively packed and opened. It has a physical presence and is bound within a specific and finite space and time between foreign and domestic dimensions. Lastly, these boxes also have a performative dimension that involves shared activities performed by specific parties – in the Central district of Hong Kong, one will likely encounter Filipina workers gathering around open boxes of varying sizes, engaged in the collaborative activity of filling in packages. One may ask a friend for a favor and hitch a small item back home. It is interesting to note that these boxes are usually packed as a group and opened as a group back home as families literally gather around the box. In an activity that mirrors Christmas mornings in western media, names are called and items are distributed as they are taken from the package.

Secondly, we are looking into the conceptual metaphor of *containment* and how this image schema makes the physical and mental model of the box effective and intuitive as a tangible and graphical interface. Johnson in his defining 1987 work, "The Body in the Mind" defines image schemas as the "continuous structure of an organizing activity", as dynamic and flexible conceptual structures [12] that evolve with the changes in how we experience and embody things in the physical world. Hurtienne also [13] writes in his 2009 dissertation that "Image schemas are multimodal and can be instantiated in different ways. This suggests that they are applicable to hardware and software user interfaces alike" and that ".. metaphorical extensions of image schemas to structure abstract concepts allow designers to convey abstract meaning in the user interface using the available spatial and physical means for input and output."

The containment image schema is one of the most common and fundamental metaphors derived from physical experience. Johnson describes containment as having these properties: an in-out relationship, boundary, and transitivity. Containers have definite boundaries that determine whether items are either inside or outside the receptacle and there is a finite limit to the amount a certain container can hold. Transitivity is how we come to conceptually understand that specific contents can belong in sets that are part of a bigger set. A pair of shoes inside a box that a person is gifted with means that that person is now in possession of the pair of shoes. Transitivity in containment can also be exemplified by a person keeping valuable belongings inside a safe located inside their house [12, 13].

These properties of containment seem mundane but in the context of the *balikbayan* box, we propose to use these principles to interpret its interactive significance. These aspects make a material artifact more effective, intuitive, and embedded in the users' daily lives.

Thirdly, we use the Family Phatic Communication design sensibilities as criteria for articulating and discussing the product attributes as a cross reference. The authors of this study identify six different sensibilities: Temporality, Expression, Connectivity, Reciprocality, and Perceivable Volume [14].

4   A Design-Led Research Process

The goal of our research is to build a deep understanding of the transnational familial relationship of Filipino migrant workers, which can shed lights on how to design for supporting communication and intimacy for this unique group of audience and, by and large, for any families who have members living far away from home. Inspired by the rich meanings and impact carried by *balikbayan* box, the research focuses on how to achieve self-expression and empathetic family communications mediated by *material objects*. Not only will the form of communication be investigated, but also the content and matter of empathetic messages in the context of a migrant family. Specifically, we are interested in what emotions and feelings are meaningful and evocative to a migrant worker employed as a domestic helper in a Hong Kong household. Likewise, we are also interested in the two-way communicative relationship as we also consider the domestic family's sentiments as the beneficiary party in the Philippines. Our research inquiry is initiated with the following research questions.

1. What problems do Overseas Filipino Workers (OFWs) face in their familial relationships?
2. What are the OFWs' experiences and feelings in packing the *balikbayan* box?
3. How do OFW mothers perform intimacy with their distanced loved ones?
4. What are the meaningful interactions performed with the items sent and received?
5. How are transnational familial relationships mediated by artifacts?

Due to the nature of the inquiry and the levels of access available to the research, qualitative methods have been the primary mode of obtaining data and insights about the problem and phenomenon. The research process went through field observation, cultural probes, semi-structured interviews, and participatory workshops in a span of 8 weeks. The first phase of the research (field observation, cultural probes, part of the interviews) aimed to broadly investigate the issue by divergence. As certain points of focus emerged, the second phase (interviews, participatory workshops) focused on convergence, culminating in the determination of certain design criteria to be used for concept development. In all research activities, we have obtained oral or written consent from our subjects and participants. For cultural probes and participatory workshop participants, we were also given permission to use their photos and drawings in our publications. To protect our subjects and participants' privacy, all names used in this paper are pseudonyms. Most conversations were done in Tagalog and some in a mix with English. All the Tagalog quotes used in this paper were all translated into English by the lead author.

4.1 Field Observation

The objective of this first engagement was to explore and make initial conversations about the behavior of packing boxes. This observation was broad, looking at the general crowd of workers gathered in the Central district of Hong Kong, as well as five separate small groups of OFW women (see Fig. 1). Some members conversed casually in the middle of packing or while relaxing within their own friend groups. One notable learning was the current service systems already in place that operate well to assist the OFWs in storing and sending their items. Being members of a foreign culture, there was also the existence of a specific vocabulary: "*Pag-iipon*" translated as "collecting" refers to the act of accumulating items for placing inside the box; "*Storage*" refers to the various warehouse and freight services that keep their accumulated items since it was rare that an employer would allow the Filipina worker to store the items in the household given Hong Kong's notorious space issues; "*Raket*"—a Filipinized version of the English "racket" referring to an informal or illegal scheme of obtaining money is a common term used for a secondary means of income, usually a buy-and-sell business.

The prime reason for sending the box is that, in these Filipino families' eyes, imported items are superior and more novel, regardless of the items themselves. Another significant observation that eventually hints at a critical point of the research insight is the existence of an informal buy-and-sell "*raket*" culture. The women engaged in these activities are particularly proud of their capabilities, talking at great lengths about the items they have sold and how this practice has saved them from the stickiest financial situations. More field observations made in a different district in Kowloon, Hong Kong also suggest that OFWs become highly engaged when they are able to pick up new skills in their daily work; for example, they would converse proudly about what they cook for their employers and sharing their cooked food to their friends in their Sunday gatherings.

Fig. 1. Field observation in the central district of Hong Kong.

4.2 Cultural Probes

The field observations not only gave us basic knowledge of the OFWs' general situations, details of their *balikbayan* box practices, as well as the highlights of their daily life, but also enabled us to get acquainted and build trust with a group of five domestic helpers. This allowed us to deploy a small set of cultural probes to the group to loosely but intimately study the deeper psyche and emotions of the OFWs. We followed the spirit of Gaver's [15] original method of cultural probes but with practical adaptations in terms of the deployment. Five different probes were designed to collect open-ended insights and raw information (see Fig. 2) about (1) their problems, experiences and feelings in Hong Kong, (2) the places that are memorable to them, (3) the items they purchase and pack, (4) their special memories in the Philippines and in Hong Kong, and (5) their daily routines and contacts. The probes aimed to collect not only texts but also images, locations, and spatial information. The cultural probes were deployed to the five Filipina domestic helpers as mentioned above: Sharon, Nora, Maricel, Vilma, and Nadine. They were a group of friends from the Ilocos region of the Philippines who spent their Sundays relaxing and chatting together. There were five types of probes given to these participants. Probes 1–4 were completed during an intensive 3-h session where the participants went through each task's instructions facilitated by the researcher. Probe 5 (Daily Diary) was left with the participants for one week, with each question to be completed as a day-to-day activity. In the following we will discuss the findings of the returned probes.

Fig. 2. Cultural probe sets

The first probe is a simple photo album intended to gather some of the most memorable experiences of our participants and the moments they choose to capture and look back on. Most of the favored images are taken in Hong Kong locations featuring the participants posing in front of aesthetically pleasing backdrops such as flowers, greenery, and other special locations wearing their Sunday best. Through this probe we found that the favorite moments of migrant workers are when they are showing themselves in fashionable, sophisticated, and beautiful ways (see Fig. 3).

Fig. 3. The images also feature themselves engaged in fancier activities – Maricel uploaded an image of herself picking out wine, while Nadine sent a photo of herself in Disneyland wearing fall clothing (whereas their Filipino counterparts at home would not be able to wear due to the all year round hot weather).

The second probe was a small, empty cardboard box and a set of paper cut-out with visuals of common gifts and items that simulate the experience of packing a box. This probe affirmed us the typical rationales of what OFWs choose to send: chocolates and coffee were always featured inside their boxes. The same colonial value of appraising "foreign" goods noted during field observation is also reflected here. However, the most critical finding is how they also yearn to make routine choices for their families: Maricel chooses to send polo shirts because she wants her children to specifically wear things that she chooses for them. Her maternal decision-making is also imbibed when she chooses to send underwear because she notes that *"panties are important for women"*. This shows us the latent need to engage in intimate decision-making in domestic affairs.

The third probe was a set of small cards for the participants to write about their conversations everyday. While many of the conversation cards featured routine "checking-up" dialogues and personal conversations that did not disclose many details, there was a lot of conversation about problems with their perfectionist employers. The most notable finding is how commonly migrant workers talk about their investments and goals back home such as land and house repairs/construction with their friends and families. Money is an important point of conversation as they speak a lot about the side-business they engage in to supplement their income.

The fourth probe was a set of maps where the participants were asked to mark specific memorable locations such as their home, favorite places, and locations they want to go to in the future. This probe's objective is to ask about where they came from, where have their treasured memories, and where do they want to go next. Many of them value their residing areas in Hong Kong as their favorites, which are specific and treasured spaces of togetherness in Hong Kong. They also have many treasured places in the Philippines and provinces that they have not yet visited. While they miss home, the most interesting finding to come forth from this probe is a desire to go even farther to countries like Australia, Japan, and Canada, citing the better wages and quality of life they might attain there. This rattles the common perception that OFWs only feel homesick and yearn only to go back home to the Philippines.

The last probe was a small written diary with daily prompts that aimed to broadly obtain information about their daily lives. The diary probe revealed that their daily lives, once thought to be rote and repetitive, was actually filled with many different activities. During their working week, OFWs get to learn how to do many things, particularly upgrading their cooking skills. The returned diaries also reveal that even if they perceive their life in Hong Kong as a life of self-sacrifice, they choose to side with and be comforted by thoughts of positivity.

4.3 Semi-structured Interviews

Before and after the cultural probes activity, we conducted two rounds of in-depth interviews. Impressed by the rich meanings and practices relating to the *balikbayan box* we observed in the field, the first round of interviews was initiated to gain a deeper understanding of the box-sending and receiving behaviors of transnational families. After we collected back the cultural probes and uncovered a wider range of findings as described above, we felt the need to conduct a second round of interviews, this time focusing on the self-expressive activities of migrant women workers and their emotions in order to build deeper insights.

Our first round of interviews, done in video calls or emails, involved six OFWs (box senders) and five additional subjects who are relatives of OFWs – either their children or extended family (box receivers). Previously, the same interview questions were also asked to five different OFW groups in Central during the field observation. Each of these interviews lasted for around 30 min to an hour. The goal of this first round of interviews was to gain in-depth information about the transnational family dynamic and their relationships, as well as how they perceive the act of *balikbayan* box sending. The interviews also intended to draw out current problems and issues within the relationship. It is necessary to point out that white-collar OFWs were also involved among the 6 interviewees, contacted through personal connections and calls-for-interview posts on Facebook.

We gathered data from conversations with all the above 16 interviewees during both rounds of interviews and grouped them into two sets: those views from the OFWs and those from the family members back at home. The key findings of the interviews showed that through the package, there is an intention to physically demonstrate where the migrant worker has been and the "imported" good things they are experiencing. These boxes are typically sent not more than twice a year. It is referred to as a "token of remembering" and a "symbol of generosity". The participants were also aware how the *balikbayan* box is an embedded part of the Filipino diasporic culture and somehow the practice of sending it has already become an unsaid expectation for the mother in a foreign country. Along this thread, a few OFWs expressed their feelings of deep burdens in the same way: "*all these [financial and material expectations] are all on me.*" Yet, they avoid passing on this feeling to their families whom they sometimes disdain if they are only approached when money is needed. On the other hand, for the OFWs, this "burden" is interestingly coupled with a newfound sense of freedom and power in the new land where they control their decisions and finances. This power is liminally expressed in how they remain consistently attuned and engaged to the routines and quotidian matters of the Philippine home, as well as how they insist on only showing their best selves in their daily interactions with their kin. They feel the need to play out their various mindsets through the objects they send and the memories they collect and send to their family. A participant noted that the box's significance was that it "showed that we are thinking about them" while another has mentioned that "it kind of gives me peace of mind knowing that they have enough supplies to last for a year.

On the other side, the families back home also expressed a two-fold relationship with the package sent. The key findings reveal that they highly enjoy the surprise factor of receiving the box – not knowing when it will arrive and its exact contents. They enjoy how the opening of the box is always a collaborative family affair where *unpacking* becomes a systematic procedure of undoing tape, taking out stuffing, and removing items piece by piece. Meanwhile, the appreciation of the receiving family is coupled with a sense of guilt and curiosity of how difficult it was to put together the package. The family members have a desire to know the struggles of the parents, but do not know how to bring the matter up without discomfort or awkwardness as one participant said: "I wish I knew what their problems were…in video calls, we never talk about problems, video calls have to be "feel good" because, the image is that you're doing well.".

4.4 Participatory Workshop (with OFWs)

At this point, we have developed a more mature understanding of our migrant Filipina workers and drawn one key insight, which is that they seek to communicate and perform not only domestic intimacy, but also self-identity in their transnational familial relationship. Self-identity is a topic not easy to talk about openly, given its personal and abstract nature. We thus considered conducting a participatory workshop to look into what constitutes self-identity for OFWs, as a workshop can provide a more intimate setting and use activities to enable participants to concretize their thoughts with visual aids. We invited three migrant Filipino workers: Bea, Angel, and Kathyrn. Bea and Angel did the workshop together in person for a session of 2 h, whereas Kathryn's workshop was conducted online via video call and lasted for an hour. In the first part of the workshop, participants were invited to talk about problems and successes in their current life, as well as their difficulties in communicating certain issues with their families back at home. In the second part of the workshop, they were invited to envision for themselves an ideal future scenario and sketch it down on paper.

Bea reflected similar themes of achievement in her narrative as she recalled the proud moment of being able to purchase her child a new phone. Kathryn also derives pride from being the chairperson of a major workers' union and that she is able to help and represent her fellow OFWs. Meanwhile, Angel mentioned that she was proud of "growing her mind" with the new skills she has learned to do in Hong Kong – including cooking and house repairs. However, all three participants brought up difficulties in communicating more difficult feelings like loneliness, homesickness, the confusions they encounter at work, the fatigue they experience that does not get recognized, and the personal yearning for prioritizing themselves for once. Bea says *"that's why I work hard here so that my children don't become like this. I know this is still an honorable living, but I still don't want this kind of life for them."*

Kathyrn had a poignant and unique perspective of being aware of the societal factors affecting her personal circumstances as a domestic worker in Hong Kong and the importance of outspoken activism in the union as a method of her self-expression, despite her parents' worries about her engaging in this activity. She says *"My mom and dad are concerned about me being an activist and union member, but I explain to them that who else will speak up for us if not ourselves?"* She also touches on her different roles as she engages with her parents' apprehension with her being a union leader. Her parents tell her *"You are not a hero…You can just be Aberdeen's mom, but you cannot be a hero."* to which Kathyrn replies *"I'm not trying to be a hero, my point is just speak up! This is not just my own struggle but everyone's struggle as well"*.

Kathryn's strong sense of role assignment and achievement is always paired with her deliberate choice to remain an activist despite her family's qualms. When asked if they felt empowered being the breadwinner in a foreign land, able to go to more developed places, Kathryn says *"For me, we are all victims of poverty, no domestic worker will ever pick being away from family but we were forced to leave. As for me, I was a painter back home, but why did I leave, I never wanted to be a domestic worker at all."*. She agrees that she feels proud of her achievements but also keenly points out that the OFW's display of a glamorous selfhood especially during the Sunday holiday is also a pretension or *"pagbabalat-kayo"*. Kathryn powerfully states that migrant workers don their best clothes and do whatever they want on Sunday to mask the less appealing sides of their migrant lives and especially to show their families that they are doing well, even if they are not.

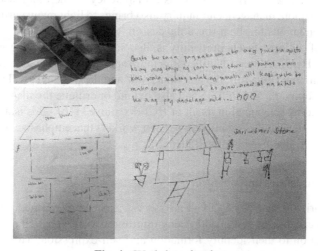

Fig. 4. Workshop sketches

When facilitated to think about and visualize the current situation and an ideal future scenario, Bea and Angel both instinctively drew house structures (see Fig. 4). Bea illustrated her long-term goal of a "*sari-sari store*" (a small corner shop selling dry goods in the neighborhood). She meticulously drew the inside of her shop, with sachets and plastic packets dangling from the structure. Angel illustrated a similar structure, a "dream" house with specific divisions and floor plans. She laughed and smiled as she planned out the inner rooms and gates of her dream house, even searching on the internet for inspiration photos. This activity affirmed the significance of the containment image schema and how the container can also allude to a long-term goal. Kathryn, on the other hand, emphasized the importance of open communication.

5   Analysis, Conceptual Framework, and Final Design Criteria

5.1   Analysis

The salient findings collected from all qualitative methods are summarized in eight coded themes grouped into three major groups that form the conceptual framework of the research. These eight code themes inform and give weight to the set of design criteria and guidelines for designing with and for migrant workers. The three major groups and eight themes are illustrated in Table 1 below:

As discussed, the design research transitions from looking into domestic intimacy to the formation of self-identity and self-expression in this inquiry about the migrant workers' communicative and phatic needs. Based on the results of the qualitative research, it can be said that self-identity consists of the positive dimension – achievements, skills, freedom, happiness, and the negative dimension – failures, frustrations, shortcomings, and vulnerabilities. A good balance of addressing both positive and negative facets in familial communication over a distance ensures the well-being of all parties involved, particularly the migrant workers'. There is transparency in the relationship and their mental states are more managed. Our inquiry also brings to light many pertinent insights about recommendations for the form of the design.

This idea of multiple facets in identity is also supported by existing work on self-identity in HCI. Henrik Åhman identified four main approaches to the self: the instrumental self, the communicative self, the emotional self and the playful self. These different dimensions are dynamic and shifting and also extend or critique the idea of the "stable, coherent, individual self found in much of HCI discourse" [16]. This is also supported by many sociological studies on migrant women workers that emphasize the importance of various role affiliations in their self identities.

5.2   Design Guidelines and Criteria

Table 1 summarizing the analysis above also serves as the basis for the following design guidelines and criteria for design addressing migrant workers' phatic family communications, in relation to their identity formation and self-expression. The guidelines are divided into criteria for design matter and design form.

The criteria for design matter concerns the meanings and values the proposed design should be able to communicate. The concept should be able to convey a sense of pride.

Table 1. Major themes and findings from research methods

Pride and Goals	Pride in foreignness and financial freedom	A desire to showcase where they've been and what they are enjoying	Pride in newfound personal and financial freedom in Hong Kong, going to foreign, fancy places	
	Pride in achievements and gaining new skills	Despite family pressure, they are able to thrive because of their skills	Pride in achievements, new skills gained, earning abilities	Personal capabilities and skills have grown in Hong Kong
		Finding ways to supplement their income with side gigs and businesses		The feeling of achievement gives satisfaction despite sadness/loneliness
	Long-term goals		The presence of long-term goals	The ideal future is the accomplishment of a long term goal/a house or store
Sadness and Passive Miscommunication	The family's intention of empathy for the mother	The family back home has an intent to know the mother's struggles		The family back home experiences some guilt, that they are a burden
		The family back home experiences some guilt, that they are a burden		
	A migrant worker's sadness, struggle & sacrifice		They self-perceive their time here as a sacrifice	There is sadness that the family does not seem to know their struggles
				Feeling deep sadness but cannot tell the family
Themes inspiring the design form	A small act of decision-making	Small acts of decision-making and hand-picking items are important	A need to assert personal choices	
	A constant and deliberate quotidian practice		A need to engage with the family in quotidian matters	A constant reminder of openness to family and employer is crucial
	Materiality & containment		Phatic engagement through objects and material things	The house is a container of aspirations and dreams

Addressing the theme of "pride and goals" in our conceptual framework, the criterion of *achievement declaration* conveys that the features and functions of a design should afford some level of displaying achievements and celebrating good moments in text, audio, or image form. The system should also convey a sense of *goal-setting* - where it can afford for users the creation, planning, and maintenance of future goals. In the context of existing HCI research, Zimmerman also identifies long-term goal setting as a consideration in designing for the self [17].

Another criterion is that the system should be embedded with *catalysts for difficult conversations*; namely, it should have mechanics to accommodate and facilitate vulnerability through the occasional introduction of uncomfortable family topics to the users of the system. Addressing the second theme "sadness and passive miscommunication" in our conceptual framework, these catalysts can be also designed in a probing, inexplicit manner, stoking *empathy* with the choice of language, time context, topic prompts written and designed to be evocative and facilitative of emotions, mental states, and life experiences.

The criterion for design form deals with the formalistic elements and features that the system should possess. Firstly we suggest the design to be *tangible & material* so as to allow for a degree of physical and material transfer or interaction, referencing from realistic objects and surfaces that users interface with in their daily lives. The second property we suggest is to use the *containment* image schema which is effective in depicting physical presence and value possession.

Lastly but importantly, one of the most reinforced criterion for design is framing the system in a *constant and quotidian* time frame dictated by routine. The interactions with the system should be a regular experience with a certain level of predictability. However, despite the quotidian nature of the interaction, some attributes of the design system can account for some level of *surprise* and *irregularity*, such as the time of arrival and the hidden digital messages embedded in each physical piece, to support an enjoyable experience. Lastly, the performance of the interaction should hover in between the *private and the communal/interpersonal*. Some activities can be done individually and some can be performed as a group.

Our design concept development began with a co-design workshop, where we attempted to conceptualize the design based on some of the key insights, with the help of a group of design students. The goal of this workshop was to gain a designerly perspective and help the research inquiry articulate the form of the design concept. The co-design workshop was also planned with 6 designers participants. There was an effort to select those designer participants who were working mothers or wives, or in distance relationships. The limitation of this method is that the point-of-view might vary from the original stakeholders. Nonetheless, we were cognizant of this and limited the objective of the co-design workshop to be largely exploratory and not definitive. They were asked to share personal narratives about their achievements and failures and from their sharings, personas were developed to help frame the design context.

The two groups chose 1 persona each to design for and generated two design concepts emphasizing different aspects of a phatic communication space. The first group came up with a small nook or corner inside the home where mothers can project different moods, roles, topics, and interests during a regular and specific time, as a nightly ritual. The second group interestingly made a shared media space using a "floating bubble" schema to represent granular thoughts and topics that were difficult for a couple to bring up in regular conversation (see Fig. 5). Similar to Bea and Angel's house metaphor, this group also useds the house image schema to contain these piecemeal thoughts.

Fig. 5. Workshop sketches

6   The Design Concept of *Bukas*

The resulting design concept development is a prototype to embody the design guidelines set forth in the previous section. Five design concept variations were deliberated on, ranging from smart labels systems, smart mirrors, mobile application, physical remote devices, and the concept chosen is the current research inquiry's best attempt at a culmination of the aforementioned design criteria.

"*Bukas*" (from the Tagalog word meaning "to open" and "tomorrow") is a tangible box artifact coupled with an augmented reality (AR) enabled mobile interface that aims to facilitate meaningful long distance family communication through a material medium. It is composed of two boxes containing seven graspable pieces each, two wireless contact chargers, and a mobile application (see Fig. 6).

Fig. 6. Components

The main idea of the concept is for the box to become a medium of slow technology [18] between the migrant worker and the distanced family by embedding messages inside the contained pieces to be created and collected during a routine of recollection that happens every night. At the end of each week, messages are collected and virtually sent through the AR patterns. OFW mothers and their families alternate the box sending and receiving process on a weekly basis.

6.1 Design of Tangible Components

The primary tangible component is a pair of box artifacts, one meant to be located with the migrant worker in Hong Kong, and the other with the family in the domestic home. Each box is designed to mimic the *balikbayan* box and is constructed with MDF board. It can be opened easily from the top with a hinged pair of lids. This box contains seven pieces of various quadrilateral figures, each with a different pattern laser cut on the surface (see Fig. 7). These pieces represent daily communication themes of the week and all seven pieces fit almost exactly to the box's inner compartment—like a 3D puzzle, with several ways to arrange them inside. The irregularity of the pieces provide variation to the experience of filling in the box and is meant to make the process of fitting in each piece more fulfilling.

Fig. 7. Tangible components

The different patterns on each piece are designed to be easily identifiable and meant to represent an abstract prompt for the family members to accomplish. The patterns also fulfill the technical function to be a unique, scannable image for the AR function to activate. The patterns are also dynamic in the sense that the topic prompt can change per pattern on a week to week basis. Moreover, the illustrated patterns are aesthetically symbolic and abstract, allowing for a degree of conceptual interpretation on the part of the user.

The smallest brick piece representing goal-setting is a special piece specifically meant for migrant workers and their families to set long-term goals that they can collaboratively contribute to over a period of time. This function is also meant to connect to an actual bank account to transfer a small amount of money to a goal fund to support this long-term goal. Each sent message using this piece slowly builds conversations around a chosen goal and enables the family to slowly build towards that target financially and cognitively.

A supplementary wireless contact charger is the secondary device meant to alert the two separated parties of one's physical presence, triggering the daily prompt to be sent to the message sender.

6.2 Design of Intangible Components

A mobile application with separate user flows for message senders and message receivers facilitates the prompt to write a nightly topic which is provided by the system. The application has 6 main functions: to answer topic prompts, to embed these answers into an AR-enabled pattern, to notify users of a receipt of a message box, to activate the AR-enabled patterns to read the messages, to connect to a bank account to transfer money, and lastly to save and re-access past received and sent message boxes. These 6 functions disclose themselves to the users in two main modes: Message Box Sending and Message Box Receiving.

Notifications deployed at different times facilitate and mark the contextual disclosure of these features. There is also a home dashboard for users to see their current status anytime, however, the main mechanic of alternative sending of message boxes week by week is fixed. Box receivers do not get to read piecemeal messages on a day-to-day basis and box senders cannot send messages without the physical piece, nor without completing all 7 topic prompts.

6.3 Interactivity

The primary physical interactivity consists of the user being able to represent messages through a graspable piece that one can hold and rotate. Another major point of interaction is the experience of puzzle-solving, putting all the pieces together to fit inside a box with finite space. Conversely, the piece-by-piece action of "unboxing" by the box receiver is also significant. This interaction takes inspiration from how the *balikbayan* box is packed to brim and is collaboratively unpacked—its contents distributed to different members of the family. There is no set order to read the messages embedded in the seven pieces. When the held message piece meets the AR-enabled mobile application, the interaction's intention is to make it seem as if the user is holding the photos embedded in the piece (see Fig. 8).

Fig. 8. Boxing and unboxing

The trigger to enable the nightly prompt notification is powered by a wireless charger that detects physical presence. The assumption is that when the distanced family member is physically present and resting while charging their phone, the migrant worker, who is far away, is made aware of this temporality and is subtly made aware of the presence of their loved one. The augmented reality function is demonstrated with a simple prototype created in CoSpaces.Edu and used with the commercially available MergeCube (see Fig. 9).

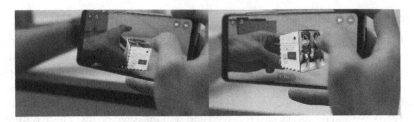

Fig. 9. Augmented reality interactivity

7 Initial User Study and Discussion

7.1 Study Set-Up

We conducted an initial user study of three participants: Sarah, Joseph, and Kamille with our design prototypes. The aforementioned names used in this paper are pseudonyms. Three participants were recruited, one migrant working mother and two of the original box receiver interviewees. Each session lasted for 45 min to one hour. Each user study session consists of two parts. In the first part, the researcher introduced the concept of Bukas and its components to the user. In this introduction, the user was also given a scenario to illustrate the use context. The scenario was narrated over video call, after which a step by step on-camera demonstration of how the tangible product – the container box with its inner pieces – is used during boxing and unboxing (Fig. 8). In the second part, we invited the user to use our online UI prototype to perform 2–3 key tasks, such as sending messages and opening the box, depending on their role: the mother or the receiving family member. When performing these tasks, if a step involved the tangible product, we would perform the steps on behalf of the user. This protocol was in fact a special, less-than-ideal arrangement for a user testing session in the COVID-19 situation.

7.2 Study Results and Improvements

During the study sessions, little clarifications were needed regarding the main functions of the product concept, with the users noting that the structure of the application and product was very comprehensive and well-structured. The positive feedback centered around the construction and design of the tangible artifact as well as the UI. They also appreciated how the product is a catalyst for prompting uncomfortable conversations, Kamille commented: *"the design encourages an old style of communication in contrast to this age of instant messages"*. She also mentioned that the idea of the presence trigger was also interesting and promoted a sense of "being" with distant loved ones. These feedback can indicate that the guidelines have achieved a certain level of efficacy. The main issues in the feedback obtained from the testers centered around three key points of improvement. First, the users were quite perceptive in mentioning the need for the topic prompts to be varied and emotionally evocative enough to cover the time frame of a transnational family's period of separation. The writing needs to be provocative and facilitative enough to address the challenge of coaxing certain emotions from stakeholders who had *"apprehensions to share deeper feelings"* according to one user. Sarah also suggested the need to *"prepare a plan on how to write these questions and topics."* This was addressed in our final design iteration by making plans on how to rotate and switch up the prompts. We also got help from a literary writer friend to rephrase the questions to be more effective. Another future plan of action is to consider the Filipino language in writing future topic prompts. In planning for the variety of topic prompts, we can divide the topics among different categories: Achievements, Identity, Loneliness, HK Culture, Availability, Problem-Solving, and Goal-Setting. We can also use McMaster's family functioning model as a potential source for new prompts.

Second, a need to recall and save messages, to recap and use for future conversations. Joseph and Kamille had noted the need *"to utilize these diaries for future daily conversations"*. This was addressed with the addition of a bookmark feature in the revision of the mobile interface.

The third major issue is more broad as it points out the need for the design solution to be situated in a service process that provides onboarding for users about the objectives and functionality of the design product. As the product is involved with highly private and potentially sensitive information, there needs to be a system set in place to assure users that it is a *"safe medium and space"* for writing. In the future iteration, this product can be a part of a larger service system or a social service or campaign.

7.3 Discussion and Reflection

Bukas serves to extend the current body of knowledge that exists in HCI that tackles relationship-mediation in family bonds. This research hopes to add the underrepresented perspective of migrant workers in the realm of interaction design and HCI. There are many points of improvement for the research and product design, beginning with the recruitment of participants. A larger sample size and stricter criteria for participants would improve the findings of the research, as currently, blue-collar and white-collar workers alike were included in the qualitative study. A stronger, more concrete framework for identity-formation could also be used to improve the topics tackled in the design matter. In terms of the form of the box, further studies need to be made to verify more image schemas and metaphors that would also be effective. The choice of patterns also needs a stronger rationale in terms of its meaning, symbolism and visual design. The current study and design concept relied greatly on the idea of materiality and tangible form, and while it proved evocative in the initial user study, a more critical and thorough user test involving an actual working prototype installed in a transnational household for an extended period of time would be the true test of efficacy. Sending tangible messages is a matter of technology and concept. However, getting migrant workers and their families to truly tap into their thoughts and emotions, reflect and recollect their self-identities and expression is the bigger challenge.

8 Conclusion and Future Work

This design research and project aims to explore the largely untapped field of migrant worker research in design and HCI. This paper provides a set of guidelines to design for the communication of migrant workers and their transnational families. A demonstrable product prototype was also produced to test the efficacy of the design criteria defined after a series of qualitative research methods. However, we are cognizant of the risks of the design research endeavor being naive. The issue of mass migration of workers from the Philippines to work as domestic helpers in other countries is not an ideal situation; it is a systemic problem with socio-political roots. *Bukas* has aimed to address a very specific need and has investigated the deeper sentiments of migrant workers, but its future direction can follow through from two distinct starting points.

First, further studies can be made in how to improve the deeper phatic communication between domestic family members and conduct experiments to verify the design criteria specified in the guidelines.

Second, a new direction can be opened transitioning from migrant worker family relationships to the larger society. Social computing and communal technologies have the opportunity to identify roles among connected individuals, highlight relationships and hierarchies. Social computing helps address and enhance the experience of connecting migrant workers towards a collective identity and goal. Further studies can move the scope to the larger community of migrant workers, promoting to individuals, a sense of inclusion in an active collective community of OFWs.

References

1. Data.gov.hk: Statistics on the number of Foreign Domestic Helpers in Hong Kong (2020). https://data.gov.hk/en-data/dataset/hk-immd-set4-statistics-fdh/resource/063e1929-107b-47ae-a6ac-b4b1ed460ac3
2. Moss, E.: 'That one day is all you have': how Hong Kong's domestic workers seized Sunday. The Guardian, 10 March 2017. https://www.theguardian.com/cities/2017/mar/10/sunday-sit-in-inside-hong-kong-weekly-domestic-worker-resistance
3. Camposano, C.C.: Balikbayan boxes and the performance of intimacy by Filipino migrant women in Hong Kong. Asian Pac. Migr. J. **21**(1), 83–103 (2012). https://doi.org/10.1177/011719681202100104
4. Hall, B.J., Garabiles, M.R., Latkin, C.A.: Work life, relationship, and policy determinants of health and well-being among Filipino domestic workers in China: a qualitative study. BMC Public Health **19**, 229 (2019). https://doi.org/10.1186/s12889-019-6552-4
5. Reyes, M.M.: Mobile Childhoods in Filipino Transnational Families (2008). https://www.unicef.org/philippines/Synthesis_StudyJuly12008.pdf
6. Asis, M.M.B., Ruiz-Marave, C.: Leaving a legacy: parental migration and school outcomes among young children in the Philippines. Asian Pac. Migr. J. **22**(3), 349–375 (2013). https://doi.org/10.1177/011719681302200303
7. Patel, D., Agamanolis, S.: Habitat: awareness of life rhythms over a distance using networked furniture (2003)
8. Judge, T., Neustaedter, C., Harrison, S., Blose, A.: Family portals: connecting families through a multifamily media space. In: Conference on Human Factors in Computing Systems – Proceedings, pp. 1205–1214 (2011). https://doi.org/10.1145/1978942.1979122
9. Wei, H., Hua, D., Blevis, E., Zhang, Z.: MemoryReel: a purpose designed device for recording digitally connected special moments for later recall and reminiscence. In: Proceedings of the 13th International Conference on Tangible, Embedded, and Embodied Interaction, pp. 135–144 (2019). https://doi.org/10.1145/3294109.3295649

10. Hassenzahl, M., Heidecker, S., Eckoldt, K., Diefenbach, S., Hillmann, U.: All you need is love: current strategies of mediating intimate relationships through technology. ACM Trans. Comput.-Hum. Interact. **19**(4) (2012). Article 30

11. Camposano, C.C.: The politics of generosity: traffic in goods, resistance, and the crafting of selves within the contemporary transnational Filipino household. Aghamtao: J. Ugnayang Pang-Aghamtao/Anthropol. Assoc. Philipp. **23**, 123–144 (2014)

12. Johnson, M.: The Body in the Mind: The Bodily Basis of Meaning, Imagination, and Reason, pp. 28–30. University of Chicago Press, Chicago (1987)

13. Hurtienne, J.: Image Schemas and Design for Intuitive Use (2009). https://doi.org/10.14279/depositonce-2753

14. Chatting, D., Kirk, D., Yurman, P., Bichard, J.-A.: Designing for family phatic communication: a design critique approach. In: Proceedings of the 2015 British HCI Conference, pp. 173–183 (2015). https://doi.org/10.1145/2783446.2783566

15. Gaver, B., Dunne, T., Pacenti, E.: Design: cultural probes. Interactions **6**(1), 21–29 (1999). https://doi.org/10.1145/291224.291235

16. Åhman, H.: Conceptualizing the self: a critical analysis of the self as a discursive trend in human-computer interaction research. Hum. Technol. **13**, 149–179 (2017). https://doi.org/10.17011/ht/urn.201711104210

17. Zimmerman, J.: Designing for the self: making products that help people become the person they desire to be. In: Proceedings of ACM Conference on Human Factors in Computing Systems, pp. 395–404 (2009). https://doi.org/10.1145/1518701.1518765

18. Hallnäs, L., Redström, J.: Slow technology – designing for reflection. Pers. Ubiquit. Comput. **5**(3), 201–212 (2001). https://doi.org/10.1007/PL00000019

The Design Intervention Opportunities to Reduce Procedural-Caused Healthcare Waste Under the Industry 4.0 Context – A Scoping Review

Pranay Arun Kumar[1] and Stephen Jia Wang[2]($\boxtimes$)

[1] Department of Postgraduate Research, School of Design, Royal College of Art,
London SW7 2EU, UK
[2] School of Design, Hong Kong Polytechnic University, Hung Hom, Kowloon, Hong Kong
stephen.j.wang@polyu.edu.hk

Abstract. The current medical device industry thrives on material redundancy and continues to advocate for a use-and-throw model of practice. Such redundancies are vital to ensure the safety of patients by preventing reinfection from reused devices, but the risks and costs of the waste generated are leaving hospitals and third-party resource handlers wary of future challenges.

The Industry 4.0 revolution has started to redefine the production and consumption models of many industries. The main advantages of adopting these methods have been increased efficiency of systems and a reduction of redundant resources. But how do these new technologies help reduce the waste generated in medical procedures? This paper scopes the opportunities that come with implementing industry 4.0 to reduce procedural caused medical waste. These challenges and opportunities have been analysed at four hierarchical levels of innovation; the system, service, procedural and product levels. The research indicates that although the adoption of industry 4.0 concepts in healthcare is contributing to a more efficient use of resources, more research is required focused specifically on its impact on the production of procedure-caused medical waste.

Keywords: Medical device design · Medical waste · Sustainability · Industry 4.0 · Advanced manufacturing

1 Introduction

The onset of the COVID 19 pandemic has brought with it an increased use of single-use disposable equipment in the healthcare industry. The production of single-use disposables has been consistently unable to meet the demand, and yet it is far too much for waste management systems to deal with (Bown 2020; Ranney et al. 2020). With the pandemic continuing to spread around the globe, a new approach is required to reduce the waste generated from the healthcare industry (Zambrano-Monserrate et al. 2020; Klemes et al. 2020).

A. Brooks et al. (Eds.): ArtsIT 2020, LNICST 367, pp. 446–460, 2021.
https://doi.org/10.1007/978-3-030-73426-8_27

This study implements a scoping review approach to explore the opportunities for implementing Industry 4.0 (I4) technologies to reduce the diagnostic, treatment and rehabilitation procedural waste. The following sections cover the background of the research by exploring various definitions of medical waste, and I4. This study has a specific focus on waste produced by medical procedures, and four aspects of I4 which can have a strong impact on reducing procedural waste; lean production systems, internet of things (IoT), artificial intelligence and additive manufacturing. Due to ... The application of these concepts in medical procedures has been reviewed from Scopus database.

There are various types of wastes produced in medical procedures, such as anatomical waste, product and packaging waste, pharmacological waste, material waste, and a waste of resources such as water, electricity, time, human resource and money. These types of waste can be attributed to various factors in a medical procedure. The product and packaging waste is often the result of how the product has been designed and used. Pharmacological waste is dependent on the use of medication as determined by the clinicians. The anatomical waste is dependent on the pathophysiology of the condition being treated and the design of the procedure. The waste of physical and human resources is also dependent on the design of the procedure and the systems within which these procedures are conducted, such as the hospital infrastructure, the financial model of operations for the hospital, and the efficiency of operations at the hospital. While design interventions may be possible at various levels of the overall healthcare system, this study focusses on interventions that are not policy driven and are achievable within the constraints of the hospital operations.

The study has been detailed in four sections covering four different levels of design intervention opportunities to reduce the procedural-caused medical waste. The first section explores the use of lean management approaches to make medical departments at healthcare facilities more efficient in delivering healthcare to patients. This covers the systems interventions that support the reduction in waste generated from medical procedures. The second section delves into the procedural-level interventions using the concept of internet of things. The third section explores the use of artificial intelligence and robotics in the delivery of healthcare services, and its impact in reducing waste from medical procedures. The fourth section explores the use of additive manufacturing in the development of products used in medical procedures. Through this review, a holistic analysis has been conducted on the scope for introducing industry 4.0 concepts in the healthcare setting to reduce medical waste from medical procedures.

1.1 Healthcare Waste and Its Causes

Healthcare waste is defined by the WHO as the waste produced by healthcare facilities (including laboratories and research centres) related to medical procedures. This also includes waste produced through healthcare related activities in households (Chartier et al. 2014). The terms healthcare waste and medical waste are often used interchangeably, and refer to the same types of waste.

The unregulated production and disposal of medical waste started with the big "plastics" explosion of the 1950s. The advent of plastics in industrial production empowered manufacturers to produce cost-effective devices which could be sterilized using Ethylene Oxide (ETO) or radiation methods. But hospitals found it cheaper to use and dispose of these devices than to sterilize and reuse them because the plastics would degrade in traditional autoclave machines, while ETO and radiation methods were expensive and inaccessible to most hospitals (Greene 1986). Today, the trend of single-use disposable products rides on the ambiguity of the safety of sterilization and reprocessing services, to ensure that infections are not re-introduced in the system. This occurs despite studies by the FDA showing there is no increased risk of infection due to the use of reprocessed devices (GAO 2008). The report reasserted that the adverse health events associated with the use of reprocessed devices were the same types and rates associated with non-reprocessed, new devices (GAO 2008). There is also an impetus for the industry to be cautiously wasteful to avoid legal implications of malpractice (Hailey et al. 2008). The result is the generation of a large amount of medical waste, often proportional to a country's GDP (Minoglou et al. 2017). Minoglou et al. (2017) observed the average amount of waste generated by a patient per hospital per day ranges from 0.44 kg in countries like Mauritius to 8.4 kg in the US.

A significant proportion of this waste is produced from medical procedures. Sa et al. (2016) conducted a surgical waste audit for hip arthroscopies and found that just 5 cases resulted in a total of 47.4 kg of waste. While 21.7 kg of that waste was biohazard, the rest was composed of sterile wraps, recyclables, non-hazardous waste and sharps (Sa et al. 2016). There is also a proportion of the waste which comes from expired or redundant inventory. In a review paper, Yazer (2018) talks about how there is a significant number of blood units collected by blood banks that get wasted due to expiration at the bank itself, or when in transit between the hospital and the blood bank. The waste produced, is not only an inefficient use of resources, but also has a financial impact on the stakeholders. In Canada, over 64,000 cases of total knee arthroplasty procedures take place annually (Yan et al. 2018). For each procedure, an average of 118g of bone cement is used, out of which 91.2g (77.2% by weight) gets wasted. This costs the Canadian Government $186 CAD per procedure, which when extrapolated for the annual number of procedures, results in a wasteful expense of almost $12 Million CAD per year (Yan et al. 2018).

In hospitals in the UK, under the NHS, decisions regarding the purchase of medical devices is on the discretion of the purchase department, on instruction of clinical staff and other users of the devices (Ison and Miller 2000). The decision to purchase a specific device is based on two criteria; the risks it poses to the patients and the users, and the price of the device. Two of the many effects not factored in this decision are; financial cost of treatment and disposal of the device, and the environmental impact of the device (Ison and Miller 2000).

When focusing on medical procedures, it has been evidenced that wasteful processes are inherently also increasing the energy and resource utilization, which can be quantified in terms of the carbon footprint generated and the toxic emissions released. Thiel et al. (2015) conducted hybrid life cycle analyses for 62 hysterectomies and found a notable environmental impact of the disposables, single-use devices, energy used for heating, ventilation, air-conditioning and the anaesthetic gases. Based on the identified culprits of emissions, they also proposed less environmentally harmful ways of providing the required care to the patient.

These environmental, financial and social problems of procedural medical waste are now being exacerbated by the COVID 19 pandemic, and call for transformative change in the way resources are used for medical procedures.

1.2   The Industry 4.0

The Industry 4.0 (I4) is believed to be the next leap in technology that will create a paradigm shift in the industrialization of our world (Lasi et al. 2014). Riding on the success of digitization in the third industrial revolution, I4 is preempted to re-define industrial production through a combination of smart objects and advanced digitization of production units. It was first announced by the German government as a key initiative towards a new industrial revolution (Ustundag and Cevikcan 2018). They imagined a future with products controlled by their own manufacturing process instead of people determining the manufacturing of products. Among the many social, economic and political advantages that this revolution brings, is the efficient use of resources. As society gears up for a shortage in supply of essential mineral ores and the impending ecological changes that are taking place, I4 can bring a stronger focus on sustainability in industrial production and consumption, while ensuring economic feasibility. This study focuses on how the fourth industrial revolution impacts the environmental sustainability of medical procedures (Lasi et al. 2014).

Sustainable industrial value creation is also believed to be one of the inherent advantages of I4 (Stock and Seliger 2016). At the macro scale, new business models focus more on selling functionality and accessibility to the consumers, rather than the tangible product itself. As companies retain ownership of their products, there will be a stronger incentive to ensure long-term use of the product before disposal. The business models will also focus more on long-term economic sustainability, consequently lengthening the value cycles of the materials used. I4 encourages closed loop product cycles, and cross-linked value creation networks, which improves the efficiency of resource usage (both material and energy). The inter-connected data streams allow horizontal integration of the product life-cycle, facilitating the interaction of various phases of product development and identification of efficient routes of value creation.

At the micro scale, there are multiple opportunities for the implementation of sustainability strategies at various stages of the product life-cycle as described below. The manufacturing units can retrofit sensors and actuators on existing machines to create Cyber-Physical Systems in which machinery can interact and communicate with each other to optimize processes. This reduces time, energy and material consumption in the manufacturing process. The role of humans will shift from machine operation to operation management. They will oversee production and identify opportunities to improve the operation flow, reduce lag time, and eliminate redundancies, all of which contributes to reducing time, human effort, energy and material usage. The role of organizations shifts to optimizing logistics for a smooth operation flow, and building the value creation network to improve end-to-end value cycles. In this entire system, the products created will be built for closed loop life cycles, encouraging, reuse and remanufacturing by implementing cradle-to-cradle principles. The usage data collected from the products will also help redesign products for better customer satisfaction, and reduce customer grievance time due to damage or bugs in the product function (Stock and Seliger 2016).

2 Method

This study uses the scoping review method as described by Arksey and O'Malley (2005). The main research question being addressed is 'How can the implementation of I4 technologies help reduce procedural caused medical waste?' Relevant published literature was sourced from SCOPUS database searches. The search criteria have been provided in Table 1. The time period used was from the proposition of I4 as a concept (Kagermann et al. 2011) until now.

Table 1. Search criteria for scoping review

Search criteria	
Databases	SCOPUS
Keywords	Industry 4.0; medical waste; medical procedure; lean system; internet of things; artificial intelligence; additive manufacturing
Type of Search	Journal articles; book chapters; conference proceedings
Languages	English
Time period	2010–2020

A total of 158 papers were identified from the search results, and 35 were found relevant to the study. The relevance was determined manually by studying the titles and abstracts of the identified papers. The identified published works were sorted based on their relevance to the role of new technologies in reducing medical waste from medical procedures. Due to the large scope of technologies found under the term of I4, studies pertaining to artificial intelligence, lean production systems, internet of things and additive manufacturing were prioritized. Papers relevant to industry 4.0 in healthcare but not focusing on the waste generated during medical procedures were not included in the review, as they are beyond the scope of this study. The results of the review have been structured to determine how interventions at various levels of a medical procedure can counter the waste generated in erstwhile procedural methods.

Table 2. Keywords searched for review

S. No.	Keywords	Total search results	Relevant results
1.	(TITLE-ABS-KEY (industry 4.0) AND TITLE-ABS-KEY (medical AND waste))	6	3
2.	(TITLE-ABS-KEY (lean AND system) AND TITLE-ABS-KEY (medical AND waste))	85	20
3.	(TITLE-ABS-KEY (internet AND of AND things) AND TITLE-ABS-KEY (medical AND waste))	18	2
4.	(TITLE-ABS-KEY (additive AND manufacturing) AND TITLE-ABS-KEY (medical AND waste))	30	6
5.	(TITLE-ABS-KEY (artificial AND intelligence) AND TITLE-ABS-KEY (medical AND waste))	19	4

3   Results - Existing Solutions and Future Prospects

This section investigates the current uses of I4 concepts in the healthcare industry, how they tackle the problem of waste generation, and future prospects of transitioning to cyber-physical systems. The section has been divided into 4 separate levels, using a top-down approach to look at system-level, procedural-level, service-level and product-level interventions to tackle waste generation using I4 (Fig. 1). As defined by Gaziulusoy and Ceschin (2016) in their Design for Sustainability (DfS) evolutionary framework, we use the first two innovation levels, namely product level and product-service system level to classify the opportunities identified in this study. We expand these two levels to distinguish procedures and systems from the products and services, as explained next. We define a product as a system of tangible and intangible elements designed to support a specific set of functions in a medical procedure. These could be surgical tools, packaging material, infrastructure connecting one product to another and softwares supporting the functionality of the products. We define a service as the interface between certain products and users that enables its use in medical procedures. Typically, services are provided by organizations or individuals in the form of access to the product functionality, repair and maintenance requirements for products and access to relevant information that is useful in a medical procedure. A medical procedure is defined as a set of tasks completed to achieve a specific diagnostic, treatment, or rehabilitation result on a patient (Becker et al. 1986). A procedure may involve the use of multiple products and services by clinicians to complete the required set of tasks for a patient. These procedures may be surgical, pharmacological, observational or a combination of the three. A system can be defined as a set of elements and the relationships between them. In this paper, we are more interested in the system that facilitates medical procedures. The system typically includes the organization responsible for the procedure, their facilities and infrastructure, and the products and services used to complete the procedure for a patient. The system-level explores uses of lean approaches to reduce waste from a systemic perspective in medical procedures. The procedural and service levels explore the interventions such as use of Internet of Things, digitization, automation and artificial intelligence in streamlining medical procedures. The product-level focuses on the role of additive manufacturing in creating products for medical procedures. Although each of the sections are interlinked, this top-down approach to the study helps identify multiple points of intervention to make the industry less wasteful.

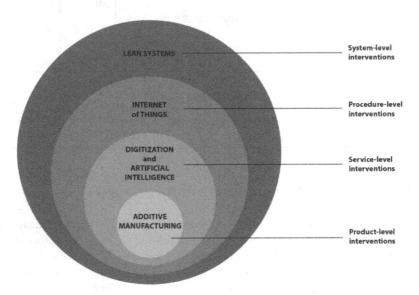

Fig. 1. The four levels of intervention to reduce procedural-caused medical waste

3.1 System Level Design Intervention Opportunities - Lean Approaches to Reducing Procedural Caused Waste

Lean production is an approach to manufacturing that adopts the philosophy of doing more with less. First witnessed in Toyota's Production System (Ohno 1988), the main purpose of this ideology is to streamline processes by eliminating various kinds of waste embedded in the system by continuously improving methods. The concept of lean thinking sits well with industry 4.0 through the creation of smart factories, connected systems and the goal of achieving efficient processes in industrial systems (Ustundag and Cevikcan 2018; Sanders et al. 2016).

A significant amount of research was found in implementing lean strategies for the reduction of procedural medical waste. The application of lean has been experimented in various medical procedures including hip fracture surgeries (Morales-Contreras et al. 2020), head and neck biopsies (Matt et al. 2014), continuous renal replacement therapy (Benfield et al. 2015) and total knee and hip replacement procedures (Gayed et al. 2013). The concept of lean is built on predictability and standardization, neither of which is yet achievable when treating individuals with unique conditions and physiologies (Edwards et al. 2012). But there is certainly a need for more efficient systems in healthcare, as Caloyeras et al. (2018) point out in their survey, which observed that nearly 15% of the time spent by physicians on work can be handled by non-physicians, and almost 10–15% of treatment provided was inappropriate. A study by Baccei et al. (2020) found that implementing a lean management approach to their musculoskeletal radiology department helped reduce expenses as well as time-frames for report submission, indicating significantly increased work efficiency in the department. Similarly observations were made in a study by Al Hroub et al. (2019), in an outpatient oncology pain clinic, by Fields et al. (2018) in a paediatric medical centre, by Sanders and Karr (2015) in an Emergency Department, and by Gjolaj et al. (2016) in an outpatient oncology infusion unit.

Overage constitutes items that are asked for by surgeons to be opened in the sterile field before a procedure, but do not get used. A study by Rigante et al. (2017) shows that overage constitutes almost 95% of the waste produced in neurointerventional procedures, evaluated at 676.49 EUR wasted per case. This is one part of medical waste that is produced purely because of probabilistic emergencies or unknowns which could be reduced with better protocols for immediate action, and better planning on procedures. A study by Lunardini et al. (2014) found that almost 40% of the instruments procured for orthopedic and neurosurgical spine cases could be removed through a lean process assessment, resulting in annual cost savings of $41,000. Similarly, Ahmadi et al. (2018) have compiled multiple gaps in knowledge in inventory management of surgical supplies, ranging from optimization methods to problems faced by practitioners. Some of their suggestions directly correlate with Industry 4.0 concepts, such as digitization, connected systems to reduce redundancy in supplies and analysing past usage statistics to efficiently prepare supplies for procedures.

The application of lean process management in medical procedures has been evidenced to reduce the dependence on instruments and material resources, along with reduced time frames for the delivery of health services and reduced costs associated with various procedures. While more research is required for the relevance on lean systems on the reduction of procedural waste, there is sufficient evidence to suggest that the application of lean management in healthcare has made significant progress in making health systems more efficient and less wasteful in time, money and efforts of health workers.

3.2 Procedure-Level Design Intervention Opportunities - Using IoT in Medical Procedures

The Internet of Things forms the basis of a connected system, where various parts of an economic chain can communicate with each other (Ustundag and Cevikcan 2018). In the industrial internet, connected systems have an important role in medical procedures.

The data generated and communicated by smart products depends upon the sensors used to collect this data, which forms the foundation of the ubiquitous computing society (Wang 2013). There has been a significant evolution in sensors over the last decade, which now enables robots to perceive information as well as, if not better than the human senses (Ustundag and Cevikcan 2018). Robots are now developed to automatically detect parts, handle them, navigate through obstacles, and complete complex movements to fulfil a task. This opens up a dialogue for robot-assisted medical procedures, especially when dealing with microscopic and nano-particles. The dexterity and precision with which robots can perform tasks, supersedes human abilities and can be constructively used for complex procedures. As summarised by Taylor et al. (2016), the role of medical robotics is not to replace clinicians, rather it is to aid them by transcending human limitations, and improving the safety, consistency, efficiency and overall quality of treatment provided.

While robots may make procedures safer and more efficient, they are not necessarily the most environmentally sustainable. A study by Woods et al. (2015) compared the carbon footprint of laparoscopy, robotically assisted laparoscopy, and laparotomy. Based on the solid waste generated and the energy consumed in each procedure, they concluded that the robotically assisted laparoscopy had a much higher carbon footprint than either of the other two (38% more than the laparoscopy and 77% more than the laparotomy).

The published sources reviewed in this study did not find specific information on the role of IoT in the reduction of procedural caused waste. The role of IoT, as reviewed in this study, is to make procedures more efficient and use technology to tackle procedures previously infeasible by human dexterity alone. This may have consequences on the waste generated, but more research is required to understand the implications of IoT on procedural caused waste.

3.3 Service-Level Design Intervention Opportunities - Digitization and AI in the Medical Industry

When it comes to patient treatment, most treatments prescribed are probabilistic and rely on the patients' response to evaluate the effectiveness of the treatment. Using data mining and artificial intelligence, it may now be possible to shift from probabilistic to definitive treatment, and allow doctors to focus more on the delivery of actual patient care (Bennett and Hauser 2013).

Imaging technologies have evolved well beyond the static imaging of X-Rays and CT scans. New imaging technology not only allows us to visualize human structures and disease states in real time, but also allows us to generatively predict the onset and spread of disease in the body. The ability to simulate disease states before the onset provides opportunities for localised rehabilitation, control and limit the disease from spreading (Dukart et al. 2013).

Data mining and predictive modelling of Electronic Health Records can help predict the optimal clinical treatment for a patient. This in turn reduces the reliance on corrective procedures, post-procedural care and treatment redundancies in cases of ineffective treatment (Bennett and Doub 2010).

The enormous amount of data generated at healthcare centres opens up multiple opportunities to use predictive analytics to reduce decompensations and hospital readmissions, estimate the risk of procedural complications (triage), and predict adverse effects such as multiple organ failures (Bates et al. 2014). These analyses can warrant timely action, and thus reduce resource consumption at hospitals.

Big data and real-time monitoring of patient data can help reduce the stress on hospitals by encouraging home care for non-critical patients. Remote monitoring of patients with wearable and implantable devices can help manage and prevent their re-hospitalization (Wang and Moriarty 2018; Arun Kumar 2014). This will benefit elderly patients by identifying both short-term critical conditions, and long-term patterns that help build personalized treatment (Grossglauser and Saner 2014).

A majority of the published research studied in the application of AI in healthcare focused on the reduction of treatment and use of healthcare facilities, and increasing the timely detection and cause of illnesses. Although the reduction of the use of healthcare facilities may suggest a reduction in resource use and waste generation, there was little information on the direct impact of AI on the reduction of procedural caused medical waste.

3.4 Product-Level Design Intervention Opportunities - Additive Manufacturing

One of the key advances in technology to reduce waste in the manufacturing process is the development of additive manufacturing. As opposed to the method of subtracting and morphing material to develop the required part, additive manufacturing uses a 3D digital model to precisely create the required part in layers of material. This not only saves material, but also enables the generation of complex structures previously not feasible using subtractive manufacturing. The reduced time required to generate a prototype, reduced labour, and the flexibility in customizing prototypes makes this technology a go-to strategy for efficient resource consumption (Gibson et al. 2015).

Additive manufacturing is now being extensively used in dentistry (Torabi et al. 2015), maxillofacial surgery (Suomalainen et al. 2015), head and neck surgery (Chan et al. 2015), correction of bone deformities (Yang et al. 2015), and plastic surgery (Choi and Kim 2015) to name a few sectors. Although the uses of additive manufacturing are plenty in the medical industry, the technology is yet to evolve to become faster, more accurate, more efficient and cheaper, for the use to be accessible to all (Martelli et al. 2016).

The use of additive manufacturing in the medical industry has been gaining speed over the last few years (Javaid and Haleem 2018). Rapid prototyping enables clinicians to not only visualize the human body, but also provide tactile insights into physiological processes and complex pathologies (Nocerino et al. 2016). This manufacturing method also helps reduce material requirements while providing the same structural strength as predicate devices (Yan et al. 2019). Despite the advances in the use of additive technologies in medical procedures, there are a number of challenges yet to be overcome. The research on manufacturing with new materials, and the high cost of AM often prevents this technology from competing with traditional manufacturing methods (Mishra et al. 2014; Garg and Mehta 2018). Even so, the publications reviewed in this study indicate that AM is one of the most promising ways forward in the reduction of procedural medical waste, and further research will only strengthen the merits of this argument.

4 Discussion and Conclusion

Healthcare systems today are far from sustainable in their practice, this includes the waste in material, waste in time, waste in expenditure and redundancies in treatment provided to the patient. With growing concerns on the environmental impacts of healthcare waste, and the concerns of exorbitant expenses by hospitals, there is a need for timely solutions to reduce the production of procedural waste in the medical industry.

As evidenced above, the application of Industry 4.0 concepts and technologies can be beneficial in reducing procedural caused medical waste, but it is important to note that the implementation of industry 4.0 can be highly complex and require huge investments of time and money. The transition to cyber-physical systems requires large infrastructural overhauls and a considerable change in mindset and behaviour of hospital staff and clinicians. A digitized system also requires ethical clearances from patients to participate and contribute their data, and health systems will need to provide adequate assurances that this data will not be misused or shared unless specifically authorized (Ustundag and Cevikcan 2018; Stock and Seliger 2016).

The concept of industry 4.0 and advanced manufacturing systems could potentially provide multiple avenues to tackle this problem at various levels. Lean production strategies are one way to streamline processes and treatment procedures and make the system more efficient. In this review, we identified four design intervention opportunities based on a variety of literature that supports the argument for a transition to industry 4.0 concepts and technologies as a means of reducing the waste generated from medical procedures. The potential applications of these design interventions can be summarized from the following three perspectives:

1. From an assistive method perspective, the seamlessly connected healthcare devices and creating cyber-physical systems in healthcare, procedures requiring skill beyond human abilities can be assisted advanced automations. Such as the assistive robots can then feed in procedure statistics and patient data through sensors back to the clinicians creating a feedback loop which allows the system, and the clinicians to learn more with every procedure.
2. From a data perspective, the digitization of systems and the use of data through artificial intelligence can shift the clinician's role from probabilistic treatment to definitive treatment. Real-time monitoring of the patient can prevent unnecessary hospitalization, provide timely treatment and reduce chances of decompensation.
3. From a manufacturing perspective, additive manufacturing has revolutionized the way in which we produce structures and parts essential for medical practice and for the wellbeing of patients. The ability to produce customized parts created for human structural reconstruction, and to use this capability in procedure simulation,

part reconstruction and even as a tool to educate future clinicians has a timely role in reducing procedure-caused medical waste and redundancies.

Yet, more research is required to quantify the benefits of cyberphysical systems in the reduction of procedural medical waste. The focus of the literature reviewed continues to be primarily about the cost incentive and the temporal efficiency of shifting to cyberphysical systems.

To summarize, this study explores the concepts of industry 4.0 that have generated significant interest in the healthcare community and can be very impactful, but Industry 4.0 is not limited to the concepts explored here. There is scope to expand on this topic and put forth many more ways in which procedural waste can be reduced in the medical industry. As we see pockets of industry 4.0 crop up in various aspects of this industry, it is important to democratize this knowledge and plan the transition in an effective manner. Multiple roadblocks are yet to be overcome in terms of data privacy, cost optimization and knowledge gaps. It could also be beneficial to develop a structured process for this transition to a smart digitized system so that adoption of new technology is simplified, and under-developed nations can leapfrog the mistakes made by developed nations to provide universal access to sustainable healthcare.

Acknowledgements. The authors would like to acknowledge the funding support for this publication, Project P0032185, the Hong Kong Polytechnic University. We would like to thank the reviewers for their relevant and detailed feedback on the initial draft of this paper.

References

Ahmadi, E., Masel, D.T., Metcalf, A.Y., Schuller, K.: Inventory management of surgical supplies and sterile instruments in hospitals: a literature review. Health Syst. **8**(2), 134–151 (2018). https://doi.org/10.1080/20476965.2018.1496875

Al Hroub, A., et al.: Improving the workflow efficiency of an outpatient pain clinic at a specialized oncology center by implementing lean principles. Asia Pac. J. Oncol. Nurs. **6**(4), 381–388 (2019)

Arksey, H., O'Malley, L.: Scoping studies: towards a methodological framework. Int. J. Soc. Res. Methodol. **8**(1), 19–32 (2005)

Arun Kumar, P.: Insulin management system for diabetic patients. In: Proceedings of the India HCI 2014 Conference on Human Computer Interaction (IndiaHCI 2014), pp. 102–107. ACM, New York (2014)

Baccei, S.J., Henderson, S.R., Lo, H.S., Reynolds, K.: Using quality improvement methodology to reduce costs while improving efficiency and satisfaction in a busy, academic muskuloskeletal radiology division. J. Med. Syst. **44**, 104 (2020). https://doi.org/10.1007/s10916-020-01569-8

Bates, D.W., Saria, S., Ohno-Machado, L., Shah, A., Escobar, G.: Big data in health care: using analytics to identify and manage high-risk and high-cost patients. Health Aff. **33**(7), 1123–1131 (2014)

Becker, E.L., Landau, S.I., Manuila, A.: The International Dictionary of Medicine and Biology. Wiley, Hoboken (1986)

Benfield, C.B., et al.: Applying lean principles to continuous renal replacement therapy processes. Am. J. Health Syst. Pharm. **72**(3), 218–223 (2015)

Bennett, C.C., Doub, T.D.: Data mining and electronic health records: selecting optimal clinical treatments in practice. In: Proceedings of the 6th International Conference on Data Mining, Las Vegas, Nevada, pp. 313–318 (2010)

Bennett, C.C., Hauser, K.: Artificial intelligence framework for simulating clinical decision-making: a Markov decision process approach. Artif. Intell. Med. **57**(1), 9–19 (2013)

Bown, C.P.: COVID-19: demand spikes, export restrictions, and quality concerns imperil poor country access to medical supplies. In: COVID-19 and Trade Policy: Why Turning Inward Won't Work, pp. 31–48. CEPR Press, London (2020)

Caloyeras, J.P., et al.: Understanding waste in health care: perceptions of frontline physicians regarding time use and appropriateness of care they and others provide. Permanente J. **22**, 17–26 (2018)

Ceschin, F., Gaziulusoy, I.: Evolution of design for sustainability: from product design to design for system innovations and transitions. Des. Stud. **47**, 118–163 (2016). https://doi.org/10.1016/j.destud.2016.09.002

Chan, H.H.L., Siewerdsen, J.H., Vescan, A., Daly, M.J., Prisman, E., Irish, J.C.: 3D rapid proto-typing for otolaryngology—head and neck surgery: applications in image-guidance, surgical simulation and patient-specific modeling. PLoS ONE **10**(9), e0136370 (2015)

Chartier, Y., et al.: Safe Management of Wastes from Health-Care Activities, 2nd edn. WHO Library, Geneva (2014)

Choi, J.W., Kim, N.: Clinical application of three-dimensional printing technology in craniofacial plastic surgery. Arch. Plast. Surg. **42**(3), 267–277 (2015). https://doi.org/10.5999/aps.2015.42.3.267

Dukart, J., et al.: Generative FDG-PET and MRI model of aging and disease progression in Alzheimer's disease. PLoS Comput. Biol. **9**(4), 1–11 (2013)

Edwards, K., Nielsen, A.P., Jacobsen, P.: Implementing lean in surgery - lessons and implications. Int. J. Technol. Manag. **57**(1/2/3), 4–17 (2012)

Fields, E., Neogi, S., Schoettker, P.J., Lail, J.: Using lean methodologies to streamline processing of requests for durable medical equipment and supplies for children with complex conditions. Healthvcare **6**(4), 245–252 (2018). https://doi.org/10.1016/j.hjdsi.2017.11.003

Garg, B., Mehta, N.: Current status of 3D printing in spine surgery. J. Clin. Orthop. Trauma **9**(3), 218–225 (2018)

GAO: REPROCESSED SINGLE-USE MEDICAL DEVICES: FDA Oversight Has Increased, and Available Information Does Not Indicate That Use Presents an Elevated Health Risk, p. 38 (2008)

Gayed, B., Black, S., Daggy, J., Munshi, I.A.: Redesigning a joint replacement program using lean six sigma in a veterans affairs hospital. JAMA Surg. **148**(11), 1050–1156 (2013)

Gibson, I., Rosen, D., Stucker, B.: Additive Manufacturing Technologies, 2nd edn. Springer, New York (2015).https://doi.org/10.1007/978-1-4939-2113-3

Gjolaj, L.N., Campos, G.G., Olier-Pino, A.I., Fernandez, G.L.: Delivering patient value by using process improvement tools to decrease patient wait time in an outpatient oncology infusion unit. J. Oncol. Pract. **12**(1), e95–e100 (2016)

Greene, V.W.: Reuse of disposable medical devices: historical and current aspects. Infect. Control **7**(10), 508–513 (1986)

Grossglauser, M., Saner, H.: Data-driven healthcare: From patterns to actions. Eur. J. Prev. Cardiol. **21**, 14–17 (2014)

Hailey, D., Jacobs, P.D., Ries, N.M., Polisena, J.: Reuse of single use medical devices in Canada: clinical and economic outcomes, legal and ethical issues, and current hospital practice. Int. J. Technol. Assess. Health Care **24**(4), 430–436 (2008)

Ison, E., Miller, A.: The use of LCA to introduce life-cycle thinking into decision-making for the purchase of medical devices in the NHS. J. Environ. Assess. Policy Manag **2**(4), 453–476 (2000)

Javaid, M., Haleem, A.: Additive manufacturing applications in medical cases: a literature based review. Alexandria J. Med. **54**(4), 411–422 (2018)

Kagermann, H., Lukas, W.D., Wahlster, W.: Industry 4.0: With the Internet of Things on the way to the 4th industrial revolution (2011). VDI Nachrichten. https://www.vdi-nachrichten.com/Tec hnik-Gesellschaft/Industrie-40-Mit-Internet-Dinge-Weg-4-industriellen-Revolution. Accessed 23 March 2019

Klemes, J.J., Fan, Y.V., Tan, R.R., Jiang, P.: Minimising the present and future plastic waste, energy and environmental footprints related to COVID-19. Renew. Sustain. Energy Rev. **127**, 109883 (2020)

Lasi, H., Fettke, P., Kemper, H.-G., Feld, T., Hoffmann, M.: Industry 4.0. Bus. Inf. Syst. Eng. **6**(4), 239–242 (2014). https://doi.org/10.1007/s12599-014-0334-4

Lunardini, D., Arington, R., Canacari, E.G., Gamboa, K., Wagner, K., McGuire, K.J.: Lean principles to optimize instrument utilization for spine surgery in an academic medical center: an opportunity to standardize, cut costs, and build a culture of improvement. Spine (Phila Pa 1976) **39**(20), 1714–1717 (2014)

Martelli, N., et al.: Advantages and disadvantages of 3-dimensional printing in surgery: a systematic review. Surgery **159**(6), 1485–1500 (2016)

Matt, B.H., Woodward-Hagg, H.K., Wade, C.L., Butler, P.D., Kokoska, M.S.: Lean six sigma applied to ultrasound guided needle biopsy in the head and neck. Otolaryngol. Head Neck Surg. **151**(1), 65–72 (2014)

Minoglou, M., Gerassimidou, S., Komilis, D.: Healthcare waste generation worldwide and its dependence on socio-economic and environmental factors. Sustainability **9**(2), 220 (2017)

Mishra, B., Ionescu, M., Chandra, T.: Additive manufacturing for medical and biomedical applications: advances and challenges. Mater. Sci. Forum **783–786**, 1286–1291 (2014)

Morales-Contreras, M.F., Chana-Valero, P., Suarez-Barraza, M.F., Diaz, A.S., Garcia, E.G.: Applying lean in process innovation in healthcare: the case of hip fracture. Int. J. Environ. Res. Public Health **17**(15), 5273 (2020)

Nocerino, E., Remondino, F., Kessler, F.B., Uccheddu, F.: 3D modelling and rapid prototyping for cardiovascular surgical planning – two case studies. In: The International Archives of the Photogrammetry, Remote Sensing and Spatial Information Sciences, Prague, Czech Republic, pp. 887–893 (2016)

Ohno, T.: Toyota Production System-Beyond Large-Scale Production. Productivity Press, Portland (1988)

Ranney, M.L., Griffeth, V., Jha, A.K.: Critical supply shortages — the need for ventilators and personal protective equipment during the Covid-19 pandemic. N. Engl. J. Med. **382**(18), e41 (2020)

Rigante, L., Moudrous, W., de Vries, J., Grotenhuis, A.J., Boogaarts, H.D.: Operating room waste: disposable supply utilization in neurointerventional procedures. Acta Neurochir. **159**, 2337–2340 (2017). https://doi.org/10.1007/s00701-017-3366-y

Sa, D., Stephens, K., Kuang, M., Simunovic, N., Karlsson, J., Ayeni, O.R.: The direct environmental impact of hip arthroscopy for femoroacetabular impingement: a surgical waste audit of five cases. J. Hip Preserv. Surg. **3**(2), 132–137 (2016)

Sanders, J.H., Karr, T.: Improving ED specimen TAT using lean six sigma. Int. J. Health Care Qual. Assur. **28**(5), 428–440 (2015). https://doi.org/10.1108/IJHCQA-10-2013-0117

Sanders, A., Elangeswaran, C., Wulfsberg, J.: Industry 4.0 implies lean manufacturing: research activities in Industry 4.0 function as enablers for lean manufacturing. J. Ind. Eng. Manag. **9**(3), 811–833 (2016)

Stock, T., Seliger, G.: Opportunities of sustainable manufacturing in Industry 4. 0. In: 13th Global Conference on Sustainable Manufacturing, vol. 40, pp. 536–541 (2016)

Suomalainen, A., Stoor, P., Mesimäki, K., Kontio, R.K.: Rapid prototyping modelling in oral and maxillofacial surgery: a two year retrospective study. J. Clin. Exp. Dent. **7**(5), e605–e612 (2015)

Taylor, R.H., Menciassi, A., Fichtinger, G., Fiorini, P., Dario, P.: Medical robotics and computer-integrated surgery. In: Siciliano, B., Khatib, O. (eds.) Springer Handbook of Robotics, pp. 1657–1684. Springer, Cham (2016). https://doi.org/10.1007/978-3-319-32552-1_63

Thiel, C.L., et al.: Environmental impacts of surgical procedures: life cycle assessment of hysterectomy in the United States. Environ. Sci. Technol. **49**, 1779–1786 (2015)

Torabi, K., Farjood, E., Hamedani, S.: Rapid prototyping technologies and their applications in prosthodontics, a review of literature. J. Dent. **16**(1), 1–9 (2015)

Ustundag, A., Cevikcan, E.: Managing the Digital Transformation. Pham, D.T. (ed.), 1st edn. Springer, Istanbul (2018)

Wang, S.J.: Fields Interaction Design (FID): The Answer to Ubiquitous Computing Supported Environments in the Post-information Age. Homa & Sekey Books, Paramus (2013)

Wang, S.J., Moriarty, P.: Big Data for Urban Health and Well-Being. In: Wang, S.J., Moriarty, P. (eds.) Big Data for Urban Sustainability. Springer, Cham (2018). https://doi.org/10.1007/978-3-319-73610-5_7

Woods, D.L., et al.: Carbon footprint of robotically-assisted laparoscopy, laparoscopy and laparotomy: a comparison. Int. J. Med. Robot. Comput. Assist. Surg. **11**(4), 406–412 (2015)

Yan, J.R., Oreskovich, S., Oduwole, K., Horner, N., Khanna, V., Adili, A.: Cement waste during primary total knee arthroplasty and its effect on cost savings: an institutional analysis. Cureus **10**(11), 1–9 (2018)

Yan, W., Ding, M., Kong, B., Xi, X., Zhou, M.: Lightweight splint design for individualized treatment of distal radius fracture. J. Med. Syst. **43**(8), 1–10 (2019). https://doi.org/10.1007/s10916-019-1404-4

Yang, M., et al.: Application of 3D rapid prototyping technology in posterior corrective surgery for Lenke 1 adolescent idiopathic. Medicine (Baltimore) **94**(8), 1–8 (2015)

Yazer, M.H.: Auditing as a means of detecting waste. International Society of Blood Transfusion Science Series **13**, 29–34 (2018)

Zambrano-Monserrate, M.A., Ruano, M.A., Sanchez-Alcade, L.: Indirect effects of COVID-19 on the environment. Sci. Total Environ. **728**, 138813 (2020)

Effects of Virtual Reality in the Area of Responsible Decision-Making Training on Adolescents

Daniel A. Muñoz[✉], Kenny K. N. Chow, and Huaxin Wei

School of Design, The Hong Kong Polytechnic University, Hung Hom, Kowloon, Hong Kong
daniel.munozprieto@connect.polyu.hk

Abstract. The number of emotional illnesses rises every year . The efforts of using HCI and VR technology to create prevention tools require to extend the design learning knowledge to provide appropriate emotional cognitive experiences. Research has shown that VR provides better engagement and improvement on basic emotional and social dimensions of learning, however, the literature shows that it is necessary for the continuous study to develop effective emotional learning experience addressed to the next generations on immersive virtual learning environment. This study aims to identify how VR experiences impact the learning of a specific emotional dimension on adolescents (responsible decision-making RDM) and identify which cognitive and experience elements have incidence in the design of the learning experience. Based on literature and theories of VR and learning sciences, we experimented using VR on learning sessions with a control group based in ethical and emotional situations using the SODAS method to learn responsible decision making. Results show that the VR group gets a higher score after the sessions, and qualitative and quantitative data reveals that learning timing, cognitive articulation, learning attribution, cognitive load, and specific emotional dimensions might be impacted by the emotional learning experience. The analyses provide helpful information for the future design of cognitive experiences on VR technology.

Keywords: Virtual reality · Cognitive experience · Interaction design

1 Introduction

Virtual reality technology (VR) has been the focus of many research disciplines that are trying to develop knowledge, analyze potential experiences, understand the effects of this technology in different fields and provide guidelines [1] for potential experiences or innovations.

While the number of emotional mental illnesses registered by year is rising, we see an educational opportunity to help the society, to address this, we look at the interaction design field and HCI technologies, to develop emotional and social prevention tools, using virtual immersive technology.

© ICST Institute for Computer Sciences, Social Informatics and Telecommunications Engineering 2021
Published by Springer Nature Switzerland AG 2021. All Rights Reserved
A. Brooks et al. (Eds.): ArtsIT 2020, LNICST 367, pp. 461–476, 2021.
https://doi.org/10.1007/978-3-030-73426-8_28

The efforts of immersive technology in mental health are numerous and in the latest years, a variety of experiments have been conducted with the purpose to understand the effects of VR technology on different emotional dimensions [2] and mental health subjects.

VR has been applied to the treatment of emotional illnesses such as anxiety, depression, stress, and cognitive rehabilitation [2]. In the social dimension, there are also experiments on behavior change and in social skills training, most of them [2] applying virtual reality exposure treatments (VRET) and some of them [3] mixing with cognitive-behavioral therapy.

This latest knowledge is settling the bases of VR technology's impact on social and emotional factors. However, a significant part of the efforts is focused on developing further palliative tools rather than proposing prevention and educational tools for mental health.

At the same time, educational VR products are in the market and emerging research is developing support, however, we observe a shortage of knowledge of VR on the design of complex cognitive experience, such as emotional education. We see that the development of IVLE's (Immersive virtual learning environment) requires to extend the knowledge production from a learning design experience side.

This study wants to extend the current knowledge from our literature review, getting the impact of the VR technology on adolescents on the responsible decision making emotional dimension of SEL, measuring learning and improvement in a mix of quantitative and qualitative data, identify cognitive and influencer factors on VR learning experience and providing knowledge-based considerations for design general and emotional learning experiences on an immersive virtual environment.

The results of this study will benefit in future design of products or services and on the research of cognitive processes on virtual learning experiences, considering factors for educational instances and helping also in the design of social and emotional training on VR platforms.

2 Literature Review

2.1 Emotional Learning

Emotional Intelligence literature [4, 5], establish a gradual development of emotional cognitive development from perception and recognition to understanding and regulation, while some literature [6] also establish that recognition and awareness of self and others is a basic emotional ability, some authors [7] complement the idea declaring that after the absorption of feelings, thoughts, and behavior will be an open space to complex emotional competences. At the same time, there are some publications [8] which declare that on emotional learning experiences it is easy to get raw knowledge about emotions but developing EI (emotional intelligence) requires deeper planned training.

A relevant perspective of emotional education is from CASEL (collaborative for academic social and emotional learning) Framework. Which divides emotional learning into 5 dimensions most of them require a diversity of cognitive articulation [9] and the learning of other basic emotions.

2.2 VR, Learning and Social Cognition

On the other hand, the immersive virtual learning environment (IVLE) creates high levels of engagement and motivation for educational experiences. Literature shows that VR can improve performance against traditional lecture dynamics. Research in the field [10] define socials and spatial discussions for virtual classrooms as an IVLE, several experiments [11, 12] declares a high knowledge absorption in virtual instruction learning experiences, and some of them connect the learning experiences with emotions on VLE, where students showed positive emotional dimensions during the performance. On the social dimension, research [3] got positive results on affective recognition but also in social attribution connecting emotional and social dimension with VR- SCT (social cognitive training) on students with high functioning autism ASD (Asperger spectrum disorder) and TOM (theory of mind).

2.3 Emotional Learning Self-regulation and Adaptation

While some studies are focused on basic emotion recognition, there are experiments on emotional adaptation and self-regulation. There is some particular experiment [13] that uses frustration game training through VR and biofeedback as a way to help participants on emotional regulation (ER) exercises. In a similar direction, spatial adaptation research [14] establishes a virtual affective architecture, using physical emotion recognition hardware to create emotional awareness and adaptation, using basic emotional concepts on adult participants. Research also discovered [15] the influence on the decision of VR on moral dilemmas and their reaction to different scenarios in adult participants.

The latest studies drive our concerns on learning virtual environments and the capabilities of VR technologies to teach beyond the basic emotional skills.

The literature of VR evidences a high number of emotional recognition and affection on experiments, however, we visualize a shortage of emotional interconnected skills revised by VR such as responsible decision making which requires the previous development of several basic emotional abilities such as empathy, ethical development, and the evaluation of consequences.

3 Hypothesis and Theoretical Background

This instance will be helpful to show how a particular educational method on VR, impacts the emotional cognitive process and provides information for further cognitive-emotional design on VR.

After literature, we understand that VR experiences have several capabilities to improve in emotional training however we want to see the effects in an interconnected emotional dimension.

Responsible decision making involves the development of different basic emotional skills. We believe that VR can simulate scenarios and create a trial environment and this could help in the learning experience of emotional cognitive processes. Particularly we think that consequential components can help in the emotional dimension of responsible decision making.

3.1 Hypothesis

1. Students who experience emotional training on responsible decision making on VR will get higher scores than students who do not experience.
2. Creating a trial environment and showing the consequences of different decisions on VR will help in the emotional cognitive process of responsible decision making on adolescents.

The analysis of this will provide light on how is the cognitive experience and which factors of the design experience require attention.

3.2 Frameworks and Scales

To develop our study we decided to use the CASEL framework, as a multidimensional emotional tool, SEL is recognized in the educational environment with validated results on emotional education and provides clear learning for each emotional dimension.

From SEL the development of responsible decision making requires

- Considering the well-being of others
- Recognizing others, one's responsibility to behave ethically
- Base decisions on safety social and ethical considerations
- Evaluating the realistic consequences of various actions
- Making constructive, safe choices for self-relationships

Under this framework and in looking for a structure for our VR stories and the flow of our activities, we consider some educational findings [16] which says that most of the responsible decision making in class tools are based in similar rationales: set objectives, collecting information, generate options, evaluate and choose. In the same light, we find a consequential model called SODAS (situation, option disadvantages, advantages, solution) based on the identification of advantages and disadvantages which will help participants in the cognitive mapping process.

From Literature [9] we find different assessments and scales on the emotional dimension of responsible decision making on direct assessments SIP-AP (social information processing) [17] a computer-based assessment, TOPS (test of problem-solving) and SLDT (social language development test) [18]. On general assessment BAR ON Multifactor[19], DESSA Deveraux Student Strengths Assessment [20], and SSIS-RS Social Skills Improvement System Rating scale [21].

A general assessment provides holistic reports of participants from different dimensions while direct assessment is more specific our criteria to choose was based like them in the case of SSIS was designed for third persons such as teachers or family express what they observe of the participant from an external perspective while BAR ON test Multifactor is a general emotional report which includes RDM but designed for the participant and not for external parts. In this case the decision to use this last to rely on the capability to create a general report which helps to see which emotional dimensions are changing in the assessment but also because they include RDM dimension with a combination of social and emotional design perspective.

4 Experiment

4.1 Participants

Around 30 volunteer students from 13 to 14 years old [22] were recruited in a public secondary school, which after a screening interview, 19 participants (4 female 15 male) matched the requirements and finished the sessions.

4.2 Procedures

Participants were separated into two groups; the control group (in the following CR) and the VR group (in the following VR). Both groups experienced ethical situations using the educational SODAS method (a situation, options, disadvantages, advantages, solution).

Our selection criteria for stories was matching the age and context of the students looking for common and realistic situations that they could be involved, and specific ethical dilemma which creates social and emotional consequences (Fig. 1).

- Story 1 "Drop out school with friends"
- Story 2 "Best friend Stealing from store"
- Story 3 "Rumor of Cheating in a relationship"

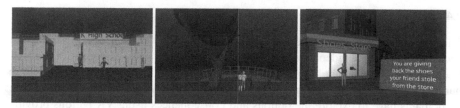

Fig. 1. VR ethical dilemmas developed for the sessions

In both groups, the situation and the options were given on the activity in the case of VR experienced on the immersive story through virtual doors which they have to explore after watch the general situation. In the case of CR, we used a traditional method based on mental simulation and imagination exercises, during which the teacher read the stories to the students while they listened and tried to imagine the situation.

In both cases a worksheet was given to fill the SODAS activity and where the situation and the options where written so they can consult after anytime they need.

4.3 Structure of the Sessions

The session was applied in a school and the two rooms are used for the sessions are belonging to the art and design department. We developed 5 sessions of around 45 min each in the following arrangement.

The first session was focused on a pre-test of responsible decision making (in the following pre-test) for this we used a general emotional assessment BAR ON Multifactor, which gives multidimensional data of emotions of the participant. The test was computer-based and made by students individually.

Sessions 2, 3 & 4, were structured firstly giving general instructions for both groups, students did not receive the worksheet until the end of the experience of the story and the options of the situation, in the case of CR students, they have to hear the story from the mediator (teacher) and the options on it and in the case of VR they have to explore all the story and all the options and then both groups received the paper sheet of SODAS situations to identify advantages and disadvantages. After identifying advantages and disadvantages, on the worksheet, we asked participants to choose an option and then we asked why you choose this option? to see if they are willing to provide arguments and reasons for their choices.

On every page, there are some questions to help students to do the metacognition process and to raise qualitative data that will be processed, the questions are "What did you learn today?", "Why that is Important for your life?". Every worksheet contains the story and the options of the session so they can back to read and consult whenever the students need it.

Session 5 was structured as a post-test a similar an arrangement using the BAR ON test but adding a survey after that about VR and the topic for the students who wanted to fill it, and is a personal appreciation about the VR elements which helps to learn responsible decision making.

4.4 Setting and Technical Considerations

The Platform used to develop the VR stories was Cospaces.edu, using a premium account, and a combination of video, audio, and interaction buttons was developed for the tasks. Each story contains neutral voice audio developed using Text to speech tools with the purpose to contextualize the situation and provide instructions to participants. Then participants have to explore the options and consequences using VR buttons provided in the scene and using the physical button of the VR headset.

The activity was developed simultaneously so the arrangement of the rooms was 9 students with 9 desks and chairs and a distance of 2 m for embodied interaction. In the CR room, we have a similar arrangement with 10 participants.

For development, we used a VR Bobo z6 headset and for participants, 10 android mobile phones and 10 with Xiaomi VR play were used with corresponding earphones so there is no sound interference with each other.

The VR stories took for students around 5 to 10 min of exploration and the language of all the activities was English except for parents' documentation and surveys, a traditional Chinese version was developed.

5   Results

5.1   Improvement Responsible Decision Making

On the pre-test, we identify a difference between CR and VR, where CR group got higher values on the BAR ON test on the RDM dimension (Std dev CR 15.34, against VR 8.71).

In the post-test, we got positive results on the VR group almost all the students show a better score than the pre-test, (Std dev. from 8,71 to 11,44), (Average score. from 58.8 to 72.4). While CR group stay or decrease their score on the post-test (Std dev. from 15,3 to 17,2) (Average score from 63.5 to 58.2). The comparison of improvement shows a significant difference between the two groups (Std. dev. CR 1,922 against VR 2,731) Fig. 2.

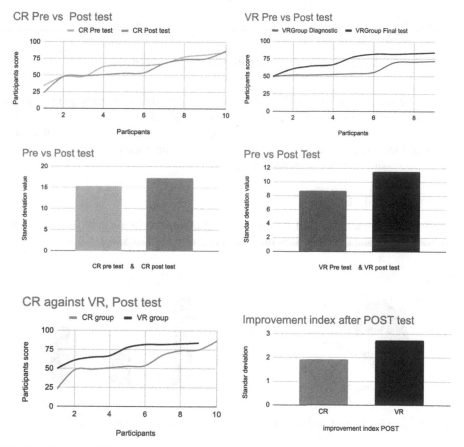

Fig. 2. CR against VR group pre and post-test and Improvement index and group comparison

To see if there is a correlation between attendance of the sessions and the result of the post-test we crossed the data of the post of each participant with the number of sessions that each of them did. CR (correlation −0,16) and VR (correlation −0,48) Fig. 3, due to the lower values, there is not a clear correlation between the attendance to the sessions and the improvement showed by the participants on RDM in the post-test. The quantitative data shows for example that some participants attend 2 of 3 sessions and have a higher score and improvement than some participants which attend all the 3 sessions, so we didn't find a proportional relation from more sessions higher score of RDM on the post-test.

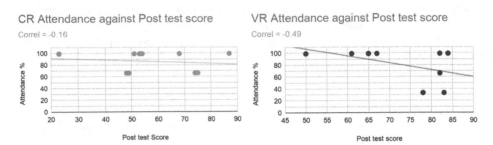

Fig. 3. Correlation between attendance and score in post test

Combination of qualitative and quantitative data show that each participant requires a different number of sessions to evidence a cognitive reflection about the emotional learning topic of RDM, while some students identify by themselves the goal of the activity and the expected learnings after one session, some students only rely on the story of the session without further analysis.

5.2 SODAS Analysis

Students on CR (Mental Simulation) did a high cognitive articulation exercise identifying more advantages and disadvantages than the VR group (515 to 328).

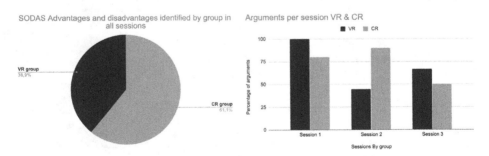

Fig. 4. Cognitive articulation of two groups and Argument per group on SODAS activity.

Immersive learning experiences could restrict the cognitive articulation process while participants identify new elements in a particular situation. However, students in the VR group were more willing to provide arguments and reasons for their SODAS choices (Session 1 and 3) Fig. 4.

5.3   Qualitative Analysis

The qualitative data contemplates analysis of the questions, "What did you learn today?" and "Why that is Important for your life?" those questions have the purpose to complement the quantitative data and understand how the participants learn after every session, see the changes during the process and get the attribution of knowledge on the different emotional dimensions of responsible decision making.

We analyzed the questions using a qualitative theming technique, where we found 5 themes for the first question (Table 1).

Table 1. Theming, learning attribution, qualitative analysis.

What did you learn today?	Why that is Important for your life?
VR and related	Responsible decision making
About themselves	About future situations
About consequences, choices, decisions, options	About success
About the topic of the session	About the topic of the session
About future situations	

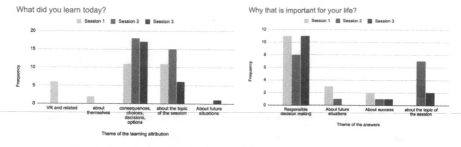

Fig. 5. Learning attribution by session qualitative theming analysis.

The first session participants reflect about VR, Responsible decision making, the topic of the session, and about themselves. The second session participants focus their reflection on learning in RDM and the topic of the session and the third session participant concentrates their reflections on RDM, The topic, and future situations.

There is a change in what the adolescents declare to learn by sessions from a technical impact of the medium and personal appreciations to a deeper understanding of the emotional decision-making area and future situations.

We identify a change of learning attribution through the question (what did you learn today?) of every session from a technical to an emotional domain, the impact of VR medium creates the first sense of attribution, participants feel they are learning about the technology after every session the impact of the VR medium was becoming lower and the impact of the content raised.

5.4 Qualitative SEL Analysis

To analyze the learning attribution of the participants and understand which emotional dimensions of responsible decision making the participants learned in the VR experience we use the SEL framework which define 5 main dimensions of responsible decision making learning from the emotional perspective:

- Considering the well-being of others
- Recognizing others, one's responsibility to behave ethically.
- Base decisions on safety social and ethical considerations.
- Evaluating the realistic consequences of various actions.
- Making constructive, safe choices for self-relationships.

We analyzed the qualitative data and the learning attribution questions using these five domains to understand which areas of learning were more impacted by the VR and CR experience.

First session participants show reflections of learning from the VR group pointing to "Recognizing others and one's responsibility" and "Evaluating realistic consequences of various actions". While CR group focus on "Base decisions on safety social and ethical consideration, and also "Evaluation of consequences of various actions.

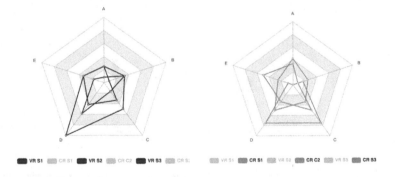

A = Considering the well being of others
B = Recognizing others, one's responsibility to behave ethically
C = Base decisions on safety social and ethical considerations
D = Evaluating the realistic consequences of various actions
E= Making constructive, safe choices for self relationships

Fig. 6. Dimension of responsible decision-making learning by session in two groups VR left CR on the right.

Second session participants show reflections of learning from the VR group pointing clearly to the "Evaluation of consequences" but also involving at least all the dimensions of learning. While CR group declares learnings in the "Well-being of others and coincidently with the other group in the evaluation of consequences.

In the third session CR group declare learnings in several areas pointing higher to "Making constructive choices for self-relationships" and " Base decisions on safety social and ethical considerations".

While the VR group present a difference in evaluating the consequences of various actions. Students on the CR group show learnings in the diversity of RDM dimensions, while students on the VR group show a clear learning trend to the "Evaluating the realistic consequences of various actions" dimension.

6 Discussion

6.1 Improvement of Responsible Decision Making

Results analysis shows that VR technology can improve the level of learning responsible decision making in post-assessment, compared with traditional methods of improvement in performance such as mental simulations and imagination exercises. A structured set of 3 sessions shows a significant difference in learning considering qualitative and quantitative data, proving our hypothesis. In terms of timing of learning our study shows that there is not a proportional relation between the number of sessions and deeper emotional learning, awareness timing or future behavioral change on RDM, even with the help of VR medium the metacognition process of RDM seems independent of every participant and might require a different number of sessions, different gaps of time to digest or supplement activities. We identify that there is an incidence in the general overall improvement of the participant, however, the timing of awareness seems independent of each adolescent and might rely on personal background dimensions rather than the VR medium and could be a matter of further research and discussion for IVLE design.

Cognitive Articulation

On the other hand, our study expresses that the identification of elements that are not on the storytelling of VR, once the participants are outside the VR environment might be affected by a lack of mental effort and that could reverberate on a shortage of cognitive articulation. Participants could rely on and what they watched on VR and decrease effort on imagining new scenarios of advantages and disadvantages.

Cognitive load theory (CLT) and prior research [23] show that on problem-solving activities there is a "completion problem effect", students with partially completed work usually learn more and perform better than fully completed work samples on future test experiences. This can explain that VR participants got better scores and lower identification of advantages and disadvantages. However, we believe that answers can be part of a deeper issue about the design of cognitive processes on immersive technology.

While our structure of tasks for VR was designed with a complementary activity after the immersive experience, intrinsic cognitive load [24, 25] factors might be playing a relevant role in the completion of tasks and the design of VR learning experiences. The complexity of emotional dimensions on VR experience (intrinsic cognitive load) might be considered also some "faded completion principles" [26] of learning and a progressive timeline of activities.

The results also show that there is a possible consequential cognition component [27] on VR which impacts the willingness or disposition to provide arguments when participants have to choose an option. We believe that VR can engage participants to elect carefully and develop consequential thinking considering future repercussions.

6.2 Learning Attribution Progression

Qualitative data frequency Fig. 5, show the learning progression with a technical attribution of learning to the technology in the first session, participants believe that they learning about technology and attribute their learning to the VR medium, however, the general and clear progression evidence that is first impact effect when participants associate their learning to responsible decision making, so we identify that there is an immediate relation of learning attribution to the VR technology.

This shows that VR technology might impact the learning attribution of emotional (or general) learnings on the experiences of the first, based in our qualitative data this impact might be different by the participant relation with the immersive technology, and a learning experience might require to monitor the learning attribution after sessions.

6.3 SEL Dimensions of Learning

Our experiment shows that CR got a diversity of emotional dimension learnings of RDM we can attribute that to the process of mental simulation. Imagination processes are less structured and involve a free flow thinking where the cognitive mapping process is less explicit and individual more than collective, each participant can visualize different situations that can get different consequences and actions, and consequently, there is a diversity of emotional dimensions.

On the VR group, the flow, the structure of the task, and the storytelling designed for the experiment were structured with a consequential component and that narrowed the absorption process [28] of participants to one of the dimensions of RDM, which is related to the realistic evaluation of consequences. This could explain the clear orientation of that SEL dimension (Fig. 6).

As our control group shows, the identification of emotional learning dimensions is affected by the freedom of thinking in the learning process, when the story is presented by VR experience to participants is already interpreted by explicit characters, environment, animations and tasks, this may reduce the intrinsic cognitive load of the responsible decision making knowledge (or any emotional knowledge) but may also reduce the diversity of knowledge attribution if the content is highly explicit or narrow.

7 Considerations for Design

A) Learning timing
    Design for emotional learning experiences on VR technologies should consider that every participant will have a different evolution of their cognitive process and the number of sessions will not be directly related to the level of emotional learning. More sessions will not always lead to deep understanding and learning.

B) Monitor Learning progression
    Because we identified an impact from VR medium in the learning attribution we believe that learning experience on VR should consider use tools to monitor the

learning attribution, understand what the people is learning and what are the incident factors on the learning experience can provide useful insight about when the participants are influenced by a first impact of the technology or not.

This is also helpful to understand the scopes of the engagement of VR technology in this context and at the same time provides feedback on the cognitive process of participants. Is relevant keep in mind the power attributed to the VR technology as a learning tool and understand that VR on emotional learning experiences might be a reason to create unexpected emotional outcomes, monitor the learning attribution in this type of training can help to elucidate the curve learning of the participants and can help to get reasons of that process.

C) Freedom of imagination in the process

From our results of the experiment, we understand that some elements such as storytelling, the way as the content are shown and structure of the task of the participants have influence in the dimensions of learning, the elements mentioned can narrow the cognitive process of participants to some specific dimensions if they are highly explicit or specific. We identify an inverse relationship between the specificity and explicitness of this element on VR learning and the diversity of the learning dimensions, from our control group which got a diversity of dimensions of learning and VR which got a narrow and specific dimension.

We believe that consider mind rooms or spaces for interpret the VR story but also consider how specific are the task of the VR experience in relation to the knowledge to achieve is relevant to give an appropriate sense of freedom for the participants.

Give for example a certain degree of interactivity in the choices of the participants and the capability to change or impact the narrative could give a different sense of freedom and create an experience with a diversity of learning dimensions. At the same time, the creation of the content should consider explicit or implicit action in the behavior of the VR characters according to every learning outcome.

D) Cognitive load

Design for IVLE should consider the intrinsic cognitive load factors of the content, divide when it's appropriate and separate by sessions and apply learning completion principles that could help to a better understanding of the content from the student perspective.

8 Conclusion

In conclusion, VR technology improved the learning of responsible decision making and could probably improve other emotional skills, combined by complementary activities, however, we identify that designing immersive virtual learning experiences should require considering several aspects which are playing a relevant role in the cognitive experience. Our contribution benefits everyone who will be in the position to design or create a cognitive experience on VR but also anyone who is looking to develop a structure for a VR experience, providing considerations to look before a development process.

8.1 Limitations

Because the similar characteristics of the sample applied to the same school in a particular place of Asia, the identified factors might reflect only the human behavior of the specific region, however, further study should involve multicultural backgrounds to see the differences and transversalities on the topic.

The school context where the participants come from have a higher relation with technology on the academic curriculum (in relation to other schools of the area), some participants have a close relationship with VR technology while others not at all, this could compromise some results shown during the experience.

The platform used to build VR experience provides non-Asian cultural avatars, this might impact the visual empathy process of some participants and some cultural attachments during the learning process.

The size of the sample should also matter to consider the results of this experiment, the behavior of the variables and the quantitative outcome could experiment changes in a different sample.

8.2 Future Work

Further work will continue elucidating the cognitive process of VR technology on training experiences, acquire and develop knowledge of how to design an appropriate VR educational experiences, (considering simple and complex skills) could evidence the factors which are playing relevant roles in the absorption process and will be one of our concerns.

We believe that further research should also consider evaluating content and cognitive load factor design during the learning process and how they may affect users in an immersive virtual learning environment.

Future work will also involve the idea to incorporate digital tools inside of IVLE to monitor the cognitive factors and also the learning attribution this could provide helpful data that can be gathered from inside of the VR experience.

References

1. Suh, A., Prophet, J.: The state of immersive technology research: a literature analysis. Comput. Hum. Behav. **86** (2018). https://doi.org/10.1016/j.chb.2018.04.019
2. Jerdan, S., Boulos, K., Maged, W., Hugo, G., Mark.: Head mounted virtual reality and mental health: critical review of current research. J. Med. Internet Res. **6**, e14 (2018). https://doi.org/10.2196/games.9226
3. Didehbani, N., Allen, T., Kandalaft, M., Krawczyk, D., Chapman, S.: Virtual reality social cognition training for children with high functioning autism. Comput. Hum. Behav. **62**, 703–711 (2016)
4. Salovey, P., Mayer, J.D.: Emotional intelligence. Imagination Cognit. Pers. **9**(3), 185–211 (1989–1990)
5. Mayer, J.D., Salovey, P., Caruso, D.R.: Models of emotional intelligence. In: Sternberg, R.J. (ed.) Handbook of Intelligence, pp. 396–420. Cambridge University Press (2000). https://doi.org/10.1017/CBO9780511807947.019

6. Goleman, D.: Emotional Intelligence: Why it Can Matter More than IQ. Bantam Books, New York (2005)
7. Frijda, N.H.: The laws of emotion. Am. Psychol. **43**(5), 349–358 (1988). https://doi.org/10.1037/0003-066X.43.5.349
8. Salovey, P., Sluyter, D.J. (eds.): Emotional Development and Emotional Intelligence: Educational Implications. Basic Books (1997)
9. Durlak, J.A., Domitrovich, C.E., Weissberg, R.P., Gullotta, T.P.: Handbook of Social and Emotional Learning: Research and Practice (2015)
10. Bailenson, J.N., Yee, N., Blascovich, J., Beall, A.C., Lundblad, N., Jin, M.: The use of immersive virtual reality in the learning sciences: digital transformations of teachers, students, and social context. J. Learn. Sci. **17**(1), 102–141 (2008)
11. Webster, R.: Declarative knowledge acquisition in immersive virtual learning environments. Interact. Learn. Environ. **24**(6), 1319–1333 (2015)
12. Allcoat, D., von Mühlenen, A.: Learning in virtual reality: effects on performance, emotion and engagement. Res. Learn. Technol. **26** (2018)
13. Rodriguez Ortega, A., et al.: A VR-based serious game for studying emotional regulation in adolescents. IEEE Comput. Graph. Appl. **35**(1), 65–73 (2015)
14. i Badia, S.B., Quintero, L.V., Cameirao, M.S., Chirico, A., Triberti, S., Cipresso, P., Gaggioli, A.: Toward emotionally adaptive virtual reality for mental health applications. IEEE J. Biomed. Health Inform. **23**(5), 1877–1887 (2018)
15. Niforatos, E., Palma, A., Gluszny, R., Vourvopoulos, A., Liarokapis, F.: Would You do it?: Enacting Moral Dilemmas in Virtual Reality for Understanding Ethical Decision-Making (2020)
16. Greenbank, P.: Initiating Change in Career Decision-making: an Action Research Approach (2010)
17. Kupersmidt, J.B., Stelter, R., Dodge, K.A.: Development and validation of the social information processing application: a web-based measure of social information processing patterns in elementary school-age boys. Psychol. Assess. **23**(4), 834 (2011)
18. Bowers, L., Huisingh, R.: Social Language Development Test (2013)
19. Bar-On, R.: The multifactor measure of performance: its development, norming, and validation. Front. Psychol. **9**, 140 (2018). https://doi.org/10.3389/fpsyg.2018.00140
20. LeBuffe, P.A., Shapiro, V.B., Robitaille, J.L.: The Devereux student strengths assessment (DESSA) comprehensive system: screening, assessing, planning, and monitoring. J. Appl. Dev. Psychol. **55**, 62–70 (2018). https://doi.org/10.1016/j.appdev.2017.05.002
21. Gresham, F.M., Elliott, S.N.: Social Skills Improvement System: Rating Scales. Pearson Assessments, Bloomington (2008)
22. Pretzlaff, R.K.: Should age be a deciding factor in ethical decision-making? Health care analysis. HCA. J. Health Philos. Pol. **13**(2) (2005). https://doi.org/10.1007/s10728-005-4475-y
23. Sweller, J.: Cognitive load theory. In: Mestre J.P., Ross, B.H. (eds.) The Psychology of Learning and Motivation: Cognition in Education, vol. 55, pp. 37–76. Elsevier Academic Press (2011). https://doi.org/10.1016/B978-0-12-387691-1.00002-8
24. Andersen, S.A.W., Mikkelsen, P.T., Konge, L., Cayé-Thomasen, P., Sørensen, M.S.: The effect of implementing cognitive load theory-based design principles in virtual reality simulation training of surgical skills: a randomized controlled trial. Adv. Simul. **1** (2016). https://doi.org/10.1186/s41077-016-0022-1
25. Zhang, L., et al.: Cognitive load measurement in a virtual reality-based driving system for autism intervention. IEEE Trans. Affect. Comput. **8**(2), 176–189 (2017). https://doi.org/10.1109/TAFFC.2016.2582490
26. Kar, N., Kar, B.: Social cognition and individual effectiveness in interpersonal scenarios: a conceptual review. J. Mental Health Hum. Behav. **22**, 27–34 (2017)

27. Sweller, J., van Merrienboer, J.J.G., Paas, F.G.W.C.: Cognitive architecture and instructional design. Educ. Psychol. Rev. **10**, 251–296 (1998). https://doi.org/10.1023/A:1022193728205

28. Glicksohn, J., Avnon, M.: Explorations in virtual reality: absorption, cognition and altered state of consciousness. Imagination Cogn. Pers. **17**(2), 141–151 (1997). https://doi.org/10.2190/FTUU-GLC5-GBT8-9RUW

Author Index

Printed in the United States
by Baker & Taylor Publisher Services